CURRENT TOPICS IN ANIMAL LEARNING:
Brain, Emotion, and Cognition

Edited by

LAWRENCE DACHOWSKI
Tulane University

CHARLES F. FLAHERTY
Rutgers—The State University

Technical Editor
Alison Hartman
Tulane University

LAWRENCE ERLBAUM ASSOCIATES, PUBLISHERS
1991   Hillsdale, New Jersey   Hove and London

Lawrence Erlbaum Associates, Inc., Publishers
365 Broadway
Hillsdale, New Jersey 07642

Library of Congress Cataloging-in-Publication Data

Current Topics in Animal Learning: brain, emotion, and cognition /
    edited by Lawrence Dachowski, Charles F. Flaherty; Technical Editor, Alison Hartman.
        p.   cm.
    Includes bibliographical references and indexes.
    ISBN 0-8058-0441-2
    1. Learning in animals—Congresses. 2. Cognition in animals—Congresses. 3. Psychology, Comparative—Congresses. 4. Learning, Psychology of–Congresses.   I. Dachowski, Lawrence. II. Flaherty, Charles F.
QL785.C87 1991
591.51—dc20   90-38864
                                                                       CIP

Printed in the United States of America
10 9 8 7 6 5 4 3 2 1

Contents

Contributors

Julia L. Bassett
Department of Behavioral Neuroscience, University of Pittsburgh
Pittsburgh, PA 15260

Theodore W. Berger
Department of Behavioral Neuroscience,University of Pittsburgh
Pittsburgh, PA 15260

Mark E. Bouton
Department of Psychology, The University of Vermont
Burlington, VT 05405

Mary M. Brazier
Department of Psychology, Loyola University
New Orleans, LA 70118

Daniel J. Calcagnetti
Department of Psychology, Emory University
Atlanta, GA

James J. Chrobak
Department of Psychology, Rutgers—The State University
New Brunswick, NJ 08903

Lawrence Dachowski
Department of Psychology, Tulane University
New Orleans, LA 70118

M. R. D'Amato
Department of Psychology, Rutgers—The State University
New Brunswick, NJ 08903

Andrew R. Delamater
Department of Psychology, Dalhousie University
Halifax, NS, Canada B3H 4J1

Michael S. Fanselow
Department of Psychology, University of California-Los Angeles
405 Hilgard Avenue, Los Angeles, CA 90024

Charles F. Flaherty
Department of Psychology, Rutgers—The State University
New Brunswick, NJ 08903

Nicholas J. Grahame
Department of Psychology, State University of New York at Binghamton
Binghamton, NY 13901

Fred J. Helmstetter
Department of Psychology, Dartmouth College
Hanover, NH

Pamela Jackson-Smith
Department of Psychology, University of Utah
Salt Lake City, UT 84112

Bruce S. Kapp
Department of Psychology, University of Vermont
Burlington, VT 05405

Vincent M. LoLordo
Department of Psychology, Dalhousie University
Halifax, NS, Canada B3H 4J1

Carrie G. Markgraf
Department of Psychology, University of Vermont
Burlington, VT 05405

Ralph R. Miller
Department of Psychology, State University of New York at Binghamton
Binghamton, NY 13901

William B. Orr
Department of Behavioral Neuroscience, University of Pittsburgh
Pittsburgh, PA 15260

Jeffrey P. Pascoe
Department of Psychology, University of Vermont
Burlington, VT 05405

John M. Pearce
School of Psychology, University of Wales
College of Cardiff, Cardiff CF1 3YG
Great Britain

David C. Riccio
Department of Psychology, Kent State University
Kent, Ohio

Rick Richardson
Department of Psychology, Princeton University
Princeton, NJ 08544

Janice N. Steirn
Department of Psychology, University of Kentucky
Lexington, KY 40506

William F. Supple
Department of Psychology, University of Vermont
Burlington, VT 05405

Peter J. Urcuioli
Department of Psychological Sciences, Purdue University
West Lafayette, Indiana 47907

Thomas J. Walsh
Department of Psychology, Rutgers—The State University
New Brunswick, NJ 08903

Amy Wilson
Department of Psychology, University of Vermont
Burlington, VT 05405

Thomas R. Zentall
Department of Psychology, University of Kentucky
Lexington, KY 40506

Preface

This book has its origins in the *1988 Flowerree Mardi Gras Symposium: Animal Learning and Conditioning*, which was held at Tulane University in New Orleans, Louisiana on February 9-10, 1988. The objective of the 1988 symposium was to give a representative sampling of contemporary research on animal learning. Our selection of areas of research to be included was guided, in part, by a description of animal learning presented by Michael Domjan (1987). At least one participant was included from each of the four research areas mentioned by Domjan: (a) learning theory, (b) comparative cognition, (c) animal models of human behavior, and (d) functional neurology.

Six of the chapters in this volume were contributed by participants at the 1988 symposium (Bouton, Zentall, Pearce, Flaherty, Dachowski, and Berger). Seven other researchers were asked to contribute chapters to this volume (Richardson, LoLordo, Miller, D'Amato, Fanselow, Kapp, and Walsh) in order to provide more complete coverage of the topics. The result is a sampling of current research on animal learning that is representative of the field, with the possible exception of animal models of human behavior where there is so much research underway in so many areas of behavior (cf. Domjan, 1987) that it would be beyond the scope of this book to give more than limited coverage.

Domjan, M. (1987). Animal learning comes of age. *American Psychologist, 42*, 556-564.

Acknowledgments

We received invaluable support and assistance during all stages of the 1988 Flowerree symposium and the preparation of the present book. The symposium was made possible by a grant from the Robert E. Flowerree Fund in Psychology of Tulane University; we wish to extend our thanks to Mr. Flowerree for his generous support of the Tulane Psychology Department. Additional financial support was received from the Graduate School Student Association of Tulane University. Numerous psychology graduate students at Tulane assisted in making the symposium a success; we particularly thank Pat Blackwell, who organized the student volunteers and helped with many other details. We also thank the faculty members of the Psychology Department at Tulane University who assisted with arrangements and gave the participants a warm welcome. Thanks also go to the chairs of the symposium sessions: Gary P. Dohanich and William P. Dunlap of Tulane University, Daniel D. Moriarty, Jr. of the University of San Diego, and Mary M. Brazier of Loyola University, New Orleans.

Preparation of the manuscript of this book was supported in part by an additional grant from the Robert E. Flowerree Fund in Psychology of Tulane University. We thank Tulane Computing Services for support in preparing the final manuscript. Our appreciation goes to Laurie Decoteau, Rebekah Green, Sandy Lin, and Mary Ann Decoteau, student assistants at Tulane Computing Services, for their careful computer editing. The assistance of Jacqueline Stroh in managing the paper work at Tulane is gratefully acknowledged. Special thanks are extended to Katherine L. Shannon of the Psychology Office at Tulane for assistance and advice at many stages of the symposium and book preparation.

Finally, we thank our wives, Meg Dachowski, Ph.D., and Mary Flaherty, for their support and patience.

Lawrence Dachowski
Charles F. Flaherty
August 1990

1 Memory Processes, ACTH, and Extinction Phenomena

Rick Richardson
Princeton University

David C. Riccio
Kent State University

That hormones can profoundly influence a number of basic behaviors is now well established. In addition to the prenatal organizational effects of hormones on the structure and function of the central nervous system (Carlson, 1981) a wide variety of activational influences can be found. For example, feeding, reproduction (Leshner, 1978; chapters 2 & 5), and maternal behavior (Rosenblatt, 1987) are all greatly affected by the animal's hormonal state. Initiation and maintenance of each of these behaviors seems to be controlled, at least in part, by one hormone or another. Until relatively recently, the role of hormones in more cognitive activities has received less emphasis. However, there is accumulating evidence that certain hormones influence various cognitive functions including attention, learning, and memory (Beckwith & Sandman, 1978; deWeid, 1970; McGaugh, 1983). One hormone that has been of particular interest in this regard is adrenocorticotropic hormone (ACTH). The effect of this hormone on learning and memory has attracted considerable attention in the last two decades (Bohus & deWeid, 1981; Riccio & Concannon, 1981).

The influence of ACTH on learning has been demonstrated in at least two very different ways. For example, some investigators have shown that exogenous ACTH influences the strength of learning while others have shown that exogenous ACTH can function as an internal cue to mediate learning across different environmental situations. As an example of the first approach, Gold and van Buskirk (1976) found that post-training injections of ACTH had a dose-dependent effect on the learning of both passive and active avoidance in rats. That is, post-training injections of low doses of ACTH enhanced the learning of these responses while high doses had the opposite effect. Gold and

1

van Buskirk (1976) suggested that post-training ACTH influenced learning by modifying memory consolidation. Other investigators have replicated these results although some have suggested that the amnestic effect produced by high doses of ACTH immediately following training is due to state-dependent learning rather than modification of memory storage processes (Izquierdo & Dias, 1983).

An example of a situation where exogenous ACTH serves as a mediating cue to establish learning to neutral environmental cues is provided by a study by Concannon, Riccio, Maloney, and McKelvey (1980). These investigators employed a "redintegration" procedure to show that animals could use the internal state produced by high levels of ACTH to associate temporally separate events. In this procedure, release of endogenous ACTH was induced in Phase 1 by subjecting rats to the stress of repeated shocks in an unpainted wooden box. Control animals were merely exposed to the chamber without being shocked. On the following day (Phase 2), all animals were exposed to the black compartment of a black-white shuttle box. Prior to being placed in the black compartment some subjects were given ACTH and others saline. Half of the animals in each drug condition had been previously shocked while the other half had not. The third phase consisted of a test for fear of the black compartment. The major outcome of this study was that only those animals that had been shocked *and* given ACTH prior to being exposed to the distinctive cues exhibited fear (as measured by avoidance of the black chamber). Concannon et al. (1980, p. 977) offered the following interpretation for their results: "It appears that an appropriate internal state can redintegrate a previous emotional response which becomes associated with contemporaneous external stimuli." That is, the high levels of ACTH present at the time of these two events allowed animals to associate exposure to the black compartment with shock—even though the two had never occurred together! This paradigm can also be viewed as a variant of higher-order Pavlovian conditioning, but with the important distinction that the transfer of fear is based upon the role of an interoceptive state (ACTH and correlated stimuli), rather than an exteroceptive signal, as the first order CS. Whatever accounts for this effect, endogenous opiate systems appear to be at least partly involved as injections of naltrexone 5 min prior to the ACTH injection completely blocked acquisition of this fear (Concannon et al., 1980; also see DeVito & Brush, 1984).

In addition to influencing learning, exogenous ACTH also appears to affect memory processes. For example, exogenous ACTH, and related peptide fragments, are effective in alleviating retention deficits produced by a wide variety of experimental treatments. Rigter, Van Riezen, and deWeid (1974) demonstrated that CO_2-induced retrograde amnesia (RA) for a passive avoidance task could be attenuated by injecting $ACTH_{4-10}$ shortly prior to the retention test. Similarly, Mactutus, Smith, and Riccio (1980) demonstrated the alleviation of hypothermia-induced RA by pretest injections of ACTH. Another situation where exogenous ACTH is effective in alleviating retention deficits comes from the work of Klein (1972) on the Kamin effect. Kamin and others (Kamin, 1957; Klein & Spear, 1970) have shown that subjects trained on an active avoidance task and then tested after an intermediate retention interval (1-6 hr) perform more poorly than subjects tested either immediately or 24 hr after training. However, Klein (1972) found that animals tested after an intermediate retention interval did not show the usual retention loss if they were injected with ACTH shortly prior to the test session. Clearly, exogenous ACTH is an effective treatment in alleviating retention deficits in a number of situations (also see Haroutunian & Riccio, 1979).

But perhaps the best known work concerning the effects of ACTH on learning and memory is the extensive series of studies by deWeid and his colleagues on the extinction of avoidance behaviors (Bohus & deWeid, 1966, 1981; deWeid, 1966). Typically, it has been reported that animals given ACTH prior to a test session are more resistant to extinction than are subjects given only the vehicle. That is, animals given ACTH prior to an extinction session continue to make the conditioned avoidance response longer than do controls. For example, deWeid (1966) trained rats on either an active avoidance task or a pole-jumping procedure. After reaching the training criterion animals were given one of a variety of treatments. For our purposes the important groups were those given ACTH or the vehicle. During subsequent extinction trials, animals given ACTH (either $ACTH_{1-39}$ or $ACTH_{1-10}$) continued to respond at a higher rate than animals given just the vehicle. These effects of exogenous ACTH on rate of extinction of the avoidance response are not due to alterations of motor activity per se, but appear to be due to some central effect. DeWeid and his colleagues have continued this line of research during the last two decades and have examined the effects of many different variables on hormonal influences on learning/memory (Bohus & deWeid, 1981).

From this extensive body of work several different mechanisms have been proposed to explain the influence of ACTH on learning/memory. A partial summary of these mechanisms include the notions that ACTH influences attentional processes (Mirsky & Orren, 1977), trial-to-trial memory (deWeid & Bohus, 1966), memory consolidation (Gold & Delanoy, 1981) or memory retrieval (Klein, 1972; Riccio & Concannon, 1981), the "motivational significance of environmental cues" (Bohus & deWeid, 1981), or that ACTH may be an attribute of memory (Bohus, 1982). Given the variety of reported effects of ACTH on learning and memory it is unlikely, as noted by Bohus and deWeid (1981), that any single explanation can account for them all. In the present chapter, however, we would like to focus on a series of experiments that were done from the perspective that ACTH (and concomitant internal changes) can be an integral component of memory.

A number of theorists have suggested that memory is best conceptualized as being comprised of many independent attributes (Spear, 1978; Underwood, 1969). This idea has proven to be quite fruitful in other areas of our work (e.g., experimentally-induced amnesia) so we decided to try to apply it to extinction. According to this view, memory consists of many different attributes, one of which is the internal state of the organism at the time of training. Furthermore, retrieval of a memory is, as stated by Spear and Mueller (1984, p. 117), ". . . governed by this simple, ancient principle: The more similar the circumstances are that comprise the episode originally learned and those present when memory retrieval is required, the greater the retention." Therefore, if during training the animal experiences high levels of ACTH, then retention will be enhanced if the animal also experiences high levels of ACTH at test. The familiar analogy used to describe this relationship involves generalization decrement. That is, if an animal is trained on some task its performance becomes degraded as the testing cues become increasingly dissimilar to those used in training. With respect to memory processes, the argument would be that retention is a direct function of the similarity of the cues present at test to those originally encoded. As the two sets of cues become more similar retention increases.

The idea that ACTH is a component of memory predicts that administration of ACTH will have quite different effects depending on when it is given. Under some circumstances, the effects of the hormone should be reflected in better performance of the original learned behavior. Consistent with this view, there is substantial evidence that exogenous ACTH prolongs the persistence during extinction of both active avoidance responding (deWeid, 1966) and conditioned taste aversions (Levine, Smotherman, & Hennesy, 1977). Also, as noted, administration of ACTH prior to testing can ameliorate retention deficits produced by amnestic agents (Keyes, 1974; Mactutus, Smith, & Riccio, 1980). On the other hand, the functional effect of enhanced memory retrieval following ACTH administration should be quite different if the experimental paradigm were re-arranged. For example, enhancing retention of the target memory during an extinction session should make that memory more susceptible to the effects of the extinction treatment. This, of course, would lead to poorer performance on a subsequent retention test. These predictions concerning the effects of exogenous ACTH on extinction of avoidance responding were tested in a series of experiments in our laboratory.

RECOVERY OF AN EXTINGUISHED AVOIDANCE RESPONSE BY ACTH

The question addressed in these initial experiments was whether injections of ACTH at the time of testing would be effective in alleviating performance decrements induced by a prior extinction session. That is, would animals that had been trained to make an avoidance response and then had that response extinguished, show stronger responding when given ACTH at testing?

As noted earlier, pre-test injections of ACTH have been found to alleviate retention deficits in a variety of situations. Although performance decrements produced by an extinction treatment are not typically thought of as being "retention" phenomena, both stimulus sampling theory (Estes, 1955) and empirical data suggest some commonalities between performance decrements resulting from manipulations involving extinction or retention loss. For example, noncontingent footshock is often used to alleviate retention deficits produced by experimentally-induced retrograde amnesia (Mactutus, Ferek, & Riccio, 1980; Miller & Springer, 1972), and it also has been shown to be effective in producing substantial recovery of an extinguished conditioned emotional response (Rescorla & Heth, 1975). However, regardless of whether performance decrements produced by extinction are viewed as "retention" losses or not, pretest injections of ACTH would increase the similarity between training and testing. The closer correspondence of stimulus conditions should promote greater retrieval which in turn should enhance performance. The focus on recovery of the extinguished memory, rather than resistance to extinction, is of course analogous to our work on the reversal of memory loss from retrograde amnesia (Mactutus, Ferek, & Riccio, 1980) or from infantile amnesia (Riccio & Haroutunian, 1979).

Another issue examined in this experiment concerned the possible time-dependent nature of any effect ACTH might have on retention. As noted earlier, administration of particular hormones (e.g., ACTH or epinephrine) immediately after training can have a profound impact on the animal's subsequent performance. However, it is typically the case that if a delay is introduced between training and hormone delivery then the hormone has no effect (Gold & van Buskirk, 1976). In the same fashion, it would seem that exogenous ACTH would influence memory retrieval only for as long as the hormone, or its internal concomitants, are present. Therefore, introducing a delay between ACTH injection and testing should lessen the effectiveness of this treatment as a reminder. Indeed, Mactutus, Smith, and Riccio (1980) found that exogenous ACTH alleviated experimentally induced amnesia if the animal was tested 0.5 hr, but not 24 hr, after hormone administration. Furthermore, it should be noted that deWeid (1966) used a long-lasting form of the peptide (containing zinc phosphate) in his experiment described earlier and even concluded "Apparently, the chronic presence of the peptide is obligatory to exert the effect" (pp. 30-31).

Passive Avoidance

In this experiment, adult male rats were trained to fear the black compartment of a black-white shuttle box (Richardson, Riccio, & Devine, 1984; Experiment 4). A Pavlovian differential conditioning procedure was used to condition fear. In this procedure animals were confined to the black side for two separate 2 min periods during which 12 inescapable footshocks were administered. All animals received an equivalent amount of exposure to the white compartment where no shock was given. A passive avoidance procedure was used to assess retention. That is, animals were placed in the white side of the shuttle box and the time taken to enter the black compartment was recorded. In this test, long latencies to enter the black compartment are indicative of good retention.

Twenty-four hours following training 3 groups of animals were given a 90 s nonreinforced exposure to the black compartment (i.e., an extinction exposure). Subjects in a fourth group did not receive any treatment on this day. Seventy-two hours after training all animals were tested for fear of the black compartment. Of the three groups that were extinguished, one was given 4 IU of ACTH (Acthar gel, Armour Pharmaceutical) and another was given the same volume of physiological saline shortly prior (15-20 min) to test. Subjects in the third extinguished group were injected with ACTH 24 hr prior to test.

As can be seen in Figure 1.1, extinguished animals given saline prior to test were quite different from the retention controls (i.e., trained but unextinguished animals). The extended nonreinforced exposure was quite effective in reducing the conditioned fear of the black compartment. Unlike the extinguished animals given saline, subjects given ACTH prior to testing were not different from the retention controls. Those rats given ACTH prior to the test were just as fearful of the black compartment as were unextinguished animals. Moreover, this was the case regardless of the interval between administration of the exogenous ACTH and test.

The results of this experiment demonstrate quite clearly that exogenous ACTH is very effective in alleviating extinction- induced decrements in avoidance behavior. Somewhat surprisingly, however, no effect of time between ACTH administration and test was seen. If the exogenous ACTH serves as a retrieval cue, then animals given ACTH should exhibit enhanced performance only for as long as the ACTH, and any correlated physiological changes, persists. As ACTH has a very short half-life (Reith & Neidle, 1981) it is hard to imagine that any stimulus properties of the hormone would persist for a 24 hour period.

In the next experiment we attempted to extend to a different task the basic finding that pretest injection of ACTH attenuates the effects of a prior extinction treatment. By using an active avoidance procedure in this experiment, rather than the passive avoidance task used before, we should be able to determine whether the observed results were due to nonspecific effects of ACTH on motor activity. If ACTH is merely influencing motor activity, then performance on the active avoidance task should not be improved (and perhaps would be made worse) by pretest injections of ACTH. However, performance on both active and passive avoidance should be improved if the ACTH is influencing some aspect of retention.

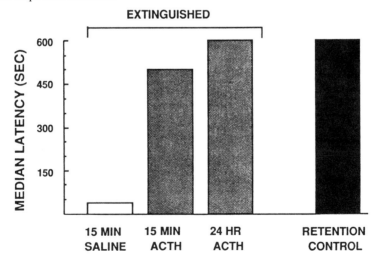

Figure 1.1. Median latency (in seconds) to enter the black compartment of a black-white shuttle box where shock had been previously administered. Performance of animals that were trained, but not extinguished, is represented by the filled bar. Performance of animals that were given ACTH prior to test are represented by the gray bars while that of animals given saline is represented by the open bar. Data redrawn from Richardson, Riccio, & Devine, 1984.

In addition, to explore more systematically the effect of the interval between hormone injection and testing, separate groups of animals were tested either 15 min, 1 day, or 7 days after exogenous administration of ACTH. In the previous experiment there was no effect of the injection-to-test interval. Perhaps that finding is restricted to the passive avoidance procedure or the intervals between injection and test were not sufficiently long. Such possibilities were examined in the active avoidance study.

Active Avoidance

Ahlers, Richardson, West, and Riccio (1989) trained adult male rats on a one-way active avoidance task. Five seconds after being placed in one side of a two compartment shuttle box the animals were shocked until they crossed into the other compartment. Training continued until animals had made 3 consecutive avoidance responses (i.e., responded in less than 5 s). On the following day this response was extinguished in some subjects. As active avoidance responses are notoriously difficult to extinguish (e.g., Solomon, Kamin, & Wynne, 1953), a response prevention procedure was used to extinguish the behavior. That is, animals were confined to the previously shocked compartment for an extended period (without shock, of course) and not allowed to make the avoidance response. This technique has repeatedly proven effective in extinguishing active avoidance responding (Baum, 1970; Mineka, 1979). Forty-eight hours after this extinction treatment animals received a subcutaneous injection of either 16 IU ACTH, an equivalent volume of the vehicle gel (obtained from Armour Pharmaceutical), or 0.9% physiological saline. In each treatment condition separate groups of animals were tested for retention of the avoidance response either 15 min, 1 day, or 7 days following the injection.

The test consisted of 10 nonreinforced trials. If an animal had not crossed into the "safe" compartment within 5s it was assigned a latency of 5s, and then placed in the safe compartment for the 15s inter-trial interval that separated all trials. In this task, as opposed to the passive avoidance procedure, short latencies are indicative of good retention. As can be seen in Figure 1.2, animals given ACTH prior to test had significantly shorter latencies to cross into the "safe" compartment than did animals given either saline or the vehicle gel. Furthermore, exogenously administered ACTH was found to be effective in alleviating extinction-induced performance decrements at all three intervals tested.

Taken together, these two experiments clearly show that exogenous ACTH is not merely influencing motor activity in these situations. When a passive avoidance test procedure was employed, ACTH increased the latency to respond, but when the task involved an active avoidance test procedure, ACTH was found to decrease latency to respond. Apparently, ACTH is influencing some central process, like memory retrieval, rather than motor activity.

Furthermore, the results of the current experiment once again show that ACTH produces a relatively long lasting recovery from extinction-induced performance decrements. ACTH given up to 7 days before the retention test had as strong an effect in attenuating the effects of the extinction treatment as did ACTH given 15 min prior to test. The stable performance of subjects given ei-

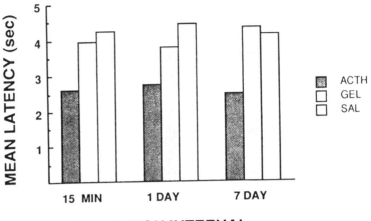

RETENTION INTERVAL

Figure 1.2. Active avoidance performance in animals tested after one of several intervals following an extinction treatment. The open bars represent the performance of animals given saline prior to test, the dark bars the performance of animals given ACTH, and the light bars the performance of animals given gel. Data redrawn from Ahlers, Richardson, West, & Riccio, 1989.

ther saline or the vehicle gel show that this long lasting effect was not due to changes in the baseline response (e.g., spontaneous recovery).

Does ACTH Have to be a Component of the Memory in Order to Attenuate Extinction-Induced Performance Decrements?

As previously stated, a basic assumption of our work is that exogenous ACTH is effective in attenuating performance decrements (due to such things as amnestic treatments or the Kamin effect) because endogenous ACTH is released at the time of training and,thus, becomes part of the original memory. If this assumption is correct then exogenous ACTH should not attenuate the effects of an extinction treatment for animals in which endogenous ACTH was not released at training. If, however, ACTH influences attentional processes or the motivational significance of environmental stimuli (see Bohus & deWeid, 1981), then it should be effective whether or not it was present at training.

To examine these issues adult male rats were trained to fear the black compartment of a black-white shuttle box with a Pavlovian differential conditioning procedure (Ahlers & Richardson, 1985). Some animals (3 groups) were given a synthetic glucocorticoid, 400 ug/kg dexamethasone phosphate (Decadron; Merck Sharp & Dohme), 2 hr prior to training. This dose of dexamethasone (DEX) has been reported as being effective in blocking the release of ACTH in rats in response to shock (Beatty, Beatty, Bowman, & Gilchrist, 1970; Kasper-Pandi, Hansing, & Usher, 1970). Therefore, ACTH *should not* be a component of the training memory for these subjects. Animals in two additional groups were given saline injections prior to training. For these subjects, ACTH *should* be a component of the training memory.

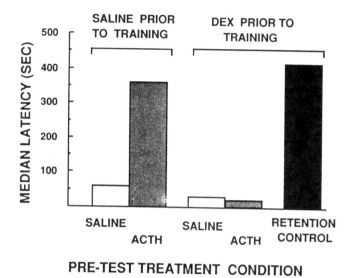

Figure 1.3. Median latency (in seconds) to enter the black compartment of a black-white shuttle box where shock had been previously administered. Performance of animals that were trained, but not extinguished, is represented by the filled bar. Performance of animals that were given ACTH prior to test are represented by the gray bars while that of animals given saline are represented by the open bars. Data redrawn from Ahlers & Richardson, 1985.

On the day following training four groups of animals received a 90 s non-reinforced extinction exposure to the black compartment. Two of these groups had been given saline prior to training while two had been given DEX. The subjects in the fifth group (which had also been given DEX prior to training) served to assess any effects of the drug on learning. These subjects were not extinguished, but were trained and tested for retention of the fear memory.

The retention test occurred 48 hours after training for all subjects. A passive avoidance procedure was again used to test retention. Fifteen minutes prior to testing two groups of animals that had undergone extinction were given 4 IU of ACTH while the other two groups of animals that had undergone the extinction treatment were given saline. One group in each of these pretest drug conditions had been given saline prior to training (so ACTH should be a component of their memory) while the other had been given DEX (so ACTH should *not* be a component of their memory). Those animals that were trained, but not extinguished, were not injected prior to test. The results of this experiment are depicted in Figure 1.3. The first two bars in this figure represent the performance of subjects given saline prior to training. The data of these two groups show that exogenous administration of ACTH shortly prior to testing alleviated the extinction-induced performance decrements. That is, animals given saline prior to test were less fearful of the black compartment than were the retention controls, but those given ACTH performed comparably to the retention control condition.

In contrast to this pattern of results, however, was the behavior of the animals given DEX prior to training. For these animals (3rd and 4th bars in Figure 1.3) pretest injection of ACTH had no effect on performance of the avoidance response. Whether these animals were given ACTH or saline they exhibited little avoidance of the black compartment. This failure of exogenous ACTH to alleviate the extinction-induced performance decrements cannot be explained by the notion that DEX prior to training interferes in some fashion with the learning of the response. The performance of those subjects given DEX prior to training, but not extinguished (5th bar in Figure 1.3), makes clear the fact that this treatment did not adversely affect learning. These findings show that it is indeed necessary for endogenous ACTH to have been released at the time of training in order for pretest injections of ACTH to attenuate performance deficits induced by extinction.

These experiments on recovery from extinction are complemented by a recent study on the role of exogenous ACTH in reversing experimentally-induced retrograde amnesia. As mentioned earlier, several investigators have found that administration of ACTH at testing substantially alleviates the memory loss produced by electroconvulsive shock or reduction of body temperature (hypothermia). The effectiveness of other reminder treatments, such as noncontingent footshock or re-exposure to the amnestic agent itself, may also depend in part on ACTH release. Accordingly, these manipulations should be less potent if endogenous ACTH is not present during the training/amnestic treatment. In order to block the release of ACTH, Santucci, Schroeder, and Riccio (1987) administered dexamethasone to rats prior to one-trial punishment training. The amnestic treatment, deep body cooling, was applied immediately after training and subjects were tested one day later. Dexamethasone had little apparent effect on retention in non-cooled animals, nor on the magnitude of amnesia in the hypothermia condition. However, the drug did blunt the effectiveness of several reminder treatments. Thus, the level of memory recovery induced by ACTH, noncontingent footshock, or re-exposure to the amnestic agent was less in subjects receiving dexamethasone prior to training than in those receiving saline. (Some reversal of amnesia, particularly with noncontingent footshock and re-cooling, might be expected, of course, on the basis of other stimulus attributes available as retrieval cues). The attenuated recovery observed by Santucci et al. (1987) is consistent with the notion that in order for exogenous ACTH to be effective as a "reminder" the hormone must also have been present during the encoding of the target memory.

SOME THEORETICAL CONSIDERATIONS

These three experiments provide strong evidence that exogenous ACTH prior to testing attenuates extinction-induced performance deficits. This basic outcome was consistent with our predictions, but as is often the case, some aspects of the findings were theoretically awkward. For example, the long term recovery from extinction produced by ACTH administration was unexpected and the mechanism involved is not yet clear. What does seem clear, however, is that our original working hypothesis, which viewed the recovery as based upon a state- dependent-like process, is untenable in light of the enhanced performance obtained 24 hr (or more) after ACTH injection. There is no evidence to suggest that the internal state produced by exogenous ACTH is still present after such long intervals, but several other possibilities can be entertained.

First, the durability of the recovery may represent a fairly direct physiological change in the organism resulting from ACTH administration. Although this interpretation is ad hoc, several recent findings do reveal surprisingly long term effects of acute hormone administration. For example, epinephrine, like ACTH, has a very limited biological half-life. However Welsh and Gold (1986) observed that epinephrine retarded the rate of onset of induced brain seizures for at least 24 hr following administration of the hormone. More directly pertinent, Hendrie (1988) has reported that a single injection of ACTH enhances the analgesic potency of morphine, and that this outcome occurred despite a three day interval between injection of the peptide and testing. Hendrie also found that ACTH impaired the development of tolerance to morphine for 12 days after administration of the hormone. While the mechanism for these persistent effects is not known either, the findings reveal another type of long term consequence of exogenous ACTH administration.

A second, behaviorally oriented, explanation for the long-term recovery focuses on the potential role of conditioning an ACTH response to implicit (contextual) cues. Thus, stimuli such as handling, which regularly precede avoidance trials during training, presumably become part of the stimulus complex associated with the elicitation of fear and ACTH release. Although these contextual cues would also be weakened during the extinction phase, their presence at the time of ACTH injection could permit rapid re-acquisition of their association with the internal attributes of fear. In the absence of further extinction trials, this conditioned association, like other learning, would persist over relatively long time intervals. At the time of testing then, the contextual cues would be expected to elicit fear and enhanced avoidance (i.e., recovery). In short, according to this learning explanation, the enduring effects of ACTH administration are mediated by stimuli common to avoidance training and the injection episode. An obvious prediction (not yet tested) is that repeated exposure to contextual cues alone (e.g., handling) following the injection would reduce or eliminate the recovery effect.

A third, and perhaps the simplest, explanation for the durable recovery from extinction is that in this situation administration of ACTH momentarily re-creates sufficient attributes of the training situation to produce retrieval of the aversion episode, much as would re-exposure to the US. For example, recovery from experimentally-induced retrograde amnesia is seen for several days following a single noncontingent footshock (Miller & Springer, 1972). More directly pertinent is a "reinstatement" finding reported by Rescorla and Heth (1975). Rats receiving a single unsignalled footshock following extinction of conditioned emotional responses showed substantial recovery of suppression to the CS when tested the next day (however, see Callan, McAllister, & McAllister, 1984). Since the internal changes produced by a brief footshock presumably do not persist for more than a few hours, the recovery of performance after long intervals appears to be based upon reactivation of critical stimulus attributes permitting subsequent retrieval of memory. Such a "priming" effect of a reminder can substantially outlast internal contextual cues. From this perspective, the question of why ACTH induces long lasting recovery from extinction may be misdirected. Perhaps the unusual outcome is that attenuation of amnesia with ACTH is so time-limited (see Mactutus, Smith, & Riccio, 1980; cf. deWeid, 1966). Obviously, extinction and amnesia involve different processes leading to degraded performance and thus what constitutes the most effective reminders in each paradigm need not be identical. As noted by Bohus (1982, p. 149) "Overall, it is not unreasonable to assume that the influences of ACTH-related peptides on preretention treatment involve different mechanisms in nonamnesic and amnesic rats."

It is worth noting that ACTH-induced recovery from extinction may share a conceptual similarity with certain findings on transfer of control of avoidance responding. In a now classic study of avoidance, Solomon and Turner (1962) showed that control of instrumental avoidance responses could be shifted to new stimuli which had acquired fear eliciting properties through strictly Pavlovian (i.e., response independent) manipulations. Presumably, conditioned fear, which provided motivational and cue functions, was established during avoidance training. Subsequent introduction of a different fear eliciting stimulus (CS+) that had never been presented during avoidance training was nevertheless sufficient to produce vigorous avoidance behaviors.

Of particular relevance to our present concerns is an important extension of that finding by Overmier and Bull (1969). These investigators eliminated the original avoidance behavior by repeated extinction trials. However, the avoidance behavior resumed when a separately conditioned Pavlovian fear-eliciting stimulus was introduced. Thus, the re-elicitation of fear (and its stimulus attributes) was capable of inducing recovery from extinction, even though the new exteroceptive stimulus (CS+) had never been a signal for avoidance. From the present perspective, exogenous administration of ACTH prior to testing would play a role similar to that of a new CS+. By reinstating the internal concomitants previously associated with avoidance responding, ACTH administration can lead to recovery of the extinguished response.

We believe that this relationship between ACTH and the recovery of fear motivated behavior may have interesting implications for clinical situations. For example, once a phobic ("fear") response has been eliminated ("extinguished") in a client, it seems plausible that an unrelated stressful event (and the release of endogenous ACTH) could lead to reinstatement of the original fear behavior. Such a relapse, while appearing to be "spontaneous" and independent of relevant stimuli, would in fact represent the role of an internal state as a cue. While the prospect that a broad range of life circumstances could undermine the therapists' (and clients') goals is discouraging, perhaps something is gained if to be forewarned is to be forearmed.

These results also share some similarity to the innovative work of Bouton and his associates on the function of context in extinction of conditioned fear stimuli (for a review see Bouton, 1988). Bouton has found that the associative value of the test context (either neutral or fear-eliciting) plays little role in the animal's response to a non-extinguished stimulus: Fear to the CS+ is about the same whether testing occurs in a fear-eliciting or neutral context. However, the test context has a critical role in the animal's response to an extinguished stimulus. That is, animals do not show fear to a previously extinguished fear stimulus if it is presented in a neutral context, but when the same extinguished stimulus is presented in a fear-eliciting context animals will display fear responses to that stimulus. Bouton maintains that an extinguished stimulus is particularly ambiguous (because of its varied history) and the animal relies on the test context to determine the stimulus's current status. In the present work, it could be said that exogenous ACTH is serving as a context to disambiguate the meaning of the black compartment. The only difficulty with this account is the failure to find an effect of time between injection of ACTH and test which this view would seem to demand.

ENHANCEMENT OF EXTINCTION BY ACTH

That ACTH is an effective reminder treatment in alleviating extinction-induced performance decrements seems clear from the studies reviewed. As stated in the Introduction, however, ACTH might cause an *enhancement* of extinction in some situations. In this section we describe research and theory exploring this possibility.

A question of continuing interest to learning theory and clinical therapy concerns how best to eliminate avoidance behavior (symptoms). Some years ago, Page and Hall (1953) and Solomon, Kamin, and Wynne (1953) independently conducted experiments in which animals that had undergone avoidance conditioning were physically prevented from making the instrumental response for several trials. During the response-prevention ("blocking") phase no US (i.e., shock) deliveries occurred. This "reality testing" technique, as Solomon et al. (1953) referred to it, proved to hasten subsequent extinction of the instrumental response. The facilitated extinction effect is robust, and a number of studies exploring the parameters of the phenomenon have been reported (Baum, 1969; for review see Mineka, 1979). One puzzling finding, difficult to incorporate into a straight-forward two-process interpretation, has been the observation of a substantial amount of fear remaining after the response prevention manipulation (Coulter, Riccio, & Page, 1969; Page, 1955). The finding that the response prevention condition has higher "residual fear" than controls after both groups have reached the same criterion for avoidance extinction, has suggested to some that processes in addition to Pavlovian fear extinction are involved (Coulter et al., 1969; Marrazo, Riccio, & Riley, 1974; for a review see Riccio & Silvestri, 1973), although this view has come under strong challenge (e.g., Bersh & Miller, 1975; Monti & Smith, 1976; Shipley, Mock, & Levis, 1971). In either event, it seems reasonable to suppose that an even greater facilitation of extinction might be achieved if the putative underlying fear motivation were further weakened. Toward that general goal several studies have administered muscle relaxants or tranquilizers to subjects prior to the blocking exposure. This approach might be thought of as akin to "counterconditioning" fear by supplanting it with the incompatible response of "relaxation." Unfortunately, neither muscle relaxants nor tranquilizers in conjunction with response prevention seem to hasten the elimination of avoidance beyond that of response prevention alone (Baum, Roy, & Leclerc, 1985; Gorman, Dyak, & Reid, 1979; Kamano, 1972).

An alternative strategy is suggested by the notion that the organism's internal state at the time of training is an important attribute of the original memory. Extinction of the fear should be increased by exposing subjects to the feared stimulus while they are in the same internal state that was present when the fear was acquired. It is certainly the case that the subject was not relaxed or "tranquil" when the memory was formed. Therefore, by coupling administration of ACTH with conditioned fear stimuli during blocking, the memorial representation of the original traumatic episode might be enhanced. This priming of memory might permit more complete extinction of fear during the CS-alone blocking exposure. One might liken this to reward magnitude contrast effects where the behavioral outcome is a function of the disparity between old and new levels of reinforcement (Flaherty, 1982). Similarly, when intense fear to a CS+ is induced but not followed by aversive consequences, perhaps the resulting extinction is greater than when a weak fear response to the stimulus is followed by nonreinforcement. Duration of extinction exposure is likely to be critical, however, as some theoretical models as well as empirical findings suggest that a very brief exposure to a fear CS may exacerbate the fear or serve as a reminder (e.g., Eysenck & Kelley, 1987; Rohrbaugh & Riccio, 1970; Silvestri, Rohrbaugh, & Riccio, 1970). It should be noted that the relationship between fear intensity during nonreinforced CS exposure and effectiveness of the extinction manipulation cannot be easily assessed in groups which receive avoidance training under different levels of shock (US), as this confounds learning strength with expression of fear.

Extinction of the Avoidance Response

In the following work, all groups received identical training so any differential weakening of performance resulting from manipulation of intensity of fear evocation in extinction cannot be attributed to differences in degree of original learning. To manipulate the severity of fear elicited during the extinction of an avoidance response, Richardson, Riccio, and Ress (1988) used injections of either epinephrine or ACTH to mimic the attributes of the original stressful learning. In one experiment, adult male rats were trained on a one-way active avoidance response. Following training, subjects in 4 groups were given an extinction treatment. Again, a response-prevention procedure was used to extinguish the active avoidance response (see p. 7). However, in this experiment the parameters for the response blocking trials were such that very little extinction was expected to result from this treatment. Shortly prior (15-20 min) to the extinction treatment animals in three groups were given either 4 IU ACTH, 8 IU ACTH, or saline. A fourth group was injected with ACTH 1 hr after the response prevention trials. A fifth and final group was not extinguished after training.

Twenty-four hours after the extinction session all animals were tested for retention of the avoidance response. During testing, animals were given 10 trials on which their latency to avoid (maximum of 5s) was recorded. No shocks occurred during test. The median latency to respond on the 10 test trials is depicted in Figure 1.4. As was expected, the parameters chosen for the response blocking trials produced very little extinction. That is, animals given saline prior to response blocking were no different from animals not given the extinction treatment at all (compare the first and fifth bars in Figure 1.4). However, if animals were given 8 IU of ACTH prior to the response blocking procedure then the effect of the extinction treatment was dramatically increased (the 3rd bar in Figure 1.4). That is, animals injected with this dose of ACTH shortly prior to the extinction treatment exhibited significantly poorer avoidance responding when tested the following day. Clearly, those animals given 8 IU of ACTH prior to the response blocking trials were more affected by the extinction treatment than were animals in any of the other groups. It would appear that the original memory was made more susceptible to the effects of the extinction treatment by virtue of the fact that it was more completely retrieved at the time of the response blocking trials. This outcome appears to bear out a recent prediction made independently by Eysenck and Kelley (1987). Focusing on the neuromodulatory effects of ACTH these investigators predicted that with appropriate parameters the hormone should facilitate the effectiveness of an extinction treatment.

Another experiment in the study by Richardson et al. (1988) attempted to determine whether ACTH enhanced the response- prevention effect by more completely weakening fear to the CS, as a two-process view might predict. Two days following the response-prevention treatment, food deprived subjects

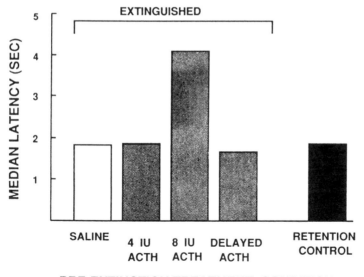

Figure 1.4. Active avoidance performance in animals following response-prevention. Performance of animals that were given ACTH are represented by the gray bars while that of animals given saline is represented by the open bar. All injections occurred 15-20 min prior to response-prevention except for one group of animals that received ACTH 1 hour following the response prevention treatment. One group of animals (represented by the filled bar) were trained, but not extinguished. Data redrawn from Richardson, Riccio, & Ress, 1988.

were tested for fear by measuring the latency with which they would return to the previously shocked compartment ("CS+") to obtain food. This residual-fear test was conducted in lieu of the avoidance response test. Although the magnitude of the difference was small, the data suggested slightly greater reduction of fear in the group receiving ACTH during blocking. That is, animals given ACTH during response blocking entered the previously shocked compartment to obtain food quicker than did the other animals.

A more detailed examination is needed of the status of Pavlovian fear, independent of the instrumental avoidance response, but the finding that extinction of avoidance can be enhanced by administration of ACTH prior to response-prevention has implications that deserve further comment and speculation. First, the outcome suggests that the effectiveness of an extinction exposure following aversive learning may depend upon the extent to which memory for the original episode is reactivated. Would a non-reinforced CS exposure be more effective as an extinction treatment if preceded by other behavioral manipulations (such as noncontingent footshock) designed to induce the internal state associated with fear conditioning? Alternatively, does an extinction exposure reduce fear more if given immediately after a traumatic episode, when memory is presumably still active, rather than after a delay? (Is there some folk wisdom in the old saw about getting right back on the horse after a fall? If so, might the value be found in the greater efficacy of extinction, rather than in preventing "incubation"?)

Second, the possible contribution of the fear state during extinction, or what might be thought of as the redintegration of the aversive memory, seems largely to have been ignored in learning research. In part, this neglect probably reflects the historical (S-R) origins of learning theory which focused on stimulus parameters such as frequency or duration of CS exposure, and, in part, on the difficulties of specification of this class of independent variable. Nevertheless, the role of the activation and expression of fear during extinction may have clinical as well as theoretical import. Foa and Kozak (1986) have recently reviewed a variety of evidence from the clinically relevant human literature showing the importance of "fear evocation" in elimination of anxiety-related disorders (but see Matthews, 1978). For example, using psychophysiological measures with mildly phobic subjects, Lang, Levin, Miller, and Kozak (1983) have found that those experiencing greater arousal during exposure to phobic material also show the most extinction. While outcomes dependent on individual difference characteristics can be difficult to interpret, the theme is at least consistent with the present experimental result.

Finally, these considerations may bear on the issue of the use of tranquilizers during psychotherapy. Previous research on drug-induced dissociation of memory ("state dependent memory") suggests that new learning achieved while the subject (client) is calmed by tranquilizers may fail to transfer to conditions without the drug, thus limiting the usefulness of potential therapeutic gains. However, as the minor tranquilizers are considered to be relatively weak state-dependent agents, dissociated learning may not be a major problem. In contrast, a very different issue is raised if the success of extinction depends upon the intensity of fear evocation. The value of confronting anxiety provoking stimuli (i.e., extinction exposure) could be compromised if the client's emotional response is attenuated by the influence of tranquilizers. Breuer and Freud's admonition with respect to their treatment of Anna O. may bear repeating: "Recollection without affect almost invariably produces no results" (Breuer & Freud, 1893, p. 6). A more contemporary version of this principle is seen in implosive therapy where Stampfl (1970, p. 200) has stated that a basic aim is to place the client in a situation involving "exposure to stimuli that will elicit negative affect."

EPILOGUE

Although this chapter has focused on ACTH and phenomena related to extinction, we view these findings as part of the more general research issue of the role of endogenous substances as cues in learning and memory retrieval. Razran's (1961) important article reviewing Soviet research on Pavlovian interoceptive conditioning called attention to the fact that mechanical and thermal stimuli could serve as CSs to elicit a variety of responses. Despite the important implication that internal stimuli could gain control over behavior, relatively little attention has been paid to other internal cues, such as hormonal changes, as associative or contextual stimuli. That hormones might be involved in learning has not been totally ignored, of course, but the major emphasis in intact animals has been on their function as unconditioned stimuli eliciting responses (e.g., Siegel, 1975) or upon their role as modulators of memory processes (McGaugh, 1983). Intriguing as these questions are, they are quite different from that of whether hormonally related stimuli function as contextual or conditioned stimuli.

Stimuli present during learning but irrelevant to the reinforcement contingencies often play an important role as "contextual cues" for memory retrieval (Spear, 1978). The phenomena of state-dependent retention (SDR) seen with many drugs provides the example "par excellence" of background interoceptive stimuli being necessary for later memory retrieval. A change in drug state between training and testing (e.g., drug to no drug) can markedly impair retention; conversely, retention is excellent when the drug states match at training and test. Since Overton's seminal contributions more than 20 years ago (Overton, 1964), an enormous research literature has developed on SDR and the related topic of drug-based discrimination learning (Overton, 1982, 1985). Although the vast majority of SDR research has been with drugs, a few studies have asked whether hormones might have state-dependent properties. One of the first such studies was reported by Stewart, Krebs, and Kaczender (1967) who showed that a steroid hormone, progesterone, could serve as a discriminative cue in a T-maze escape task. Ebner, Richardson, and Riccio (1981) later extended this finding to a state-dependent paradigm. Rats conditioned to fear distinctive apparatus cues after administration of progesterone failed to passively avoid these cues 24 hrs later unless reinjected with the hormone. Under similar conditions insulin has recently been found to have state dependent effects (Santucci, Schroeder, Reister, & Riccio, 1986). With respect to stress-hormones, Gray (1975) provided evidence that exogenous ACTH during training had a state-dependent effect. As mentioned earlier, Izquierdo and his colleagues (Izquierdo, 1984) have shown that state-dependent modulation of memory can occur even post-training, if ACTH or epinephrine are administered immediately after the training trial.

These studies reveal that hormones, like drugs, can function as internal contextual cues. However, the doses used were typically at a more pharmacological than physiological level. Thus, an intriguing question remains: Does dissociative memory also result from naturally occurring shifts in hormonal states? To date, there is little evidence that naturally occurring hormonal changes produce SDR effects. Using stages of the estrus cycle, or stages of pregnancy, as endogenous sources of incongruity between training and testing, Ebner et al. (1981) failed to find convincing evidence of memory dissociation for fear conditioning (see also Morilak, Orndoff, Riccio, & Richardson, 1983). As this negative finding may have been at least partly due to the strong emotional reaction to footshock, Costanzo, Riccio, and Kissinger (1987) used a taste conditioning task in which the target flavor was paired with quinine to induce a shift in preference. Some evidence of reduced retention was found when a mismatch in estrous cycles at training and testing was induced, but the effect was quite weak. The clearest examples of the potential SDR effects of naturally occurring hormonal changes can be found in the waxing and waning of retention reported with circadian rhythms (Holloway & Wansley, 1973; Stroebel, 1967) and in the Kamin effect (Kamin, 1957; Klein & Spear, 1970) although non-hormonal variables are probably involved as well.

Although much remains to be done it is clear that an animal's hormonal state has an important role in learning and memory. How organisms adjust to changing environmental contingencies and how they "update" their memories for aversive episodes can be greatly influenced by their internal state. A more complete understanding of how these internal states influence such cognitive activities as learning and memory will have profound theoretical and practical implications.

ACKNOWLEDGMENTS

This research was supported by NIMH grant MH 37535 to D.C.R. During preparation of this chapter R.R. was supported by U.S. Public Health Services Grant MH-01562 to Byron A. Campbell.

REFERENCES

Ahlers, S.T., & Richardson, R. (1985). Administration of dexamethasone prior to training blocks ACTH-induced recovery of an extinguished avoidance response. *Behavioral Neuroscience, 99*, 760-764.

Ahlers, S.T., Richardson, R., West, C., & Riccio, D.C. (1989). ACTH produces long-lasting recovery following partial extinction of an active avoidance response. *Behavioral and Neural Biology, 51*, 102-107.

Baum, M. (1969). Extinction of an avoidance response: Some parametric investigations. *Canadian Journal of Psychology, 23*, 1-10.

Baum, M. (1970). Extinction of avoidance responding through response prevention (flooding) in rats. *Psychological Bulletin, 74*, 276-284.

Baum, M., Roy, S., & Leclerc, R. (1985). Failure of a peripheral muscle relaxant (suxomethonium bromide) to increase the efficacy of flooding (response prevention) in rats. *Behavioral Research & Therapy, 23*, 361-364.

Beatty, P.A., Beatty, W.B., Bowman, R.E., & Gilchrist, J.C. (1970). The effects of ACTH, adrenalectomy and dexamethasone on the acquisition of an avoidance response in rats. *Physiology & Behavior, 5*, 939-944.

Beckwith, B.E., & Sandman, C.A. (1978). Behavioral influences of the neuropeptides ACTH and MSH: A methodological review. *Neuroscience and Biobehavioral Reviews, 2* , 311-338.

Bersh, P., & Miller, S.K. (1975). The influence of shock during response prevention upon resistance to extinction of an avoidance response. *Animal Learning & Behavior, 3*, 140-142.

Bohus, B. (1982). Neuropeptides and Memory. In R.L. Isaacson & N.E. Spear (Eds.), *The expression of knowledge.* New York: Plenum.

Bohus, B., & deWeid, D. (1966). Inhibitory and facilitory effect of two related peptides on extinction of avoidance behavior. *Science, 153*, 318-320.

Bohus, B., & deWeid, D. (1981). Actions of ACTH- and MSH-like peptides on learning, performance, and retention. In J.L. Martinez, Jr., R.A. Jensen, R.B. Messing, H. Rigter, & J.L. McGaugh (Eds.), *Endogenous peptides and learning and memory processes.* New York: Academic Press.

Bouton, M.E. (1988). Context and ambiguity in the extinction of emotional learning: Implications for exposure therapy. *Behavioral Research & Therapy, 26*, 137-149.

Breuer, J., & Freud, S. (1893). On the psychical mechanism of hysterical phenomena: Preliminary communication. In *The standard edition of the complete psychological works of Sigmund Freud*, Vol. II. London: The Hogarth Press.

Callan, E.J., McAllister, W.R., & McAllister, D.E. (1984). Investigations of the reinstatement of extinguished fear. *Learning and Motivation, 15*, 302-320.

Carlson, N.R. (1981). *Physiology of behavior.* Boston, MA: Allyn and Bacon.

Concannon, J.T., Riccio, D.C., Maloney, R., & McKelvey, J. (1980). ACTH mediation of learned fear: Blockade by naloxone and naltrexone. *Physiology & Behavior, 25*, 977- 979.

Costanzo, D., Riccio, D.C., & Kissinger, S. (1987). State-*dependent retention produced with estrus in rats.* Paper presented at the annual meeting of the Midwestern Psychological Association, Chicago, IL.

Coulter, X., Riccio, D.C., & Page, H.A. (1969). Effects of blocking an instrumental avoidance response: Facilitated extinction but persistence of "fear." *Journal of Comparative and Physiological Psychology, 68*, 377-381.

DeVito, W.J., & Brush, F.R. (1984). Effects of ACTH and vasopressin on extinction: Evidence for opiate mediation. *Behavioral Neuroscience, 98*, 59-71.

deWeid, D. (1966). Inhibitory effects of ACTH and related peptides on extinction of conditioned avoidance behavior in rats. *Proceedings of the Society for Experimental Biology and Medicine, 122*, 28-32.

deWeid, D. (1970). Peptides and behavior. *Life Sciences, 20*, 195-204.

deWeid, D., & Bohus, B. (1966). Long term and short term effects on retention of a conditioned avoidance response in rats by treatment with long acting pitressin and α MSH. *Nature, 212*, 1484-1486.

Ebner, D.L., Richardson, R., & Riccio, D.C. (1981). Ovarian hormones and retention of learned fear in rats. *Behavioral and Neural Biology, 33*, 45-58.

Estes, W.K. (1955). Statistical theory of spontaneous recovery and regression. *Psychological Review, 62*, 145-154.

Eysenck, H.J., & Kelley, M.J. (1987). The interaction of neurohormones with Pavlovian A and Pavlovian B conditioning in the causation of neurosis, extinction, and incubation of anxiety. In G. Davey (Ed.), *Cognitive processes and Pavlovian conditioning in humans.* New York: John Wiley.

Flaherty, C.F. (1982). Incentive contrast: A review of behavioral changes following shifts in reward. *Animal Learning & Behavior, 10,* 409-440.

Foa, E.B., & Kozak, M.J. (1986). Emotional processing of fear: Exposure to corrective information. *Psychological Bulletin, 99,* 20-35.

Gold, P.E., & Delanoy, R.L. (1981). ACTH modulation of memory storage processing. In J. Martinez, R.A. Jensen, R.B. Messing, H. Rigter, & J.L. McGaugh (Eds.), *Endogenous peptides and learning and memory processes.* New York: Academic Press.

Gold, P.E., & van Buskirk, R.B. (1976). Enhancement and impairment of memory processes with post-trial injections of adrenocorticotropic hormone. *Behavioral Biology, 16,* 387- 400.

Gorman, J.E., Dyak, J.D., & Reid, L.D. (1979). Methods of deconditioning persisting avoidance: Diazepam as an adjunct to response prevention. *Bulletin of the Psychonomic Society, 14,* 46-48.

Gray, P. (1975). Effect of adrenocorticotropic hormone on conditioned avoidance in rats interpreted as state dependent learning. *Journal of Comparative and Physiological Psychology, 88,* 281-284.

Haroutunian, V., & Riccio, D.C. (1979). Drug-induced "arousal" and the effectiveness of CS exposure in the reinstatement of memory. *Behavioral and Neural Biology, 26,* 115-120.

Hendrie, C.A. (1988). ACTH: A single pretreatment enhances the analgesic efficacy of and prevents the development of tolerance to morphine. *Physiology & Behavior, 42,* 41-45.

Holloway, F.A., & Wansley, R.A. (1973). Multiple retention deficits at periodic intervals after passive avoidance learning. *Science, 80,* 208-210.

Izquierdo, I. (1984). Endogenous state dependency: Memory depends on the relation between the neurohumoral and hormonal states present after training and at the time of testing. In G. Lynch, J.L. McGaugh, & N.M. Weinberger (Eds.), *Neurobiology of learning and memory.* New York: Guilford.

Izquierdo, I., & Dias, R.D. (1983). Memory as a state dependent phenomenon: Role of ACTH and epinephrine. *Behavioral and Neural Biology, 38,* 144-149.

Kamano, D.K. (1972). Using drugs to modify the effect of response prevention on avoidance extinction. *Behavioral Research & Therapy, 10,* 367-370.

Kamin. L.J. (1957). Retention of an incompletely learned avoidance response. *Journal of Comparative and Physiological Psychology, 50,* 457-460.

Kasper-Pandi, P., Hansing, R., & Usher, D.R. (1970). The effect of dexamethasone blockade of ACTH release on avoidance learning. *Physiology & Behavior, 5,* 361-363.

Keyes, J.B. (1974). Effects of ACTH on ECS-produced amnesia of a passive avoidance task. *Physiological Psychology, 2,* 307- 309.

Klein, S.B. (1972). Adrenal-pituitary influence in reactivation of avoidance-memory in the rat after intermediate intervals. *Journal of Comparative and Physiological Psychology, 79,* 341-359.

Klein, S.B., & Spear, N.E. (1970). Forgetting by the rat after intermediate intervals ("Kamin effect") as retrieval failure. *Journal of Comparative and Physiological Psychology, 71,* 165-170.

Lang, P.J., Levin, D.N., Miller, G.A., & Kozak, M.J. (1983). Fear behavior, fear imagery, and the psychophysiology of emotions: The problem of affective response integration. *Journal of Abnormal Psychology, 92,* 276-306.

Leshner, A. I. (1978). *An introduction to behavioral endocrinology.* New York: Oxford University Press.

Levine, S., Smotherman, W.P., & Hennesy, J.W. (1977). Pituitary-adrenal hormones and learned taste aversion. In L.H. Miller, C.A. Sandman, & A.J. Kastin (Eds.), *Neuropeptide influence on the brain and behavior.* New York: Raven Press.

Mactutus, C.F., Ferek, J.M., & Riccio, D.C. (1980). Amnesia induced by hyperthermia: An unusually profound, yet reversible, memory loss. *Behavioral and Neural Biology, 30,* 260-277.

Mactutus, C.F., Smith, R.F., & Riccio, D.C. (1980). Extending the duration of ACTH-induced memory reactivation in an amnestic paradigm. *Physiology & Behavior, 24,* 541-546.

Marrazo, M.J., Riccio, D.C., & Riley, J. (1974). Effects of Pavlovian conditioned stimulus-unconditioned stimulus pairings during avoidance response-prevention trials in rats. *Journal of Comparative and Physiological Psychology, 86,* 96-100.

Matthews, A. (1978). Fear-reduction research and clinical phobias. *Psychological Bulletin, 85,* 390-404.

McGaugh, J.L. (1983). Hormonal influences on memory. *Annual Review of Psychology, 34,* 297-323.

Miller, R.R., & Springer, A.D. (1972). Induced recovery of memory in rats following electroconvulsive shock. *Physiology & Behavior, 8,* 645-651.

Mineka, S. (1979). The role of fear in theories of avoidance learning, flooding, and extinction. *Psychological Bulletin, 86,* 985-1010.

Mirsky, A.F., & Orren, M.M. (1977). Attention. In L.H. Miller, C.A. Sandman, & A.J. Kastin (Eds.), *Neuropeptide influences on the brain and behavior.* New York: Raven Press.

Monti, P.M., & Smith, N.F. (1976). Residual fear of the conditioned stimulus as a function of response prevention after avoidance or classical defensive conditioning in the rat. *Journal of Experimental Psychology: General, 105,* 148-162.

Morilak, D.A., Orndoff, R.K., Riccio, D.C., & Richardson, R. (1983). Persistence of flavor neophobia as an indicator of state-dependent retention induced by pentobarbital, stress, and estrus. *Behavioral and Neural Biology, 38,* 47-60.

Overmier, J.B., & Bull, J.A. (1969). On the independence of stimulus control of avoidance. *Journal of Experimental Psychology, 79,* 464-467.

Overton, D.A. (1964). State-dependent or "dissociated" learning produced with pentobarbital. *Journal of Comparative and Physiological Psychology, 57,* 3-12.

Overton, D.A. (1982). Memory retrieval failures produced by changes in drug states. In R.L. Isaacson & N.E. Spear (Eds.), *The expression of knowledge.* New York: Plenum.

Overton, D.A. (1985). Contextual stimulus effects of drugs and internal states. In P.D. Balsam & A. Tomie (Eds.), *Context and learning.* Hillsdale, NJ: Lawrence Erlbaum Associates.

Page, H.A. (1955). The facilitation of experimental extinction by response prevention as a function of the acquisition of a new response. *Journal of Comparative and Physiological Psychology, 48,* 14-16.

Page, H.A., & Hall, J.F. (1953). Experimental extinction as a function of prevention of a response. *Journal of Comparative and Physiological Psychology, 46,* 33-44.

Razran, G. (1961). The observable unconscious and the inferable conscious in current Soviet psychophysiology: Interoceptive conditioning, semantic conditioning, and the orienting reflex. *Psychological Review, 68,* 81-147.

Reith, M.E.A., & Neidle, A. (1981). Breakdown and fate of ACTH and MSH. *Pharmacology & Therapeutics, 12,* 449-461.

Rescorla, R.A., & Heth, C.D. (1975). Reinstatement of fear to an extinguished conditioned stimulus. *Journal of Experimental Psychology: Animal Behavior Processes, 1,* 88-96.

Riccio, D.C., & Concannon, J.T. (1981). ACTH and the reminder phenomena. In J. Martinez, R.A. Jensen, R.B. Messing, H. Rigter, & J.L. McGaugh (Eds.), *Endogenous peptides and learning and memory processes.* New York: Academic Press.

Riccio, D.C., & Haroutunian, V. (1979). Some approaches to the alleviation of ontogenetic memory deficits. In N.E. Spear & B.A. Campbell, (Eds.), *Ontogeny of learning and memory.* Hillsdale, NJ: Lawrence Erlbaum Associates.

Riccio, D.C., & Silvestri, R. (1973). Extinction of avoidance behavior and the problem of residual fear. *Behavior Research & Therapy, 11,* 1-9.

Richardson, R., Riccio, D.C., & Devine, L. (1984). ACTH-induced recovery of extinguished avoidance responding. *Physiological Psychology, 12,* 184-192.

Richardson, R., Riccio, D.C., & Ress, J. (1988). Extinction of avoidance through response prevention: Enhancement by administration of epinephrine or ACTH. *Behavior Research & Therapy, 26,* 23-32.

Rigter, H., Van Riezen, H., & deWeid, D. (1974). The effects of ACTH- and vasopressin-analogues on CO_2-induced retrograde amnesia in rats. *Physiology & Behavior, 13,* 381-388.

Rohrbaugh, M., & Riccio, D.C. (1970). Paradoxical enhancement of learned fear. *Journal of Abnormal Psychology, 75,* 210-216.

Rosenblatt, J. (1987). Biologic and behavioral factors underlying the onset and maintenance of maternal behavior in the rat. In N.A. Krasnegor, E.M. Blass, M.A. Hofer, & W.P. Smotherman (Eds.), *Perinatal development: A pychobiological perspective.* Orlando, FL: Academic Press.

Santucci, A., Schroeder, H., & Riccio, D.C. (1987). *Suppression of ACTH release blocks memory recovery from hypothermia-induced retrograde amnesia in rats.* Paper presented at the annual meeting of the Eastern Psychological Association, Arlington, VA.

Santucci, A., Schroeder, H., Reister, R., & Riccio, D.C. (1986). *Insulin-induced state dependent retention in rats.* Paper presented at the annual meeting of the Midwestern Psychological Association, Chicago, IL.

Shipley, R.H., Mock, L.A., & Levis, D.J. (1971). Effects of several response prevention procedures on activity, avoidance responding, and conditioned fear in rats. *Journal of Comparative and Physiological Psychology, 77,* 256-270.

Siegel, S. (1975). Conditioning insulin effects. *Journal of Comparative and Physiological Psychology, 89,* 189-199.

Silvestri, R., Rohrbaugh, M., & Riccio, D.C. (1970). Conditions influencing the retention of learned fear in young rats. *Developmental Psychobiology, 2,* 389-395.

Solomon, R.L., Kamin, L.J., & Wynne, L.C. (1953). Traumatic avoidance learning: The outcomes of several extinction procedures with dogs. *Journal of Abnormal and Social Psychology, 48,* 291-302.

Solomon, R.L., & Turner, L.H. (1962). Discriminative classical conditioning in dogs paralyzed by curare can later control discriminative avoidance responses in the normal state. *Psychological Review, 69*, 202-219.

Spear, N.E. (1978). *The processing of memories: Forgetting and retention*. Hillsdale, NJ: Lawrence Erlbaum Associates.

Spear, N.E., & Mueller, C.W. (1984). Consolidation as a function of retrieval. In H. Weingartner & E.S. Parker (Eds.), *Memory consolidation: Psychobiology of cognition*. Hillsdale, NJ: Lawrence Erlbaum Associates.

Stampfl, T.C. (1970). Implosive therapy: An emphasis on covert stimulation. In D.J. Levis (Ed.), *Learning approaches to therapeutic behavior change*. Chicago: Aldine.

Stewart, J., Krebs, W.H., & Kaczender, E. (1967). State- dependent learning produced with steroids. *Nature (London), 216*, 1223-1224.

Stroebel, C.F. (1967). Behavioral aspects of circadian rhythms. In J. Zubin & H.F. Hunt (Eds.), *Comparative psychopathology*. New York: Grune & Stratton.

Underwood, B.J. (1969). Attributes of memory. *Psychological Review, 76*, 559-573.

Welsh, K.A., & Gold, P.E. (1986). Epinephrine proactive retardation of amygdala-kindled epileptogenesis. *Behavioral Neuroscience, 100*, 236-245.

2 Context and Retrieval in Extinction and in Other Examples of Interference in Simple Associative Learning

Mark E. Bouton
University of Vermont

The goal of this chapter is to link together several separate issues in the study of associative learning. One issue is the interpretation of extinction, the loss of responding that occurs when a conditioned stimulus (CS) is presented without the unconditioned stimulus (US) many times following conditioning. A second is how the background of stimulation, or "context," controls behavior in Pavlovian conditioning situations. One of the chapter's main messages is that context and extinction are intimately interrelated. I will suggest that the subject's knowledge about the current context is the main determinant of behavior in extinction, and that the context acts by signaling or retrieving the current relation between the CS and the US. Another major message is that what we know about the relation between context and extinction can be applied to a larger set of problems of which extinction is only an example. I will suggest that the context may play the same role in any Pavlovian "interference paradigm" in which a CS is associated with different events in different phases of the experiment.

Extinction is one of the most fundamental problems in conditioning theory, and there is no shortage of ideas about how it works. However, many views of extinction assume that it involves some degree of unlearning. If conditioning creates a CS-US association, then it is convenient to assume that extinction either destroys that association (e.g., Rescorla & Wagner, 1972) or destroys some aspect of it (e.g., Rescorla & Heth, 1975). However, I will emphasize data indicating that at least some of the original learning survives even prolonged extinction procedures. Under certain conditions the subject will respond as if the CS is still associated with the US. Behavior evoked by an extinguished CS is in fact bi-stable. It is therefore reasonable to suppose that the subject retains memories of both conditioning and extinction in a long-term memory store. What determines behavior in extinction is which memory is accessed or retrieved. After extinction, the CS has two available "meanings," and therefore properties resembling those of an ambiguous word (Bouton, 1984, 1988; Bouton & Bolles, 1985): The response it evokes pivots crucially on its current context (e.g., grizzly bear vs. bear fruit). In what follows, I hope to show that this view can accomodate several interesting features of extinction and perhaps other interference paradigms.

Extinction became a focus of the work in my laboratory as we studied the role of context in determining performance in aversive conditioning. Typically, we used conditioned suppression procedures in which a CS was paired with mild footshock in rats, and its ability to evoke "fear" was indexed by its ability to suppress an operant lever-pressing baseline reinforced by food. The contexts were operationally defined as the apparatuses in which the events were presented; these differed in their location in the lab and in their visual, olfactory, and tactile respects. Such contexts can be strong determinants of the fear the CS evokes; the question is how they actually work. In most of the phenomena we were concerned with, it was sensible to assume that the context was simply a second stimulus present in compound with the target CS (e.g., Rescorla & Wagner, 1972). If CS-context compounds work the way ordinary compounds are expected to (e.g., Rescorla & Wagner, 1972), then the strength of the context's association with the US should summate with that of the CS to generate performance. This view was consistent with the energizing role that earlier theories of conditioned performance had given context (e.g., Asratyan, 1965; Konorski, 1967; Spence, 1956).

Our results, however, quickly led us to question the summation rule. Demonstrable context-US associations were neither necessary (Bouton & King, 1983; Bouton & Swartzentruber, 1986) nor sufficient (Bouton, 1984; Bouton & King, 1986) for the context to affect performance to the CS. And equally significant, extinguished CSs, as opposed to CSs that had never been extinguished, seemed especially sensitive to the influence of the context. We thus arrived at a somewhat different view of how both context and extinction operate. In what follows I will first review the role of context in extinction, and then discuss the possible mechanisms of contextual control. I will then ask what it all may tell us about the role of context in conditioning in general.

REINSTATEMENT OF EXTINGUISHED FEAR BY CONTEXT-US ASSOCIATIONS

One of the first extinction phenomena we examined was "reinstatement" (e.g., Rescorla & Heth, 1975). In this paradigm, simple exposure to the US alone after extinction can partially restore fear of an extinguished CS. Reinstatement is an example of a phenomenon which suggests that the original learning is not completely lost during extinction; conditioned performance can return via simple presentation of the US. Rescorla and Heth (1975; see also Rescorla &

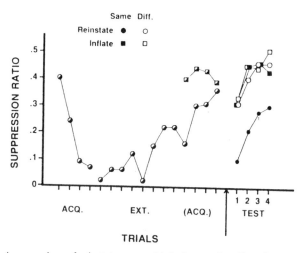

Figure 2.1. A comparison of reinstatement and inflation, or the effect of contextual condition-ing on extinguished and nonextinguished CSs (circles and squares, respectively). Following the initial conditioning or conditioning plus extinction treatment (i.e., at arrow), groups re-ceived USs in a context that was either the same as (Same) or different from (Diff) the context of final testing (shown at right). The suppression ratio is the number of lever-press responses recorded during the CS divided by the sum of that number and responses during an equal period prior to the CS. Adapted from Bouton (1984, Experiment 5), but reprinted from Bouton (1988). Copyright 1988 by Pergamon Journals Ltd. Reprinted by permission of the publisher.

Cunningham, 1977, 1978) suggested that the US presentations reinstate re-sponding by strengthening a memory of the US that was weakened, or perhaps forgotten, during extinction. But there is little evidence that the US representa-tion is ever weakened in extinction. For example, extinction of one CS does not weaken the responding evoked by another CS associated with the same US (Bouton & King, 1983; Kasprow, Schachtman, Cacheiro, & Miller, 1984; Richards & Sargent, 1983). Furthermore, we soon discovered that the rein-statement depends strongly on conditioning of the context that occurs during exposure to the US (Bouton, 1984; Bouton & Bolles, 1979b; Bouton & King, 1983, 1986). It is new contextual associations, rather than simple exposure to the US, that produce reinstatement of extinguished fear.

There is now a fair amount of evidence to support the contextual condi-tioning account of reinstatement. In fear conditioning, the effect does not occur unless the USs are presented in the context in which the CS is going to be tested (Bouton, 1984; Bouton & Bolles, 1979b; Bouton & King, 1983, 1986); the same USs delivered in an irrelevant context have no effect on responding to the CS. In addition, extensive exposure to the context alone following presen-tation of the US can reduce reinstatement (Bouton & Bolles, 1979b). Further, independent measures of contextual fear have confirmed that the US presenta-tions do condition new context-US associations, and that the strength of those associations correlates with, and can thus predict, the strength of reinstated fear of the CS (Bouton, 1984; Bouton & King, 1983). In a newly "dangerous" con

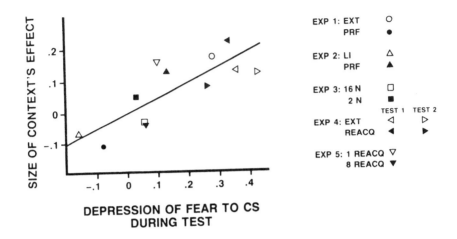

Figure 2.2. The results of five experiments on the effects of contextual conditioning on per-formance to CSs with different conditioning histories. Conditioning treatments examined are listed at right (EXT = extinction, PRF = partial reinforcement, LI = latent inhibition, N = non-reinforced trials embedded as runs in partial reinforcement, REACQ = reacquisition). Contex-tual conditioning was manipulated after the conditioning treatment by exposing groups to USs in either the test context or a different context prior to testing. For each treatment, the size of contextual conditioning's augmenting effect on performance to the CS is plotted as a function of the degree to which CS performance was otherwise depressed during testing (e.g., by extinction). From Bouton and King (1986). Copyright 1986 by the American Psychologi-cal Association. Reprinted by permission of the publisher.

text, the extinguished CS again arouses fear (see Bouton & Peck, 1989, for compatible evidence from appetitive conditioning).

This view of reinstatement is consistent with the effects of compounding extinguished CSs with other excitors after extinction. Generally speaking, when an extinguished CS is presented against an excitatory background, it evokes fear again. Reberg (1972) found that a CS extinguished many trials be-yond the point at which it became behaviorally "silent" evoked fear again when it was tested in compound with a moderately excitatory CS. And Hendry (1982) found that two excitors that were separately conditioned and then sepa-rately extinguished (for 96 extinction trials) still evoked fear when they were tested together. Clearly, a CS can still retain excitatory power even after fairly extensive extinction. The picture that emerges is that extinction yields a CS with bistable, volatile power. In fact, the unstable nature of the extinguished CS could be taken as a central feature of extinction.

We learned more about reinstatement, and about the relation between con-text and extinction, when we examined performance to *nonextinguished* CSs in an excitatory context (Bouton, 1984; Bouton & King, 1986). In a manner sim-ilar to reinstatement, one can expose the subject to USs alone following a simple conditioning procedure. Surprisingly, here strong context-US associa-tions very often have no impact on performance to the CS. For example, in the inflation paradigm (Rescorla, 1974), the CS is initially paired with a weak US, and then the animal is separately exposed to stronger USs. In a final test, exposure to the stronger USs can be shown to enhance, or inflate, fear of the CS. Our work with reinstatement suggested that context-US associations produced during US exposure could summate with the CS to produce the effect. However, neither delivering the larger USs in an irrelevant context (Bouton, 1984, Experiment 1) nor extinguishing the context following US exposure (Bouton, 1984, Experiment 2) reduced inflation. The results were striking, because both manipulations can abolish reinstatement, and because separate measures of contextual fear indicated that they had been successful at reducing extant context-US associations. Groups that differed substantially in contextual fear did not differ in their fear of the CS. It was as if contextual conditioning had no impact on the response to the CS.

We soon found that the discrepant effects of contextual conditioning on CS-performance were linked to extinction. In the experiment shown in Figure 2.1 (Bouton, 1984, Experiment 5), two sets of groups arrived at a common level of conditioned responding via different routes prior to a final test. One set (circles) initially received CS-US pairings and then extinction trials that did not completely eliminate fear. The other set (squares) received only four conditioning trials with a weak US; pilot work had indicated that this treatment would produce a weak level of suppression similar to that in the other groups at the end of extinction. The two sets of groups were then divided in two, and one group from each condition received four relatively intense USs in either the context which was to be used the next day for testing (Group Same), or in an irrelevant context (Group Diff). The design allowed us to see how comparable amounts of contextual fear (produced by identical exposure to shock and confirmed via an independent measure) influenced fear of extinguished and nonextinguished CSs that entered testing evoking similar amounts of fear. The results, shown at right in Figure 2.1, were clear: Fear of the extinguished CS was strongly affected by contextual fear, but fear of the nonextinguished CS was not. For the nonextinguished CS, strong contextual fear was not sufficient to affect performance to the CS. The performance-enhancing effects of contextual fear were specific to the extinguished CS.

Figure 2.2 summarizes the results of a series of experiments that followed up on these findings (Bouton & King, 1986). In each experiment, we compared the effects of contextual fear on responding to CSs that had received conditioning treatments involving both reinforced and nonreinforced trials. As before, contextual fear was manipulated following conditioning by further exposure to the US in either the test or an irrelevant context. Figure 2.2 presents the most important generalization from the series: The best predictor of whether performance to a CS would be augmented by context-US associations was the degree to which performance was otherwise "depressed" from its earlier maximum, that is, under the influence of extinction. CSs with any of a variety of conditioning histories that did not leave the CS at least partially extinguished were not affected by context-US associations. Context-US associations thus appear to work by restoring responding that has been depressed by extinction. In a sense they retrieve a memory of conditioning that has been suppressed in performance by extinction (cf. Kaplan & Hearst, 1985).

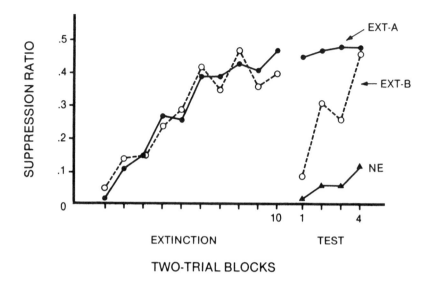

Figure 2.3. The renewal effect in conditioned suppression. Conditioning (not shown) initially occurred in Context A; extinction trials (left) occurred in either Context A (Group Ext-A) or Context B (Group Ext-B). At right, the groups received final extinction tests of the CS in Context A. Group NE had received no extinction prior to the final test. From Bouton and King (1983, Experiment 1). Copyright 1983 by the American Psychological Association. Reprinted by permission of the publisher.

The results of the line of research that began with our work on reinstatement suggest that performance in the presence of a CS that is under the influence of extinction is almost peculiarly augmented by context-US associations (cf. Balaz, Capra, Hartl, & Miller, 1981). Two points should be emphasized here. First, some remnant of conditioning clearly remains following extinction; it is easily revealed when the CS is presented in an excitatory context. Second, if the CS is not under the influence of extinction, context-US associations may not otherwise be sufficient to affect performance to a CS. One can begin to see why I believe that context and extinction are interrelated, and why we have become skeptical of the view that CS and context simply summate to generate behavior.

RENEWAL OF EXTINGUISHED FEAR WITH
A CHANGE OF CONTEXT

There is another phenomenon which, like reinstatement, suggests that responding to an extinguished CS is dependent on its context. If a CS is paired with a US in one context (Context A) and then presented alone repeatedly so as to extinguish fear in another (Context B), responding to the CS is "renewed" when the CS is removed from the extinction context and tested back in Context A (e.g., Bouton & Bolles, 1979a; Bouton & King, 1983; Bouton & Swartzentruber, 1989). Renewal can also occur if testing occurs in a third, neutral con

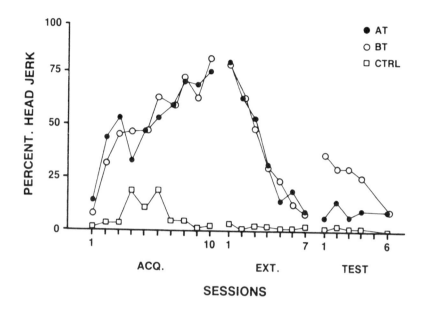

Figure 2.4. The renewal effect in appetitive conditioning. Conditioning (left) occurred in Context A; Groups AT and BT received tone-food pairings while CTRL received the same events in an explicitly unpaired manner. In extinction (middle), Groups AT and BT received tones alone in Context A or Context B, respectively; half of Group CTRL received similar trials in A and the other half received them in B. During testing (right), all groups received further extinction tests of the tone in Context A. Percentage head jerk is the percentage of time-sampled observations in the CS that were scored as head jerk, a response of the rat to auditory cues associated with food. From Bouton and Peck (1989, Experiment 1). Copyright 1989 by the Psychonomic Society. Reprinted by permission of the publisher.

text (Bouton & Bolles, 1979a; Bouton & Swartzentruber, 1986, see also 1989, Experiment 3). Although a return to the original conditioning context probably produces the strongest renewal (see Bouton & Swartzentruber, 1986), a switch out of the extinction context can suffice. The loss of responding that occurs in extinction may thus depend partly on learning about the extinction context.

Figures 2.3 and 2.4 illustrate renewal in two different conditioning preparations. Figure 2.3 (Bouton & King, 1983, Experiment 1) shows the phenomenon in conditioned suppression, where conditioning was created by pairing a 60-s tone with footshock and indexed by the ability of the CS to suppress operant baseline responding. Figure 2.4 (Bouton & Peck, 1989, Experiment 1) shows it in an appetitive conditioning situation in which conditioning was created by pairing a 10-s tone with food pellets and indexed by the observation of "head jerking," a response of the rat to auditory CSs associated with food (e.g., Holland, 1977, 1979). In either preparation, a context switch following conditioning had no effect on conditioned responding, a finding consistent with the notion that nonextinguished stimuli are less dependent on context (see also Kaye, Preston, Szabo, Druiff, & Mackintosh, 1987; Lovibond, Preston, & Mackintosh, 1984, for similar results). In contrast, returning the CS to Context A following extinction in Context B caused a robust renewal of conditioned responding during the final tests.

The similarity of the results in aversive and appetitive conditioning encourages the view that the renewal effect is general across response systems; it has also occurred in operant conditioning (Welker & McAuley, 1978) and in taste aversion learning (e.g., Archer, Sjoden, Nilsson, & Carter, 1979). It may also be produced by several types of contexts. For example, renewal occurs when drug states are arranged to provide a context for extinction. Cunningham (1979) found that rats extinguished under the influence of alcohol showed renewed fear when tested without the drug. We have recently observed a similar effect when fear extinction is combined with the tranquilizers chlordiazepoxide (librium) and diazepam (valium) (Bouton, Kenney, & Rosengard, 1990).

In principle, of course, the CS is always embedded in a new context during extinction. An especially interesting one may be provided by the passage of time. Spontaneous recovery, in which the response recovers naturally when time elapses following extinction (e.g., Pavlov, 1927), is essentially the renewal effect that occurs when the CS is tested outside its temporal extinction context. Extinction is thus inherently context specific. The subject may always learn some version of "the CS means no US *now*." The loss of responding that occurs in extinction is clearly not a matter of unlearning. It is more like a context discrimination problem.

MECHANISMS OF CONTEXTUAL CONTROL

The mechanisms underlying the renewal effect thus need to be considered in more detail. The effect can be cast in the terms of mainstream compound conditioning theory (e.g., Rescorla & Wagner, 1972). Context A might acquire context-US associations during conditioning, and Context B might acquire inhibitory associations when it is nonreinforced in compound with the CS during extinction. The latter might inhibit fear during extinction, and "protect" the CS from total associative loss (e.g., Soltysik, Wolfe, Nicholas, Wilson, & Garcia-Sanchez, 1983). Either type of association would be expected to summate with direct CS-US associations to generate contextual control of performance.

Though perhaps plausible in principle, this analysis runs into significant problems. For example, since Context A ostensibly begins extinction with direct associations with the US, one might wonder why the animals did not respond more in Context A than Context B during the extinction phases shown in Figures 2.3 and 2.4. Perhaps more importantly, there is no evidence that the contexts acquire associations that can be demonstrated independently of the renewal effect they are supposed to explain (Bouton & King, 1983). For example, Context A does not arouse fear on its own in our procedures, even when it is assessed with multiple techniques (Bouton & King, 1983). Exposure to the contexts alone, which should weaken context-US associations, does not abolish the renewal effect (Bouton & King, 1983, Experiment 3; see also Lovibond et al., 1984, Experiment 1b), and has no effect on the results when manipulated experimentally (Bouton & Peck, 1989, Experiment 2; see also Bouton & Swartzentruber, 1986, Experiment 3). And even when we set out to make context-US associations especially strong by alternating sessions containing CS-US pairings in Context A and CSs alone in Context B, the two contexts fail to control behavior on their own, fail to summate with other CSs, and fail to affect learning to other CSs in ways that traditional excitors and inhibitors do (Bouton & Swartzentruber, 1986). Demonstrable context-US associations thus do not appear to be *necessary* for the context to affect performance to a CS. When these results are combined with evidence that context-US associations are not *sufficient* to control performance (Bouton, 1984; Bouton & King, 1986; see above), one must question the view that performance is a simple function of direct context-US associations.

A related possibility is that renewal and other context discriminations are controlled by configural conditioning. Unique cues (e.g., Rescorla, 1973) emerging from the CS-context combinations could acquire excitatory or inhibitory associations themselves. However, two lines of evidence question their importance in our experiments. First, as noted above, there is no loss of responding when the tone is switched to Context B following conditioning in Context A (Bouton & King, 1983; Bouton & Peck, 1989; Bouton & Swartzentruber, 1986); one might expect a generalization decrement if unique cues control performance. Similar results also obtain when total darkness provides the CS; it is difficult to see how darkness could generate unique perceptual cues in different contexts (e.g., Bouton & Swartzentruber, 1989). Second, the context's control of responding to one CS can transfer to a separate CS. In a recent experiment, we reinforced and nonreinforced a tone in Contexts A and B, respectively, and concurrently treated a light-off CS similarly in Contexts C and D (Swartzentruber & Bouton, 1988). During a final test, Context A facilitated suppression to the light-off, suggesting that Context A had acquired an ability to facilitate that transcended its unique combination with the tone. The key to producing such transfer appears to be discrimination training with the transfer target (cf. Bouton & King, 1983; Bouton & Swartzentruber, 1986). The important point is that the data suggest little role for unique cue conditioning in our laboratory.

Thus the action of context in renewal and other discriminations (Bouton & Swartzentruber, 1986) does not appear to depend on direct associations with the US. We have suggested that contexts work instead by signaling or retrieving whole CS-US associations (Bouton & Bolles, 1985; see also Estes, 1973; Spear, e.g., 1973). The context of conditioning may signal the CS-US association, while the context of extinction may signal a representation of extinction. The analogy to ambiguous words (Bouton, 1984, 1988; Bouton & Bolles, 1985) is again appropriate: When a verbal context disambiguates the meaning of an ambiguous word, it actually selects among the word's own multiple associations with other objects or concepts. The function of the context in extinction is to signal the CS's current association with the US.

This action of contexts resembles that of *occasion setters* (e.g., Holland, 1983, 1985; Ross & Holland, 1981) and *facilitators* (e.g., Rescorla, 1985), stimuli which have received some attention recently. Like our contexts, occasion setters modulate responding to upcoming target CSs in a manner that seems independent of their direct associations with the US. Like our contexts, they may not control much responding on their own, and instead act largely to enable the target CS-US association (e.g., Rescorla, 1985; Ross & Holland, 1981). They also have unusual "summation" properties when they are compounded with new target CSs. Like our contexts (Bouton & King, 1983; Bouton & Swartzentruber, 1986; Swartzentruber & Bouton, 1988), occasion setters do not readily affect performance to separately-trained targets (Holland, 1983; Holland & Lamarre, 1984; Lamarre & Holland, 1985; Rescorla, 1985) unless those targets have either been extinguished (Rescorla, 1985) or trained in a separate occasion-setting discrimination (Davidson & Rescorla, 1986; Lamarre & Holland, 1987). Contexts and occasion setters may convey similar information. In dissertation research that is currently in progress, Dale Swartzentruber has found that punctate occasion setters can "block" (Kamin, 1968) the acquisition of control by Context A in an AT+/BT- discrimination paradigm. Simple punctate excitors do not (cf. Ross & LoLordo, 1986; LoLordo & Ross, 1987). Contexts and occasion setters may both act as conditional cues signaling associations to other stimuli.

This sort of explanation of the renewal effect was rejected prematurely by Lovibond et al. (1984). These investigators found that renewal did not occur in experiments designed to equate Contexts A and B on their direct associations with the US. The renewal effect was initially replicated; for example, a tone paired with shock in Context A showed renewed suppression in A following extinction in Context B. However, in other experiments, when the tone was conditioned in Context A, a second CS (a light) was also conditioned in Context B; when the tone was extinguished in B, the light was extinguished in A. The light's converse treatment eliminated renewal when the tone was finally returned to Context A; this suggested that renewal otherwise depends on differences in A's and B's associative values. The problem with this inference is that the light's treatment would also affect the occasion setting abilities of A and B. For example, Rescorla (1986) has since shown that extinction of a second CS (i.e., the light) in compound with a positive occasion setter (i.e., Context A) can eliminate the occasion setter's ability to facilitate responding to its original target (i.e., renewal to the tone in Context A). Like the renewal effect itself, the results of Lovibond et al. are consistent with *either* the associative or occasion setting views of context. They cannot distinguish between them.

Taken as a whole, the evidence weighs against the assumption that context-US associations are necessary and sufficient to affect CS-performance. It is therefore not unreasonable to suppose that contexts control responding to CSs embedded in them through a mechanism other than summation. Most of the data are consistent with the view that contexts work by retrieving, signaling, or setting the occasion for CS-US associations. This is the fundamental role of context in controlling performance in extinction.

CONTEXT IN OTHER FORMS OF PAVLOVIAN INTERFERENCE

Extinction is just one example of a paradigm in which the CS is associated with different events in different phases of the experiment. Table 2.1 lists several others. Because each is formally similar to proactive and retroactive interference designs in human verbal learning, I will refer to them as "interference paradigms." In many of these situations, the Phase 1 treatment produces negative transfer, or proactive interference, with the development of responding in Phase 2. This is not universally true, however, and this is not the sense of the term "interference" that I wish to convey here.

TABLE 2.1
Interference paradigms in Pavlovian learning

	Phase 1	Phase 2	(Phase 3)
Latent inhibition	T-	T-shock	
Hall-Pearce negative transfer	T-shock	T-SHOCK!	
Learned irrelevance	T/shock (uncorr.)		T-shock
Aversive-appetitive transfer	T-shock	T-food	
Appetitive-aversive transfer	T-food	T-shock	
Reacquisition following extinction	T-shock	T-	T-shock
Extinction	T-shock	T-	

Note: T refers to a hypothetical tone CS.

Latent inhibition is probably the most intensively studied example of interference in Pavlovian learning: Initial exposure to the CS alone can interfere with the occurrence of conditioned responding when the CS is subsequently paired with the US (e.g., Lubow, 1973). But there are of course others. A similar effect can occur when the CS is initially paired with a weak US and then paired with a stronger one in Phase 2; initial CS-weak US pairings can produce negative transfer with Phase 2 (e.g., Hall & Pearce, 1979). Initial uncorrelated pairings of CS and US may likewise interfere with responding during subsequent pairings (e.g., Baker & Mackintosh, 1977; Mackintosh, 1973). And CS-shock pairings also interfere with responding that develops during CS-food pairings (e.g., Krank, 1985; Scavio, 1974). CS-food pairings preceding CS-shock pairings meet my definition of interference, although in this case Phase 1 training often facilitates responding in Phase 2 (DeVito & Fowler, 1982; Scavio & Gormezano, 1980). Reacquisition, where CS-US pairings are resumed following extinction, also fits the present definition, and I will discuss this paradigm in detail later because it brings extinction into contact with the other forms of interference very clearly.

Extinction itself is placed at the bottom of the list because one rarely finds it associated with phenomena like latent inhibition. Yet the formal similarity among the paradigms encourages the view that similar mechanisms might operate within them. If what we know about extinction applies to other forms of interference, then we should remain open to the possibility that interference generally presents itself as a retrieval problem to the subject. As we found in extinction, memories of both phases may be retained and available in long-term memory. Those memories may then be retrieved, or signaled, by appropriate retrieval cues like the context. And importantly, *performance* during interference may therefore depend on which of the two available memories is currently active or retrieved. Negative transfer, when it occurs, can thus result from the retrieval of incompatible information.

Similar views have been presented by Spear (1981) and by Tulving and Psotka (1971) for interference in animal learning and human verbal learning, respectively. It is an unusual approach, however. Theories of interference have usually focused on the learning or encoding that occurs during Phase 2. For example, latent inhibition (along with most of the other effects listed in Table 2.1) is typically assumed to occur because of reduced attention to the CS (e.g., Lubow, Weiner, & Schnur, 1981; Mackintosh, 1975) or reduced processing of the CS in short-term or working memory (Pearce & Hall, 1980; Wagner, 1978, 1981), either of which would reduce the amount of learning possible during Phase 2. We saw the same bias in thinking about extinction, where it has been convenient to emphasize *un*learning. But that emphasis is misleading. The original material is still in memory after extinction; it is simply less likely to be retrieved. And similarly, there is evidence to suggest that Phase 2 is in fact learned in the latent inhibition paradigm: If a "reminder treatment" is administered after conditioning, evidence of learning may be revealed (Kasprow, Catterson, Schachtman, & Miller, 1984; cf. Kraemer & Roberts, 1984). Extinction can be characterized as a retrieval problem, and it may be fruitful to think of other interference paradigms the same way.

Consistent with this framework, the context may have a ubiquitous role in interference. Research in several laboratories has now established that latent inhibition depends substantially on context. If the context is switched between Phases 1 and 2, interference with the acquisition of responding in Phase 2 is strongly attenuated (e.g., Channell & Hall, 1983; Hall & Channell, 1985; Hall & Minor, 1984; Lovibond et al., 1984; Swartzentruber & Bouton, 1986; but see Baker & Mercier, 1982). The right-hand panel of Figure 2.5 illustrates this finding with an experiment conducted in my laboratory (Swartzentruber & Bouton, 1986, Experiment 2). The conditioning and extinction trials shown occurred in Context A. Previously, Group AT- had received 66 nonreinforced tones in the same context, while Group BT- had received the same treatment in Context B; actual exposure to the two contexts had been equated. Group BT- thus received the tone in a new context at the outset of conditioning, and as the figure suggests, conditioned suppression was ultimately more substantial in this group. The left-hand panel shows two groups that had received the same tones in Contexts A or B, except that each of these had terminated in a weak and brief footshock US (0.4-mA, 0.5-s). The conditioning trials shown involved a stronger US (0.8-mA, 1-s); these groups thus underwent the Hall-Pearce negative transfer treatment described previously. As in latent inhibition, a context switch prior to Phase 2 attenuated interference (Group BT+). Context thus plays a similar role in latent inhibition and Hall-Pearce negative transfer.

Other data suggest that the context is also involved in the other paradigms listed in Table 2.1. Recent experiments on learned irrelevance suggest that a context switch between Phases 1 and 2 may attenuate that effect (Matzel, Schachtman, & Miller, 1988; see also Kaye et al., 1987; Tomie, 1981; Tomie, Murphy, Fath, & Jackson, 1980), although it probably does not eliminate the effect completely (Matzel et al., 1988). In preliminary experiments employing our observational method, Charles Peck and I have observed a role for context in aversive-appetitive and appetitive-aversive transfer. When tone-shock pairings preceded tone-food pairings, a context switch between phases reduced the usual interference with the development of appetitive head jerking (cf. Kaye et al., 1987). When tone-food pairings preceded tone-shock pairings, the effect of a context switch between phases was not as clear, but a return to the context of appetitive training after aversive training was complete yielded renewed appetitive behavior to the CS. Finally, a role for context in reacquisition has recently been established in experiments that I will describe in the next section (Bouton & Swartzentruber, 1989). To summarize, the context may play a role in interference that goes beyond its role in extinction.

The models of Wagner (e.g., Wagner, 1978, 1981) anticipate the effects of context switches on responding in many of these paradigms. Both of these

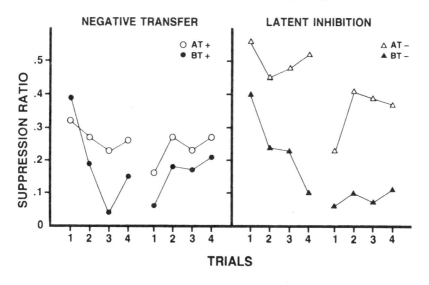

Figure 2.5. Effect of a context switch on latent inhibition (right) and Hall-Pearce negative transfer (left). Trials shown occurred in Context A; in each panel the group designated by open symbols had received previous exposure to the CS in Context A while closed symbols had received exposure in a different context (Context B). For latent inhibition groups, the CS had been nonreinforced; for negative transfer groups the CS had been paired with a weak US. The first four trials shown in each panel were paired with a strong US and the second four trials were nonreinforced. From Swartzentruber and Bouton (1986, Experiment 2). Copyright 1986 by Academic Press. Reprinted by permission of the publisher.

models propose that the subject learns to associate the CS (as well as the US) with its context during Phase 1. In effect the context comes to signal the CS, thereby habituating the surprisingness of the CS, and thus the degree to which it is active (Wagner, 1981) or rehearsed (Wagner, 1978) in short-term memory during subsequent trials. Because learning about the CS depends directly on such activation, context-CS associations would reduce the degree to which the CS could enter into future associations. A context switch between phases would dishabituate the surprise value of the CS. Through this mechanism, the models predict the context-specificity of many of the interference phenomena described above. But predicting the phenomena is not necessarily the same as explaining them accurately. Context switch effects are often interpreted in Wagner's terms, but they are equally consistent with the view that the context functions to signal or retrieve a CS-US relation that interferes with performance corresponding to Phase 2.

There are reasons to favor the retrieval hypothesis over the habituation view. One major problem with the habituation mechanism is that it has been difficult to confirm empirically. Habituation as observed in several response systems does not appear to be affected by context switches or by other manipulations of context (e.g., Baker & Mercier, 1982; Churchill, Remington, & Siddle, 1987; Hall & Channell, 1985; Leaton, 1974; Marlin & Miller, 1981). We have investigated the issue in my own laboratory by monitoring the habituation of the unconditional suppression of lever-pressing produced by our tone and light-off stimuli; a role for context has not emerged (Bouton, 1987; Bouton, Okun, & Swartzentruber, 1989). The data are consistent between laboratories and across response systems. Taken as a group, they suggest that context-specific habituation may be a risky concept on which to base the explanation of interference.

It is possible that simple measures of unconditional responding to a stimulus are less sensitive to context-specific habituation than is the rate with which the stimulus can become conditioned. However, habituation has been dissociated from latent inhibition, at least, in a way that begins to make this view implausible (Hall & Channell, 1985; Hall & Schachtman, 1987). When the context is switched, latent inhibition is reduced while habituation of an orienting response to the CS is unchanged (Hall & Channell, 1985). Conversely, when time is permitted to pass between Phase 1 and Phase 2, habituation is reduced while latent inhibition is unchanged (Hall & Schachtman, 1987). Overall, the data suggest that it may be time to seek other mechanisms besides habituation as the mechanism of Pavlovian interference. Retrieval of Phase 1 information is a strong alternative.

Interference in non-Pavlovian paradigms is also compatible with the retrieval notion. In both verbal interference in humans and discrimination reversals in animals, memories corresponding to both phases (or word lists) remain available, ready to be retrieved, in a long-term memory store. In verbal interference, memory of the List 1 material can be cued by the original learning context after List 2 material has been memorized (e.g., Greenspoon & Ranyard, 1957), a finding analogous to our renewal effect in extinction. In addition, recall for the original words can be reinstated by introducing retrieval cues such as category labels (Tulving & Psotka, 1971) and can show spontaneous recovery when time elapses following learning of List 2 (e.g., Postman, Stark, & Fraser, 1968; Underwood, 1948a, 1948b). In animal discrimination reversal learning, Phase 1 performance likewise increases with the passage of time following Phase 2 (Burr & Thomas, 1972; Spear, Gordon, & Chiszar, 1972; Spear, Smith, Bryan, Gordon, Timmons, & Chiszar, 1980). And perhaps more to the point, Phase 1 performance can be renewed when the subject is returned to the Phase 1 context following the completion of Phase 2 (Spear et al., 1980; Thomas, McKelvie, Ranney, & Moye, 1981). Such results suggest that the context of Phase 1 can generate negative transfer by retrieving Phase 1 information even after Phase 2 has been encoded. Overall, the data are remarkably consistent with the effects we have observed in extinction. Is it possible we have emphasized the wrong mechanisms in explaining other examples of Pavlovian interference?

SLOW REACQUISITION FOLLOWING EXTINCTION

The retrieval view of interference is consistent with the results of recent research on reacquisition following extinction. In this paradigm, the CS is first paired with the US, then presented alone in extinction, and ultimately paired with the US again in a final phase. Figure 2.6 presents results from the last phase of one of our experiments on this problem (Bouton, 1986, Experiment 2). In the phase shown at left, Group Control received tone-shock pairings for the first time; the tone was actually paired with shock on every other trial. (This group had previously received one nonreinforced tone designed to habituate unconditional suppression to it.) The two remaining groups had previously

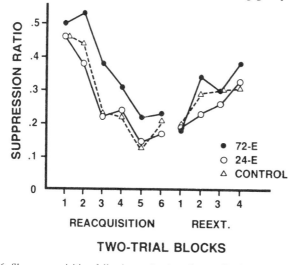

Figure 2.6. Slow reacquisition following extinction. Groups 72-E and 24-E had previously received eight conditioning trials followed by either 72 or 24 extinction trials. Group Control had received no conditioning or extinction. From Bouton (1986, Experiment 2). Copyright 1986 by Academic Press. Reprinted by permission of the publisher.

received eight tone-shock pairings followed by different amounts of extinction; Group 24-E received 24 extinction trials and Group 72-E received 72. During reconditioning, Group 24-E was statistically indistinguishable from Group Control. But Group 72-E acquired significantly *less* conditioned suppression than Group Control. Extensive extinction training thus retarded the development of suppression during reacquisition. Extinction, like initial nonreinforcement of the CS in latent inhibition, can interfere with subsequent conditioning.

These results contrast with conventional wisdom about reacquisition, which is often assumed to occur very rapidly. That wisdom seems compatible with reinstatement and renewal, which indicate that the CS retains excitatory power after extinction. Why shouldn't relearning therefore be rapid? The answer is that responding should indeed recover rapidly with procedures that promote retrieval of a memory of conditioning. Responding does reappear quickly in many reacquisition procedures (e.g., Frey & Butler, 1977; Frey & Ross, 1968; Hoehler, Kirschenbaum, & Leonard, 1973; Konorski & Szwejkowska, 1950, 1952a, 1952b; Smith & Gormezano, 1965). But note that it might do so for several reasons. If the procedure allows time to elapse between the end of extinction and the beginning of reacquisition, responding could reappear at the start through spontaneous recovery (e.g., Frey & Ross, 1968; Hoehler et al., 1973; Smith & Gormezano, 1965). And if a reacquisition procedure reintroduces cues that were uniquely associated with conditioning, such cues could cause rapid recovery by producing a renewal effect. Given the short intertrial intervals that are commonly used in the reacquisition literature, the after-effects of recent USs might often provide such cues. The point is that responding can return readily in reacquisition studies without truly rapid relearning (see Frey & Butler, 1977, for a related discussion). From the retrieval view of extinction, one would expect acquisition-like responding in procedures that cue a memory of conditioning. But one might likewise expect extinction-like responding, and therefore slow reacquisition, in procedures that cue a memory of extinction.

The results of a recent set of experiments (Bouton & Swartzentruber, 1989) are consistent with this view. In one experiment (Experiment 2), we produced either acquisition-like or extinction-like responding during reacquisition with appropriate manipulations of the context. The experimental design, summarized in Table 2.2, was a 2 x 2 factorial in which reacquisition was conducted in a context that was (a) the same or different as the context of conditioning, and/or (b) the same or different as the context of extinction. All groups initially received eight conditioning trials with the light-off CS in Context A. Extinction then occurred in Context A for two groups (Groups AAA and AAB, where the letters refer to the contexts of conditioning, extinction, and reacquisition) and Context B for the two remaining groups (Groups ABB and ABA). There were seven extinction sessions, each containing 12 trials, for a total of 84 extinction trials. Exposure to the two contexts was controlled throughout the experiment by alternating sessions between contexts as shown in Table 2.2. In the final phase, one group from each extinction condition received reconditioning in the extinction context (Groups AAA and ABB) while the other group (ABA and AAB) received reconditioning in the other, non-extinction context. During reacquisition, odd-numbered trials were reinforced while even-numbered trials were nonreinforced.

The results of each reacquisition trial are shown in Figure 2.7. The results of the first trial (shown separately at left) were informative; bear in mind that suppression on this trial occurred prior to delivery of the first US of the phase. Group ABA had received conditioning in Context A, extinction in Context B, and now received the CS again in Context A for the first time since conditioning. The substantial suppression shown by Group ABA (but none of the other groups) is another demonstration of the renewal effect. Renewal here is instructive because it occurred after a lengthy extinction procedure (84 trials) that also

TABLE 2.2

Design of Bouton and Swartzentruber (1989) Experiment 2

Phase

Group	Conditioning	Extinction	Reconditioning
AAA	AL+, B-	AL-, B-	AL+
ABB	AL+, B-	BL-, A-	BL+
ABA	AL+, B-	BL-, A-	AL+
AAB	AL+, B-	AL-, B-	BL+

Note: A and B refer to contexts (where A is the context of conditioning); L refers to a house-light-termination CS; + and - designates sessions in which trials were reinforced or nonreinforced. Conditioning and extinction consisted of several repetitions of the "cycles" shown. See text for other details.

involved extensive exposure to Context A without the US. It suggests that the memory of conditioning is still available, and cueable, after an extinction procedure that can generate slow reacquisition. And note that it would be possible to mistake the strong suppression shown by Group ABA throughout the phase as evidence of rapid reacquisition following extinction.

The remainder of Figure 2.7 suggests that suppression was reacquired least successfully when reacquisition was conducted in the context of extinction (Groups AAA and ABB, the open symbols). Put another way, reacquisition was relatively rapid when the CS was removed from the extinction context. Note that this was true for Group AAB (solid circles), which received reacquisition in Context B after both conditioning and extinction had been conducted in Context A. Although Group AAB began the phase with little initial suppression, reacquisition in this group was more rapid than in the groups that were not switched out of the extinction context. Slow reacquisition is thus at least partly controlled by the extinction context. A parsimonious way to view the complete pattern of results is to note that while retrieval of the acquisition memory causes the renewal effect, retrieval of the extinction memory may cause slow reacquisition.

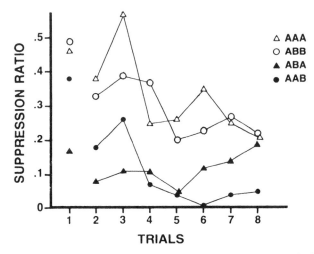

Figure 2.7. Results of the reacquisition phase of the experiment summarized in Table 2.2. Letters in group designations correspond to the contexts of conditioning, extinction, and reacquisition (respectively). The first trial (shown separately at left) occurred just prior to the first US delivered in the phase; note the renewal effect in Group ABA. Open symbols received reacquisition in the context of extinction while closed symbols received it in a different context. From Bouton and Swartzentruber (1989, Experiment 2). Copyright 1989 by the American Psychological Association. Reprinted by permission of the publisher.

There are other ways to account for the role of the extinction context. According to the habituation view reviewed above (Wagner, 1978, 1981), the subject might form context-CS associations during extinction that could habituate activation of the CS in short-term memory. Such habituation would reduce learning about the CS during reacquisition; a context switch would cause dishabituation and thus improve that learning. Recall, however, that there is little evidence in the literature that habituation is specific to its context. With habituation parameters similar to those used here in extinction, we have not observed dishabituation with a context switch (Bouton, Okun, & Swartzentruber, 1989). And perhaps most important, the results of a final reacquisition experiment suggest that slow reacquisition occurs because the extinction context can interfere with *performance*, rather than learning, during reconditioning.

The experiment in question (Bouton & Swartzentruber, 1989, Experiment 3) asked whether the context of extinction could interfere with reacquisition performance even after reacquisition had clearly been learned and encoded. Four groups went through conditioning, extinction, reconditioning, and then a final test. The two target groups received initial conditioning in Context A, and then 72 extinction trials in either Context B (Group Ext-B) or Context C (Group Ext-C). As usual, exposure to Contexts B and C was equated by alternating sessions of exposure to each during the extinction phase. The remaining two groups (LI-B and LI-C) received a latent inhibition treatment which consisted of comparable nonreinforced exposure to the CS in Context B or C, respectively, without initial conditioning. (These animals also received the same initial exposures to the CS in Context A, but without the US.) In a reconditioning phase that followed extinction, all groups were returned to Context A, where they now received eight CS-shock pairings; for Groups Ext-B and Ext-C, this was a reacquisition treatment, while for Groups LI-B and LI-C this was the first experience with conditioning. In a final test, the groups were tested for suppression in Context B, the context where Group Ext-B had received extinction. If the extinction context controls slow reacquisition by interfering with reacquisition performance, we might expect reduced suppression in Group Ext-B during this test.

Figure 2.8 summarizes the results. The last two-trial blocks of extinction (or CS pre-exposure) are shown at left; the reconditioning trials conducted in Context A are shown at center. Note that suppression was renewed upon return to the conditioning context in the Groups Ext-B and Ext-C; once again, the memory of conditioning was available and retrieved after fairly substantial extinction. The latent inhibition groups of course started with relatively little suppression, but acquired an amount comparable to that of the other groups by the end of the phase.

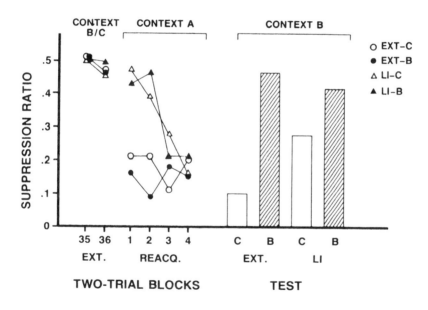

Figure 2.8. Contextual cueing of interference in reacquisition and latent inhibition. Group designations refer to extinction or latent inhibition treatments and the contexts in which these occurred (Contexts B or C). Groups in the extinction condition had initially received conditioning in Context A (not shown). The last trial-blocks of extinction or CS preexposure are shown at left; middle represents trials on which the CS was then paired with the US in Context A. Bars at right indicate suppression on the first trial of a final test of the CS in Context B, the context in which Groups Ext-B and LI-B had received nonreinforcement of the CS during extinction or CS preexposure, respectively. From Bouton and Swartzentruber (1989, Experiment 3). Copyright 1989 by the American Psychological Association. Reprinted by permission of the publisher.

The major results from the final test are shown at right. Even on the first test trial, the group that received testing in its extinction context (Group Ext-B) showed a marked and complete recovery of extinction performance. The group that had received equivalent extinction in a different context (Ext-C) did not. In effect, Group Ext-B demonstrated a renewal of extinction performance following reacquisition. This result strongly suggests that the context of extinction can interfere with reacquisition performance, as opposed to reacquisition learning, by cueing performance appropriate to extinction. In the terms of the retrieval framework, the extinction context may interfere with reacquisition performance because it retrieves a representation of extinction. Slow reacquisition may thus be evident in performance because the context retrieves conflicting information.

The results shown in Figure 2.8 also suggest that a similar mechanism may play a role in other paradigms. When Group LI-B was returned to Context B, the context in which it had received nonreinforced exposure to the CS prior to conditioning, performance corresponding to nonreinforcement was renewed in comparison to a group that had received preexposure in a different context (Group LI-C). This result suggests that latent inhibition, like slow reacquisition, might result from the retrieval of a representation of nonreinforcement. A similar effect was reported in earlier latent inhibition experiments that were flawed by a lack of context counterbalancing and/or equation of exposure to the contexts (Bouton & Bolles, 1979a, Experiment 4; Dexter & Merrill, 1969; Wright, Skala, & Peuser, 1986; see also Anderson, O'Farrell, Formica, & Caponigri, 1969). The results shown in Figure 2.8 may put the earlier findings on firmer ground, although I would note that they are not always easy to obtain. Lovibond et al. (1984) reported trouble finding the effect in two well-controlled experiments, although they actually had some evidence of it in both.[1] I have also obtained mixed results in experiments which, like Lovibond et al.'s, involved fewer initial nonreinforced trials than the 72 used in the Figure 2.8 experiment (Bouton, 1987). It is possible that the behavioral effects of an initial memory of nonreinforcement may be less salient than those of a more recent conditioning phase (see Kraemer & Roberts, 1984). However, retrieval of a nonreinforcement memory could easily be involved during the early trials of conditioning, where latent inhibition is often most strongly observed. Our re-

---

[1] Lovibond et al. (1984) tested the effect with a tone and a light CS in both experiments. In Experiment 2, the data were reported collapsing over tone and light. Here a significant effect [F (1,28) = 4.6, tabled p value < .05] was overlooked because the authors evaluated planned comparisons (p. 364) with a post hoc method that apparently adjusted error rate over all phases of the experiment (instead of the test phase alone). In Experiment 3, the authors noted that the effect was significant with the light, but dismissed it on the grounds that the light could have been perceived as a somewhat different stimulus in the two contexts. This possibility is plausible given the light CS used, but it does not make the effect go away. Some stimulus, such as the unique attributes of the light in the preexposure context, appears to have cued preexposure. Lovibond et al.'s data are not convincing as null results.

sults suggest that contextual retrieval of conflicting information may provide a general mechanism for negative transfer in Pavlovian interference.

Other data argue against two alternative performance interference mechanisms. It is worth repeating that an extinction context could in principle attenuate performance if it became inhibitory during extinction. However, recall that previous data, in addition to other data actually obtained in our reacquisition experiments (see Bouton & Swartzentruber, 1989, Experiment 3), suggest that an extinction context's ability to cue extinction performance is not the result of demonstrable inhibitory conditioning (Bouton & King, 1983; Bouton & Swartzentruber, 1986). (Note also that the effect in latent inhibition lies beyond the scope of this mechanism because the context of preexposure was never associated with nonreinforcement of an excitatory CS or the offset of a US, conditions almost universally required by current theories for the development of inhibition.) A second possible mechanism is suggested by the more recent version of Wagner's CS-activation model (i.e., SOP, Wagner, 1981). If the context is associated with the CS during extincton or CS preexposure, its ability to prime the CS in memory (specifically, to put CS elements in A2 rather than A1) could interfere with the CS's ability to activate the representation of the US, and thus cause performance interference. Note, however, that this effect is merely a new consequence of the familiar context-specific habituation mechanism that I have already described. As such, it is challenged by data suggesting that habituation does not depend on the context (e.g., Baker & Mercier, 1982; Bouton, 1987; Bouton, Okun, & Swartzentruber, 1989; Churchill et al., 1987; Hall & Channell, 1985; Leaton, 1974; Marlin & Miller, 1981). In total, the results may be most consistent with the view that slow reacquisition, and perhaps other interference effects, occur because the context retrieves conflicting information.

The cueing effects evident in Figure 2.8, where a return to the Phase 1 context renewed Phase 1 performance even following the completion of Phase 2, actually provide additional information about interference. Successful cueing of Phase 1 after Phase 2 is complete requires that Phase 1 information actually survive Phase 2. In principle, retrieval interference could produce negative transfer even if the Phase 1 memory were eventually modified during Phase 2. Yet Phase 1 information often does appear to survive: The Phase 1 cueing effect has been obtained in slow reacquisition (Figure 2.8), latent inhibition (e.g., Figure 2.8), discrimination reversal learning (Spear et al., 1980; Thomas et al., 1981), and proactive interference in human verbal learning (Greenspoon & Ranyard, 1957). Charles Peck and I have also obtained preliminary evidence of it in both aversive-appetitive and appetitive-aversive transfer. Such effects are formally identical to the renewal effect in extinction (e.g., Bouton & Bolles, 1979a; Bouton & King, 1983). The observation of renewal in any interference paradigm suggests that the animal may retain some record of its mixed history of experience with the CS (see Bouton & Bolles, 1985).

In some ways, it is not surprising to find the retrieval of an extinction representation operating as the mechanism of slow reacquisition. We have seen that a memory corresponding to conditioning has always been available in memory, but not manifest in behavior, through the course of extinction.

Knowledge of the CS-US association has been invisible all along. We have come full circle. Extinction, renewal, reinstatement, and slow reacquisition are all part of the same retrieval problem.

SUMMARY AND CONCLUSIONS

A major message of this chapter is that extinction performance depends fundamentally on which of two available representations is active or retrieved. If one takes an extinguished CS and creates conditions that retrieve a memory of conditioning, the animal will respond as if it is in conditioning. This is reinstatement, renewal, and perhaps spontaneous recovery. On the other hand, if one creates conditions that retrieve a memory of extinction, the subject will respond as if it is in extinction. This is the mechanism of slow reacquisition. Conditioning and extinction are both learned and representations of them are both retained; performance depends on which is retrieved. This view rejects a role for unlearning in extinction. It accepts the behaviorally bi-stable nature of an extinguished CS as one of its most fundamental properties. And it also implies a pivotal role for context that may go beyond its simple associations with the CS and US. Although extinction could be viewed as a retrieval problem even if the context worked via simple associations, the data suggest instead that it plays a superordinate, relation-signaling role.

Can this view be applied to other forms of interference? Its most important implication is that contexts (and perhaps other retrieval cues) can determine performance by signaling or retrieving representations of the CS's different associative relations. As discussed above, contextual stimuli do appear to play a general role in interference, a role not anticipated by some models (e.g., Mackintosh, 1975; Pearce & Hall, 1980). The alternative view that the context might affect encoding (Wagner, 1978, 1981) has encountered significant problems recently. And perhaps most important, evidence from several paradigms (e.g., slow reacquisition) suggests that negative transfer can be created by contextual-cueing of information yielding performance interference, rather than encoding interference, during Phase 2 (Bouton & Swartzentruber, 1989; Greenspoon & Ranyard, 1957; Spear et al., 1980; Thomas et al., 1981; see also Bouton & Bolles, 1979a, Experiment 4; Dexter & Merrill, 1969; Wright et. al., 1986). There is a certain appeal to putting all interference phenomena into one framework instead of explaining each with separate mechanisms. This is not to say that attention, inhibitory conditioning, and motivational competition mechanisms cannot play a role. But it may be fruitful to recognize the similarity, rather than dissimilarity, of the paradigms.

There are at least two issues that might stand in the way of accepting retrieval as a general mechanism of interference. The first is the problem of representation. The recent production of good evidence of occasion setting (e.g., Holland, 1983, 1985; cf. Rescorla, 1985) makes the view that contexts retrieve representations of CS-US and CS-no US relations (e.g., Bouton & Bolles, 1985; Estes, 1973; Spear, 1973) plausible. But if latent inhibition is due to retrieval interference, then what exactly is being retrieved? There is a reluctance to accept the possibility that representations can be formed in the absence of reinforcers, or take the form of anything other than associations. What is associated with the CS in latent inhibition? We know that it is not "no US," at least not in the sense that true conditioned inhibitors signal "no US," because the animal has not received the US yet and because latent inhibitors differ from the true inhibitors that develop when the US is actually presented in the background (e.g., Reiss & Wagner, 1972; Rescorla, 1971). One alternative is that latent inhibition may involve retrieval of a representation of a CS meaning nothing. Rescorla and his associates (e.g., Rescorla & Durlach, 1981) have provided evidence that animals can construct fairly rich representations of to-be-conditioned stimuli in the absence of reinforcers. Phase 1 of the latent inhibition paradigm could thus involve the construction of a reasonably detailed representation of the CS. If that representation lacked the features that distinguish excitors and inhibitors (e.g., associations with "US" or "no US"), negative transfer with excitatory or inhibitory learning would be possible. A complete resolution of the representation problem will require a better idea of how excitation and inhibition are themselves represented in the memory system.

The second obstacle to the retrieval view is the long-standing interest in processes like attention (e.g., Lubow et al., 1981; Mackintosh, 1975), rehearsal (e.g., Wagner, 1978, 1981), and associability (e.g., Pearce & Hall, 1980). As applied to negative transfer, each of these processes assumes that poor responding during Phase 2 reflects poor *learning*. Yet I know of no evidence that directly supports this assumption. The few experiments that have addressed it have actually provided evidence of good learning that is not manifest in performance (Kasprow et al., 1984; Kraemer & Roberts, 1984). In the case of extinction, a similar emphasis on *un*learning rather than performance processes has proven oversimple and misleading. To some extent the emphasis on learning processes in interference is based more on theoretical convenience (and inertia) than on hard evidence.

There is, in contrast, evidence that orienting responses (ORs) to the CS that might index attention or associability do change in an orderly manner during CS exposure and conditioning (e.g., Kaye & Pearce, 1984). Such evidence eliminates any circularity of constructs like attention and associability, but it does not necessarily establish associability as the cause of negative transfer. The causal relation has become even more difficult to establish now that the decline in the OR that occurs during CS preexposure has been doubly dissociated from latent inhibition (Hall & Channell, 1985; Hall & Schachtman, 1987). Still, the approach has led to the discovery of new negative transfer effects that are not obviously handled by the retrieval view (e.g., Swan & Pearce, 1988). It would be a mistake to reject attention and associability outright as possible explanations of interference.

The issue is partly one of generality. When will attention and associability be more important than the retrieval processes that have been suggested here? When will there be overlap? Can retrieval of Phase 1 information interfere with encoding as well as performance during Phase 2? The research reviewed in this chapter suggests a fairly general role for context in Pavlovian interference. It also suggests that the retrieval processes we believe may operate in extinction may have considerable generality across the different interference paradigms.

ACKNOWLEDGMENT

Preparation of this chapter was supported by Grant BNS 86-07208 from the National Science Foundation. I thank A. G. Baker, Geoffrey Hall, and Dale Swartzentruber for commenting on an earlier version of the manuscript.

REFERENCES

Anderson, D. C., O'Farrell, T., Formica, R., & Caponigri, V. (1969). Preconditioning CS exposure: Variation in place of conditioning and of presentation. *Psychonomic Science, 15*, 54-55.

Archer, T., Sjoden, P. O., Nilsson, L. G., & Carter, N. (1979). Role of exteroceptive background context in taste-aversion conditioning and extinction. *Animal Learning & Behavior, 7*, 17-22

Asratyan, E. A. (1965). *Compensatory adaptations, reflex activity, and the brain.* Oxford: Pergamon Press.

Baker, A. G., & Mackintosh, N. J. (1977). Excitatory and inhibitory conditioning following uncorrelated presentations of the CS and UCS. *Animal Learning & Behavior, 5*, 315-319.

Baker, A. G., & Mercier, P. (1982). Prior experience with the conditioning events: Evidence for a rich cognitive representation. In M. L. Commons, R. J. Herrnstein, & A. R. Wagner (Eds.), *Quantitative analyses of behavior: Acquisition* (pp. 117-144). Cambridge, MA: Ballinger.

Balaz, M. A., Capra, S., Hartl, P., & Miller, R. R. (1981). Contextual potentiation of acquired behavior after devaluing direct context-US associations. *Learning and Motivation, 12*, 383-397.

Bouton, M. E. (1984). Differential control by context in the inflation and reinstatement paradigms. *Journal of Experimental Psychology: Animal Behavior Processes, 10*, 56-74.

Bouton, M. E. (1986). Slow reacquisition following the extinction of conditioned suppression. *Learning and Motivation, 17*, 1-15.

Bouton, M. E. (1987). *Context, encoding, and retrieval in latent inhibition.* Unpublished manuscript.

Bouton, M. E. (1988). Context and ambiguity in the extinction of emotional learning: Implications for exposure therapy. *Behaviour Research and Therapy, 26*, 137-149.

Bouton, M. E., & Bolles, R. C. (1979a). Contextual control of the extinction of conditioned fear. *Learning and Motivation, 10*, 445-466.

Bouton, M. E., & Bolles, R. C. (1979b). Role of conditioned contextual stimuli in reinstatement of extinguished fear. *Journal of Experimental Psychology: Animal Behavior Processes, 5*, 368-378.

Bouton, M. E., & Bolles, R. C. (1985). Contexts, event-memories, and extinction. In P. D. Balsam & A. Tomie (Eds.), *Context and learning* (pp. 133-166). Hillsdale, NJ: Lawrence Erlbaum Associates.

Bouton, M. E., Kenney, F. A., & Rosengard, C. (1990). State-dependent fear extinction with two benzodiazepine tranquilizers. *Behavioral Neuroscience, 104*, 44-55.

Bouton, M. E., & King, D. A. (1983). Contextual control of the extinction of conditioned fear: Tests for the associative value of the context. *Journal of Experimental Psychology: Animal Behavior Processes, 9*, 248-265.

Bouton, M. E., & King, D. A. (1986). Effect of context on performance to conditioned stimuli with mixed histories of reinforcement and nonreinforcement. *Journal of Experimental Psychology: Animal Behavior Processes, 12,* 1-12.

Bouton, M. E., Okun, K., & Swartzentruber, D. (1989). *Lack of a role of context in habituation after few and many habituation trials.* Manuscript in preparation.

Bouton, M. E., & Peck, C. A. (1989). Context effects on conditioning, extinction, and reinstatement in an appetitive conditioning preparation. *Animal Learning & Behavior, 17,* 188-198.

Bouton, M. E., & Swartzentruber, D. (1986). Analysis of the associative and occasion-setting properties of contexts participating in a Pavlovian discrimination. *Journal of Experimental Psychology: Animal Behavior Processes, 12,* 333-350.

Bouton, M. E., & Swartzentruber, D. (1989). Slow reacquisition following extinction: Context, encoding, and retrieval mechanisms. *Journal of Experimental Psychology: Animal Behavior Processes, 15,* 43-53.

Burr, D. E. S., & Thomas, D. R. (1972). Effect of proactive inhibition upon the postdiscrimination generalization gradient. *Journal of Comparative and Physiological Psychology, 81,* 441-448.

Channell, S., & Hall, G. (1983). Contextual effects in latent inhibition with an appetitive conditioning procedure. *Animal Learning & Behavior, 11,* 67-74.

Churchill, M., Remington, B., & Siddle, D. A. T. (1987). The effects of context change on long-term habituation of the orienting response in humans. *Quarterly Journal of Experimental Psychology, 39B,* 315-338.

Cunningham, C. L. (1979). Alcohol as a cue for extinction: State dependency produced by conditioned inhibition. *Animal Learning & Behavior, 7,* 45-52.

Davidson, T. L., & Rescorla, R. A. (1986). Transfer of facilitation in the rat. *Animal Learning & Behavior, 14,* 380-386.

DeVito, P. L., & Fowler, H. (1982). Transfer of conditioned appetitive stimuli to conditioned aversive excitatory and inhibitory stimuli. *Learning and Motivation, 13,* 135-154.

Dexter, W. R., & Merrill, H. K. (1969). Role of contextual discrimination in fear conditioning. *Journal of Comparative and Physiological Psychology, 69,* 677-681.

Estes, W. K. (1973). Memory and conditioning. In F. J. McGuigan & D. B. Lumsden (Eds.), *Contemporary approaches to conditioning and learning* (pp. 265-286). Washington, DC: Winston.

Frey, P. W., & Butler, C. S. (1977). Extinction after aversive conditioning: An associative or nonassociative process? *Learning and Motivation, 8,* 1-17.

Frey, P. W., & Ross, L. E. (1968). Classical conditioning of the rabbit eyelid response as a function of interstimulus interval. *Journal of Comparative and Physiological Psychology, 65,* 246-250.

Greenspoon, J., & Ranyard, R. (1957). Stimulus conditions and retroactive inhibition. *Journal of Experimental Psychology, 53,* 55-59.

Hall, G., & Channell, S. (1985). Differential effects of contextual change on latent inhibition and on the habituation of an orienting response. *Journal of Experimental Psychology: Animal Behavior Processes, 11,* 470-481.

Hall, G., & Minor, H. (1984). A search for context-stimulus associations in latent inhibition. *The Quarterly Journal of Experimental Psychology, 36B,* 145-169.

Hall, G., & Pearce, J. M. (1979). Latent inhibition of a CS during CS-US pairings. *Journal of Experimental Psychology: Animal Behavior Processes, 5,* 31-42.

Hall, G., & Schachtman, T. R. (1987). Differential effects of a retention interval on latent inhibition and the habituation of an orienting response. *Animal Learning & Behavior, 15*, 76-82.

Hendry, J. S. (1982). Summation of undetected excitation following extinction of the CER. *Animal Learning & Behavior, 10*, 476-482

Hoehler, F. K., Kirschenbaum, D. S., & Leonard, D. W. (1973). The effects of overtraining and successive extinctions upon nictitating membrane conditioning in the rabbit. *Learning and Motivation, 4*, 91-101.

Holland, P. C. (1977). Conditioned stimulus as a determinant of the form of the Pavlovian conditioned response. *Journal of Experimental Psychology: Animal Behavior Processes, 3*, 77-104.

Holland, P. C. (1979). The effects of qualitative and quantitative variation in the US on individual components of Pavlovian appetitive conditioned behavior in rats. *Animal Learning & Behavior, 7*, 424-432.

Holland, P. C. (1983). "Occasion-setting" in conditional discriminations. In M. L. Commons, R. J. Herrnstein, & A. R. Wagner (Eds.), *Quantitative analyses of behavior: Discrimination processes (Vol. 4)* (pp. 183-206). New York: Ballinger.

Holland, P. C. (1985). The nature of conditioned inhibition in serial and simultaneous feature negative discriminations. In R. R. Miller & N. E. Spear (Eds.), *Information processing in animals: Conditioned inhibition* (pp. 267-297). Hillsdale, NJ: Lawrence Erlbaum Associates.

Holland, P. C., & Lamarre, J. (1984). Transfer of inhibition after serial and simultaneous feature negative discrimination training. *Learning and Motivation, 15*, 219-243.

Kamin, L. J. (1968). "Attention-like" processes in classical conditioning. In M. R. Jones (Ed.), *Miami symposium on the prediction of behavior: Aversive stimulation* (pp. 9-31). Miami, FL: University of Miami Press.

Kaplan, P. S., & Hearst, E. (1985). Contextual control and excitatory versus inhibitory learning: Studies of extinction, reinstatement, and interference. In P. D. Balsam & A. Tomie (Eds.), *Context and learning* (pp. 195-224). Hillsdale, NJ: Lawrence Erlbaum Associates.

Kasprow, W. J., Catterson, D., Schachtman, T. R., & Miller, R. R. (1984). Attenuation of latent inhibition by a post-acquisition reminder. *Quarterly Journal of Experimental Psychology, 36B*, 53-63.

Kasprow, W. J., Schachtman, T. R., Cacheiro, H., & Miller, R. R. (1984). Extinction does not depend upon degradation of event memories. *Bulletin of the Psychonomic Society, 22*, 95-98.

Kaye, H., & Pearce, J. M. (1984). The strength of the orienting response during Pavlovian conditioning. *Journal of Experimental Psychology: Animal Behavior Processes, 10*, 90-109.

Kaye, H., Preston, G., Szabo, L., Druiff, H., & Mackintosh, N. J. (1987). Context specificity of conditioning and latent inhibition: Evidence for a dissociation of latent inhibition and associative intereference. *Quarterly Journal of Experimental Psychology, 39B*, 127-145.

Konorski, J. (1967). *Integrative activity of the brain.* Chicago: University of Chicago Press.

Konorski, J., & Szwejkowska, G. (1950). Chronic extinction and restoration of conditioned reflexes. I. Extinction against the excitatory background. *Acta Biologiae Experimentalis, 15*, 156-170.

Konorski, J., & Szwejkowska, G. (1952a). Chronic extinction and restoration of conditioned reflexes III. Defensive motor reflexes. *Acta Biologiae Experimentalis, 16,* 91-94

Konorski, J., & Szwejkowska, G. (1952b). Chronic extinction and restoration of conditioned reflexes IV. The dependence of the course of extinction and restoration of conditioned reflexes on the "history" of the conditioned stimulus (the principle of the primacy of the training). *Acta Biologiae Experimentalis, 16,* 95-113.

Kraemer, P. J., & Roberts, W. A. (1984). The influence of flavor preexposure and test interval on conditioned taste aversions in the rat. *Learning and Motivation, 15,* 259-278.

Krank, M. D. (1985). Asymmetrical effects of Pavlovian excitatory and inhibitory aversive transfer on Pavlovian appetitive responding and acquisition. *Learning and Motivation, 16,* 35-62.

Lamarre, J., & Holland, P. C. (1985). Acquisition and transfer of feature- negative discriminations. *Bulletin of the Psychonomic Society, 23,* 71-74.

Lamarre, J., & Holland, P. C. (1987). Transfer of inhibition after serial feature negative discrimination training. *Learning and Motivation, 18,* 319-342.

Leaton, R. N. (1974). Long-term retention of the habituation of lick suppression in rats. *Journal of Comparative and Physiological Psychology, 87,* 1157-1164.

LoLordo, V. M., & Ross, R. T. (1987). Role of within-compound associations in occasion setting: A blocking analysis. *Journal of Experimental Psychology: Animal Behavior Processes, 13,* 156-167.

Lovibond, P. F., Preston, G. C., & Mackintosh, N. J. (1984). Context specificity of conditioning, extinction, and latent inhibition. *Journal of Experimental Psychology: Animal Behavior Processes, 10,* 360-375.

Lubow, R. E. (1973). Latent inhibition. *Psychological Bulletin, 79,* 398-407.

Lubow, R. E., Weiner, I., & Schnur, P. (1981). Conditioned attention theory. In G. H. Bower (Ed.), *The psychology of learning and motivation (Vol. 15)* (pp. 1-49). New York: Academic Press.

Mackintosh, N. J. (1973). Stimulus selection: Learning to ignore stimuli that predict no change in reinforcement. In R. A. Hinde & J. Stevenson-Hinde (Eds.), *Constraints on learning* (pp. 75-100). New York: Academic Press.

Mackintosh, N. J. (1975). A theory of attention: Variations in the associability of stimuli with reinforcement. *Psychological Review, 82,* 276-298.

Marlin, N. A., & Miller, R. R. (1981). Associations to contextual stimuli as a determinant of long-term habituation. *Journal of Experimental Psychology: Animal Behavior Processes, 7,* 313-333.

Matzel, L. D., Schachtman, T. R., & Miller, R. R. (1988). Learned irrelevance exceeds the sum of CS-preexposure and US-preexposure deficits. *Journal of Experimental Psychology: Animal Behavior Processes, 14,* 311-319.

Pavlov, I. P. (1927). *Conditioned reflexes.* (G. V. Anrep, Trans.) London: Oxford University Press.

Pearce, J. M., & Hall, G. (1980). A model for Pavlovian learning: Variations in the effectiveness of conditioned but not of unconditioned stimuli. *Psychological Review, 87,* 532-552.

Postman, L., Stark, K., & Fraser, J. (1968). Temporal changes in interference. *Journal of Verbal Learning and Verbal Behavior, 7,* 672-694.

Reberg, D. (1972). Compound tests for excitation in early acquisition and after prolonged extinction of conditioned suppression. *Learning and Motivation, 3,* 246-258.

Reiss, S., & Wagner, A. R. (1972). CS habituation produces a "latent inhibition effect" but no active "conditioned inhibition". *Learning and Motivation, 3*, 237-245.

Rescorla, R. A. (1971). Summation and retardation tests of latent inhibition. *Journal of Comparative and Physiological Psychology, 75*, 77-81.

Rescorla, R. A. (1973). Evidence for "unique stimulus" account of configural conditioning. *Journal of Comparative and Physiological Psychology, 85*, 331-338.

Rescorla, R. A. (1974). Effect of inflation of the unconditioned stimulus value following conditioning. *Journal of Comparative and Physiological Psychology, 86*, 101-106.

Rescorla, R. A. (1985). Conditioned inhibition and facilitation. In R. R. Miller & N. E. Spear (Eds.), *Information processing in animals: Conditioned inhibition* (pp. 299-326). Hillsdale, NJ: Lawrence Erlbaum Associates.

Rescorla, R. A. (1986). Extinction of facilitation. *Journal of Experimental Psychology: Animal Behavior Processes, 12*, 16-24.

Rescorla, R. A., & Cunningham, C. L. (1977). The erasure of reinstated fear. *Animal Learning & Behavior, 5*, 386-394.

Rescorla, R. A., & Cunningham, C. L. (1978). Recovery of the US representation over time during extinction. *Learning and Motivation, 9*, 373-391.

Rescorla, R. A., & Durlach, P. J. (1981). Within-event learning in Pavlovian conditioning. In N. E. Spear & R. R. Miller (Eds.), *Information processing in animals: Memory mechanisms* (pp. 81-112). Hillsdale, NJ: Lawrence Erlbaum Associates.

Rescorla, R. A., & Heth, C. D. (1975). Reinstatement of fear to an extinguished conditioned stimulus. *Journal of Experimental Psychology: Animal Behavior Processes, 1*, 88-96.

Rescorla, R. A., & Wagner, A. R. (1972). A theory of Pavlovian conditioning: Variations in the effectiveness of reinforcement and nonreinforcement. In A. H. Black & W. F. Prokasy (Eds.), *Classical conditioning II: Current research and theory* (pp. 64-99). New York: Appleton-Century-Crofts.

Richards, R. W., & Sargent, D. M. (1983). The order of presentation of conditioned stimuli during extinction. *Animal Learning & Behavior, 11*, 229-236.

Ross, R. T., & Holland, P. C. (1981). Conditioning of simultaneous and serial feature-positive discriminations. *Animal Learning & Behavior, 9*, 293-303.

Ross, R. T., & LoLordo, V. M. (1986). Blocking during serial feature-positive discriminations: Associative versus occasion setting functions. *Journal of Experimental Psychology: Animal Behavior Processes, 12*, 315-324.

Scavio, M. J. (1974). Classical-classical transfer: Effects of prior aversive conditioning upon appetitive conditioning in rabbits. *Journal of Comparative and Physiological Psychology, 86*, 107-115.

Scavio, M. J., & Gormezano, I. (1980). Classical-classical transfer: Effects of prior appetitive conditioning upon aversive conditioning in rabbits. *Animal Learning & Behavior, 8*, 218-224.

Smith, M., & Gormezano, I. (1965). Effects of alternating classical conditioning and extinction sessions on the conditioned nictitating membrane response of the rabbit. *Psychonomic Science, 3*, 91-92.

Soltysik, S. S., Wolfe, G. E., Nicholas, T., Wilson, W. J., & Garcia-Sanchez, J. L. (1983). Blocking of inhibitory conditioning within a serial conditioned stimulus-conditioned inhibitor compound: Maintenance of acquired behavior without an unconditioned stimulus. *Learning and Motivation, 14*, 1-29.

Spear, N. E. (1973). Retrieval of memory in animals. *Psychological Review, 80*, 163-194.

Spear, N. E. (1981). Extending the domain of memory retrieval. In N.E. Spear & R. R. Miller (Eds.), *Information processing in animals: Memory mechanisms* (pp. 341-378). Hillsdale, NJ: Lawrence Erlbaum Associates.

Spear, N. E., Gordon, W. C., & Chiszar, D. A. (1972). Interaction between memories in the rat: Effect of degree of prior conflicting learning on forgetting after short intervals. *Journal of Comparative and Physiological Psychology, 78*, 471-477.

Spear, N. E., Smith, G. J., Bryan, R., Gordon, W., Timmons, R., & Chiszar, D. (1980). Contextual influences on the interaction between conflicting memories in the rat. *Animal Learning & Behavior, 8*, 273-281.

Spence, K. W. (1956). *Behavior theory and conditioning.* New Haven: Yale University Press.

Swan, J. A., & Pearce, J. M. (1988). The orienting response as an index of stimulus associability in rats. *Journal of Experimental Psychology: Animal Behavior Processes, 14*, 292-301.

Swartzentruber, D., & Bouton, M. E. (1986). Contextual control of negative transfer produced by prior CS-US pairings. *Learning and Motivation, 17*, 366-385.

Swartzentruber, D., & Bouton, M. E. (1988). Transfer of positive contextual control across different conditioned stimuli. *Bulletin of the Psychonomic Society, 26*, 569-572.

Thomas, D. R., McKelvie, A. R., Ranney, M., & Moye, T. B. (1981). Interference in pigeons' long-term memory viewed as a retrieval problem. *Animal Learning & Behavior, 9*, 581-586.

Tomie, A. (1981). Effect of unpredictable food on the subsequent acquisition of autoshaping: Analysis of the context-blocking hypothesis. In C. M. Locurto, H. S. Terrace, & J. Gibbon (Eds.), *Autoshaping and conditioning theory* (pp. 181-215). New York: Academic Press.

Tomie, A., Murphy, A. L., Fath, S., & Jackson, R. L. (1980). Retardation of autoshaping following pretraining with unpredictable food: Effects of changing the context between pretraining and testing. *Learning and Motivation, 11*, 117-134.

Tulving, E., & Psotka, J. (1971). Retroactive inhibition in free-recall: Inaccessibility of information available in the memory store. *Journal of Experimental Psychology, 87*, 1-8.

Underwood, B. J. (1948a). Retroactive and proactive inhibition after five and forty-eight hours. *Journal of Experimental Psychology, 38*, 29-38.

Underwood, B. J. (1948b). "Spontaneous" recovery and verbal associations. *Journal of Experimental Psychology, 38*, 429-439.

Wagner, A. R. (1978). Expectancies and the priming of STM. In S. H. Hulse, H. Fowler, & W. K. Honig (Eds.), *Cognitive processes in animal behavior* (pp. 177-209). Hillsdale, NJ: Lawrence Erlbaum Associates.

Wagner, A. R. (1981). SOP: A model of automatic memory processing in animal behavior. In N. E. Spear & R. R. Miller (Eds.), *Information processing in animals: Memory mechanisms* (pp. 5-47). Hillsdale, NJ: Lawrence Erlbaum Associates.

Welker, R. L., & McAuley, K. (1978). Reductions in resistance to extinction and spontaneous recovery as a function of changes in transportational and contextual stimuli. *Animal Learning & Behavior, 6*, 451-457.

Wright, D. C., Skala, K. D., & Peuser, K. A. (1986). Latent inhibition from context-dependent retrieval of conflicting information. *Bulletin of the Psychonomic Society, 24*, 152-154.

3 Event Revaluation Procedures and Associative Structures in Pavlovian Conditioning

Andrew R. Delamater
Vincent M. LoLordo
Dalhousie University

Associationism has long attempted to decompose experience into its basic elements. Historically, it was assumed that knowledge of what elements become connected and how they become connected would ultimately inform us about how experience gives rise to streams of thoughts, feelings, and behaviors.

The introspectionists were probably the first psychologists to practice this analytical approach within an experimental setting, classifying experience into fundamental sensations and feelings in an attempt to "recreate" perception and memory. Külpe and his followers, however, discovered that much of what goes on during thought is not available to introspection, but rather happens "instantaneously" as a result of our prior attitudes (determining tendencies), which are not reducible to images (see Boring, 1950; Külpe in Mandler & Mandler, 1964). In other words, there is directedness in thought which is itself imageless. Instead of regarding the basic structure of experience as most fundamental, Külpe and the Würzburg school placed process at the core of the problem.

Early animal learning theorists were also strongly influenced by associationism's search for structure. Perhaps one of the most divisive and long-lasting debates in the study of animal learning centered around what the association consisted of. On the one hand, physiology-minded theorists regarded stimuli and their cortical representations to be directly involved in associative connections (e.g., Konorski, 1948; Pavlov, 1927). On the other hand, more behavior-minded theorists linked the response directly to the stimulus, bypassing any reduction to physiology (e.g., Thorndike, 1911; Watson, 1913, 1916). Motivation theorists added to the account of learning some form of motive, be it in the form of a central physiological state (e.g., Konorski, 1967) or in the form of an undetected response or stimulus (e.g., Hull, 1943).

It is interesting to consider why the S-S/S-R issue became the basis of so much dispute. Perhaps each camp of theorists was convinced that acceptance of the other camp's claim meant giving up their own more basic assumptions about science and the organism (see Kendler, 1952). For example, theorists who identified the S-R bond as the unit saw it as their task to re-create, via empiricism, more complicated forms of behavior as chains of S-R units. These theorists perceived themselves as obeying the methodological rules of associationism. Tolman's views of the organism became identified with the S-S approach. Influenced by the earlier Gestalt or even earlier vitalistic school (Boakes, 1984), Tolman thought the learning theorist's task was not to re-create, via associative chains, more complex behavior, but rather to account for complex behavior in terms of teleological explanation that involves, among other things, purposive behavior and stimulus expectations (Tolman, 1925a, 1925b, 1932, 1933a; see also Boden, 1972). Consequently, the S-S/S-R controversy amounted to asking, on the surface, whether the reinforcing stimulus or the unconditioned response was the more fundamental element of associations, or more implicitly, whether one was an associationist who emphasized empiricism or a vitalist who emphasized teleology.

This difference in style is perhaps similar to the difference mentioned earlier between those theorists interested in structure and those interested in process. The Würzburg school broke from orthodox structural psychology because they noticed that thought was directed by something which was not itself reducible to the sensory elements of which associations consisted. Instead, a process, an attitude, was that "something" which interacts with the basic structures of the mind. In the same vein, Tolman saw behavior as directed not by a chain of reflexes but by a process, specifically a "purpose," which interacts with basic psychological structures (i.e., stimulus expectations arising from S-S associations).

Today, we recognize that both structure and process play a role in psychological explanation. The question for the psychology of learning is not whether the association is S-S or S-R. It seems likely that animals learn about stimuli, responses, and motives. The primary issues concern identifying the variety of associative structures mediating learning and performance, identifying the conditions under which particular elements become part of an associative structure, identifying what processes interact with associative structures to determine the significance of stimuli and their effects on behavior, and understanding the nature of those interactions.

We will begin by reviewing results collected from experiments that have used the reinforcer revaluation procedure, and we will ask how well these results can be explained by existing theories of associative structure (e.g., Konorski, 1967). The reinforcer revaluation procedure involves manipulating the value of the reinforcer or unconditioned stimulus (UCS) after the initial conditioning phase, but before retesting the conditioned strength of the conditioned stimulus (CS). Such a manipulation can be construed as changing the value of the reinforcer but not its stimulus properties. If revaluation affects the magnitude of the conditioned response (CR) on a subsequent test trial, then the conditioned stimulus must have been associated with the stimulus properties of the UCS during conditioning. If the conditioned response is insensitive to reinforcer devaluation, then it may be that stimulus properties of the reinforcer do not get learned about, and by default that the response evoked by the reinforcer or the motivational properties of the reinforcer do (see Rozeboom, 1958; Tolman, 1933b).

The issue of process is more difficult to address than the issues of structure. We will approach it by extending our analysis to cover procedures that have manipulated aspects of the conditioning situation other than the reinforcer after the initial learning phase. Such procedures include those used to examine "reinstatement," "reminder," "retrospective," and "comparator" effects. Having discussed a structural framework for interpreting reinforcer revaluation results, we will be in a position to ask how well a purely structural theory explains results from these other post-conditioning event revaluation procedures.

Traditionally, structural approaches have said little about the processes of learning, such as those involved in acquisition, retention, and performance. Process approaches, on the other hand, usually have not made assumptions about associative structure. A comprehensive theory of associative learning is one which blends our knowledge of associative structures with the knowledge we have obtained about basic processes. This review can be seen as an attempt at identifying types of associative structures and interacting processes of Pavlovian learning, and identifying the constraints that a theory must face in attempting to integrate structure with process.

REINFORCER REVALUATION EXPERIMENTS

Post-conditioning manipulations of the reinforcer have been carried out in several different paradigms—for example, rat and pigeon autoshaping, non-signal directed appetitive conditioning, conditioned emotional response (CER), conditioned punishment, conditioned analgesia, and conditioned taste aversion (CTA). The kinds of manipulations performed on the UCS were designed to investigate representational theories of classical conditioning (e.g., Konorski, 1967; Rescorla, 1973; see also Dickinson, 1980; Mackintosh, 1983).

Briefly, representational theories assume that stimulus "representations" become associated. The evocation of a UCS memory is further assumed to result in the performance of some overt or covert response (e.g., fear or hunger). By this account, a manipulation that would "deflate" or "inflate" the UCS memory should affect the magnitude of the conditioned response. Investigators have attempted to deflate the UCS memory, following a conditioning phase, through UCS habituation procedures, manipulations of UCS intensity, manipulations of motivational state, or counterconditioning procedures. Inflation has been attempted through manipulations of UCS intensity and motivational state.

Post-Conditioning Exposures to the Same UCS Used in Conditioning

Rescorla (1973) noted that habituating rats to a loud noise UCS following conditioning attenuated the strength of a CER previously conditioned with that same noise. While bar pressing for food, rats learned that a flashing light preceded the 112 dB noise UCS (two trials were spaced over an hour period). Then, the experimental group received 72 unsignaled noise presentations at a rate of 12/hr either on- or off-baseline (in different experiments), whereas the controls received no noise. When the CS was subsequently presented in a simple extinction test, there was less suppression of responding over trials in the experimental group than in the control, although the groups did not differ on the first test trial. In a further experiment, Rescorla demonstrated that a tone as well as a light CS was sensitive to noise habituation, but this time the effect was present only early in extinction. The magnitude of the effects reported were relatively small, although statistically reliable. Attenuation of the CR was far from complete, as there was still considerable suppression. In a similar experiment Rescorla (1974) found that weak shocks presented after conditioning attenuated the CER previously conditioned with shocks of the same intensity.

There was no independent estimation of habituation in these experiments. Without such an assessment of habituation (or of other revaluation procedures) the interpretive difficulty arises from trying to distinguish an incomplete effect of complete reinforcer revaluation from the effect of an incomplete revaluation of the reinforcer. The consequences of this point will be discussed later.

In another CER experiment Randich and Haggard (1983) reported that a large number of post-conditioning shocks are required to obtain an effect of habituation. In one of their studies, unsignalled post-conditioning shocks (1-mA, .8-s) were distributed at the same rates as in conditioning (3/session). Ten such sessions, but not one or five sessions, resulted in less suppression in extinction, relative to a no post-conditioning shock control group. However, Randich and Rescorla (1981) found that even a few post-conditioning shocks would attenuate the magnitude of a CER previously conditioned with the same shocks, if the interval between post conditioning shocks and the test trial was only 12 min, instead of the 1 day used in the other studies. Using a very short interval between the last shock and the test trial may allow short-term habituation of the response to shock to affect the magnitude of the CR.

On the other hand, Ayres and Benedict (1973) found no effect of post-conditioning shocks on the conditioned suppression of licking. Rats received pairings of a tone with a 1.6-mA, 2-s foot shock off-baseline. Unsignalled shocks were delivered at a higher rate than during conditioning but with the same intensity as in conditioning. When the animals licked sucrose from a dipper in a different chamber, the tone suppressed licking in the post-shock and no post-shock groups equally well throughout the six extinction trials. Miller and Schachtman (1985) similarly reported no attenuation of conditioned lick suppression after post-conditioning shocks were delivered at a higher rate than during conditioning. Their test, however, consisted of only one test trial.

In a conceptually similar study which used a conditioned punishment test, Sherman (1978) reported failures of post-conditioning effects when the shocks used during conditioning and post-conditioning treatments were weak but of long duration, (.4 mA, 2-s long). Sherman suggested that the failure of post-conditioning shocks to reduce CR magnitude might be attributed to the greater severity of shocks in his study, compared to Rescorla's which were .5-s, .5-mA. This suggestion can be interpreted as a claim that stronger shocks yield less habituation. Ayres and Benedict used strong shocks, so this suggestion could also account for their results.

Under certain conditions, the strength of a conditioned taste aversion appears sensitive to post-conditioning UCS injections. Mikulka, Leard, and Klein (1977) paired a palatable sucrose solution with a large dose of LiCl (3-mEq) on one trial and then administered the same dose of LiCl (or saline) on a subsequent day. On a subsequent two-bottle test trial the LiCl post-exposed group drank more sucrose (pitted against water) than the controls, which consumed a moderate amount. In subsequent experiments, Mikulka et al. (1977) reported better attenuation of the aversion, measured on a one-bottle test, if more LiCl injections were administered following conditioning. When more conditioning trials were given (i.e., with a stronger aversion conditioned), the attenuation effect seemed harder to obtain, even with many LiCl post-exposures.

Colby and Smith (1977) obtained a devaluation effect even when the aversion conditioned to saccharin was strong (three aversion trials with 3-mEq were administered). Similarly, more LiCl post-exposures led to more of an attenuated aversion, which could only be seen after several two-bottle (saccharin vs water) extinction trials. Additionally, Colby and Smith provided some independent evidence for LiCl habituation. In a no-taste-aversion control group receiving 10 LiCl exposures following saccharin-saline pairings, consumption of saccharin in the tests was enhanced, compared to groups receiving 1 or 5 LiCl post-exposures. This could reflect an elimination, via habituation, of poison-enhanced neophobia (see Domjan, 1975).

Several experiments, however, reported no sensitivity to post-conditioning administrations of the UCS. Riley, Jacobs and LoLordo (1976) conditioned a strong aversion to saccharin using a moderate-strong dose of LiCl (1.8-mEq). Following 5 post-conditioning LiCl exposures, these rats did not drink any more saccharin in a one-bottle test than a group that received physiological saline following conditioning. More interestingly, a group that received successively lower doses of LiCl (1.8, 1.2, .8, .4, and .1-mEq) during the post-exposure phase also showed no enhanced saccharin consumption during the test. During the single, one-bottle test, less than 5 ml was consumed by all three groups. Similarly, Holman (1976) found no evidence that 8 LiCl post-conditioning exposures (approximately 3-mEq) attenuated a strong taste aversion. In this test, saccharin was presented in one bottle over repeated test trials; extinction was obtained over 8 test trials but there was no difference in the rate of extinction between the LiCl and the saline post-exposure groups. Brookshire and Brackbill (1976) conditioned a weak saccharin aversion with apomorphine hydrochloride over six conditioning trials, and then found that 10 subsequent apomorophine injections only weakly (but not significantly by their statistical test) enhanced saccharin intake over three saccharin versus water tests. In this experiment the weak effect could be due to substantial drug habituation occurring during the six conditioning trials, as suggested by their rapidly asymptoting acquisition data.

The aforementioned data suggest that to maximize the likelihood of a post-exposure effect with the CTA procedure: (1) the initial taste aversion should be only moderate in strength, (2) many UCS injections should be administered following the conditioning phase (as with shocks in CER), and (3) the effect of post-conditioning UCSs should be assessed with repeated two-bottle tests. Furthermore, use of a moderate or weak dose of the drug UCS should lead to greater habituation, thus increasing the likelihood of a post-exposure effect.

Having said this, one marked discrepancy remains. Mikulka et al. (1977) and Riley et al. (1976) conducted experiments yielding equally strong aversions in control groups. Yet after a similar number of post-conditioning exposures to LiCl Mikulka et al. found a reduction in the CTA in the experimental group, whereas Riley et al. did not. Riley et al. used a 4-day inter-injection interval during post-exposure, whereas Mikulka et al. used a shorter two-day interval, which might have produced greater habituation of the aversive reaction to LiCl. Moreover, if the sucrose used as the CS by Mikulka et al. was more desirable than the saccharin used by Riley et al., then any manipulation which weakened the aversion would be more likely to show up in the sucrose consumption data.

In summary, although UCS devaluation effects, through habituating the UCS, do not always occur, there do seem to be ideal conditions under which UCS habituation can be observed to attenuate the CR. For example, many post-conditioning UCS exposures help, especially when the UCS itself is relatively weak. Also, the effect may be seen under testing conditions which are sensitive to small differences in the strength of conditioned responding. These procedural constraints may suggest that the UCS devaluation effect is weak. However, this conclusion need not be made when we consider that habituation was rarely assessed independently. The weak effects may therefore reflect weak UCS revaluations. Without appropriate independent assessments this conclusion cannot be rejected. Sometimes investigators have used the fact that UCS exposures proactively attenuate subsequent conditioning to indicate habituation, but this measure is complicated by other explanations for that phenomenon (e.g., Randich & LoLordo, 1979; also see Dacanay & Riley, 1982). A more promising approach may be to look for habituation of responses evoked by the UCS, such as the evoked startle response in the case of loud noise or shock UCSs.

Post-Conditioning Exposures to a Less Intense UCS

Another way to deflate the UCS following conditioning is to present a weaker version of the UCS after the conditioning phase. It has been assumed that this weaker UCS somehow replaces the intense UCS memory with a weaker UCS memory, which, when subsequently evoked by the CS produces a "weaker" response (Rescorla & Heth, 1975).

Randich and his colleagues (Randich & Haggard, 1983; Randich & Rescorla, 1981; Randich & Ross, 1985) have used this procedure with fairly consistent results. Randich and Haggard (1983) found that 10 sessions of post-exposure to a less intense shock (.5 mA, .8-s relative to a 1-mA, .8-s conditioning shock) attenuated the level of conditioned fear (CER) produced by the CS, and enhanced the rate of extinction. These effects, however, were not any stronger than similar effects occurring in a group that received post-conditioning shocks of the same intensity used during conditioning. On the other hand, Randich and Rescorla observed greater deflation when the post-conditioning shock was less intense (.23-mA, .5-s) than that used in conditioning (.5-mA, .5-s) compared to when the same intensity was maintained. The magnitude of the CER across the first four extinction test trials was smaller in the .23 mA group than in the .5 mA group, which in turn was smaller than the CER in the no-shock group.

The results of these two experiments can be explained on the basis of the amounts of habituation they produced. Randich and Haggard administered 10 sessions of post-conditioning exposure to shock, permitting so much habituation in the unchanged intensity group that it would be difficult to see an effect of substituting a memory of a weaker shock for a memory of a stronger one in the decreased intensity group. On the other hand, Randich and Rescorla gave only two post-conditioning shocks. This treatment would be expected to produce no more than a moderate amount of habituation, so that the effect of replacing the memory of the conditioning shock with that of the weaker post-conditioning one would be manifested in less suppression on test trials in the reduced intensity group.

The memory replacement analysis also applies to some results reported by Hendersen (1985), who used parameters similar to those of Randich and Rescorla (1981) but with licking rather than bar-pressing as an appetitive baseline. Reducing shock intensity following conditioning appeared to attenuate lick suppression on a subsequent test trial, compared to the performance of a control group. Moreover, attenuation of the CR was quite marked in a group that had a sixty-day retention interval between conditioning and the post-conditioning shocks. This result suggests that older memories of shock intensity are more easily replaced than newer ones, given presentation of a weaker shock than that used in conditioning.

The magnitude of the deflation effect cannot be determined in these studies. For instance, the deflation manipulation may have reduced conditioned fear to a level that would be equivalent to the amount of fear supportable by the weaker UCS, say, when it is used to condition a stimulus in a naive group. This outcome would be consistent with the memory replacement notion. On the other hand, it seems possible that the reduction will never be complete, that is, the group receiving weak post-conditioning shocks may still demonstrate more fear than a group only receiving conditioning with the weak shock. This result would be incompatible with the claim that the new memory completely replaces the old, but would be compatible with an averaging model.

It may be pointed out here that not all experiments attempting to deflate the UCS memory with presentations of weaker UCSs have been successful.

The study of Riley et al. (1976), described earlier, failed to observe attenuation of a taste aversion when progressively weaker dosages of LiCl were presented after the conditioning phase. It may be recalled, however, that the habituation effects with the taste aversion paradigm were highly sensitive to procedural variations. Similarly, under nonoptimal training and testing conditions, then, it may be difficult to observe an effect of presenting weaker UCSs. In this particular experiment, recall that a strong aversion had been conditioned, only one extinction test was given, and this test used a relatively insensitive one-bottle procedure.

Post-Conditioning Exposures to a More Intense UCS

Post-conditioning UCSs can also be made more intense. Given the effects of presenting weaker UCSs after conditioning, post-exposure to a more intense UCS should, according to a memory replacement analysis, enhance the strength of the CR. Several experimenters, but not all, have found this result.

Rescorla (1974) was the first to demonstrate a shock intensity-dependent enhancement of CER. After conditioning fear to a tone CS with a .5-mA, .5-s foot-shock, either no shocks, 1-mA, or 3-mA shocks were delivered. Each of these post-conditioning shocks was signalled by a flashing light. When the tone was subsequently presented several times without shock, both the 1-mA and 3-mA shock groups revealed increased conditioned suppression. The 1 mA group, however, did not differ from the no shock group at the very start of extinction testing. Also, since groups only receiving conditioning with either 1-mA or 3-mA shocks were not included, we have no way of knowing how complete these inflation effects were. Using a conditioned punishment test procedure, Sherman (1978) also demonstrated an inflation effect when post-conditioning shocks were more intense than those used during conditioning.

Bouton and Bolles (1985) presented data indicating that the inflation effect does not depend upon presenting the post-conditioning shocks in the same context used in extinction testing, and that inflation is only weakly attenuated by signalling the post-conditioning shocks. Following fear conditioning to a tone (paired with a .5-mA, .5-s shock), different groups either received many unsignalled 3-mA shocks in the same context that conditioning occurred in, received the shocks in a different context, or received no post-conditioning shocks. Both post shock groups showed enhanced suppression to the tone throughout extinction testing, although the effects did not always show up immediately. Even though context-escape measures revealed more context fear in the same group than in the different group, there was no difference in fear to the CS in the two groups.

In an experiment described earlier, Hendersen (1985) also gave rats two post-conditioning shocks more intense than those used in conditioning. These shocks occurred either 24 hrs or 60 days after conditioning, and were followed on the same day by a test of the CS's ability to suppress licking. There was only a hint of an inflation effect in the 24-hr group, but a marked increase in lick suppression was observed in the 60-day group. As in the case of deflation, it seems that old memories of shock intensity are more easily replaced than newer ones, given presentation of stronger shocks than that used in conditioning.

Randich and Rescorla (1981) report that time, as well as increasing shock intensity, contributes to the inflation effect. Rats that received tone-shock conditioning and then a CS test immediately following conditioning showed less conditioned suppression than a group experiencing a 24-hr wait before testing. Further, this time-enhanced suppression was attenuated if the same shock used in conditioning was presented 12 min before the CS test. If a stronger shock was presented 12 min before CS extinction testing, then extinction of the CER took longer than in a group receiving the same 24-hr wait but not receiving any post-conditioning shocks. Thus, it appears that time since shock is a variable that may make it difficult to interpret inflation or, especially, deflation effects. For example, decreasing the shock intensity after conditioning may not always produce a weak shock memory at the time of testing. Appropriate controls, however, allow one to easily evaluate the contribution of time.

In another study Randich and Haggard (1983) reported that increasing the shock intensity after conditioning attenuated the amount of CER shown in extinction relative to a group not receiving any post-conditioning shocks. Three groups of rats received many shocks during ten post-conditioning sessions, with shock weaker than, the same as, or stronger than conditioning shocks. A fourth group did not receive any post-conditioning shocks. On the first trial of an extinction test session, the three post-shock groups displayed an intensity-dependent alleviation of suppression relative to the control group. The strongest post-exposure shocks resulted in the least suppression. If either inflation or habituation of the UCS representation, or the two effects in combination, were mediating these effects, then there should have been greater suppression in the group receiving stronger shocks than in the group receiving weaker shocks. Over the next two extinction test trials, the groups that had received either the same or less intense shocks following conditioning showed extremely rapid extinction rates, whereas the intense shock post-exposure group showed no evidence of extinction but remained less suppressed than no-shock controls. Given the large number of post-conditioning exposures to shock in this experiment, we must assume very considerable habituation in all experimental groups. If we further assume that habituation was inversely related to UCS intensity, then this might explain why the group exposed to stronger shocks extinguished more slowly than the other two shock groups. Adding the memory replacement assumption doesn't change this prediction, so long as habituation is assumed to be the stronger of the two effects.

Miller and Schachtman (1985) briefly reported a failure to obtain inflation using a lick-suppression procedure. Their experiment included only one test trial.

Post-Conditioning Manipulations of Motivational State

Holland and Rescorla (1975) reported that food satiation following appetitive conditioning attenuated the amount of conditioned responding and facilitated extinction of the CR. A tone had been paired with food in food-deprived rats; then half of the rats were allowed to eat ad lib for four days. When the tone was subsequently presented without reinforcement, it elicited less activity in the satiated rats than in the deprived ones. Holland (1981) replicated this finding for each of three components of the activity measure: startle, magazine behavior and head jerk. These effects were large, but incomplete. Early in extinction testing the tone still elicited more responses than late in testing. There was no group that had been conditioned while sated; thus it is difficult to assess the "completeness" of the effect of satiation.

Using a within-subject autoshaping procedure with rats, Cleland and Davey (1982) demonstrated similar sensitivity of the CR to reinforcer satiation. Two retractable levers were inserted into the chamber prior to milk and food pellets, respectively. Following satiation to both food and milk, the frequency of consummatory responses directed towards the levers (e.g., mouthing, licking, biting, or pawing) was reduced to near-zero levels. However, preparatory behaviors, such as orienting and sniffing, were either increased or not affected by the satiation manipulation.

Recently, Ramachandran and Pearce (1987) have shown that motivationally-induced reinforcer revaluation effects can be produced by removing an irrelevant drive. Goal-directed responses conditioned to a light by food when rats were hungry and thirsty, were slow to be acquired and fast to extinguish, relative to rats that were only hungry. The irrelevant thirst drive affected performance, rather than the ability of the rats to learn, since rats conditioned while both hungry and thirsty displayed extinction levels when tested while only hungry that were similar to those of rats both conditioned and tested while hungry. Further, the irrelevant thirst drive did not generally depress performance. Rats trained while hungry and tested while thirsty displayed more responses in extinction than rats trained while hungry but tested while sated (to both food and water). Thus the suppressive effects of the irrelevant thirst drive depend upon interactions between thirst and hunger, and the outcome of this interaction may be seen as influencing the value of the food UCS representation.

Several plausible interpretations, different from those suggested by Rozeboom (1958), may account for revaluation effects when motivational state is altered. State-dependent learning (e.g., Overton, 1971), learning of conditional relations where motivational state functions as a "modulator" (Rescorla, 1985) or a cue (Davidson, 1987), and general depressive effects of performance by changes in motivation are just some mechanisms that do not assume that motivational changes alter the UCS representation. A study of Zener's (1937) is relevant to this point. In his experiment dogs were trained to expect two different types of food, given different signals (a bell or light). When he subsequently selectively satiated his dogs to only one of the reinforcers, salivary CRs were selectively reduced (see also Holman, 1980). Similarly, Stanhope (1989) trained hungry and thirsty pigeons to expect food after one keylight and water after another. When they were subsequently satiated on either food or water there was greater suppression of the piegons' keypeck CRs to the CS correlated with the satiated reinforcer than to the one correlated with the deprived reinforcer. Under such conditions one may be more confident that the motivational effects observed are UCS-specific, and are not the result of a general motivational, performance, or modulator mechanism.

Recently Fedorchak and Bolles have also conducted a selective satiation experiment (1987; see also Deems, Oetting, Sherman, & Garcia, 1986). They mixed one flavor (e.g., orange) with calorie-rich ethanol (or sometimes sugar water) and mixed another flavor (e.g., grape) with a non-nutritive, but palatable, saccharin solution. While hungry, the rats were given free access to each solution on alternate days. The rats were then given a choice between the orange and grape flavors (in the absence of their associates). When the rats were tested while food deprived, they strongly preferred the flavor that had been paired with the calorie-rich ethanol. But when they were tested under free feeding and drinking conditions, they displayed no preference for one flavor over the other. Other groups tested while hungry indicated that the saccharin-paired and ethanol-paired flavors were preferred to a flavor simply paired with water, indicating that conditioning to both tastes had occurred. Moreover, vis-a-vis water, testing under *ad lib* feeding conditions reduced the preference for the ethanol-paired flavor, but not the preference for the saccharin-paired flavor. Thus this experiment demonstrates selective satiation both between and within groups (see also Holland, 1988).

Selective effects of motivational shifts upon conditioned responding have also been reported when a specific hunger for one of the reinforcers used to established conditioned responding has been induced following a conditioning phase. Rescorla and Freberg (1978) have shown that after rats were depleted of sodium they preferred a quinine solution to water if in an earlier conditioning phase the quinine solution had been mixed with sodium chloride. Fudim (1978) and Berridge and Schulkin (1989) have gone on to show that inducing a sodium need selectively enhanced preference for tastes that had previously been paired with sodium chloride and not for tastes paired with a sugar solution.

In the Berridge and Schulkin experiment, under ad lib food and water conditions citric acid and quinine hydrochloride solutions were paired (in a counterbalanced fashion) with either sodium chloride or fructose tastes that served as the UCSs. Rats were then tested under normal ad lib conditions or after a sodium need was induced by injections of furosemide. In a two-bottle preference test under normal conditions, the rats showed no preference for either the citric acid or the quinine solution. However, when tested while sodium depleted the rats consumed the same amount of the fructose-paired taste, but increased their intake of the sodium chloride-paired taste. In addition, this taste elicited more ingestive taste reactivity responses while the rats were sodium depleted, indicating that its hedonic evaluation was also enhanced by the motivational shift.

In what may be considered a procedure that combines elements of the selective satiation and deprivation designs just mentioned, Dickinson and Dawson (1987) have also recently provided evidence for selective effects of a motivational shift using more conventional appetitive Pavlovian conditioning procedures. In their experiment, rats were trained while hungry to expect free food pellets in the presence of a 2-min light, to expect free deliveries of a sugar solution in the presence of a 2-min tone, and to expect the delivery of food pellets if they pressed a lever that was present during 2-min periods in the absence of the Pavlovian CSs. The effectiveness of these Pavlovian cues for sugar or food on lever pressing was then tested in an extinction session where some of the rats were maintained hungry and others were made thirsty. For the rats shifted to thirst, food is no longer relevant and should therefore lose its motivational significance, but sugar water is relevant and should gain new motivational significance. In this test session, the thirsty rats lever pressed more in the presence of the CS for sugar than in the CS for food, and the hungry rats responded equally in the presence of the two CSs. Dickinson and Dawson asserted that the induction of thirst selectively enhanced the (Pavlovian) conditioned motivational state evoked by the CS for sugar solution, which in turn facilitated the prepotent instrumental behavior (e.g., Rescorla & Solomon, 1967).

The results of the experiments in this section suggest that Pavlovian CS-evoked reinforcer representations are sensitive to shifts in motivational states. Moreover, this sensitivity can be selective. Shifts in motivation that decrease the value of UCS1, but not UCS2, (e.g., Stanhope, 1989) depress the representations evoked by CSs that have been paired with UCS1, but not the representations evoked by CSs paired with UCS2. Shifts in motivation that increase the value of UCS1, but not UCS2 (e.g., Berridge & Schulkin, 1989), enhance the representations evoked by CSs that have been paired with UCS1, but not those evoked by CSs paired with UCS2. This conclusion argues against the possibilities that shifts in motivation affect conditioned responding by generally influencing performance or by removing conditional cues (e.g., Davidson, 1987; Rescorla, 1985).

In our opinion the experiments on motivational shifts described above can be more readily explained in S-S than in S-R terms. Consider the experiment by Berridge and Schulkin, in which rats repeatedly received infusions of one taste paired with sodium chloride and another paired with fructose, while they were maintained on ad lib sodium-free food and water. When the two taste CSs were infused while the rats were sodium depleted, the palatability of the NaCl-paired taste was enhanced. The S-S account maintains that the CS taste and the taste of NaCl become associated under ad lib conditions, so that when the rat is tested sodium depleted the CS taste evokes the representation of the taste of NaCl. Sodium depletion unconditionally increases the incentive value of the taste of NaCl (e.g., Wolf, Schulkin, & Simpson, 1984), therefore the incentive value of the CS should also be increased.

To explain the same outcome, an S-R view would have to assert that the mixture containing sodium chloride evokes some affective response even under ad lib conditions, and that the CS taste becomes associated with that response. Sodium depletion would then have to enhance the positive affective value of that response, for example, as might happen if the response had an inhibitory effect on the aversive state of Na depletion. This account seems less parsimonious than the S-S account. Moreover, in an experiment similar to that of Berridge and Schulkin (1989), Rescorla and Freberg (1978) found that separate presentation of NaCl between the conditioning and sodium depletion phases reduced the preference for the NaCl-paired flavor when the rats were subsequently tested sodium depleted. This result is also easier to explain in S-S than S-R terms.

If one accepts these arguments, it might still be that they apply only to the case where CS and UCS are presented simultaneously. We don't believe that this is so, in light of Dickinson and Dawson's (1987) results, which were obtained with exteroceptive CSs that preceded the food pellets and sucrose solution UCSs in a delay conditioning procedure. The S-S account of these results parallels, up to a point, the aforementioned account of the sodium depletion experiment. The state of thirst enhances the incentive value of the oral stimuli that had been experienced when the rat drank sucrose. By virtue of evoking a UCS representation with enhanced incentive value, the CS for sugar solution became a more effective Pavlovian CS in test. This was reflected, not by a change in the incentive value of the CS itself as in the experiments with flavor cues, but by an increase in the CS's ability to motivate appetitive instrumental behavior.

Counterconditioning Studies

In an appetitive conditioning procedure one obvious counterconditioning manipulation is to condition an aversion to the appetitive UCS (e.g., food or palatable solutions). Although procedures exist for counterconditioning shock by pairing it with food (Pearce & Dickinson, 1975), this procedure has not been used to evaluate deflation effects in aversive conditioning (but see Ross, 1986).

Holland and Rescorla (1975) investigated the effects of appetitive-to-aversive counterconditioning on activity conditioning to an auditory CS. After establishing activity CRs to a tone, they paired their food UCS with high-speed rotation and established a mild aversion. Before the first nonreinforced tone test, rats that experienced food-rotation pairings ate approximately half as many food pellets as rats receiving only rotation after conditioning. During the tone test, the aversion group was less active than the no-aversion group early in testing and their activity CRs appeared to be lost more quickly. It may be noted that a group receiving conditioning with the mildly aversive food was not included to assess the magnitude of the deflation effect. The aversion was then subsequently extinguished, and in another pellet consumption test the aversion-extinction group ate more pellets. This group was also more active in the presence of the tone in another test.

In a related set of experiments, Holland and Straub (1979) showed that establishing a food pellet aversion with LiCl pairing after tone-pellet conditioning had no deleterious effects on tone-elicited "activity" CRs, but pairings of pellet and rotation did. A more detailed behavioral analysis indicated that magazine behavior, such as snout in the feeding trough, was reduced nearly to nonconditioning-baseline levels by pellet-LiCl pairings after conditioning, but startle and head-jerk CRs were unaffected. Food-rotation pairings completely reduced (to near-baseline levels) tone-elicited conditioned startle and head-jerk responses, but only partially reduced magazine behaviors occurring towards the end of the CS. Pellet consumption data further indicated that although the food aversions showed only moderate transfer from the home cages to the testing apparatus, the food aversion conditioned by LiCl was stronger than the rotation-induced aversion as measured against the control groups that received only LiCl and rotation without food pellets.

If head-jerk and startle responses may be considered as "preparatory" CRs, since they occur early in the CS and are diffuse or non-directed, and mazagine responses as consummatory CRs, because they occur later in the CS and are directed (see also Boakes, 1979), then the incompleteness of the deflation effect, in the case of pellet-LiCl, could be explained by the selective reduction of consummatory CRs, with residual preparatory CRs remaining intact (recall that Cleland & Davey (1982) observed a similar pattern, in which consummatory CRs were more sensitive than preparatory CRs, following satiation on the food pellet or milk UCS).

How then, might we explain the greater decrement in preparatory CRs than in consummatory CRs when rotation was the counterconditioning agent? Following Holland and Straub (1979), it might be supposed that the two classes of behavior are supported by different aspects of the food UCS, and that those aspects might be differentially affected by rotation and LiCl. Specifically, suppose rotation, but not LiCl injection, induces dizziness. If conditionable, this state might compete more effectively with such preparatory responses as startle and head jerk than with consummatory responses like standing motionless in front of the food magazine with nose or head within the magazine.

In another related experiment, Cleland and Davey (1982) demonstrated that both consummatory and preparatory CRs elicited by the sudden appearance of a response lever were reduced (or completely eliminated) if the taste used to condition these CRs was paired with LiCl following lever-autoshaping. The right lever was paired with, and the left lever unpaired with, milk delivered to a liquid trough. Following the final conditioning session, in which there was good evidence for discriminative responding, and following each of two more home cage milk presentations, the rats were administered either a moderate-strong dose of LiCl or saline. The levers were then presented in discrete trials over two sessions without milk. The LiCl rats showed a greater reduction in the percentage of trials on which they oriented towards, sniffed, and licked the milk-paired lever than the saline rats, and the amount of magazine approach behavior was reduced. Thus, similar to Holland and Straub (1979), consummatory CRs were reduced or, in the case of licking, eliminated by the LiCl counterconditioning treatment. In addition, however, preparatory responses (sniffing, lever orienting) were reduced by pairing the taste with LiCl. In this experiment, head-jerks were not measured but lever-orienting responses were similar, by definition, to Holland and Straub's startle response. The failure to find selective persistence of preparatory CRs in Cleland's and Davey's experiment could be related to the establishment of a strong aversion. Such an aversion may not only reduce consummatory CRs, by altering the value of the milk, but it may also reduce any preparatory CRs. There is reason to believe that the aversion to milk in this experiment might be stronger than the aversion to pellets in Holland and Straub (1979); Cleland and Davey poisoned the rats after consumption of milk in the experimental chamber, whereas Holland and Straub administered the LiCl after pellets were consumed in the home cage.

Similar to imposing motivational state changes following conditioning to deflate the UCS, a counterconditioning procedure sometimes produces both strong and weak sensitivity to this deflation. Residual conditioned responding can be understood in terms of differential suppressive effects upon preparatory and consummatory response systems. If the counterconditioning procedure dramatically changes the value of the UCS (e.g., as indicated by a strong taste aversion), then preparatory and consummatory CRs will be greatly if not completely reduced. However, sometimes characteristics of the counterconditioning UCS seem to be important in determining which response system may be primarily affected by the counterconditioning procedure.

Summary of Reinforcer Revaluation Experiments

Altering the value of the UCS used to support first-order conditioning seems to reliably affect the responses that manifest that conditioning. However, no one procedure has consistently produced complete revaluation effects. This is not surprising, since we do not know how complete the revaluation treatments themselves were in altering the value of the UCSs. It becomes important, for example, to develop a measure of habituation that is independent of the conditioning procedure that the treatment is presumed to affect. It is hard to know whether altering the motivational state should completely reduce the value of the UCS. In order to assess the completeness of a motivational change it would be useful to know how much conditioning could be supported by food, for example, in a sated rat. In assessing the completeness of a counterconditioning manipulation, the amount of conditioning supportable by a counterconditioned UCS would serve as a good control. In addition, the completeness of inflation and deflation manipulations when increasing and decreasing, respectively, UCS intensity can easily be assessed with the appropriate controls.

Complete revaluation effects may be taken as support of the view that only sensory aspects of the conditioned and conditioning stimuli enter into the association, that is, that the learning is S-S. When no effect of revaluation occurs, assuming that the revaluation treatment was effective, this would be grounds for believing that the association did not involve sensory aspects of the reinforcer, and thus involved a response, whether central or peripheral. And finally, when partial effects of revaluation are observed this could mean that both sensory and non-sensory components of the reinforcer entered the association. This last conclusion seems to best fit at least some of the first-order Pavlovian conditioning data reviewed here (e.g., Cleland & Davey, 1982; Holland & Straub, 1979). In these experiments, sometimes different response systems were affected differently by the revaluation treatment. This finding raises questions regarding the associative structure that is assumed to underlie the observed behavior.

To see more clearly how revaluation treatments might alter conditioned responding, we can evaluate one representational theory in some detail and ask whether it can accommodate the empirical observations. Consider Konorski's system (1967), in which both specific sensory and more general motivational (or affective) components of the UCS are assumed to independently enter into associations with a CS. Under normal conditions, the specific sensory aspects of the UCS representation are thought to control highly specific, directed, consummatory responses; whereas, more general motivational aspects of the UCS representation are thought to control diffuse, nondirected, preparatory responses. It is also assumed that the two systems interact; conditioned elicitation of a consummatory response depends upon the activation of the motivational system.

Consider now what might happen following UCS habituation. When a UCS (like loud noise) is presented, we suppose that both the sensory and motivational aspects of this event will be processed. After repeatedly presenting the UCS, however, we may suppose that the UCS is still perceived, that is, the sensory aspects of the stimuli are still processed (maybe at a somewhat reduced level). The most significant result of UCS habituation, however, may be indicated by the reduced ability (or complete inability, if habituation has been complete) of the UCS to result in affective processing. Accordingly, activation of the sensory representation of the UCS, whether this activation be unconditioned or conditioned, will no longer result in further affective processing. One obvious consequence of this is that preparatory responses will be reduced, since these responses are presumed to directly depend upon the amount of activity in the motivational system. An indirect consequence is that consummatory responses, as well, will be reduced, since this response system is also dependent, more indirectly, upon the amount of activity in the motivational system.

Notice, however, that, according to Konorski, when a CS has become associated with a UCS the CS has acquired the capacity to *independently* evoke sensory and affective representations of that UCS. Thus, whereas the evoked sensory representation of the UCS will no longer be affectively processed after UCS habituation, the CS still independently produces activity in the motivational system. This independent source of "excitation" then could produce, on its own, preparatory responses, and it could also enable the evoked sensory representation to elicit some level of consummatory responses. Thus, UCS habituation, even when it is complete, should never completely eliminate conditioned responding. However, since the total amount of activity in the motivational system after habituation, all of which arises directly from the CS, would be smaller than that produced at the end of conditioning, when such activity arose both directly from the CS and from the CS-evoked sensory representation of the UCS, there should be some reduction in the strength of both preparatory and consummatory CRs.

A similar analysis can be applied to UCS devaluation when it occurs with a change in motivational state. When the rat becomes sated, for example, the sensory characteristics of food should lose their positive affect. This assumption receives some empirical support from work which demonstrates that tastes paired with the end of a satiating meal tend to become less preferred (e.g., Booth, 1972). But since the CS has independently been associated with sensory and motivational aspects of the UCS, then the CS may still be expected to evoke these representations. The total amount of activity in the motivational system (arising from both the UCS sensory representation and the CS itself) has been reduced, so both preparatory and consummatory CRs should be reduced. We assume that when the rat is sated a CS still has the ability to make it hungry even when the UCS cannot (see Weingarten, 1983). Unconditioned stimulus devaluation with this method should at best, only attenuate, but not eliminate, conditioned responding. The data fit this characterization reasonably well . Holland and Rescorla (1975) reported that preparatory conditioning with food declined at a faster rate in extinction in the sated animals. Cleland and Davey (1982), in addition, found that consummatory, but not preparatory, responses declined following satiation. Konorski's account can accommodate the last result if we assume that consummatory responses require more conditioned affect (motivation) than preparatory responses.

An analysis in the spirit of Konorski of UCS revaluation effects produced with counterconditioning procedures is slightly more complex, requiring an additional mechanism. During counterconditioning we might think of the original UCS as a new "CS" which comes to be associated with both the sensory and motivational aspects of the new UCS (e.g., sucrose may be associated with both stomach pains and nausea). When the original CS (e.g., a tone that was previously paired with sucrose) is subsequently presented, it will evoke both sensory and motivational representations that were appropriate to the original UCS. But because of counterconditioning, the sensory representation of the original UCS will now activate a sensory representation of the new counterconditioning UCS as well as a motivational representation of that UCS, which is opposed to the motivational state that was part of the original UCS representation. The presence of two oppositely valenced motivational activations may result in motivational antagonism (see also Dickinson & Dearing, 1979). In our example, if the aversive motivation is enough to completely antagonize the appetitive motivation, then this should completely eliminate both appetitive preparatory and consummatory CRs, and if there is "extra" aversive motivation then aversive preparatory or consummatory CRs may even be seen. On the other hand, if there is not enough aversive motivation to antagonize the appetitive motivation evoked by the CS, then this incomplete antagonism should result in only an attenuation of conditioned responding to the CS.

Consider now how presentation of less intense or more intense UCSs following conditioning would affect the associative structure assumed to mediate conditioning. Consider the experiment by Bouton and Bolles (1985), in which inflation resulted from post-exposure to 3-mA shock after conditioning with .5-mA shock. If the sensory representations of those two shock intensities are very different, as seems likely, then it is not immediately obvious why the memory of the 3-mA shock should replace the memory of the 0.5-mA shock. Would a qualitatively different event that is as aversive as the 3-mA shock have the same effect? If so, then it seems unreasonable to assert that the inflation (or deflation) effect results from the sensory representation of the conditioning UCS having new affective consequences as a result of post-exposure. If not, then similarity of the sensory representations of the conditioning and post-exposure UCSs must be important. This should be the case even when the change in UCS is a marked change in intensity. For example, the effect of increasing or decreasing UCS intensity after conditioning may have to be modelled in terms of how many sensory features are shared by the conditioning and post-exposure UCSs.

One outcome that makes more sense if we consider the similarity factor was observed by Hendersen, who found stronger inflation and deflation effects with a 60-day interval between conditioning and post-exposure than with a one-day interval. If over the 60 days the rats forgot some of the distinctive features of the conditioning shock, so that the two shocks became more similar, this outcome would follow.

It should be noted that, according to Konorski (1967), an additional factor also affects the outcomes of experiments in which UCS intensity is changed during post-exposure. In his view the CS was also directly associated with the motivational aspect of the conditioning UCS. This source of motivational activation should be "protected" from any changes occurring during the revaluation phase, and should, in general, lead us to expect that these kinds of revaluation effects would never be complete.

In this summary, so far, we have shown how motivational processes may interact with representational structures to modulate performance. We have tried to indicate how UCS revaluation techniques may be effective within this scheme. We have suggested that revaluation techniques may never completely eliminate the CR, especially if the CS has independent input into the motivational system, or if there is incomplete antagonism of opposing motivational states, or if response systems differ in their sensitivities to changes in motivation.

REINSTATEMENT OF PAVLOVIAN CONDITIONING

Procedurally, "reinstatement" can be observed if presentation of a UCS following extinction of a CS reestablishes a CR to the extinguished CS. Encouraged by Konorski's representational theory and confirming evidence from some of the revaluation experiments reported above, Rescorla and Heth (1975) proposed a representational theory of extinction which also readily accounted for reinstatement. They supposed that through the course of extinction the associative bond presumed to connect internal representations of the CS and UCS became degraded, and, more importantly, the UCS representation weakened. Consequently, the effect that a reinstating UCS has on the UCS representation following extinction was seen as directly analogous to the effect that an inflating UCS has on the UCS representation following conditioning, that is, it somehow replaces the UCS memory.

Rescorla and Heth demonstrated reinstatement by showing that shocks (signalled or not) presented after extinction of the CS's ability to suppress food-reinforced lever pressing had the effect of reestablishing suppression to the CS on subsequent nonreinforced test presentations. An unpaired control group also receiving additional shocks did not show any suppression, and a group not receiving additional shocks showed no evidence of spontaneous recovery of suppression. Additional experiments showed that loud noise and shock could be interchanged in their abilities to serve as conditioning and reinstating UCS, and that reinstatement was most easily seen if suppression to the CS had been reduced by pairing the CS with a weaker intensity shock (a procedure thought to leave intact the associative bond while weakening only the UCS memory) rather than by simple extinction.

Bouton and Bolles' (1979) investigation of reinstatement focused on the role played by the context. In their procedure extinction of conditioned suppression and nonreinforced presentations of the CS in a later test phase occurred in a context which was very different from the context in which the CS was paired with shock. For one group reinstating shocks were delivered in the extinction (and test) context, whereas another group received reinstating shocks in the conditioning context (not the test context). Reinstatement of conditioned suppression was seen only in the group which was tested in the context where reinstating shocks had been delivered. Subsequent experiments also showed that nonreinforced exposures to the reinstatement context following the presentation of reinstating shocks, but before testing, eliminated the reinstatement effect that otherwise was observed. Bouton and King (1983) and Bouton (1984) provided additional evidence that reinstatement is highly positively correlated with the amount of fear evoked by the test context, as assessed by their context-preference measure (i.e., a measure that records the latency to escape from an aversive context).

The Bouton and Bolles experiments are not consistent with the analysis of reinstatement given by Rescorla and Heth (1975). Rescorla and Heth's memory inflation account of reinstatement makes no allowance for context dependence. Instead, the Bouton and Bolles experiments provide data suggesting that reinstatement results from simple summation of the ambient context fear with a presumed sub-threshold level of CS fear. This sum could result in a supra-threshold level of fear in the presence of the CS.

Bouton and King (1986), however, presented data suggesting that context-CS summation may not be the only mechanism involved in reinstatement. In their experiments, unlike Bouton's earlier ones, extinction of conditioned suppression occurred in the same context as conditioning and test. Reinstatement shocks were then delivered for some rats in the same context used for conditioning and subsequently for testing, or in a different context. In addition, other groups of rats received the CS partially reinforced with shock before receiving shocks in either of the two contexts. Suppression appeared to be reinstated in both extinction groups, with the group receiving testing in the reinstatement context evidencing more suppression. The groups that had received partial reinforcement, on the other hand, showed no such differential effect of context but sometimes appeared to show evidence of enhanced levels of suppression relative to their baselines at the end of conditioning. Context preference scores revealed clear context discrimination in both the extinguished and the partially reinforced groups. In another experiment groups receiving nonreinforced exposures of the CS *prior* to conditioning, (latent inhibition) also showed no differential effect of context. Following the latent inhibition treatment and conditioning, groups received additional shocks in either the same or different context as was used during conditioning and would be used for testing. Both of these groups appeared to display enhanced levels of suppression relative to the conditioning phase baseline, but there was no evidence for greater enhancement of suppression in the group that was tested in the same context in which reinstating shocks occurred. These data contrasted with the context preference scores, which showed that the same group was quicker to escape the test environment than the different group.

Finally, Bouton found that groups given conditioning, extinction, and then extensive reacquisition training before receiving shocks in either the same context to be used in testing or a different one, showed no differential effects of context, nor did they show enhanced levels of suppression relative to their conditioning phase baselines. These data occurred in spite of clear context discriminations, as indicated by the context preference measure.

The failures of the context in the partial reinforcement, the latent inhibition, and the reacquisition groups to differentially control CS suppression are outcomes that are not anticipated by a straightforward context summation view of reinstatement. It is not clear, for instance, why fearful contexts should summate differentially with CSs that are equivalent in terms of the amount of suppression conditioned to them but that differ in their reinforcement histories. Instead, Bouton and Bolles (1985) asserted that contexts may be especially effective in modulating the effects of CSs that have "ambiguous" reinforcement histories. Under such a view it would have to be assumed that for a stimulus to be considered "ambiguous" it would have to have a mixed history of whatever processes mediate acquisition and extinction, for example, conditioned excitation and inhibition. The context could then serve to "disambiguate" the CS, for example, by calling up the memory of acquisition. This disambiguating role of context is most easily seen in the "renewal" experiment. For example, Bouton and King (1983) found that following acquisition of conditioned suppression, if extinction occurred in a context other than the conditioning context, then when the rats were subsequently tested in the conditioning context conditioned suppression was renewed. The contexts in this procedure may be seen as evoking the separate mechanisms of conditioning and extinction. That is, instead of the effects of conditioning and extinction combining to produce the net effect of the CS, as traditional theory would assert (e.g., Rescorla & Wagner, 1972), whether the CS activates the UCS representation or the no UCS representation depends upon the context, which acts as a conditional cue. The extinction context should thus control the CS-activation of mechanisms of inhibition, and the conditioning context should control the CS-activation of mechanisms of excitation (see Bouton & Swartzentruber, 1989).

Lovibond, Preston, and Mackintosh (1984) suggested that the greater conditioned suppression in test in Group Different than in Group Same observed by Bouton and King (1983; see also Bouton & Bolles, 1979) reflected differences in the associative strengths of both test context and CSs in the two groups rather than conditional cue learning. The test context had greater associative strength in Group Different because it had not been extinguished in that group. Moreover, since the extinction context was associatively neutral at the start of extinction for Group Different, it should have become inhibitory during extinction, and thus partially protected the CS from extinction (Rescorla & Wagner, 1972). In test both context and CS should have been more excitatory in Group Different, and the summation of the two effects should have resulted in greater suppression in that group. Thus the renewal effect does not require conditional cue learning.

To support their claim, Lovibond et al. conducted an experiment in which Group Same received conditioning to tone in one context, and conditioning to light in a second. Then each CS was extinguished in its conditioning context. Finally each was tested in the same context. Group Different received the same treatment in the conditioning and test phases, but the assignment of discrete cues to contexts was reversed in the extinction phase. In this experiment, which ensures that the familiarity and associative strength of the two contexts are equated in the two groups, Group Different (extinguished in a context different from the one in which it was conditioned and tested) showed no more renewal of the CR than Group Same (conditioned, extinguished, and tested all in one context).

Bouton and Swartzentruber (1986; see also Bouton & Peck, 1989) advanced a different interpretation of the absence of a renewal effect in Group Different of the experiment by Lovibond et al. They suggested that each context becomes a positive conditional cue or occasion setter (e.g., Holland, 1985) in phase one, but loses this property in the second phase, because the other discrete cue is non-reinforced in its presence during that phase. This account seems plausible, and thus we are left with two quite different explanations of the renewal effect observed by Bouton and King (1983) and absence of such an effect in the experiment by Lovibond et al. (1984).

Even if we accept the assertion that renewal occurs because the conditioning context acquires an occasion setting or conditional cue function, the reinstatement (after extinction) experiments demand a different explanation. This is so because in neither the Bouton and Bolles (1979) nor Bouton and King (1986) experiments was it true that both: (1) conditioning and extinction occurred in different contexts, and (2) the test occurred in the conditioning context. In the absence of these two features, the test context cannot selectively retrieve the conditioning memory. So Bouton and King (1986) suggested instead that context fear acted as a retrieval cue for the memory of acquisition, at least when the CS was ambiguous. This is close to saying that contextual fear acts as a positive occasion setter. But recall that conditioning and extinction occurred in the same context in the Bouton and King (1986) experiment. Moreover, there should have been more context fear at the start of the extinction session than at the start of the conditioning session. So contextual fear should have evoked the memory of extinction.

From a different theoretical perspective, Miller and his colleagues have been investigating similar sets of procedures that bear on what processes are involved in reinstatement, and more generally, in any post-conditioning stimulus manipulation. Using a latent inhibition procedure somewhat similar to that used by Bouton and King (1986), Kasprow, Catterson, Schachtman, and Miller (1984) found evidence for recovery of conditioning to a latently inhibited CS following presentation of the UCS. Thirsty rats drank water from a tube in each of two contexts and then received nonreinforced exposures to a white noise CS followed by noise-shock pairings (on different days) in one of the contexts. Subsequently, some rats received a few unsignaled shocks in the conditioning context. After two lick-recovery days in each context, the rats' 25th lick in the context *not* used for conditioning and post-conditioning shocks produced the noise, which remained on until the 50th lick had been recorded. The group receiving additional shocks took longer to complete these 25 licks than a group that had not received additional shocks or a group that had received additional shocks following unpaired presentations of noise and shock. The enhancement of conditioned suppression observed here was complete, as the run latency for the group given post-conditioning shocks was as long as the latency for a group receiving no nonreinforced noise presentations before conditioning (i.e., a continuous reinforcement procedure). Additional shocks had no effect on this continuous reinforcement group. Thus, like Bouton and King (1986), Kasprow et al. found that additional shocks delivered in a context other than the testing context may serve to enhance conditioning of a latently inhibited CS. However, this "other" context was the conditioning context in the experiment by Kasprow et al., but a different context in Bouton and King.

In a different study, Balaz, Gutsin, Cacheiro, and Miller (1982) reported that additional shocks enhanced the level of fear that was conditioned to a "blocked" stimulus, that is, "unblocking" was produced. A tone that was paired with shock apparently interfered with subsequent conditioning of a flashing light when the two were presented together and paired with shock. When shocks were delivered in a different context after conditioning, this treatment enhanced the level of lick suppression subsequently controlled by the flashing light, even though testing occurred in the conditioning context. The effect seemed to depend upon associative factors, since additional shocks did not influence response to the flashing light if it had been previously unpaired with shock. The effect also seemed to depend upon the flashing light undergoing a blocking procedure; if independent tone-shock conditioning had not preceded tone+flashing light compound conditioning, then no enhancement of fear to the light was produced by additional shocks. This outcome could, however, reflect ceiling effects. Finally, the enhancement effect reported here could also be produced by exposing the rat to either the conditioning context alone or the flashing light (i.e., the blocked stimulus) alone in a context other than the conditioning context. In a related experiment, Kasprow, Cacheiro, Balaz, and Miller (1982) found that two nonreinforced exposures of an otherwise "overshadowed" flashing light in a context different from the conditioning context could enhance the level of lick suppression controlled by the flashing light when it was later tested in the conditioning context.

These data seem to be consistent with a view of associative processing that Miller and his colleagues are developing (Miller, Kasprow, & Schachtman, 1986). They distinguish between *manifest* associative learning and *nonretrieved* associative learning. When performance does not reflect what an animal has learned, for example, this might reflect the fact that the relevant association, or component thereof, has simply not been retrieved. The failures we see with procedures such as overshadowing and blocking might be at least partly understood in this way. The use of appropriate retrieval cues might, consequently, tend to alleviate the performance and/or learning failures we see. Since it is unclear which cues could function to retrieve associations, a good first guess might be the cues present during the initial conditioning. This would help explain why exposures to the conditioning context, to the UCS, or to the

CS itself in a different context, resulted in recovery of latently inhibited, over-shadowed, and blocked associations (see Balaz et al., 1982; Kasprow et al., 1982; Kasprow, Catterson et al., 1984). But retrieval is not enough to account for these effects because the "reminder" treatments in these experiments all occurred 24 hr before the tests were made. Miller and Schachtman (1985) further assumed that a retrieved association can undergo further associative rehearsal, which is assumed to produce a more "permanent" memory trace. We can understand the reinstatement phenomenon on the basis of this scheme if we assume that UCSs following extinction can retrieve the extinguished CS-UCS association and promote further rehearsal (of the excitatory relationship).

On this account, it can be seen that the success of reinstatement would depend upon the extent of extinction. If the CS is fully extinguished, for example, then we might assume that inhibitory relations have combined with the existing excitatory relations to produce a net value near zero (see for instance, Konorski, 1948). Presentation of the UCS might selectively retrieve the excitatory relation, because the UCS was present during conditioning and not extinction. Additional rehearsal, however, may not be sufficient to overcome the strong contribution made by the inhibitory relation established during an extensive extinction treatment. In other words, the CS would still have a net value near zero.

Schachtman, Brown, and Miller (1985) using a taste aversion learning paradigm, have tried reinstating an extinguished taste aversion after partial and extensive extinction. Groups received saccharin either paired or unpaired with an injection of LiCl. One pair of groups then drank saccharin on each of three days for 10 min without receiving LiCl. By the end of this extinction treatment, the groups still differed in their saccharin intake. Subsequently, these two groups received an injection of LiCl in a different environment. During the test exposure to saccharin, conducted in the conditioning and extinction environment, only the paired group drank less than they had on the previous extinction trial. Meanwhile, the second pair of experimental and control groups went on to drink saccharin without LiCl on three more occasions before receiving a reinstating LiCl injection in the novel context. These additional extinction trials erased the difference in saccharin consumption between these two groups. On the test trial, neither group drank less saccharin than they had on the last extinction trial, that is, there was no reinstatement.

In a related series of studies, Bouton (1982) could not find any evidence for reinstatement of an extinguished taste aversion. Unlike the Schachtman et al. (1985) study, in the Bouton study conditioning occurred in one context, but extinction and reinstating UCS presentations occurred in the test context. Another difference was that Bouton gave between 5 and 7 extinction trials, enough to result in no difference in saccharin consumption (measured in a one-bottle test) between the groups by the end of extinction.

In experiments where UCSs are presented during extinction, for example if UCSs are unpaired with the CS, then reinstating UCSs might be expected to be ineffective as they should retrieve and promote rehearsal of both excitatory and inhibitory relations. To our knowledge, this test of the Miller and Schachtman (1985) notions has not been made, (however, see Bouton & King 1986; Durlach 1986; Lindblom & Jenkins, 1981 for related findings).

In summary, reinstatement effects result from several different learning processes. There are cases in which the context appears to summate with an extinguished CS to produce the effect (e.g., Bouton, 1984; Bouton & Bolles, 1979). But "simple" context summation cannot account for all the data, since partially reinforced, latently inhibited, and extinguished but then extensively reconditioned CSs do not show this test-context specific enhancement (e.g., Bouton & King, 1986). However, the latently inhibited (and perhaps also the partially reinforced) CS does show an enhancement effect that is not test-context specific. The latter effect also seems to be related to the recoveries obtainable in the blocking and overshadowing procedures. The treatments that led to these recoveries did not have to occur in the test context, but recovery did seem to be induced by stimuli that were part of the stimulus complex that had been present during acquisition. The retrieval and rehearsal processes used to account for these effects may also contribute to the context-general *reinstatement* effects explored above (Bouton & King, 1986; Schachtman et al., 1985; see also Bouton & Peck, 1989).

There may be contextual constraints determining the effectiveness of retrieval cues in reinstatement experiments (see Kasprow, Catterson et al., 1984). For a cue to serve a retrieval function, it should be part of, or related to, the set of stimulus conditions of acquisition (see Miller & Schachtman, 1985) but not extinction. This constraint allows the retrieval-rehearsal view to account for the apparent test-context specificity shown with the reinstatement of extinguished CRs. If it can be assumed that presenting the UCS in the conditioning context will be more effective at retrieving the acquisition experience (i.e., the excitatory CS-UCS relation) than presenting the UCS in a different context, then the UCS presented in the same context should produce more reinstatement (Bouton & King, 1986). Alternatively, perhaps the effects of rehearsal are more pronounced on the subsequent test day because the rehearsal and test contexts are the same. Perhaps rehearsal in the conditioning context, rather than somewhere else, makes the conditioning context a more effective retrieval cue on the test day. However, it remains unclear on this account why under similar conditions, the latent inhibition procedure should show no context-specific enhancement (Bouton & King, 1986; Kasprow, Catterson et al., 1984). This effect of conditioning history clearly needs to be considered for the retrieval-rehearsal model to have any generality.

Instead of asking when retrieval cues are differentially effective, we could ask when retrieval cues are not effective at all. Additional shock UCSs had no enhancing effect on the CER controlled by a CS that had undergone extinction and then reacquisition, even though suppression was not complete (Bouton & King, 1986). Furthermore, Balaz et al. (1982) and Kasprow, Catterson et al. (1984) included control groups that received continuous reinforcement (in the former, a flashing light was compounded with a tone and in the later, the flashing light, by itself, was paired with shock). In neither of these procedures did additional shocks enhance the lick suppression scores. Finally, Kasprow et al. (1982) found in one of their control groups that the flashing light CS when presented by itself had no observable retrieval-rehearsal effects if it had been conditioned singly. However, before concluding that responses to these continuously reinforced CSs or other unambiguous stimuli are not affected by retrieval cues, it would have to be shown that such null outcomes were not the result of ceiling effects. In addition, it might prove useful to know whether trace conditioned CSs or weakly conditioned CSs similarly show no sensitivity to reminder manipulations.

OTHER EXTINCTION EFFECTS

Rescorla and Cunningham (1977, 1978) introduced another procedure designed to demonstrate that reinstatement of extinguished fear resulted from UCS memory deflation and inflation mechanisms. Two CSs were reinforced with shock, and then one was extinguished. Unsignalled reinstating shocks were then presented. Before testing the extinguished CS, however, the nonextinguished CS was presented without reinforcement. Nonreinforced exposure to the additional CS was shown to "erase" the reinstatement effect otherwise shown to the extinguished CS. This effect was shown to be sensitive to the time intervening between nonreinforced presentations of the nonextinguished CS and testing of the previously extinguished CS, with the effect disappearing with increasing time intervals (i.e., days). These data are consistent with Rescorla and Heth's (1975) earlier ideas about extinction involving a degradation of the UCS memory. That is, a reinstatement-produced inflated UCS memory may have been deflated again following nonreinforced presentation of the other CS. The authors also raised the possibility, consistent with Randich and Rescorla's (1981) later finding, that the UCS memory may inflate with time.

Subsequent assessments of the memory inflation model of extinction, as we saw in the previous section, have not encouraged this view. Several experimenters, using conditioned suppression procedures, have independently determined that extensive extinction experience with one CS does not alleviate fear evoked by another CS, despite the other CS being conditioned with the same UCS (Bouton & King, 1983; Kasprow, Schachtman, Cacheiro, & Miller, 1984; Matzel, Schachtman, & Miller, 1985; Richards & Sargent, 1983). Even when two of three CSs had been extinguished, this experience produced no alleviation of suppression to the third, either on the first trial or throughout extinction testing (Richards & Sargent, 1983).

Effects of extinction of one CS upon responding to another CS have been demonstrated using a related procedure, though. If the two CSs are conditioned in a simultaneous compound, as in an overshadowing procedure, then extinction of one of these CSs has been shown to enhance aversive conditioning to the other CS (Kaufman & Bolles, 1981; Matzel, et al., 1985; Matzel, Shuster, & Miller, 1987, but see Schweitzer & Green, 1982). In the Kaufman and Bolles study, a weak light was compounded with a white noise stimulus and the two were paired with foot shock in two groups. A control group received only noise-shock pairings. One of the compound groups subsequently received nonreinforced presentations of the light. Conditioned freezing elicited by the noise CS was then assessed in an extinction test. Overshadowing of noise by light was indicated by quick extinction of freezing during noise in the light-noise group relative to the noise-only group. However, the overshadowing group that also received light extinction before noise testing froze as much to the noise CS as the noise-only group did.

Perhaps the most interesting implication of the Kaufman and Bolles (1981) result is that elements of a stimulus compound may interact in ways that seem very different from how stimulus interactions have typically been understood, that is, in terms of mechanisms of associative competition (Rescorla & Wagner, 1972) or within-compound associations (Rescorla, 1981).

This effect was replicated and extended by Matzel et al. (1985). Using both lick suppression and the traditional CER procedure, Matzel et al. obtained the Kaufman and Bolles effect by extinguishing the auditory element of an auditory-visual compound after initial compound conditioning. In addition, the effect was obtained only if the suppressive effect of the auditory stimulus had extinguished. A group that received relatively few extinction trials to the auditory stimulus did not display enhanced fear to the visual CS when tested after nonreinforcement of the auditory CS. Since a few presentations of a retrieval cue usually suffice, this failure indicates that a retrieval-rehearsal process, which operated in some procedures reviewed earlier, is not working to produce the result. Furthermore, the enhancement effect depended upon extinction of an auditory CS that accompanied the visual CS during compound conditioning. In a group that separately received aversive conditioning to a clicker CS and a tone-flashing light compound CS, fear conditioned to the clicker was subsequently extinguished. Extinction of the clicker had no effect on the amount of fear controlled by the visual CS when the latter was presented alone. However, the group receiving tone extinction again displayed enhanced fear to the light relative to the no-extinction control group (i.e., the overshadowing group).

Matzel, Shuster, and Miller (1987) extended this research to the case where the overshadowing stimulus preceded the overshadowed one on compound trials; a 10-sec tone and 5-sec flashing light terminated as shock was presented. Following compound conditioning, light controlled less suppression of licking than in a control group which had been conditioned to light alone. This overshadowing effect was completely eliminated if the conditioned effect of tone was extinguished between the compound conditioning and test phases. Thus the effect of extinguishing the overshadowing stimulus was stronger than that observed by Matzel et al. (1985), perhaps because the use of simultaneous compounds in the earlier study permitted the formation of within-compound associations, which would work against the observed effect.

In conceptually similar experiments, but using the blocking rather than the overshadowing design, Rescorla (1981) and Robbins (1988a) failed to find evidence that extinction of one element of a reinforced compound stimulus strengthened subsequent responding to the other element.

In Rescorla's experiment pigeons were shown two different line orientation stimuli, each reliably followed by the food UCS. Then a color was added to each line orientation, color and line occupying halves of a divided pigeon key, and reinforcement continued as before. Thus each bird received two blocking treatments concurrently. Next, one line orientation was extinguished, and the other reinforced, until the rates of pecking at the two orientations differed markedly. In a subsequent test the rate of pecking was significantly higher for the color whose paired orientation had subsequently been reinforced, a result opposite those just described. Rescorla attributed this result to the formation of a within-compound association between each line orientation cue and the color which accompanied it.

Robbins (1988a) attempted to minimize the role of within-compound associations in a formally similar experiment by compounding stimuli with different spatial characteristics and different onset times, and by providing presentations of the individual "blocking" stimuli intermixed with the compound trials. Pigeons received two diffuse CSs, each followed by food after half its presentations. Then a different keylight was added during the last 5 sec of each 15-sec diffuse stimulus, and reinforcement continued as before. The diffuse stimuli also continued to be presented by themselves, and were reinforced on 50% of those presentations. Then one diffuse stimulus was extinguished, whereas the other continued to be reinforced. The effect of this manipulation upon responding to the two key lights was assessed in a session in which each keylight was reinforced separately, as was a third keylight which had never accompanied any other stimulus, and had been reinforced on 50% of its presentations. In this test both keylights which had been trained in compound with a diffuse CS evoked less pecking than the control keylight, but did not differ from each other. Furthermore, a subsequent summation test revealed that the two keylights were equally excitatory. This result challenges the results from Miller's laboratory only if it could be demonstrated that differential reinforcement of the two diffuse cues had been effective. This was accomplished by showing that the diffuse cue that had been extinguished was less effective in promoting second-order conditioning to a new keylight.

Rescorla (1981) and Robbins (1988a) relied on within-group comparisons of the effects upon subsequent responding to the blocked stimuli of reinforcing one blocking stimulus versus presenting, but not reinforcing, another. There was no control group in which no stimulus presentations intervened between compound conditioning and test. Suppose such a control would have responded less frequently to the test stimuli than did the groups actually run by Robbins and by Rescorla. In that case, the data could be explained by a retrospective effect of the kind observed by Kaufman and Bolles acting along with a strong within-compound effect in Rescorla's experiment, and with a weaker within-compound effect in Robbins' study.

Alternatively, perhaps retrospective effects have been observed in overshadowing but not in blocking experiments because only in the former case are the effects of each CS upon the other reciprocal. This is pure speculation, because none of the experiments have tested for reciprocal effects.

CONTINGENCY EXPERIMENTS

Another class of experiments bears a formal similarity to the Kaufman and Bolles (1981) experiment. When a positive contingency between some CS and UCS is established, one can think of the CS and context interacting in the same way that two discrete CSs interact in an overshadowing experiment. Then the analogue to the Kaufman and Bolles experiment is one in which p(UCS|no CS) is subsequently decreased, for example, by context extinction. The effect of the CS is then assessed.

This is only one kind of experiment in which p(UCS|no CS) is altered following establishment of a contingency between CS and UCS. That contingency can be positive, zero, or negative, and after any of these p(UCS|no CS) can either be increased or decreased, prior to a test of CS.

Increasing p(UCS|no CS): Effects on Positive Contingency Learning

Jenkins and Lambos (1983; Experiment 2) obtained an effect of increasing the food rate following initial autoshaping. Three groups of pigeons received partially reinforced key light-food pairings (with food occurring at a rate of 120 feedings/hr in CS), a procedure which engendered key-pecking. Two groups then received 15 or 21 days in which unsignalled food was presented at a rate of 120 feedings/hr. The three groups then received a zero-contingency treatment in which the occurrence of food was equiprobable in the presence and absence of the CS. In this zero-contingency phase, initially there was no difference between the groups' rates of key pecking. However, with continued exposure all groups displayed extinction, and groups which had received separate unsignalled feedings extinguished at a much faster rate than controls.

In contrast to this finding, Kaplan and Hearst (1985) reported that autoshaped approach to a key light, as well as key pecking, is insensitive to subsequent unsignalled feedings. After establishing strong approach to a 10-s key light that was always followed by food, separate groups either received exposure to the chamber without key lights or feedings, or they received unsignalled feedings delivered on variable-time (VT) 148-s, 74-s, or 37-s schedules. When the CS was subsequently presented without food, the groups did not differ in terms of their approach measure or their rate of key pecking, both of which were high. Further, the groups displayed no decline in either measure over 32 nonreinforced trials, indicating that little or no extinction had taken place.

Several differences between the procedures of Jenkins and Lambos (1983) and Kaplan and Hearst (1985) are worth noting. First, since Kaplan and Hearst (1985) observed no extinction in any group, it may be that with further extinction trials they would have observed differences in rate of extinction like those seen by Jenkins and Lambos. Second, in terms of the relation between p(UCS|CS) and p(UCS|no CS), Kaplan and Hearst's manipulation was much weaker than that of Jenkins and Lambos, and would be expected to produce a smaller decrement in conditioned responding.

Similarly, Miller and Schachtman (1985), using a conditioned lick suppression paradigm, reported no alleviation of conditioned suppression following a treatment in which the p(UCS|no CS) was increased to a value greater than p(UCS|CS) had been during conditioning. A noise was partially reinforced by foot shock in the first phase of their experiment. Shocks were then delivered at a high rate in the absence of the noise in the conditioning context, and in another context no shocks or CSs were delivered. Subsequently, when the thirsty animals drank water from a spout in the non-shock context and the noise suddenly sounded, their lick suppression scores for this one-trial test were no different from those of a group that never received additional shocks in the conditioning context. This finding is similar to one reported by Ayres and Benedict (1973), who demonstrated with a lick suppression procedure that following excitatory conditioning with an intense shock UCS, additional unsignalled shocks delivered at the same rate had no effect on the amount of suppression over six extinction trials, even though both experimental and no post-conditioning shock control groups showed considerable extinction. This result contrasts most strongly with Jenkins and Lambos (1983), since in both studies UCSs were administered at a high rate following conditioning, in order to make the p(UCS|no CS) equal to the value of p(UCS|CS) during conditioning. Moreover, in these studies extinction was observed. It is conceivable that, because Ayres and Benedict used intense shocks, sensitization occurred and masked the effects of the contingency manipulation. Alternatively, it may be that the 100% reinforcement used in training by Ayres and Benedict made the CR less sensitive to the effects of post-conditioning UCSs than the 40% reinforcement used by Jenkins and Lambos (see Granger & Schlimmer, 1986).

Ayres and Benedict's result is in contrast to the habituation effects reported by Rescorla (1973, 1974) and others. Should the latter results be interpreted in contingency terms? We think not, because the post-conditioning manipulations left p(UCS|no CS) still far smaller than p(UCS|CS) had been during conditioning.

One could also increase p(UCS|no CS) after a negative contingency had been established. No experiments have been conducted to determine whether conditioned inhibition would be enhanced by this manipulation.

Decreasing p(UCS|no CS): Effects on Positive Contingency Learning

This procedure has not received much experimental attention. Kaplan and Hearst (1985) have reported no effect of context extinction on key-pecking or approach behavior. Unfortunately, in their study the pigeons were approaching and pecking the key at very high rates prior to context extinction, making it difficult to measure enhancement.

Balsam (1984) exposed pigeons to repeated pairings of a keylight and food, with an intertrial interval so short that very little autoshaped keypecking occurred. Following extensive context extinction, when the CS was again presented in that context it evoked more pecking than it had during conditioning.

In what may be considered a conceptually similar procedure, Matzel, Brown, and Miller (1987) investigated the effects of context extinction in a UCS preexposure paradigm. Three groups of rats received shocks in the conditioning context prior to conditioning. Of these, only two subsequently received context-extinction treatments, one occurring before conditioning and the other occurring after conditioning had taken place. The fourth group received shock preexposures in a different context. These treatments resulted in a context-specific preexposure effect which was abolished by context extinction, whether it occurred before conditioning or, most interestingly, after conditioning (and before another test). It appears that decreasing p(UCS|no CS) after conditioning may affect the behavior arising from a positive contingency procedure, at least as revealed in a paradigm that produces interference with conditioning to the target CS.

This conclusion receives additional support from an experiment reported by Kaplan and Hearst (1985), which also shows an effect of context extinction upon a "degraded" conditioned stimulus. In this experiment, after pigeons had acquired high levels of key-light approach responses, resulting from explicitly paired presentations of the key-light with food, they were exposed to an explicitly unpaired procedure until they demonstrated withdrawal from the key-light. Pigeons that next received context extinction actually approached the key-light in a subsequent nonreinforced CS test. Pigeons which had received either no context extinction or extinction of a context other than the training context still showed withdrawal during this nonreinforced CS test.

It is perhaps worth pointing out that although these experiments tend to support the general claim that decreasing p(UCS|no CS) following conditioning enhances the relative importance of p(UCS|CS) established during conditioning, the result has not been investigated in the simpler procedure where a weak positive contingency has been established, for example, by setting p(UCS|CS) = .6 and p(UCS|no CS) = .3.

Decreasing p(UCS|no CS): Effects on Negative and Zero Contingency Learning

Kasprow, Schachtman, and Miller (1987) demonstrated that following negative contingency learning, decreasing the p(UCS|no CS) attenuated the amount of inhibition revealed in a summation test. During conditioning in context A, shocks were occasionally paired with a noise CS, but they occurred much more frequently in the absence of the CS. This noise passed the summation and retardation tests for inhibition when compared with appropriate controls (see Miller & Schachtman, 1985; Schachtman, Brown, Gordon, Catterson, & Miller, 1987). Subsequently, a clicker was paired with shock in context C. Some rats were then simply exposed to context A without shocks or CSs, while the others remained in their home cages. When the clicker and noise in compound were then subsequently superimposed onto a baseline level of water licking in a neutral context B, more suppression occurred in the group that had been exposed (without being shocked) to the shock context, suggesting that the noise was less inhibitory in this group.

In a second experiment the same authors showed that extinction of the conditioning context after a negative contingency treatment and several CS-UCS pairings resulted in an increase in the lick-suppressive effect of the CS. Moreover, extinction of a control context in which unsignalled UCSs had previously been presented did not have this effect on responding to the CS. This result is also compatible with the claim that reducing the associative strength of the conditioning context decreases the inhibitory effect of a CS from a negative contingency treatment (also see Schachtman et al., 1987, Experiment 3).

Recently Robbins (1988a, Experiment 1), using the pigeon autoshaping preparation, obtained results which are discrepant with those of Kasprow et al. (1987). Birds were conditioned to peck a reference stimulus, a horizontal line

(H), in the test context. Then they received zero-contingency training with two other keylights, red (R) in context one, and green (G) in context two. One of the contexts was then extinguished over a number of sessions, whereas unsignalled grain UCSs were presented at a rate twice that of conditioning in the other. The effects of this manipulation were assessed in several ways. First red and green were presented in the test context. A summation test followed, in which response rates to H, RH, and GH were compared. Finally there was a retardation of conditioning test. Activity measured at the start of the sessions indicated that the pigeons discriminated the reinforced and extinguished contexts. There was no difference between the rate of pecking R and the rate of pecking G in the test context, nor did the two stimuli have different effects in the summation test. Both reduced responding to H. Furthermore, responses to the two CSs did not differ in the retardation test. Thus there was no evidence that reducing the associative strength of the conditioning context results in an increase in the CR to a zero-contingency CS.

The results of Kasprow et al. (1987) and Robbins are difficult to reconcile, as subsequent papers by Miller, Schachtman and Matzel (1988) and Robbins (1988b) indicate. It may be that the discrepant results hinge on the difference between zero-contingency and negative contingency treatments, or between the autoshaping and lick suppression procedures. Moreover, the crucial comparisons in the two experiments are different; Kasprow et al. compared a group that received post-conditioning deflation of context with a group that received no treatment of that context, whereas Robbins compared inflation of one context with deflation of another in the same group. These outcomes are not directly contradictory, and both can be accounted for if within-compound associations and comparator processes are acting concurrently. Of course, the magnitudes of these two sorts of processes, and the factors which affect them, would have to be determined before such a resolution would be meaningful.

Using withdrawal as an index of negative contingency learning, Kaplan (1985) and Kaplan and Hearst (1985) found that context extinction eliminated withdrawal conditioned to the key-light. Although these results can be understood in terms of the general principle that the performance of an inhibitory CR depends upon concurrent excitation (Rescorla, 1979), the results of Kasprow, Schachtman, and Miller (1987), because they assessed their effects with a summation test, are less readily accounted for in this way.

Summary of Contingency Experiments

Although the evidence is far from conclusive, three sorts of contingency manipulations have produced some outcomes compatible with retrospective effects. Jenkins and Lambos (1983) found that increasing p(UCS|no CS) following conditioning attenuated conditioned pecking that had been established through a positive contingency between keylight and food. Although this outcome is consistent with retrospection, it is also consistent with the view that presentation of free food conditioned responses to context that subsequently competed with the keypeck.

Decreasing p(UCS|no CS) after positive contingency training seems to strengthen excitatory CRs (e.g., Kaplan & Hearst, 1985; Matzel et al., 1987) whereas the same manipulation after negative contingency training seems to attenuate inhibitory CRs (Kasprow et al., 1987; Schachtman et al., 1987). These outcomes cannot be explained in terms of competing responses. The first is formally similar to the outcome of the Kaufman and Bolles (1981) overshadowing experiment, and like that outcome, suggests a retrospective effect. That is, both of these outcomes require some mechanism whereby the current associative status of the stimulus which has just been manipulated, such as context (the comparator in Miller's terms), is compared with the status of the discrete CS, with the result of that comparison ultimately determining the strength of the CR (see Miller's comparator hypothesis; Miller & Schachtman, 1985; also see Gibbon & Balsam, 1981; Jenkins, Barnes, & Barrera, 1981 for a view in which test stimuli are the comparators). To the extent that these phenomena occur reliably, they present a challenge to current structural views of simple associative learning.

STRUCTURES AND PROCESSES INVOLVED IN PAVLOVIAN CONDITIONING

How are we to envision an associative theory which addresses the different kinds of experimental findings reviewed above? For instance, how may we understand the relation between retrieval, reinstatement, and contingency effects on the one hand, and habituation, inflation, and deflation effects on the other?

As noted earlier, the above types of experiment have been designed as investigations of representational and contingency theories. If we are right in equating the emphasis on representations with a "structural" approach and an emphasis on retrospective effects with a "process" approach, then we are faced with the challenge of incorporating process into a structural theory.

How can the processes that seem to be necessitated by the results described in this paper be integrated with a structural model? Consider first the retrospection experiment by Kaufman and Bolles (1981). The traditional account would assert that the CR to the target CS reflects only the degree of activation of the UCS representation by the target CS. This won't do; in its simplest form this account predicts no difference between the groups. Moreover, if within-compound associations between target and reference stimuli are added, then, as Kaufman and Bolles pointed out, the traditional account incorrectly predicts stronger CRs in the control group. The associative status of target and reference stimuli thus must somehow be compared.

It seems unlikely that the basis of this comparison process is the level of activation of the UCS representation. If target presentation activated the UCS representation to a certain extent and also activated the reference stimulus, which in turn activated the (same) UCS representation to a certain extent, then there should have been summation of the two amounts of UCS activation, again predicting a result opposite to that observed.

What, then, might be compared? Perhaps the animal compares the degree of activation of representations of the target-UCS association and the reference-UCS association. These two terms are distinct, and thus there is no reason to expect that they will summate, as is necessarily the case for two concurrent activations of the same UCS representation. How are these relations activated?

The best suggestion might be that the target CS activates the target CS-UCS association, and also activates the representation of the reference stimulus, which in turn activates the reference CS-UCS association. Alternatively, context might activate both associations. However, in that case context would also activate other CS-UCS associations formed in that context, which have been shown not to be involved in the comparator process (Matzel et al., 1985). This is not to deny contextual evocation of CS-UCS associations, but rather to say that such would not be critical in producing this effect.

In the control group we may suppose that the activation of the reference-UCS association is strong enough, compared to the activation of the target stimulus-UCS association, to produce overshadowing. To predict the behavior of the experimental group, the strength of activation of the target CS-UCS association must be compared with the strength of activation of some weighted combination of the reference CS-UCS association formed during conditioning and the reference CS-no UCS association formed during extinction. Furthermore, if we think of the comparison as an ordered operation, for example, division or subtraction, then the system must "tag" the stimulus actually being presented as the target, so that it won't be calculating x/y instead of y/x or x-y instead of y-x.

On this sort of account the response to the target CS is a function of the comparison process. However, since this account retains the assumptions of the traditional model, presentation of the target CS is concurrently activating the UCS representation—both directly and through the mediation of the reference stimulus. As noted earlier, this mechanism predicts greater responding in the control group. Clearly, unless we reject the traditional assumptions, what is needed are rules which specify the relative contributions of the retrospective and traditional mechanisms.

Consider next the reinstatement experiment by Bouton and King (1986), in which reinstating shocks presented in the same context used for conditioning and test, but not shocks administered in a different context, enhanced suppression to a CS that had been conditioned and then partially extinguished, but not to one that had been partially reinforced.

Let's assume that all groups acquire CS-UCS and CS-no UCS associations. When rats which had been conditioned and then extinguished receive UCSs in the reinstatement phase, the CS-UCS association is selectively activated, since CS-UCS trials, but not CS alone trials, had been temporally proximate to UCS presentations. Moreover, it is reasonable that shock in a different context is a somewhat different stimulus, and thus is less effective in activating the CS-UCS association. Why should the pattern of activation be different for the partial reinforcement group? Because both CS-UCS and CS alone trials had been temporally proximate to UCSs.

One could abandon the assumption that the UCS was differentially effective in the two reinstatement contexts and still produce the same pattern of activation by assuming that context also activates the CS-UCS and CS-no UCS associations in the groups given UCSs in the conditioning context. Thus, in that group "CS-UCS" is activated by both UCS and context, and "CS-no UCS" only by context. In the group given UCSs in the different context, "CS-

UCS" would be activated by UCS, but "CS-no UCS" would not be activated. To predict the appropriate pattern of activation across these two groups, particular assumptions about the combination rules for sources of activation would have to be made (e.g., a multiplicative rule).

It is interesting to consider the last possibility in the context of recent research on occasion setting (e.g., Holland, 1985; Rescorla, 1985). What we have just described can be called a temporal contiguity rule for describing when stimuli evoke associations between other stimuli and reinforcers. Whether this is the correct rule remains to be seen; some may not like the implication that the same learning about the feature occurs in serial conditioning and serial feature positive discrimination training.

How does the appropriate pattern of activation on the reinstatement day produce the observed responses to the CS during test? The standard answer is "rehearsal," which could be equated with the claim that the strength of the associations activated by the CS will be proportional to the strength of their activation on the reinstatement day. The observed CR then depends on the difference between (or ratio of) the level of activation of the "CS-UCS" and "CS-no UCS" associations evoked by CS in the various groups.

The foregoing is not meant to be a theory of Pavlovian conditioning. Instead, it is an illustration of some of the problems faced by an account which proposes to combine structure and process. If retrieval and retrospective effects can be obtained reliably, then a theory which includes only excitatory and inhibitory links between representations will have to be supplemented by another level of processing, involving the evocation of CS-UCS relations which are then compared or combined in various ways. This enriched system includes subsystems which have opposing effects, at least in some experiments. Rules for specifying the relative contributions of the subsystems will have to be worked out. Alternatively, one could attempt to do without the traditional level of analysis. But then explanation of "lower-level" phenomena like inflation and deflation effects becomes a problem.

REFERENCES

Ayres, J.J.B., & Benedict, J.O. (1973). US-alone presentations as an extinction procedure. *Animal Learning and Behavior*, *1*, 5-8.

Balaz, M.A., Gutsin, P., Cacheiro, H., & Miller, R.R. (1982). Blocking as a retrieval failure: Reactivation of associations to blocked stimuli. *Quarterly Journal of Experimental Psychology*, *34B*, 99-113.

Balsam, P.D. (1984). Bringing the background to the foreground: The role of contextual cues in autoshaping. In M. Commons, R. Herrnstein, & A.R. Wagner (Eds.), *Quantitative analyses of behavior: Volume 3: Aquisition.* Cambridge, MA: Ballinger.

Berridge, K.C., & Schulkin, J. (1989). Palatability shift of a salt-associated incentive during sodium depletion. *Quarterly Journal of Experimental Psychology*, *41B*, 121-138.

Boakes, R.A. (1979). Interactions between type I and type II processes involving positive reinforcement. In A. Dickinson & R.A. Boakes (Eds.), *Mechanisms of learning and motivation* (pp. 233-268). Hillsdale, NJ: Lawrence Erlbaum Associates.

Boakes, R. (1984). *From Darwin to behaviourism*. Cambridge: Cambridge University Press.

Boden, M.A. (1972). *Purposive explanation in psychology*. Cambridge, MA: Harvard University Press.

Booth, D.A. (1972). Conditioned satiety in the rat. *Journal of Comparative and Physiological Psychology*, *81*, 457-471.

Boring, E.G. (1950). *History of experimental psychology (2nd ed.)*. New York: Appleton-Century-Crofts.

Bouton, M.E. (1982). Lack of reinstatement of an extinguished taste aversion. *Animal Learning and Behavior*, *10*, 233-241.

Bouton, M.E. (1984). Differential control by context in the inflation and reinstatement paradigms. *Journal of Experimental Psychology: Animal Behavior Processes*, *10*, 56-74.

Bouton, M.E., & Bolles, R.C. (1979). Role of conditioned contextual stimuli in reinstatement of extinguished fear. *Journal of Experimental Psychology: Animal Behavior Processes*, *5*, 368-378.

Bouton, M.E., & Bolles, R.C. (1985). Contexts, event-memories, and extinction. In P.D. Balsam & A. Tomie (Eds.), *Context and learning*, (pp. 133-166). Hillsdale: NJ: Lawrence Erlbaum Associates.

Bouton, M.E., & King, D.A. (1983). Contextual control of the extinction of conditioned fear: Tests for the associative value of the context. *Journal of Experimental Psychology: Animal Behavior Processes*, *9*, 248-265.

Bouton, M.E., & King, D.A. (1986). Effect of context on performance to conditioned stimuli with mixed histories of reinforcement and nonreinforcement. *Journal of Experimental Psychology: Animal Behavior Processes*, *12*, 4-15.

Bouton, M.E., & Peck, C.A. (1989). Context effects on conditioning, extinction, and reinstatement in an appetitive conditioning preparation. *Animal Learning & Behavior*, *17*, 188-198.

Bouton, M.E., & Swartzentruber, D. (1986). Analysis of the associative and occasion-setting properties of context participating in a Pavlovian discrimination. *Journal of Experimental Psychology: Animal Behavior Processes*, *12*, 333-350.

Bouton, M.E., & Swartzentruber, D. (1989). Slow reaquistion following extinction: Context, encoding, and retrieval mechanisms. *Journal of Experimental Psychology: Animal Behavior Processes*, *15*, 43-53.

Brookshire, K.H., & Brackbill, R.M. (1976). Formation and retention of conditioned taste aversions and UCS habituation. *Bulletin of the Psychonomic Society*, *7*, 125-128.

Cleland, G.G., & Davey, G.C.L. (1982). The effects of satiation and reinforcer devaluation on signal-centered behavior in the rat. *Learning and Motivation*, *13*, 343-360.

Colby, J.J., & Smith, N.F. (1977). The effect of three procedures for eliminating a conditioned taste aversion in the rat. *Learning and Motivation*, *8*, 404-413.

Dacanay, R.J., & Riley, A.L. (1982). The UCS preexposure effect in taste aversion learning: Tolerance and blocking are drug specific. *Animal Learning and Behavior*, *10*, 91-96.

Davidson, T.L. (1987). Learning about deprivation intensity stimuli. *Behavioral Neuroscience*, *101*, 198-208.

Deems, D.A., Oetting, R.L., Sherman, J.E., & Garcia, J. (1986). Hungry, but not thirsty, rats prefer flavors paired with ethanol. *Physiology and Behavior*, *36*, 141-144.

Dickinson, A. (1980). *Contemporary animal learning theory.* Cambridge: Cambridge University Press.

Dickinson, A., & Dawson, G. (1987). Pavlovian processes in the motivational control of instrumental performance. *Quarterly Journal of Experimental Psychology, 39B,* 201-213.

Dickinson, A., & Dearing, M.F. (1979). Appetitive-aversive interactions and inhibitory processes. In A. Dickinson & R.A. Boakes (Eds.), *Mechanisms of learning and motivation* (pp. 203-233). Hillsdale, NJ: Lawrence Erlbaum Associates.

Domjan, M. (1975). Poison-induced neophobia in rats: Role of stimulus generalization of conditioned taste aversions. *Animal Learning and Behavior, 3,* 205-211.

Durlach, P. (1986). Explicitly unpaired procedure as a response elimination technique in autoshaping. *Journal of Experimental Psychology: Animal Behavior Processes, 12,* 172-185.

Fedorchak, P.M., & Bolles, R.C. (1987). Hunger enhances the expression of calorie- but not taste-mediated conditioned flavor preferences. *Journal of Experimental Psychology: Animal Behavior Processes, 13,* 73-79.

Fudim, O.K. (1978). Sensory preconditioning of flavors with a formalin-produced sodium need. *Journal of Experimental Psychology: Animal Behavior Processes, 4,* 276-285.

Gibbon, J., & Balsam, P. (1981). Spreading association in time. In C.M. Locurto, H.S. Terrace, & J. Gibbon (Eds.), *Autoshaping and conditioning theory.* New York: Academic Press.

Granger, R.H., Jr., & Schlimmer, J.C. (1986). The computation of contingency in classical conditioning. In G. H. Bower (Ed.), *The psychology of learning and motivation* (Vol. 20, pp. 137-192). New York: Academic Press.

Hendersen, R.W. (1985). Fearful memories: The motivational significance of forgetting. In F.R. Brush & J.B. Overmier (Eds.), *Affect, conditioning, and cognition: Essays on the determinants of behavior.* Hillsdale, NJ: Lawrence Erlbaum Associates.

Holland, P.C. (1981). The effect of satiation after first and second-order appetitive conditioning. *Pavlovian Journal of Biological Science, 16,* 18-24.

Holland, P.C. (1985). The nature of conditioned inhibition in serial and simultaneous feature negative discriminations. In R.R. Miller & N.E. Spear (Eds.), *Information processing in animals: Conditioned inhibition* (pp. 267-297). Hillsdale, NJ: Lawrence Erlbaum Associates.

Holland, P.C. (1988). Excitation and inhibition in unblocking. *Journal of Experimental Psychology: Animal Behavior Processes, 14,* 261-279.

Holland, P.C., & Rescorla, R.A. (1975). The effect of two ways of devaluing the unconditioned stimulus after first- and second-order appetitive conditioning. *Journal of Experimental Psychology: Animal Behavior Processes, 1,* 355-363.

Holland, P.C., & Straub, J.J. (1979). Differential effects of two ways of devaluing the unconditioned stimulus after Pavlovian appetitive conditioning. *Journal of Experimental Psychology: Animal Behavior Processes, 5,* 65-78.

Holman, E.W. (1976). The effect of drug habituation before and after taste aversion learning in rats. *Animal Learning and Behavior, 4,* 329-332.

Holman, E.W. (1980). Irrelevant-incentive learning with flavors in rats. *Journal of Experimental Psychology: Animal Behavior Processes, 6,* 126-136.

Hull, C.L. (1943). *Principles of behavior.* New York: Appleton-Century-Crofts.

Jenkins, H.M., & Lambos, W.A. (1983). Tests of two explanations of response elimination by noncontingent reinforcement. *Animal Learning and Behavior, 11*, 302-308.

Jenkins, H.M., Barnes, R.A., & Barrera, F.J. (1981). Why autoshaping depends on trial spacing. In C.M. Locurto, H.S. Terrace, & J. Gibbon (Eds.), *Autoshaping and conditioning theory,* (pp. 255-284). New York: Academic Press.

Kaplan, P.S. (1985). Explaining the effects of relative time in trace conditioning: A preliminary test of a comparator hypothesis. *Animal Learning and Behavior, 13*, 233-238.

Kaplan, P.S., & Hearst, E. (1985). Contextual control and excitatory versus inhibitory learning: Studies of extinction, reinstatement, and interference. In P.D. Balsam & A. Tomie (Eds.), *Context and learning* (pp. 195-224). Hillsdale, NJ: Lawrence Erlbaum Associates.

Kasprow, W.J., Cacheiro, H., Balaz, M.A., & Miller, R.R. (1982). Reminder-induced recovery of associations to an overshadowed stimulus. *Learning and Motivation, 13*, 155-166.

Kasprow, W.J., Catterson, D., Schachtman, T.R., & Miller, R.R. (1984). Attenuation of latent inhibition by post-acquisition reminder. *Quarterly Journal of Experimental Psychology, 36B*, 53-63.

Kasprow, W.J., Schachtman, T.R., Cacheiro, H., & Miller, R.R. (1984). Extinction does not depend upon degradation of event memories. *Bulletin of the Psychonomic Society, 22*, 95-98.

Kasprow, W.J., Schachtman, T.R., & Miller, R.R. (1987). The comparator hypothesis of conditioned response generation: Manifest conditioned excitation and inhibition as a function of relative excitatory associative strengths of CS and conditioning context at the time of testing. *Journal of Experimental Psychology: Animal Behavior Processes, 13*, 395-406.

Kaufman, M.A., & Bolles, R.C. (1981). A nonassociative aspect of overshadowing. *Bulletin of the Psychonomic Society, 18*, 318-320.

Kendler, H.H. (1952). "What is learned?" A theoretical blind alley. *Psychological Review, 59*, 269-277.

Konorski, J. (1948). *Conditioned reflexes and neuron organization.* Cambridge: Cambridge University Press.

Konorski, J. (1967). *Integrative activity of the brain.* Chicago: University of Chicago Press.

Lindblom, L.L., & Jenkins, H.M. (1981). Responses eliminated by non-contingent reinforcement recovery in extinction. *Journal of Experimental Psychology: Animal Behavior Processes, 7*, 175-190.

Lovibond, P.F., Preston, G.C., & Mackintosh, N.J. (1984). Context specificity of conditioning, extinction, and latent inhibition. *Journal of Experimental Psychology: Animal Behavior Processes, 10*, 360-375.

Mackintosh, N.J. (1983). *Conditioning and associative learning.* Oxford: Oxford University Press.

Mandler, J.M., & Mandler, G. (1964). *Thinking: From association to Gestalt.* New York: Wiley.

Matzel, L.D., Brown, A.M., & Miller, R.R. (1987). Associative effects of US preexposure: Modulation of conditioned responding by an excitatory training context. *Journal of Experimental Psychology: Animal Behavior Processes, 13*, 65-72.

Matzel, L.D., Schachtman, T.R., & Miller, R.R. (1985). Recovery of an overshadowed association achieved by extinction of the overshadowing stimulus. *Learning and Motivation, 16*, 398-412.

Matzel, L.D., Shuster, K., & Miller, R.R. (1987). Covariation in conditioned response strength between stimuli trained in compound. *Animal Learning and Behavior, 15,* 439-447.

Mikulka, P., Leard, B., & Klein, S. (1977). Illness-alone exposure as a source of interference with the acquisition and retention of a taste aversion. *Journal of Experimental Psychology: Animal Behavior Processes, 3,* 189-201.

Miller, R.R., Kasprow, W.J., & Schachtman, T.R. (1986). Retrieval variability: Sources and consequences. *American Journal of Psychology, 93,* 145-218.

Miller, R.R., & Schachtman, T.R. (1985). Conditioning context as an associative baseline: Implications for response generation and the nature of conditioned inhibition. In R.R. Miller & N.E. Spear (Eds.), *Information processing in animals: Conditioned inhibition.* Hillsdale, NJ: Lawrence Erlbaum Associates.

Miller, R.R., Schachtman, T.R., & Matzel, L.D. (1988). Testing response generation rules. *Journal of Experimental Psychology: Animal Behavior Processes, 14,* 425-429.

Overton, D.A. (1971). Discriminative control of behavior by drug states. In T. Thompson & R. Pickins (Eds.), *Stimulus properties of drugs.* New York: Appleton-Century-Crofts.

Pavlov, I.P. (1927). *Conditioned reflexes* (G.V. Anrep, Trans.). Oxford: Oxford University Press.

Pearce, J.M., & Dickinson, A. (1975). Pavlovian counterconditioning: Changing the suppressive properties of shock by association with food. *Journal of Experimental Psychology: Animal Behavior Processes, 1,* 170-177.

Ramachandran, R., & Pearce, J.M. (1987). Pavlovian analysis of interactions between hunger and thirst. *Journal of Experimental Psychology: Animal Behavior Processes, 13,* 182-192.

Randich, A., & Haggard, D. (1983). Exposure to the unconditioned stimulus alone: Effects upon retention and acquisition of conditioned suppression. *Journal of Experimental Psychology: Animal Behavior Processes, 9,* 147-159.

Randich, A., & LoLordo, V.M. (1979). Associative and nonassociative theories of the UCS preexposure phenomenon: Implications for Pavlovian conditioning. *Psychological Bulletin, 86,* 523-548.

Randich, A., & Rescorla, R.A. (1981). The effects of separate presentations of the US on conditioned suppression. *Animal Learning and Behavior, 9,* 56-64.

Randich, A., & Ross, R.T. (1985). Contextual stimuli mediate the effects of pre- and postexposure to the unconditioned stimulus on conditioned suppression. In P.D. Balsam & A. Tomie (Eds.), *Context and learning* (pp. 105-132). Hillsdale, NJ: Lawrence Erlbaum Associates.

Rescorla, R.A. (1973). Effect of US habituation following conditioning. *Journal of Comparative and Physiological Psychology, 82,* 137-143.

Rescorla, R.A. (1974). Effect of inflation of the unconditioned stimulus value following conditioning. *Journal of Comparative and Physiological Psychology, 86,* 101-106.

Rescorla, R.A. (1979). Conditioned inhibition and extinction. In A. Dickinson & R.A. Boakes (Eds.), *Mechanisms of learning and motivation: A memorial volume to Jerzy Konorski.* Hillsdale, NJ: Lawrence Erlbaum Associates .

Rescorla, R.A. (1981). Within-signal learning in autoshaping. *Animal Learning and Behavior, 9,* 245-252.

Rescorla, R.A. (1985). Conditioned inhibition and facilitation. In R.R. Miller & N.E. Spear (Eds.), *Information processing in animals: Conditioned inhibition* (pp. 299-326), Hillsdale, NJ: Lawrence Erlbaum Associates.

Rescorla, R.A., & Cunningham, C. (1977). The erasure of reinstated fear. *Animal Learning and Behavior*, 5, 396-394.

Rescorla, R.A., & Cunningham, C. (1978). Recovery of the US representation over time during extinction. *Learning and Motivation*, 9, 373-391.

Rescorla, R.A., & Freberg, L. (1978). The extinction of within- compound flavor associations. *Learning and Motivation*, 9, 411-427.

Rescorla, R.A., & Heth, C.D. (1975). Reinstatement of fear to an extinguished conditioned stimulus. *Journal of Experimental Psychology: Animal Behavior Processes*, 1, 88-96.

Rescorla, R.A., & Solomon, R.L. (1967). Two-process learning theory: Relationship between Pavlovian conditioning and instrumental learning. *Psychological Review*, 74, 151-182.

Rescorla, R.A., & Wagner, A.R. (1972). A theory of Pavlovian conditioning: Variations in the effectiveness of reinforcement and nonreinforcement. In A.H. Black & W.F. Prokasy (Eds.), *Classical conditioning II: Current research and theory*, (pp. 64-99). New York: Appleton-Century-Crofts.

Richards, R.W., & Sargent, D.M. (1983). The order of presentation of conditioned stimuli during extinction. *Animal Learning and Behavior*, 11, 229-236.

Riley, A.L., Jacobs, W.J., & LoLordo, V.M. (1976). Drug exposure and the acquisition and retention of a conditioned taste aversion. *Journal of Comparative and Physiological Psychology*, 90, 799-807.

Robbins, S.J. (1988a). Role of context in performance on a random schedule in autoshaping. *Journal of Experimental Psychology: Animal Behavior Processes*, 14, 413-424.

Robbins, S.J. (1988b). Testing response generation rules: A reply to Miller, Schachtman and Matzel (1988). *Journal of Experimental Psychology: Animal Behavior Processes*, 14, 430-432.

Ross, R.T. (1986). Pavlovian second-order conditioned analgesia. *Journal of Experimental Psychology: Animal Behavior Processes*, 12, 32-39.

Rozeboom, W.W. (1958). "What is learned?" - An empirical enigma. *Psychological Review*, 65, 22-33.

Schachtman, T.R., Brown, A.M., Gordon, E., Catterson, D., & Miller, R.R. (1987). Mechanisms underlying retarded emergence of conditioned responding following inhibitory training: Evidence for the comparator hypothesis. *Journal of Experimental Psychology: Animal Behavior Processes*, 13, 310-322.

Schachtman, T.R., Brown, A.M., & Miller, R.R. (1985). Reinstatement-induced recovery of a taste-LiCl association following extinction. *Animal Learning and Behavior*, 13, 223-227.

Schweitzer, L., & Green, L. (1982). Reevaluation of things past: A test of the "Retrospection hypothesis" using a CER procedure with rats. *Pavlovian Journal of Biological Science*, 17, 62-68.

Sherman, J.E. (1978). US inflation with trace and simultaneous fear conditioning. *Animal Learning and Behavior*, 6, 463-468.

Stanhope, K.J. (1989). Dissociation of the effect of reinforcer type and response strength on the force of a conditioning response. *Animal Learning and Behavior*, 17, .

Thorndike, E.L. (1911). *Animal intelligence*. New York: Macmillan.

Tolman, E.C. (1925a). Behaviorism and purpose. *The Journal of Philosophy*, 22, 36-41.

Tolman, E.C. (1925b). Purpose and cognition: The determiners of animal learning. *Psychological Review*, 32, 285-297.

Tolman, E.C. (1932). *Purposive behavior in animals and men*. New York: Century.

Tolman, E.C. (1933a). Sign-gestalt or conditioned reflex? *Psychological Review*, *40*, 391-411.
Tolman, E.C. (1933b). Gestalt and sign-gestalt. *Psychological Review*, *40*, 246-255.
Watson, J.B. (1913). Psychology as the behaviorist views it. *Psychological Review*, *20*, 158-188.
Watson, J.B. (1916). The place of the conditioned reflex in psychology. *Psychological Review*, *23*, 89-116.
Weingarten, H.P. (1983). Conditioned cues elicit feeding in sated rats: A role for learning in meal initiation. *Science*, *220*, 431-433.
Wolf, G., Schulkin, J., & Simpson, P.D. (1984). Multiple factors in the satiation of salt appetite. *Behavioral Neuroscience*, *98*, 661-673.
Zener, K. (1937). The significance of behavior accompanying conditioned salivary secretion for theories of the conditioned response. *American Journal of Psychology*, *50*, 394-403.

4   Expression of Learning

Ralph R. Miller
Nicholas J. Grahame
State University of New York at Binghamton

The modification of behavior as a consequence of prior experience is the central concern of learning theory. Yet, as the name itself suggests, learning theory has historically emphasized the acquisition of information, to the relative neglect of the postacquisition processes that translate acquired knowledge into behavior.[1] The working assumption of most students of learning was that what a subject did was an accurate reflection of what the subject had learned. This assumption was successfully challenged by Tolman (e.g., 1932) and his colleagues who demonstrated that a well trained animal would not manifest its acquired knowledge unless there was concordance between the available reinforcer and the animal's motivational state. Although these observations served as the basis for proposing a distinction between learning variables and performance variables, in practice the only widely accepted examples of performance variables were the very same internal and external motivational factors which first

---

[1] The historical roots for this bias are complex and can be traced at least as far back as the British Empiricists of the eighteenth and nineteenth centuries. In reaction to this great concern with acquisition processes, one of the central tenets of the cognitive revolution in experimental psychology has been a greater emphasis of postacquisition processing of information than is provided by conventional learning theory. Unfortunately, this desirable reorientation has frequently been accompanied by a dilution of the high value that learning theory traditionally has accorded parsimony. The orientation of the present authors is to retain the parsimony of traditional learning theory to the extent possible while accommodating recent data suggesting that interesting things happen to information after acquisition.

gave rise to the learning-performance distinction. Currently, the working assumption in the research laboratory is still that behavior is an accurate reflection of learning, only now with the proviso that the subject is appropriately motivated at the time of testing.

As an example of the theoretical bias of the field toward explaining behavioral deficits in terms of acquisition failures, we should briefly consider the phenomenon of state-dependent learning. State-dependent learning refers to the superior performance seen when the subject is in a drug-induced state during the test trial that is similar to the drug-induced state in which the subject was trained (e.g., Overton, 1964). As the subject's behavior yields evidence of the original training when the conditions of testing are similar to those of training, learning must have taken place. Yet, only recently have researchers begun to call the phenomenon state-dependent retrieval rather than state-dependent learning (e.g., Riccio & Ebner, 1981).

The present chapter reviews three factors beyond the traditional motivational ones that can influence the behavioral expression of acquired knowledge. Latent learning in Tolman's day was demonstrated by altering performance variables (i.e., for Tolman, motivational variables) after an unsuccessful test trial and causing the subject to manifest its knowledge in the absence of additional relevant training. The research that is described in the present chapter uses the same general strategy.

RETRIEVAL CUES AND REMINDERS

It has long been recognized that performance on a test trial depends heavily upon the retrieval cues present during the trial (e.g., Spear, 1973; Tulving, 1974). The working assumption has been that the best retrieval cues are those that were present during training. In the learning literature, the decrement in performance that arises as the mismatch between training and test stimuli increases is referred to as stimulus generalization decrement. As retrieval cues that are poorly selected with respect to the original training cues will result in poor performance despite adequate acquisition with respect to the original training cues, the quality of retrieval cues has appropriately come to be regarded as a performance variable.

Not only is the quality of retrieval cues critical to the current test trial, it often influences performance on subsequent test trials (i.e, hypermnesia in humans, see Roediger & Payne, 1982). Essentially, successful retrieval of acquired information, without the subject receiving new information that could promote new learning (i.e., feedback), appears capable of initiating further processing of the information which renders it more retrievable on subsequent trials. For example, we trained rats in a complex maze and found that exposures to the reinforcer outside of the maze or to the start box of the maze could reduce the rate of subsequent errors when these exposures occurred near the middle of the training sequence, that is, during *apparent* acquisition (Miller, 1982). We speculated that in this situation early training trials provided information about the prevailing contingencies of reinforcement and later training trials primarily provided an opportunity for the subject to further process the information so as to enhance its subsequent retrievability.

Although it is widely assumed that the best retrieval cues are those stimuli that were present during training, this maxim is subject to qualification. Specifically, stimuli more intense or more prolonged than those of initial training might be expected to be inferior retrieval cues as a result of generalization decrement. However, such cues often prove to be superior elicitors of target behavior. Presumably this potential arises from their greater power as reactivators of memory (i.e., they appear to elevate the stimulus generalization gradient) and/or greater behavioral activation (akin to Hull's [1952] concept of stimulus intensity dynamism). The superiority of more intense or prolonged retrieval cues is particularly evident when there is a deficit in responding due to impaired retrieval. Thus, in the framework of Pavlovian conditioning, post-training exposure to the unconditioned stimulus (US) alone, the conditioned stimulus (CS) alone, or training context precludes relevant new learning, but under certain circumstances can improve subsequent responding to the CS.

When the US is used as such a reminder cue, it is ordinarily administered outside the test context in order to avoid the formation of context-US associations that could sum with CS-US associations at the time of testing. The enhancement in conditioned responding that is often obtained when the US is used as a reminder cue might be mediated by an upward revaluation of the US representation (see Delamater & LoLordo, chap. 3 in this volume). However, the effectiveness of the CS and training context as reminder agents is not subject to a revaluation interpretation. Brief posttraining exposure to the CS or training context has little effect on responding to an already effective CS (i.e., a CS that elicits a robust conditioned response), and extended exposure to an already functional CS ordinarily causes a decrement in responding to the CS, that is, extinction. In practice, if exposure to the same CS that served as a reminder cue is continued, extinction does occur (Gordon, Smith, & Katz, 1979). CS-induced reminder effects require an appropriately small number of CS presentations in order to minimize the effects of CS extinction.

Retrograde amnesia. Administration of various disruptive physiological manipulations soon after training can interfere with subsequent performance based upon that training. For example, electroconvulsive shock administered within ten seconds of a training trial renders the training trial ineffective (Chorover & Schiller, 1965). Traditionally, this behavioral deficit has been attributed to an acquisition failure arising from the electroconvulsive shock obliterating the active neural representation of the training event before a less vulnerable, inactive representation of the training event can be formed (McGaugh, 1966). Yet, the observation of recovery from retrograde amnesia in rats as a consequence of either reminder trials with the reinforcer (e.g., Miller & Springer, 1972) or reminder trials with the discriminative stimulus from training (Miller, Ott, Berk, & Springer, 1974) indicates that the behavioral deficit was not due to an acquisition failure. Recovery without additional relevant training suggests that the information provided by training was in fact encoded within the amnesic animal, but that prior to the reminder treatment it was not manifest. (For a review of other research that supports the retrieval failure interpretation of retrograde amnesia see Miller & Marlin, 1979.)

Blocking. Blocking refers to the deficit in conditioned responding seen when a potential CS is paired with a US in the presence of a second CS that was previously paired with the US. The phenomenon of blocking has been central to the formulation of most modern theories of learning (e.g., Mackintosh, 1975; Pearce & Hall, 1980; Rescorla & Wagner, 1972). Although there has been considerable disagreement concerning the processes underlying this behavioral deficit, all of these theorists have concurred in regarding it as an acquisition failure. The only question has been why acquisition failed. However, Balaz, Gutsin, Cacheiro, and Miller (1982; also see Schachtman, Gee, Kasprow, & Miller, 1983), using rats in a conditioned lick suppression task, found that a blocked response can be recovered by a posttraining reminder treatment consisting of brief exposure to either the blocked CS, the US (outside of the test context), or the training context (see Fig. 4.1). In each instance, control groups were included which demonstrated that the enhanced re-

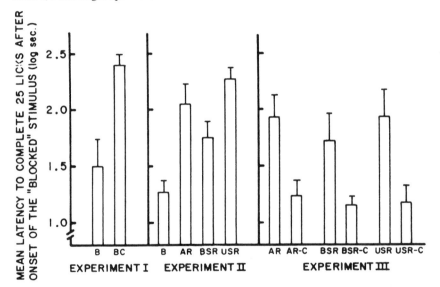

Figure 4.1. Mean latencies to complete 25 licks in the presence of the blocked stimulus (flashing light). Higher scores represent greater evidence of learning. Experiment 1 demonstrates blocking (Group B) relative to control subjects (Group BC) for which the blocking stimulus (tone) was not previously made excitatory. Experiment 2 illustrates recovery from blocking in animals that received as reminder treatments either exposure to the apparatus cues (Group AR), brief exposure to the blocked stimulus (Group BSR), or additional presentations of the footshock US (Group USR), all relative to animals subjected to blocking without any reminder treatment (Group B). In the latter two cases, the reminder treatment was administered outside the context that was used for training and testing. Experiment 3 determined that the apparent reminder-induced recovery from blocking observed in Experiment 2 was specific for blocked stimuli and not seen in animals for which the flashing light was not a blocked stimulus despite equivalent reminder treatments with the apparatus cues (Group AR-C), blocked stimulus (Group BSR-C), or the US (Group USR-C). Brackets depict standard errors. From Balaz, Gutsin, Cacheiro, and Miller (1982). Copyright 1982 by the Experimental Psychology Society. Reprinted with permission.

sponding depended upon the target CS having been blocked. Such a recovery of the blocked association is inconsistent with the view that blocking is an acquisition failure. We must conclude that blocking is apparently in part or total a performance failure.

Overshadowing. Overshadowing refers to the deficit in responding to a potential CS that is seen when that CS during training is presented in compound with a second potential CS (one that is more salient than the first CS) relative to responding to the first CS when it is trained in the absence of another CS. As in the case of blocking, there are a variety of theories to explain overshadowing, all of which assume that overshadowing is the consequence of an acquisition failure. Several interpretations of overshadowing have been proposed. For example, Rescorla and Wagner (1972) hypothesized that the more salient stimulus (higher alpha value in the Rescorla-Wagner formulation) quickly accrues associative strength on the first few training trials and then on subsequent trials blocks further learning of the association between the less salient CS and the US. Alternatively, Mackintosh (1975) suggested that the overshadowing stimulus, as the best predictor of the US, distracts the subject from the target CS. Despite such major differences in interpretation, both of these models assume that the overshadowing deficit is the result of an acquisition failure.

In contradiction of this assumption, Kasprow, Cacheiro, Balaz, and Miller (1982) found that posttraining presentation of the US outside of the test context restored responding to the first CS without influencing responding to that CS in appropriate control subjects. As the reminder treatment precluded relevant new learning, the observed recovery of responding to the overshadowed CS indicates that overshadowing at least in part is a performance failure rather than an acquisition failure. This conclusion is corroborated by the finding of Kraemer, Lariviere, and Spear (1988) that under certain conditions, rats will exhibit spontaneous recovery from overshadowing. Spontaneous recovery from overshadowing is particularly interesting in that it provides an example of recovery from overshadowing that precludes even the most subtle arguments that recovery from overshadowing is the result of unintended relevant new learning or reevaluation of the US representation.

Latent Inhibition. The CS-preexposure effect (also known as latent inhibition) refers to the deficit in responding to a CS that occurs when the subject has been repeatedly exposed to the CS without reinforcement prior to the pairings of the CS and US that constitute training. As with the preceding behavioral deficits, there are several hypotheses concerning the bases of the CS preexposure effect (e.g., DeVietti et al., 1987; Lubow, Weiner, & Schnur, 1981; Pearce & Hall, 1980; Wagner, 1978); however, all of these hypotheses assume that the deficit is due to an acquisition failure. Inconsistent with this view is the observation by Kasprow, Catterson, Schachtman, and Miller (1984) that a US reminder treatment outside of the test context between the CS-US pairings and testing can restore responding by rats to the CS (see Fig. 4.2). These researchers interpreted the observed recovery of responding as evidence that latent learning had taken place during the CS-US pairings and

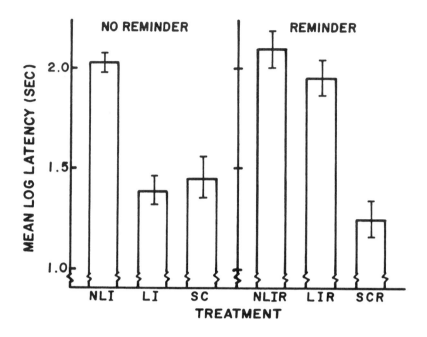

Figure 4.2. Mean latencies to complete 25 licks in the presence of the CS (white noise). Groups LI and SC received nonreinforced pretraining exposures to the CS (latent inhibition) in contrast to Group NLI which did not. Then Groups LI and NLI received pairings of the CS and footshock whereas Group SC experienced these stimuli unpaired. Reminder treatment consisted of two footshocks administered outside the context used for training and testing. Brackets depict standard errors. From Kasprow et al. (1984). Copyright 1984 by the Experimental Psychology Society. Reprinted with permission.

that the reminder treatment facilitated later retrieval of the CS-US association, but their data are also interpretable in terms of upward revaluation of the US representation at the time of the reminder treatment compensating for an acquisition failure. However, no enhancement of responding was seen as a result of reminder treatment following CS-US pairings in control subjects that had not received pretraining exposure to the CS. Additionally, paralleling the case of overshadowing, the latent learning view of the CS-preexposure effect is supported by the observation of spontaneous recovery from the CS preexposure deficit with increasing intervals between the CS-US pairings and testing (Kraemer & Roberts, 1984).

Most of the traditional interpretations of latent inhibition view the responding deficit as arising from a lack of attention to the CS during the CS-US pairings and differ only in the factor responsible for the diminution in attention to the CS (e.g., DeVietti et al., 1987; Lubow et al., 1981; Pearce & Hall, 1980). If an attentional framework is retained, reminder-induced and spontaneous recovery from latent inhibition would suggest that attention is not essential for acquisition, but rather is necessary for ease of later utilization of the acquired information. The idea that attention during acquisition primarily influences not acquisition, but some later stage of information processing is foreign to most models of animal learning, but is a rather popular notion among students of attention in humans (e.g., Kantowitz, 1985).

Implications of Reminder Effects. The preceding examples demonstrate that numerous behavioral deficits traditionally regarded as arising from a lack of acquisition are reversible without the occurrence of relevant new learning. That is, latent associations were present during the behavioral deficit observed on the initial test trial. A more extensive list of such reversible deficits in acquired behavior can be found in Miller, Kasprow, and Schachtman (1986). Collectively, these instances of enhanced performance indicate that many deficits of associative responding are actually performance failures rather than acquisition failures. Our own theoretical bias has been to refer to behavioral deficits that are reversible without further training as retrieval failures. But in view of how misleading it has proven to prematurely label these behavior deficits as acquisition failures, it might be equally misleading to label them as retrieval failures at this time rather than temporarily settling for a more empirical description such as performance failures. Performance failure here is intended to encompass any behavioral deficit that does not arise from an acquisition failure, whereas retrieval failure denotes one specific source of performance failure.

RESPONSE RULES AND THE COMPARATOR HYPOTHESIS

The retrieval process is but one of several seemingly essential stages of information processing that have been neglected as a result of the disproportionate attention researchers have bestowed upon acquisition. Another process in need of illumination is that of response generation. Most theories of learning assume that responding to a CS is a direct reflection of the associative strength of the CS, that is, they assume implicitly if not explicitly that there is a linear relationship between associative strength and conditioned responding, provided that motivational factors are equated.

Proposing response rules more complex than monotonicity or linearity may appear unparsimonious. However, such rules can serve two important functions. First, they can illuminate certain behavioral phenomena that are inexplicable in terms of any of the prevailing acquisition-oriented theories. Second, they can offer alternative explanations of behavioral phenomena that are successfully addressed by prevailing models of acquisition. This would devalue the unique empirical support claimed by some models of acquisition, and thereby render viable simpler models of acquisition that were previously rejected because they could not explain these phenomena in terms of acquisition. In essence, nontrivial response rules permit a shifting of part of the explanatory burden from models of acquisition to models of response generation.

The Comparator Hypothesis. We will use the comparator hypothesis (Miller & Matzel, 1988; Miller & Schachtman, 1985) to illustrate the potential explanatory power of a nontrivial response rule. The comparator hypothesis posits first that conditioned responding is not only directly related to

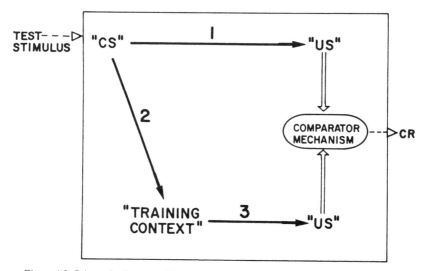

Figure 4.3. Schematic diagram of the comparator process. Numbers 1, 2, and 3 denote the three associations assumed to underlie the comparison process: CS-US, CS-context, and context-US. Conditioned responding is presumed to be directly related to the US representation activated by the CS and inversely related to the US representation activated by the representation of the training context.

the associative strength of the CS, but also is inversely related to the associative strength of other stimuli that were present *during training* of the CS (i.e., comparator stimuli, which include but are not restricted to contextual cues). Second, the comparator hypothesis posits that this comparison occurs at the time of testing, even if testing occurs outside of the training context. The bases for these two assumptions come from numerous experiments—some of which are reported by Kasprow, Schachtman, and Miller (1987) and Miller and Schachtman (1985).

The processes assumed to underlie the comparator hypothesis are depicted in Figure 4.3. Presentation of the CS on the test trial reactivates a representation of the US based upon the CS-US association. Additionally the CS presentation serves to reactivate the CS-training context association. The active representation of the training context in turn reactivates a representation of the US based upon the training context-US association. Responding to the CS is then determined by a comparison of the two US representations, one based on the CS and the other based upon the CS's comparator stimuli, which in this case are assumed to be the background cues of the training context. Thus, there are three critical associations: CS-US, CS-training context, and training context-US.[2] To demonstrate the potential explanatory power of response rules, here

----

[2] The comparator hypothesis has much in common with the model of learning proposed by Gibbon and Balsam (1981). See Miller and Matzel (1988) for a discussion of the similarities and differences between the two models.

we will describe some experiments conceived in the framework of the comparator hypothesis in which latent associations were unmasked, following termination of training with the CS, by treatment in which neither the CS nor the US was presented.

The US Preexposure Effect. If prior to CS-US pairings subjects are exposed to the US in the absence of a punctate signal, more CS-US pairings will be necessary in order to obtain conditioned responding to the CS than if the US pretraining exposures had not occurred. This retardation of conditioned responding is referred to as the US preexposure effect. The usual interpretation of this phenomenon is that the unsignaled USs make the context excitatory and during the subsequent CS-US pairings the context blocks acquisition of a CS-US association. The evidence cited to support this interpretation is that retardation can be eliminated by either extinction of the context or a change in context between US preexposure and the CS-US pairings (e.g., Randich & LoLordo, 1979). It should be noted that, as is typical in the field, the behavioral deficit was assumed to be an acquisition failure and the experiments performed were designed with the thought of supporting rather than disproving this assumption.

An alternate interpretation of the US preexposure effect is that it is a performance failure arising from the action of the comparator process at the time of testing. Specifically, the training context, which presumably acts as the comparator stimulus for the CS, is more excitatory at the time of testing than it would have been if the unsignaled USs had not occurred. Hence, responding to the CS fails to occur despite formation of a CS-US association. This view is as consistent with the beneficial effects of extinguishing the context or switching contexts before the CS-US pairings as is the blocking of acquisition interpretation. Moreover, the comparator view of the US preexposure effect makes the unique prediction that extinction of the context used for the CS-US pairings after the CS-US pairings should also attenuate the US preexposure deficit.

Exactly such an effect has been obtained by Matzel, Brown, and Miller (1987) using a conditioned lick suppression task with rats. The results of this study are illustrated in Figure 4.4. Groups +A, +A/b, and +A/a initially received unsignaled footshock in Context A; Group +C experienced equivalent unsignaled footshock in Context C. Then all subjects received CS-US pairings in Context A. Additionally, Group +A/b had Context A extinguished before the CS-US pairings, whereas Group +A/a had Context A extinguished after the CS-US pairings. Testing for fear of the CS occurred in a neutral context in which no CS or US presentations had previously occurred, thereby precluding any differential fear of the training context from summing with fear of the CS at the time of testing. Extinction of the training context either before or after CS training eliminated the US preexposure deficit. Moreover, a second experiment reported in the same paper demonstrated that this effect of posttraining contextual extinction is specific to extinction of the CS training context as opposed to extinction of an excitatory context in which the CS had not been trained. Notably, a blocking interpretation of the US preexposure effect predicts that extinction of the training context after the CS-US pairings should not influence responding to the CS. The findings of Matzel et al. (1987) indicate that learning took place during the CS-US pairings and that this association was masked by the excitatory value of the training context.

Overshadowing. In the preceding example with US preexposure, the training context served as the comparator stimulus for the CS. For purposes of contrast, the present example, which concerns overshadowing, was selected to demonstrate how punctate stimuli present during CS training can act as comparator stimuli for a CS. In contradiction to the previously described prevailing views of overshadowing which are couched in the framework of acquisition failure, the comparator hypothesis suggests that the simultaneous presentation of the overshadowing and overshadowed stimuli during training cause them to later serve as comparator stimuli for each other. In the comparator framework, if the overshadowing stimulus has a higher asymptote for associative strength than does the overshadowed stimulus, responding to the overshadowed stimulus should be greatly attenuated despite the presence of an appreciable association between the overshadowed CS and the US. Alternatively, if the overshadowed and overshadowing stimuli have similar associative asymptotes but the overshadowing stimulus accrues associative strength faster than the overshadowed stimulus, overshadowing should appear as the two stimuli diverge in associative value. Then after the overshadowing stimulus has reached its associative asymptote, the overshadowed stimulus should be able to continue to gain associative strength over additional trials on which the compound CS is reinforced. Data have been reported consistent with this prediction that overshadowing should decrease over large numbers of reinforced trials with the compound stimulus (Bellingham & Gillette, 1981).

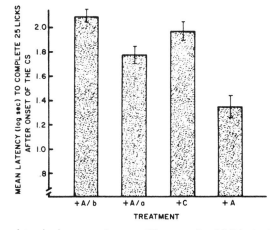

Figure 4.4. Mean latencies in a neutral context (B) to complete 25 licks in the presence of the CS (noise). Groups +A, +A/b, and +A/a received unsignaled USs (footshocks) in Context A, whereas Group +C received unsignaled USs in Context C. All subjects then received CS-US pairings in Context A as part of a retardation test. Group A+/ b had Context A extinguished before the CS-US pairings while Group A+/a had Context A extinguished after the CS-US pairings. Lower scores indicate greater retardation of conditioned lick suppression. Brackets depict standard errors. From Matzel et al. (1987). Copyright 1987 by the American Psychological Association. Reprinted with permission.

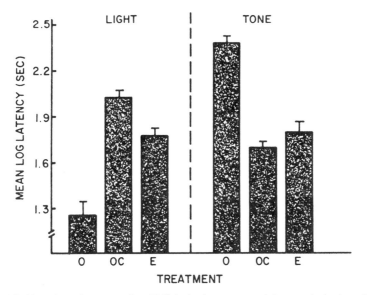

Figure 4.5. Mean latencies to complete 25 licks in the presence of the overshadowing stimulus (tone) and the overshadowed stimulus (light). Group O demonstrates overshadowing, Group OC represents acquisition to the light when it is trained in the absence of the tone, and Group E illustrates responding after overshadowing and subsequent extinction of the tone. Brackets depict standard errors. From Matzel et al. (1985). Copyright 1985 by Academic Press. Reprinted with permission.

In either case, if the overshadowing stimulus has its effect upon the overshadowed stimulus at the time of testing as suggested by the comparator hypothesis, extinction of the overshadowing stimulus after completion of training should attenuate the behavioral deficit called overshadowing. Using rats, data consistent with this prediction were reported by Kaufman and Bolles (1981), who monitored activity as a behavioral measure, and Matzel, Schachtman, and Miller (1985; also see Matzel, Shuster, & Miller, 1987), who monitored suppression of drinking as a behavioral measure. The results of the Matzel et al. (1985) study are depicted in Figure 4.5. In another experiment in this series, it was demonstrated that this means of unmasking overshadowed associations required that the extinguished stimulus be the overshadowing stimulus as opposed to an unrelated excitatory stimulus.

The data just reviewed suggest that overshadowing is a failure in response generation that arises from the comparator process. This appears to contrast with our retrieval failure interpretation of the previously described effects of reminder treatment upon overshadowing. One means of reconciling these two interpretations is to assume that a US reminder facilitates retrieval of the association between the overshadowed stimulus and the US more than it facilitates retrieval of either the association between overshadowed stimulus and the overshadowing stimulus or the association between the overshadowing stimulus and the US. Logically, it seems plausible that a US reminder would enhance retrieval of both associations to the US but not the association between the overshadowed stimulus and overshadowing stimulus. Judgement of this supposition awaits further research, but for the present, both of these means of un-masking overshadowed associations yield evidence supporting the view that overshadowing is due at least in part to something other than an acquisition failure.

The fact that we have been able to achieve a posttraining reduction of overshadowing by both reminder treatment and extinction of the overshadowing stimulus suggests some similarity between these seemingly diverse techniques for enhancing behavior. By intent, we have avoided proposing a specific mathematical relationship for the comparison between the CS and its comparator stimulus. However, if a reminder treatment is assumed to enhance by a fixed percentage both the effective (i.e., retrievable) comparator-US association and the effective CS-US association, improved responding to the CS would be predicted by a difference rule for the comparison, but not by a ratio rule. Although we think it potentially misleading to advocate a specific mathematical relation for the comparison between a CS and its comparator stimulus on the basis of existing data, for reasons such as this we favor a difference rule over a ratio rule such as that proposed by Gibbon and Balsam (1981) based on scalar expectancy theory.

Conditioned Inhibition. The comparator hypothesis views all associations as positive and regards behavior indicative of conditioned inhibition (i.e, retardation of responding and negative summation) as the consequence of a CS-US excitatory association that is weaker than the excitatory association between the CS's comparator stimulus and the US. Conversely, behavior indicative of conditioned excitation is assumed to arise from administering a test for excitation with a CS when the CS-US association is not weaker than the association between the CS's comparator stimulus and the US. Thus, when the strength of the CS-US association is roughly equivalent to the strength of the comparator-US association, the CS might be expected to pass tests for both inhibition and excitation.

Consistent with this possibility, Matzel, Gladstein, and Miller (1988) have recently presented data demonstrating that, after weak negative contingency training during which the CS was reinforced 33% of the time and the absence of the CS was reinforced 67% of the time, the very same stimulus was capable of passing a test for excitation as well as retardation and summation tests for inhibition. This demonstration that conditioned excitation and conditioned inhibition are not mutually exclusive is contrary to the widely accepted view of the Rescorla-Wagner (1972) model that conditioned excitation and conditioned inhibition are opposite ends of the same associative continuum. However, a little reflection on the nature of excitatory and inhibitory tests makes clear that these tests measure rather different attributes of a stimulus and there is no reason beyond theoretical bias to assume that empirically defined excitation and inhibition are mutually exclusive.

The comparator hypothesis takes the view that excitatory responding to a CS is inversely related to the associative value of the CS's comparator stimulus. Thus, posttraining reduction in the associative strength of the comparator stimulus should augment excitatory responding to the CS. This is exactly what was reported in the preceding examples with the US preexposure effect and overshadowing. A parallel effect is predicted in the case of conditioned inhibition. In the framework of the comparator hypothesis, the training context plays the role of the comparator stimulus as a result of negative contingency training (i.e., +/X-) and the punctate excitor A plays the primary role of the comparator stimulus as a result of A+/AX- Pavlovian inhibition training. As a result of either type of conditioned inhibition training with Stimulus X, there ought to be a second-order excitatory association between Stimulus X and US (+) that is mediated by the conditioned excitor with which Stimulus X was trained (i.e., Stimulus A in the case of A+/AX- and the training context in the case of +/X-). Additionally, if the putative inhibitor were ever reinforced during training, there will likely also be a first-order excitatory association between Stimulus X and the US. Consequently, if these two sources of excitation are strong enough, extinction of Stimulus X's comparator stimuli might reveal these excitatory associations.

Hallam, Matzel, Sloat, and Miller (1989) used a conditioned lick suppression task to test the possibility that extinguishing the comparator stimulus for a conditioned inhibitor would transform the inhibitor into a conditioned excitor. They initially gave rats Pavlovian inhibition training in which Stimulus A was reinforced 100% of the time and the AX compound was reinforced 25% of the time. Training with these parameters resulted in passage of retardation and summation tests for conditioned inhibition and failure of a test for conditioned excitation. But when Stimulus A was extinguished following the completion of conditioned inhibition training, Stimulus X was found not only to fail the two inhibitory tests, but also to support weak but significant excitatory responding. Notably, such results require the use of parameters that minimize within-compound associations between the inhibitor and the excitor used in inhibitory training. Otherwise decreased inhibition as a consequence of extinguishing the excitor can be masked by an accompanying loss of second-order excitation mediated by the excitor. The situation is indeed similar to that of overshadowing as described previously, except in the case of Pavlovian inhibition the conditioned inhibitor presumably has accrued less excitatory associative strength than has the typical overshadowed stimulus.

Generality. All of the data from our laboratory in support of the comparator hypothesis has used rats in conditioned suppression situations. This invites questions about the generality of the reported phenomena. However, other laboratories using different species and tasks have obtained similar results. For example, posttraining extinction of the training context has been found to decrease inhibition produced through negative contingency training using pigeons in an autoshaping task (Kaplan & Hearst, 1985) and rats in a conditioned taste aversion task (Best, Dunn, Batson, Meachum, & Nash 1985).

In rejecting traditional views of conditioned inhibitors such as those that attribute negative associative strengths to inhibitors (Rescorla & Wagner, 1972), we have an obligation to offer alternative explanations of behavioral phenomena that ordinarily have been explained in terms of negative associative strengths. The three most notable phenomena of this sort are retardation, summation, and superconditioning.

Retardation refers to an inhibitor requiring more CS-US pairings to elicit excitatory responding than does an otherwise equivalent neutral stimulus. Schachtman, Brown, Gordon, Catterson, and Miller (1987) have demonstrated that at least part of the resultant retardation following inhibitory training arises from the CS's comparator stimulus gaining strong excitatory strength during inhibitory training and the associative strength of the CS having to rise above this value during the CS-US pairings that constitute the retardation test before conditioned responding will be evidenced.

Superconditioning refers to the enhanced responding seen to a CS that is reinforced in the presence of a conditioned inhibitor. Navarro-Guzman, Hallam, Matzel, and Miller (1989) have found that superconditioning is the result of the inhibitor being a less effective overshadowing stimulus than the equivalent stimulus without inhibitory training. Thus, superconditioning does not appear to be a result of the inhibitor having negative associative strength, but rather is a product of the inhibitor having reduced associability.

Inhibitory summation refers to the reduced responding to an established excitor seen when the excitor is presented in compound with a conditioned inhibitor relative to when the excitor is presented alone. At the present time, the best explanation of inhibitory summation that avoids attributing negative associative strength to putative inhibitors appears to be the view that inhibitors, in addition to their direct associations to USs and their training contexts, also have a modulatory influence on retrieval of, and/or response generation based on, associations between other conditioned excitors and the US in question, that is, negative occasion setting (Holland, 1985; Rescorla, 1987). More research is needed to evaluate this proposition.

An anomalous phenomenon in the inhibition literature is the fact that posttraining presentations of a conditioned inhibitor alone (i.e., operational extinction) does not reduce the inhibitory potential of the CS as predicted by the Rescorla-Wagner (1972) model (Zimmer-Hart & Rescorla, 1974). The comparator hypothesis not only predicts no loss of inhibition as a result of CS alone presentations, but additionally predicts that if the inhibitor has latent first- or second-order excitatory value, CS alone presentations will *increase* the inhibitory potential of the CS as a result of decreasing the excitatory associative strength of the CS relative to its comparator stimulus. Exactly such an effect has been reported by several laboratories (DeVito & Fowler, 1987; Holland & Gory, 1986; Miller & Schachtman, 1985).

Evaluation of the Comparator Hypothesis. The preceding examples of the comparator process all involved modification of the associative status of a CS's comparator stimulus following completion of CS training. This was done to provide phenomena that are predicted uniquely by the comparator hypothesis. The comparator hypothesis also predicts similar effects when the associative status of the comparator stimulus is altered before or during CS training; however, various models of acquisition also predict these latter effects. Although further experimentation has to be performed to distinguish between acquisition and comparator explanations phenomena that appear amenable to both acquisition and comparator explanations, models of acquisition that posit new processes purely for the purpose of explaining these phenomena are particularly suspect. The comparator hypothesis is needed to explain the effects of comparator stimuli revaluations after the completion of CS training; hence, no new principle is required to explain similar effects before and during CS training. To the extent that the comparator hypothesis of response generation is embraced, simpler models of *learning* may be possible. As an extreme case (too extreme, but food for thought), we might consider the possibility that acquisition depends on mere contiguity and responding depends on contingency. More realistically, the comparator hypothesis is a response rule that in principle can be wedded to any rule for acquisition.

The comparator hypothesis predicts that associative deflation (extinction) of a CS's comparator stimulus before, during, or after CS training will increase excitatory responding and decrease behavior indicative of inhibition. These predictions of the comparator hypothesis concerning the effects of deflating the CS's comparator stimulus following CS training are unique to the comparator hypothesis and, by and large, have been supported. Additionally, the comparator hypothesis predicts that associative inflation of the CS's comparator stimulus before, during, or after CS training will decrease excitatory responding and increase behavior indicative of inhibition. The part of this prediction that is unique to the comparator hypothesis concerns the effects of comparator modification following CS training, and it is here that a major failing of the comparator hypothesis appears to arise. To date, across a broad range of tasks we have seen no effect on responding to the CS of posttraining inflation of the CS's comparator stimulus. If this failure proves reliable, the comparator hypothesis is in need of major revision. However, the problem of posttraining inflation of comparator stimuli not withstanding, the comparator hypothesis has proven to be and continues to be a useful heuristic tool, which is the primary purpose of any model. More to the point, the comparator hypothesis has been presented here not to proselytize for the comparator hypothesis per se, but rather to illustrate the potential explanatory power of response rules that rise above linear mapping of reactivated associations into behavior.

Contrast Effects. Contrast effects refer to modulation of performance by task motivation relative to the motivation underlying tasks similar in space, time, or action (see Dachowski & Brazier, chap. 10 in this volume; Flaherty, chap. 9 in this volume). They are ordinarily obtained by alternating between two motivational circumstances or by studying the effect of a prior motivational experience upon a subsequent task (e.g., Crespi, 1942). Despite a decided difference in the terminologies used to discuss contrast and comparator effects, the motivational view of contrast effects has much in common with the comparator hypothesis. Alternately stated, the comparator hypothesis implies that all acquired behavior is modulated by contrast effects. Contrast effects have traditionally been studied in instrumental situations, whereas the comparator hypothesis was initially developed for Pavlovian situations. Collectively, contrast effects and the comparator hypothesis appear to apply the same principle of relative motivation to both types of acquired behavior.

Interestingly, there does not appear to be a reported instance of a heightened motivational experience between training and testing having a deleterious contrast effect on test performance. Hence, it is even possible that the clearest failure of the comparator hypothesis, that is, the lack of effect of posttraining inflation of the comparator stimulus, is paralleled by an absence of the analogous contrast effect.

APPROPRIATENESS OF RESPONSE MEASURES

The preceding sections of this chapter discussed how acquired associations can be masked by factors that we have conceptualized as retrieval failures and response rule processes. A further factor that can mask associations is the selection of the response to be monitored as an indication of learning having occurred. There are many responses that can be recorded and obviously they are not all equally sensitive to the association of interest. Although this principle has long been recognized, researchers began to appreciate the full implications of it only with Holland's (1977) seminal experiments which demonstrated the importance of this point by recording multiple behavioral measures simultaneously and showing their differential sensitivity as indicators of particular associations.

We have recently entertained the possibility that the differential effectiveness of various responses as indicators of learning might tell us something about underlying associative structure. Specifically, we considered the possibility that the apparent inferiority of simultaneous conditioning relative to short-delay forward conditioning reflected a performance failure rather than an acquisition failure. Early attempts at revealing otherwise latent simultaneous associations by either reminder techniques or comparator manipulations proved unsuccessful (Matzel, Castillo, & Miller, 1988). Consequently, we considered the hypothesis that the apparent weakness of simultaneous conditioning was due to the experimenter recording anticipatory responses appropriate for CSs that *predict* the US, rather than "simultaneous" responses appropriate for CSs that might be expected to *accompany* the US.

To investigate this hypothesis, we (Matzel, Held, & Miller, 1988) attempted to create a forward (serial) link between an otherwise neutral stimulus (S1) and another CS (S2) that was presented simultaneously with the US. Thus, S1 should have had a forward relationship with the US which was mediated by S2, and consequently S1 might support an anticipatory conditioned response. The central study in this series employed a sensory preconditioning procedure. In Phase 1, Stimulus S1 consistently preceded Stimulus S2 for all the rats that served as subjects. In Phase 2, S2 was paired with the US (footshock) in either a forward or simultaneous fashion. Testing for conditioned suppression found excitatory responding to the forward S2 but not the simultaneous S2, consistent with many prior observations that forward conditioning is manifestly superior to simultaneous conditioning. However, on the critical test, S1 was found to elicit equal responding regardless of the temporal relationship between S2 and the US (see Fig. 4.6). Moreover, control groups indicated that responding to S1 depended upon S2 being paired with the US.

Our interpretation of these observations and the results of several related studies was that an association had been formed between the simultaneous S2 and the US, but our behavioral measure was inappropriate to index this associ-

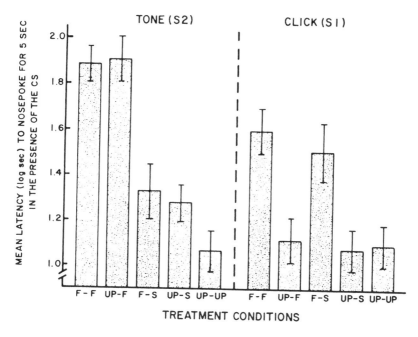

Figure 4.6. Mean latency to drink (nosepoke in a cull containing a lick tube) for five cumulative seconds. In the group designations, the symbols before the dash indicates the relationship of S1 to S2 in Phase 1 and the symbols following the dash indicate the relationship of S2 to the US in Phase 2. F = forward, S = simultaneous, and UP = unpaired. The critical group is Group F-S, which received S1-S2 forward pairings in Phase 1 and S2-US simultaneous pairings in Phase 2. Brackets depict standard errors. From Matzel, Held, and Miller (1988). Copyright 1988 by Academic Press. Reprinted with permission.

ation. Seemingly, those CSs that announce an impending US can elicit an anticipatory response, whereas those CSs that effectively say that the US should be occurring now do not elicit anticipatory responses. This implies that an acquired association is more than a simple link between a CS representation and a US representation. Rather, the association must additionally encode something about the temporal relationship between the CS and the US. This view adds complexity to what is learned, but at the same time allows a simpler model of the acquisition process in that there is no longer a need to explain why forward CS-US pairings result in associations superior to those produced by simultaneous or backward pairings. If simultaneous pairings are found to produce substantial acquisition, as is suggested here, renewed attention to contiguity as a necessary and sufficient condition for acquisition of associations would be in order.

In contrast to the view of simultaneous conditioning presented here, Rescorla (1980) has suggested that the inferiority of simultaneous conditioning is due to the US distracting the subject from the CS. In support of this position, Rescorla demonstrated in a sensory preconditioning preparation that simultaneous S1-S2 pairings in Phase 1 result in good conditioned responding to S1 after S2 has been paired with the US in a forward fashion during Phase 2.

According to Rescorla, S1 and S2 are weaker stimuli than the US; consequently neither is apt to greatly distract the subject from the other stimulus. Although this explanation is fully consistent with Rescorla's observations, so is the view that he obtained responding to S1 because S1 had a forward relationship with the US representation, a relationship mediated by the simultaneous association between S1 and S2 and the forward association between S2 and the US. Moreover, Rescorla's hypotheis concerning the US distracting the subject from simultaneous CSs, although compatible with Rescorla's data, cannot account for the responding seen by Matzel, Held, and Miller (1988) to S1 when S1 and S2 had a forward relationship in Phase 1 and S2 and the US had been presented simultaneously in Phase 2 because, according to Rescorla, no S2-US association should have been acquired.

Matzel, Held, and Miller (1988) also performed a backward conditioning experiment using the same basic sensory preconditioning procedure described above and found that a CS presented with a backward relationship to the US could not support appreciable excitatory responding, whereas a stimulus that had a forward relationship to the CS that had been backward paired with the US did elicit excitatory responding. This view of backward conditioning is compatible with the weak excitatory responding seen to backward CSs after a small number of pairings (Shurtleff & Ayres, 1981) and the inhibitory properties of backward CSs seen after many pairings (Moscovitch & LoLordo, 1968; Rescorla & LoLordo, 1965) if it is assumed that the basic associative link can be learned in fewer trials than the specific temporal relationship between the elements.

CONCLUSIONS

Bases of Enhanced Performances. Each of the behavior deficits discussed above were reduced through manipulations that minimized the possibility of relevant new learning. Our working assumption has been that in each instance complete, full-strength, CS-US associations were formed during training, but for one reason or another these associations were masked. One viable alternative to this view is that the latent associations in question were complete, but weak rather than full-strength, and that the behavior-enhancing posttraining treatments in some manner strengthened the existing associations. In this latter framework, the initial weak association provides the basic information that is strengthened by posttraining treatment.

At this stage of our knowledge, we cannot empirically differentiate between these two possibilities. Our assumption that the latent associations were full strength is predicated on the view that molar associations arise from the collective action of all-or-none atomistic associations between attributes (i.e., elements) of the CS and attributes of the US. The assumed all-or-none nature of these atomistic associations would preclude individual atomistic associations from being strengthened without relevant new learning. One possible means of action of the behavior-enhancing treatments, particularly reminder treatments, is that reactivation of event representations by the recovery treatment might allow the creation of redundant representations of already existing, full strength, atomistic associations, thereby facilitating later attempts at retrieval. In contrast, the view that our behavior-enhancing treatments strengthen existing weak associations suffers from the fact that no mechanism(s) has been proposed by which the various performance-enhancing treatments might act to strengthen associations.[3]

Implications for Contiguity Theory. The three techniques for revealing latent associations reviewed in this chapter converge on the conclusion that many associative behavior deficits ordinarily attributed to acquisition failures arise not from acquisition failure but from some problem in postacquisition processing of the target information. This not only raises questions concerning the critical postacquisition processes, some of which have been introduced in the preceding discussion, but it also is grounds for reexamining the appropriateness of models of learning (in the narrow sense) that were developed in part in order to explain these specific behavioral deficits that are now seen to be performance failures rather than acquisition failures. With less to explain, simpler models of learning than those currently in fashion become viable. Contiguity theory, although surely an oversimplification even in light of the type of phenomena described in this chapter, may merit a revival for its heuristic value. This would appear particularly appropriate, as contingency effects and the consequences of compounding stimuli during training which were the primary bases for the rejection of contiguity theory in the late 1960s now appear to have part or all of their origins in various posttraining phases of information processing. Alternately put, contiguity might be the basis of learning, whereas contingency might be the basis of responding.

The present emphasis on postacquisition information processing is not unique to the present authors. The need to devote greater attention to these processes was one of the incentives for the development of modern cognitive psychology (e.g., Anderson, 1983). Learning theory, with its generally commendable emphasis on minimizing theoretical constructs, has been slower to acknowledge the importance of postacquisition information processing. However, Wagner's (1981) SOP model stands as an example of a "learning" theory that recognizes the importance of postacquisition information processing. Additionally, theories of contrast (see Dachowski & Brazier, chap. 10 in this volume; Flaherty, chap. 9 in this volume) have historically been concerned with postacquisition processes. More recently, posttraining revaluation of stimuli (see Delamater & LoLordo, chap. 3 in this volume) has also stimulated interest in postacquisition processing of information. None of this is to suggest that acquisition processes are not important. Rather, there is a need to recognize that each of the steps in processing information is potentially subject to modulation, and a mind set to focus on only one step, such as acquisition, in

---

[3] If "strengthening" an existing association means increasing redundant representations of the association, the difference between the view that the latent associations are full strength and that they are weak would appear to be a semantic one hinging on what we mean by full strength. Beyond this semantic distinction, further consideration of the view that the present behavior deficits arise from weak associations requires a clear definition of what is meant by a "weak" association.

the overall sequence of processing acquired information is apt to be highly misleading.

ACKNOWLEDGMENTS

This chapter was prepared with the support of NIMH Grant 33881 and NSF Grant BNS 86-00755. The content is based in part on an invited lecture delivered at the 1988 meeting of the Eastern Psychological Association in Buffalo, NY. Thanks are due Steve C. Hallam, Susan L. Priore, and Todd Schachtman for their comments on an early draft of the manuscript. The ideas presented here were developed over several years with important contributions by Wesley Kasprow, Louis Matzel, and Todd Schachtman.

REFERENCES

Anderson, J.R. (1983). *The architecture of cognition.* Cambridge, MA: Harvard University Press.

Balaz, M.A., Gutsin, P., Cacheiro, H., & Miller, R.R. (1982). Blocking as a retrieval failure: Reactivation of associations to a blocked stimulus. *Quarterly Journal of Experimental Psychology, 34B,* 99-113.

Bellingham, W.P., & Gillette, K. (1981). Attenuation of overshadowing as a function of nondifferential compound conditioning trials. *Bulletin of the Psychonomic Society, 18,* 218-220.

Best, M.R., Dunn, D.P., Batson, J.D., Meachum, C.L., & Nash, S.M. (1985). Extinguishing conditioned inhibition in flavour-aversion learning: Effects of repeated testing and extinction of the excitatory element. *Quarterly Journal of Experimental Psychology, 37B,* 359-378.

Chorover, S.L., & Schiller, P.H. (1965). Short-term retrograde amnesia in rats. *Journal of Physiological and Comparative Psychology, 59,* 73-78.

Crespi, L.P. (1942). Quantitative variation of incentive and performance in the white rat. *American Journal of Psychology, 55,* 467-517.

DeVietti, T.L., Bauste, R.L., Nutt, G., Barrett, O.V., Daly, K., & Petree, A.D. (1987). Latent inhibition: A trace conditioning phenomenon? *Learning and Motivation, 18,* 185-201.

DeVito, P.L., & Fowler, H. (1987). Enhancement of conditioned inhibition via an extinction treatment. *Animal Learning and Behavior, 15,* 448-454.

Gibbon, J., & Balsam, P. (1981). Spreading association in time. In C.M. Locurto, H.S. Terrace, & J. Gibbon (Eds.), *Autoshaping and conditioning theory* (pp. 219-253). New York: Academic Press.

Gordon, W.C., Smith, G.J., & Katz, D.S. (1979). Dual effects of response blocking following avoidance learning. *Behavior Research and Therapy, 17,* 479-487.

Hallam, S.C., Matzel, L.D., Sloat, J., & Miller, R.R. (1989). *Excitation and inhibition as a function of posttraining extinction of the excitatory cue used in Pavlovian inhibitory training.* Manuscript submitted for publication.

Holland, P.C. (1977). Conditioned stimuli as a determinant of the form of the Pavlovian conditioned response. *Journal of Experimental Psychology: Animal Behavior Processes, 3,* 77-104.

Holland, P.C. (1985). The nature of conditioned inhibition in serial and simultaneous feature negative discriminations. In R.R. Miller & N. E. Spear (Eds.), *Information processing in animals: Conditioned inhibition* (pp. 267-297). Hillsdale, NJ: Lawrence Erlbaum Associates.

Holland, P.C., & Gory, J. (1986). Extinction of inhibition after serial and simultaneous feature negative discrimination training. *Quarterly Journal of Experimental Psychology, 38B*, 245-265.

Hull, C.L. (1952). *A behavior system*. New Haven, CT: Yale University Press.

Kantowitz, B.H. (1985). Channels and stages of human information processing: A limited analysis of theory and methodology. *Journal of Mathematical Psychology, 29*, 135-173.

Kaplan, P.S., & Hearst, E. (1985). Excitation, inhibition, and context: Studies of extinction and reinstatement. In P.D. Balsam & A. Tomie (Eds.), *Context and learning* (pp. 195-224). Hillsdale, NJ: Lawrence Erlbaum Associates.

Kasprow, W.J., Cacheiro, H., Balaz, M.A., & Miller, R.R. (1982). Reminder-induced recovery of associations to an overshadowed stimulus. *Learning and Motivation, 13*, 155-166.

Kasprow, W.J. Catterson, D., Schachtman, T.R., & Miller, R.R. (1984). Attenuation of latent inhibition by postacquisition reminder. *Quarterly Journal of Experimental Psychology, 36B*, 53-63.

Kasprow, W.J., Schachtman, T.R., & Miller, R.R. (1987). The comparator hypothesis of conditioned response generation: Manifest conditioned excitation and inhibition as a function of relative excitatory associative strengths of CS and conditioning context at the time of testing. *Journal of Experimental Psychology: Animal Behavior Processes, 13*, 395-406.

Kaufman, M.A., & Bolles, R.C. (1981). A nonassociative aspect of overshadowing. *Bulletin of the Psychonomic Society, 18*, 318-320.

Kraemer, P.J., Lariviere, N.A., & Spear, N.E. (1988). Expression of a taste aversion conditioned with an odor-taste compound: Overshadowing is relatively weak in weanlings and decreases over a retention interval in adults. *Animal Learning and Behavior, 16*, 164-168..

Kraemer, P.J., & Roberts, W.A. (1984). The influence of flavor preexposure and test interval on conditioned taste aversions in rats. *Learning and Motivation, 15*, 259-278.

Lubow, R.E., Weiner, I., & Schnur, P. (1981). Conditioned attention theory. In G.H. Bower (Ed.), *The psychology of learning and motivation* (Vol. 15, pp. 1-49). New York: Academic Press.

Mackintosh, N.J. (1975). A theory of attention: Variations in the associability of stimuli with reinforcement. *Psychological Review, 82*, 276-298.

Matzel, L.D., Brown A.M., & Miller, R.R. (1987). Associative effects of US preexposure: Modulation of conditioned responding by an excitatory training context. *Journal of Experimental Psychology: Animal Behavior Processes, 13*, 65-72.

Matzel, L.D., Castillo, J., & Miller, R.R. (1988). Contextual modulation of simultaneous associations. *Bulletin of the Psychonomic Society, 26*, 371-374.

Matzel, L.D., Gladstein, L., & Miller, R.R. (1988). Conditioned excitation and conditioned inhibition are not mutually exclusive. *Learning and Motivation, 19*, 99-121.

Matzel, L.D., Held, F.P., & Miller, R.R. (1988). Information and expression of simultaneous and backwards associations: Implications for contiguity theory. *Learning and Motivation, 19*, 317-344.

Matzel, L.D., Schachtman, T.R., & Miller, R.R. (1985). Recovery of an overshadowed association achieved by extinction of the over-shadowing stimulus. *Learning and Motivation, 16*, 398-412.

Matzel, L.D., Shuster, K., & Miller, R.R. (1987). Covariation in conditioned response strength between elements trained in compound. *Animal Learning and Behavior, 15,* 439-447..

McGaugh, J.L. (1966). Time-dependent processes in memory storage. *Science, 153,* 1351-1358.

Miller, R.R. (1982). Effects of intertrial reinstatement of training stimuli on complex maze learning in rats: Evidence that "acquisition" curves reflect more than acquisition. *Journal of Experimental Psychology: Animal Behavior Processes, 8,* 86-109.

Miller, R.R., Kasprow, W.J., & Schachtman, T.R. (1986). Retrieval variability: Sources and consequences. *American Journal of Psychology, 99,* 145-218.

Miller, R.R., & Marlin, N.A. (1979). Amnesia following electroconvulsive shock. In J.F. Kihlstrom & J.F. Evans (Eds.), *Functional disorders of memory* (pp. 143-178). Hillsdale, NJ: Lawrence Erlbaum Associates.

Miller, R.R., & Matzel, L.D. (1988). The comparator hypothesis: A response rule for the expression of associations. In G.H. Bower (Ed.), *The psychology of learning and motivation, Vol. 22* (pp. 51-92). Orlando, FL: Academic Press.

Miller, R.R., Ott, C.A., Berk, A.M., & Springer, A.D. (1974). Appetitive memory restored after electroconvulsive shock in the rat. *Journal of Physiological and Comparative Psychology, 87,* 717-723.

Miller, R.R., & Schachtman, T.R. (1985). Conditioning context as an associative baseline: Implications for response generation and the nature of conditioned inhibition. In R.R. Miller & N.E. Spear (Eds.), *Information processing in animals: Conditioned inhibition* (pp. 51-88). Hillsdale, NJ: Lawrence Erlbaum Associates.

Miller, R.R., & Springer, A.D. (1972). Induced recovery of memory in rats following ECS. *Physiology and Behavior, 8,* 645-651.

Moscovitch, A., & LoLordo, V.M. (1968). Role of safety in the Pavlovian backward fear conditioning procedure. *Journal of Comparative and Physiological Psychology, 66,* 673-678.

Navarro-Guzman, J.I., Hallam, S.C., Matzel, L.D., & Miller, R.R. (1989). Superconditioning and overshadowing. *Learning and Motivation, 20,* 130-152.

Overton, D.A. (1964). State dependent or "dissociated learning produced with pentobarbital. *Journal of Physiological and Comparative Psychology, 57,* 3-12.

Pearce, J.M., & Hall, G. (1980). A model for Pavlovian conditioning: Variations in the effectiveness of conditioned but not unconditioned stimuli. *Psychological Review, 87,* 332-352.

Randich, A., & LoLordo, V.M. (1979). Preconditioning exposure to the unconditioned stimulus affects the acquisition of a conditioned emotional response. *Learning and Motivation, 10,* 245-277.

Rescorla, R.A. (1980). Simultaneous and successive associations in sensory preconditioning. *Journal of Experimental Psychology: Animal Behavior Processes, 6,* 207-216.

Rescorla, R.A. (1987). Facilitation and inhibition. *Journal of Experimental Psychology: Animal Behavior Processes, 13,* 250-259.

Rescorla, R.A., & LoLordo, V.M. (1965). Inhibition of avoidance behavior. *Journal of Comparative and Physiological Psychology, 59,* 406-412.

Rescorla, R.A., & Wagner, A.R. (1972). A theory of Pavlovian conditioning: Variations in the effectiveness of reinforcement and nonreinforcement. In A.H. Black & W.F. Prokasy (Eds.), *Classical conditioning II: Current research and theory* (pp. 64-99). New York: Appleton-Century-Crofts.

Riccio, D.C., & Ebner, D.L. (1981). Postacquisition modification of memory. In N.E. Spear & R.R. Miller (Eds.), *Information processing in animals: Memory mechanisms* (pp. 291-317). Hillsdale, NJ: Lawrence Erlbaum Associates.

Roediger, H.L., & Payne, D.G. (1982). Hypermnesia: The role of repeated testing. *Journal of Experimental Psychology: Learning, Memory, and Cognition, 8,* 66-72.

Schachtman, T.R., Brown, A.M., Gordon, E., Catterson, D., & Miller, R. R. (1987). Mechanisms underlying retarded emergence of conditioned responding following inhibitory training: Evidence for the comparator hypothesis. *Journal of Experimental Psychology: Animal Behavior Processes, 13,* 310-322.

Schachtman, T.R., Gee, J-L., Kasprow, W.J., & Miller, R.R. (1983). Reminder-induced recovery from blocking as function of the number of compound trials. *Learning and Motivation, 14,* 154-164.

Shurtleff, D., & Ayres, J.J.B. (1981). One-trial backward excitatory fear conditioning in rats: Acquisition, retention, extinction, and spontaneous recovery. *Animal Learning and Behavior, 9,* 65-74.

Spear, N.E. (1973). Retrieval of memories in animals. *Psychological Review, 80,* 163-194.

Tolman, E.C. (1932). *Purposive behavior in animals and men.* New York: Century.

Tulving, E. (1974). Cue-dependent forgetting. *American Scientist, 62,* 74-82.

Wagner, A.R. (1978). Expectancies and priming in STM. In S.H. Hulse, H. Fowler, & W.K. Honig (Eds.), *Cognitive processes in behavior* (pp. 177-209). Hillsdale, NJ: Lawrence Erlbaum Associates.

Wagner, A.R. (1981). SOP: A model of automatic memory processing in animal behavior. In N.E. Spear & R.R. Miller (Eds.), *Information processing in animals: Memory mechanisms* (pp. 5-47). Hillsdale, NJ: Lawrence Erlbaum Associates.

Zimmer-Hart, C.L., & Rescorla, R.A. (1974). Extinction of a Pavlovian conditioned inhibitor. *Journal of Comparative and Physiological Psychology, 86,* 837-845.

5   Memory Strategies in Pigeons

Thomas R. Zentall
University of Kentucky

Peter J. Urcuioli
Purdue University

Pamela Jackson-Smith and Janice N. Steirn
University of Kentucky

Among procedures used in the study of animal memory, perhaps the most widely used is the delayed matching to sample or delayed conditional discrimination task (see e.g., Cumming & Berryman, 1965; D'Amato, 1973; Roberts, 1972; Zentall & Hogan, 1977). In a delayed conditional discrimination, reinforcement is provided for a response to stimulus X (but not to stimulus Y) if both were preceded by stimulus A, and reinforcement is provided for a response to stimulus Y (but not to stimulus X) if both were preceded by stimulus B. Thus the comparison or test stimulus (X or Y) to which a response will be reinforced is conditional on the prior presence of a particular initial or sample stimulus (A or B).

A delay between the sample and comparison stimuli means that subjects must retain some information through the retention interval in order to perform accurately when the test stimuli are presented. The question of interest here is: what is the nature of the information remembered during the delay? Generally speaking, the memory code can take one of two forms. First, and most intuitively, it can consist of some representation of the previously presented sample stimulus. Such a "retrospective" memory code (Honig & Thompson, 1982) is consistent with traditional theories of animal memory, such as trace decay theory (Roberts & Grant, 1974), and interference theory (see Zentall & Hogan, 1977).

Alternatively, the sample may be "translated" into a representation of the test stimulus to which a response will later be made. According to this view, a representation of the correct comparison (rather than a representation of the sample) is retained during the delay. If the animal retains a representation of the correct comparison (or other future events), then it is using a "prospective" memory code (Honig & Thompson, 1982).

The idea that one might encode a future course of action is implicit in our everyday notions of human memory. We are often said to anticipate future events and "plan ahead" or "plan what to do" (see, for example, Tversky, 1969, for an experimental demonstration of this type of memory encoding).

Recently, it has been suggested that animal memory may also involve prospective codes under certain conditions (Grant, 1981; Honig & Thompson, 1982; Roitblat, 1980, 1984; Wasserman, 1986). The purpose of the research described in this chapter is to specify the conditions that might encourage animals to code retrospectively versus prospectively in delayed conditional discriminations.

According to Honig and Thompson (1982), prospective coding should be most likely to occur whenever the prospective information (or memory) load is less than the retrospective load. In the simplest case, memory load can be defined as the number of stimuli to be remembered. Later in this chapter we will examine the development of memory strategies in a task in which number of stimuli to be remembered is manipulated. But one can also define memory load in terms of the difficulty in remembering a single stimulus. For example, Honig and Thompson have noted that in the simple delayed response discrimination (responses following a delay are reinforced if the predelay stimulus was S+ but not if it was S-) the memory code can consist of an instruction, either "peck" or "don't peck," whereas in the more difficult delayed conditional discrimination, the memory code must include the identity of a particular stimulus (e.g., "peck red" or "peck green"). These authors have argued that it is more difficult to remember a code that involves an arbitrary external stimulus, than to remember an instruction, "peck" or "don't peck." In other words, the "peck" and "don't peck" codes are easier to discriminate from each other than the "red" and "green" codes. According to Honig and Thompson, the difference in discriminability or memorability between the memory codes in these two tasks accounts for the differences in delay accuracy. To test this hypothesis, we will examine the effect on delay performance of stimulus discriminability.

One can also view memory load as being a function of the number of stimuli with which the to-be-remembered stimulus may be confused. For example, the more stimuli there are in the set of potential stimuli to be remembered, the greater the likelihood that a particular memory code will be replaced by one of the other (i.e., incorrect) codes. Thus we will also explore effects on delay performance of varying the number of stimuli in the sample and comparison sets.

In this chapter we will describe results we have obtained in an attempt to assess the memory processes used by pigeons. In this research we have used two methodologies. The first involves the delayed conditional discrimination task, already described. The second involves an analog of the radial arm maze task developed by Olton and Samuelson (1976) for use with rats. With both of these methodologies we are asking, under what conditions pigeons' memory is based on retrospective vs. prospective codes.

CODING IN DELAYED CONDITIONAL DISCRIMINATIONS

Our first series of experiments assessed the effect on delayed conditional discrimination performance of two variables that should presumably affect retrospective or prospective memory load. We assumed that if pigeons' memory in a delayed conditional discrimination is predominantly retrospective, then manipulation of the memory load associated with the sample stimuli should affect performance to a greater degree than similar manipulation of the memory load associated with the comparison stimuli. Conversely, if pigeons' memory is predominantly prospective, the greater effect should be obtained by manipulation of the memory load associated with the comparison stimuli.

In Experiment 1 we examined how the discriminability of the sample and comparison stimuli affected performance. In Experiment 2 we manipulated the number of stimuli in the sample and comparison sets. And finally, in Experiment 3 we explored possible interactions between stimulus discriminability and number.

Stimulus Discriminability

The purpose of Experiment 1 (Urcuioli & Zentall, 1986, Experiment 2) was to manipulate the discriminability of both the sample and comparison stimuli to see whether either or both would affect performance of the delayed conditional discrimination. For example, if pigeons use a strictly retrospective coding process, one would predict that manipulation of sample discriminability would result in poorer delay performance when the samples are less discriminable than when they are more discriminable, but manipulation of comparison discriminability would not have any affect on delay performance. On the other hand, if pigeons use a strictly prospective coding process, as some claim (e.g., Grant, 1982; Roitblat, 1980; Santi & Roberts, 1985), then manipulation of sample discriminability should have little affect on pigeons' delay performance, but manipulation of comparison discriminability should result in poorer delay performance when the comparisons are less discriminable than when they are more discriminable. Finally, if pigeons are capable of using both retrospective and prospective coding processes, one might see poorer delay performance only when both samples and comparisons are less discriminable. When samples are more discriminable than comparisons, they would retrospectively code the easier to remember samples, whereas when comparisons are more discriminable than samples, they would prospectively code the easier to remember comparisons. Thus if both coding processes can be used, we should expect to find an interaction between sample and comparison discriminability.

In Experiment 1, discriminability was manipulated by using either more discriminable hues or less discriminable lines. Farthing, Wagner, Gilmour, and Waxman (1977) reported that vertical and horizontal lines were harder to discriminate, and when trained to comparable levels of 0-delay performance were forgotten faster (i.e., showed a steeper decline in performance with increasing delay) than were red and green hues.

Four groups of pigeons were initially trained on a 0-delay conditional discrimination with either lines or hues as samples and either lines or hues as comparisons. For the hue-hue group (H-H) both the samples and comparisons were red (R) and green (G) hues. For the hue-line group (H-L) the samples were R and G hues and the comparisons were vertical (V) and horizontal (H) lines. For the line-hue (L-H) group the samples were V and H lines and the comparisons were R and G hues. Finally, for the line-line group (L-L) both the samples and comparisons were V and H lines. This 2 x 2 design allowed us to independently determine the effect of sample and comparison discriminability on delayed conditional discrimination performance. Each pigeon was trained on the 0-delay task to a criterion of five out of six consecutive sessions at or above 90% correct responding. All pigeons were then tested with mixed delays of 0, 0.5, 1.0, 2.0, and 4.0 s.

Acquisition data from Experiment 1 indicated that both sample and comparison discriminability affected the rate of acquisition. The H-H group learned the 0-delay task fastest, the L-L group learned the task slowest, and the H-L and L-H groups fell in between. The delay data indicated, however, that only sample discriminability affected level of performance. The retention functions relating performance level to delay interval indicated there was a significantly higher level of performance when the initial stimuli were hues than when they were lines, however, a similar analysis of the comparison stimulus dimension effect yielded nonsignificant results. In addition, a significant group x delay interval interaction was found. Results from Experiment 1 are presented in Figure 5.1.

Under the present conditions, pigeons trained with a delayed conditional discrimination appear to retrospectively code a representation of the sample stimulus during the delay, independently of the discriminability of the comparison stimuli. Such coding occurs in spite of the fact that, in the case of the L-

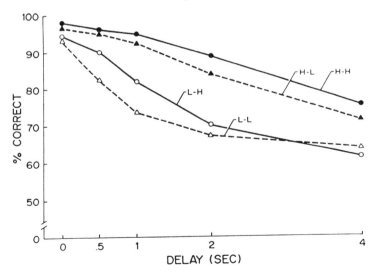

Figure 5.1. Retention gradients for the four groups in Experiment 1 averaged over the last 10 delay sessions. (Urcuioli & Zentall, 1986. Copyright 1986 by the American Psychological Association. Reprinted by permission.)

H group, it is likely that a prospective memory strategy would have led to a higher level of performance (based on the reported finding that hues are easier to remember than lines, see Farthing et al., 1977).

Number of Stimuli

In Experiment 2 (Zentall, Jagielo, Jackson-Smith, & Urcuioli, 1987) we attempted to vary the memory load by manipulating, independently, the number of stimuli in the sample and comparison sets. We reasoned that as the number stimuli in the set increased, so should the interference or confusion among them. Four groups of pigeons were trained on a 0-delay conditional discrimination task. For all groups a single sample and pair of comparisons were presented on each trial. The groups differed in the number of different stimuli from which the sample could be drawn during a session (two or four) and the number of comparison stimuli from which the comparisons could be drawn during a session (two or four). These variables were factorially combined such that the 2-2 group had two samples and two comparisons, the 2-4 group had two samples and four comparisons, the 4-2 group had four samples and two comparisons, and the 4-4 group had four samples and four comparisons. The pool of sample and comparison stimulus sets were vertical and horizontal lines and circle and triangle shapes. Wherever appropriate, the stimuli were counterbalanced

TABLE 5.1
Trial Types for the Four Training Groups from Experiment 2

	Group		
2-2	2-4	4-2	4-4
V(VH)	V(VH)	V(VH)	V(VH)
H(HV)	H(HV)	H(HV)	H(HV)
	V(TC)	T(VH)	T(TC)
	H(CT)	C(HV)	C(CT)
	OR		
T(TC)	T(TC)	T(TC)	T(TC)
C(CT)	C(CT)	C(CT)	C(CT)
	T(VH)	V(TC)	V(VH)
	C(HV)	H(CT)	H(HV)

Note: V = vertical lines, H = horizontal lines, T = triangle, C = circle. The first letter represents the sample stimulus and the two letters in parentheses represent the comparison stimuli. The first letter in parentheses is the correct comparison for that trial type.

across birds within a group. The trial types for each group are summarized in Table 5.1. After each bird reached the criterion level of performance, it was tested with mixed delays of 0, 1.0, 2.0, and 4.0 s.

Acquisition was affected by both the of number of sample and comparison stimuli. The 2-2 group learned fastest, the 4-4 group slowest, and the 2-4 and 4-2 groups were in between. The mixed-delay test data, however, indicated that only the number of *comparison* stimuli affected performance. The 2-2 and 4-2 groups both performed significantly better than the 2-4 and 4-4 groups. Performance by each group on test sessions is presented in Figure 5.2.

The results of Experiment 2 thus provide a quite different picture of coding strategies than the results of the first experiment. In Experiment 1 pigeons showed evidence of retrospective coding but no evidence of prospective coding, whereas pigeons showed evidence of prospective but not retrospective coding in Experiment 2. The purpose of Experiment 3 was to try to determine why the manipulations of stimulus discriminability and number produced such different results.

In Experiment 3 (Zentall, Urcuioli, Jagielo, & Jackson-Smith, 1989, Experiment 2) we varied both stimulus discriminability and number in the same design to see how the two dimensions would interact in controlling pigeons' delayed conditional discrimination performance.

There were four main groups in Experiment 3 (2-2, 2-4, 4-2, and 4-4). For the 2-2 group, half the pigeons were trained with hues as sample and comparison stimuli and half with lines. For the 2-4 group, half the pigeons were

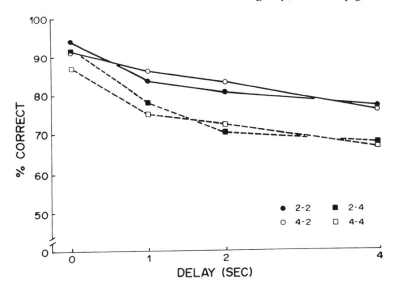

Figure 5.2. Retention gradients for the four groups in Experiment 2 averaged over all delay sessions. (Zentall, Jagielo, Jackson-Smith, & Urcuioli, 1987. Copyright 1987 by Academic Press. Reprinted by permission.)

trained with hues as samples and half with lines, and they all received both hues and lines as comparisons. For the 4-2 group, half the birds were trained with hues as comparisons and half with lines, and they all received hues and lines as samples. All the birds in the 4-4 group were trained with both hues and lines as samples and comparisons. The trial types for each of these groups are summarized in Table 5.2. Again, all birds were trained with a 0-s-delay task and tested with a mixed-delay task.

An analysis of the retention data shown in Figure 5.3 indicated that there was a small, nonsignificant effect of number of comparison stimuli, and no effect of number of sample stimuli. Thus the presence of highly discriminable hue stimuli (like those used in Experiment 1), reduced the effect of number of comparison stimuli seen in Experiment 2.

Examination of the data by trial type for each group indicated that the stimulus-discriminability variable had apparently masked some of the between-group effects in all four groups. For the 2-2 and 2-4 groups the sample-stimulus-dimension effect was between subgroups that had hues as samples vs. those that had lines as samples. For the 4-2 and 4-4 groups the sample-stimulus-dimension effect was a within-subject hue vs. line stimulus effect. For none of the groups was the comparison-stimulus-dimension effect significant. Thus these data support the conclusions reached following Experiment 1, that the pigeons were retrospectively coding the sample stimuli during the retention interval. The test data, plotted separately for each of the training groups, appear in Figure 5.4.

TABLE 5.2
Trial Types for the Four Training Groups in Experiment 3

2-2	2-4	4-2	4-4
R(RG)	R(RG)	R(RG)	R(RG)
G(GR)	G(GR)	G(GR)	G(GR)
	R(VH)	V(RG)	V(VH)
	G(HV)	H(GR)	H(HV)

OR

2-2	2-4	4-2	4-4
V(VH)	V(VH)	V(VH)	V(VH)
H(HV)	H(HV)	H(HV)	H(HV)
	V(RG)	R(VH)	R(RG)
	H(GR)	G(HV)	G(GR)

Note: V = vertical lines, H = horizontal lines, R = red, G = green. The first letter represents the sample stimulus, and the two letters in parentheses represent the comparison stimuli. The first letter in parentheses is the correct comparison for that trial type.

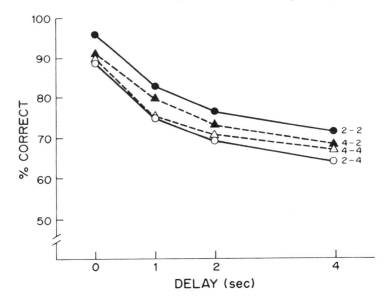

Figure 5.3. Retention gradients for the four groups in Experiment 3 averaged over all delay sessions. (Zentall, Urcuioli, Jagielo, & Jackson-Smith, 1989. Copyright 1989 by the Psychonomic Society. Reprinted by permission.)

How can the interpretation of these data be reconciled with those from Experiment 2 in which prospective coding was inferred from retention data obtained from groups exposed to the identical sample-comparison mapping used in Experiment 3 (i.e., one-to-one for the 2-2 and 4-4 groups, one-to-many for the 2-4 group, and many-to-one for the 4-2 group)? One hypothesis is that highly discriminable hue samples trigger a retrospective coding strategy in pigeons, independently of the number of comparison stimuli involved in the task (at least up to four). If this hypothesis is correct, then a reanalysis of the overall group data might uncover an effect of number of comparison stimuli if one considers data only from those trials involving line samples. These data are presented in Figure 5.5, and the analysis does, in fact, yield a significant effect of number of comparison stimuli. Thus these results suggest that memory strategy can be affected by the relative salience of the sample stimuli.

There is also some evidence in the results of Experiment 3 for another type of prospective coding effect. As can be seen in Figure 5.4, the magnitude of the sample-stimulus-dimension effect was smaller for the 4-2 group than for any of the other three groups. A separate analysis performed on the data from the 4-2 and 4-4 groups (which could be compared by ignoring the comparison-dimension effect) resulted in a significant interaction between sample dimension and group. The mean difference in level of performance between trials with hue samples and trials with line samples (averaged over the four retention intervals) was quite different for the two groups (20.9% correct for the 4-4 group and 5.7% correct for the 4-2 group). Apparently the difference in memorability between hue and line samples was greatly reduced for the 4-2 group.

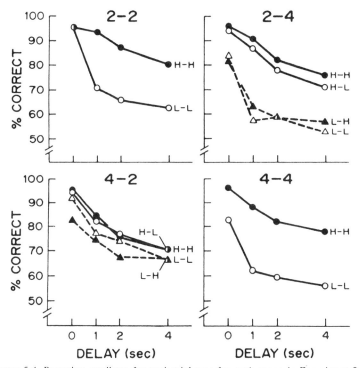

Figure 5.4. Retention gradients for each trial type for each group in Experiment 3 averaged over all delay sessions. The two-letter trial designations correspond to type of initial stimulus (hues, H, or lines, L) followed by type of comparison stimulus (hues, H, or lines, L). (Zentall, Urcuioli, Jagielo, & Jackson-Smith, 1989. Copyright 1989 by the Psychonomic Society. Reprinted by permission.)

One explanation for this finding may be that the many-to-one mapping of samples onto comparisons in the 4-2 group encouraged the pigeons to use the same memory code for the two samples paired with the same comparison. For example, the birds may have treated the vertical and red samples (both associated with a vertical comparison) as "Sample A" and the horizontal and green samples (both associated with a horizontal comparison) as "Sample B." Common coding of stimuli has been previously shown to occur when two highly distinctive samples are both associated with the same reinforcing outcome. For example, Edwards, Jagielo, Zentall, and Hogan (1982) trained pigeons on a hue matching-to-sample task with differential outcomes associated with red and green matching responses. The pigeons were then trained on a shape matching-to-sample task, also with differential outcomes of the same type used in the hue matching task. When the pigeons were transferred to mixed-dimension trials (i.e., trials with a hue sample and line comparisons or a line sample and hue comparisons), the birds indicated that "appropriate" hue-line and line-hue associations already existed. Thus it appears that pigeons in the Edwards et al.

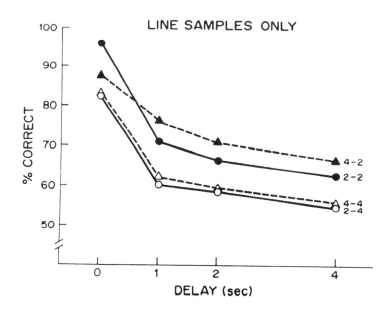

Figure 5.5. Retention gradients involving only line-sample-trials data for the four groups in Experiment 3 averaged over all delay sessions. (Zentall et al., 1989. Copyright 1989 by the Psychonomic Society. Reprinted by permission.)

study learned to code each sample in terms of its associated outcome, and that outcome expectancy served as a mediator between the sample from one dimension and the correct comparison from the other dimension. In Experiment 3, having pairs of samples associated with the same correct comparison may have produced a similar "acquired equivalence of cues" (see Lawrence, 1949; McIntire, Cleary, & Thompson, 1987), thus reducing the effective differences in discriminability between sample stimuli within each pair.

If common coding does occur in the 4-2 group, then one should be able to demonstrate positive transfer from one task to another based on the common code. We have recently confirmed this prediction by first training pigeons on a many-to-one (4-2) task with hue and line samples and a common set of line comparisons, and then training them to respond to a new set of comparisons (e.g., shapes) in Phase 2 with only the hue samples from Phase 1. Then, in Phase 3, the pigeons were tested with the line samples from Phase 1 and the shape comparisons from Phase 2. In Phase 3, when the correct sample-comparison associations in Phase 3 were compatible with the hypothesized common codes, transfer performance was significantly better (74.2% correct) than when the associations were incompatible with the hypothesized common codes (44.8% correct). It thus appears that one can encourage pigeons to commonly code two very different stimuli (a hue and a line orientation) by training them to associate both stimuli with the same comparison stimulus outcome.

If common coding does occur in the 4-2 task, it clearly must involve an anticipatory process because the only event that can be responsible for the common coding of samples is the common correct comparison. But this antic-ipatory process appears to be different from the prospective coding of individual comparison stimuli described earlier. If the common code were a representation of the correct comparison, one might expect, in the experiment just described, that the samples presented in Phase 3 would evoke representations of the cor-rect comparisons from Phase 1 (rather than those from Phase 2) and if so, posi-tive transfer should not have been found.

SPATIAL LEARNING TASK

Spatial learning tasks provide an alternative to delayed conditional discrimina-tions for the study of memory in animals. Rats, for example, show remarkable memory when they perform the radial arm maze task developed by Olton and Samuelson (1976). In the radial arm maze, rats successively choose from among, say, eight arms with all arms initially baited. Errors are defined as a second entry into an arm (i.e., entry into an unbaited arm). Rats typically learn this task quickly and often make fewer than one error per trial after only about two weeks of training with one trial per day.

Because memory load with the radial arm maze task varies as a function of the number of choices already made, this task is well suited for the study of memory strategies. If one interrupts the series of choices on a given trial by inserting a delay at some point between choices, and then compares accuracy of subsequent choices as a function of different points of delay interpolation, one can discriminate between different coding strategies. For example, if the animal only remembers the choices it has already made (retrospective coding), then one would expect greater disruption in performance the later the delay is interpo-lated in the sequence of choices because memory load increases with the num-ber of choices already made. On the other hand, if the animal only remembers the choices yet to be made (prospective coding), then one would expect there to be an inverse relation between the point of delay interpolation and errors (the more choices already made, the smaller the memory load and the better perfor-mance should be). Finally, the animal could use a combination of coding strategies to keep memory load at a minimum. The animal could use retrospec-tive coding early in a trial and prospective coding later. Such a combined strat-egy would result in greatest disruption in performance when the delay is inter-polated at about the midpoint of the trial.

In a study with rats, Cook, Brown, and Riley (1985) found that rats do, in fact, use a combination strategy. Error rates were low when the delay was in-terpolated early in the choice sequences, increased until half the choices had been made, and then decreased from that point on. Apparently, the rats retro-spectively coded choices already made until the number of prior choices equalled the number of choices remaining, and then prospectively coded the re-maining choices. This represents an efficient memory strategy because it min-imizes the memory load throughout the trial.

A number of techniques have been used to study spatial memory in pi-geons. Some have used modified versions of the rat maze (Bond, Cook, & Lamb, 1981; Roberts & Van Veldhuizen, 1985), whereas others have used an open-field analog of the radial arm maze (Spetch & Edwards, 1986; Spetch &

Honig, 1988). Wilkie and Kennedy (1985) recently reported an operant analog of the maze in which the first peck to each of three lit response keys was reinforced on each trial but repeat pecks were never reinforced. We trained pigeons on a five-choice version of the Wilkie and Kennedy (1985) task, in order to explore the pigeon's coding strategies (Zentall, Steirn, & Jackson-Smith, 1990). During initial acquisition, we manipulated a number of variables expected to affect level of performance. We then interpolated delays of gradually increasing duration at different points in the trial to see if a similar inverted U shaped function relating errors to point of delay interpolation would appear.

When rats perform a radial arm maze task, there is good evidence that they base their spatial memory on the extra-maze cues associated with each choice (Suzuki, Augerinos, & Black, 1980; see Spetch & Honig, 1988 for similar data with pigeons). More distinctive cues yield better performances. In the present experiment similar effects were examined using the operant-analog task.

One variable we manipulated was the spatial arrangement of the keys. For some birds the five keys were arranged close together in a horizontal row (linear condition). For other birds, four keys were placed at the corners of a square (12.7 cm on a side) and a fifth key was placed in the center of the square (matrix condition). By spatially separating the keys in the latter condition, we hoped to increase their distinctiveness relative to the linear array.

A second variable manipulated was the presence vs. absence of nonspatial cues on the response keys. For half of the pigeons in each group all the keys were white; for the others, each key was a different color.

All five keys were lit at the start of each trial and five consecutive pecks to any one of them resulted in food reinforcement and the offset of all keys for 3 s. When the keys came back on, five consecutive pecks to any key not yet pecked resulted in reinforcement. Five pecks to a key already pecked resulted only in 3 s of key offset. The trial ended when all five keys had been pecked. A 60 s intertrial interval (ITI) separated the 10 trials that comprised a session for each bird. A bright house light during the ITI signalled that the trial was over.

Acquisition Results

Acquisition data (mean errors per trial in blocks of three sessions) for this experiment appear in Figure 5.6. In interpreting these data, note that a random selection of response keys with no memory from choice to choice (i.e., random sampling with replacement) would produce an expected error rate of approximately 6.4 errors per trial. In fact, mean errors started out well above chance for all groups. Apparently, pigeons, unlike rats, are predisposed to repeat a previously reinforced choice more often than would be expected by chance. Over the course of training, errors for the linear-hues group dropped to about three per trial, whereas they never dropped much below six per trial for the linear-white group. Apparently, the added hues facilitated acquisition in the linear condition. Spatial separation of the five keys also facilitated acquisition as can be seen by comparing the matrix-white group to the linear-white group. The combination of spatial separation and added hues (i.e., the matrix-hues condition), however, did not further facilitate acquisition relative to the matrix-white or linear-hues conditions.

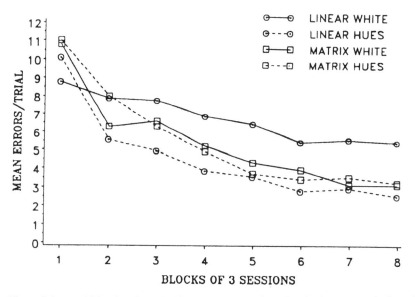

Figure 5.6. Acquisition functions, in blocks of three sessions, for the four groups in Experiment 4.

Acquisition was continued until a criterion of three consecutive sessions with an average of three or fewer errors per trial was reached. Because birds in the linear-white condition were performing so poorly, we increased the number of consecutive responses that defined a choice for half the birds in this group. For three of the six birds in the linear-white condition the response requirement was increased to 10 for 10 sessions and then to 20 for an additional 10 sessions. No consistent differences in level of performance were found with this response requirement manipulation. Apparently, any facilitation of acquisition due to increased "exposure" to chosen keys was offset by the added delay required to complete the response.

Delay Results

As birds reached criterion on the task they were transferred to sessions with interpolated delays. (All birds reached criterion within 110 sessions, except one from the linear-white 5-response group that was dropped from the study.) In each delay session, two trials involved no delay and two trials each involved delay following the first, second, third, and fourth correct choices. The point of delay interpolation was randomly assigned to trials within a session. Delays started at 15 s and were increased every 10 sessions through 1020-s delays. Starting with the next delay (1200 s), sessions were reduced to five trials per day (four delay and one control trial) and the number of sessions at each delay was increased to 20. (The progression of delays was 15, 30, 60, 90, 120, 150, 180, 210, 240, 300, 360, 420, 480, 600, 720, 840, 1020, 1200, 1500, 1800, 2400, 3600 s.)

Birds in the linear-white 5-response group performed poorly throughout testing. The two remaining birds in this condition made an increasing number of errors with increasing delay, not only on delay trials but also on no-delay (control) trials. The two remaining linear-white/5- response birds were dropped from the study (one at 180 s and the other at 210 s) when their control-trial errors averaged more than 4.0 per trial over a block of 10 sessions.

The linear-white 20-response group, on the other hand, showed excellent performance on both delay and control trials. Errors on control trials decreased with increasing time on the task and leveled off at just over one error per trial. Errors on delay trials actually decreased with increasing delay to less than two errors per trial over delays between 210 and 420 s before they began to increase again with longer delays. Thus although the increase in responses from 5 to 20 that defined a choice had little affect on performance during acquisition, it did improve delay performance considerably. Data from the linear-white groups appear in Figure 5.7 (squares for the 5-response group, triangles for the 20-response group).

Performance by the linear-hues group was also better than performance by the linear-white (5-response) group. Thus the benefit of having hues on the keys extended beyond its effects during acquisition. Data from the linear-hues group also appear in Figure 5.7. The benefit of adding distinctive hues to the keys (circles) is somewhat less than that of increasing the choice response requirement from 5 to 20 responses (triangles). Thus both distinctive hues and increased responses per choice facilitated performance of the linear task, but the latter had a more pronounced effect.

Performance by the matrix-groups shows that, although there was no effect of adding hues during acquisition, they did facilitate delay performance relative to white keys (hexagons vs. diamonds in Figure 5.7). The effect of adding

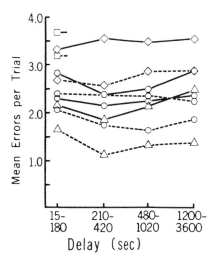

Figure 5.7. Delay and control functions for the linear and matrix groups. The linear-white 5-response group is represented by squares, the linear-white 20-response group by triangles, the linear-hues group by circles, the matrix-white group by diamonds, and the matrix-hues group by hexagons. Solid lines represent performance on delay trials and dashed lines represent performance on control trials.

hues in the matrix condition was somewhat smaller, however, than it was in the linear condition (squares vs. triangles). Over the first block of delays (15-180 s), the difference in delay-trial performance between the linear-white (5-response) group and the linear-hues group was 1.40 errors, whereas it was only .51 errors between the matrix-white and matrix-hues groups.

The effect of spatial separation of response keys can also be seen in Figure 5.7. As was the case during acquisition, when no distinctive stimuli were present on the keys, separating the response keys facilitated task performance, especially on control trials (control performance by the matrix-white group was better than performance by the linear-white 5-response group). When distinctive stimuli were present on the keys, however, separating the response keys provided no added benefit. In fact, performance by the linear-hues group was somewhat better than performance by the matrix-hues group.

Examination of Figure 5.7 indicates that the pigeons performed quite well on delay trials, overall, even when the delays were as long as 20 min to 1 hr. A measure of memory loss in this radial arm analog task is the difference in performance between delay and control trials. If one pools across groups and delays, the average memory loss was about half an error per trial. Memory loss functions (the difference in performance between delay and control trials) at each block of delays is presented in Figure 5.8. Memory loss for the linear groups shows a progressive increase with increasing delay. For the matrix

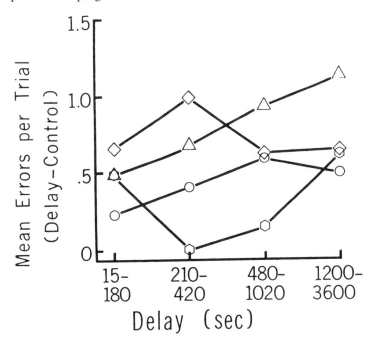

Figure 5.8. Memory loss functions (delay errors minus control errors) for the linear-white (triangles), linear-hues (circles), matrix-white (diamonds), and matrix-hues (hexagons) groups.

groups, however, memory loss was more variable; there was actually little or no memory loss over the middle range of delays. It may be that the combination of key separation provided by the matrix panel together with the distictive hues largely eliminated delay errors once the birds had learned how to handle delay trials and before the delays got really long. The fact that control errors were higher for the matrix groups than for the linear groups, however, suggests that other (nonmemory) factors may also be involved (e.g., hue and position preferences that appeared to disrupt performance overall).

Although it is difficult to interpret the relatively constant level of performance with increasing delay shown in Figures 5.7 and 5.8 (because delay duration was confounded with practice), the relatively high level of performance at long delays is nonetheless remarkable when compared with performance obtained with more typically used pigeon memory tasks. Following extensive training on a delayed matching-to-sample (DMTS) task, for example, performance accuracy can be maintained at above-chance levels with delays of up to about 60 s (Grant, 1976). More typically, however, performance falls to chance within about 10 s (see e.g., Cumming & Berryman, 1965). It is likely that the spatial nature of the present task accounts for the superior working memory found in this experiment. If so, then the spatial task may well be better suited for analyzing pigeons' memory strategies than DMTS.

Point of Delay Interpolation Results

The primary purpose of the radial arm maze analog experiment was to determine whether or not errors would vary as a function of point of delay interpolation (PDI) in a similar fashion with pigeons as with rats. Cook et al. (1985) found an inverted U shaped error function with increasing PDI, suggesting that the rats retrospectively coded choices already made early in the trial and prospectively coded choices yet to be made late in the trial. Results of the present experiment indicated that pigeons too, can use a mixed retrospective-prospective coding strategy that minimizes memory load at each point of delay interpolation.

The mean adjusted error score used as a measure of differential performance at various PDIs involved delay trial errors attributable to the delay, corrected for opportunity at each PDI (see Cook et al., 1985 for a complete discussion of this adjusted error score). As these scores remained relatively stable over sessions, adjusted error scores were pooled over delays.

For the matrix-white group performance was good when the delay was interpolated after the first choice but was much worse when the delay occurred after the second correct choice. Thus the birds appeared to be retrospectively coding their early choices. When the delay was interpolated after the third choice, however, performance was at about the same level as it was after the second choice. Such a finding would be expected if the pigeons had shifted from a retrospective to a prospective coding strategy because the retrospective memory load following two correct choices should be about the same as the prospective memory load following three correct choices. Finally, when the delay was interpolated after the fourth correct choice, performance improved, as would be expected if the pigeon maintained a prospective memory code for choices yet to be made. PDI functions for the matrix-white group appear in Figure 5.9 (solid lines).

For the matrix-hues group the shape of the PDI function was quite similar to that of the matrix-white group. Again, it appeared that the pigeons were retrospectively coding following the first two correct choices but were prospectively coding following the third and fourth correct choices. The PDI functions for the matrix-hues group also appear in Figure 5.9 (dashed lines).

The PDI functions for the linear birds were generally not as consistent across birds as were those of the matrix birds. However, with the exception of one bird, their error functions increased and then decreased as a function of increasing PDI and adjusted errors were higher at both PDI positions 2 and 3 than at positions 1 and 4, evidence that these birds, too, shifted from retrospective to prospective coding with increasing PDI. The PDI functions for the linear-white (solid lines) and linear-hues (dashed lines) groups are presented in Figure 5.10.

Thus pigeons in the four groups that were tested at extended delays appeared to retrospectively code choices made early in the trial and prospectively code choices yet to be made late in the trial.

Cook et al. (1985) have argued that what appears to be evidence for prospective coding (i.e., declining adjusted errors at PDIs late in the trial) may, in fact, result from a shift in the criterion for making a choice from a liberal decision rule early in the trial when the probability of making a correct choice is high, to a conservative decision rule late in the trial when the probability of making a correct choice is considerably lower. In support of this criterion-shift hypothesis, when performance on control trials was corrected for opportunity

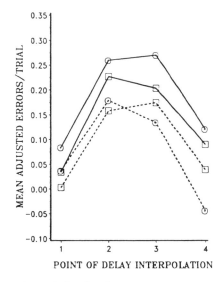

Figure 5.9. Point of delay interpolation functions (delay was presented after 1, 2, 3, or 4 correct choices) for individual birds in the matrix-white (solid lines) and matrix-hues (dashed lines) groups. Adjusted errors/trial are errors attributable to the delay, corrected for opportunity.

to make an error, a sharp drop in error rate was consistently found following the fourth correct choice. On the other hand, the fact that the adjusted error score is based on the difference between delay and control errors should do much to remove criterion-shift effects from the adjusted error scores. Thus there is reason to believe that the downturn in adjusted errors that occurred following the fourth correct choice in the present experiment was reflective of a true shift in memory strategy and not simply to an increase in the care with which choices were made as the trial progressed.

The results of the present spatial memory study suggest that (a) pigeons can shift their coding strategy within a trial to optimize their memory load, (b) distinctive visual cues (i.e., adding distinctive colors to the response alternatives) or distinctive spatial cues (i.e., spatially separating the response alternatives) can facilitate acquisition and delay performance of this radial arm maze analog task for pigeons, and (c) increasing the number of responses required for each choice clearly facilitates memory performance. Finally, the high level of performance by pigeons on this spatial task with long interpolated delays (up to 1 hr) suggests that this may be an ideal task with which to study other aspects of pigeon memory, for example, directed forgetting, and retroactive and proactive interference effects.

CONCLUSIONS

Data from the present set of experiments indicate that pigeons can use both retrospective and prospective memory codes depending on the demands of the task. In the case of delayed conditional discrimination learning, when stimuli presented prior to the retention interval are highly discriminable, pigeons tend

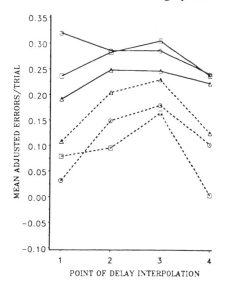

Figure 5.10. Point of delay interpolation functions for individual birds in the linear-white (solid lines) and linear-hues (dashed lines) groups.

to code them retrospectively. When these initially-presented stimuli are not so discriminable, however, pigeons will code the comparison stimuli prospectively. Thus memory load, as defined either by stimulus discriminability or by stimulus number, appears to determine memory strategy. In the case of the radial-arm-maze analog, memory strategy appears to be determined by memory load within a trial, as defined by the number of stimuli to be remembered.

There is now considerable evidence that pigeons can not only use prospective memory strategies, but that they can select a particular memory strategy according to the anticipated demands of the task. An important challenge that remains is to be able to specify the characteristics of the memory code. Are the codes direct representations of external stimuli or do they perhaps take the form of idiosyncratic mediators better suited for maintenance over delays? The data reported from the experiment that used the many-to-one procedure suggest that pigeons are capable of commonly coding stimuli that are highly distinctive and physically unrelated, based solely on their association with a common correct comparison stimulus. But as noted earlier, it is not likely that the common code is simply a prospective representation of the correct comparison. Determination of the characteristics of memory codes will undoubtedly require great patience and ingenious experimental designs, but now that there is considerable evidence for the existence of a variety of different types of memory code in animals, we should be prepared to extend that investigation to the identification of those memory codes.

ACKNOWLEDGMENTS

The research presented here was supported by Grant MH 35378 from the National Institutes of Health to TRZ and Grant BNS 8418275 from the National Science Foundation to TRZ and PJU.

REFERENCES

Bond, A. B., Cook, R. G., & Lamb, M. R. (1981). Spatial memory and the performance of rats and pigeons in the radial-arm maze. *Animal Learning and Behavior, 9*, 575-580.

Cook, R. G., Brown, M. F., & Riley, D. A. (1985). Flexible memory processing by rats: Use of prospective and retrospective information in the radial maze. *Journal of Experimental Psychology: Animal Behavior Processes, 11*, 453-469.

Cumming, W. W., & Berryman, R. (1965). The complex discriminated operant: Studies of matching-to-sample and related problems. In D. I. Mostofsky (Ed.), *Stimulus generalization* (pp. 284-330). Stanford, CA: Stanford University Press.

D'Amato, M. R. (1973). Delayed matching and short-term memory in monkeys. In G. H. Bower (Ed.), *The psychology of learning and motivation: Advances in research and theory* (Vol. 7, pp. 227-269). New York: Academic Press.

Edwards, C. A., Jagielo, J. A., Zentall, T. R., & Hogan, D. E. (1982). Acquired equivalence and distinctiveness in matching-to-sample by pigeons: Mediation by reinforcer-specific expectancies. *Journal of Experimental Psychology: Animal Behavior Processes, 8*, 244-259.

Farthing, G. W., Wagner, J. M., Gilmour, S., & Waxman, H. M. (1977). Short-term memory and information processing in pigeons. *Learning and Motivation, 8,* 520-532.

Grant, D. S. (1976). Effect of sample presentation time on long-delay matching in the pigeon. *Learning and Motivation, 7,* 580-590.

Grant, D. S. (1981). Short-term memory in the pigeon. In N. E. Spear & R. R. Miller (Eds.), *Information processing in animals: Memory mechanisms* (pp. 227-256). Hillsdale NJ: Lawrence Erlbaum Associates.

Grant, D. S. (1982). Prospective versus retrospective coding of samples of stimuli, responses, and reinforcers in delayed matching with pigeons. *Learning and Motivation, 13,* 265-280.

Honig, W. K., & Thompson, R. K. R. (1982). Retrospective and prospective processing in animal working memory. In G. H. Bower (Ed.), *The psychology of learning and motivation* (Vol. 16, pp. 239-283). New York: Academic Press.

Lawrence, D. H. (1949). Acquired distinctiveness of cues: I. Transfer between discriminations on the basis of familiarity with the stimulus. *Journal of Experimental Psychology, 39,* 770-784.

McIntire, K. D., Cleary, J., & Thompson, T. (1987). Conditional relations by monkeys: Reflexivity, symmetry, and transitivity. *Journal of the Experimental Analysis of Behavior, 47,* 279-285.

Olton, D. S., & Samuelson, R. J. (1976). Remembrance of places past: Spatial memory in rats. *Journal of Experimental Psychology: Animal Behavior Processes, 2,* 97-116.

Roberts, W. A., & Grant, D. S. (1974). Some studies of short-term memory in the pigeon with presentation time precisely controlled. *Learning and Motivation, 5,* 393-408.

Roberts, W. A., & Van Veldhuizen, N. (1985). Spatial memory in pigeons on the radial arm maze. *Journal of Experimental Psychology: Animal Behavior Processes, 11,* 241-260.

Roitblat, H. L. (1980). Codes and coding processes in pigeon short-term memory. *Animal Learning and Behavior, 8,* 341-351.

Roitblat, H. L. (1984). Representations in pigeon working memory. In H. L. Roitblat, T. G. Bever, & H. S. Terrace (Eds.), *Animal cognition* (pp. 79-97). Hillsdale, NJ: Lawrence Erlbaum Associates.

Santi, A., & Roberts, W. A. (1985). Prospective representation: The effects of varied mapping of sample stimuli to comparison stimuli and differential trial outcomes on pigeons' working memory. *Animal Learning and Behavior, 13,* 103-108.

Spetch, M. L., & Edwards, C. A. (1986). Spatial memory in pigeons (*Columba livia*) in an open-field feeding environment. *Journal of Comparative Psychology, 100,* 266-278.

Spetch, M. L., & Honig, W. K. (1988). Characteristics of pigeons' spatial working memory in an open field task. *Animal Learning and Behavior, 16,* 123-131.

Suzuki, S., Augerinos, G., & Black, A. H. (1980). Stimulus control of spatial behavior on the eight-arm maze in rats. *Learning and Motivation, 11,* 1-18.

Tversky, B. (1969). Pictorial and verbal encoding in a short-term memory task. *Perception and Psychophysics, 6,* 225-233.

Urcuioli, P. J., & Zentall, T. R. (1986). Retrospective coding in pigeons' delayed matching-to-sample. *Journal of Experimental Psychology: Animal Behavior Processes, 12,* 69-77.

Wasserman, E. A. (1986). Prospection and retrospection as processes of animal short-term memory. In D. F. Kendrick, M. E. Rilling, & M. R. Denny (Eds.),

Theories of animal memory (pp. 53-75). Hillsdale, NJ: Lawrence Erlbaum Associates.

Wilkie, D. M., & Kennedy, D. (1985). Intrusion of stereotyped responding in pigeon spatial memory tasks. *Behavioural Processes, 11*, 159-169.

Zentall, T. R., & Hogan, D. E. (1977). Short-term proactive inhibition in the pigeon. *Learning and Motivation, 8*, 367-386.

Zentall, T. R., Jagielo, J. A., Jackson-Smith, P., & Urcuioli, P. J. (1987). Memory codes in pigeon short-term memory: Effects of varying the number of sample and comparison stimuli. *Learning and Motivation, 18*, 21-33.

Zentall, T. R., Steirn, J. N., & Jackson-Smith, P. (1990). Memory strategies in pigeons' performance of a radial-arm-maze analog task. *Journal of Experimental Psychology: Animal Behavior Processes, 16*, 358-371.

Zentall, T. R., Urcuioli, P. J., Jagielo, J. A., & Jackson-Smith, P. (1989). Interaction of sample dimension and sample-comparison mapping on pigeons' performance of delayed conditional discriminations. *Animal Learning and Behavior, 17*, 172-178.

6 The Acquisition of Concrete and Abstract Categories in Pigeons

John M. Pearce
University of Wales, College of Cardiff

At least some animals share with humans the ability to react differently to stimuli that belong to different categories. In a study by Herrnstein, Loveland, and Cable (1976), for instance, pigeons were trained to discriminate between photographic slides on the basis of whether or not they contained a picture of a tree. Once this discrimination had been learned, it transferred readily to novel slides. This outcome has been shown to have considerable generality. It has been revealed with such diverse categories as water, a specific person, fish, cars, letters of the alphabet, chairs, and even a cartoon character—Charlie Brown (e.g., Bhatt, Wasserman, Reynolds, & Knauss, 1988; Cerella, 1980; Herrnstein et al. 1976; Herrnstein & deVilliers, 1980; Morgan, Fitch, Holman & Lea, 1976). Moreover, the ability to categorize is not confined to pigeons, it has also been shown with monkeys (D'Amato & Van Sant, 1988; Roberts & Mazmanian, 1988; Schrier, Angarella, & Povar, 1984; Schrier & Brady, 1987), quail (Kluender, Diehl, & Killeen, 1987), chickens (Ryan, 1982), and a parrot (Pepperberg, 1983).

In these studies, the solution to the categorization problem presumably rests with identifying whether or not an instance contains a particular feature, or set of features. The presence of a branch, say, could be used to classify an instance as a tree (see D'Amato & Van Sant, 1988; Herrnstein, 1984, 1985; Lea, 1984; Schrier et al., 1984). Humans, however, are able to solve a rather different sort of categorization problem, in which the members of both categories share the same features. Reed (1972), for example, showed students cartoon drawings of faces which belonged to two categories. The faces from one category, on average, had smaller foreheads, eyes closer together, and shorter noses than those from the other category. It is important to note that for any given feature the distribution of values for the two categories overlapped, so that it was not possible to perform accurately on this task simply by attending to a single feature. Nonetheless, with practice the students were able to identify correctly the category to which an item belonged, even when it was novel. See also Hayes-Roth and Hayes-Roth (1977), Neumann (1977), and Posner and Keele (1968, 1970) for related studies.

In view of the upsurge of interest in categorization by animals, it is perhaps surprising to discover that there have been no attempts to determine whether or not they can solve this second type of problem. Accordingly, the initial experiments to be reported examine the performance of pigeons on a task that is similar in principle to that employed by Reed (1972). Since the subjects were able to categorize the training patterns successfully, additional experiments are described that evaluate a variety of theoretical interpretations for their performance. It is argued that none of these interpretations is adequate, and in the final section an alternative interpretation of categorization is presented.

A DEMONSTRATION OF CATEGORIZATION

The apparatus used in all the experiments consisted of standard pigeon test chambers which were modified to accommodate a color microtelevision. The screen of the television was located behind a clear Perspex response key. Computer generated patterns were presented on the screen, and two examples are shown in Figure 6.1. Each pattern consisted of three vertical colored bars (yellow, red, and white, going from left to right) presented against a blue background and within a rectangular frame consisting of a white line. For the purposes of the computer program, the bars were measured in units that were equivalent to 0.5 cm on the television screen. The width of each bar was 0.8 units and their maximum height was 7 units, which was also the height of the frame. For the first experiment the patterns were constructed according to two criteria. The combined height of the bars for each member of the short category

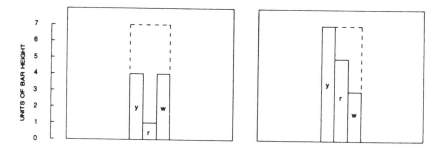

Figure 6.1. Examples of a short, 4-1-4, and a tall, 7-5-3, pattern used in the initial experiments. The bars were yellow (y), red (r), and white (w). They were presented within a frame provided by a white line (dotted line) and against a blue background. From Pearce (1988). Copyright 1988 by Oxford University Press. Reprinted by permission.

was always 9 units, with each bar never deviating from its mean height of 3 by more than 2 units. A similar constraint applied to all members of the tall category, except that the combined bar height was always 15 units, and the mean height of each bar was 5 units. An example of a short pattern is 4-1-4 (left-hand panel) and of a tall pattern is 7-5-3 (right-hand panel), where the numbers refer, respectively, to the height of the left, center, and right bars. The construction of the patterns was therefore such that there were certain heights of each bar that occurred on both reinforced and nonreinforced trials. As with the study by Reed (1972), therefore, it is not possible to solve this discrimination simply by attending to a specific dimension.

The method of training was autoshaping, with patterns from both categories being presented for 10 sec in a randomly determined sequence. The offset of members of the short category was always followed by food, while members of the tall category were followed by nothing. If pigeons can discriminate between these categories then eventually they should peck the response key rapidly in the presence of the short but not the tall patterns.

There were two groups of four pigeons in Experiment 1. Group Category received the training just described, with 18 patterns in each category. These patterns were also shown to Group Random, but the delivery of food was not signalled by a particular category. Instead, 9 short and 9 tall patterns were consistently paired with food, while the remaining patterns were followed by nothing. The results are portrayed in Figure 6.2 which shows for each group, in two-session blocks, the mean rate of responding elicited by the patterns that signalled the occurrence or nonoccurrence of food. Turning first to Group Category, it is apparent that as training progressed the discrimination was mastered. Eventually, the rate of responding during the short patterns was substantially faster than during the tall patterns. This was true for all members of the group in each of the last eight sessions. One explanation for this successful discrimination is that the patterns were treated as if they were unrelated and subjects learned about the significance of each one. By itself, however, this explanation is unlikely to be correct since such a strategy was also available to Group Random, which failed to learn the discrimination. It thus appears that like humans, pigeons can discriminate between categories that share common features, the properties of which vary with overlapping distributions.

Further support for this conclusion comes from a session in which occasional test trials, involving novel short and tall patterns, were intermixed with the normal training trials for Group Category. Whenever a novel short pattern was presented it elicited a rate of responding that was equivalent to that for the familiar short patterns and, likewise, there was no difference between the effects of novel and familiar tall patterns. These results indicate that as a result of their original training, subjects were able to categorize correctly the novel patterns.

Despite the success of this experiment, it would be unjustifiable to conclude that the discrimination was solved on the basis of the information provided by the varying bar heights. A less interesting interpretation is that the subjects failed to detect the differences among the members of the two categories and were responding simply on the basis of some feature that was con-

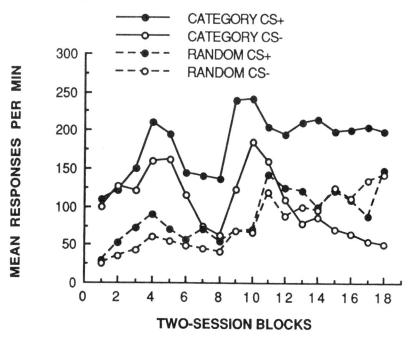

Figure 6.2. The mean rates of responding in the presence of patterns that signalled either the occurrence (CS+) or nonoccurrence (CS-) of food in Group Category and Group Random of Experiment 1.

stant within a category. For example, the area of blue background was the same for all short patterns, and for all the tall ones, so that the discrimination could be construed as being between two different intensities of blue illumination. Fortunately a number of findings suggest that this interpretation is incorrect.

In the second experiment, a group of eight pigeons was trained in a very similar manner to that just described for Group Category. Once the discrimination had reached a stable asymptote, two novel patterns were presented during the course of a normal training session. One of these patterns was of the form 4-4-4, while the other was of the form 6-0-6. These patterns were selected because the area of blue background in each was the same and according to the above interpretation, they should have elicited the same rate of responding. This prediction was not confirmed. The left-hand pair of histograms in the left-hand panel of Figure 6.3 shows the rate of responding recorded during the test session to the short (+) and tall (-) training patterns. It is quite apparent that at this point in the experiment subjects were discriminating between the two categories. Moreover, this discrimination was reflected in the level of responding to the two test patterns, as shown in the right-hand pair of histograms. Responding was found to be substantially, and significantly faster during the 4-4-4 than the 6-0-6 pattern. An explanation for this finding will be considered later; for the present these results are of interest because they indi-

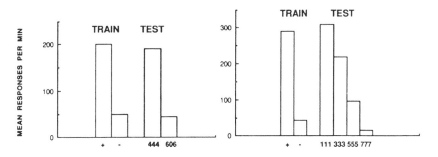

Figure 6.3. The mean rates of responding to the short (+) and the tall (-) training patterns and to the test patterns employed for Experiment 2 (left-hand panel). The right-hand panel shows the results for the training and test patterns employed in Experiment 3.

cate that it is not just the area of blue background that determines performance in the presence of a pattern.

A PROTOTYPE ANALYSIS

In the study by Reed (1972), an additional finding was that the students were able to categorize faces that they had not seen before. Furthermore, he reported that the accuracy of this performance was highest when the test item corresponded to the average of the training faces for a given category. This effect is not unusual and has been reported with a variety of stimuli (Fried & Holyoak, 1984; Hayes-Roth & Hayes-Roth, 1977; Homa, Sterling, & Trepel, 1981; Neumann, 1977; Omohundro, 1981; Posner & Keele, 1968, 1970).

To explain this type of result it has been proposed that exposure to the members of a category results in the development of a prototype that reflects their central tendency. The prototype is then assumed to be used in judgments as to which category a new instance belongs. When the new instance bears a close resemblance to the prototype then it is more likely to be classified correctly than when the resemblance is slight (Franks & Bransford, 1971; Fried & Holyoak, 1984; Homa et al., 1981; Reed, 1972). The purpose of the next two experiments was to determine whether the formation of a prototype underlies the ability of pigeons to discriminate between the short and tall categories.

For Experiment 3, a single group (n=8) received discrimination training between the short and tall categories. When the rate of responding during the short patterns was substantially greater than during the tall patterns, test trials with the four novel patterns, 1-1-1, 3-3-3, 5-5-5, 7-7-7, were introduced. It is reasonable to assume that the 3-3-3 and 5-5-5 patterns are closely related to the central tendencies of the short and tall categories. Accordingly, if the formation of prototypes is responsible for the successful categorization of the short and tall patterns, then it is likely that subjects will respond very rapidly during the 3-3-3 pattern and very slowly during the 5-5-5 pattern. One reason for including the remaining patterns was to assess the effects of introducing novel patterns which bore little resemblance to the average of the training stimuli.

The results of these test sessions are presented in the right- hand panel of Figure 6.3. The left-hand pair of histograms shows the mean rate of responding in the presence of the reinforced short (+) and the nonreinforced tall (-) training patterns. As in the first experiment, subjects eventually displayed a clear discrimination between the categories. The right-hand histograms show the outcome of the generalization tests. Contrary to the predictions derived from the prototype analysis, the discrimination between the 3-3-3 and 5-5-5 patterns was not particularly good. Indeed, numerically it was inferior to that between the training patterns, and statistically, responding during the 3-3-3 pattern was significantly slower than during the 1-1-1 pattern, while during the 5-5-5 pattern it was significantly faster than during the 7-7-7 pattern.

To the extent that response rate can be used to indicate the accuracy of classification, these results provide no support for the idea that the formation of a prototype is responsible for the discrimination between the short and tall categories. Such an idea leads to the prediction that the clearest discrimination will be between instances that correspond to the averages of the training patterns. But it is quite apparent that the best discrimination was between items that represented the extremes of the dimensions on which the two categories were based.

One way of reconciling these findings with those obtained with humans is by considering the way the generalization of excitation and inhibition might influence the outcome of the final test. The performance on that test is reminiscent of demonstrations of positive and negative peak shift found in operant discriminations (e.g., Guttman, 1965; Hanson, 1959). Traditionally, peak shift is attributed to the interaction between excitatory and inhibitory generalization gradients (Mackintosh, 1974; Rilling, 1977) and this account can be applied to the present findings. That is, prototypes for the short and tall categories may have been formed, and been responsible for the successful discrimination. However, the generalization of excitation and inhibition associated with these representations might have interacted in such a way (Spence, 1937) as to result in the highest rate of responding to a pattern that is shorter than the 3-3-3 pattern, and the lowest rate of responding to a pattern that is taller than the 5-5-5 pattern. Thus while the previous experiment provides no support for the suggestion that pigeons form a prototype as a result of certain sorts of discrimination training, they do not allow us to reject this idea. Experiment 4 examines an alternative means for assessing the role of prototypes in categorization.

Thirty-two pigeons were trained initially with patterns belonging to the short category signalling food, and patterns belonging to the tall category signalling nothing. They were then divided into four groups, of equal sizes, for four sessions of extinction. Groups 1-1-1 and 3-3-3 received repeated nonreinforced exposure, respectively, to the 1-1-1 and 3-3-3 patterns which were both novel at the outset of this stage. Group Short received nonreinforced exposure to all the members of the short category, and Group 4-3-2 received extinction trials with a single training pattern, 4-3-2. The main question of interest was how these extinction trials would influence responding when the subjects were again exposed to the short category. To answer this question all subjects received 10 nonreinforced trials with members of the short category; followed by a recovery test in which they were reintroduced to the category discrimination.

If the ability to discriminate between the categories depends upon the formation of a prototype, then it is likely that responding to the short category will be considerably disrupted by extinction trials with a stimulus that corresponds to the prototype. On this basis, therefore, it would be predicted that the subsequent exposure to the short category will result in a lower rate of responding after extinction trials with the 3-3-3 than 1-1-1 pattern. Since in this experiment, the test trials for the four groups were conducted with the same stimuli, the interaction of excitatory and inhibitory gradients is unlikely to result in one group responding more vigorously than another. Consequently, the design of this experiment may be better suited than its predecessor to look for any special properties that may be conferred upon the 3-3-3 pattern.

The initial discrimination training progressed normally, so that by the final session of training there was a significant difference between the rates of responding during the short and tall categories for each of the four groups (see the left-hand panel of Figure 6.4). The results to the right of this panel depict the decline in responding to the patterns presented to the various groups during the four sessions of extinction. The next panel shows the effects of this treatment for the 10 trials of the test session when all subjects were exposed to short patterns without food. It is evident that the different extinction treatments had the same effect of virtually abolishing responding to the short category. This effect was not so apparent in Group 4-3-2, nonetheless the level of responding in this group did not differ significantly from that recorded in the other groups. The right-hand panel of the figure summarizes the effects of reintroducing the discrimination. All groups responded more vigorously on the reinforced trials with the short patterns, than the nonreinforced trials with the tall patterns. But overall, responding was significantly slower in Group Short than in any other group.

Once again, these results lend no support to the suggestion that the formation of a prototype is responsible for the successful discrimination between the short and tall categories. If this account were correct, the most disruptive effect of the extinction trials should have been with the 3-3-3 pattern. In fact, the treatment with this stimulus was no more disruptive than with the 1-1-1 pattern, and less disruptive than exposure to all the short training patterns. Future research may reveal support for a prototype account of categorization by animals, but on the basis of the present results success in this respect would seem to be unlikely.

At a theoretical level, the failure to find any evidence that pigeons form prototypes may not be too surprising. A number of authors have questioned whether humans form prototypes (e.g., Estes, 1986; Medin & Schaffer, 1978; Hintzman, 1986), proposing instead that they retain information about all the training patterns. The fact remains, however, that after they have been trained with a category, humans may respond in a special way to an instance that represents the average or central tendency of the training items. The results described here have failed to replicate this effect. Whether this is because of an

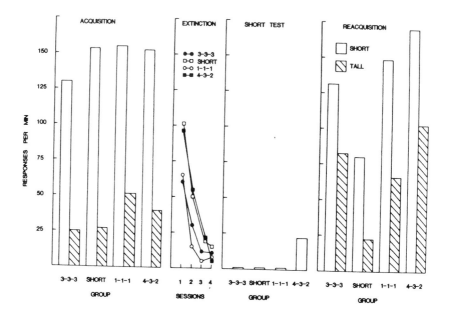

Figure 6.4. The mean rates of responding recorded for the four groups during the various stages of Experiment 4.

inadequacy in the experimental design, or whether it reflects some fundamental difference between the categorization processes of humans and pigeons remains to be seen.

The results from this experiment also bear on the suggestion, raised earlier, that subjects are insensitive to the variations among the patterns within a category. If this were correct, then the different extinction treatments for Groups Short and 3-3-3 should have had the same effect. Instead, the results from the reintroduction of the discrimination, indicate that subjects belonging to Group Short detected at least some of the differences among the patterns presented during the extinction stage.

A FEATURE ANALYSIS

According to a number of theories of learning, when a complex stimulus is used for conditioning, the elements of which it is composed separately enter into associations with the unconditioned stimulus (Pearce & Hall, 1980; Rescorla & Wagner, 1972). The strength of performance is then said to be determined by the combined associative strength of all the elements that are present on a trial. When applied to the above experiments this approach implies that as training progressed, representations of the different heights of the bars would individually enter into separate associations with the US. An important assumption of these theories is that the elements must compete for their associative strength, and the most successful will be those that are the most reliable predictors of the trial outcome. In the foregoing experiments there was, necessarily, a direct relationship between the height of a bar and the likelihood of it being followed by food. Such a relationship ensures that the associative strength of a short bar will be greater than of a tall bar and this would account for the different response rates between the two categories.

It is also possible to understand from this perspective the outcome of the test trials in Experiment 3. Since bars with a height of 1 unit will possess greater associative strength than those of 3 units, responding should be more rapid during the 1-1- 1 than 3-3-3 pattern; likewise, the weaker associative strength of bars with a height of 7 than 5 units would account for the difference in response rates to the 7-7-7 and 5-5-5 patterns. The purpose of the experiments to be described in this section is not to show that this account is wrong. Rather, they demonstrate that at least certain aspects of performance on categorization tasks are not readily explained by such an elemental approach.

Experiment 5 is based on the design of the previous experiments and initially involved training a single group to discriminate between the short and tall categories. Once this discrimination had been mastered, the eight birds received a number of test trials at irregular intervals during an otherwise normal training session. The patterns presented for the test trials were modified versions of two short (2-2-5 and 3-1-5) and two tall (6- 4-5 and 4-7-4) training patterns. Specifically, for each pattern the bars were separated by a gap of 1 unit. This resulted in the white bar remaining in the center of the screen, but the red and yellow bars were displaced towards their respective sides. The blue background occupied the space between the bars.

The important results from the test session are shown in Figure 6.5. The left-hand pair of histograms indicate that, as a result of the initial discrimination training, responding in the presence of the two selected short training patterns (+) was substantially faster than during the two selected tall training patterns (-). This discrimination, however, was disrupted considerably by the modification to these patterns. The right- hand pair of histograms show that separating the bars of the two short patterns resulted in a substantial decrease in responding, while this manipulation had the opposite effect on responding during the tall patterns.

The reason for conducting this test was to discover the effects of manipulating features that are irrelevant to the solution to the discrimination. According to elemental theories of conditioning, such features ultimately should exert relatively little control over responding. Since the height of the bars indicates the trial outcome, it follows that the irrelevant features relating to the position of the bars will gain little associative strength and separating them should have little impact on responding. But the results have shown that this manipulation had a profound effect. It might be argued that this finding is of relatively slight importance, reflecting nothing more than a generalization decrement brought about by the change in the patterns. However, this suggestion leads to the ex-pectation that the effect of the manipulation should be the same on the patterns

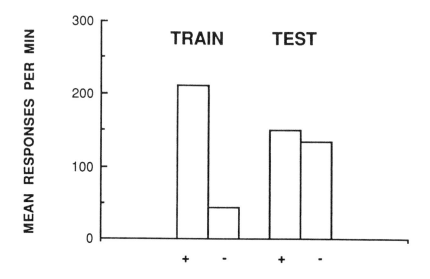

Figure 6.5. The mean rates of responding in Experiment 5 to two short (+) and two tall (-) patterns when they were presented in the normal manner with the bars adjacent (train), and when they were presented with a gap between the bars (test).

from both categories, which was clearly not the case. It also fails to explain the mechanisms that were responsible for producing the decrement.

It would be foolish to propose that these findings lie beyond the scope of an elemental interpretation. By making the appropriate assumptions about certain features gaining excitatory or inhibitory properties, it is doubtless possible to explain the outcome of the experiment. Nonetheless, the results suggest that irrelevant features may play an important role in determining performance, and this conclusion does not follow readily from the sort of account that is under consideration.

Instead of learning about the significance of the most relevant features, the results imply that discrimination training results in the retention of information about the shapes created by the training patterns. This conclusion is also suggested by the next experiment which uses different patterns than the previous studies.

In Experiment 6, a single group of 8 pigeons was given discrimination training with four patterns. Patterns 3-6-4 and 7-3-5 were consistently paired with food, while patterns 3-3-4 and 7-6-5 were never followed by food. The reason for selecting these patterns was that none of them contained a feature that uniquely signalled the trial outcome. For each of the three bars, a given height was followed by food on half the occasions on which it occurred. Hence if the only means that animals have at their disposal for solving discriminations is by learning about those elements that reliably signal the outcome of a trial, then they should find this discrimination insoluble. The left-hand panel of Figure 6.6 indicates, however, that the discrimination was mastered with little difficulty. From Session 5 onwards, the rate of responding was significantly faster during the reinforced than nonreinforced patterns. This outcome again suggests that instead of learning the significance of individual elements, it is the overall shape of a pattern that indicates to a subject whether or not food will be delivered. Specifically, in the present experiment, food was presented only after patterns in which the center bar was either lower or higher than both the side bars.

Further evidence that the shape of the patterns was important to the solution of the discrimination comes from an additional stage of the experiment. After the original training, the procedure was changed so that in each session 40 different patterns were presented. They were all based on the four training patterns but the height of each bar was increased or reduced by a maximum of 2 units. In addition, the 20 patterns based on the 3-6-4 and the 7-3-5 originals retained the overall shape of both sides being either lower or higher than the center bar. None of the remaining patterns was of these shapes. Food was signalled by variants of the 3-6-4 and 7-3-5 patterns, and the selection of bar height ensured that no single feature could indicate the trial outcome.

The right-hand side of Figure 6.6 shows that the effects of the original training transferred reasonably well to the novel patterns. In fact, responding to the patterns paired with food was significantly faster than to the others, even in the first session of this stage. The implication of these findings is that as a result of their original training, the pigeons categorized the new patterns on the basis of their overall configuration or shape. The way in which this was

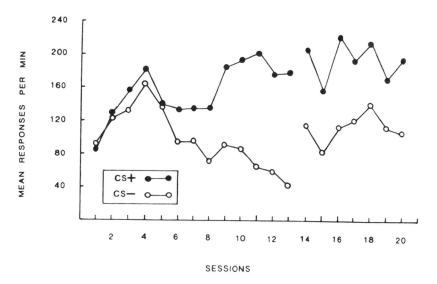

Figure 6.6. The left-hand side shows the mean rate of responding by a group of pigeons in the presence of two patterns, 3-6-4 and 7-3-5, that signalled food (S+) and two, 3-3-4 and 7-6-5, that signalled nothing (S-) in Experiment 6. The mean rates of responding during the patterns based on these training stimuli is shown in the right-hand side. From Pearce (1988). Copyright 1988 by Oxford University Press. Reprinted by permission.

achieved remains to be considered. For the present, this conclusion is important because it indicates that categorization can take place even when it is impossible to identify physical features that by themselves indicate to which category an instance belongs.

Before leaving this feature approach to categorization, we should explore the implications of a modification to the Rescorla-Wagner (1972) suggested by Gluck and Bower (1988). They have proposed that any complex stimulus will excite a number of sensory nodes which can enter into associations with the outcome of a trial. These nodes correspond to all the different physical features of which the stimulus is composed, as well as to all the possible combinations of these features. Since, in the previous experiment it is possible to identify combinations of features that are unique to the reinforced and nonreinforced trials, it is easy to see how its results can be explained by this sort of model. However, there are good reasons for questioning Gluck and Bower's (1988) proposal. First, it predicts that for the stimuli employed in the present study, each pattern will excite an extremely high number of nodes. Even this number is likely to be slight, however, in comparison to all the nodes that, theoretically, will be excited by a photograph of the sort used in the studies by Herrnstein et al. (1976). It is fair to ask, therefore, whether the proposal by Gluck and Bower (1988) is realistic. Of course, the number of nodes excited by a pattern could be reduced if it is assumed to be composed of only a few features. But then this highlights one major weakness of a feature analysis: there does not exist a theory which allows us to specify the features that will be selected to represent a stimulus. The second problem is that Gluck and Bower (1988) do not indicate the way in which the nodes corresponding to configural features are generated. What, for example, is responsible for the existence of a node that is sensitive to two short bars separated by a tall bar? Until these shortcomings are overcome, it will at least be worthwhile exploring alternative explanations for the findings reported in this chapter.

A RELATIONAL ANALYSIS

One interpretation of the results from the previous experiment is that they depend upon relational learning. During the first stage of the experiment subjects may have perceived that the center bar was lower than the side bars in the 7-3-5 pattern, and higher than the side bars in the 3-6-4 pattern. Once these relationships have been perceived, and associated with food, then the original discrimination could be solved. Moreover, this learning should permit accurate categorization as soon as subjects were exposed to the 40 novel patterns. Because of its important theoretical implications, the next two experiments explore the possibility that animals can categorize on the basis of relational information.

In the next experiment, Experiment 7, discrimination training was conducted with patterns composed of two vertical bars (see Figure 6.7). The heights of the bars varied from trial to trial; when they were both of equal height (*same* category) then they were followed by food, but when they were of different heights (*different* category) then they were followed by nothing. One way of solving this discrimination is to focus on the relationship between the

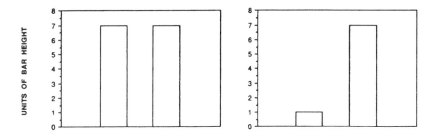

Figure 6.7.Examples of two patterns employed in a study to determine if pigeons can discriminate between categories with bars of either the same or different heights (Experiment 7). The yellow bars were presented against a blue background and were separated by a distance of 1.3 units.

bars. If pigeons can perceive this relationship, and if they can associate it with the outcome of a trial, then responding during members of the same category should eventually be faster than during the different category.

Two groups of 8 pigeons were used for this study. Group Variable was exposed to the seven possible patterns with bars of equal height, and to 13 patterns containing bars of different heights. Group Instance was shown four patterns: the two depicted in Figure 6.8, 7-7 and 1-7, and their counterparts, 1-1 and 7-1. For both groups, food was presented after members of the same but not the different category, and there was an equal number of reinforced and non-reinforced trials in each session.

The results of the 20 sessions of this training are shown in the left-hand panel of Figure 6.8. It is quite clear from the upper panel, which shows the results for Group Variable, that for these subjects the discrimination was insoluble. In contrast, the lower panel shows that Group Instance was able to solve the discrimination, but not particularly well. During the final four sessions the rate of responding during the same patterns was significantly faster than during the different patterns for this group. For the final 10 sessions of the experiment the bars were placed side-by-side in the center of the screen. There was no sign of any improvement in the performance of Group Variable, even though this manipulation had a substantial influence on Group Instance. In every session of this stage, all subjects in the latter group responded more rapidly during the same than the different category.

The clear implication of the results from Group Variable is that pigeons did not categorize the patterns according to the relationship that exists between their elements. Although the results of Group Instance may seem to be inconsistent with this conclusion, the use of a limited number of patterns may have allowed subjects to associate each one with its outcome, rather than learn about the significance of the relationship between the bar heights.

On the basis of informal experiments with university students, and a six-year old girl, the results from Group Variable were completely unexpected. When they were shown the problem for this group, and had to predict whether

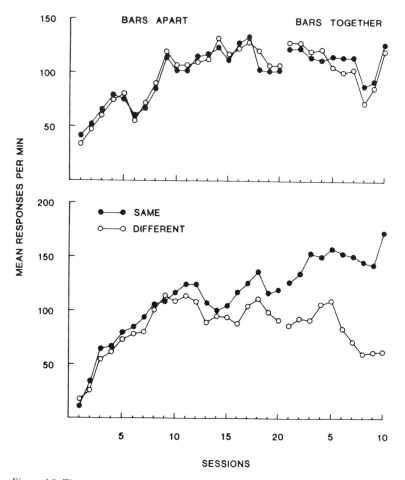

Figure 6.8. The mean rate of responding to reinforced same patterns and to nonreinforced different patterns for Group Variable (upper panel) and Group Instance (lower panel) of Experiment 7. During the first 20 sessions the gaps were separated, but for the remaining 10 sessions they were adjacent. From Pearce (1988). Copyright 1988 by Oxford University Press. Reprinted by permission.

or not food would be presented after a pattern, then every person tested was able to respond correctly within a few trials. Moreover, the correct predictions were based upon the relationship between the bars. There is no denying that there are differences between the intellectual processes of pigeons and people. Even so, the ease with which the latter solved the discrimination led me to believe that it should also be solved by the former. Indeed this belief was so strong that it led to the design of one further experiment.

The rationale behind Experiment 8 was to introduce subjects gradually to the same-different categorization task, in the hope that this would encourage them to use a relational rule to solve it. The discrimination training passed through several stages, and started with the bars together. At first, training was conducted with adjacent bars and just four patterns, 1-1, 7-7, 7- 1, and 1-7. Gradually, additional patterns were introduced so that eventually all the patterns that were shown to Group Variable in the second stage of the previous study were employed. The left half of the left-hand panel of Figure 6.9 shows the effects of this training. It is apparent that by session-block 20, responding was substantially faster during the 7 same than the 20 different patterns. This discrimination, however, is of little theoretical significance because there was no need to rely upon the relationship between the bars in order to solve it. Instead, the presence or absence of a discontinuity at the top of the bars provided a physical feature that could be used to indicate to which category an instance belonged.

Additional training was therefore given in which the bars were gradually separated, thus destroying the feature that might have been relied upon when the bars were adjacent. The remainder of the left-hand panel shows that this manipulation did not disrupt the discrimination, even though the bars were eventually separated by a gap of more than 1 cm. By adopting a different training technique, it has thus proved possible to teach pigeons a discrimination that was insoluble for Group Variable in the previous study. To what extent has this technique encouraged the use of a relational rule?

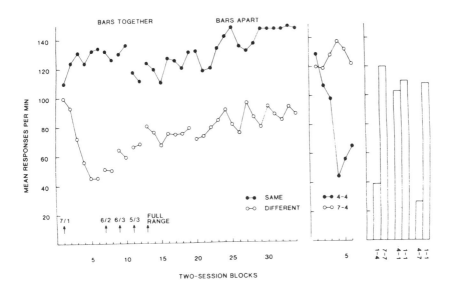

Figure 6.9. The results of Experiment 8. The left-hand panel shows the mean rate of responding to members of the same and different categories during the initial discrimination training, the information above the abscissa shows the sessions on which different patterns were introduced (e.g., 7/1 indicates the introduction of the patterns 7-7, 1-1, 1-7, 7-1 on Session 1). The center panel shows the effects of the reversal training, and the right-hand panel indicates the mean rate of responding to individual test patterns in the final three sessions.

To answer this question a further stage of training was included in the experiment. For 12 reversal sessions, conditioning consisted of trials in which a single same pattern, 4-4, was followed by nothing and a single different pattern, 7-4, was followed by food. Not surprisingly, this training was effective and resulted in a substantially slower rate of responding during the same than the different pattern (see the center panel of Figure 6.9). In each of the last three reversal sessions, test trials were conducted in which members of the same and different categories were presented. If success on the original discrimination depended upon learning about the significance of the relationship between the bars, then the training with the 4-4 and 7-4 patterns might be expected to reverse this learning (Lea, 1984; Robbins, Barresi, Compton, Furst, Russo, & Smith, 1978). That is, reinforced trials with the 7-4 pattern should teach subjects that bars of a different height signal food, and the nonreinforced trials with the 4-4 pattern should teach them that bars of the same height signal nothing. Accordingly, on the test trials, if this interpretation is correct, the rate of responding during the different patterns should be substantially faster than during the same patterns.

The pairs of histograms in the right-hand panel of Figure 6.9 show the mean rates of responding during the same and different test patterns that were presented in successive test sessions. In the first and third sessions the rate of responding during the 7-7 and 1-1 test patterns was significantly faster than during the 1-4 and 4-7 patterns, which indicates that the reversal training had relatively little impact on these members of the same and different categories. In the second test session responding to the 1-1 test pattern was again rapid, but this was also true for the 4-1 test pattern.

The fact that the reversal training substantially influenced responding to only the 4-1 pattern, lends little support to the relational analysis. Nonetheless, it might be argued that during the reversal stage subjects associated the relationship of "left bar taller than right" with food and that this was responsible for the high rate of responding elicited by the 4-1 test pattern. If this were the case, then we should expect that a relational manner of encoding information would also be used for the other pattern presented during reversal training, 4-4, and this should result in a slow rate of responding to the test patterns, 1-1 and 7-7. In fact, there was very little evidence of such generalization. Moreover, the failure to find any other clear evidence of relational learning in these experiments makes this interpretation implausible.

One interpretation for the previous results might be that subjects employed one strategy for solving the original discrimination, and another for the reversal training. For example, they may have relied upon the relationship between the bars when a large number of patterns was employed, but for the reversal stage they may simply have associated each pattern with its outcome. One problem with this account is that is provides no justification for why the different strategies should be adopted. And another problem is that it leads to the incorrect prediction that the experimental group in Experiment 1 should have solved the discrimination. On the whole, therefore, there seems to be little reason for believing that relational learning is responsible for successful performance on the categorization tasks considered in this chapter.

Before leaving this discussion, some comment is needed concerning the failure to find any clear indication that the relationship between the heights of the bars played a role in categorization. The implication of this finding is that, at best, pigeons have considerable difficulty in solving relational discriminations. It is of interest to note that a similar conclusion has been reached by both Wilson, Mackintosh, and Boakes (1985), and by D'Amato, Salmon, and Colombo (1985) when considering the results from matching and oddity problems. Whether or not this means that pigeons are incapable of solving relational problems remains to be seen. For the present, the reported results strongly suggest that when for humans there exists an obvious relational solution to a problem, pigeons are extremely reluctant to adopt it.

A STIMULUS GENERALIZATION MODEL FOR CATEGORIZATION

The experiments described in this chapter have shown that pigeons are able to categorize patterns composed of vertical bars. The purpose of this section is to present a model that can explain these findings. In essence, it is assumed that animals remember each pattern to which they have been exposed, and the unconditioned stimulus (US) with which it was associated. Performance in the presence of any pattern is then determined by its similarity to the memories of patterns shown on previous trials. There are a number of models of categorization based upon these principles (e.g., Estes, 1986; Hintzman, 1986; Medin & Schaffer, 1978) but the one to be developed here is based upon a theory that is specifically concerned with Pavlovian conditioning (Pearce, 1987, 1988).

According to Pearce (1987), conditioning results in an excitatory association being formed in long term memory (LTM) between the US, and the entire pattern of stimulation that constitutes the conditioned stimulus (CS) that precedes it. If on the next trial there is no change in the pattern of stimulation, then the previously formed association will be strengthened further. But if this pattern should change, even slightly, then a new association will be formed. During the course of conditioning with the members of a category, therefore, a large number of CS- US associations will be formed, each one relating to a specific instance of the category. On every trial, the pattern that is presented is assumed to be stored temporarily in a buffer while it is compared with all the representations in LTM. If the pattern is similar to a representation then it will activate the representation strongly, but if they are different then the degree of activation will be slight. Once it is activated, a representation will excite the US representation with which it is associated to a degree that is determined by the level of its activation and the strength of the CS-US association. The strength of the CR is then held to be directly related to the extent to which the US representation is activated. These ideas, as they relate to the procedure employed in the first experiments, are presented pictorially in the upper part of Figure 6.10. The figure shows a test item stored in a buffer while it is being compared with all the representations in LTM. Some of the representations belong to the short category ($S_1....S_n$) and are associated with food.

To understand the effects of discrimination training, suppose that conditioning has been conducted with a number of patterns, all paired with a US.

When a new pattern is introduced, it will bear some similarity to, and hence activate, the representations of these patterns and elicit a CR. If the new stimulus is not paired with the US, then it is assumed to enter into an association with a no-US representation, the function of which is to inhibit the arousal of the US representation and weaken the CR it normally elicits (Konorski, 1967; Pearce & Hall, 1980). Thus in the initial experiments, the nonreinforced trials will result in representations of the tall patterns being associated with a no-food representation (see the lower half of Figure 6.10). With continued training, the tall patterns will arouse increasingly greater levels of activity in the no-food representation until a point will be reached where it suppresses completely the concurrently excited food representation and a CR will not be recorded. Essentially, then, the proposal is that discrimination learning will result in a generalization gradient of excitation around the short patterns, and of inhibition around the tall patterns. The level of responding in the presence of any stimulus will then be determined by the interaction of these gradients. In the following discussion the application of these principles to the different patterns that were employed will be considered in separate sections.

Experiments 1-5

The foregoing discussion has already shown the way the model accounts for the successful discrimination between patterns from the short and tall categories.

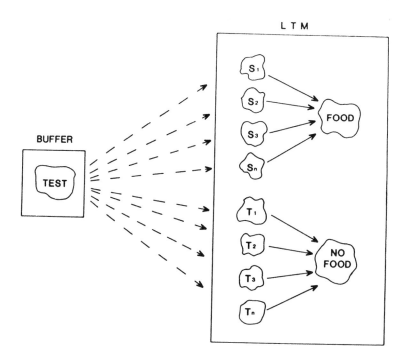

Figure 6.10. A model for categorization by pigeons: for explanation see text.

There remain, however, the results from the generalization tests in these experiments to consider. In one test it was found that the rate of responding to the 1-1-1 pattern was faster than to the 3-3-3 pattern, and that the 7-7-7 pattern elicited a lower response rate than the 5- 5-5 pattern. At first sight these results may seem to be inconsistent with the views presented above. The 1-1-1 pattern can be considered to be less similar to the short training patterns than the 3-3-3 pattern, and this might be expected to ensure that responding was slower to the 1-1-1 than the 3-3-3 pattern. But it must be appreciated that the test trials were conducted after the completion of discrimination training. If this training resulted in bell-shaped gradients of excitation and inhibition around the training patterns (e.g., Spence, 1937) then, in the same way that peak shift is explained (e.g., Mackintosh, 1974) it follows that responding on test trials with a 1-1-1 pattern will be more vigorous than with a 3-3-3 pattern. Furthermore, this account also leads to the prediction that the 7-7-7 pattern will result in slower responding than with a 5-5-5 pattern. Pearce (1988) provides a more detailed discussion of these results.

A major problem for this type of account is to specify the way in which the similarity between two patterns is computed. In the first experiments it could have been determined by the average heights of the bars, but this is not the only possibility. Similarity judgments could equally well have been based upon the area occupied by the bars, or by the amount of blue background surrounding them. The adoption of any of these would lead to the short and tall patterns being ordered in the same way along a continuum and thus account for many of the results from experiments involving the short-tall discrimination.

Some of the results from these experiments, however, force us to refine our views on the way in which similarity might be computed. For example, it was discovered that after discrimination training with the short and tall patterns, test trials revealed a higher rate of responding with the 4-4-4 than 6-0-6 pattern. On the measures just considered, these patterns are equivalent and should have elicited similar response rates. Perhaps, then, another dimension, such as shape, also influences the judgments of similarity between stimuli. It seems likely that the shape created by the 4-4-4 pattern will bear a closer resemblance to the shapes of the short training patterns than the 6-0-6 pattern and this would result in the former test pattern eliciting the higher response rate.

Experiment 6

Further evidence that shape may play a role when judging the similarity of patterns comes from the sixth experiment. Initially training was conducted with 3-6-4 and 7-3-5 patterns signalling food, and the 3-3-4 and 7-6-5 patterns being followed by nothing. Then, in the next stage, a large number of patterns based on the original shapes was introduced. Those with a center bar that was either taller or shorter than both side bars were followed by food, while the other patterns were followed by nothing. For this stage of the experiment, the average bar height of the patterns paired with food varied from 2.7 to 5.3 units, while for the others the range was from 1.7 to 7.0 units. Given such overlap it is most unlikely that average bar height provided the dimension which allowed such successful generalization from the first to the second stages of the experiment. On the other hand, it is quite plausible that it was the shape of the patterns that determined the similarity between them.

This suggestion, that shape can play a prominent role in generalization, raises the issue of identifying the way in which different shapes are compared. Unfortunately this is not an easy issue to resolve. The results of the same-different experiments make it unlikely that patterns are encoded and compared on the basis of relational information. And the problems encountered by a template matching account (see Smith & Medin, 1981), make this approach unattractive. Referring to common features between patterns is also difficult, because the design of the stimuli in Experiment 6 was such that any given feature (more specifically bar height) was present on an equal number of reinforced and nonreinforced trials. Perhaps the safest, and certainly the easiest, approach for the present is to acknowledge that shape is an important dimension for generalization (see Sutherland & Mackintosh, 1971). It can then be left to the future, and to students of perception, to reveal how animals judge the similarity of different shapes.

Experiments 7 and 8

The results from the last two experiments can also be understood if it is accepted that animals remember the significance of each training pattern. Consider first the procedure for the control group of Experiment 7. Reinforced trials will result in separate associations being formed between the 7-7 and 1-1 patterns and food while the remaining trials will result in the 1-7 and 7-1 patterns being associated with the effects of nonreinforcement. Note, however, that the height of each bar in a reinforced pattern is the same as the height of its counterpart in a nonreinforced pattern, but it is different than the height of its counterpart in the other reinforced pattern. Accordingly, the generalization between the categories is likely to be high, and this would account for the slow appearance of the discrimination during the first stage of training.

Turning to the results of the experimental group for this stage, the use of a larger number of patterns will ensure that there will be at most only a few presentations of each pattern in a session. As a consequence, insufficient trials may have been given to these subjects to allow learning to reach asymptote for all of the patterns. Perhaps, then, if further training had been given, or a different training technique adopted, then this group would also have mastered the discrimination. The results of the final experiment support this suggestion. In this experiment, which resulted in different levels of responding to the same and different categories, two manipulations were employed that might be expected to facilitate learning about the individual patterns: they were introduced gradually, and there were many more trials than in the previous study.

The majority of the results of the reversal test in the final experiment are also consistent with this analysis. Once subjects have learned the significance of each pattern, then reversing the significance of two patterns is unlikely to exert much influence upon responding elicited by the remainder. In support of this prediction it was found that the reversal training did not markedly influence responding during 5 of the 6 patterns that were selected for the test sessions.

The fact that responding to one of these patterns was affected by the reversal stage, however, does pose a problem for this account. One solution is to return to the possibility that the shape of a pattern is an important dimension for determining its similarity to other patterns. The single pattern that was influenced by the reversal training was 1-4, which was of similar shape to the 4-7 pattern (short bar on the left tall bar on the right) that was paired with food for the reversal stage. Alternatively, generalization between the 4-7 and 1-4 patterns might have occurred because they both contain a yellow bar, the top of which has an area of unbroken blue background to the left.

Concluding Comments

The previous discussion highlights the problems of identifying the dimension along which generalization between two patterns can take place. However, that such a discussion is being considered emphasizes the importance of the overall conclusion suggested by the experiments reported in this chapter. Successful discrimination between different categories of patterns depends upon the retention of information about many of the instances used for training. Once this conclusion is accepted, then a number of interesting questions are raised. One is whether or not animals store information about every pattern, or just a selected few. On the one hand, it seems unlikely that they would distinguish between such similar patterns as 5-4 and 4-3, say; but the fact that reversal training with a 4-4 pattern did not markedly influence responding to either a 7-7 or a 1-1 pattern in the test sessions of Experiment 8 indicates that relatively specific information is retained about individual patterns.

One objection to this stimulus generalization approach is that by proposing that animals remember each training pattern, it poses an intolerable burden on the pigeon's memory. There are, however, at least two reasons for not taking this objection too seriously. In a study by Vaughan and Greene (1984), pigeons were shown to be quite capable of discriminating between two sets of randomly selected photographs. Each set contained 160 different photographs, and there was no indication that the upper limit of the memory capacity of the subjects had been reached. In view of this finding, the underlying assumptions of the stimulus generalization model may not be too unreasonable. The second reason relates to a finding by Bhatt et al. (1988). They used a large number of photographs to train pigeons to discriminate between different categories. When, at the end of training, test trials were given, it was found that novel instances were categorized less accurately than those presented repeatedly during training. Such an outcome can readily be explained if animals remember many of the training patterns.

Finally, there is the question of whether the principles developed above, to explain categorization with patterns, apply to studies using photographs of what have been referred to as natural categories (e.g., Herrnstein et al., 1976). The tremendous complexity of the photographs means that it will not be easy to test predictions from a stimulus generalization model with this sort of training material. Nonetheless, there is no reason in principle why the present approach should not be applied to these examples. But even if it does turn out to be inappropriate, this discovery will be valuable in pointing to the way in which learning about natural categories is unique.

ACKNOWLEDGMENTS

This chapter was written while the author was on study leave in the Department of Psychology at Duke University. I am very grateful to this department for the generous provision of facilities. I am also grateful to Louis Collins, Rama Ganesan, and Jacky Swan for their comments concerning this work. Funds for the experiments were provided by a grant from the United Kingdom Science and Engineering Research Council.

REFERENCES

Bhatt, R.S., Wasserman, E.A., Reynolds, W.F., & Knauss, K.S. (1988). Conceptual behavior in pigeons: Categorization of both familiar and novel examples from four classes of natural and artificial stimuli. *Journal of Experimental Psychology: Animal Behavior Processes, 14,* 219-234.

Cerella, J. (1980). The pigeon's analysis of pictures. *Pattern Recognition, 12,* 1-6.

D'Amato, M.R., Salmon, D.P., & Colombo, M. (1985). Extent and limits of the matching concept in monkeys (*Cebus apella*). *Journal of Experimental Psychology: Animal Behavior Processes, 11,* 35-51.

D'Amato, M.R., & Van Sant, P. (1988). The person concept in monkeys (*Cebus apella*). *Journal of Experimental Psychology: Animal Behavior Processes, 14,* 43-55.

Estes, W.K. (1986). Memory storage and retrieval processes in category learning. *Journal of Experimental Psychology: General, 115,* 155-174.

Franks, J.J., & Bransford, J.D. (1971). Abstraction of visual patterns. *Journal of Experimental Psychology, 90,* 65-74.

Fried, L.S., & Holyoak, K.J. (1984). Induction of category distributions: A framework for classification learning. *Journal of Experimental Psychology: Learning, Memory, and Cognition, 10,* 234-257.

Gluck, M.A., & Bower, G.H. (1988). Evaluating an adaptive network model of human learning. *Journal of Memory and Language, 27,* 166-195.

Guttman, N. (1965). Effects of discrimination training on generalization measured from the positive baseline. In D. Mostofsky (Ed.) *Stimulus generalization* (pp.210-217). Stanford: Stanford University Press.

Hanson, H.M. (1959). Effect of discrimination training on stimulus generalization. *Journal of Experimental Psychology, 58,* 321-334.

Hayes-Roth, B., & Hayes-Roth, F. (1977). Concept learning and the recognition and classification of exemplars. *Journal of Verbal Learning and Verbal Behavior, 16,* 321-338.

Herrnstein, R.J. (1984). Objects, categories, and discriminative stimuli. In H.T. Roitblat, T.G. Bever, & H.S. Terrace (Eds.), *Animal cognition* (pp.263-276). Hillsdale, NJ: Lawrence Erlbaum Associates.

Herrnstein, R,J. (1985). Riddles of natural categorization. *Philosophical Transactions of the Royal Society of London, B308,* 129-144.

Herrnstein, R.J., & deVilliers, P.A. (1980). Fish as a natural category for people and pigeons. In G.H.Bower (Ed.), *The psychology of learning and motivation,* Volume *14,* (pp. 59-95). New York: Academic Press.

Herrnstein, R.J., Loveland, D.H., & Cable, C. (1976). Natural concepts in pigeons. *Journal of Experimental Psychology: Animal Behavior Processes, 2,* 285-301.

Hintzman, D.L. (1986). 'Schema abstraction' in a multiple trace memory. *Psychological Review, 93,* 411-428.

Homa, D., Sterling, S., & Trepel, L. (1981). Limitations of exemplar- based generalization and the abstraction of categorical information. *Journal of Experimental Psychology: Human Learning and Memory, 6,* 418-439.

Kluender, K.R., Diehl, R.L., & Killeen, P.R. (1987). Japanese quail can learn phonetic categories. *Science, 237,* 1195-1197.

Konorski, J. (1967). *Integrative activity of the brain.* Chicago: University of Chicago Press.

Lea, S.E.G. (1984). In what sense do pigeons learn concepts? In H.T.Roitblat, T.G. Bever, & H.S. Terrace (Eds.), *Animal cognition* (pp.263-276). Hillsdale, NJ: Lawrence Erlbaum Associates.

Mackintosh, N.J. (1974). *The psychology of animal learning.* London: Academic Press.

Medin, D.L., & Schaffer, M.M. (1978). Context theory of classification learning. *Psychological Review, 85,* 207-238.

Morgan, M.J., Fitch, M.D., Holman, J.G., & Lea, S.E.G. (1976). Pigeons learn the concept of an "A". *Perception, 5,* 57-66.

Neumann, P.G. (1977). Visual prototype information with discontinuous representation of dimensions of variability. *Memory and Cognition, 5,* 187-197.

Omohundro, J. (1981). Recognition vs. classification of ill- defined category exemplars. *Memory and Cognition, 9,* 324-331.

Pearce, J.M. (1987). A model of stimulus generalization for Pavlovian conditioning. *Psychological Review, 94,* 61-73.

Pearce, J.M. (1988). Stimulus generalization and the acquisition of categories by pigeons. In L.Weiskrantz (Ed.), *Thought without language* (pp. 132-152). Oxford: Oxford University Press.

Pearce, J.M., & Hall, G. (1980). A model for Pavlovian learning: Variations in the effectiveness of conditioned but not unconditioned stimuli. *Psychological Review, 82,* 532-552.

Pepperberg, I.M. (1983). Cognition in the African grey parrot: Preliminary evidence for auditory/vocal comprehension of the class concept. *Animal Learning and Behavior, 11,* 179-185.

Posner, M.I., & Keele, S.W. (1968). On the genesis of abstract ideas. *Journal of Experimental Psychology, 77,* 353-363.

Posner, M.I., & Keele, S.W. (1970). Retention of abstract ideas. *Journal of Experimental Psychology, 83,* 304-308.

Reed, S.K. (1972). Pattern recognition and categorization. *Cognitive Psychology, 3,* 382-407.

Rescorla, R.A., & Wagner, A.R. (1972). A theory of Pavlovian conditioning: Variations in the effectiveness of reinforcement and nonreinforcement. In A.H. Black & W.F. Prokasy (Eds.), *Classical conditioning II: Current research and theory,* (pp.64-99). New York: Appleton-Century-Crofts.

Rilling, M. (1977). Stimulus control and inhibitory processes. In W.K. Honig, & J.E.R. Staddon (Eds.), *Handbook of operant behavior* (pp.432-480). Englewood Cliffs, NJ: Prentice-Hall.

Robbins, D., Barresi, J. Compton, P., Furst, A., Russo, M., & Smith, M.A. (1978). The genesis and use of exemplar vs. prototype knowledge in abstract category learning. *Memory and Cognition, 6,* 473-480.

Roberts, W.A., & Mazmanian, D.S. (1988). Concept learning at different levels of abstraction by pigeons, monkeys, and people. *Journal of Experimental Psychology: Animal Behavior Processes, 14,* 247-260.

Ryan, C.W.E. (1982). Concept formation and individual recognition in the domestic chicken (*Gallus gallus*). *Behavior Analysis Letters, 2*, 213-220.

Schrier, A.M., Angarella, R., & Povar, M.L. (1984). Studies of concept formation by stumptailed monkeys: Concepts humans, monkeys, monkeys, and letter *A*. *Journal of Experimental Psychology: Animal Behavior Processes, 10*, 564-584.

Schrier, A.M., & Brady, P.M. (1987). Categorization of natural stimuli by monkeys (*Macaca mulatta*): Effects of stimulus set size and modification of exemplars. *Journal of Experimental Psychology: Animal Behavior Processes, 13*, 136-143.

Smith, E.E., & Medin, D.L. (1981). *Categories and concepts*. Cambridge, MA: Harvard University Press.

Spence, K.W. (1937). The differential response in animals to stimuli varying within a single dimension. *Psychological Review, 44*, 430-444.

Sutherland, N.S., & Mackintosh, N.J. (1971). *Mechanisms of animal discrimination learning*. New York: Academic Press.

Vaughan, W.,Jr., & Greene, S.L. (1984). Pigeon visual memory capacity. *Journal of Experimental Psychology: Animal Behavior Processes, 10*, 256-271.

Wilson, B., Mackintosh, N.J., & Boakes, R.A. (1985). Matching and oddity learning in the pigeon: Transfer effects and the absence of relational learning. *Quarterly Journal of Experimental Psychology, 37B*, 295-312.

7 Comparative Cognition: Processing of Serial Order and Serial Pattern

M. R. D'Amato
Rutgers—The State University

The present chapter has three aims. The first is to describe our recent efforts devoted to analyzing the mechanisms employed by cebus monkeys when learning a serial order task. This development begins with a description of some important characteristics of the serial learning achieved by monkeys. In search of persuasive evidence that cebus monkeys are capable of extracting positional information from serially ordered events, we are led to a pair of wild-card experiments and subsequently to a phenomenon much studied in humans—the symbolic distance effect. The second objective may be viewed as an exercise in comparative cognition. I will try to show that although pigeons, like monkeys, can learn four- and five-item series to respectable levels of accuracy, they do so by quite different means. Third in order of listing though not in actual sequence, I will provide an illustration of the possibility of using results from relatively simple tasks to predict species' differences on more complex tasks. Finally, the chapter closes with some observations regarding the capacity of animals for processing serial pattern, a much more demanding task than dealing with serial order.

ASSOCIATIVE TRANSITIVITY IN MONKEYS AND PIGEONS

Our interest in serial learning sprang from what might appear on the surface as an unlikely source—associative transitivity. To describe the latter paradigm, monkeys were trained on a conditional matching task with cues A1 and A2 as the sample stimuli and with B1 and B2 as the comparison stimuli. When A1 was presented as the sample, the monkeys had to respond to B1; with A2 as the sample, they had to respond to B2. When these relations were well learned, a second matching task was introduced in which B1 and B2 were the samples, with two new items, C1 and C2, serving as the comparison stimuli. Responding to C1 was correct when B1 was the sample, and responding to C2 was correct for sample B2. The subjects were then tested on a third conditional matching task in which A1 and A2 were the samples and C1 and C2 were the comparison stimuli. The question of interest was whether the monkeys would treat the test situation as a new conditional matching task or whether they would spontaneously respond to C1 when A1 appeared as the sample and to C2 when the sample was A2.

The results were clean cut (D'Amato, Salmon, Loukas, & Tomie, 1985, Experiment 2). Although comparison stimuli C1 and C2 were never before experienced with samples A1 and A2, the four monkeys responded as though they had little doubt that comparison stimulus C1 went with sample A1 and that C2 went with sample A2. The relevant data appear in Figure 7.1, which is based on percentage of correct responses on each 24-trial positive or negative transitivity test. On the positive transitivity test, the monkeys were reinforced for responding to C1 when A1 was the sample and to C2 when the sample was

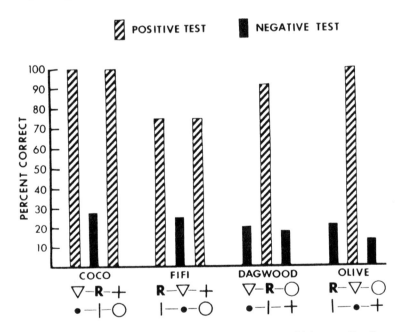

Figure 7.1. Performance on the 24-trial positive and negative transitivity tests. For Coco, triangle and dot served as samples in the first matching task, with red disk and vertical line as the comparison stimuli; the associative relations are shown by the horizontal lines. In the second matching task, red disk and vertical line were the samples, with the plus stimulus and circle as the associated comparison stimuli. During the test sessions, triangle and dot were the samples, while the comparison stimuli were plus and circle. In the positive test, Coco was reinforced for responding to plus when triangle was the sample and to circle when the sample was the dot; the reverse contingencies held for the negative transitivity test.

A2; on the negative transitivity test, the reinforcement contingencies were just the reverse. The order in which the three tests were given was balanced across the four subjects, as were the critical stimulus relations. Performance on the positive transitivity tests averaged 91.7% correct, compared to only 22.4% correct on the negative tests. Considering only the first 12 trials of each test session, the corresponding values were 90.6% versus 11.5% correct.

We labelled this inferential-like behavior *associative transitivity* to distinguish it from *inferential transitivity*, a more complex cognitive activity much investigated in children. Discussion of the relation between the two processes will be deferred until later. The important issue for the present is to account for the monkeys' test behavior.

Our interpretation was that when, say, sample A1 was presented on a test trial, there was of course no direct basis on which the subjects could choose between comparison stimuli C1 and C2. However, owing to prior training on the first matching task, sample A1 elicited an internal representation of its correlated comparison stimulus, B1. This activated representation then functioned as a surrogate sample, and, because of the prior training on the second conditional matching task, it elicited a response to comparison stimulus C1. Our view, in short, was that the associative transitivity displayed by the monkeys was mediated by activated representations of stimuli B1 and B2, which served as the functional sample stimuli during the test trials.

But why implicate internal representations to account for associative transitivity? Why not attribute the monkeys' test behavior to direct stimulus-response associations, uncomplicated by mediating representations? There are several reasons for our decision, perhaps the most important of which is that this alternate interpretation carries the implication that associative transitivity should be displayed by any organism capable of acquiring the first and second conditional matching tasks. This seems not to be the case. We trained and tested pigeons with procedures very comparable to those employed with the monkeys. The birds learned the two matching tasks to high levels of accuracy, but they showed no sign of associative transitivity (D'Amato et al., 1985, Experiment 3).

The capacity for associative transitivity appears linked to the ability to form well-integrated internal representations of the sample and comparison stimuli, which, in turn, may require more highly developed cortical structures than are found in pigeons. The following observation is relevant to this point. In an identity matching task, a familiar sample stimulus can be presented extremely briefly to monkeys with little, if any, decrement in performance, even with long retention intervals (D'Amato & Worsham, 1972). In contrast, the matching performance of pigeons remains dependent on sample duration even when there is virtually no retention interval and the sample stimuli are highly familiar (see D'Amato & Salmon, 1984; Grant, 1976). These results suggest that monkeys and pigeons differ importantly in their ability to develop highly integrated representations of the sample stimuli that can be fully activated by very minimal input.

SERIAL LEARNING BY PIGEONS AND MONKEYS

It occurred to us that the internal representations that apparently played a central role in associative transitivity might also be important agents in other, more complex, behaviors. Serial order learning seemed a promising candidate. Straub and Terrace (1981) had reported that pigeons were capable of learning four-item series to a rather high level of accuracy. In their study four colors were presented on projectors simultaneously, and the birds had to learn to peck the colors in a particular order, which will be referred to as ABCD. All stimuli remained present until the series was completed or until an error occurred. Errors could be committed by jumping forward in the sequence (e.g., ABD) or by retracing (e.g., ABA).

After learning the four-item sequence, the birds were given a pair-wise test in which only two of items were presented on each trial; the subjects' task was to respond to the test items in the order that was appropriate for the original sequence. The birds performed well on five of the six pairs; however, their performance on the interior pair, BC, was below chance expectation. This result, in addition to other aspects of their data, seems at odds with the authors' suggestion that the pigeons had made use of an internal representation of the four elements of the series. Had they developed a well-integrated and accessible internal representation of the series, their performance on pair BC should have been significantly above chance.

Five-Item Series Performance: Monkeys Versus Pigeons

In any case, if competence in learning about sequences of stimuli is related to a species' ability to form functional internal representations of the stimuli, given the associative transitivity results, monkeys should fare much better than pigeons in this enterprise. We therefore trained four monkeys on a five-item serial learning task, which will be referred to as ABCDE, and after acquisition, we probed them with a pair-wise test (D'Amato & Colombo, 1988b). Figure 7.2 presents the test results, along with those reported by Terrace (1987) for pigeons that had learned a similar five-item task. Both the monkey and pigeon subjects received only eight trials on each of the 10 test pairs. Note that there was little difference between the monkeys' and pigeons' performance on pairs that included either the first or last items of the series. There was, however, a large and consistent difference on the interior pairs, BC, BD, and CD. Also note that the pigeons' performance on these pairs is consistently below chance expectation (50% correct).

Our interpretation of the monkeys' competence on the interior test pairs is that by the end of acquisition they had developed an internal representation of the series which could be accessed during the pair-wise test to position properly the two items of a test pair. Presumably, they accessed their representation at item A and progressed from one represented item to the next until they found a matching item in the stimulus display. One implication of this account is that response latency to the first item of a test pair ought to increase the further along in the series that the first item is located. For example, response latency

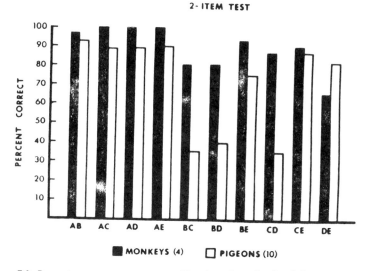

Figure 7.2. Percentage correct responses achieved on the pair-wise (2-item) test by the four monkeys of the D'Amato and Colombo (1988b) study and the 10 pigeons of Terrace's (1987) experiment on each of the 10 test pairs generated by the ABCDE series. Only eight trials were given with each test pair.

to item B in the pair BD ought to be shorter than the latency to item C in pair CD.

Figure 7.3 presents first-item response latency for all test pairs that were responded to correctly, arranged in order of the sequential position of the first item (A, B, C, or D). Also shown in the figure are similar values calculated from data provided by Terrace, which were based on the five pigeons of his Group I (Terrace, 1987). For the monkey subjects, first-item response latency was strongly dependent on first-item position; all four monkeys displayed the relationship, which was highly reliable. Clearly, there was no such dependence in the case of the pigeons.

Another implication of the internal representation hypothesis is that second-item response latency ought to increase as the number of missing items separating the first and second items increases, so that, for example, response latency to item C ought to be greater for test pair AC than for pair BC. The reason, of course, is that the larger the number of intervening missing items, the more time will be spent consulting the internal representation of the series. As Figure 7.4 shows, this prediction was borne out for the monkeys. Again, the relationship was highly significant and held for all four subjects. It clearly is absent in the data of the Group I pigeons of the Terrace (1987) study.

Implications for Representational Competence

The response accuracy results of the pair-wise test coupled with the relations obtained for first- and second-item response latencies provide strong support for the notion that the monkeys had developed a functional internal representation

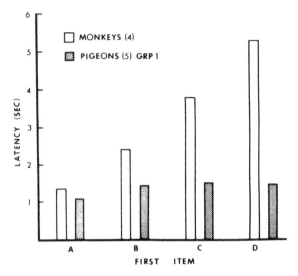

Figure 7.3. First-item response latency on each of the 10 test pairs plotted as a function of the location of the first item. The monkey data come from D'Amato and Colombo (1988b); the pigeon results are based on the five Group I subjects of the Terrace (1987) study.

of the series, which, among other things, enabled them to respond appropriately when confronted with only two of the series' items. By the same token, these assessments provide no evidence for a similar mechanism in pigeons. But how, then, were pigeons able to learn four- and five-item series? We have suggested that they accomplish such feats by means of discriminative processes that do not require elaborate internal representations (D'Amato & Colombo, 1988b).

In brief, we think it possible that a sequence of conditional discriminations underlies pigeons' serial learning. Onset of the stimulus array serves as a discriminative stimulus to peck item A; pecking A in turn serves as the cue to peck B, and so forth. Thus pigeons have little trouble with test pairs that include item A but they fail on the interior test pairs because the needed discriminative stimulus of pecking the previous item is missing. As shown in Figure 7.2, however, Terrace's (1987) pigeons also performed well with test pairs that included the terminal item, E. A possible explanation of this finding is that throughout training the birds were never reinforced for pecking item E first following onset of the stimulus display. Although the same contingency was in effect for items B, C, and D, the special status of the terminal item, namely, that reinforcers were presented only after responses to it, could have made this contingency more salient than first responses to items B-D. As a result, onset of the stimulus array may have developed into a powerful inhibitory stimulus with regard to pecking item E.

Pigeons may also learn something about the temporal ordering of the series items, in the sense of discriminating the relative temporal distance that separates each item from reinforcement. Assuming this to be the case, it would

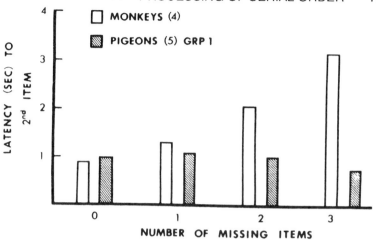

Figure 7.4. Second-item response latency on each of the 10 test pairs plotted as a function of the number of intervening missing items. The monkey data come from D'Amato and Colombo (1988b); the pigeon results are based on the five Group I subjects of the Terrace (1987) study.

explain their below-chance performance on the interior test pairs. Given the test pair BD, for example, they may have preferred pecking item D to pecking B because on correct trials D was closer in time to delivery of the reinforcer than was item B.

To summarize the development thus far, the different competence of monkeys and pigeons with regard to associative transitivity suggested to us that these species differ in their capacity to form well-integrated internal representations that can serve functional roles in guiding behavior. This interpretation was assessed within a more complex task, serial learning, and detailed analysis of performance on pair-wise tests provided confirming evidence. I should make it clear that the claim is not that pigeons are incapable of forming internal representations of stimuli. Rather it is that their representations, compared to those of monkeys, are less well-developed, less able to become integrated portrayals of complex external episodes, and more restricted in the number that can be maintained at any one time. As a consequence, their internal representations are more limited than those of monkeys with regard to the degree that they can construct and support complex behaviors.

THE MONKEY'S KNOWLEDGE OF ORDINAL POSITION

The Associative Chain Theory

The internal representation of the five-item series acquired by the monkeys could consist of the separate representation of each item organized as an associative chain, which may be symbolized as $a \rightarrow b \rightarrow c \rightarrow d \rightarrow e$, where the letters a-e refer to the internal representations of items A-E. An organized representation of this minimal structure, which will be referred to as the *associative chain theory*, appears sufficient to account for the results obtained on the pair-wise test. The monkeys could have accessed their representation of the series at a and associatively progressed through the item representations until they found a matching stimulus among the displayed items. The first- and second-item response latency relationships discussed above are also easily accounted for by such a mechanism.

Still, the question arises as to whether the associative chain account is adequate as a complete characterization of the monkey's capacity for representing sequential information. According to this view, a subject responds correctly to item B simply because the representational component *a* elicits *b*. The subject need not have any knowledge of the ordinal position of the item, for example, that B comes before items C, D, and E. Slamecka (1985) has pointed out that such theories, which have been advanced to account for rote serial learning in humans, eliminate the need for assuming that subjects acquire order information. "It is associations that are literally acquired rather than some abstract knowledge of what follows what" (1985, p. 417). Nevertheless, in learning a serial order task humans often acquire order, or positional, information, the alphabet being a conspicuous example (Lovelace & Snodgrass, 1971). Do monkeys have this capacity?

The Single-Wild-Card Experiment

To address this issue we modified the serial learning paradigm by introducing a new stimulus item, referred to as a wild card (W), that could substitute for any one of the regular items (D'Amato & Colombo, 1989). For example, on a certain proportion of trials the wild-card item substituted for item B; to be correct on such trials, the monkeys had to respond to the five items in the order AWCDE. In effect, this procedure created five additional five-item series, WBCDE through ABCDW. Our view was that, although the associative chain theory could in principle accommodate acquisition of the wild-card sequences, its task would be considerably more complicated because of the multiple associations that would have to be formed between the wild card and the baseline items (A-E).

Assume, for example, that a subject has responded correctly to the first three items of the ABWDE series. Because item W precedes items D and E equally often in the wild-card sequences, the strength of the W→D and W→E associations should be approximately equal. To avoid the resulting implication of large numbers of incorrect W→E transitions, the associative chain theory would have to assume that the remote forward association B→D was sufficiently strong to "prime" item D and thus encourage responding to D. However, a strong B→D remote association will cause trouble when it comes to properly locating the wild card, as it will compete with the B→W association. Indeed, it is not at all clear how the latter association can develop in the first place, given the existence of the B→D remote association before introduction of the wild card. The same difficulties obviously arise for the WBCDE and AWCDE wild-card sequences. Interestingly, because in the ABCDW sequence correct positioning of the wild card does not depend on remote associations and no transition from the wild card to a baseline item is required, the associative chain theory would predict that this sequence will generate the best wild-card performance.

Actually, two different wild card items were employed, referred to as items X and Y. The three monkey subjects had been in the D'Amato and Colombo (1988b) study and were therefore well versed on the ABCDE series. Wild card training was begun with the three-item series (ABC), followed by the four-item and finally the five-item task. In each case, the subjects were trained with one wild card and then the second, with the appropriate baseline sequence (ABC, ABCD, or ABCDE) interspersed among the wild-card trials. Figure 7.5 presents the performance of the monkeys on the five-item baseline and wild-card sequences during the last 10 of the 25 sessions that they received with each wild card. The results are averaged over the three subjects and the two wild cards. Each session contained 20 baseline trials and 20 wild-card trials; the wild-card trials consisted of four each of the five wild-card sequences.

The mean percentage of correct wild-card sequences was 59.7, which is rather impressive considering that in order for a wild-card trial to be counted as correct, the entire sequence had to be responded to correctly. If we assume that the monkeys positioned the wild card by chance alone and that when they guessed correctly they completed the entire trial, their expected performance on wild-card trials would be only 20% correct. The difference between the latter and the actual value is statistically reliable.

It is apparent from Figure 7.5 that, contrary to the prediction of association chain theory, sequence ABCDW did not generate the best wild-card performance. The only consistent positional effect was that performance was lowest when the wild card substituted for item B.

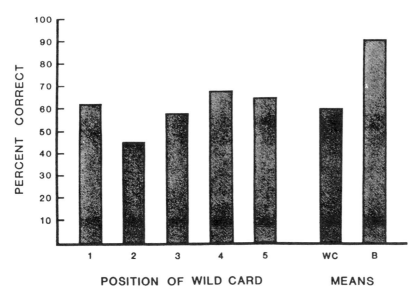

Figure 7.5. Mean percentages of correct wild card (WC) and baseline (B) trials for the three monkeys of the experiment appear in the right portion of the figure. A breakdown of wild-card performance in terms of the ordinal position of the wild card in the five-item series is shown in the left portion.

Performance on the interspersed baseline trials was much higher than that achieved on wild-card sequences, which, of course, was to be expected. Apart from the fact that the monkeys had far greater experience with the baseline series than with the wild-card sequences, wild-card items were subject to diverse sources of errors that did not apply to baseline items. For example, there was some physical similarity between each wild card and one of the baseline items; also, having no unique position in the series, wild-card items were subject to proactive interference effects from previous trials that did not apply to baseline items. We were able to estimate the level of wild-card performance that would have been achieved if the only errors committed by the monkeys on such trials arose from transitions to and from the wild card. This value turned out to be 76.8% correct, substantially above the obtained 59.6%.

The Double-Wild-Card Experiment

In a follow-up study (D'Amato & Colombo, 1989, Experiment 2), we confronted the associative chain theory with a more difficult challenge. Wild cards X and Y were presented on the same trial, creating 10 double-wild-card sequences. In six sequences the two wild cards were separated by at least one baseline item (e.g., AWCDW) and in the other four they were contiguous (e.g., AWWDE). The two wild-card positions could be filled in either order (wild card X first or Y first), but returning to the wild card previously responded to was treated as a backward error.

If the monkeys operated in accordance with the associative chain account, they should find the double-wild-card sequences virtually unmanageable. Consider the contiguous wild-card trials (e.g., AWWDE). To account for a transition from the first to the second wild card, an association between the two wild cards, either $X \rightarrow Y$ or $Y \rightarrow X$, would have to be assumed. Initially no such association exists, and its development should be difficult because, owing to the previous single-wild-card training, each wild card is presumably associated to each of the baseline items. Worse still, if the two wild cards were to become associated, this relation would cause serious interference on non-contiguous wild-card trials, in which one or more baseline items separate the two wild cards. It follows from this analysis that competent performance on contiguous wild-card trials should be accompanied by strongly unidirectional responding to the two wild cards. Also implied is an inverse relation between performance on contiguous and on non-contiguous wild-card trials, which would seriously limit the overall level of competence that could be achieved on double-wild-card trials.

Two of the three previous subjects, Fifi and Goldy, served in this experiment and they each received only 460 trials of double-wild-card training, 46 trials on each of the 10 double-wild-card sequences. Over the final two sessions, which included six trials with each of the 10 double-wild-card sequences, Fifi averaged 58.3% correct on the double-wild-card trials, with Goldy reaching 60.0% correct. These values are only moderately lower than the levels reached in the single-wild-card sessions shown in Figure 7.5. If we assume that the monkeys guessed the serial position of the wild cards and that when they guessed correctly they got the entire trial correct, the expected performance level on double-wild-card trials is 10% correct. The difference between mean performance on the last two double-wild-card sessions and the latter value is statistically reliable.

Figure 7.6 presents the percentages of correct double-wild-card trials for sequences in which 0, 1, 2, or 3 baseline items separated the two wild cards. These data are based on the last 10 training sessions, during which each of the 10 wild-card sequences was presented a total of 30 times. Note that there is little difference between Fifi's performance on contiguous wild-card trials (0 items separating the wild cards) and on trials where 1, 2, or 3 baseline items intervened between the two wild cards. Although Goldy reached a higher level of accuracy when the wild cards were separated by 2 or 3 baseline items, her performance was virtually identical when the wild cards were contiguous or separated by a single baseline item. There is little in these data to support the associative chain theory's prediction of an inverse relation between performance on contiguous and non-contiguous double-wild-card sequences. Finally, detailed examination of the contiguous wild-card trials failed to provide evidence of a strong unidirectional associative linking of the two wild cards.

The results produced by the single- and double-wild-card experiments do not support the associative chain theory as a complete account of our monkeys' competence for dealing with serially ordered events. They therefore provide indirect evidence that the monkeys were capable of extracting some information regarding the ordinal positions of the baseline items, information that enabled them to insert the wild cards in their proper positions at a level of accuracy much higher than seems plausible from the associative chain account.

A "SYMBOLIC" DISTANCE EFFECT IN MONKEYS

As already stated, the results from the wild-card studies provide only indirect evidence that our monkeys are capable of extracting positional information

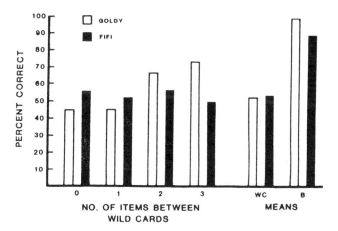

Figure 7.6. Mean percentages of correct double-wild-card (WC) and baseline (B) trials for each monkey of the study appear in the right portion of the figure. A breakdown of double-wild-card performance in terms of the number of baseline items that separated the two wild cards is shown in the left portion.

from serially ordered events. By enlisting a robust and general phenomenon that emerges when humans judge linearly ordered stimuli—the *symbolic distance effect*, or more simply, the *distance effect*—we recently approached this issue in a different, and perhaps more direct, way.

Nature and Relevance of the Distance Effect

In a remarkably wide variety of situations, human subjects are faster to judge which member of a pair has more (or less) of the attribute along which the test items are ordered the greater the difference (distance) that separates the two items. For example, asked to choose the larger member of the pair, response latency will be longer for fox/dog than for fox/sheep or for fox/cow (Kerst & Howard, 1977). If subjects are trained that Mary is prettier than Jane, that Jane is prettier than Nancy, and so forth for several pairs of individuals, when later tested on all possible pairings, they will judge remote pairs faster than contiguous pairs, even though they received no training whatsoever with the former pairs (e.g., Potts, 1974). It should be mentioned that this frequently used training-test procedure is actually a transitive inference paradigm.

A distance effect has also been obtained with serially organized stimuli or events, for example, letters of the alphabet (e.g., Hamilton & Sanford, 1978; Lovelace & Snodgrass, 1971). Such results indicate that, in humans at least, arbitrary items that are associatively related, which is to say, items that do not share a common attribute, are also subject to the distance effect phenomenon.

To accommodate the distance effect, many theorists assume that on a test trial the subject extracts positional information regarding the location of each target item (see Holyoak & Patterson, 1981). The distance effect is generated in large measure by the fact that the more distant the two items, the easier, and therefore the faster, one can obtain this information and execute the required discrimination. Accounting for the distance effect by means of associative chaining is generally regarded as implausible because of the implication that the effect is due solely to the fact that the greater the separation between the items of a pair, the faster a serial scan will locate the first item (Banks, 1977). Manifestation of the distance effect therefore appears to provide reasonably strong evidence that subjects have extracted positional information without associatively scanning the items.

When subjects are taught the ordering of the adjacent stimuli in a pretest training phase, the distance effect is usually accompanied by a nonmonotonic or an inverted-U function relating response latency to adjacent pairs of contiguous items. Trained with pairs AB, BC, CD, and DE, for example, response latency is usually lower on pairs AB and DE and higher on the interior pairs, both during the training and the testing phases (see Banks, 1977). Confidence that common underlying processes mediate the distance effect in humans and in animals would be heightened, therefore, if animals that displayed the distance effect also manifested a similar nonmonotonic latency function.

Returning to our serial learning task, a distance effect would be observed if, on a pair-wise test, response latency to item B decreased across pairs BC, BD, and BE, and across pairs CD and CE. Pairs that included item A might not show a distance effect because of the very short response latencies likely to be elicited by that item. To determine whether the pair-wise test data presented in Figure 7.3 might harbor a distance effect, we examined first-item response latencies for all 10 test pairs. There was little sign of a distance effect. Response latency to item B did not depend on the location of the second item, and the same was true for response latency to item C. Nor were first-item response latencies generated by pairs of adjacent items (AB, BC, CD, and DE) related by a nonmonotonic function.

The Distance-Effect Experiment

On reflection, however, we realized that the monkeys' prolonged previous training on the ABCDE series probably mitigated against observing a distance effect. Trial after trial the monkeys were required to start at item A and progress item by item through the series, which probably encouraged an associative chain mode of processing. As already described, the usual procedure in related studies of the distance effect is to train subjects on adjacent pairs and then assess their performance on these and remote pairs. This procedure, which is quite the reverse of our own, clearly does not bias the subject in the direction of associative chaining. Interestingly, there is some evidence that squirrel monkeys display a distance effect when trained on adjacent pairs before testing (McGonigle & Chalmers, 1986).

We therefore recruited Fifi and Goldy, who had served in the wild-card experiments, and Jane, who had been a subject in the D'Amato and Colombo (1988b) study, for training on the adjacent pairs AB, BC, CD, and DE (D'Amato & Colombo, 1990). For each subject the stimuli that served as A, B, C, D, and E were the very same that formed the ABCDE series, so that the paired relations were by no means novel. To increase experimental precision, the stimuli were presented only on the upper two of the five stimulus projectors, and, of course, the left/right configuration of the items of a pair varied from trial to trial. Consistent with the earlier pair-wise test, the monkeys' task was to respond to the first item of each pair. However, second-item responses were not required, and the display was turned off after execution of the first response.

Goldy received two 40-trial training sessions, which were followed by ten 40-trial test sessions, equally divided among the 10 test pairs. Fifi and Jane received 14 training sessions, and two 10-session blocks of test sessions. The performance of all subjects was very high during the last 10 test sessions, averaging 97% correct.

Figure 7.7 presents the main results of the study, based on correct trials only. Average response latencies on the adjacent pairs during training (pretest) and during testing are shown in the left panel. The pretest data come from the last training session; the test results are based on the final 10 test sessions. A statistically significant nonmonotonic function was obtained on the adjacent pairs during both the training and the test phases. Of much greater consequence a reliable distance effect emerged for the BC, BD, BE pairs. And as evaluated by a paired t test, the difference between pairs BC and BD was significant, which is important because these are interior pairs. In addition, all subjects re-

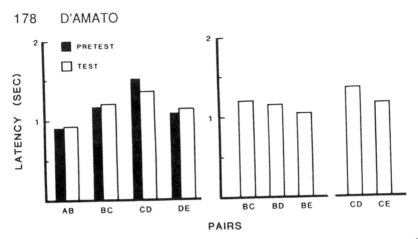

Figure 7.7. The left panel shows, for the three monkeys of the experiment, mean response latency on the four adjacent-item pairs during the last session of training (pretest) and during the subsequent 10 test sessions. The latency data in the right panel also come from the test sessions and reveal that response latency decreased with increasing remoteness of the second item from the first, i.e., the distance effect.

sponded faster to pair CE than to CD, but owing to the variability of the magnitude of the differences and the small number of subjects, the group result was not significant. As expected, response latency to pairs which included item A were uniformly low.

Individual-subject analyses were consistent with the group results. All subjects produced a reliable nonmonotonic function across the four adjacent pairs during the pretest session and two did so during the test. For Goldy and Jane the decline in latency across pairs BC, BD, and BE was statistically reliable, as was the decline across pairs CD and DE. For Fifi, the first comparison was marginally significant, but the second fell far short.

These results suggest the following conclusions. First, it appears that a distance effect, much like that observed in human subjects, was displayed by the monkeys: nonmonotonic functions relating response latency to successive adjacent pairs were obtained, and decreasing response latency with increasing remoteness of the test pair emerged clearly in two of the three monkeys. Second, manifestation of the distance effect is solid evidence that the monkeys possessed information regarding the ordinal position of the series' items. Rather than being generated by an associative scan through the series, this information resides in each item itself, much like the letter R directly conveys information regarding its ordinal position in the alphabet without our having first to scan through the alphabet from an earlier letter.

Finally, monkeys apparently can use either positional information or associative scanning to locate the items of a series. Prolonged recent experience in running off the series from beginning to end seems to bias the subjects towards the associative scanning processing mode. However, not much training on adjacent pairs is required to shift the monkeys' processing to positional information, which suggests that the latter might ordinarily be the preferred mode. Humans also shift between the two modes. For example, we often engage in associative scanning to distinguish between letters of the alphabet that lie close together (Hamilton & Sanford, 1978).

REPRESENTATION OF ORDINAL INFORMATION

How information regarding the ordinal positions of seriated items is internally represented is an interesting and important issue. Representing items ordered either associatively or by relational means as a spatial array seems to be a leading candidate (Holyoak & Patterson, 1981; McGonigle & Chalmers, 1986). Apparently, the basic function served by this transformation is to allow direct processing of an attribute of items (ordinal information) that could otherwise be accessed only serially. Suppose, for example, that the only representation available for the alphabet were an associative chain of the letters, from A to Z. To determine the relative position of two letters, no matter how separated they might be one would have to associatively scan the chain until one or both items was reached. On the other hand, with the alphabet represented as a spatial array, perhaps linearly from left to right, the relative position of a letter is directly available (though, of course, with limited precision). Left-right (or ends-inward) scanning is no more necessary for this judgment than it is for determining that a chair is in the center of our field of view and not at the extreme right.

Another advantage of the spatial array representation of ordinal information is its potential for parallel processing. Extrapolating from spatial perception, simultaneous assessment of the positional status of two spatially represented items seems entirely reasonable. Holyoak and Patterson (1981), for example, assume that subjects employ some degree of parallel processing in locating target items in the spatial array.

Associative Versus Inferential Transitivity

As was indicated earlier, many studies of the distance effect in adult humans have used an inferential transitivity design. Subjects learn, for example, that B is prettier than A, C is prettier than B, and so on. When confronted with the test pair BD, the subject chooses D as prettier, presumably on the basis of logical inference. That is, if the subject understands the relation holding between B and C and between C and D, that D is prettier than B follows by logical necessity.

No such necessity attended the performance of our monkeys in their pairwise tests, as the items were only associatively related. Nor could logical considerations have dictated the behavior of McGonigle and Chalmers' (1977) squirrel monkeys, who were trained on the five two-stimuli conditional discriminations A-/B+, B-/C+, C-/D+, and D-/E+.[1] In a subsequent test based on

---

[1] The discriminative stimuli were differently colored containers that either contained lead shot or were empty. For example, if in the A-/B+ discrimination A- was an empty red can and B+ a white weighted can, in the B-/C+ discrimination B- would be the white can now empty and C+ would be weighted and, say, blue. Thus although the items of a training pair were different in weight, their weight status was not defined in relative terms but absolutely, either heavy or light. It is not clear

all possible 10 pairs, their performance on remote pairs was as inferential-like as that of six-year-old children trained with adjacent pairs linked by a "taller-than" relation (Bryant & Trabasso, 1971). These same monkeys apparently also displayed a distance effect (see McGonigle & Chalmers, 1986).

The preceding considerations raise the following question. How does one account for similar transitive performance and a qualitatively similar distance effect in such different preparations—adult human subjects who have a logical relation at their disposal to construct linear order and nonhuman primates, who must resort to lesser, presumably associative, means? A reasonable answer is that in both cases the subjects have access to a spatial representation of the ordered items. It is this representation, queried on the pair-wise test, that produces both transitive behavior and the distance effect, perhaps in the manner described by Holyoak and Patterson (1981). Working within a broader theoretical context than the present one, McGonigle and Chalmers (1986) have advanced a similar view in some detail.

As was pointed out earlier, transitive performance can be accommodated by the associative chain account. It is possible, therefore, that primates will display transitive behavior even though a spatial representation of the associatively ordered items is, for one reason or another, lacking. However, when transitivity and the distance effect are both in evidence, a common genesis of both phenomena—namely, a spatial representation of item order—seems a more reasonable interpretation.

The major difference between humans and primates probably lies in the processes used to create the seriation that the spatial representation reflects. When items are linked by relations, humans can employ logical inference to impose order on the experimental items; for nonhuman primates, item seriation is associatively driven. The role of associations in constructing item order is obvious enough in our serial learning studies, but they probably also were a critical agent in the McGonigle and Chalmers (1977) experiment and in Gillan's 1981 study, which employed chimpanzees.

Consider the two conditional discriminations B-/C+, and C-/D+; obviously, the animal must process both stimuli of a discrimination before it can make an appropriate response. When learning the first conditional discrimination, it very likely will often scan from stimulus B to C, visually, and possibly also with overt responses. Consequently, the sight of B should elicit anticipation of C. On the other hand, stimulus C will not evoke anticipation of B, or at least not to the same strength, inasmuch as an association in that direction lacks functionality. Moreover, there is evidence that monkeys do not form backward associations in any strength (D'Amato et al., 1985). Similarly, per-

---

why transitive inference should be expected in such a situation; rather, the subjects might become confused by the two different weights assigned to the interior items and ignore them. Gillan (1981) reported inference-like behavior in chimpanzees without the use of a correlated weight cue, which also questions the functionality of the latter. Chalmers and McGonigle (1984), who it should be noted have consistently interpreted their monkeys' transitive behavior in non-inferential terms, acknowledged this problem but did not think it crucial.

ception of stimulus C in the discrimination C-/D+ should elicit the anticipation of D, without the reverse occurring to any significant degree. Granting the squirrel monkey the capacity to form functional representations of stimuli, given sufficient training on the four adjacent-item conditional discriminations, the associations just described could easily become linked into an associative structure resembling that developed in our serial learning task.

To state the preceding line of argument more succinctly, the major difference between humans and nonhuman primates with regard to the distance effect and transitive performance appears to reside in the means by which seriation of the experimental items is accomplished. Humans often employ logical inference for this purpose, while primates depend on something akin to associative transitivity.

Of course, there is no reason why associative transitivity should not also operate in humans, particularly in young children. Because the adjacent items are distinctively labelled as well as being linked by relations, studies of transitive inference allow for seriation both by logical inference and associatively. Distinguishing between the contributions of associative transitivity and logical inference is often not an easy task (Breslow, 1981), though the triadic tests reported by McGonigle and Chalmers (1986) seem a promising tool for this purpose.

Knowledge of Ordinal Position in Other Species

The capacity to extract ordinal information from sequential events has been examined in a number of species other than primates. For example, knowledge of ordinal position has been attributed to pigeons for three-item sequences (e.g., Roitblat, Scopatz, & Bever, 1987; Terrace, 1986). We have expressed some reservation regarding these claims, largely because of the absence of more than one interior item (D'Amato & Colombo, 1989); still, such a capacity might lie within the pigeon's grasp.

Acquisition of ordinal information has also been reported for rats trained in a runway with a sequence of different reward magnitudes (e.g., Roitblat, Pologe, & Scopatz, 1983). Recently, Capaldi and Miller (1988) have gone further and advanced rather strong claims regarding the ability of rats to count reinforcing events. My impression is that their results can be accommodated by assuming that, for each specific sequence of rewarded and nonrewarded trials, an associative chain of the series was constructed, which the rats then converted into a spatial representation. By accessing such representations appropriately, the rats could easily keep track of their position in a particular series, much as they are able to negotiate a radial-arm maze effectively by means of a related representation ("cognitive map"). One implication of the parallel drawn is that variables known to affect performance accuracy on the radial-arm maze, such as lesions of the hippocampus (e.g., Becker, Walker, & Olton, 1980), should have a parallel effect on the rat's "counting" behavior. Attributing to the rat a capacity for abstract counting may not, therefore, be necessary at this time.

Knowledge of ordinal position no doubt often plays an important role in the development of complex discriminative behaviors. Comprehension of artificial language by the sea lion (Schusterman & Krieger, 1984) and the dolphin

(Herman, Richards, & Wolz, 1984) are instructive examples. In both cases, the animals are sensitive to "word" order, that is, to syntax, which implies that their knowledge of ordinal position is substantial. Obviously, the same observation applies to language-competent apes (e.g., Savage-Rumbaugh, 1988).

PROCESSING OF SERIAL PATTERN BY ANIMALS

A sequence in which all items possess a common attribute that can vary in extent has the potential of conveying more than ordinal information. Confronted with such a sequence, it is possible for a subject to learn something about the magnitudes of the series' items and perhaps how the magnitudes are interrelated, that is, learn about the serial pattern of the sequence. The transitive inference studies of the distance effect may be interpreted as a special case of serial pattern learning, in the sense that the human subjects deduced a pattern of increasing magnitude of an attribute across a series of items on the basis of incomplete information. On the other hand, serial learning studies such as our own provide no opportunity for serial pattern learning, inasmuch as the individual items of the series are unrelated.

Since many species of animals apparently are capable of acquiring ordinal information, a natural question is whether their serial processing ability extends to serial pattern detection. This issue has been addressed in a number of ways, of which I will discuss only two, tonal pattern perception and, in an entirely different modality, reward-magnitude pattern perception.

Tonal Pattern Perception

I have recently reviewed several studies from our laboratory aimed at demonstrating in monkeys tonal pattern perception of non-species-specific acoustic stimuli (D'Amato, 1988). Despite an early promising result (D'Amato & Salmon, 1982), all subsequent assessments proved negative. Even monkeys who had an enormous amount of experience discriminating, matching, and remembering acoustic stimuli appeared unable to learn the tonal patterns of simple ascending and descending sequences of tones (D'Amato & Colombo, 1988a). Songbirds, too, seem remarkably insensitive to the tonal patterns of non-species-specific stimuli. (For a more optimistic assessment, see Hulse & Page, 1988.)

In short, given the rich auditory communication systems of many species of animals, it is quite surprising that thus far only meager evidence for tonal pattern perception in animals has been scraped together. Perhaps detection of tonal pattern draws on cognitive capacities that are also involved in language competence and therefore requires a degree of abstraction that exceeds the available resources of most animals (D'Amato, 1988).

Reward-Magnitude Pattern Perception

It has been claimed that rats trained on a sequence of trials in which reward magnitude (number of food pellets) decreases monotonically across the series of trials learn this fact, which is encoded as a "rule" (e.g., Hulse & Dorsky, 1979). Note that such a rule—which may be expressed as $E(i + 1) < E(i)$, where the latter term refers to the reward magnitude on Trial i—represents a level of abstraction beyond that required for serial pattern perception itself. Thus a rat could represent the pattern of a monotonically decreasing five-trial sequence by encoding four decreases in reward magnitude, without taking the extra step of collapsing the separate discriminations into a single generalized relation.

In any case, do the available data require the assumption that rats learn such rules or even that they learn patterns of reward magnitude? I think not. The reason is that a simpler interpretation has not been ruled out, namely, that what rats learn about is the *sequence* of reward magnitudes, not their *pattern*. To illustrate this distinction for the case of tonal pattern perception, suppose monkeys are trained on a sequence of three tones: 500, 1000, and 500 Hz. Suppose further that tests show that they respond to that sequence but not to the other seven three-item sequences that can be constructed with the 500- and 1000-Hz tones. It does not follow from these results that the monkeys have necessarily learned the tonal pattern of the sequence. They could have learned only the position and absolute frequency of each tone. To establish relational learning, appropriate transposition tests in which all frequencies are increased or decreased proportionally are required (D'Amato, 1988).

The same argument applies to reward-magnitude pattern learning. Granting that rats can extract positional information regarding the reward conditions of the trials of a sequence, they clearly could associate each position of the sequence with a specific magnitude of reward (see Roitblat et al., 1983). It is possible that these associations mediate many of the results taken as evidence of reward-magnitude pattern perception. To implicate reward pattern perception unambiguously, appropriate transposition tests analogous to those required for demonstrating tonal pattern perception should be conducted.

SUMMARY

It is evident from the above discussion that the ability to construct spatial representations of associatively ordered events can significantly extend the cognitive reach of animals. Stating the function of spatial representations in more general terms, they allow random access to ordered items (or representations thereof) that otherwise could be accessed only serially. Any mechanism having this property could serve as well. How such mechanisms are realized structurally and the extent of their representation in various species are interesting questions for future research.

ACKNOWLEDGMENT

The author's research described in this chapter was supported by grants from the National Science Foundation. I am grateful for the assistance provided by Michael Colombo.

REFERENCES

Banks, W. P. (1977). Encoding and processing of symbolic information in comparative judgments. In G. H. Bower (Ed.), *The psychology of learning and mo-*

tivation: Advances in theory and research (Vol. 11, pp. 101-159). New York: Academic Press.

Becker, J. T., Walker, J. A., & Olton, D. S. (1980). Neuroanatomical bases of spatial memory. *Brain Research, 200,* 307-320.

Breslow, L. (1981). Reevaluation of the literature on the development of transitive inferences. *Psychological Bulletin, 89,* 325-351.

Bryant, P. E., & Trabasso, T. (1971). Transitive inference and memory in young children. *Nature, 232,* 456-458.

Capaldi, E. J., & Miller, D. J. (1988). Counting in rats: Its functional significance and the independent cognitive processes that constitute it. *Journal of Experimental Psychology: Animal Behavior Processes, 14,* 3-17.

Chalmers, M., & McGonigle, B. (1984). Are children any more logical than monkeys on the five-term series problem? *Journal of Experimental Child Psychology, 37,* 355-377.

D'Amato, M. R. (1988). A search for tonal pattern perception in cebus monkeys: Why monkeys can't hum a tune. *Music Perception, 5,* 453-480.

D'Amato, M. R., & Colombo, M. (1988a). On tonal pattern perception in monkeys (Cebus apella). *Animal Learning & Behavior, 16,* 417-424.

D'Amato, M. R., & Colombo, M. (1988b). Representation of serial order in monkeys (Cebus apella). *Journal of Experimental Psychology: Animal Behavior Processes, 14,* 131-139.

D'Amato, M. R., & Colombo, M. (1989). Serial learning with wild card items by monkeys *(Cebus apella)*: Implications for knowledge of ordinal position. *Journal of Comparative Psychology, 103,* 252-261.

D'Amato, M.R., & Colombo, M. (1990). The symbolic distance effect in monkeys *(Cebus apella). Animal Learning and Behavior, 18,* 133-140.

D'Amato, M. R., & Salmon, D. P. (1982). Tune discrimination in monkeys (Cebus apella) and in rats. *Animal Learning & Behavior, 10,* 126-134.

D'Amato, M. R., & Salmon, D. P. (1984). Cognitive processes in cebus monkeys. In H. L. Roitblat, T. G. Bever, & H. S. Terrace (Eds.), *Animal cognition* (pp. 149-168). Hillsdale, NJ: Lawrence Erlbaum Associates.

D'Amato, M. R., Salmon, D. P., Loukas, E., & Tomie, A. (1985). Symmetry and transitivity of conditional relations in monkeys (Cebus apella) and pigeons (Columba livia). *Journal of the Experimental Analysis of Behavior, 44,* 35-47.

D'Amato, M. R., & Worsham, R. W. (1972). Delayed matching in the capuchin monkey with brief sample durations. Learning and Motivation, 3, 304-312.

Gillan, D. J. (1981). Reasoning in the chimpanzee: II. Transitive inference. *Journal of Experimental Psychology: Animal Behavior Processes, 7,* 150-164.

Grant, D. S. (1976). Effect of sample presentation time on long-delay matching in the pigeon. *Learning and Motivation, 7,* 580-590.

Hamilton, J. M. E., & Sanford, A. J. (1978). The symbolic distance effect for alphabetic order judgements: A subjective report and reaction time analysis. *Quarterly Journal of Experimental Psychology, 30,* 33-43.

Herman, L. M., Richards, D. G., & Wolz, J. P. (1984). Comprehension of sentences by bottlenosed dolphins. *Cognition, 16,* 129-219.

Holyoak, K. J., & Patterson, K. K. (1981). A positional discriminability model of linear-order judgments. *Journal of Experimental Psychology: Human Perception and Performance, 7,* 1283-1302.

Hulse, S. H., & Dorsky, N. P. (1979). Serial pattern learning by rats: Transfer of a formally defined stimulus relationship and the significance of nonreinforcement. *Animal Learning & Behavior, 7,* 211-220.

Hulse, S. H., & Page, S. C. (1988). Toward a comparative psychology of music perception. *Music Perception, 5*, 427-452.

Kerst, S. M., & Howard, J. H., Jr. (1977). Mental comparisons for ordered information on abstract and concrete dimensions. *Memory & Cognition, 5*, 227-234.

Lovelace, E. A., & Snodgrass, R. D. (1971). Decision times for alphabetic order of letter pairs. *Journal of Experimental Psychology, 88*, 258-264.

McGonigle, B. O., & Chalmers, M. (1977). Are monkeys logical? *Nature, 267*, 694-696.

McGonigle, B., & Chalmers, M. (1986). Representations and strategies during inference. In T. Myers, K. Brown, & B. McGonigle (Eds.), *Reasoning and discourse processes* (pp. 141-164). London: Academic Press.

Potts, G. R. (1974). Storing and retrieving information about ordered relationships. *Journal of Experimental Psychology, 103*, 431-439.

Roitblat, H. L., Pologe, B., & Scopatz, R. A. (1983). The representation of items in serial order. *Animal Learning & Behavior, 11*, 489-498.

Roitblat, H. L., Scopatz, R. A., & Bever, T. G. (1987). The hierarchical representation of three-item sequences. *Animal Learning & Behavior, 15*, 179-192.

Savage-Rumbaugh, S. (1988). A new look at ape language: Comprehension of vocal speech and syntax. In D. W. Leger (Ed.), *Nebraska symposium on motivation, 1987* (Vol. 35, pp.201-255). Lincoln: University of Nebraska Press.

Schusterman, R. J., & Krieger, K. (1984). California sea lions are capable of semantic comprehension. *The Psychological Record, 34*, 3-23.

Slamecka, N. J. (1985). Ebbinghaus: Some associations. *Journal of Experimental Psychology: Learning, Memory, and Cognition, 11*, 414-435.

Straub, R. O., & Terrace, H. S. (1981). Generalization of serial learning in the pigeon. *Animal Learning & Behavior, 9*, 454-468.

Terrace, H. S. (1986). A nonverbal organism's knowledge of ordinal position in a serial learning task. *Journal of Experimental Psychology: Animal Behavior Processes, 12*, 203-214.

Terrace, H. S. (1987). Chunking by a pigeon in a serial learning task. *Nature, 325*, 149-151.

8 Parallels Between the Behavioral Effects of Dimethoxy-ß-Carboline (DMCM) and Conditional Fear Stimuli

Michael S. Fanselow
University of California-Los Angeles

Fred J. Helmstetter
Dartmouth College

Daniel J. Calcagnetti
Emory University

Recent progress in our understanding of the γ-aminobutyric acid (GABA) receptor complex may have implications for the analysis of fear and anxiety. Our purpose in this chapter is threefold; 1) to describe some relevant concepts about the action of substances that modulate GABAergic transmission focusing upon a particular ß-carboline, methyl 6,7-dimethoxy-4-ethyl-ß-carboline-3-carboxylate (DMCM), 2) to discuss experimental evidence from our laboratory suggesting that administration of DMCM results in behavioral effects that roughly parallel those found in Pavlovian fear conditioning and 3) briefly consider the possibility that an endogenous substance functioning like DMCM is involved in normal Pavlovian fear conditioning.

MECHANISM OF ACTION AND BEHAVIORAL EFFECTS OF ß-CARBOLINES

There are several reasons why a survey of current topics in animal learning such as that represented in this volume should include a chapter dealing with the GABA receptor complex. GABA is considered to be the major inhibitory neurotransmitter in the mammalian central nervous system. Thus it is not surprising that pharmacological agents that influence GABA systems appear to have a wide range of behavioral effects including a potent influence on motivational/emotional processes. There is a high density of GABA receptors in anatomical regions related to anxiety (Niehoff & Kuhar, 1983; Young & Kuhar, 1980). In addition, at the molecular level the function of this receptor complex challenges previous thinking about how a single receptor site may influence neural transmission. The GABA Receptor complex contains separate recognition sites (receptors) for two classes of substances each of which has a different but interacting function (for review see Martin, 1987). GABA and related compounds bind to one of these recognition sites (ß-subunit), while the second site (α-subunit) is occupied by benzodiazepines and related compounds (see Figure 8.1).

Recently, the structure of the receptor complex has been worked out to the point that its DNA sequence has been determined allowing the use of gene splicing techniques to successfully clone the functional receptor complex into a species of toad that has no endogenous GABA receptors (Schofield et al., 1987). The receptor complex is known to consist of 4 monomeric units. Each unit harbors three areas which serve a different function that consist of a chloride channel, a GABA-binding site and a benzodiazepine (BZP)-binding site.

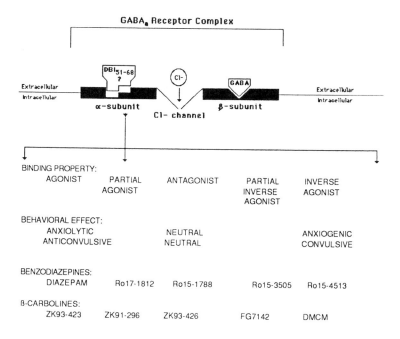

Figure 8.1 illustrates the GABA receptor complex which is made up of two receptor sites (α and β subunits) and a chloride ionophore. The endogenous ligand for the β subunit is GABA, which causes the ionophore to permit passage of Cl- ions from outside the cell. One putative endogenous ligand for the α-subunit may be a fragment of the peptide Diazepam Binding Inhibitor (DBI; Ferrero, Conti-Tronconi, & Guidotti, 1986). The α-subunit regulates the frequency of ionophore openings. Agents that bind with the α-subunit act along a continuum of agonist to antagonist to inverse agonist. The behavioral effects of these agents vary in a manner that is related to their binding property. Exogenous ligands for the α-subunit may be benzodiazepines or β-carbolines.

When GABA occupies the ß-subunit the chloride channel opens. The influx of chloride ions causes GABA's post synaptic inhibitory effects. The efficacy of chloride ion influx is regulated by what is happening at the α-subunit or BZP recognition site. Occupation of the BZP site modulates the opening of the chloride channel that occurs in response to GABA binding at its receptor. Hence, the efficacy of GABA to regulate the chloride channel is affected by the presence of BZPs at the receptor complex.

Pharmacological agents that interact with the BZP receptor lie on a functional continuum ranging from agonist to inverse agonist (Little, Nutt & Taylor, 1987; Martin, 1987). The classic benzodiazepines, such as diazepam and chlordiazepoxide, are agonists that increase the frequency of chloride channel opening; the resulting behavioral effects are caused by a facilitation of GABA's inhibitory actions. In an attempt to find an endogenous ligand for the benzodiazepine receptor, Braestrup and his colleagues (e.g., Braestrup, Nielsen, Honore, Jensen, & Petersen, 1983; Braestrup, Nielsen, & Olsen, 1980) found that a ß-carboline, ß-carboline-3-carboxylic acid ethyl ester, could bind to the α-subunit but appeared to exert actions contrary to those of previously studied benzodiazepine ligands. Subsequently, it has been determined that these substances, which have been labelled inverse agonists, have effects opposite to those of agonists. They reduce the post-synaptic inhibitory effects of GABA by reducing the frequency of chloride channel openings that occur in response to occupation of the ß-subunit by GABA. In the middle of the continuum are antagonists. These substances also bind to the α-subunit. While BZP antagonists block the actions of both agonists and inverse agonists, they are functionally neutral. For example, the benzodiazepine Ro15-1788 (ethyl-8-fluoro-5,6 -dihydro -5- methyl -6- oxo- 4H-imidazo (1,5a) (1,4) benzodiazepine -3- carboxylate) binds to the BZP receptor with high affinity and will block the behavioral and physiological effects of both agonists and inverse-agonists at this receptor (Hunkeler et al., 1981). Recently, an array of substances with both benzodiazepine and ß-carboline structures have been synthesized that run the full continuum of binding properties from agonist to antagonist to inverse agonist actions. Relevant examples are provided in Figure 8.1. Thus GABA acts as the neurotransmitter at its receptor site but its action is modulated in a bidirectional manner by substances, that are not transmitters in the classical sense, acting at a separate but coupled receptor site. Together these two recognition sites constitute the GABA receptor complex.

The arsenal of drugs acting at the BZP receptor makes available pharmacological tools to determine the behavioral importance of the GABA receptor complex. For example, the behavioral effects of BZP ligands, like the ß-carbolines, may be conceptualized along a continuum that parallels the continuum of binding properties (see Figure 8.1). Classic agonist effects produced by drugs like diazepam are displayed by the ß-carboline, ZK93-423, that include sedative (Stephens, Kehr, Schneider, & Schmiechen, 1984), hyperphagic (Cooper, 1986), anxiolytic (Lal & Emmett-Oglesby, 1983) and anticonvulsant effects (Cooper, 1986). Whereas the ß-carboline ZK93-426 is relatively neutral in producing behavioral effects at low doses (Braestrup, Honore, Nielsen, Petersen, & Jensen, 1984; Cooper, 1986; Stephens, Kehr & Duka, 1986), it acts as an antagonist given the presence of BZP agonists or inverse-agonists.

The ß-carboline inverse-agonists, the most potent of which is DMCM, produce effects that appear to be the reverse of those of agonists. In rats, DMCM dose-dependently produces convulsions (Petersen, 1983), and anorexia/hypophagia (Cooper, 1986). With the procedures used to document the anxiolytic effects of benzodiazepine agonists, the inverse agonists have been purported to be anxiogenic. For instance, they enhance the effects of punishment on conflict tests (Stephens & Kehr, 1985). Inverse-agonists range from high to low efficacy (i.e., partial to full). FG7142 is called a partial inverse-agonist with low efficacy partly because it is less potent when compared to a full inverse-agonist like DMCM. For example, acute systemic injection of both FG7142 and DMCM produce convulsions in mice beginning within 10 min of administration that last approximately 10 min. However, the dose required to achieve this effect with FG7142 (20 mg/kg) was 10 times that of DMCM (2 mg/kg; Rodgers & Randall, 1987).

The most well known and clinically utilized behavioral consequence of benzodiazepine agonist administration is to quell anxiety. If benzodiazepine inverse agonists invariably produce opposite effects it might be expected that they would generate or potentiate anxiety. Data supporting this prediction has lead to the labelling of these substances as anxiogenic. One of the more interesting illustrations of the anxiogenic properties of inverse agonists comes from test trials on humans (Dorow, Horowski, Paschelk, Amin, & Braestrup, 1983). Five male volunteers were given oral doses of FG7142. In two out of twelve trials, reports of severe anxiety-like symptoms were obtained. One volunteer was unable to speak, close his eyes, lie down or even sit still. Blood pressure, heart rate and muscle tension all increased. Growth hormone, prolactin and cortisol levels were elevated. The second subject showed similar reactions although he was able to speak in terse but coherent phrases. The symptoms were alleviated by injection of the benzodiazepine agonist, lormetazepam. This subject later described his sensations as an impending fear of death or annihilation. Consistent effects have been seen in several animal models. In the four plate test, mice are placed in a chamber containing a floor made up of four metal squares. Locomotion is measured in terms of the number of crosses from plate to plate. Shock is administered to punish moving from one plate to the next. DMCM, at doses that did not affect unpunished locomotion, enhanced the suppressing effects of punishment (Stephens & Kehr, 1985). The amount of social interaction in rats is sensitive to the level of situational anxiety; reducing anxiety enhances social interaction and visa versa (File & Baldwin, 1987). FG7142 decreases social interaction in this test, an effect that is reversed by the antagonist Ro15-1788 (File & Pellow, 1984). Another line of evidence was provided by Gardner and Budhram (1987), who found that stress-induced ultrasounds of rat pups were enhanced by DMCM. The purpose of the experiments described in this chapter was to further characterize the anxiogenic-like properties of inverse agonists. We used DMCM, which is the most potent full inverse agonist presently available, to see if it produced behaviors that parallel those produced by stimuli that had undergone Pavlovian fear conditioning.

There is an obvious difference between generating fear with an environmental stimulus such as a Pavlovian Conditional Stimulus (CS) and a pharmacological stimulus such as DMCM. If a localizable light is paired with electric shock, fear produced by the CS is tied to a discrete object. However, the fear generated by an anxiogenic drug may not be attached to any specifiable environmental object. Rather, it may be a more generalized situational fear. There is the possibility that such a variation in the source of fear may translate into differences in the behavioral topography through which that fear is expressed. One strategy to minimize the potential of problems in this regard is to compare the behavioral sequelae of DMCM administration to conditioning procedures that produce situational fear. That seemed to be natural for our laboratory as we have been examining the behavioral responses of rats to shock associated situational or contextual cues for a number of years (e.g., Fanselow, 1980; Fanselow & Tighe, 1988). For example, if a rat is returned to an environment in which it previously received electric footshock the rat's behavior is characterized by freezing and a reduction in sensitivity to painful stimuli (Fanselow & Baackes, 1982). Freezing is one of the rats species-specific defensive reactions and is characterized by an immobile crouching posture. Both the freezing and the analgesia are completely dependent on the presence of the environmental cues associated with shock and should be considered conditional responses (e.g., Fanselow, 1984). The question raised here is, would the behavioral responses of rats to DMCM mimic their reactions to shock-associated situational cues?

EXPERIMENTS

DMCM and Freezing

The first experiment examined DMCM's ability to modulate freezing conditioned to contextual cues by footshock (see Fanselow, 1980 for more details). On the first day of the experiment, rats were placed in an observation chamber, where they were given 3 shocks (.5 mA, .5 s) spaced 20 s apart. The next day the rats were given two injections intraperitoneally (ip); the first was either the benzodiazepine antagonist Ro15-1788 (7 mg/kg, ip) or its vehicle. The second injection was either DMCM (0.8 mg/kg, ip) or its vehicle given in a factorial combination with the first. The rats were replaced in the observation chamber 10 min later and observed for freezing during an 8-min session. The mean percent time spent freezing for each of the four groups is presented in Figure 8.2. A 2x2 analysis of variance (ANOVA) indicated a reliable interaction ($F(1,16)=5.04$, $p<.04$). When the first injection was vehicle, DMCM enhanced conditioned freezing ($F(1,16)=8.72$, $p<.01$). However, when the animals were pretreated with Ro15-1788, DMCM did not reliably affect freezing ($F(1,16)<1$). Ro15-1788 had no effect on its own ($F(1,16)=1.85$, $p>.19$). Thus, DMCM enhanced the freezing response elicited by conditional fear stimuli. As this enhancement is attenuated by Ro15-1788, it is likely that the effect is mediated at the benzodiazepine receptor. While the above experiment showed that DMCM influenced the freezing produced by an already conditioned fear, it seemed more interesting and important to determine if DMCM could elicit freezing behavior in the absence of any stimuli for conditioned fear. To do this rats were run through the test portion of the last design without a conditioning day. Again the animals were given two injections in a factorial de-

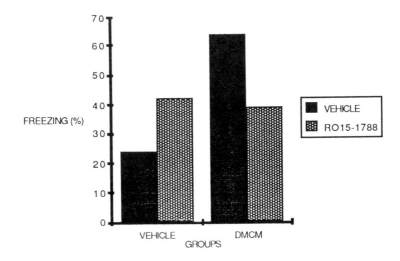

Figure 8.2 shows the percentage of an 8 min observation period that rats spent freezing as a function of treatment with DMCM (0 or 0.8 mg/kg, ip) and Ro15-1788 (0 or 7 mg/kg, ip). The vehicle for all drugs was DMSO. The rats received shock, in the observation chamber, 24 h earlier.

sign. The first was either DMCM (1.25 mg/kg) or a placebo; the second was diazepam (2.5 mg/kg) or placebo. Ten min following injection the rats were placed in the observation chamber and observed for freezing behavior. The animals did not receive shock in this design. The means of the four groups are presented in Figure 8.3. ANOVA indicated a reliable interaction (F(1,20)=4.69, p<.04). The animals that received two placebo injections did not freeze, as is typical of nonshocked rats. Rats treated only with DMCM froze reliably more than any of the other groups (Fs≥5.08, p<.03), none of which differed from each other (Fs<1). Thus DMCM elicited freezing even in nonshocked rats and diazepam reversed this effect. In a follow-up experiment we employed the same design but substituted the antagonist ZK93-426. DMCM again produced freezing and the effect was completely blocked by ZK93-426. Thus it seems that in rats that are not given any environmental stimuli which provoke fear, this inverse agonist can generate species specific defensive reactions, apparently mediated through an action at the benzodiazepine receptor.

DMCM and the Open Field

Another experimental procedure that may serve as an assay of situational fear is the open field test (Archer, 1973, 1974; Walsh & Cummins, 1976). Often, defecation and reduced locomotion in an open field are taken as indices of fear. Therefore, the next experiment examined the effects of two doses of DMCM (1 or 2.5 mg/kg, ip) on rats placed in a large open field. The floor of the open field was marked by a grid and locomotion was scored as the number of lines of the grid the animal crossed. Freezing was also scored. The data are presented in Figure 8.4. Overall ANOVA indicated reliable between group differences for

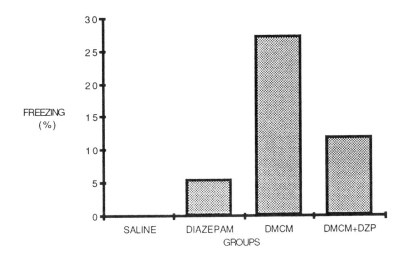

Figure 8.3 illustrates the percentage of an 8 min observation period that unshocked rats spent freezing as a function of treatment with DMCM (1.25 or 0 mg/kg in acidified water vehicle, ip) and diazepam (2.5 or 0 mg/kg in injectible Hoffmann-La Roche Vehicle, ip).

line crossings (F(2,12)=4.0, p<.05), defecation (F(2,12)=3.86, p=.05), and freezing (F(2,12)=6.56, p<.05). The 1 mg/kg dose decreased line crossings, but increased both freezing and defecation. These observations are consistent with the hypothesis that the 1 mg/kg dose of DMCM provokes a fear-like state in the open field. The high dose produced similar effects on line crossings and freezing but did not increase defecation. However, interpretation of the observations at this dose was complicated by the occurrence of tremors and motor interference. Our results in the open field are consistent with Huttunen and Myers (1986) finding that another ß-carboline, 1,2,3,4-tetrahydro-ß-carboline hydrochloride increases freezing in the open field when injected directly into the hippocampus.

DMCM and Analgesia

A number of stressful manipulations including conditional fear produce a reduction in sensitivity to painful stimuli. Most relevant to the present case is that contextual stimuli associated with an electric shock produce analgesia (Fanselow & Baackes, 1982). There have been several reports that benzodiazepine agonists block the analgesia produced in stressful situations including "social defeat" (Rodgers & Randall, 1987b), innately recognized predators (Kavaliers, 1988), exposure to electric tail-shock (Doi & Sawa, 1980) and warning stimuli predicting a series of electric shocks (Willer & Ernst, 1986). We have demonstrated that three benzodiazepine agonists (diazepam, chlor-

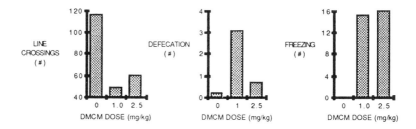

Figure 8.4 displays the frequency of three dependent measures taken simultaneously from rats in an open field as a function of DMCM dose. Tween 80 was added to DMCM and then ultrasonically dispersed in water.

diazepoxide and midazolam) block the analgesia produced by contextual fear stimuli (Fanselow & Helmstetter, 1988). It seems likely that benzodiazepines are most effective in preventing or reversing analgesia in situations where anxiety or fear is producing the changes in pain sensitivity. Since fear provoking stimuli produce analgesia and benzodiazepine agonists block the analgesia, it might be expected that BZP inverse agonists like DMCM would have effects opposite to agonists and similar to fear stimuli and thus, produce analgesia.

In our laboratory, analgesia is assessed by a suppression of the behaviors (paw licking and lifting) produced by a subcutaneous (sc) injection of a small amount of a dilute formalin solution into a hind paw (Fanselow, 1984; Fanselow & Baackes, 1982). For this experiment, rats were first injected sc with formalin (.05 ml, 15%) under the dorsal surface of the right hind paw. Twenty min later they were injected ip with DMCM (0, .5, 1, 1.5 mg/kg, ip). Ten min after DMCM injection they were placed in the observation chamber and scored for formalin-induced paw licking and lifting. Freezing behavior was also recorded. As can be seen in Figure 8.5, formalin-related behavior decreased linearly with dose ($F(1,21)=7.81$, $p<.02$), while freezing showed a linear increase ($F(1,21)=16.91$, $p<.001$). Thus there is some similarity between the behavior of rats that have previously been shocked in an observation chamber and nonshocked rats treated with DMCM, in so far as freezing and analgesia are concerned. It seems likely that the anxiolytic effects of benzodiazepines are mediated through an interaction with various forebrain structures that have been implicated in the experience of emotion. Radiolabelled benzodiazepines bind with relatively high densities in limbic structures such as the hippocampus and amygdala (Young & Kuhar, 1980) and microinjection of diazepam into the area of the amygdala reduces the analgesia and freezing produced by shock-associated contextual stimuli (Helmstetter, Leaton, Fanselow, & Calcagnetti, 1988). Possibly the anxiogenic actions of DMCM are to some extent related to the promotion of activity in these structures. In support of this, Ableitner and Herz (1987) reported that administration of DMCM and FG7142 results in a dramatic increase in the rate of local cerebral glucose utilization in the limbic sys-

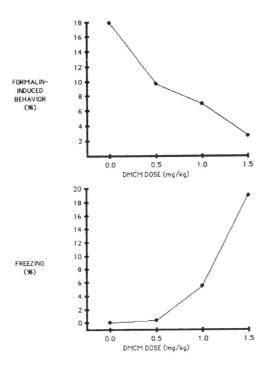

Figure 8.5 displays freezing and formalin-induced recuperative behaviors scored simultaneously in rats treated with various doses of DMCM. DMCM was suspended in water by adding Tween 80 and sonicating).

tem. In addition, intra-hippocampal injection of ß-carbolines has been reported to evoke defensive freezing behavior in rats (Huttunen & Myers, 1986). Based on the evidence for the involvement of these central structures in the anxiogenic effects of DMCM, we wished to further characterize this compound's analgesic effects by examining central administration of DMCM. Therefore, rather than systemic DMCM, the drug was injected directly into the cerebral ventricles. In order to extend the generality of DMCM's analgesic effects, rather than using the formalin test, the hot plate test was employed. Pavlovian conditional fear stimuli cause an elevated paw lick latency on this test (MacLennan, Jackson & Maier, 1980)

In the first of these experiments, the dose-effect relationship for DMCM when administered directly into the ventricular system was determined. Anesthetized rats were implanted with cannula into the right lateral ventricle. They were given a minimum of 10 days to recover from this surgery. On the test day they were given an intra-cerebro-ventricular (icv) injection of DMCM (0, .5, 1, 2.5, 10, or 20 µg/rat) and 20 min later they were placed on a 52 °C hot plate.

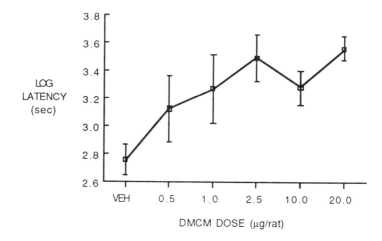

LOG
LATENCY
(sec)

DMCM DOSE (µg/rat)

Figure 8.6 shows the dose response function for the analgesic effects of DMCM (dissolved in acidified sterile water) on the hotplate. The data are the natural logarithm of the latency to paw lick.

The latency to lick a paw was recorded. If the rat did not lick in 90 s it was removed and given a latency score of 90 s. Figure 6 presents the mean latency to lick. As the concentration of DMCM increased, so did the animal's latency to respond to the thermal stimulation. Analysis of variance indicated that increases in paw lick latencies were linearly related to the dose of DMCM, $F(1,39) = 15.05$, $p < .001$. In order to confirm that the analgesia produced by DMCM was mediated by benzodiazepine receptors, a 5 µg dose of DMCM was administered in factorial combination with the selective BZP receptor antagonist, Ro15-1788. Animals were tested on the hot plate 20 min after drug injection. As can be seen in Figure 8.7, central injection of DMCM at 5 µg again produced an elevation of paw lick latency relative to vehicle injected controls, $F(1,14) = 4.75$, $p < .05$. This increase was reversed by ip administration of Ro15-1788. Interestingly, the group receiving both DMCM and Ro15-1788 had the lowest average latency. Paw lick responding in the DMCM/Ro15 group was significantly lower than that of all other treatment groups ($p < .05$). Rodgers and Randall (1987a) using the radiant heat tail-flick test reported that, in mice, DMCM produces an analgesia that is reversed by Ro15-1788. Similarly, conditional fear-induced analgesia has been reported using this test (Chance, 1980; Watkins, Cobelli, & Mayer, 1982). Therefore, with three commonly used assays of pain sensitivity (tail-flick, hot-plate & formalin) it has been shown that DMCM produces analgesia. Since all three assays have been used to demonstrate conditional fear-induced analgesia, the parallel between the behavioral sequelae of DMCM and contextual-fear is striking.

Analgesia in response to stress is in many cases produced via the release of endogenous opioid peptides (Terman, Shavit, Lewis, Cannon, & Liebeskind, 1984), and a good deal of evidence indicates that analgesia produced by condi-

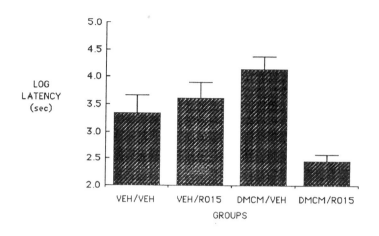

Figure 8.7 indicates that the analgesia produced by the 5 µg/rat (icv) dose of DMCM (in acidi-fied sterile water) is reversed by Ro15-1788 (ultrasonic suspension with Tween 80) adminis-tered ip. The data are the log latency to lick a paw following placement on the hotplate.

tional fear stimuli is nearly always opioid in nature (Watkins & Mayer, 1982). If DMCM were acting on some central system involved in the expression of fear or anxiety that corresponds at least in part to the system(s) responsible for the expression of conditional analgesia, then the analgesia produced by DMCM should also depend on the action of endogenous opioids. Therefore, the ability of the opioid antagonist naltrexone, which completely reverses conditional analgesia (Helmstetter & Fanselow, 1987), was tested for its ability to reverse the analgesia produced by central injection of DMCM.

Rats were given DMCM (20 µg/rat) or vehicle icv. This was followed by an ip injection of naltrexone (5 mg/kg) or placebo. Twenty min after icv injection the rats were given the hot plate test. Other procedural details were similar to those of the last experiment. The mean lick latencies are presented in Figure 8.8. Naltrexone did not effect baseline lick latencies in the vehicle treated animals ($F(1,17)<1$). DMCM elevated lick latencies relative to the vehicle controls ($F(1,17)=7.09$, $p<.02$). Rats treated with both DMCM and naltrexone did not differ from the vehicle controls, $F(1,17)=1.81$, $p>.19$). Thus DMCM produced analgesia and this analgesia was somewhat attenuated by naltrexone. Naltrexone's ability to block the analgesia produced by DMCM indicates that endogenous opioids play some role in this effect.

DMCM and the Acoustic Startle Response

When a loud auditory stimulus is presented to a rat in the presence of a cue that predicts shock, the amplitude of the animal's startle response is greater than in the presence of a "neutral" cue (Brown, Kalish, & Farber, 1951; Davis & As-trachan, 1978). This potentiation of startle by shock associated stimuli is as-sumed to reflect selective activation of a central fear-like motivational process (Davis, 1986). Evidence for this account includes the fact that a variety of

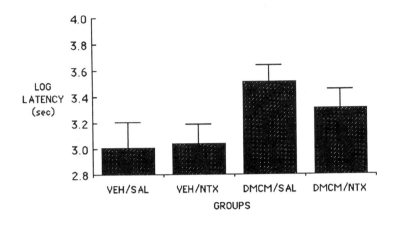

Figure 8.8 shows the log latency of rats to lick a paw following placement on a hotplate as a function of treatment with DMCM (0 or 20 μg, icv in acidified water) and naltrexone (5 or 0 mg/kg, ip in saline).

fear/anxiety reducing manipulations block potentiated startle without changing baseline reactivity (see Davis, 1986). Administration of BZP receptor agonists, for example, selectively block the potentiating effect of a shock associated light (Davis, 1979). Therefore, we tested the ability of DMCM to mimic the effects of fear producing signals on acoustic startle in the rat. If this benzodiazepine inverse-agonist promotes rather than reduces activity in the same central nervous system structures responsible for fear-potentiated startle through modulation at the BZP receptor, DMCM should enhance acoustic startle amplitude.

In the first experiment, three doses of DMCM within the range found effective in earlier studies were administered to naive rats 20 min before being placed in an apparatus designed to measure acoustic startle (see Leaton & Borszcz, 1985 for details). Animals received 50 presentations of a 125 dB / 100 msec burst of white noise at 1 min intervals. The output of a transducer, mounted under the apparatus, which was directly proportional to the amplitude of the startle response served as the dependent measure. The data shown in Figure 8.9 indicate that rather than increasing startle amplitude, as would be consistent with a purely anxiogenic effect of DMCM, the drug actually decreased startle, although the effect does not seem dose related. A repeated measures analysis of variance using averages based on ten-trial blocks indicated a statistically marginal main effect for drug group, $F(3,16) = 2.87$, $p < .07$, and a significant main effect for trial block, $F(4,64) = 3.84$, $p < .01$. The group by trial interaction was not significant. When startle amplitudes for the first ten trials were subjected to a separate analysis of variance both the group main effect ($F(3,16) = 3.84$, $p < .03$) and the trial main effect ($F(9,144) = 3.21$, $p < .01$) were reliable. Thus DMCM appears to produce a depression of the acoustic

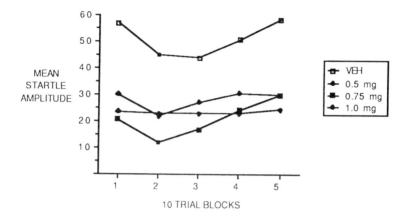

Figure 8.9 shows acoustic startle amplitude as a function of DMCM dose. The vehicle was acidified water.

startle response that does not interact with repeated stimulus presentations or time (see Davis, 1980 for a discussion of other compounds that decrease the amplitude of acoustic startle).

It is possible that DMCM reduces startle via some action at BZP receptor sites other than those responsible for the modulation of freezing and analgesia. BZP receptors in the periphery, for example, have been implicated in some of the sedative and muscle relaxant effects of BZP agonists and often cause behavioral reactions that are different from the effects of those produced at central BZP receptors (Drugan, Basile, Crawley, Paul, & Skolnick, 1987; File & Lister, 1983). To minimize the possibility of this result being due to a population of receptors outside the central nervous system, the effects of DMCM administered icv on acoustic startle were determined. The design of this experiment was essentially the same as previously described except that animals prepared with chronic ventricular cannula now received either 20 μg of DMCM or its vehicle 20 min prior to exposure to 30 presentations of the startle stimulus. Central administration of DMCM also depressed acoustic startle (see Figure 8.10). A drug x trials analysis of variance indicated significant suppression, $F(1,10) = 11.61$, $p < .01$, but no main effect for trial, or drug by trial interaction. Thus it appears that DMCM's ability to modulate startle amplitude is mediated by some central nervous system mechanism.

Repeated administration of BZP ligands will in many cases alter their effectiveness. Importantly, daily injections of BZP agonists often result in tolerance to their sedative and anticonvulsant effects first, followed after continued administration by tolerance to their anxiety-related effects (File, 1985). If the suppressant effect of DMCM on acoustic startle occurred by some mechanism that is similar to that responsible for the sedative effects of BZP agonists, then after repeated administration DMCM may loose its ability to suppress startle. A preliminary study to look at this possibility, using two

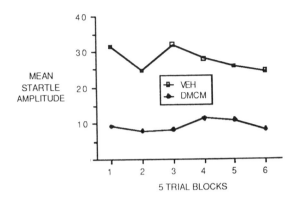

Figure 8.10 shows acoustic startle amplitude following icv administration of DMCM. The vehicle was acidified sterile water.

groups of rats that were used in another experiment, was conducted. In that other study, one group had received a single daily injection of DMCM at a dose that has been shown to suppress startle (.75mg) while the other group received comparable injections of the vehicle on each of 8 consecutive days. All animals received a single .5 mA /.5 footshock each day. On the following day (Day 9) animals were given the same drug treatment they had been receiving in the other study and were placed in the startle chamber and tested as in the previous experiment. The data in Figure 8.11 indicate that DMCM was able to suppress startle amplitude in animals after chronic treatment to about the same extent as in naive animals (see above). This impression was supported by an analysis of variance that indicated a main effect for drug, $F(1,10) = 11.38$, $p <$ .01, but no effect of trials or drug by trial interaction. It is clear from these results that DMCM suppresses the acoustic startle response; a result directly opposite to that typically found with conditional fear stimuli. This surprising

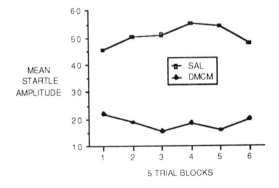

Figure 8.11 shows the effects of DMCM on startle in rats that were chronically treated with DMCM. The drug was prepared in acidified water.

result can not be easily dismissed as artifactual because it was found in several experiments following both systemic, icv and chronic administration. Furthermore, while reports of potentiation typically use a light CS, potentiation is also found with conditioned contextual stimuli (Melia, Campeau, & Davis, personal communication).

ENDOGENOUS INVERSE AGONIST LIGANDS AS MEDIATORS OF CONDITIONAL FEAR

A question of considerable interest is what natural purpose do benzodiazepine receptors serve in animals that have not been treated with pharmacological agents? One intriguing possibility would be if an endogenous inverse agonist mediated the production of fear. This hypothesis predicts that fear producing stimuli lead to the release of natural ligands for the benzodiazepine receptor and these ligands, because they act as inverse agonists, generate the responses recognized as fear. While no endogenous benzodiazepine ligand has been conclusively identified, several candidates have been suggested (Braestrup et al., 1980; Ferrero et al., 1986; Ferrero, Santi, Conti-Tronconi, Costa, & Guidotti, 1985; Guidotti et al., 1983) and these seem to act as inverse agonists. There is a relatively straightforward test of this hypothesis. Benzodiazepine antagonists should antagonize the effects of endogenous ligands just as they do exogenous ligands. If a natural inverse agonist mediated fear-related behaviors such as freezing, then a benzodiazepine antagonist should reduce such behaviors. The data shown in the first experiment described actually provided a test of this hypothesis. As can be seen in Figure 8.2, rats that were freezing because they received shock previously, evidenced no alteration in the level of freezing because of the antagonist Ro15-1788. It is not reasonable to argue that our dose of Ro15-1788 was insufficient as it completely reversed the effects of the very potent inverse agonist DMCM. As a further test of this prediction rats were given one shock a day (1 mA, .75 s) over 9 days. To provide an index of the acquisition of fear conditioning there was a three min observation period prior to

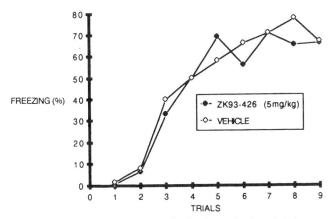

Figure 8.12 shows the percentage of a 3 min preshock period that rats spent freezing over 9 conditioning days. Rats were given ip injections of the BZP receptor antagonist ZK93-426 or its vehicle. Tween 80 was added to the drug and then it was ultrasonically dispersed in water.

shock delivery. Half the rats received the antagonist ZK93-426 (5 mg/kg) at a dose we previously found to completely block the effects of DMCM; the other half received vehicle. The data are presented in Figure 8.12. ZK93-426 never affected freezing. While this is a null result, several aspects of the finding make it convincing. First, at no point, neither when freezing was low nor when it was asymptotic, did ZK93-426 have an effect. Additionally, the dose was one that completely reversed the effects of DMCM; indeed it was sufficient to protect animals against lethal doses of the ß-carboline. Finally, the design was such that any effects whether they were on learning of the fear, performance of the fear, or both should have been detected, but none were. Thus our work with benzodiazepine antagonists provides no support for the idea that a natural inverse agonist-like ligand is a critical mediator of conditional fear. Nonetheless, there seems to be some correspondence between the behavioral effects of DMCM and the behaviors generated by Pavlovian fear stimuli. DMCM can enhance performance of the freezing response conditioned by shock. By itself, DMCM can provoke freezing and cause a reduction in pain-related behaviors similar to that of conditional fear-induced analgesia. This pattern of findings is consistent with the suggestion that administration of inverse agonists of the benzodiazepine receptor can result in a fear-like state as well as enhance an already conditioned fear. Perhaps the natural function of the benzodiazepine receptor may be more to modulate then to mediate fear. It may be interesting to examine the effects of benzodiazepine antagonists in Pavlovian conditioning preparations where learned cues act as modulators rather than as direct generators of conditioned behavior such as Pavlovian inhibition and occasion setting (e.g., Holland, 1984; Rescorla, 1984).

Finally, the parallels between the effects of DMCM and Pavlovian fear were less than perfect. This was most notable in the acoustic startle preparation, where DMCM had the opposite effect from that expected for a fear producing agent. Another less than perfect parallel was that naltrexone, which can block conditional analgesia at relatively low doses, only weakly attenuated the analgesia produced by DMCM. This lack of a perfect parallel may be due to the fact that the GABA receptor complex is involved in far more than just the modulation of fear/anxiety. Indeed, between 30 to 60% of all synapses are believed to involve GABA (for review see Martin, 1987). Thus there is concern as to whether the differences between our fear conditioning preparations and our effects of DMCM are caused by the influence of DMCM on other response systems or if DMCM influences anxiety indirectly through its action on other response systems.

ABBREVIATIONS

BZP (benzodiazepine)
DMCM (6,7-dimethoxy-4-ethyl-β-carboline-3-carboxylic acid methyl ester).
ZK93-426 (5-isopropoxy-4-methyl-β-carboline-3-carboxylic acid ethyl ester)
GABA (γ-aminobutyric acid)
Ro15-1788 (ethyl-8-fluoro-5,6-dihydro-5-methyl-6-oxo-4H imidazo(1,5a)(1,4) benzodiazepine-3-carboxylate)

ACKNOWLEDGMENTS

This research was supported by National Science Foundation grant # BNS-8606787 to MSF. We thank the following for their generous gifts: Dr. D. N. Stephens of Schering, Berlin for DMCM and ZK93-426. Drs. W. Haefely, M. Da Prada and R. Eigenmann, of Hoffmann-La Roche, Basel, Switzerland, for Ro15-1788. Naltrexone was provided by the National Institute on Drug Abuse. Diazepam was purchased from Sigma chemicals. We appreciate the assistance of R. L. Calcagnetti throughout this research.

REFERENCES

Ableitner, A. & Herz, A. (1987). Changes in local cerebral glucose utilization induced by the ß-carbolines FG 7142 and DMCM reveal brain structures involved in the control of anxiety and seizure activity. *Journal of Neuroscience, 7*, 1047-1055.

Archer, J. (1973). Tests for emotionality in rats and mice: A review. *Animal Behaviour, 21*, 205-235.

Archer, J. (1974). Sex differences in the emotional behavior of three strains of laboratory rat. *Animal Learning & Behavior, 2*, 43-48.

Braestrup, C., Honore, T., Nielsen, M., Petersen, E. N., & Jensen, L. H. (1984). Ligands for benzodiazepine receptors with positive and negative efficacy. *Pharmacology, Biochemistry and Behavior, 33*, 859-862.

Braestrup, C. Nielsen, M., Honore, T., Jensen, L. H., & Petersen, E. N. (1983). Benzodiazepine receptor ligands with positive and negative efficacy. *Neuropharmacology, 22*, 1451-1457.

Braestrup, C., Nielsen, M., & Olsen, C.E., (1980). Urinary and brain B-carboline-3-carboxylates as potent inhibitors of brain benzodiazepine receptors. *Proceedings of the National Academy of Sciences USA, 77*, 2288-2292.

Brown, J.S. , Kalish, H.I., & Farber, I.E. (1951). Conditional fear as revealed by the magnitude of startle response to an auditory stimulus. *Journal of Experimental Psychology, 41*, 317-327.

Chance, W.T. (1980). Autoanalgesia: Opiate and nonopiate mechanisms. *Neuroscience & Biobehavioral Reviews, 4*, 55-67.

Cooper, S. J. (1986). ß-Carbolines characterized as benzodiazepine receptor agonists and inverse agonists produce bi-directional changes in palatable food consumption. *Brain Research Bulletin, 17*, 627-637.

Davis, M. (1979). Diazepam and Flurazepam: Effects on conditioned fear as measured with the potentiated startle paradigm. *Psychopharmacology, 62*, 1-7

Davis, M. (1980). Neurochemical modulation of sensory-motor reactivity: Acoustic and tactile startle reflexes. *Neuroscience and Biobehavioral Reviews, 4*, 241-263.

Davis, M. (1986). Pharmacological and anatomical analysis of fear conditioning using the fear-potentiated startle paradigm. *Behavioral Neuroscience, 100*, 814-824.

Davis, M., & Astrachan, D. I. (1978). Conditioned fear and startle magnitude: Effects of different footshock and backshock intensities in training. *Journal of Experimental Psychology: Animal Behavior Processes, 4*, 95-108.

Doi, T., & Sawa, N. (1980). Antagonistic effects of psycholeptic drugs on stress-induced analgesia. *Archives of International Pharmacodynamics and Therapeutics, 247*, 264-274.

Dorow, R., Horowski, R., Paschelke, G., Amin, M., & Braestrup, C., (1983). Severe anxiety induced by FG 7142, a B-Carboline ligand for benzodiazepine receptors. *Lancet, ii*, 98-99.

Drugan, R.C., Basile, A.S., Crawley, J.N., Paul, S.M., & Skolnick, P., (1987). "Peripheral" benzodiazepine binding sites in the Maudsley Reactive rat: Selective decrease confined to peripheral tissues, *Brain Research Bulletin, 18*, 143-145.

Fanselow, M.S. (1980). Conditional and unconditional components of post-shock freezing. *Pavlovian Journal of Biological Sciences, 15*, 177-182.

Fanselow, M.S. (1984). Shock-induced analgesia on the Formalin Test: Effects of shock severity, naloxone, hypophysectomy and associative variables. *Behavioral Neuroscience, 98*, 79-95.

Fanselow, M. S. & Baackes, M. P. (1982). Conditioned fear-induced opiate analgesia on the formalin test: Evidence for two aversive motivational systems. *Learning & Motivation, 13*, 200-221.

Fanselow, M.S. & Helmstetter, F.J., (1988). Conditional analgesia, defensive freezing & benzodiazepines. *Behavioral Neuroscience, 102*, 233-243.

Fanselow, M.S., & Tighe, T.J., (1988). Contextual conditioning with massed versus distributed unconditioned stimuli in the absence of explicit conditional stimuli. *Journal of Experimental Psychology: Animal Behavior Processes, 14*, 187-199.

Ferrero, P., Conti-Tronconi, B., & Guidotti, A. (1986), DBI, an anxiogenic neuropeptide found in human brain. In G. Biggio & E. Costa (Eds), *GABAergic Transmission and Anxiety*, (pp. 177-185). New York: Raven Press.

Ferrero, P., Santi, M. R., Conti-Tronconi, B., Costa, E., & Guidotti, A., (1985). Study of an octadecaneuropeptide derived from diazepam binding inhibitor (DBI): Biological activity and presence in rat brain. *Proceedings of the National Academy of Sciences, U.S.A., 83*, 827-831.

File, S.E. (1985). Tolerance to the behavioral effects of benzodiazepines. *Neuroscience and Biobehavioral Reviews, 9*, 113-121.

File, S. E., & Baldwin, H.A. (1987). Effects of B-carbolines in animal models of anxiety, *Brain Research Bulletin, 19*, 293-299.

File, S. E., & Lister, R. G. (1983). The anxiogenic action of Ro-5-4864 is reversed by phenytoin. *Neuroscience Letters, 35*, 93-96.

File, S. E., & Pellow, S. (1984). The anxiogenic action of FG 7142 in the social interaction test is reversed by chlordiazepoxide and Ro15-1788 but not CGS 8216. *Archives of International Pharmacodynamics and Therapeutics, 271*, 198-205.

Gardner, C. R., & Budhram, P., (1987). Effects of agents which interact with central benzodiazepine binding sites on stress-induced ultrasounds in rat pups. *European Journal of Pharmacology, 134*, 275-283.

Guidotti, A., Forchetti, C. M., Corda, M. G., Konkel, D., Bennet, C. D., & Costa, E. (1983). Isolation, characterisation and purification to homogeneity of an endogenous polypeptide with agonistic action on Benzodiazepine receptors. *Procedings of the National Academy of Science U.S.A., 80*, 3531-3535.

Helmstetter, F. J., & Fanselow, M. S. (1987). Effects of naltrexone on learning and performance of conditional fear-induced freezing and opioid analgesia. *Physiology and Behavior, 39*, 501-505.

Helmstetter, F. J., Leaton, R. N., Fanselow, M. S., & Calcagnetti, D. J. (1988). The amygdala is involved in the expression of conditional analgesia. *Society for Neuroscience: Abstracts, 14*, 1227.

Holland, P. C. (1984). Differential effects of reinforcement of an inhibitory feature after serial and simultaneous feature negative discrimination training. *Journal of Experimental Psychology: Animal Behavior Processes, 10*, 461-475.

Hunkeler, W., Mohler, H., Pieri, L., Pole, P., Bonetti, E. P., Cumin, R., Schaffner, R., & Haefely, W. (1981). Selective antagonists of benzodiazepines. *Nature, 290*, 514-516.

Huttunen, P., & Myers, R.D. (1986). Tetrahydro-B-Carboline micro-injected into the hippocampus induces an anxiety-like state in the rat. *Pharmacology Biochemistry and Behavior, 24*, 1733-1738.

Kavaliers, M. (1988). Brief exposure to a natural predator, the short-tail weasel, induces benzodiazepine sensitive analgesia in white-footed mice. *Physiology & Behavior, 43*, 187-193.

Lal, H., & Emmett-Oglesby, M. W. (1983). Behavioral analogues of anxiety. Animal models. *Neuropharmacology, 22*, 1423-1441.

Leaton, R.N., & Borszcz, G.S. (1985). Potentiated startle: Its relation to freezing and shock intensity in rats. *Journal of Experimental Psychology: Animal Behavior Processes. 11*, 421-428.

Little, H. J., Nutt, D. J., & Taylor, S. C. (1987). Kindling and withdrawal changes at the benzodiazepine receptor. *Journal of Psychopharmacology, 1*, 35-46.

MacLennan, A.J., Jackson, R.L., & Maier, S.F. (1980). Conditioned analgesia in the rat. *Bulletin of the Psychonomic Society, 15*, 387-390.

Martin, I. L. (1987). The benzodiazepines and their receptors: 25 years of progress. *Neuropharmacology, 26*, 957-970.

Niehoff, D., & Kuhar, M.J., (1983). Benzodiazepine receptors: Localization in rat amygdala. *Journal of Neuroscience, 3*, 2091-2097.

Petersen, E. N. (1983). DMCM: a potent convulsive benzodiazepine receptor ligand. *European Journal of Pharmacology, 94*, 117-124, .

Rescorla, R. A. (1984). Inhibition and facilitation. In R. R. Miller & N. E. Spear (Eds.), *Information processing in animals: Conditioned inhibition* (pp. 299-326). Hillsdale, NJ: Lawrence Erlbaum Associates.

Rodgers, R. J., & Randall, J. I. (1987a). Are the analgesic effects of social defeat mediated by benzodiazepine receptors? *Physiology and Behavior, 41*, 279-289.

Rodgers, R. J., & Randall, J. I. (1987b). Benzodiazepine ligands, nociception and 'defeat' analgesia. *Psychopharmacology, 91*, 305-315.

Schofield, P.R., Darlison, M.G., Fujita, N., Burt, D.R., Stephenson, F.A., Rodriguex, H., Rhee, L.M., Ramachandran, J., Reale, V., Glencorse, T.A., Seeburg, P.H., & Barnard, E.A. (1987). Sequence and functional expression of the GABA receptor shows a ligand-gated receptor super-family, *Nature, 328*, 221-227.

Stephens, D.N., & Kehr, W. (1985). B- Carbolines can enhance or antagonize the effects of punishment in mice, *Psychopharmacology, 85*, 143-147.

Stephens, D. N., Kehr, W., & Duka, T. (1986). Anxiolytic and anxiogenic ß-carbolines: Tools for the study of anxiety mechanisms. In G. Biggio & E. Costa (Eds), *GABAergic transmission and anxiety* (pp. 91-106). New York: Raven Press.

Stephens, D. N., Kehr, W., Schneider, H. H., & Schmiechen, R. (1984). ß-carbolines with agonistic and inverse agonistic properties at benzodiazepine receptors of the rat. *Neuroscience Letters, 47*, 333-338.

Terman, G. W., Shavit, Y., Lewis, J. W., Cannon, J. T., & Liebeskind, J. C. (1984). Intrinsic mechanisms of pain inhibition: Activation by stress. *Science, 226*, 1270-1277.

Walsh, R. N. & Cummins, R. A. (1976). The open-field test: A critical review. *Psychological Bulletin, 83*, 482-504.

Watkins, L.R., Cobelli, D.A., & Mayer, D.J. (1982). Classical conditioning of front paw and hind paw footshock induced analgesia (FSIA): Naloxone reversibility and descending pathways. *Brain Research, 243*, 119-132.

Watkins, L. R., & Mayer, D. J. (1982). Organization of endogenous opiate and nonopiate pain control systems. *Science, 216*, 1185-1192.

Willer, J. C., & Ernst, M. (1986). Somatovegetative changes in stress-induced analgesia in man: An electrophysiological and pharmacological study. *Annals of the New York Academy of Sciences, 467*, 256-272.

Young, W.S., & Kuhar, M.J. (1980). Radiohistichemical localization of benzodiazepine receptors in rat brain. *Journal of Pharmacology and Experimental Therapeutics, 212*, 337-346.

9 Incentive Contrast and Selected Animal Models of Anxiety

Charles F. Flaherty
Rutgers—The State University

The first section of this chapter will be concerned with a pharmacological analysis of negative contrast in consummatory behavior. In the second section the pharmacological profile of negative contrast will be compared to those obtained in three selected animal models of anxiety—operant conflict, punished drinking, and potentiated startle.

The term *contrast effect* refers to an exaggeration of the effect of reward on behavior when an animal experiences two or more rewards (Dunham, 1968). Contrast effects are pervasive in animal behavior, occurring in operant tasks, mazes, runways, electrical stimulation of the brain, and consummatory behavior. All that seems to be necessary is the opportunity for animals to experience two or more reward levels, within certain parametric constraints, and an experiment appropriately designed to measure the contrast effects (Bitterman, 1975; Flaherty, 1982; Mackintosh, 1974; McSweeney, 1982; Mellgren, 1972; Williams, 1983).

The experiments to be considered in this chapter are, for the most part, concerned with successive negative contrast. Rats shifted from a large to a small reward in a runway generally show an abrupt decrement in running speed to a level slower than that of animals that have experienced only the lower level of reward (e.g., Crespi, 1942; Daly, 1974; Gonzalez, Gleitman, & Bitterman, 1962). It is the slower running by the shifted animals, as compared to the unshifted animals, that is referred to as a successive negative contrast effect (SucNCE). Successive negative contrast generally dissipates after a number of trials, depending upon other parameters of the experiment. The degree of successive negative contrast varies directly with the degree of difference between preshift and postshift reward (Crespi, 1942; DiLollo & Beez, 1966; Gonzalez et al., 1962) and inversely with the time between the last experience with the preshift reward and the first experience with the postshift reward (E. J. Capaldi, 1972; Gleitman & Steinman, 1964; Gonzalez, Fernhoff, & David, 1973).

CONTRAST EFFECTS IN CONSUMMATORY BEHAVIOR

Successive negative contrast also occurs in consummatory behavior. For example, rats given access to 32% sucrose for five minutes a day consume more than rats given access to 4% sucrose. If the 32% group is shifted to 4% sucrose there is a precipitous decline in lick frequency to a level substantially below that of animals maintained on the 4% sucrose solution. This negative contrast effect typically diminishes in degree over a three or four day postshift period (Lombardi & Flaherty, 1978; Vogel, Mikulka & Spear, 1968). As is the case with contrast obtained in runway behavior, degree of contrast in consummatory behavior varies directly with the degree of difference between preshift and postshift sucrose (Flaherty, Becker & Osborne, 1983) and inversely with the length of the retention interval between the preshift and postshift periods (Ciszewski & Flaherty, 1977; Flaherty & Lombardi, 1977). Contrast is obtained in free-feeding as well as deprived animals. The principal difference between the two conditions seems to be faster recovery from contrast in deprived animals (Riley & Dunlap, 1979).

Negative contrast in consummatory behavior also occurs if a sucrose solution is adulterated with quinine (Flaherty & Rowan, 1989b), and with shifts in the concentration of saccharin solutions. But whether or not contrast is obtained in the latter procedure may critically depend on the degree of difference between the two solutions and also possibly on the absolute values of the solutions selected (Flaherty & Rowan, 1986; Vogel et al., 1968). Particularly robust contrast effects may be obtained by shifting rats from sucrose solutions (20% or 32%) to a saccharin solution (0.15%) (Flaherty, Weaver, & Rowan, 1990).

The SucNC procedure may be regarded as one which involves a comparison process on the part of the animal; one which demonstrates psychological relativity; and one which may serve as an animal model of disappointment.

Basic Data

In the typical experiment, one group of rats is given access to a 32% sucrose solution and another group access to a 4% sucrose solution for five minutes each day for ten days. Over the following four days both groups are given the 4% sucrose.

As illustrated in Figure 9.1, the 32% group generally consumes more than the 4% group during the preshift period. The shift to 4% leads to a precipitous decrease in lick frequency to a level approximating that of animals given a 2% sucrose solution. Rats typically recover from negative contrast in three to five days. However, if the experiment is conducted in an open field, contrast is more enduring and the decrease in licking is accompanied by an increase in activity (rearing and ambulation). Other behaviors, such as grooming and passive

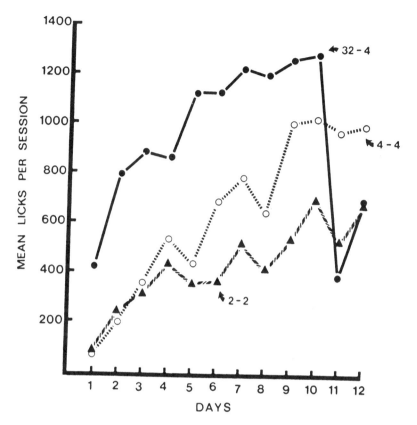

Figure 9.1. Mean lick frequency over the preshift period (Days 1-10) and postshift period (Days 11 and 12) as a function of sucrose concentration and concentration shift. In the post-shift period, the animals that had received the 32% concentration were shifted to 4% sucrose. The 4% and 2% groups remained under their original conditions. (From Flaherty, Becker, & Pohorecky, 1985).

sitting are not increased (e.g., Flaherty, Blitzer, & Collier, 1978; Flaherty, Powell, & Hamilton, 1979; Flaherty, Troncoso, & Deschu, 1979).

Interpretation

One interpretation of SucNC is that the decline in licking is due to a generalization decrement or neophobic process. That is, the postshift solution is not "worse" than the preshift solution, it is just different. The analogy in instrumental learning would be training an animal to run in a white runway and then shifting the animal to a black runway. You would expect a decrement in running because the animal had not been trained to run in a black runway (E.D. Capaldi, 1978). This interpretation portrays negative contrast as a largely passive response to stimulus change.

However, the data suggest that contrast involves more than this. The effect of adding a novel stimulus, a loud tone, coincident with the shift in sucrose so-

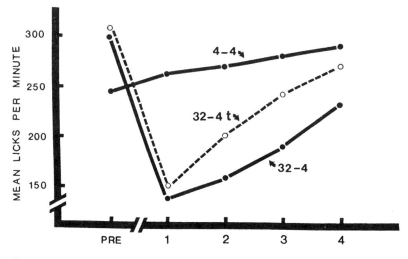

Figure 9.2. Mean lick frequency on terminal preshift day (PRE) and daily postshift sessions (1-4) in unshifted animals (4-4), shifted animals (32-4) and shifted animals with a novel tone added coincident with the shift (32-4t). (From Lombardi & Flaherty, 1978).

lutions is illustrated in Figure 9.2. The novel tone had no influence on the shifted animals on the first postshift day, but the tone reliably reduced the degree of contrast on subsequent postshift days (Lombardi & Flaherty, 1978). Additional experiments showed that a novel tone did not influence unshifted animals, nor did it influence animals given access to a 2% sucrose solution, a condition which produces lick frequencies approximately equivalent to that of the shifted animals on the first postshift day.

These results suggest that novelty is not a principal cause of contrast since added novelty, the tone, served to reduce contrast, not increase it. Furthermore, the control conditions suggest that the tone does not increase licking because of some energization effect, or rate-dependent energizing effect, since the lick rates of the 4% controls and the 2% controls were not affected by the tone. The data are most compatible with the assumption that the shifted group actively inhibits licking and the novel tone serves as a disinhibitor in the Pavlovian fashion (Black, 1968). Thus, negative contrast seems to be an active and not a passive process.

It also seems to be aversive—at least as indicated by levels of the stress hormone corticosterone. As shown in the left panel of Figure 9.3, there was no elevation in corticosterone on the first day after a shift from 32% to 4% sucrose, but there was a substantial elevation on the second postshift day (right panel). Separate groups of animals were used for the first and second postshift day measurements. Note also that an additional group, which received 2% sucrose, was included as a lick-rate control (Flaherty, Becker, & Pohorecky, 1985). These results suggest that a downshift in sucrose concentration is stressful (cf. Daly, 1974), but perhaps only on the second day after the shift.

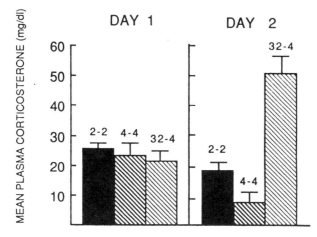

Figure 9.3. Corticosterone levels taken five minutes after session end on either the first or second postshift day in shifted (32-4), unshifted (4-4), and unshifted lick frequency (2-2) groups (From Flaherty, Becker, & Pohorecky, 1985).

If reward downshift is stressful, and if the stress is causally related to the behavioral aspects of contrast, then drugs that serve to alleviate stress might also alleviate contrast. Evidence that this would be the case has been obtained previously in studies of contrast effects in instrumental responding (Ridgers & Gray, 1973; Rosen, Glass, & Ison, 1967; Rosen & Tessel, 1970).

We found that the administration of the anxiolytic chlordiazepoxide (CDP) will eliminate SucNC when the drug is administered on the second postshift day (Flaherty, Lombardi, Wrightson, & Deptula, 1980). Contrast returns on the third postshift day, when the drug is no longer administered. This effect is dose-dependent, with a dose of 6 mg/kg, but not 4 mg/kg, being effective in reliably reducing contrast (Figure 9.4). Further dose/response data will be considered below.

Similar results have been obtained with other benzodiazepine tranquilizers such as midazolam (Becker, 1986) and flurazepam (unpublished experiments). Our interpretation of these data is that contrast, at least on the second postshift day, involves an emotional response that is causally related to degree of contrast.

However, the benzodiazepine tranquilizers have a number of effects in addition to anxiety reduction. They are muscle relaxants, anti-convulsants, sedatives, and, most importantly for our interests, they are appetite stimulants (e.g., Cooper & Estall, 1985). Is it possible that the enhanced recovery from contrast that we interpret as an anxiolytic effect is really only a reflection of the appetite stimulating aspects of the benzodiazepines?

There are several controls for this possibility. One is the unshifted 4% animals that are injected with the drug. If the effect of the tranquilizers was simply to increase sucrose consumption, then this group should be affected as much as the shifted group and, thus, there would be no contrast reduction. But this is not the case; the rats shifted from 32% to 4% sucrose show a much

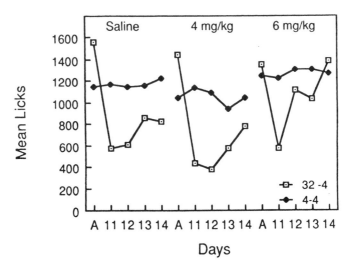

Figure 9.4. Administration of 6 mg/kg, but not 4 mg/kg, of chlordiazepoxide on the second postshift day (Day 12) reliably reduces contrast.

greater increase in lick frequency than the rats that have been maintained on 4% sucrose. Thus, there is something special about the shift that determines the effectiveness of CDP.

There are also cases in which CDP is ineffective in reducing contrast but, in some of these cases, it does have an appetite stimulating effect—suggesting that the two effects are not necessarily related.

The first case involves contrast in free-feeding rats. As illustrated in Figure 9.5, the injection of CDP on the second postshift day did not reduce contrast in free-feeding rats even though it increased intake—it did so equally in shifted and unshifted animals. Apparently, the animals must be in a state of deprivation in order for CDP to reduce contrast.

A second situation is presented in Figure 9.6. Illustrated here are the effects of chlordiazepoxide on the Syracuse High Avoidance (SHA) and Syracuse Low Avoidance (SLA) rats. These rats were from strains bred by Brush (1985) for avoidance performance. There is some evidence that the poor avoidance rats are high in emotionality and the good avoidance rats low in emotionality (Brush, 1985). In our laboratory, the SLA rats showed a significantly larger contrast effect than the SHA rats and CDP was differentially effective in the two strains. The drug substantially and reliably reduced contrast in the SLA animals but had no effect at all in the SHA animals (Flaherty & Rowan, 1989a).

The next two examples are derived from contrast procedures different from successive negative contrast. The first of these we term *simultaneous contrast*. If rats are given repeated and alternating brief access periods to solutions of 32% sucrose and 4% sucrose, they will consume more 32% than they will if only the 32% is available, and less 4% than they will if only the 4% is available (Flaherty & Largen, 1975).

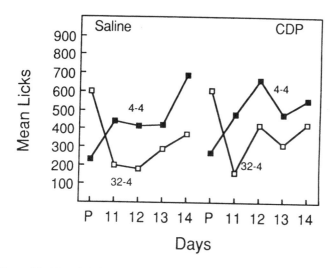

Figure 9.5. The administration of chlordiazepoxide (8 mg/kg) on the second postshift day (Day 12) to free-fed rats reliably increased sucrose intake in both shifted and unshifted animals but did not differentially reduce contrast (unpublished data.) The same dose eliminated contrast in deprived animals (e.g., Flaherty et al., 1980).

These positive and negative contrast effects are apparent in Figure 9.7 which, reading from left to right, illustrates lick frequency for 32% when it is alternated with 4%, lick frequency for 32% when it is presented alone, lick frequency for 4% when it is presented alone, and lick frequency for 4% when it is alternated with 32%. This figure illustrates both positive contrast (32-4 > 32-32) and negative contrast (4-32 < 4-4).

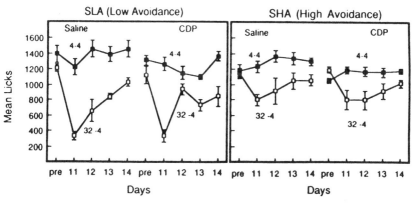

Figure 9.6. Effect of chlordiazepoxide (8mg/kg), injected on Day 12, the second postshift day, on contrast in Syracuse High Avoidance (SHA) and Syracuse Low Avoidance (SLA) rats. The SHA group showed a reliably smaller contrast effect, and one that was uninfluenced by the drug (From Flaherty & Rowan, 1989a).

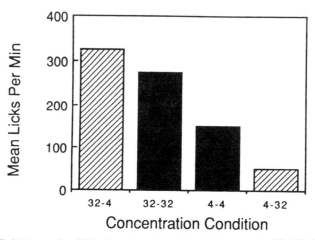

Figure 9.7. Lick rate for 32% when the alternative bottle contains 4% (32-4), etc., in a "simultaneous" contrast paradigm (see Flaherty & Largen, 1975). Both positive and negative contrast effects are typically obtained using this procedure of rapid and repeated alternation between two solutions.

These contrast effects may be importantly related to adaptation of the taste receptors (e.g., Bartoshuk & Gent, 1984). That is, the sensory stimulation provided by 4% sucrose which immediately follows adaptation to 32% may be different from the sensory stimulation provided by 4% applied to unadapted taste receptors.

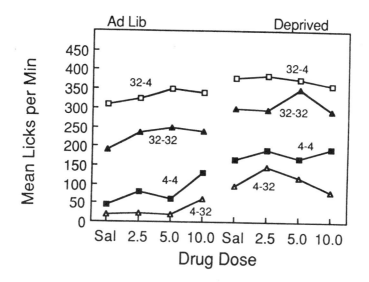

Figure 9.8. Effect of chlordiazepoxide (2.5, 5.0 or 10.0 mg/kg on simultaneous contrast. The drug did not reliably affect contrast in either free-fed or deprived rats (from Flaherty et al., 1977).

The simultaneous negative contrast effect (SimNCE) obtained with this procedure is not affected by the same disinhibitory stimulus that reduces successive negative contrast (Lombardi & Flaherty, 1978). As illustrated in Figure 9.8, SimNCE is also not affected by CDP in doses of 2.5, 5, or 10 mg/kg in either ad-lib or deprived animals—even though the drug tended to have an appetite-stimulating effect (Flaherty, Lombardi, Kapust, & D'Amato, 1977). Thus, this is another case in which consummatory behavior is suppressed and this suppression is not alleviated by a tranquilizer.

A similar finding has been obtained in yet another contrast paradigm—one that we term *anticipatory contrast*. In this paradigm rats are given single daily pairings of a 0.15% saccharin solution and a 32% sucrose solution. Typically, the animals are given access to the saccharin solution for a three minute period, then there is a break of 15 seconds, and then they have access to the preferred 32% sucrose solution. Because they experience this sequence only once each day, there is no opportunity for the sensory effects of the sucrose to influence the responsivity of the taste receptors to the saccharin solution. A control group is given access to the saccharin solution twice.

As shown in the left panel of Figure 9.9, the intake of the initial saccharin solution is suppressed in the saccharin-sucrose group compared to the saccharin-saccharin group (Flaherty & Rowan, 1988). Other studies have shown that this suppression does not occur if the second substance is 2% sucrose, which is not preferred to the saccharin solution. Also, degree of suppression is inversely related to length of the intersolution interval (Flaherty & Checke, 1982).

Anticipatory contrast has been interpreted as indicating that the animals learn the sequential relationship between the first and the second substances and

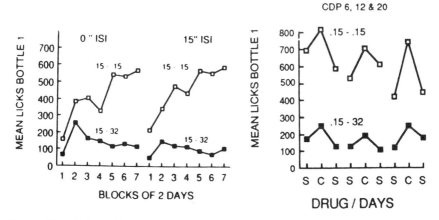

Figure 9.9. Left Panel. Mean lick frequency for a 0.15% saccharin solution when it preceded either 0.15% saccharin (.15-.15) or 32% sucrose (.15-32). The intersolution interval (ISI) of zero or 15 seconds had no effect on degree of suppression of saccharin intake in the .15-32 condition. Right Panel. Continuation of same animals with the ISI conditions collapsed. The rats were injected with either saline (S) or chlordiazepoxide (C) in a series of three-day drug cycles in which the drug dose was increased (6, 12, or 20 mg/kg) (from Flaherty & Rowan, 1988).

that this association, once formed, leads to the anticipation of the preferred second substance (Flaherty & Grigson, 1988; Flaherty & Rowan, 1986). The suppression of intake of the predictive saccharin solution is, we believe, not related to a negative emotion, as is successive negative contrast, but is instead related to the anticipation of a hedonically preferred substance. The anticipation of a caloric load is probably not an important factor in this procedure since anticipatory contrast also occurs when both the first and second substances are saccharin (Flaherty & Rowan, 1986), although the effect is greater in the saccharin-sucrose procedure.

The effects of CDP on anticipatory contrast are illustrated in the right hand panel of Figure 9.9. These data represent a continuation of the experiment shown in the left panel. The drug treatments were administered in three-day blocks. The first and third days of each cycle were saline control days; on the second day of each cycle the animals were injected with CDP (6, 12, and 20 mg/kg). In between each cycle the animals were given a day off. There was no tendency for the drug to reduce the anticipatory contrast effect—even though there was a clear and reliable appetite-stimulating effect of the drug (Flaherty & Rowan, 1988). The drug doses used in this experiment were more than enough to completely eliminate successive negative contrast. A similar lack of effect of CDP on anticipatory contrast was recently obtained with the Maudsley reactive and Maudsley nonreactive rats (Rowan, 1988).

Thus, of three contrast procedures, successive, simultaneous, and anticipatory, CDP is effective in alleviating only successive negative contrast. These data suggest that something other than the appetite-stimulating effects of the benzodiazepine tranquilizers are responsible for the contrast-reducing properties of the drugs. Our hypothesis is that the successive negative contrast procedure involves an aversive emotional state, perhaps something akin to disappointment, but that the simultaneous and anticipatory procedures do not involve such a state.

The Process of Recovery from Contrast

The drug data considered in regard to the successive contrast procedure thus far have been concerned with the effects of administering CDP on the second postshift day. There is a difference in the effectiveness of the drug on the first and second postshift days. Recall that the presentation of a novel tone has a disinhibitory effect on the second and subsequent postshift days (Figure 9.2) and that corticosterone is elevated on the second postshift day but not on the first postshift day (Figure 9.3). It happens that CDP is ineffective on the first postshift day. The drug, injected on Day 1 postshift, generally has an appetite-stimulating effect, but does not reduce contrast. However, CDP injected on the second postshift day statistically eliminates contrast (see Figure 9.10).

We have investigated several possible reasons for this difference in the effectiveness of CDP across the first two postshift days. One possibility is that the drug effects are due to the differential retention interval between the last preshift day and the first and second postshift days. In order for the animals to show a contrast effect they must be able to compare the postshift solution with

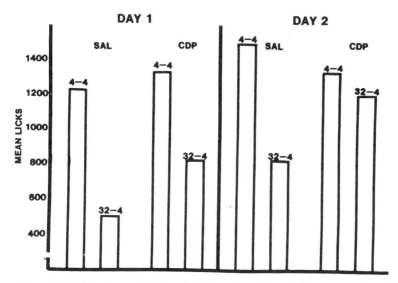

Figure 9.10. Chlordiazepoxide (8 mg/kg) injected on either the first or second postshift day. The drug had no effect on the first day, but reliably reduced contrast when injected for the first time on the second postshift day (from Flaherty et al., 1980).

the *memory* of the preshift solution (Spear, 1967). On the second postshift day there has been a 48 hour retention interval in regard to the last experience with the preshift solution whereas there has been only a 24 hour interval on the first

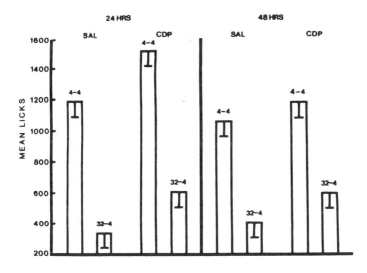

Figure 9.11. Chlordiazepoxide (8 mg/kg) injected on the first postshift day, which came either 24 or 48 hours after the last experience with the preshift solution. The drug did not reliably reduce contrast under either condition (from Flaherty, Grigson, & Rowan, 1986).

postshift day. Perhaps CDP is effective on the second postshift day because the contrast is weaker due to a less effective comparison with the memory of the preshift solution.

In order to test this possibility we conducted an experiment in which the first postshift day was given either 24 or 48 hours after the last preshift day. The results of this experiment(illustrated in Figure 9.11) show that CDP did not reduce contrast under either condition, although it did have an appetite-stimulating effect (Flaherty, Grigson & Rowan, 1986). Thus, retention interval is not responsible for the differential effectiveness of CDP on the first and second postshift days.

Another possibility is that the animals must have some experience with the postshift solution before the CDP becomes effective. What we term the first and second postshift day is somewhat arbitrary since it is based on our procedure of giving the animals access to the sucrose solutions for only five minutes per day.

In the next experiment we gave the rats access to the postshift solution for 20 minutes on the first postshift day. Thus, we included all four postshift "days", in a manner of speaking, into the first experience with the postshift solution. Lick frequency was then recorded on a minute to minute basis in animals injected with either saline or CDP (8 mg/kg). The results of this experiment showed that the drug was ineffective during the first five minutes of exposure but, in the second five minute period, CDP reliably reduced contrast

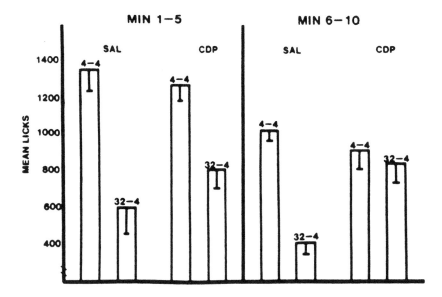

Figure 9.12. Chlordiazepoxide (8 mg/kg) reduced contrast in the second five minute period of exposure (right panel), but not in the first five minute period (left panel). The drug was administered 30 minutes prior to the start of the session (from Flaherty, Grigson & Rowan, 1986).

(see Figure 9.12). Similar results were obtained in a replication of this experiment (Flaherty et al., 1986).

To summarize the data thus far, the successive negative contrast effect that occurs when rats are shifted from 32% to 4% sucrose may be reduced by a novel tone and eliminated by CDP, but both of these treatments are effective only on the second postshift day. The shift also elevates corticosterone levels, but again only on the second postshift day. The failure of CDP to affect contrast on the first postshift day seems unrelated to a retention-interval factor, but it may be related to the amount of experience that the subjects have with the postshift solution.

One hypothesis as to why this pattern of results is obtained is that the downshift in sucrose concentration triggers a sequence of psychological processes. First, the rats must detect that a change has taken place. This detection must involve a comparison of the postshift solution with the memory of the preshift solution. Second, an evaluation must be made. The postshift solution is not only different, it is less sweet—poorer in a hedonic sense—than the preshift solution. These processes may require time and experience with the postshift solution. Third, once the evaluation is made, the animals may enter a conflict stage—oscillating between consuming the postshift solution because of its absolute rewarding properties (animals will consume a substantial amount of 4% sucrose), or avoiding it because of its poor relative rewarding properties, in comparison to the memory of the 32% solution.

It is perhaps during this conflict stage that contrast is aversive and during this stage that the benzodiazepines are effective in reducing contrast. It is interesting that most animal models of anxiety, the procedures that have been developed to screen potential anxiolytics, involve an explicit conflict procedure—often between obtaining food and receiving shock concurrently.

In order to test the memory/recognition-time aspect of this hypothesis, we conducted experiments in which the animals were given an initial period (prior to preshift training) of experience with the 4% sucrose solution. Some animals were given a period of either four or ten days with the 4% sucrose, then the usual 10-day preshift period and then were shifted to 4% again. Other animals were given prior experience with the 4% sucrose in the context of the simultaneous contrast procedure (alternating 32% and 4%) for three days prior to preshift training. The assumption in these experiments was that the prior experience with the postshift shift solution would facilitate recognition time and, perhaps, hasten the development of conflict and, thereby, the point of effectiveness of CDP. On the first postshift day, half of each group was injected with CDP (10 mg/kg) and half with saline. In no case did CDP lead to a reliable reduction of contrast even though the prior training experience (in the case of the 10-day pre-exposure condition) did lead to a smaller contrast effect on the first postshift day (Flaherty, Grigson, & Lind, 1990).

These data signal a flaw in the initial hypothesis. That is, the data suggest that the failure of CDP to be effective on the first postshift day may not be due to an initial period of detection and evaluation during which CDP plays no role. Another explanation for the inactivity of CDP on the first postshift day must be sought.

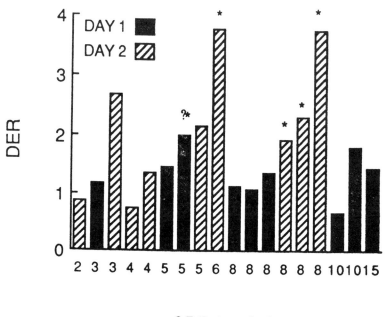

CDP (mg/kg)

Figure 9.13. Drug Effectiveness Ratios (DER) for different doses of chlordiazepoxide administered on either the first or second postshift day in various experiments (see text).

However, before coming to a conclusion regarding the inactivity of CDP on the first postshift day additional dose/response data were collected. In two experiments, the effects of 3-, 5-, 10-, and 15-mg/kg of CDP administered on the first postshift day were examined. Although one of these experiments indicated that a low dose of CDP (5 mg/kg) might have a marginally reliable effect on the first postshift day, this was not replicated in an additional experiment (Flaherty, Grigson, & Lind, 1990). Thus, there seems little doubt that CDP is considerably more effective in reducing SucNC in consummatory behavior when administered for the first time on the second postshift day than when administered on the first postshift day. In fact, there is scant evidence that it has a reliable effect at all on the first day whereas the drug, in an appropriate dose, will statistically eliminate contrast on the second postshift day.

One method of illustrating this difference is shown in Figure 9.13 in which Drug Effectiveness Ratios (DERs) are presented for the several doses of CDP used on the first and second postshift days across a number of experiments. The DER accounts for preshift differences in lick frequency by examining postshift data in terms of proportions (P) of preshift values (i.e., Day 11/(day 10 +Day 11) or Day 12/(Day 10 + Day12)). The effectiveness of the drug is then examined by obtaining a ratio of the difference between saline injected unshifted and shifted animals and drug injected unshifted and shifted animals:

$$DER = \frac{(P(\text{unshifted saline}) - P(\text{shifted saline}))}{(P(\text{unshifted drug}) - P(\text{shifted drug}))}$$

The greater the effect of the drug in reducing contrast, the larger the DER. It is apparent from Figure 9.13 that CDP is considerably more potent on the second postshift day.

If the results of the pretreatment experiments suggest that it is not a recognition/evaluation process that accounts for the lag in the effectiveness of CDP in reducing contrast, what remains as a possibility? The dose/response data give no indication that a higher dose of CDP is more likely to be effective. Indeed, the animals given a 15 mg/kg dose, the highest investigated, showed some signs of sedation (Flaherty, Grigson, & Lind, 1990). It is not the difference in passage of time per se between the first and second postshift days because CDP is ineffective whether the first postshift day is given 24 or 48 hours following the last experience with the preshift solution (Flaherty et al., 1986). It also seems unlikely that the ineffectiveness of CDP on the first postshift day is due to there being a greater stress response on this day. The indication from corticosterone measures, at least, suggests that the second day is stressful, whereas the first postshift day is not (Flaherty et al., 1985).

A possible interpretation of the lag in the effectiveness of CDP is the following. The drug does not become effective until an endogenous recovery processes is underway. Behavioral evidence derived from minute-by-minute recording of lick frequency indicates that recovery does not normally begin until the second postshift day (Meinrath & Flaherty, 1987, 1988) or until the fourth to sixth minute of continuous exposure (Flaherty et al., 1986). Recovery (consuming the 4% solution—the only available solution) is probably driven by the deprivation condition of the animal since free-fed animals are slow to recover (Riley & Dunlap, 1979) and CDP is apparently ineffective in such animals (unpublished data).

The initial response to reward reduction may involve a rejection of the new reward and a search for the old reward. Indeed, one of the earliest explanations for negative contrast in maze behavior was that the rats' entries into blind alleys subsequent to reward downshift were not errors but rather represented searching or exploratory responses (Elliott, 1928). A similar interpretation may apply to the consummatory contrast procedure since rats downshifted in sucrose concentration show substantial increases in ambulation and rearing (Flaherty et al., 1978; Flaherty, Powell, & Hamilton, 1979), behaviors often associated with exploration. Furthermore, if a novel source of sucrose is placed in an open field concurrently with the shift, the downshifted animals (as well as the controls) quickly sample from the novel source. However, if the novel source is the same concentration as the postshift solution, the shifted rats tend to return to the original location (Flaherty et al., 1978). In a recently completed experiment, we found that rats shifted in the context of an eight-arm radial maze showed large and enduring contrast effects and the decrease in licks was accompanied by an abrupt increase in entries to the seven-arms that did not contain sucrose during the preshift period (see Figure 9.14)

The interpretation of contrast in terms of an initial "search" stage may have ecological validity in the sense that foraging animals may form an expectancy of the average level of "reward" available to them and they may leave a particular location if the reward available there falls below the expectation (Pyke, 1978; Waddington & Heinrich, 1981). The failure of CDP to have a substantial effect on contrast on the first postshift day may be because there is no conflict involved in this initial reaction to reward reduction. It is only after the animals has obtained sufficient information indicating that there is no bet-

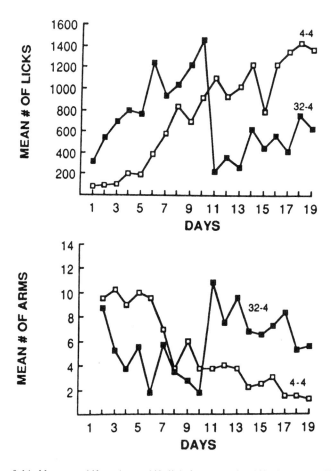

Figure 9.14. Mean preshift and postshift lick frequency in shifted and unshifted rats (top panel) and frequency of entry into arms that did not contain sucrose (bottom panel). The experiment was conducted in an eight-arm radial maze with only one arm containing the sucrose solution (Flaherty, Rothberg, & Noctor, 1990).

ter source of nutrition available than the postshift reward that conflict arises and only at this point that CDP becomes effective.

Although the data may be open to several interpretations, there is some evidence that benzodiazepines may increase exploratory behavior (Crawley, 1981; File, 1985; Pellow & File, 1986). If this were to prove to be the case, then, on the basis of the above hypothesis, circumstances might be found in which the same dose of CDP would enhance contrast initially after a reward reduction and subsequently accelerate recovery from contrast after the exploratory phase of the response to reward shift was completed. This hypothesis remains to be tested.

There is another approach to these results, one involving the neurochemical effects of the benzodiazepine tranquilizers. A principal effect of the benzodiazepines is the potentiation of the effectiveness of the inhibitory neurotransmitter gamma-amino-butyric acid (GABA). The benzodiazepines do this by binding to a specific benzodiazepine receptor which is closely allied with the GABA receptor. When GABA is released by the presynaptic neuron it binds to its receptor and opens Cl- ionophores, thereby hyperpolarizing the postsynaptic neuron. If a benzodiazepine is bound to its receptor, it potentiates the effects of GABA on the Cl- ionophore, thereby enhancing the inhibitory effects of GABA (e.g., Costa, 1983; also see Fanselow, Helmstetter, & Calcagnetti, Chap. 8 in this volume).

The relevance of this is that the benzodiazepines are neuromodulators, not neurotransmitters. That is, in the absence of GABA, the benzodiazepines do not, in and of themselves, affect the Cl- ionophore. Thus, the benzodiazepines would not be expected to have an effect in the absence of GABA.

It is possible, then, that the occurrence of a contrast effect triggers an endogenous recovery process that involves GABA and, until this recovery process is underway, the benzodiazepines are without effect. The Day 1-Day 2 postshift data may mean that the recovery process requires a period of some five minutes of experience with the postshift solution, *and* a search of the environment that indicates the continued absence of the preshift reward, before recovery is initiated.   This hypothesis is speculation at this time, but it is potentially testable. For example, GABA agonists (e.g., muscimol) should tend to produce recovery on the first postshift day. The hypothesis also suggests a variety of experiments which manipulate conditions of environmental novelty and exploration, conditions of deprivation, and drug administration on the first and second postshift days. The hypothesis also suggests connections to loss of valued objects in humans, where the first response is often directed toward "recapture" of the lost object or denial that it is lost (e.g., Klinger, 1975).

Pharmacological Profile

Thus far, the effects of the benzodiazepine tranquilizers on contrast have been considered. A variety of other drugs has also been examined and the results of these experiments suggest that drugs that function as tranquilizers in humans are the most potent alleviators of contrast—other classes of drugs often being totally ineffective.

Listed in Table 9.1 is a variety of drugs that we have found effective in reducing contrast and a number of drugs that we have found to be ineffective.

Although many of these drugs are broad spectrum—influencing more than one neural system, this profile suggests research directions for the further investigation of the neurochemical and psychological processes involved in contrast. For example, the three benzodiazepines (CDP, midazolam, flurazepam), the barbiturate sodium amobarbital, and ethanol, all potentiate GABA (e.g., Burch & Ticku, 1980; Nestoros, 1980; Skolnick, Paul, & Barker, 1980), a fact which suggests a role for GABA in contrast recovery, as mentioned above. The effects of several of these drug classes will be considered below in preparation for an examination of the relationship between contrast and selected animal models of anxiety.

Sodium Amobarbital. Sodium amobarbital reduced SucNC in a dose-dependent manner when given acutely during the postshift stage (Flaherty,

TABLE 9.1

LIST OF DRUGS FOUND TO BE EFFECTIVE OR INEFFECTIVE IN REDUCING NEGATIVE CONTRAST IN THE CONSUMMATORY NEGATIVE CONTRAST PROCEDURE. DATA REFER TO DRUG ADMINISTRATION (mg/kg) ON THE SECOND POSTSHIFT DAY. * INDICATES EFFECTIVE DOSE.

EFFECTIVE DRUGS	INEFFECTIVE DRUGS
Chlordiazepoxide (2, 4, 6*, 8*, 10*)	Imipramine (8, 16)
Midazolam (.25, .5, 1.0*, 1.25*, 2.0*)	
Flurazepam (5, 10, 20*)	
	Chlorpromazine (1, 3, 5,)
Sodium Amobarbital (15, 17.5*, 20)	Haloperidol (.1, .5, 1.0)
Ethanol (250, 500, 750*, 1000* 1500, 2000	Amphetamine (.125, .25)
	Naloxone (.25, .5, 1.0)
Morphine (.5, 1, 2, 4*, 8*, 16)	Methysergide (3,6,12)
	Buspirone (.125, .25, .5, 1, 2, 15)
Cyproheptadine (3*, 6, 12)	
Cinanserin (5, 10*, 15*, 20)	Gepirone (5, 10)
	Propranolol (5, 10)
	Clonidine (.00312, .00625 .0125, .025, .05)
	Scopolomine (.25, .5, 1.0)
	Pyrilamine (3, 6)
	Ketanserin (2,8)
	Ritanserin (.63, 2.5)
	PCPA (150, 300)

Becker, & Driscoll, 1982; Flaherty & Driscoll, 1980). Unlike CDP, amobarbital was equally effective when administered for the first time on either the first or second postshift day, but the degree of contrast reduction was considerably less than that produced by CDP. Amobarbital was not effective when given during both the preshift and postshift periods and it was not effective in the simultaneous contrast procedure.

Ethanol. The administration of ethanol reliably reduced negative contrast in a dose dependent manner (Becker & Flaherty, 1982, 1983). The effects of a 1.00 g/kg dose of a 15% ethanol solution, injected on the second postshift day, are illustrated in Figure 9.15. Contrast was reliably reduced, but not statistically eliminated. Unlike the benzodiazepines, no dose of ethanol that we investigated was effective enough to completely eliminate contrast—the higher doses producing motor incoordination in both shifted and unshifted rats. Ethanol and CDP also influenced contrast in an additive fashion. That is, marginally effective doses of CDP (4 mg/kg) and ethanol (0.50 g/kg) given together substantially reduced contrast (Becker & Flaherty, 1983). This combined effect of the two drugs on contrast mirrors a significant clinical problem—the use of alcohol and tranquilizers concurrently. Like the benzodiazepines, ethanol seems to be ineffective when administered on the first postshift day (Becker & Flaherty, 1983).

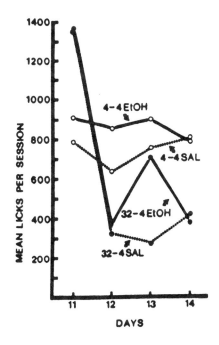

Figure 9.15. Effect of a 1.0 g/kg dose of ethanol (15%) administered on the second postshift day (Day 13, in this case) in shifted (32-4) and unshifted (4-4) rats. Contrast was reliably reduced by the ethanol (from Becker & Flaherty, 1982).

Dopaminergic Agents. The ineffective drugs chlorpromazine and haloperidol (Flaherty, Becker, & Checke, unpublished data) function as dopamine antagonists, whereas amphetamine (also ineffective) is a dopamine agonist. Chlorpromazine has also been found ineffective in runway contrast (Roberts & Pixley, 1965; Rosen & Tessel, 1970). The fact that none of these drugs influence contrast suggests that dopaminergic systems may not play a major role in contrast—an outcome that is somewhat surprising since dopamine has been implicated as a mediator of reward, at least in the case of brain stimulation (e.g., Wise, 1978). However, all of these drugs have complex effects behaviorally and neurochemically, including the reduction of sucrose intake per se, and it would be premature to completely exclude dopaminergic involvement in contrast at this point (cf. Phillips & LePiane, 1986; Royall & Klemm, 1981).

Noradrenergic Agents. Imipramine, an anti-depressant, blocks the reuptake of norepinephrine, thus increasing concentration at the postsynaptic membrane. But imipramine, whether administered chronically or acutely, has no effect on SucNC (Becker & Flaherty, unpublished data), nor on simultaneous contrast (Flaherty et al., 1977). Norepinephrine antagonists also do not affect contrast. Propranolol is a beta-adrenergic blocker and clonidine is an alpha-2 agonist (which generally lead to antagonistic effects on norepinephrine release). Neither of these influences contrast, (Flaherty, Grigson, & Demetrikopoulos, 1987; Flaherty & Rowan, unpublished data), suggesting that noradrenergic mechanisms may not be involved in contrast.

These results are particularly interesting since one of the more elaborate models of anxiety (Gray, 1982), suggests a major role for norepinephrine. To the extent that negative contrast functions as a model of anxiety, our data are inconsistent with Gray's model. Gray also argues that the hippocampal-septal area of the brain is a principal nodal point in an anxiety circuit, but we have found that lesions of either structure have no affect on negative contrast in consummatory behavior (Flaherty, Capobianco, & Hamilton, 1973; Flaherty, Powell, & Hamilton, 1979; Flaherty, Rowan, Emerich, & Walsh, 1989). However, it must be stated that the boundary conditions of Gray's theory may not include the consummatory contrast procedure. The theory was developed to explain anxiety and it is not clear yet the extent to which SucNC involves "anxiety". Also, Gray specifically states that his theory applies to anticipatory or conditioned forms of behavior, not to primary or unconditioned responses. Thus, the initial response to reward reduction would not be included in the domain of Gray's theory. Whether the recovery stages should or should not be is not clear at this point. Finally, Gray's theory was developed from data derived from instrumental responding, not consummatory responding. There is not a one-to-one correspondence between the two. For example, the ease with which SucNC occurs in consummatory behavior following a shift in sucrose concentration stands in contradistinction to the apparent absence of SucNC in runway behavior when the concentration of sucrose is shifted (e.g., Burns, Lorig, & McCrary, 1986; Flaherty, & Caprio, 1976; Flaherty, Riley, & Spear, 1973; Rosen & Ison, 1965; Spear, 1965; Shanab, France, & Young, 1975). There is also the possibility that the effects of damage to the hippocampus may lead to different effects in instrumental as compared to consummatory contrast (cf. Flaherty et al., 1989; Franchina & Brown, 1971).

Serotonergic Agents. The neuropharmacology of serotonin is becoming increasingly complex as a variety of receptor subtypes are discovered and receptor-specific agents developed (e.g., Green, 1985). The effect of serotonergic agents on contrast is also complex and not well understood. For example, methysergide, cinanserin, and cyproheptadine are generally regarded as nonspecific serotonin antagonists, yet they have different effects on contrast—cyproheptadine and cinanserin reduce contrast whereas methysergide has no effect (Becker, 1986). In these studies, the drugs were administered only on the second postshift day.

Buspirone, a selective $5\text{-}HT_{1A}$ agonist, also has no effect on contrast (Flaherty, Grigson, Demetrikopoulos, Weaver, et al., 1990). In this case, the drug has been investigated over a wide dose range on both the first and second postshift days, and both following acute and chronic (20 days prior to the shift) administration. The failure of buspirone to affect contrast is interesting in that it has had anxiolytic effects in several animals models of anxiety, but not all (see below).

Anti-depressants such as imipramine also have substantial serotonergic activity. For example, imipramine inhibits serotonin binding at re-uptake sites (Briley, 1985). Chronic treatment with anti-depressants, including imipramine, leads to a decrease in the number of serotonin receptors (Ogren & Fuxe, 1985). The failure to find an effect of acute imipramine administration on contrast again questions the role of 5-HT mechanisms (Becker & Flaherty, unpublished data). However, the meaning of the chronic aspects of this study are not clear since the drug was administered for seven days only and current evidence suggests that a period of two to three weeks of imipramine administration is necessary before a decrease in 5-HT receptors is obtained (Ogren & Fuxe, 1985).

Morphine. The opiate agonist morphine has small, but statistically reliable contrast-reducing effects (Rowan & Flaherty, 1987). The opiate antagonist naloxone blocks the effects of morphine but appears to have no intrinsic effect on contrast. Unlike CDP and ethanol, but like the barbiturate sodium amobarbital, morphine appears to be equally effective on the first and second postshift days. The actions of drugs specific for different opiate receptor subtypes remain to be investigated.

Acetylcholine. The only specific cholinergic drug investigated thus far is the antagonist scopolamine and it has no influence on contrast (Becker, 1986; Flaherty & Meinrath, 1979).

Histamine. Similarly, only one histaminergic drug has been studied— the antagonist pyrilamine has no effect on contrast (Becker, 1986).

Quantitative Effects. An appreciation of the relative magnitude of the influence produced by some of the effective and ineffective drugs may be gained from an examination of Figure 9.16, in which Drug Effectiveness Ratios (cf. Figure 9.13) are presented for the most effective dose of each drug investigated. The larger the ratio, the greater the effect on contrast.

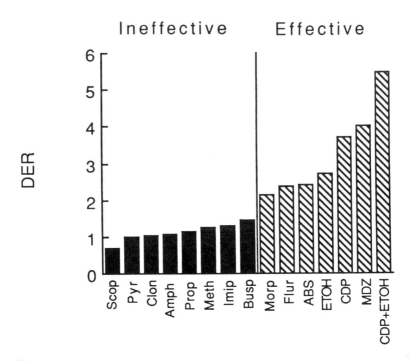

Figure 9.16. Drug Effectiveness Ratios (DER) for the most effective dose of a series of effec-tive and ineffective drugs administered on the second postshift day (see Figure 9.13 and related text for derivation of DER values). The CDP plus ethanol values were 4.0 mg/kg CDP and 0.50 g/kg ethanol.

SELECTED ANIMAL MODELS OF ANXIETY

Although the behavioral pharmacology of negative contrast is incomplete, some insight into the psychology and neurochemistry of contrast may be obtained by comparing the existing data with those obtained in animal models of anxiety.

Generally speaking, an animal model of anxiety is a situation in which behavior that has been suppressed by some experimenter-contrived conflict situation (e.g., concurrent punishment and reward) is released from that suppression by a drug that reduces anxiety in humans (see File, 1987; Gray, Davis, Feldon, Rawlins, & Owens, 1981; Iversen, 1983; Lal & Emmett-Oglesby, 1983; Sepinwall, 1985; and Treit, 1985, for further discussions of the concept of an animal model of anxiety). There are well over 20 such situations that have been used at one time or another. Some of these are listed in Table 9.2.

Three of these models will be examined for comparison purposes—the punished drinking test, the operant conflict test, and the potentiated startle test. This will not be an exhaustive review of the behavioral pharmacology of these procedures, but rather an examination of the effects of those drugs that have been used thus far in the contrast procedure.

TABLE 9.2

SOME ANIMAL MODELS OF ANXIETY

Operant Conflict Punished Drinking	Extinction Negative Contrast
Potentiated Startle	Partial Reinforcement Acquisition Effect
Conditioned Taste Aversion Defensive Burying	Partial Reinforcement Extinction Effect
Social Interaction	Partial Punishment Effect
Novel Food Consumption Food in a Novel Context	Exploration Four Plate Test Crawley Test
Passive Avoidance One-Way Avoidance Two-Way Avoidance Escape	Staircase Test Elevated Plus Maze Hypertonic Saline Test
	PTZ Test

Punished Drinking

In the punished drinking test rats are given some minimal experience with a water deprivation schedule, then after a 23 hr period of water deprivation they are given access to water from a drinking tube. After a given number of licks or a brief access time, subsequent licks are shocked. The number of licks made during the shock period by drugged and undrugged rats is used to determine the anxiolytic efficacy of a drug (Vogel, Beer, & Clody, 1971).

A number of variations of this procedure are used, often incorporating signaled and unsignaled shock periods to allow for a better assessment of the effect of a drug on drinking per se and not just drinking when a shock is present (e.g., Commissaris & Rech, 1982; Kilts, Commissaris, & Rech, 1981; Pich & Samanin, 1986; Soderpalm & Engel, 1988). The punished drinking procedure is simple, fast, and widely used as an anxiolytic screen in the pharmaceutical industry. The theory behind this test is that the animals are placed in a conflict situation—a conflict between the availability of needed water and the response contingent shock associated with that water.

Operant Conflict

The operant conflict test developed by Geller and Seifter (e.g., 1960) is also widely used as an anxiolytic screen. The procedure involves a multiple schedule which typically consists of a period of variable interval 2 min (VI-2) schedule of reinforcement which alternates with a period of continuous reinforcement (CRF) plus shock punishment. Variations on this basic procedure include modifications of the schedules, usually in the direction of using a low fixed ratio (FR) punishment contingency and/or the inclusion of a time-out (TO) period in addition to the two reinforcement periods. Also, the shock intensity is often adjusted for each animal to insure a baseline level of responding from which measurable deviations produced by a drug treatment may be obtained (cf. Howard & Pollard, 1977).

The theory is that the animals are placed in a conflict—they "...must balance the positive features of ... reward payoff against the negative features of accepting pain shocks" (Geller & Seifter, 1960, p 483). A "good" anxiolytic should increase responding during the shock component without affecting responding during the non-punished component or the TO component.

Potentiated Startle

The final model to be considered, the potentiated startle test, is quite different from the other paradigms in that it probably does not involve a conflict component. Instead, this procedure, which has been extensively investigated by Davis (e.g., Davis, Hitchcock, & Rosen, 1988), involves a Pavlovian fear conditioning paradigm.

The basic behavior of interest is the animal's startle response to a brief, loud sound. In Davis's procedure, animals are first conditioned by pairing a light with a shock for a number of trials. The effect of this conditioning is then measured by preceding some noise presentations by the light. The basic result is that the startle amplitude is enhanced when the light precedes the noise. Controls for conditioning include the use of paired and unpaired light-shock groups.

COMPARATIVE DRUG EFFECTS

Presented in Table 9.3 is a listing of the drugs that have been investigated in consummatory contrast and a comparison of the effectiveness of these drugs in contrast and in the three animal models of anxiety described above. The data from which this table was drawn are described below.

Benzodiazepines, Ethanol, and Barbiturates

Punishment-suppressed drinking is alleviated by CDP (6 - 40 mg/kg) and other benzodiazepines (e.g., Colpaert, Meert, Niemegeers, & Janssen, 1985; Goldberg, Salama, Patel, & Malick, 1983; Kilts et al., 1981; Vogel et al., 1971); by sodium amobarbital (3-10 mg/kg) and other barbiturates (Kilts et al., 1981; Vogel et al., 1971); but not by ethanol—in a dose range of from 30 - 2,000 mg/kg of a 10% solution (Kilts et al., 1981).

TABLE 9.3

Paradigm Comparisons. (+) indicates antianxiety effect; (-) indicates no antianxiety effect; (?) indicates unknown; (+/-) indicates contradictory results.

	Negative Contrast	Punished Drinking	Potentiated Startle	Operant Conflict
Benzodiazepines	+	+	+	+
Barbiturates	+	+	+	+
Ethanol	+	-	+	+/-
Morphine	+	?	+	+/-
5-HT Antagonists	+/-	+/-	-	+/-
Buspirone	-	+/-	+	+/-
Neuroleptics	-	+/-	-	-
NE Antagonists	-	?	+	+/-
ACH Antagonists	-	-	?	?

Benzodiazepines also have anticonflict activity in the Geller-Seifter procedure, with CDP being effective at doses as low as 2.5 mg/kg orally (Cook & Sepinwall, 1975). Barbiturates also have anti-punishment effects (Cook & Davidson, 1973; Geller & Seifter, 1960), but the effects of ethanol are inconsistent (Cook & Davidson, 1973; Geller, Bachman, & Seifter, 1963; Sepinwall & Cook, 1978), although there are some situations in which ethanol is effective (e.g., Cook & Davidson, 1973, p. 333).

Potentiated startle is reduced by the benzodiazepines diazepam and flurazepam (Davis, 1979a), by sodium amytal (Chi, 1965), and by ethanol (Williams, described in Miller & Barry, 1960).

Thus, the benzodiazepines and barbiturates have consistent anxiolytic effects in contrast and in the three comparison models, whereas the effects of ethanol are somewhat model specific.

Morphine

The antipunishment effects of morphine in operant conflict are limited or nonexistent (Sepinwall & Cook, 1978), but the drug is effective in reducing potentiated startle (Davis, 1979b). As in contrast, naloxone antagonized the effect of morphine but did not itself affect potentiated startle (Davis, 1979b). Considering that the effects of morphine in contrast, though reliable, are small, and that they are marginal at best in the Geller-Seifter procedure, current evidence indicates that a morphine-related endogenous opiate system may not be importantly involved in conflict situations, although it may have some role to play in non-conflict fear systems.

Serotonergic Agents

The effects of serotonergic agents on punished drinking are mixed. Boast, Popick, Stone, and Kalinsky (1985) reported that cyproheptadine (10 and 30 mg/kg), cinanserin (3 and 30 mg/kg), and methysergide (3 and 30 mg/kg) all had anticonflict effects. However, Kilts et al. (1981) reported that methysergide (1-10 mg/kg) was ineffective in their modification of the Vogel procedure and cinanserin (10 - 100 mg/kg) was also ineffective except for a 56 mg/kg dose.

The results obtained with serotonin antagonists in operant conflict have also been mixed. Cinanserin has been reported to have an anxiolytic effect at doses of 15 mg/kg (the same dose that is effective in contrast), but not at higher and lower doses (Cook & Sepinwall, 1975). However, Geller, Hartmann, and Croy (1974, as reported in Gardner, 1985) found that a 60 mg/kg dose was effective, but lower doses were not. Also, low doses of methysergide have been reported effective, but a 10 mg/kg dose ineffective (Cook & Sepinwall, 1975). However, using different procedural parameters, Stein, Wise, and Beluzzi (1975) reported that 10 mg/kg had an anti-punishment effect. In a variation of the Geller-Seifter procedure (e.g., an FR rather than a VI reinforced period with interspersed periods of signaled CRF punishment), cinanserin was found effective at 56 mg/kg, but not at lower doses, and methysergide (1-18 mg/kg) was found to be ineffective (Kilts et al., 1981). In a different modification of the basic Geller-Seifter procedure, Hodges, Green, and Glenn (1987) found anxiolytic effects with both peripheral (2.5 and 5.0 mg/kg) and intra-amygdala administration of methysergide.

Cyproheptadine has been found to have small but reliable anticonflict effects (Sepinwall & Cook, 1980), but Gardner (1985, p. 297) suggests that these could be due to direct effects of the drug on a chloride ionophore linked to GABA, rather than through a serotonergic mechanism.

The variations among these, and other, studies (cf. Gardner, 1985, 1986; Kilts et al., 1981) in the effectiveness of 5-HT antagonists suggests that procedural factors, such as the schedules used, shock intensity, pre-injection time, etc., may interact with drug and drug dose in determining the anticonflict activities of these 5-HT antagonists. In addition, the different antagonists used in the above studies may be active in different brain regions (e.g., Moret, 1985) and/or on different 5-HT receptor subtypes (e.g., Ogren & Fuxe, 1985; Sills, Wolfe, & Frazer, 1984). In this regard, it is interesting that Sills et al. (1984, Table 2) reported that methysergide, which is inactive in contrast, may be somewhat specific for 5-HT$_1$ receptors in the frontal cortex, whereas cinanserin and cyproheptadine, which were active in contrast, are non-specific. There is also some indication that methysergide may be particularly effective at a subtype of the 5-HT$_1$ receptor—the 5-HT$_{1c}$ receptor (Peroutka, 1986). However, this issue is not yet resolved since there is also evidence that methysergide is a non-specific antagonist (e.g., Lucki, Nobler, & Frazer, 1984; Shearman & Tolcsavi, 1987).

In the case of potentiated startle, the antagonists cinanserin (10 mg/kg) and cyproheptadine (5 mg/kg) are ineffective (Davis, Hitchcock, & Rosen, 1988).

Imipramine

The anti-depressant imipramine affects adrenergic and serotonergic neurotransmitter systems. Its serotonergic effects are principally to block re-uptake of serotonin at presynaptic sites (Briley, 1985).

As in contrast, imipramine has been found to be ineffective (1-10 mg/kg) in the drinking-conflict procedure (Kilts et al., 1981), and, over a wide range of doses, in operant conflict (Cook & Davidson, 1973) as in general are other antidepressants with serotonergic activity (Gardner, 1985, p. 303).

Imipramine also did not reduce potentiated startle when given acutely (5 or 10 mg/kg), chronically (10 mg/kg), or both (Cassella & Davis, 1985).

Buspirone

Buspirone is a 5-HT$_{1A}$ agonist and, as such, should have an inhibitory effect on serotonin. The effects of buspirone on punished drinking are unclear. Buspirone has been found effective in several studies (e.g., Eison, Eison, Stanley, & Riblet, 1986; Riblet, Taylor, Eison, & Stanton, 1982; Taylor et al., 1984; Weissman et al., 1984), but totally ineffective (in the same dose ranges) in others (e.g., Gardner, 1986; Goldberg et al., 1983; see also Johnston & File, 1986; Sepinwall, 1985). There is some indication that buspirone might be more likely to be found effective under conditions of a reversed light/dark cycle (Eison et al., 1986) and when subjects that lick at a low rate are dropped from the experiment.

Buspirone is largely ineffective in operant conflict when rats are used (e.g., Gardner, 1986; but see Porter, Johnson, & Jackson, 1985, for contrary evidence), but it may or may not be effective in monkeys (Sepinwall, 1985; Weissman et al., 1984), and it may have anxiolytic properties in pigeons (Barrett, Witkin, & Mansbach, 1984), which are probably not due to its dopaminergic actions (Witkin & Barrett, 1986).

Both buspirone and its analog gepirone reduced the magnitude of potentiated startle (Kehne, Cassella & Davis, 1988). However, the effects of buspirone in this paradigm may not be related to its effects on serotonergic systems (Davis, Cassella & Kehne, 1988; Davis, Hitchcock & Rosen, 1988).

Dopaminergic Agents

The neuroleptic haloperidol has been found to have an anticonflict effect in punished drinking in low doses (0.05, 0.10 mg/kg)(Pich & Samanin, 1986), but the neuroleptic chlorpromazine (0.1 - 3.0 mg/kg) increased suppression (Kilts et al., 1981). Amphetamine has been found to have no effect (Vogel et al., 1971) or to increase suppression in the punished drinking procedure (Ford, Rech, Commissaris, & Meyer, 1979).

Amphetamine is generally ineffective in selectively alleviating punishment-suppressed responding in the operant conflict task (e.g., Geller & Seifter, 1960; Cook & Davidson, 1973). There are, however, a few circumstances in which small anti-conflict effects of amphetamine have been observed. These include situations in which shock intensity was low or situations in which the animals were not food deprived (see Sepinwall & Cook, 1978, for a review).

Promazine, chlorpromazine, and haloperidol are ineffective in alleviating punished responding and, in fact, generally decrease overall responding (Geller & Seifter, 1960; Cook & Davidson, 1973; Morse, 1964). The failure of these three compounds and the failure of amphetamine to have clear and consistent effects suggests a negligible role for dopaminergic mechanisms in conflict-related behavior.

Noradrenergic Agents

Clonidine has been reported to have an anxiolytic effect on punished drinking when administered in a low dose (6.25 ug/kg), but a propunishment effect at higher doses (12.5 and 25.0 ug/kg) in a modified Vogel test (Soderpalm & Engel, 1988). However, these data should be interpreted with caution since the rats were offered a glucose solution in this experiment and a study of simple intake of an 8% sucrose solution revealed parallel effects of clonidine (increase with a 6.25 ug/kg dose and decreases with the two higher doses) in a situation that involved no shock or apparent conflict (Flaherty & Grigson, in press).

In the operant conflict procedure, the results obtained with noradrenergic agents other than imipramine have been mixed. For example, the alpha$_2$ agonist clonidine has been reported to be effective in this model (Bullock, Kruse, & Fielding, 1978; Kruse, Theurer, Dunn, Novick, & Shearman, 1980), but the beta-adrenergic antagonist propranolol is ineffective (McMillan, 1973; Robichaud, Sledge, Hefner, & Goldberg, 1973; Sepinwall, Grodsky, Sullivan, & Cook, 1973; Wise, Berger, & Stein, 1973). However, as was the case with buspirone, there is some evidence that propranolol may be effective as an anxiolytic in pigeons (Durel, Krantz, & Barrett, 1986). Although noradrenergic agents do not have major effects in contrast or operant conflict situations, they may be effective in some other anxiety or "panic-attack" models (e.g., Chopin, Pellow, & File, 1986; Mason & Fibiger, 1979; Soderpalm & Engel, 1988).

Clonidine (10 - 40 ug/kg) decreased potentiated startle but propranolol (20 mg/kg) had only a partial antagonistic effect (Davis, Redmond, & Baraban, 1979).

Cholinergic Agents

As was the case in contrast, the anticholinergic scopolamine (0.2-0.8 mg/kg) has no effect on punished drinking (Vogel et al., 1971).

SUMMARY AND CONCLUSIONS

The pharmacological analysis of contrast and the comparison of these data with the three selected animal models of anxiety lead to several conclusions.

1. The successive negative contrast paradigm is differentially sensitive to drugs, with recognized tranquilizers being particularly effective in alleviating contrast.

2. The successive negative contrast paradigm may be psychologically complex, with different processes involved in the occurrence of contrast and recovery from contrast.

3. Behavioral suppression brought about by other consummatory contrast paradigms, such as simultaneous and anticipatory contrast, will not yield the same drug profile as successive negative contrast and probably involves still different psychological processes.

4. One clear aspect of the comparison of successive negative contrast with the three animal models of anxiety is that the benzodiazepines and barbiturates are universally effective, in a qualitative sense, in reducing the effects of the aversive situation—whether it be loss of reward, punished consummatory or operant responding, or energized startle. This universality suggests the possibility of a common element in the various paradigms—as different as they are behaviorally. These data also suggest the possibility that GABA transmission plays some role in this common element.

5. It is also clear that neuroleptics, amphetamine, and imipramine are by and large without effect in all the models. One implication of at least some of these data is that dopaminergic systems are not strongly involved in relativity or anxiety processes. If this proved to be the case, it would be surprising given the evidence for dopamine involvement in other aspects of reward.

6. There is the possibility that serotonergic agents may distinguish contrast from other models. However, the data are as yet insufficient to draw definite conclusions. Buspirone is clearly ineffective in contrast while effective in potentiated startle. But the effects obtained with buspirone in the other two models reviewed here are mixed. Similarly, the effects obtained with classic 5-HT antagonists in all models are mixed except potentiated startle, where they are apparently ineffective.

7. Noradrenergic antagonists are ineffective in ameliorating contrast and not particularly effective in other models with the possible exception of potentiated startle.

8. The data are sparse, but there is little evidence of cholinergic involvement in these models.

9. There is the possibility that potentiated startle is moderated by a wider class of drugs than the other three paradigms. It is tempting to speculate that this difference might be related to different psychological processes—such as conditioned arousal or fear in the startle paradigm, but conflict-related processes in the other paradigms.

10. Overall, the data suggest that the comparison of pharmacological profiles in animal models of emotional responsivity may reveal different combinations of emotional/neurochemical substrates of behavior. Continued work may lead to a behavioral and pharmacological separation among emotional states such as fear, anxiety, and disappointment.

ACKNOWLEDGMENTS

The preparation of this manuscript was aided by a grant from the National Institute of Mental Health (MH 40489) and by a Charles and Johanna Busch Memorial Grant.

I am very grateful to the following graduate students, who conducted much of the research described in this paper: Howard Becker, Susan Checke, Patricia Grigson, Scott Lind, Bruce Lombardi, Anne Meinrath, and Grace Rowan. I thank Patricia Grigson and Grace Rowan for their comments on an earlier version of this chapter.

REFERENCES

Barrett, J.E., Witkin, J.M., & Mansbach, R.S. (1984). Behavioral and pharmacological analysis of buspirone. *Federation Proceedings, 43*, 931.

Bartoshuk, L.M., & Gent, J.F. (1984). Taste mixtures: An analysis of synthesis. In D. Pfaff (Ed.), *Taste, olfaction and the central nervous system* (pp. 210-232). New York: Rockefeller University Press.

Becker, H.C. (1986) Comparison of the effects of the benzodiazepine midazolam and three serotonin antagonists on a consummatory conflict paradigm. *Pharmacology, Biochemistry & Behavior, 24*, 1057-1064.

Becker, H.C., & Flaherty, C.F.(1982). Influence of ethanol on contrast in consummatory behavior. *Psychopharmacology, 77*, 253-258.

Becker, H.C., & Flaherty,C.F. (1983) Chlordiazepoxide and ethanol additively reduce gustatory negative contrast. *Psychopharmacology, 80*, 35-37.

Bitterman, M.E. (1975). The comparative analysis of learning. *Science, 188*, 699-709.

Black, R.W. (1968). Shifts in magnitude of reward and contrast effects in instrumental and selective learning: A reinterpretation. *Psychological Review, 75*, 114-126.

Boast, C., Popick, F., Stone, G., & Kalinsky, H. (1985). Positive correlation between serotonin antagonism and anticonflict activity. *Society for Neuroscience Abstract, 128*.9.

Briley, M. (1985). Imipramine binding: its relationship with serotonin uptake and depression. In A.R. Green (Ed.). *Neuropharmacology of Serotonin.* Oxford: Oxford University Press.

Brush, F.R. (1985). Genetic determinants of avoidance learning: mediation by emotionality? In F.R. Brush & B. Overmier (Eds.), *Affect, conditioning and cognition* (pp. 27-42). Hillsdale, NJ: Lawrence Erlbaum Associates.

Bullock, S.A., Kruse, H., & Fielding, S. (1978). The effect of clonidine on conflict behavior in rats: Is clonidine an anxiolytic agent? *Psychopharmacologist, 20*, 223.

Burch, T.P., & Ticku, M.K. (1980). Ethanol enhances 3H diazepam binding at the benzodiazepine-GABA-receptor-ionophore complex. *European Journal of Pharmacology, 67*, 325-326.

Burns, R.A., Lorig, T. S., & McCrary, M. D. (1986). Reduction of sucrose reward to smaller and nonreward levels without contrast effects. *The Journal of General Psychology, 113*, 97-102.

Capaldi, E.D. (1978). Effects of changing alley color on the successive negative contrast effect. *Bulletin of the Psychonomic Society, 12*, 69-70.

Capaldi, E.J. (1972). Successive negative contrast effect: Intertrial interval, type of shift, and four sources of generalization decrement. *Journal of Experimental Psychology, 96*, 433-438.

Cassella, J.V., & Davis, M. (1985). Fear-enhanced acoustic startle is not attenuated by acute or chronic imipramine treatment in rats. *Psychopharmacology, 87*, 278-282.

Chi, C.C. (1965). The effect of amobarbital sodium on conditioned fear as measured by the potentiated startle response in rats. *Psychopharmacologia, 7*, 115-122.

Chopin, P., Pellow, S., & File, S.E. (1986). The effects of yohimbine on exploratory and locomotor behavior are attributable to its effects at noradrenaline and not at benzodiazepine receptors. *Neuropharmacology*, *25*, 53-57.

Ciszewski, W.A., & Flaherty, C.F. (1977). Failure of a reinstatement treatment to influence negative contrast. *American Journal of Psychology, 90*, 219-229.

Colpaert, F.C., Meert, T.F., Niemegeers, C.J.E., & Janssen, P.A.J. (1985). Behavioural and 5-HT antagonist effects of ritanserin: A pure and selective antagonist of LSD discrimination in rat. *Psychopharmacology*, *86*, 45-54.

Commissaris, R.L., & Rech, R.H. (1982). Interactions of metergoline with diazepam, quipazine, and hallucionogenic drugs on a conflict behavior in the rat. *Psychopharmacology*, *76*, 282-285.

Cook, L., & Davidson, A.B. (1973). Effects of behaviorally active drugs in a conflict procedure in rats. In S. Garattini, E. Mussini, & L.O. Randall (Eds.). *The benzodiazepines* (pp.327-345). New York: Raven Press.

Cook, L., & Sepinwall, J. (1975). Psychopharmacological parameters and methods. In L.Levi (Ed.), *Emotions—their parameters and measurement* (pp. 379-404). New York: Raven Press.

Cooper, S.J., & Estall, L.B. (1985). Behavioral pharmacology of food, water and salt intake in relation to drug actions at benzodiazepine receptors. *Neuroscience & Biobehavioral Reviews*, *9*, 5-19.

Costa, E. (Ed.). (1983). *The Benzodiazepines: From Molecular Biology to Clinical Practice.* New York: Raven Press.

Crawley, J.N. (1981). Neuropharmacologic specificity of a simple animal model for the behavioral actions of benzodiazepines. *Pharmacology Biochemistry & Behavior*, *15*, 695-699.

Crespi, L.P. (1942). Quantitative variation in incentive and performance in the white rat. *American Journal of Psychology*, *55*, 467-517.

Daly, H.B. (1974). Reinforcing properties of escape from frustration. In G.H. Bower (Ed.), *The psychology of learning and motivation* (Vol. 8, pp.187-231). New York: Academic Press.

Davis, M. (1979a). Diazepam and flurazepam: Effects on conditioned fear as measured with the potentiated startle paradigm. *Psychopharmacology*, *62*, 1-7.

Davis, M. (1979b). Morphine and naloxone: Effects on conditioned fear as measured with the potentiated startle paradigm. *European Journal of Pharmacology*, *54*, 341-347.

Davis, M., Cassella, J.V., & Kehne, J.H. (1988). Serotonin does not mediate anxiolytic effects of buspirone in the fear-potentiated startle paradigm: Comparison with 8-OH-DPAT and ipsapirone. *Psychopharmacology*, *94*, 14-20.

Davis, M., Hitchcock, J.M., & Rosen, J.B. (1988). Anxiety and the Amygdala: Pharmacological and anatomical analysis of the fear-potentiated startle paradigm. In G. Bower (Ed.), *The psychology of learning and motivation* (Vol. 21; pp. 263-305). New York: Academic Press.

Davis, M., Redmond, D.E., Jr., & Baraban, J.M. (1979). Noradrenergic agonists and antagonists: Effects on conditioned fear as measured by the potentiated startle paradigm. *Psychopharmacology*, *65*, 111-118.

DiLollo, F.D., & Beez, V. (1966). Negative contrast effect as a function of magnitude of reward decrement. *Psychonomic Science*, *5*, 99-100.

Dunham, P.J. (1968). Contrast conditions of reinforcement: A selective critique. *Psychological Bulletin*, *69*, 295-315.

Durel, L.A., Krantz, D.S., & Barrett, J.E. (1986). The antianxiety effect of beta blockers on punished responding. *Pharmacology Biochemistry & Behavior*, *25*, 371-374.

Eison, A.S., Eison, M.S., Stanley, M., & Riblet, L.A. (1986). Serotonergic mechanisms in the behavioral effects of buspirone and gepirone. *Pharmacology Biochemistry & Behavior*, *24*, 701-707.

Elliott, M.H. (1928). The effect of change of reward on maze performance of rats. *University of California Publications in Psychology*, *4*, 19-30.

File, S.E. (1985). What can be learned from the effects of the benzodiazepines on exploratory behavior? *Neuroscience & Biobehavioral Reviews*, *9*, 45-54.

File, S.E. (1987). The contribution of behavioral studies to the neuropharmacology of anxiety. *Neuropharmacology*, *26*, 877-886.

Flaherty, C.F. (1982) Incentive contrast: A review of behavioral changes following shifts in reward. *Animal Learning & Behavior*, *10*, 409-440.

Flaherty, C.F., Becker, H.C., & Driscoll, C. (1982). Conditions under which amobarbital sodium influences consummatory contrast. *Physiological Psychology*, *10*, 122-128.

Flaherty, C.F., Becker, H.C., & Osborne, M. (1983). Negative contrast following regularly increasing concentrations of sucrose solutions: Rising expectations or incentive averaging? *The Psychological Record*, *33*, 415-420.

Flaherty, C.F., Becker, H.C., & Pohorecky,L. (1985). Correlation of corticosterone elevations and negative contrast varies as a function of postshift day. *Animal Learning Behavior*, *13*, 309-314.

Flaherty, C.F., Blitzer, R., & Collier, G.H. (1978). Open field behaviors elicited by reward reduction. *American Journal of Psychology*, *91*, 429-433.

Flaherty, C.F., Capobianco, S., & Hamilton, L.W. (1973). Effect of septal lesions on retention of negative contrast. *Physiology & Behavior*, *11*, 625-631.

Flaherty, C.F., & Caprio, M. (1976). Dissociation between instrumental and consummatory measures of contrast. *American Journal of Psychology*, *89*, 485-498.

Flaherty, C.F., & Checke, S. (1982). Anticipation of incentive gain. *Animal Learning & Behavior*, *10*, 177-182.

Flaherty, C.F., & Driscoll, C. (1980). Amobarbital sodium reduces successive gustatory contrast. *Psychopharmacology*, *69*, 161-162.

Flaherty, C.F., & Grigson, P.S. (in press). The effects of clonidine on sucrose intake and on water intake vary as a function of dose, deprivation condition and duration of exposure. *Pharmacology Biochemistry & Behavior*.

Flaherty, C.F., & Grigson, P.S. (1988). From contrast to reinforcement: Role of response contingency in anticipatory contrast. *Journal of Experimental Psychology: Animal Behavior Processes*, *14*, 165-176.

Flaherty, C.F., Grigson, P.S., & Demetrikopoulos, M.K. (1987). Effect of clonidine on negative contrast and novelty-induced stress. *Pharmacology Biochemistry & Behavior*, *27*, 659-664.

Flaherty, C.F., Grigson, P. S., Demetrikopoulos, M.K., Weaver, M. S., Krauss, K. L., & Rowan, G. A. (1990). Effect of serotonergic drugs on negative contrast in consummatory behavior. *Pharmacology Biochemistry and Behavior*, *36*, 799-806.

Flaherty, C.F., Grigson, P.S., & Lind, S. (1990). Chlordiazepoxide and the moderation of the initial response to reward loss. *Quarterly Journal of Experimental Psychology*, *42 B*, 87-105.

Flaherty, C.F., Grigson, P.S., & Rowan, G.A. (1986). Chlordiazepoxide and the determinants of contrast. *Animal Learning & Behavior*, *14*, 315-321.

Flaherty, C.F., & Largen, J. (1975). Within-subjects positive and negative contrast effects. *Journal of comparative and Physiological Psychology*, *88*, 653-664.

Flaherty, C.F., & Lombardi, B.R. (1977). Effect of prior differential taste experience on the retention of taste quality. *Bulletin of the Psychonomic Society, 9,* 391-394.

Flaherty, C.F., Lombardi, B.R., Kapust, J., & D'Amato, M.R. (1977). Incentive contrast uninfluenced by extended testing, imipramine, or chlordiazepoxide. *Pharmacology Biochemistry & Behavior, 7,* 315-322.

Flaherty, C.F., Lombardi, B.R., Wrightson, J., & Deptula, D. (1980). Conditions under which chlordiazepoxide influences successive gustatory contrast. *Psychopharmacology, 67,* 269-23.

Flaherty, C.F., & Meinrath, A.B. (1979). Influence of scopolamine on sucrose intake under absolute and relative test conditions. *Physiological Psychology, 7,* 412-418.

Flaherty, C.F., Powell, G., & Hamilton, L.W. (1979). Septal lesion, sex, and incentive shift effects on open field behavior of rats. *Physiology & Behavior, 22,* 903-909.

Flaherty, C.F., Riley, E.P., & Spear, N.E. (1973). Effects of sucrose concentration and goal units on runway behavior in the rat. *Learning and Motivation, 4,* 163-175.

Flaherty, C.F., Rothberg, H., & Noctor, N.C. (1990). [Contrast in a radial-arm maze]. Unpublished raw data.

Flaherty, C.F., & Rowan, G.A. (1986). Successive, simultaneous and anticipatory contrast effects in the consumption of saccharin solutions. *Journal of Experimental Psychology: Animal Behavior Processes, 12,* 381-393.

Flaherty, C.F., & Rowan, G.A. (1988). Effect of intersolution interval, chlordiazepoxide, and amphetamine on anticipatory contrast. *Animal Learning & Behavior, 16,* 47-52.

Flaherty, C.F., & Rowan, G.A. (1989a). Rats selectively bred to differ in avoidance behavior also differ in response to novelty stress, in glycemic conditioning, and in reward contrast. *Behavioral and Neural Biology, 51,* 145-164.

Flaherty, C.F., & Rowan, G.A. (1989b). Negative contrast in the consumption of sucrose and quinine-adulterated sucrose solutions. *Journal of the American College of Nutrition, 8,* 47-55.

Flaherty, C.F., Rowan, G.A., Emerich, D., & Walsh, T. (1989). Effects of intrahippocampal administration of colchicine on incentive contrast and on radial maze performance. *Behavioral Neuroscience, 103,* 319-328.

Flaherty, C.F., Troncoso, B., & Deschu, N. (1979). Open field behaviors correlated with reward availability and reward shift in three rat strains. *American Journal of Psychology, 92,* 385-400.

Flaherty, C.F., Weaver, M., & Rowan, G.A. (1990). [Contrast following shifts in saccharin concentration.] Unpublished raw data.

Ford, R.D., Rech, R.H., Commissaris R.L., & Meyer, L.Y. (1979). Effects of acute and chronic interactions of diazepam and d-amphetamine on punished behavior of rats. *Psychopharmacology, 65,* 197-204.

Franchina, J.J., & Brown, T.S. (1971). Reward magnitude shift effects in rats with hippocampal lesions. *Journal of Comparative and Physiological Psychology, 76,* 365-370.

Gardner, C.R. (1985). Pharmacological studies of the role of serotonin in animal models of anxiety. In A. R. Green (Ed.), *Neuropharmacology of serotonin.* Oxford: Oxford University Press.

Gardner, C.R. (1986). Recent developments in 5HT-related pharmacology of animal models of anxiety. *Pharmacology Biochemistry & Behavior, 24,* 1479-1485.

Geller, I, Bachman, E., & Seifter, J. (1963). Effects of reserpine and morphine on behavior suppressed by punishment. *Life Sciences, 4,* 226-231.

Geller, I., & Seifter, J. (1960). Effects of meprobamate, barbiturates, d-amphetamine and promazine on experimentally-induced conflict in the rat. *Psychopharmacologia, 1,* 482-492.

Gleitman, H., & Steinman, F. (1964). Depression effect as a function of retention interval before and after shift in reward magnitude. *Journal of Comparative and PHysiological Psychology, 57,* 158-160.

Goldberg, M.E., Salama, A.I., Patel, J.B., & Malick, J.B. (1983). Novel non-benzodiazepine anxiolytics. *Neuropharmacology, 22,* 1499-1504.

Gonzalez, R.C., Fernhoff, D., & David, F.G. (1973). Contrast, resistance to extinction and forgetting in rats. *Journal of Comparative and Physiological Psychology, 84,* 562-571.

Gonzalez, R.C., Gleitman, H., & Bitterman, M.E. (1962). Some observations on the depression effect. *Journal of Comparative and Physiological Psychology, 55,* 578-581.

Gray, J.A. (1982). *The neuropsychology of anxiety.* New York: Oxford University Press.

Gray, J.A., Davis, N., Feldon, J., Rawlins, J., & Owens, S.R. (1981). Animal models and anxiety. *Progress in Neuropsychopharmacology, 5,* 143-157.

Green, A.R. (1985). *Neuropharmacology of serotonin.* Oxford: Oxford University Press.

Hodges, H., Green S., & Glenn, B. (1987). Evidence that the amygdala is involved in benzodiazepine and serotonergic effects on punished responding but not on discrimination. *Psychopharmacology, 92,* 491-504.

Howard, J.L., & Pollard, G.T. (1977). The Geller conflict test: A model of anxiety and a screening procedure for anxiolytics. In I. Hanin & E. Usdin (Eds.), *Animal models of psychiatry and neurology* (pp. 269-278). Oxford: Pergamon Press.

Iversen, S. (1983). Animal Models of anxiety. In M.R. Trimble (Ed.), *Benzodiazepines divided.* (pp. 87-89). New York: Wiley.

Johnston, A.L., & File, S.E. (1986). 5-HT and anxiety: Promises and pitfalls. *Pharmacology Biochemistry & Behavior, 24,* 1467-1470.

Kehne, J.H., Cassella, J.V., & Davis, M. (1988). Anxiolytic effects of buspirone and gepirone in the fear-potentiated startle paradigm. *Psychopharmacology, 94,* 8-13.

Kilts, C.D., Commissaris, R.L., & Rech, R.H. (1981). Comparison of anti-conflict drug effects in three experimental animal models of anxiety. *Psychopharmacology, 74,* 290-296.

Klinger, E. (1975). Consequence of commitment to and disengagement from incentives. *Psychological Review, 82,* 1-25.

Kruse, H., Theurer, R., Dunn, W., Novick, J., & Shearman, G.T. (1980). Attenuation of conflict-induced suppression by clonidine: Indication of anxiolytic activity. *Drug Development Research, 1,* 137-143.

Lal, H., & Emmett-Oglesby, M.W. (1983). Behavioral analogues of anxiety. *Neuropharmacology, 22,* 1423-1441.

Lombardi, B.R., & Flaherty, C.F. (1978). Apparent disinhibition of successive but not of simultaneous negative contrast. *Animal Learning & Behavior, 6,* 30-42.

Lucki, I., Nobler, M.S., & Frazer, A. (1984). Differential actions of serotonin antagonists on two behavioral models of serotonin receptor activation in the rat. *Journal of Pharmacology and Experimental Therapeutics, 228,* 133-139.

Mackintosh, N.J. (1974). *The psychology of animal learning*. London: Academic Press.

Mason, S.T., & Fibiger, H.C. (1979). Current concepts I. Anxiety: The locus coeruleus disconnection. *Life Sciences, 256*, 2141-2147.

McMillan, D.E. (1973). Drugs and punished responding: IV. Effects of propranolol, ethchlorynol and chloral hydrate. *Research Communications in Chemical Pathology and Pharmacology, 1*, 167-174.

McSweeney, F.K. (1982). Positive and negative contrast as a function of component duration for key pecking and treadle pressing. *Journal of the Experimental Analysis of Behavior, 37*, 281-293.

Meinrath, A.B., & Flaherty, C.F. (1987). Preweanling handling influences open-field behavior, but not negative contrast or sucrose neophobia. *Animal Learning & Behavior, 15*, 83-92.

Meinrath, A.B., & Flaherty, C.F. (1988). Effect of varied taste experience on negative contrast in consummatory behavior. *American Journal of Psychology, 101*, 87-96.

Mellgren, R.L. (1972). Positive and negative contrast effects using delayed reinforcement. *Learning and Motivation, 3*, 185-193.

Miller, N.E., & Barry, H. III. (1960). Motivational effects of drugs: Methods which illustrate some general problems in psychopharmacology. *Psychopharmacology, 1*, 169-199.

Moret, C. (1985). Pharmacology of the serotonin autoreceptor. In A.R. Green (Ed.). *Neuropharmacology of Serotonin*, pp.21-49 Oxford: Oxford University Press.

Morse, W.H. (1964). Effect of amobarbital and chlorpromazine on punished behavior in the pigeon. *Psychopharmacologia, 6*, 286-294.

Nestoros, J.N. (1980). Ethanol specifically potentiates GABA-mediated neurotransmission in feline cerebral cortex. *Science, 209*, 708-710.

Ogren, S., & Fuxe, K. (1985). Effects of antidepressant drugs on serotonin receptor mechanisms. In A.R. Green (Eds.). *Neuropharmacology of serotonin* (pp. 131-180). Oxford: Oxford University Press.

Pellow, S., & File, S.E. (1986). Anxiolytic and anxiogenic drug effects on exploratory activity in an elevated plus-maze: A novel test of anxiety in the rat. *Pharmacology Biochemistry & Behavior, 24*, 525-529.

Peroutka, S.J. (1986). Pharmacological differentiation and characterization of 5-HT_{1A}, 5-HT_{1B}, and 5-HT_{1C} binding sites in rat frontal cortex. *Journal of Neurochemistry, 47*, 529-540.

Phillips, A.G., & LePiane, F.G. (1986). Effects of pimozide on positive and negative incentive contrast with rewarding brain stimulation. *Pharmacology Biochemistry & Behavior, 24*, 1577-1582.

Pich, E.M., & Samanin, R. (1986). Disinhibitory effect of buspirone and low doses of sulpiride and haloperidol in two experimental anxiety models in rats: Possible role of dopamine. *Psychopharmacology, 89*, 125-130.

Porter, J.H., Johnson, D.N., & Jackson, J.Y. (1985). Anxiolytic testing of buspirone in rodents. *Society for Neuroscience Abstracts*, No. 126.11.

Pyke, G.H. (1978). Optimal foraging: Movement patterns of bumblebees between infloresences. *Theoretical Population Biology, 13*, 72-98.

Riblet, L.A., Taylor, D.P., Eison, M.S., & Stanton, H.C. (1982). Pharmacology and neurochemistry of buspirone. *Journal of Clinical Psychiatry, 43*, 11-16.

Ridgers, A., & Gray, J.A. (1973). Influence of amylobarbitone on operant depression and elation effects in the rat. *Psychopharmacologia, 32*, 265-270.

Riley, E.P., & Dunlap, W.P. (1979). Successive negative contrast as a function of deprivation condition following shifts in sucrose concentration. *American Journal of Psychology, 92,* 59-70.

Roberts, W.A., & Pixley, L. (1965). The effect of chlorpromazine on the depression effect. *Psychonomic Science, 3,* 407-408.

Robichaud, R.C., Sledge, K.L., Hefner, M.A., & Goldberg, M.E.(1973). Propranolol and chlordiazepoxide on experimentally induced conflict and shuttle box performance in rodents. *Psychopharmacologia, 32,* 157-160.

Rosen, A.J., Glass, D.H., & Ison, J.R. (1967). Amobarbital sodium and instrumental performance changes following reward reduction. *Psychonomic Science, 9,* 129-130.

Rosen, A.J., & Ison, J.R. (1965). Runway performance following changes in sucrose rewards. *Psychonomic Science, 2,* 335-336.

Rosen, A.J., & Tessel, R.E. (1970). Chlorpromazine, chlordiazepoxide and incentive shift performance in the rat. *Journal of Comparative and Physiological Psychology, 72,* 257-262.

Rowan, G.A. (1988). *The behavior of the Maudsley reactive and Maudsley nonreactive rats in three incentive contrast paradigms and several tests of emotionality.* Unpublished dissertation, Rutgers University.

Rowan, G.A., & Flaherty, C.F. (1987). Effect of morphine on negative contrast in consummatory behavior. *Psychopharmacology, 93,* 51-58.

Royall, D.R., & Klemm, W.R. (1981). Dopaminergic mediation of reward:evidence gained using a natural reinforcer in a behavioral contrast paradigm. *Neuroscience Letters, 21,* 223-229.

Sepinwall, J. (1985). Behavioral effects of antianxiety agents: Possible mechanisms of action. In L.S. Seiden and R.L. Balster (Eds.), *Behavioral pharmacology: The current status* (pp. 181-203). New York: Alan R. Liss, Inc.

Sepinwall, J., & Cook, L. (1978). Behavioral pharmacology of antianxiety drugs. In L.L. Iversen, S.D. Iversen & S.H. Snyder (Eds.). *Handbook of psychopharmacology* (Vol. 13, pp. 345-393). New York: Plenum Press.

Sepinwall, J., & Cook, L. (1980). Relationship of gamma-aminobutyric acid (GABA) to antianxiety effects of benzodiazepines. *Brain Research Bulletin, 5,* 839.

Sepinwall, J., Grodsky, F.S., Sullivan, J.W., & Cook, L. (1973). Effects of propranolol and chlordiazepoxide on conflict behavior in rats. *Psychopharmacologia, 31,* 375-382.

Shanab, M.E., France, J., & Young, T. (1975). Negative contrast effect obtained with downshifts in magnitude but not concentration of solid sucrose reward. *Bulletin of the Psychonomic Society, 5,* 429-432.

Shearman, G.T., & Tolcsavi, L. (1987). Effect of selective $5-HT_3$ receptor antagonists ICS 205-930 and MDL 72222 on 5-HTP-induced head shaking and behavioral symptoms induced by 5-methoxy-N,N,dimethyltryptamine in rats: Comparison with some other 5-HT receptor antagonists. *Psychopharmacology, 92,* 520-523.

Sills, M.A., Wolfe, B.B., & Frazer, A. (1984). Determination of selective and nonselective compounds for the $5-HT_{1A}$ and $5-HT_{1B}$ receptor subtypes in rat frontal cortex. *Journal of Pharmacology and Experimental Therapeutics, 231,* 480-487.

Skolnick, P., Paul, S.M., & Barker, J.L. (1980). Pentobarbital potentiates GABA-enhanced (^{3}H)-diazepam binding to benzodiazepine receptors. *European Journal of Pharmacology, 65,* 125-127.

Soderpalm, B., & Engel, J.A. (1988). Biphasic effects of clonidine on conflict behavior: Involvement of different alpha-adrenoceptors. *Pharmacology Biochemistry & Behavior, 30,* 471-477.

Spear, N.E. (1965). Replication report: Absence of a successive contrast effect on instrumental running behavior after a shift in sucrose concentration. *Psychological Reports, 16,* 393-394.

Spear, N.E. (1967). Retention of reinforcer magnitude. *Psychological Review, 74,* 216-234.

Stein, L., Wise, C.D., & Beluzzi, J.D. (1975). Effects of benzodiazepines on central serotonergic mechanisms. In E. Costa & P. Greengard (Eds.). *Mechanism of action of benzodiazepines* (pp. 29-44). New York: Raven Press.

Taylor, D.P., Eison, A.S., Eison, E.S., Riblet, L.A., Temple, D.L., & Van der Maelen, C.P. (1984). Biochemistry and pharmacology of the anxioselective drug buspirone. *Clinical Neuropharmacology, 7,* Supplement 1, 25-32.

Treit, D. (1985). Animal models for the study of anti-anxiety agents: A review. *Neuroscience and Biobehavioral Reviews, 9,* 203-222.

Vogel, J.R., Beer, B., & Clody, D.E. (1971). A simple and reliable conflict procedure for testing antianxiety agents. *Psychopharmacologia, 21,* 1-7.

Vogel, J.R., Mikulka, P.J., & Spear, N.E. (1968). Effects of sucrose and saccharin concentrations on licking behavior in the rat. *Journal of Comparative and Physiological Psychology, 66,* 661-666.

Waddington, K.D., & Heinrich, B. (1981). Patterns of movement and floral choice by foraging bees. In A.C. Kamil & T.D. Sargent (Eds.), *Foraging behavior: Ecological, ethological, and psychological approaches.* New York: Garland STPM Press.

Weissman, B.A., Barrett, J.E., Brady, L.S., Witkin, J.M., Mendelson, W.B., Paul, S.M., & Skolnick, P. (1984). Behavioral and neurochemical studies on the anticonflict actions of buspirone. *Drug Development Research, 4,* 83-93.

Williams, B.A. (1983). Another look at contrast in multiple schedules. *Journal of the Experimental Analysis of Behavior, 39,* 345-384.

Wise, C.D., Berger, B.D., & Stein, L. (1973). Evidence of alpha-noradrenergic reward receptors and serotonergic punishment receptors in the rat brain. *Biological Psychiatry, 6,* 3-21.

Wise, R.A. (1978). Catecholamine theories of reward: A critical review. *Brain Research, 152,* 215-247.

Witkin, J.M., & Barrett, J.E. (1986). Interaction of buspirone and dopaminergic agents on punished behavior of pigeons. *Pharmacology Biochemistry & Behavior, 24,* 751-756.

10 Consummatory Incentive Contrast: Experimental Design Relationships and Deprivation Effects

Lawrence Dachowski
Tulane University

Mary M. Brazier
Loyola University, New Orleans

In an early study of incentive contrast, Elliott (1928) trained experimental rats to run a maze for bran mash, a highly preferred reward. When these animals were switched to sunflower seed reward they made more errors and ran more slowly than control rats who had been trained from the start with sunflower seeds. This study of incentive contrast has a number of interesting features. First, there was a qualitative change in the reward, from one that was highly preferred to one that was less preferred. Second, a comparison of contrast (i.e., experimental postshift) data was made with data from a control condition to determine if incentive contrast had occurred. In this case, the contrast data were compared to data gathered from a control group of animals who had been run on the same days as the shifted group. Finally, the two incentive conditions were given to the experimental group animals in separate phases of the experiment, so that any contrast exhibited must have been based on a comparison by the experimental animals of the second-phase incentive condition with the previously experienced first-phase condition.

This chapter will begin by looking at various incentive contrast designs in terms of what dimension of the incentive is varied, how the control comparison is made, and whether the contrasting incentives are presented in the same phase or separate phases of the experiment. The various types of incentive contrast design which could be used and some of the implications of using different designs will be systematically considered in light of these three dimensions. We will then look at a procedure that has been extensively employed by Flaherty, contrast in licking behavior with shifts in sucrose solution concentration (See Flaherty, chap. 9 in this volume). Data will be presented from Tulane University that might shed some light on the boundary conditions under which contrast phenomena have been found using this procedure. The implications of our results for an explanation of the mechanisms which underlie this class of phenomena will be discussed.

The incentive contrast literature has been reviewed by a number of scientists (Black, 1968; Cox, 1975; Dunham, 1968; Flaherty, 1982; Rashotte, 1979; Williams, 1983). Although this chapter may suggest certain new approaches to the next reviewer of this literature, a review will not be attempted here.

TAXONOMY OF INCENTIVE CONTRAST DESIGNS

Psychology has not been taxonomically oriented for most of its development in the twentieth century. Schemes for classifying conditioning and learning experiments, however, have occasionally been useful. For instance, Rescorla and Solomon's (1967) article on the interaction between Pavlovian conditioning and instrumental learning was unusually influential. A taxonomy of instrumental conditioning procedures (Woods, 1974) seems to have had some heuristic value (e.g., Tryon, 1976). A taxonomy of incentive contrast experiments based on a few design and procedural dimensions will be presented which, in a similar manner, may be useful in organizing the large incentive contrast literature.

Traditional Terminology

It is desirable for any new system to allow the continued employment of current, commonly used, terminology. Discrete-trials contrast experiments in which two incentive conditions (usually two reward sizes) are given in separate phases are traditionally (e.g., Flaherty, 1982) called successive contrast studies. Elliott's (1928) experiment used this design. When the different rewards are presented within the same phase, usually in an irregular or mixed order, they are called simultaneous contrast studies. In the simultaneous designs there are distinctive exteroceptive cues correlated with the different rewards, that is, a discrimination procedure is used. Distinctive exteroceptive cues ordinarily are not explicitly introduced in successive contrast studies. Behavior of the contrast group is compared with behavior of a non-contrast control group. In each case, if the behavior of the contrast group is greater than the control data, then a positive contrast effect (PCE) has occurred; if it falls below the control performance, then a negative contrast effect (NCE) has occurred.

Behavioral contrast experiments are either treated as a third type of design, or are excluded from reviews (such as Flaherty's, 1982) that are confined to the discrete-trials (i.e., non-Skinnerian) contrast literature. Behavioral contrast experiments are typically conducted with a free-responding operant task, with distinctive exteroceptive cues correlated with two or more schedule components that are mixed together within the same phase ("multiple schedule"). They thus are similar in terms of cues and same-phase presentation to simultaneous contrast as described in the preceding paragraph. After establishing a baseline during nondifferential reinforcement on the two components, the rate of reinforcement is changed on one of the components, and the occurrence of contrast is evaluated by comparing the rate of responding on the unchanged component with the baseline level on that component for the same animal.

The taxonomic system presented here is compatible with the earlier terminology in that two of the cells correspond to the successive and simultaneous contrast paradigms. In addition, behavioral contrast is seen to correspond to yet another cell, which promises the advantage of uniting this Skinnerian contrast literature with that which developed outside the Skinnerian tradition.

Dimensions for Classifying Experimental Designs[1]

This system for classifying contrast experiments is based on two dimensions: the phase(s) in which different incentives are presented, and the control comparison used to evaluate the contrast. There is a noticeable influence of Dunham's (1968, p. 297) discussion of contrast procedure terminology on our taxonomy.

Phase relations. The first distinction in the current taxonomic system is between experiments in which, as in successive contrast, the two incentive conditions are presented in separate phases of the experiment, and those in which the different incentives alternate or are otherwise mixed together within the same phase, as in simultaneous contrast designs. This feature is referred to as "same-phase" versus "separate-phase" designs in Table 10.1.

Control comparisons. The second major dimension for classifying incentive contrast designs is the type of control comparison. By definition, incentive contrast means performance different than that obtained under some non-contrast control condition. The successive contrast design usually includes one or more unshifted control groups, and data from the post-shift phase of the experimental group(s) are compared with data from corresponding trials of the control groups. This is designated "Between-groups" control comparison in Table 10.1. The obvious other possibility would be comparison with other, non-contrast, data from the same subjects, designated "Within-subject." This use of each subject as its own control allows experiments with N=1, or powerful within-subjects statistical analysis. The possible importance of this control comparison dimension is suggested by the fact that experimental findings sometimes depend critically on the nature of the experimental design (Grice, 1966).

Crespi's (1942) frequently-cited study (which introduced the terms "elation" and "depression" for the PCE and NCE, respectively), is not an adequate PCE experiment in terms of our view of control comparisons. If Crespi intended this to be a separate-phase between-groups PCE experiment (as was the NCE portion of Crespi, 1942), then it is flawed by the lack of an unshifted large-reward control group. If it is construed as a separate-phase within-subject study, which is plausible given Crespi's comparison of postshift results against preshift data, then a valid criticism is the one levelled by Spence (1956, p. 130), namely, "that the asymptote of performance had not been attained at

---

[1] We thank Glenn Phelps for useful suggestions about this taxonomic system for incentive contrast research designs. He should not, however, be blamed for any shortcomings in this presentation.

the time of shift and that the subjects were merely responding at a higher level because of the additional training." The problem is more serious than Spence indicated, however, because the preshift data Crespi chose for this comparison were from a different group than the one which was shifted; even if an asymptote had been reached by this control group it still would not permit a within-subjects analysis. The Crespi PCE demonstration is not a flawed experiment in our view; it is no experiment at all because it controls for neither between-subject sampling error nor for variations between occasions.

We do not wish to imply that a separate-group control comparison *and* stable preshift baselines both are necessary in the ideal contrast study. By the present analysis of control aspects, either one or the other would be sufficient (cf. Black, 1968, p. 116).

Although not part of the design taxonomy presented in Table 10.1, the relationship of the incentives of the control condition in same-phase contrast experiments should be considered. For example, McSweeney and Norman (1979) distinguished between two definitions of behavioral contrast. An "intraschedule" definition requires equal baseline rates of reinforcement. By comparison, any change in the rate of responding on an unchanged component, when the other component has a change in reinforcement, is called "interschedule" behavioral contrast, without regard to whether the reinforcement rates of the components were equal during the control phase. McSweeney and Norman recommended that the two definitions of behavioral contrast be distinguished to avoid empirical and theoretical confusion. Our preference would be to use only the intraschedule approach because the control data under equal reinforcement should be free of contamination by any possible contrast effect. The interschedule definition might label a change in behavior as contrast when the control data themselves are affected by contrast. Under either definition of behavioral contrast, of course, a stable asymptote should be achieved in the control phase before a change is introduced.

The traditional successive contrast design, such as that used by Elliott (1928) with separate phases and between-groups comparisons, is in the upper left quadrant of Table 10.1. Simultaneous contrast (e.g., Bower, 1961) with incentive variation in the same phase and a separate control group is in the lower left quadrant. Behavioral contrast experiments, of which there are numerous examples (e.g., King & McSweeney, 1987; Reynolds, 1961; Williams, 1988), fall in the lower right quadrant.

The upper right quadrant corresponds to an interesting design which does not seem to have been used very often. In this case, different incentives would be given to the subject(s) in separate phases of the experiment, but comparison would be made to data from the same subject(s) in an earlier period when the same incentive was given but no contrast was possible. This seems to require at least a three phase design: a control phase, in which a certain level of the incentive is given, a second phase, in which a different incentive value is experienced, and finally a third phase in which the subject(s) would be returned to the original incentive value. A comparison of response measures from the first and third phases would indicate if the intervening second-phase experience changed

TABLE 10.1

Traditional Incentive Contrast Designs and Examples Classified by the Proposed Taxonomic System

Incentive Change	Control Comparison	
	Between-groups	Within-subjects
Separate Phase	"Successive contrast" Elliott (1928)	Gandelman & Trowill (1969)
Same Phase	"Simultaneous Contrast" Bower (1961)	"Behavioral Contrast" Reynolds (1961)

the organism's reaction to the third-phase level of the incentive. This three-phase approach has, in fact, been employed in experiments that Flaherty (1982, pp. 425-426) reviewed under "Saccharin Elation Effect."

Incentive dimensions. The incentive dimension which may be varied is not represented in Table 10.1. There are a number of possibilities:

1. Reward magnitude or amount;
2. Reward quality (such as taste or texture);
3. Delay of reward;
4. Percentage or schedule of reinforcement;
5. Duration of reward;
6. Deprivation level.

The first two of these incentive variables are confounded in most studies of reward quality contrast. For example, in the Elliott (1928) study, it may be that the mash was not only qualitatively different from the sunflower seeds (and more attractive to the rats), but it may also have provided better nutrition than the sunflower seeds; thus it may have been a study of the contrast achieved with simultaneous shifts in both amount and quality of reward. Indeed, there is a basic definitional problem involved in quality shift experiments. More preferred incentives may be inherently more reinforcing (e.g., drive reducing). This is seen most clearly in sucrose shift studies with hungry rats, where the higher concentration sucrose solutions yield more calories as well as tasting different, and there is no way to know certainly whether the contrast effects reported are attributable to the hedonic or caloric variable. This confound may be avoided in sucrose shift studies by using animals that are not food deprived. Shifts in non-nutritive sweeteners should also avoid this confound.

Delay and schedule of reward are variables that do not pose any intrinsic confound problems. With regard to schedule contrast experiments, a possible virtue of the proposed taxonomy is that it makes explicit that schedule contrast research and the use of a behavioral contrast design are logically independent. Even though studies in the Skinnerian ("experimental analysis of behavior") tradition usually used the behavioral contrast design to study schedule contrast, the correlation of this design with this incentive dimension may be regarded as a historical accident rather than a logical necessity.

The last two incentive variables are possibly less clear-cut than the others because each one may be intrinsically confounded with one of the other reward variables. Duration of reward may be viewed just as another way to manipulate reward amount, which seems to be implicitly the approach sometimes used in Skinner box research (Bonem & Crossman, 1988), or it may be regarded as a variable in its own right (Czeh, 1954; Dachowski, 1968).

Shift in the degree of deprivation does sometimes produce contrast effects (E. D. Capaldi, 1973; but also see Hovancik, 1978). To the extent that the incentive or reinforcement value of a reward may be affected by changes in the drive for that reward, these could also be regarded as incentive contrast experiments. If one chooses to conceptualize energizing effects of deprivation (e.g., D in Hull's 1943 theory) separately from the incentive-enhancing effects (e.g., effects on K, Black, 1965), then all deprivation shift experiments would seem to have these two effects of deprivation change confounded.

There is also a potential design limitation on deprivation shift experiments. With ordinary deprivation procedures it is not possible to have more than one drive level within a single day; thus drive contrast studies can use same-phase designs only if, within a phase, each component at a given drive level is 24 hours or longer in duration.

For instance, one trial might be given per day either just before or just after the animal's normal daily feeding, resulting in either 0-hr or 24-hr deprivation on each trial. These high and low drive trials could alternate regularly or randomly in the experimental condition of a same phase experiment. None of the published drive shift studies used this procedure, however.

Variables Not Part of the Taxonomy

It might be worthwhile to point out some things that are not part of this taxonomy. The use of free responding in a Skinner box for behavioral contrast studies as compared to the discrete-trial procedures in most simultaneous or successive contrast studies does not, a priori, have to be an essential difference in incentive contrast designs. This means that it may, in principle, be possible for the behavioral contrast literature to be fully integrated with the body of discrete-trials results. This is a pre-judgement on our part, and may turn out to be untenable; empirical data could overrule our judgement. It might be challenging for researchers to attempt to replicate behavioral contrast results in discrete-trials tasks, and to replicate simultaneous and successive contrast results in the Skinner box. Only if the data are not functionally equivalent would there be a reason to incorporate this task distinction into a taxonomy of incentive contrast.

Within reasonable limits, the same argument can apply to the type of response required; running, swimming, climbing, manipulandum operation, or consummatory behavior do not necessarily produce differences (cf. Padilla, 1971). Where there seem to be empirical differences based on the response-type variable, an examination of specific methodological details may be fruitful.

Species of subjects, it is suggested, need not be a dimension of the taxonomy. Species differences have often been confounded with apparatus and design (viz. pigeons used in Skinner box behavioral contrast studies and rats used in runway incentive contrast experiments), but species effects are of interest in their own right, and could usefully be explored in each of the contrast paradigms. Bitterman and his associates have studied a few types of incentive contrast in different species (e.g., Couvillon & Bitterman, 1984; Papini, Mustaca, & Bitterman, 1988). A desirable but relatively unusual approach is to study one type of contrast in two species within the same experiment; Dougan, Farmer-Dougan, and McSweeney (1989) have done this with rats and pigeons in a behavioral contrast experiment.

Examples

For each of the four paradigms defined in Table 10.1, an attempt was made to find at least one published example of contrast for each of the six incentive dimension that might be varied. For most of the twenty-four possible contrast situations the earliest and/or the most-typical examples known to the authors are listed. There remain several instances, noted below, where no examples are known to the authors; these may be regarded as challenges to future reviewers of this literature to find already published examples, or challenges to researchers to perform new experiments to fill the vacant cells.

Separate phase, between-groups. This design has been used in studies of reward magnitude, quality, delay, and schedule contrast and deprivation contrast. Mellgren (1972) found both positive and negative contrast with shifts in magnitude of food reward in an experiment which employed a constant 20 sec delay of reinforcement. In addition to the previously cited study by Elliott (1928), reward quality contrast has been studied in the runway with changes in sucrose concentration by Homzie and Ross (1962). Marx (1969) reported positive contrast in bar press latencies when rats were shifted from plain food pellets to 32% sucrose pellets. Incentive contrast with shifts in delay of reward were found by McHose and Tauber (1972). Shifts in percentage of reinforcement have produced both positive (Leung & Jensen, 1968) and negative (Seybert, 1979) contrast. Schedule contrast also was examined by Stevenson and Black (1985, experiment 2) using this design. Negative deprivation-shift contrast was demonstrated by E. D. Capaldi (1973) with this design. There do not seem to be any published studies of contrast in duration of reinforcement using this design.

Separate phase, within-subject. Studies that used three or more phases (two or more shifts) in successive reward magnitude contrast could be considered to fall in this category (e.g., Maxwell, Calef, Murray, Shepard, & Norville, 1976; R. Weinstock, 1971). Although statistical comparisons of third phase (post-shift) data with first phase baseline data of the same subjects are not generally reported in these studies, examination of graphs suggests that, in at least some of the experiments of this type, positive or negative contrast occurred.

As mentioned above, the "saccharin elation effect" studies (e.g., Gandelman & Trowill, 1969) fall in this design category with shifts in quality of reward. Stevenson and Black (1985, experiment 1) used this design to look for schedule contrast. Apparently there are no published reports of this design used to look for contrast effects with shifts in delay or duration of reward, or with shifts in deprivation.

Same phase, between-groups. Bower (1961) and others (e.g., Mellgren & Dyck, 1974) have used this approach to study reward magnitude contrast. Contrast with different delays of reward have also been examined with this design (e.g., Beery, 1968). A number of studies (e.g., Henderson, 1966) have looked for schedule or percentage contrast with this paradigm. There does not seem to have been any runway research of reward delay or quality contrast using this approach; consummatory contrast studies with this design will be discussed below. Apparently no deprivation contrast studies have used this approach.

Same phase, within-subject. In a runway-shuttling task Padilla (1971) found evidence for reward magnitude (as well as schedule) contrast with a design of this type. Jaffe (1973) examined quality of reward contrast (reward pellets with added quinine or sucrose, or nothing added) in an experiment designed like the traditional behavioral contrast experiment except that baseline data were obtained after subjects already had some experience with different reward schedules on the two components. Behavioral contrast has been studied with shifts in delay of reinforcement (e.g., Richards & Hittesdorf, 1978; Wilkie, 1972). The most common incentive manipulation, of course, has been schedule of reinforcement (e.g., Reynolds, 1961). Merigan, Miller, and Gollub (1975) looked for behavioral contrast with shifts in reward duration. Apparently no deprivation contrast studies have used this approach.

CONSUMMATORY CONTRAST

Simultaneous and Successive Contrast

Most studies which varied concentration of sucrose solution and looked for contrast in lick rate data (e.g., Vogel, Mikulka, & Spear, 1968) have used the separate-phase between-groups paradigm (successive contrast). For example, the drug studies carried out by Flaherty and his associates (e.g., Flaherty, in press; Flaherty, chap. 9 in this volume) most commonly used this design. The "simultaneous contrast" studies (e.g., Flaherty & Largen, 1975; Flaherty & Rowan, 1986) used chambers with two drinking tubes to allow alternation of two different solutions within each daily session, making this a same-phase design. Control comparisons were sometimes performed between groups (e.g., Flaherty & Largen, 1975, Experiment 3) and sometimes within subjects (e.g., Flaherty & Rowan, 1986, Experiment 2).

When one examines the many variations in procedure that have been used in consummatory contrast, however, it is apparent that some of the distinctions discussed so far are not essential characteristics of the various paradigms. When repeated successive contrast is studied there must be more than two phases to the experiment. For example, Riley and Dunlap (1979) trained rats preshift for 12 days, downshifted experimental animals for four days, retrained for three more days, and finally downshifted again for four days (Phase 1). A double alternation procedure has two days of training alternating with two days of downshift; single alternation of incentive from one day to the next is the next step along this continuum (e.g., Flaherty, Becker, & Checke, 1983, Experiment 3). Finally, there may be two or more alternations of the different incentive conditions within a daily session (e.g., Flaherty & Largen, 1975). This last procedure would normally be considered as simultaneous contrast or behavioral contrast, depending on the control comparison, but in fact it differs from the double or single alternation studies only on the quantitative dimensions of inter-component times. It may be that what really distinguishes the successive contrast experiments from the other designs is the presence or absence of exteroceptive cues correlated with the different incentive values. The separate-phase studies usually do not have such discriminative cues, while the same-phase experiments do.

While explicit exteroceptive stimuli are used to differentiate conditions in most same-phase experiments, they seem to be absent in one sub-group—those conducted by Flaherty and Largen (1975) with alternating drinking tubes within each daily session. However, the position of the tube is a cue, at least within a given day. Also, the very first lick may provide the subject with a highly salient sweetness stimulus indicating whether the higher or lower concentration incentive is available from that tube. In this sense one of the relevant incentive dimensions might itself constitute a signal for differential consummatory behavior for that substance.

If we define a part of an experiment in which the incentive remains the same as a "component," we can describe repeated shift studies in terms of the number of components experienced by the subjects, and the time between components.

The similarity to behavioral contrast is especially striking in the within-subject studies, because, in addition to the design similarities, licking is a free-responding behavior just as bar pressing or key pecking is (cf. Flaherty, Clancy, & Kaplan 1981). In addition, the first taste at each drinking tube, as discussed above, may serve the same role as the cues correlated with the different components of the multiple schedule used in behavioral contrast experiments.

Flaherty's belief that sensory adaptation or sensory contrast is involved in simultaneous consummatory contrast (Flaherty & Avdzej, 1974) may be more a matter of short inter-component intervals (Flaherty & Rowan, 1986), rather than an essential aspect of the design. Consummatory contrast studies using other designs but with short inter-component intervals may also demonstrate incentive contrast based at least in part on sensory contrast.

Anticipatory Contrast

Another design in which effects probably depend crucially on inter-component interval length is anticipatory consummatory contrast. In most studies of anticipatory contrast (e.g., Flaherty & Checke, 1982) a 0.15% saccharin solution is followed by a 32% sucrose solution each day; after several days of training lick rates on the first solution are less than a control group that receives only the saccharin. Lucas, Gawley, and Timberlake (1988) have reported that anticipatory contrast is found with an inter-component interval of 16 minutes but not 32 minutes when testing is done in an apparatus similar to the home cages or when daily feeding of maintenance rations occurs relatively long (90 min) after the second component for the day. When testing in a relatively brightly illuminated apparatus with maintenance feeding soon (5 min) after the second component, anticipatory contrast was found with a 32 minute inter-component interval. Thus, anticipatory negative contrast was a joint function of inter-component time and testing conditions. The fact that Lucas et al. (1988) discuss anticipatory contrast within the framework of optimal foraging theory raises the interesting question of whether one might explain incentive contrast in terms of foraging theory, or explain the foraging data in terms of known incentive contrast principles. One might invoke the marginal value theorem of Charnov (cf. Timberlake, Gawley, & Lucas, 1987) to predict negative anticipatory contrast. But that theorem would only predict that the effect will occur, without specifying the mechanism mediating it. Lucas et al. (1988) noted that the competing response foraging hypothesis of Timberlake et al. (1987) cannot be operating in anticipatory contrast. Perhaps it would be a more fruitful strategy to develop a theory of the mechanism(s) producing incentive contrast independent of foraging theories, and then one could non-circularly use such mechanisms to account for anticipatory contrast when it is demonstrated in foraging behavior.

The strong effect of the second component on anticipatory contrast (Flaherty & Rowan, 1985) seems analogous to the importance of the component "that was to follow" (Williams & Wixted, 1986). Especially when a within-subjects analysis of anticipatory contrast is conducted (Flaherty & Rowan, 1985), the similarity to behavioral contrast is particularly striking. Investigation of this area of consummatory contrast might yield to an approach employing the three component design of Williams.

Anticipatory contrast experiments may be viewed as paradigmatically continuous with successive and simultaneous experiments if one focuses on quantitative variations in intercomponent intervals. Viewed from this standpoint, the interval preceding the critical (e.g., saccharin) component is long (one day) compared to the interval following the critical component (e.g., seconds or minutes).

TULANE UNIVERSITY STUDIES OF CONSUMMATORY CONTRAST

The studies of consummatory contrast at Tulane University have been concerned with the durability of negative consummatory contrast and the effects of food deprivation on successive contrast.

Negative Consummatory Contrast

Both of these concerns are apparent in the dissertation of Edward P. Riley (Riley & Dunlap, 1979). In Phase 1 half of the rats were maintained at 80% of their pre-deprivation weight while the other animals had food and water continuously available in the home cage. Within each deprivation condition one group of rats always received 4% sucrose solution during the 5 min in the apparatus, while the other rats received 32% sucrose for 12 days and then were shifted to 4% for 4 days. Successive negative contrast, that is, lower number of licks for shifted rats than 4% control group animals, was found in food deprived and non-deprived rats. The size of the negative contrast effect (NCE) was about the same for both deprivation conditions on the first postshift day; as often reported with successive contrast in hungry animals (e.g., Flaherty, Becker, & Checke, 1983, Experiment 1), the NCE diminished over the four postshift days as the lick rate of the deprived experimental subjects increased,

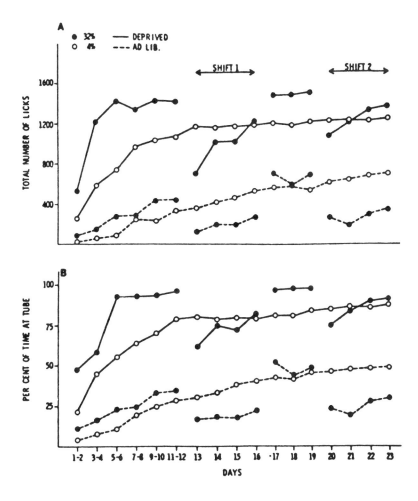

Figure 10.1. The mean number of licks (panel A) and time spent at the tube (panel B) for daily 5 min sessions for food deprived and nondeprived (ad lib) rats as a function of sucrose concentration. From Riley and Dunlap (1979, p. 62). Copyright 1979 by the University of Illinois Press. Reprinted by permission.

but the NCE continued at the same level for the four postshift days for the nondeprived rats. These data are shown in Figure 10.1. The experimental animals were retrained for three days with 32% sucrose, and then downshifted again. Control animals were always given 4% sucrose to lick. The difference in durability of NCE is even more striking than after the first downshift. The NCE is virtually nonexistent for the deprived animals by the second postshift day, while the NCE in the nondeprived (ad lib) subjects remains large over the 4 days. The findings for the deprived animals have since been confirmed by Flaherty, Becker, and Checke (1983, Experiments 1 and 2).

Riley and Dunlap (1979) then performed two more retrainings and downshifts, once with all rats nondeprived and then with all rats deprived. The results (see Figure 10.2) were durable contrast with nondeprived animals and very transitory contrast with deprived animals, and no interaction with prior deprivation condition. That is, the effect of deprivation on NCE pattern was strictly a function of the current deprivation level, and was not influenced by previous deprivation history. The lower panels of Figures 10.1 and 10.2 show virtually the same patterns of results for the dependent variable of time spent at the drinking tube. This dependent measure was obtained in most of the Tulane studies reported here. It will not be reported again because, except for a few trivial exceptions, the time at tube measure paralleled the lick rate data in both general nature of the effects and statistical significance.

Durability of Negative Consummatory Contrast

The Riley and Dunlap (1979) study demonstrated consummatory NCEs in nondeprived animals which lasted at least four days and which recurred undiminished for four downshifts. The next study attempted to determine how many postshift days it would take for the NCE to diminish in nondeprived animals. We also wanted to determine if NCEs would continue to reappear with more than four downshifts. This study, performed with the assistance of Michael McNichols (Dachowski & Dunlap, 1976), used three groups of ten nondeprived rats each: a control group which always received 4% sucrose; a group which received 32% sucrose for 13 days, followed by 11 days of 4% sucrose; and a group which received 13 days of 32% sucrose followed by 11 days alternating between 4% and 32% (a total of 6 downshifts). The NCEs were durable beyond our expectations. The single downshift group continued licking significantly below the control group for all 11 postshift days. The alternating group licked significantly below the control group on each downshift day, and did not significantly differ from the single downshift group's performance on those days (see Figure 10.3). Findings similar to the NCEs of the alternating condition have since been reported with deprived animals by Flaherty, Becker, and Checke (1983, Experiment 3).

We decided to replicate these results and attempt to extend them by looking at the durability of NCE in nondeprived animals in yet another way (Dachowski, Piazza, & Dunlap, 1981). The same three-group design was used as in the previous study (with 9 rats per group). Fifteen days of preshift training were given before licking behavior stabilized. The first postshift period

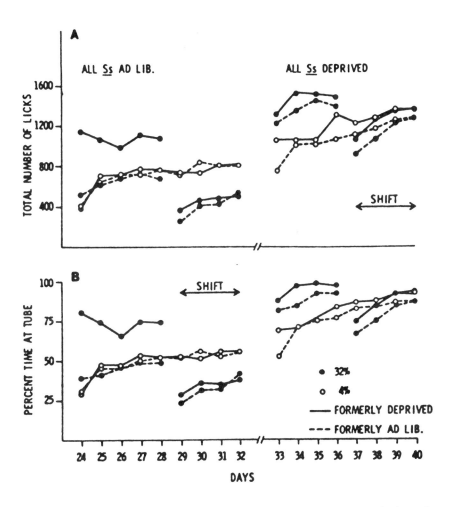

Figure 10.2. Lick rates (panel A) and time spent at the tube (panel B) with all animals nonde-prived (ad lib) and then all animals food deprived. From Riley and Dunlap (1979, p. 66). Copyright 1979 by the University of Illinois Press. Reprinted by permission.

lasted 10 days, allowing five downshifts for the alternating group. As in the previous study, NCE was found for all 10 days for the single-downshift group, and on each downshift day the alternating group exhibited NCEs which were not significantly different than those of the single-downshift group on those days (see Figure 10.4). A 78-day vacation was then introduced, during which the animals continued to receive food and water ad lib in their individual home cages, and were occasionally handled.

Two animals died during the vacation period, one each from the control and alternating groups. When testing was resumed under the same treatment for each group as prevailed before the vacation, the single-downshift and alternating groups continued to show NCEs as before. Eight days of post-vacation treatment were given. Only the NCEs over the last four days reached marginal statistical significance ($p = .055$); evidently the NCEs on the first four days were affected by the rather low performance of the 4% control group and increased variability in all groups. Apparently the long vacation induced a nonspecific disorganization of behavior for many of the rats which lowered mean lick rates and increased individual difference variability, but which did not affect their basic reaction to the sucrose solutions.

The durability of the NCE of the single downshift group is remarkable, considering that these rats had not had contact with the 32% solution for 95 days by the last day of the experiment. This is markedly different than the situation with food deprived rats when a retention interval is introduced between the last preshift day and the first postshift day in consummatory contrast studies. Retention periods of 17 days (Flaherty, Capobianco, & Hamilton, 1973) and 32 days (Gordon, Flaherty, & Riley, 1973), but not 10 days (Flaherty & Lombardi, 1977), prevent the occurrence of consummatory NCE. It is unknown whether the difference between the effect of retention intervals and the

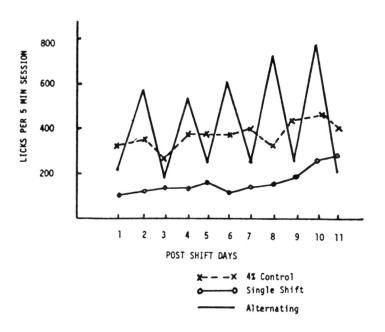

Figure 10.3. Mean lick rates per daily 5 min session during the second (postshift) phase for a control group given 4% sucrose solution on all days, an experimental group shifted from 32% to 4% sucrose, and a group shifted from 32% to alternation between 4% and 32% sucrose (Dachowski & Dunlap, 1976).

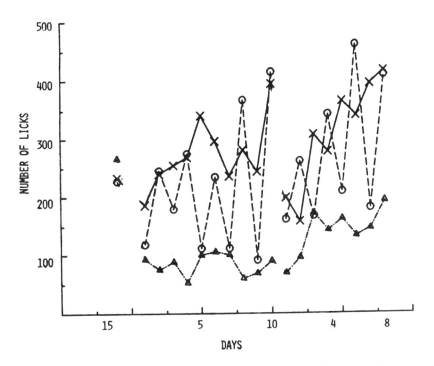

Figure 10.4. Mean number of licks on the last preshift day (Day 15), ten postshift days, and eight post-vacation days (Dachowski, Piazza, & Dunlap, 1981). Solid lines with Xs represent data of the 4% control group, triangles are for the group that was trained with 32% sucrose solution and received 4% solution on all postshift days, and circles are for the group trained with 32% solution and alternated between 4% and 32% on postshift days.

effect of the 78-day vacation is a matter of the deprivation level or the placement of the retention/vacation period. Additional research would be needed to decide between these two hypotheses. It may be that the introduction of the vacation after several postshift days on which the NCE was manifest allowed that lower level of responding to be conditioned to the entire experimental context in a micro-molar fashion such that, when rats from this group were returned to the testing situation, they reproduced their low (NCE) level of behavior. This seems to be a more plausible explanation than deprivation level.

Symmetrical Consummatory Contrast Effects

A continuing empirical concern about the contrast literature has been the difficulty of demonstrating symmetrical contrast effects, that is finding a PCE as well as an NCE (Flaherty, 1982). This difficulty has been attributed to a ceiling effect (Bower, 1961) whereby large reward control conditions generate such high levels of performance that it is difficult for upshifted groups significantly to surpass them. Relatively low deprivation has been suggested (e.g., Shanab & Ferrell, 1970) as a way of avoiding the ceiling effect by lowering performance of all subjects, including those in the control group. Flaherty (1982) has pointed out that data from runway studies (e.g., Benefield, Oscos, & Ehrenfreund, 1974) do not support the value of this suggestion. Consummatory contrast studies using within-subject designs found either a larger PCE under low deprivation (Panksepp & Trowill, 1971), or no difference in magnitude of the PCE (Flaherty & Largen, 1975), but PCEs were found in the higher deprivation conditions. Food deprivation appeared to eliminate the saccharin elation effect (Ashton, Gandelman, & Trowill, 1970) which usually is found in nondeprived rats (e.g., Gandelman & Trowill, 1969). No previous studies investigated the effect of food deprivation on the successive consummatory PCE with between-subjects control comparisons.

We decided to conduct a study (Brazier & Dachowski, 1987) using a factorial combination of preshift (4% and 32%) and postshift (4% and 32%) sucrose solutions. All rats were maintained with food and water continuously available except for the daily 5-min experimental sessions. This design allowed us to look for the PCE and NCE in nondeprived animals. As can be seen in Figure 10.5, no PCE was obtained; rats shifted from 4% to 32% sucrose failed to reach the level of licking of the unshifted 32% control group. The apparent convergence of performance of these groups on the last (tenth) postshift day seems mainly a matter of poorer performance of the control group on that day. A statistically significant NCE was found on the first four postshift days. The finding of a relatively durable NCE was in agreement with the results of Riley and Dunlap's (1979) nondeprived groups.

The Tulane studies reported above differed in procedure in one possibly important detail from the procedure usually followed by Flaherty in his successive consummatory contrast studies: the timing of the 5 min daily session began with the placement of the rat in the licking box, rather than with the first

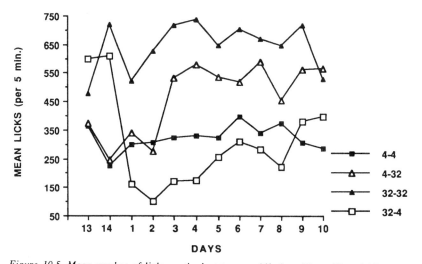

Figure 10.5. Mean number of licks on the last two preshift days (Days 13 and 14) and ten postshift days (Brazier & Dachowski, 1987). Group designations refer to sucrose concentrations received during the preshift and postshift phases, respectively; for example, the 4-32 group received 4% sucrose preshift and 32% sucrose postshift.

lick (e.g., Flaherty, Becker, & Osborne, 1983). The final Tulane study followed the usual Flaherty procedure; the 5 min interval was timed from the first lick.

In her dissertation Brazier (1986) used a repeated shift design in which the experimental group of rats received two days of exposure to 32% sucrose, followed by two days exposure to 4% sucrose, and so forth, alternating every two days. Control groups were always maintained on either 4% or 32% to check for NCE and PCE, respectively. Flaherty, Becker, and Checke (1983, Experiment 3) found both PCE and NCE using this approach with deprived rats. Their PCEs were statistically significant on the first and second upshifts (Days 5 and 6, and 8 and 9) only; the reduction in positive contrast on the later shifts seemed to be a matter of increased responding by control animals rather than a reduction in the effect of the upshifts. Their NCEs were greater on the first day of each downshift, tending to diminish on the second day of each downshift. We combined this three group design with two levels of deprivation (90% of predeprivation body weight and nondeprived) to determine if these effects would occur equally in deprived and nondeprived animals.

The data from the three deprived groups of this six-group experiment, shown in Figure 10.6, agree with those reported by Flaherty et al. (1983). NCEs were found on the first day of every downshift from 32% to 4% sucrose relative to the 4% sucrose control group and were statistically significant. The apparent NCEs on the second day of each downshift were smaller, and were

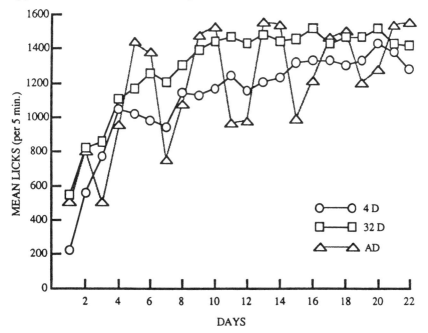

Figure 10.6. Mean number of licks of deprived subjects shifted every two days between 32% and 4% sucrose solutions (AD), and subjects always receiving 4% (4D) or 32% (32D) sucrose (Brazier, 1986).

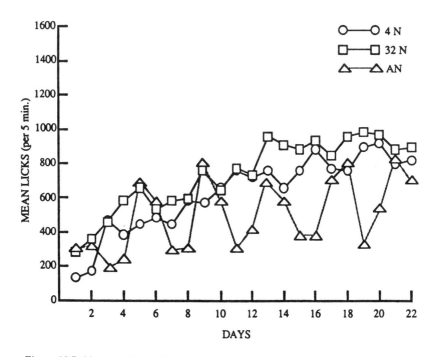

Figure 10.7. Mean number of licks of nondeprived subjects shifted every two days between 32% and 4% sucrose solutions (AN), and subjects always receiving 4% (4N) or 32% (32N) sucrose (Brazier, 1986).

significant in shifts 3 and 5 only. Some PCE relative to the 32% control group was present on all upshifts, most pronounced on shifts 1, 2, 3, and 5, but was statistically significant only on the first day of the first upshift.

The data from the nondeprived groups, shown in Figure 10.7, resembles those from Brazier's master's thesis with nondeprived rats, discussed above, in that: 1) NCEs were found with each downshift; 2) the NCEs were enduring and significant on the second day of each downshift, and appeared undiminished (except for the last downshift) across shifts; and, 3) there was no evidence of PCEs.

Subsequent observations were made while all of the animals received the nondeprived maintenance condition (Brazier, 1988). The data followed the now-familiar pattern for nondeprived subjects: no PCE, and durable NCEs (see Figure 10.8). All groups performed essentially the same regardless of prior deprivation history, except that previously deprived animals licked at higher overall rates than animals which had never been deprived (but the rate differences were not statistically significant). This difference may have been produced by residual body weight differences, as weights of previously deprived groups remained significantly below the weights of never-deprived groups even though they received 24 days of continuous access to food and water. These residual lick-rate differences apparently did not modify the typical nondeprived pattern of consummatory contrast. These results are similar to those reported by Riley and Dunlap (1979) discussed above with regard to NCEs.

With regard to the lack of PCEs in nondeprived animals, it should be noted that Rabiner, Kling, and Spraguer (1988) reported substantial and enduring PCEs with nondeprived rats; their procedure was substantially different from ours with regard to several details. Saccharin was used rather than sucrose, and daily sessions were 30 min long rather than 5 min.

Taken together, the Tulane studies show large, recurring, and durable NCEs in nondeprived animals. The NCE can persist through a long vacation interpolated between postshift sessions. Only deprived rats exhibited a PCE in these studies, all of which used between-group control comparisons.

SUMMARY AND CONCLUSIONS

Two theoretically important findings in consummatory contrast have been regularly reported in animals under food-deprivation conditions: 1) The size of consummatory successive negative contrast decreases on the second postshift day (or by the third 5 min segment of a 20 min postshift session, Flaherty, Grigson, & Rowan, 1986, Experiments 2a and 2b). 2) Certain drugs, particularly chlordiazepoxide (CPD), further decrease the NCE on the second postshift day, as discussed by Flaherty (chap. 9 in this volume).

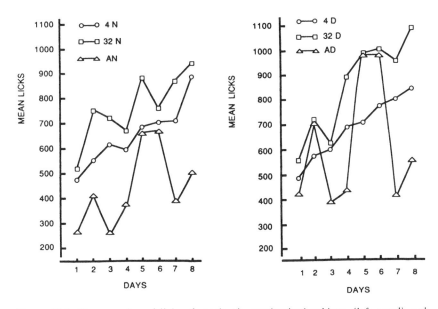

Figure 10.8. Mean number of licks of previously nondeprived subjects (left panel) and previously deprived subjects (right panel) when all subjects received the nondeprived maintenance condition (Brazier, 1988). Triangles are for subjects shifted every two days between 32% and 4% sucrose solutions (groups AD and AN), squares are for subjects always receiving 32% sucrose (groups 32 D and 32 N), and circles are for subjects always receiving 4% sucrose (groups 4 D and 4 N).

The absence of the first of these effects in nondeprived animals is now well established (Brazier, 1986; Brazier, 1988; Brazier & Dachowski, 1987; Dachowski & Dunlap, 1976; Dachowski et al., 1981; Riley & Dunlap, 1979). Figure 9.5 of Flaherty (chap. 9 in this volume) shows the absence of both of these effects in nondeprived rats. That is, on the second postshift day, nondeprived rats receiving the control injections (saline) did not show a particular decrease of NCE on that day, and nondeprived animals injected with CDP similarly did not decrease their NCE. It can be noted that both the subjects shifted from 32% to 4% sucrose, and those always receiving the 4%, showed a nonspecific increase in drinking on the day that they received CDP.

There is a third, probably related, difference between the first and second postshift day in deprived rats. Blood plasma corticosterone levels are elevated on the second, but not the first, postshift day for rats which demonstrate negative consummatory contrast (Flaherty, Becker, & Pohorecky, 1985). This last result presumably shows that a downshift in sucrose concentration is stressful, but perhaps only on the second day. It is tempting to speculate that plasma corticosterone elevation might also fail to appear in nondeprived rats on the second postshift day, but no data on this point are currently available.

Taken together, this pattern of deprivation effects suggests that something fundamentally different happens during the second day of successive consummatory NCE than on the first day for food deprived rats, and this difference does not exist for nondeprived animals. We believe that the NCE procedure seems to produce, for whatever reason, a strong tendency for the downshifted animals to lick less of the 4% sucrose solution, but by the second day in deprived animals this tendency is in strong conflict with the tendency to lick the 4% sucrose based on the need for calories (cf. Flaherty & Rowan, 1986, p. 390). This conflict is stressful, and the resolution of this conflict is facilitated by CDP. Whether CDP facilitates this resolution by acting directly on the conflict, or whether it works through stress or emotion reduction, may be answered through further research.[2]

This account of the consummatory NCE in deprived animals is supported by the pattern of conditions under which CDP does *not* affect the NCE. As mentioned above, the CDP effect is absent in nondeprived animals (Flaherty, this volume). It also is absent in the simultaneous consummatory NCE (Flaherty, Lombardi, Kapust, & D'Amato, 1977) and the anticipatory NCE (Flaherty & Rowan, 1988). In each of these cases, the results are consistent with the view that there will be an effect of CDP only if there is conflict based on a continuing need for calories and the availability of calories. Likewise, even in deprived rats it would be expected that NCEs resulting from shifts in a nonnutritive substance such as saccharin should not be affected by CDP. Re-

---

[2] The elimination or reduction of NCE by certain brain lesions (cf. Becker, Jarvis, Wagner, & Flaherty, 1984) may not have the same basis as the reduction of NCE by CDP. The brain lesions may have their effect on whatever processes cause NCE on the first exposure to the lower sucrose concentration, and thus need not be involved in the conflict hypothesized to mediate second-day effects.

cently reported results (Weaver, Rowan, & Flaherty, 1989) confirm this prediction.

There remains the question of the causal mechanism for consummatory contrast when it does occur. We hypothesize that, under either food deprived or nondeprived conditions, the NCE is the result of a hedonic devaluation of the less sweet solution based on a comparison with a cognitive representation (cf. Spear, 1967) of the sweeter solution. This representation may be a memory, whether controlled by classical conditioned stimulus relationships or by other means (cf. Flaherty & Rowan, 1986). A parallel with certain posttraining revaluations of stimuli discussed by Delamater and LoLordo (chap. 3 in this volume) is apparent. Perhaps the comparator hypothesis (Miller & Grahame, chap. 4 in this volume), by means of its response evocation rule, can provide the mechanism for prediction of reduced responding in this situation.

When inter-component times are short (e.g., less than a few minutes, as in Flaherty & Largen, 1975), there is a sensory contrast effect that adds to any cognitively mediated hedonic effect. This sensory contrast should tend to produce a PCE with short inter-component times, regardless of deprivation level. With longer inter-component times, apparently only deprived animals show a consummatory PCE. Why this should be so is unclear, but the evidence that Amsel frustration is similarly related to deprivation condition (Dunlap & Frates, 1970) is consistent with the notion that emotional factors have a special role in consummatory PCE at longer inter-component intervals. On the other hand, Rabiner et al. (1988) suggest that the pattern of their findings, which included PCEs in nondeprived animals, provide evidence against an emotional theory such as Crespi's (1942) elation and depression, as well as against Solomon and Corbit's (1974) opponent process theory.

The wealth of information on consummatory NCEs encourages a limited range of explanatory speculation regarding the causal basis for the effects observed under various experimental procedures (cf. Flaherty & Rowan, 1986). Explaining why the PCE is found under a more limited set of conditions is more difficult because, ironically, the difficulty of demonstrating PCEs means that there are much less data available on which to base our theories.

ACKNOWLEDGMENTS

This research was supported in part by a Biomedical Sciences Support Grant from PHS to Tulane University. Preparation of this manuscript was supported in part by the Robert E. Flowerree Fund in Psychology of Tulane University. We thank W. J. Hansche for computer assistance, and Roy Fowler for help with apparatus improvements and maintenance. The authors thank Charles F. Flaherty, Michelle LeDuff, and Meg Dachowski for their comments on an earlier version of this chapter.

REFERENCES

Ashton, A. B., Gandelman, R., & Trowill, J. A. (1970). Effect of food deprivation upon elation of saccharin drinking following a temporary shift to water. *Psychonomic Science, 21*, 5-6.

Becker, H. C., Jarvis, M., Wagner, G., & Flaherty, C. F. (1984). Medial and lateral amygdala lesions differentially influence contrast with sucrose solutions. *Physiology & Behavior, 33*, 707-712.

Beery, R. G. (1968). A negative contrast effect of reward delay in differential conditioning. *Journal of Experimental Psychology, 77*, 429-434.

Benefield, R., Oscos, A., & Ehrenfreund, D. (1974). Role of frustration in successive positive contrast. *Journal of Comparative and Physiological Psychology, 86*, 648-651.

Black, R. W. (1965). On the combination of drive and incentive motivation. *Psychological Review, 72*, 310-317.

Black, R. W. (1968). Shifts in magnitude of reward and contrast effects in instrumental and selective learning: A reinterpretation. *Psychological Review, 75*, 114-126.

Bonem, M., & Crossman, E. K. (1988). Elucidating the effects of reinforcement magnitude. *Psychological Bulletin*, 104, 348-362.

Bower, G. H. (1961). A contrast effect in differential conditioning. *Journal of Experimental Psychology, 62*, 196-199.

Brazier, M. M. (1986). Effects of repeated shifts on positive and negative contrast in consummatory behavior in deprived and non-deprived rats. (Doctoral dissertation, Tulane University, 1986.) *Dissertation Abstracts International, 47*, 3142B.

Brazier, M. M. (1988). *Effects of present and former deprivation condition on consummatory contrast following repeated shifts in sucrose concentration.* Paper presented at the meeting of the Southern Society for Philosophy and Psychology, Miami, FL.

Brazier, M. M., & Dachowski, L. (1987). *Successive contrast effects in non-deprived rats following shifts in sucrose concentration.* Paper presented at the meeting of the Midwestern Psychological Association, Chicago, IL.

Capaldi, E. D. (1973). Effect of shifts in body weight on rats' straight alley performance as a function of reward magnitude. *Learning and Motivation, 4*, 229-235.

Couvillon, P. A., & Bitterman, M. E. (1984). The overlearning-extinction effect and successive negative contrast in honeybees (*Apis mellifera*). *Journal of Comparative Psychology, 98*, 100-109.

Cox, W. M. (1975). A review of recent incentive contrast studies involving discrete-trial procedures. *Psychological Record, 25*, 373-393.

Crespi, L. P. (1942). Quantitative variation of incentive and performance in the white rat. *American Journal of Psychology, 55*, 467-517.

Czeh, R. S. (1954). *Response strength as a function of the magnitude of the incentive and consummatory time in the goal box.* Unpublished master's thesis, State University of Iowa, Iowa City, IA.

Dachowski, L. (1968). Effects of reward magnitude and duration on runway performance. *Psychological Reports, 23*, 769-770.

Dachowski, L., & Dunlap, W. P. (1976). *Durable negative contrast with repeated shifts in sucrose concentration.* Paper presented at the meeting of the Psychonomic Society, St. Louis, MO.

Dachowski, L., Piazza, C., & Dunlap, W. P. (1981). *Effects of motivation and 78-day vacation on negative contrast.* Paper presented at the meeting of the Psychonomic Society, Philadelphia, PA.

Dougan, J. D., Farmer-Dougan, V. A., & McSweeney, F. K. (1989). Behavioral contrast in pigeons and rats: A comparative analysis. *Animal Learning and Behavior, 17*, 247-255.

Dunham, P. J. (1968). Contrasted conditions of reinforcement: A selective critique. *Psychological Bulletin, 69*, 295-315.

Dunlap, W. P., & Frates, S. B. (1970). Influence of deprivation on the frustration effect. *Psychonomic Science, 21*, 1-2.

Elliott, M. H. (1928). The effect of change of reward on the maze performance of rats. *University of California Publications in Psychology, 4*, 19-30.

Flaherty, C. F. (1982). Incentive contrast: A review of behavioral changes following shifts in reward. *Animal Learning and Behavior, 10*, 409-440.

Flaherty, C. F. (in press). Effects of anxiolytics and antidepressants on extinction and negative contrast. In S. E. File (Ed.), *International encyclopedia of pharmacology and therapeutics: Psychopharmacology of anxiolytics and antidepressants*. New York: Pergamon.

Flaherty, C. F., & Avdzej, A. (1974). Bidirectional contrast as a function of rate of alternation of two sucrose solutions. *Bulletin of the Psychonomic Society, 4*, 505-507.

Flaherty, C. F., Becker, H. C., & Checke, S. (1983). Repeated successive contrast in consummatory behavior with repeated shifts in sucrose concentration. *Animal Learning and Behavior, 11*, 407-414.

Flaherty, C. F., Becker, H. C., & Osborne, M. (1983). Negative contrast following regularly increasing concentrations of sucrose solutions: Rising expectations or incentive averaging? *Psychological Record, 33*, 415-420.

Flaherty, C. F., Becker, H. C., & Pohorecky, L. (1985). Correlation of corticosterone elevation and negative contrast varies as a function of postshift day. *Animal Learning and Behavior, 13*, 309-314.

Flaherty, C. F., Capobianco, S., & Hamilton, L. W. (1973). Effect of septal lesions on retention of negative contrast. *Physiology and Behavior, 11*, 625-631.

Flaherty, C. F., & Checke, S. (1982). Anticipation of incentive gain. *Animal Learning and Behavior, 10*, 177-182.

Flaherty, C. F., Clancy, J. A., & Kaplan, P. S. (1981). Behavioral contrast in rats with an operant licking response. *Bulletin of the Psychonomic Society, 17*, 269-272.

Flaherty, C. F., Grigson, P. S., & Rowan, G. A. (1986). Chlordiazepoxide and the determinants of negative contrast. *Animal Learning and Behavior, 14*, 315-321.

Flaherty, C. F., & Largen, J. (1975). Within-subjects positive and negative contrast effects in rats. *Journal of Comparative and Physiological Psychology, 88*, 653-664.

Flaherty, C. F., & Lombardi, B. R. (1977). Effect of prior differential taste experience on retention of taste quality. *Bulletin of the Psychonomic Society, 9*, 391-394.

Flaherty, C. F., Lombardi, B. R., Kapust, J., & D'Amato, M. R. (1977). Incentive contrast uninfluenced by extended testing, imipramine, or chlordiazepoxide. *Pharmacology, Biochemistry, & Behavior, 7*, 315-322.

Flaherty, C. F., & Rowan, G. A. (1985). Anticipatory contrast: Within-subjects analysis. *Animal Learning and Behavior, 13*, 2-5.

Flaherty, C. F., & Rowan, G. A. (1986). Successive, simultaneous, and anticipatory contrast in the consumption of saccharin solutions. *Journal of Experimental Psychology: Animal Behavior Processes, 12*, 381-393.

Flaherty, C. F., & Rowan, G. A. (1988). Effect of intersolution interval, chlordiazepoxide, and amphetamine on anticipatory contrast. *Animal Learning & Behavior, 16*, 47-52.

Gandelman, R., & Trowill, J. A. (1969). Effects of reinforcement shifts upon subsequent saccharin consumption. *Psychonomic Science, 15*, 25.

Gordon, W. C., Flaherty, C. F., & Riley, E. P. (1973). Negative contrast as function of the interval between pre-shift and post-shift training. *Bulletin of the Psychonomic Society, 1*, 25-27.

Grice, G. R. (1966). Dependence of empirical laws upon the source of experimental variation. *Psychological Bulletin, 66*, 488-498.

Henderson, K. (1966). Within-subjects partial-reinforcement effects in acquisition and in later discrimination learning. *Journal of Experimental Psychology, 72*, 704-713.

Homzie, M. J., & Ross, L. E. (1962). Runway performance following a reduction in the concentration of a liquid reward. *Journal of Comparative and Physiological Psychology, 55*, 1029-1033.

Hovancik, J. R. (1978). The effect of deprivation level during noncontingent pairings and instrumental learning on subsequent instrumental performance. *Learning and Motivation, 9*, 1-15.

Hull, C. L. (1943). *Principles of behavior*. New York: Appleton-Century.

Jaffe, M. L. (1973). The effects of lesions in the ventromedial nucleus of the hypothalamus on behavioral contrast in rats. *Physiological Psychology, 1*, 191-198.

King, G. R., & McSweeney, F. K. (1987). Contrast during multiple schedules with different component response requirements. *Animal Learning and Behavior, 15*, 97-104.

Leung, C. M., & Jensen, G. D. (1968). Shifts in percentage of reinforcement viewed as changes in incentive. *Journal of Experimental Psychology, 76*, 291-296.

Lucas, G. A., Gawley, D. J., & Timberlake, W. (1988). Anticipatory contrast as a measure of time horizons in the rat: Some methodological determinants. *Animal Learning and Behavior, 16*, 377-382.

Marx, M. H. (1969). Positive contrast in instrumental learning from qualitative shift in incentive. *Psychonomic Science, 16*, 254-255.

Maxwell, F. R., Calef, R. S., Murray, D. W., Shepard, J. C., & Norville, R. A. (1976). Positive and negative successive contrast effects following multiple shifts in reward magnitude under high drive and immediate reinforcement. *Animal Learning and Behavior, 4*, 480-484.

McHose, J. H., & Tauber, L. (1972). Change in delay of reinforcement in simple instrumental conditioning. *Psychonomic Science, 27*, 291-292.

McSweeney, F. K., & Norman, D. M. (1979). Defining behavioral contrast for multiple schedules. *Journal of the Experimental Analysis of Behavior, 32*, 457-461.

Mellgren, R. L. (1972). Positive and negative contrast effects using delayed reinforcement. *Learning and Motivation, 3*, 185-193.

Mellgren, R. L., & Dyck, D. G. (1974). Reward magnitude in differential conditioning: Effects of sequential variables in acquisition and extinction. *Journal of Comparative and Physiological Psychology, 86*, 1141-1148.

Merigan, W. H., Miller, J. S., & Gollub, L. R. (1975). Short-component multiple schedules: Effects of relative reinforcement duration. *Journal of the Experimental Analysis of Behavior, 24*, 183-189.

Padilla, A. M. (1971). Analysis of incentive and behavioral contrast in the rat. *Journal of Comparative and Physiological Psychology, 75*, 464-470.

Panksepp, J., & Trowill, J. A. (1971). Positive and negative contrast in licking with shifts in sucrose concentration as a function of food deprivation. *Learning and Motivation, 2*, 49-57.

Papini, M. R., Mustaca, A. E., & Bitterman, A. E. (1988). Successive negative contrast in the consummatory responding of didelphid marsupials. *Animal Learning & Behavior, 16*, 53-57.

Rabiner, D. L., Kling, J. W., & Spraguer, P. A. (1988). Modulation of taste-induced drinking: The effects of concentration shifts and drinking interruptions. *Animal Learning and Behavior, 16*, 365-376.

Rashotte, M. E. (1979). Reward training: Contrast effects. In M. E. Bitterman, V. M. LoLordo, J. B. Overmier, & M. E. Rashotte (Eds.), *Animal learning: Survey and analysis* (pp. 195-239). (v.19 in NATO advanced studies institutes series: Series A, Life Sciences). New York: Plenum Press.

Rescorla, R. A., & Solomon, R. L. (1967). Two-process learning theory: Relationships between Pavlovian conditioning and instrumental learning. *Psychological Review, 74*, 151-182.

Reynolds, G. S. (1961). Behavioral contrast. *Journal of the Experimental Analysis of Behavior, 4*, 57-71.

Richards, R. W., & Hittesdorf, W. M. (1978). Inhibitory stimulus control under conditions of signalled and unsignalled delay of reinforcement. *Psychological Record, 28*, 615-625.

Riley, E. P., & Dunlap, W. P. (1979). Successive negative contrast as a function of deprivation condition following shifts in sucrose concentration. *American Journal of Psychology, 92*, 59-70.

Seybert, J. A. (1979). Positive and negative contrast effects as a function of shifts in percentage of reward. *Bulletin of the Psychonomic Society, 13*, 19-22.

Shanab, M. E., & Ferrell, H. J. (1970). Positive contrast obtained in the Lashley maze under different drive conditions. *Psychonomic Science, 20*, 31-32.

Solomon, R. L., & Corbit, J. D. (1974). An opponent-process theory of motivation: I. Temporal dynamics of affect. *Psychological Review, 81*, 119-145.

Spear, N. E. (1967). Retention of reinforcer magnitude. *Psychological Review, 74*, 216-234.

Spence, K. W. (1956). *Behavior theory and conditioning.* New Haven: Yale University Press.

Stevenson, M. K., & Black, R. W. (1985). Incentive value of free-response reward schedules. *American Journal of Psychology, 98*, 333-352.

Timberlake, W., Gawley, D. J., & Lucas, G. A. (1987). Time horizons in rats foraging for food in temporally separated patches. *Journal of Experimental Psychology: Animal Behavior Processes, 13*, 302-309.

Tryon, W. W. (1976). Models of behavior disorder: A formal analysis based on Woods's taxonomy of instrumental conditioning. *American Psychologist, 31*, 509-518.

Vogel, J. R., Mikulka, P. J., & Spear, N. E. (1968). Effects of shifts in sucrose and saccharine concentrations on licking behavior in the rat. *Journal of Comparative and Physiological Psychology, 66*, 661-666.

Weaver, M., Rowan, G.A., & Flaherty, C. F. (1989, March). *Effects of chlordiazepoxide on contrast following shifts in saccharin concentration.* Paper presented at the meeting of the Southern Society for Philosophy and Psychology, New Orleans, LA.

Weinstock, R. B. (1971). Preacquisition exploration of the runway in the determination of contrast effects in the rat. *Journal of Comparative and Physiological Psychology, 75*, 107-115.

Wilkie, D. M. (1972). The peak shift and behavioral contrast: Effects of discrimination training with delayed reinforcement. *Psychonomic Science, 26*, 257-258.

Williams, B. A. (1983). Another look at contrast in multiple schedules. *Journal of the Experimental Analysis of Behavior, 39,* 345-384.

Williams, B. A. (1988). The effects of stimulus similarity on different types of behavioral contrast. *Animal Learning and Behavior, 16,* 206-216.

Williams, B. A., & Wixted, J. T. (1986). An equation for behavioral contrast. *Journal of the Experimental Analysis of Behavior, 45,* 47-62.

Woods, P. J. (1974). A taxonomy of instrumental conditioning. *American Psychologist, 29,* 584-597.

11 Multiple Memory Systems of the Mammalian Brain Involved in Classical Conditioning

Theodore W. Berger
Julia L. Bassett
William B. Orr
University of Pittsburgh

Experimental Strategies for Investigating the Neurobiological Basis of Learning: The Model Systems Approach

During the 1960s, a consensus developed that identification of the neurobiological basis of learning was a sufficiently complex problem that it required an experimental strategy very different than had been used previously. It was proposed that a major focus of research involve the use of "model systems," characterized as animal preparations which exhibit simple, highly stereotypic reflexes amenable to learning-dependent modification through controlled experimental conditions, for example, habituation, sensitization, and classical conditioning paradigms (Cohen, 1969; Crow & Alkon, 1980; Kandel & Spencer, 1968; Thompson et al., 1976; Thompson & Spencer, 1966; Weinberger, Diamond, & McKenna, 1984; Woody, 1974). The rationale was that experimenter-determined, phasic presentation of conditioning stimuli would facilitate identification of sensory pathways transmitting information about the environmental events controlling behavior. Likewise, the simplified nature of the behavior would facilitate identification of the motor pathways mediating the reflex and conditioned responses. Points of convergence between sensory and motor circuitry would identify synapses where neural plasticity underlying learned behavior first occurred. Such "primary sites" of plasticity then could be subjected to biochemical and molecular analyses to reveal the mechanisms responsible for information storage in the nervous system.

This experimental strategy, implemented over the course of the last two decades, has been remarkably successful. In particular, the use of invertebrate preparations has allowed the identification and detailed study of several mechanisms of synaptic plasticity believed to underlie non-associative and associative forms of learning (Alkon, 1979; Crow & Forrester, 1986; Gingrich & Byrne, 1987; Klein & Kandel, 1980). Extension of the same experimental strategy to vertebrate and mammalian preparations has been more difficult, because of the larger size and greater complexity of neuronal systems of higher species and the reduced accessibility of their neurons. Nonetheless, there has been notable success in identifying candidate mechanisms of learning-induced synaptic plasticity in vertebrates (Disterhoft, Coulter, & Alkon, 1986; Glanzman & Thompson, 1980; Mamounas, Thompson, Lynch, & Baudry, 1984; Swartz & Woody, 1979; Vrenson & Cardozo, 1981), as well as in localizing possible primary sites of synaptic plasticity for further study (Berger & Weisz, 1987; Davis, Gandelman, Tischler, & Gandelman, 1982; Diamond & Weinberger, 1986; Greenough, Larson, & Withers, 1985; Kraus & Disterhoft, 1982; LeDoux, 1987; Thompson, 1986; Wall, Gibbs, Broyles, & Cohen, 1985). Although there can be little doubt that at least the initial stage of extending the model systems strategy to vertebrate and mammalian species has been successful, it has become equally clear that there are a number of principles of nerve cell function that are expressed uniquely in higher species. These principles relate not to functioning at a molecular level, but to functioning at a system level[1]. As a result, it also is becoming apparent that a more complete understanding of these principles will require an experimental strategy which is radically different than the model systems approach, and which already has begun to evolve.

Multiple Memory Systems of the Mammalian Brain

One of the characteristics of the mammalian brain that distinguishes it from lower species is that learning and memory functions are mediated by several anatomically discrete systems, each responsible for the acquisition and/or storage of a different class of learned behaviors. For example, studies of human amnesia have shown that the hippocampus and adjacent limbic brain regions are essential for the formation of long-term memories of names and facts (Cohen & Squire, 1980; Zola-Morgan, Squire, & Amaral, 1986). In lower mammals an analogous specialization is expressed in the necessity of the hippocampus for learning higher-order associations, such as those related to conditional discriminations or reversal of a previously learned discrimination (Berger & Orr, 1983; Fagan & Olton, 1986; Hirsh, 1974; Loechner & Weisz, 1987; O'Keefe & Nadel, 1975; Port & Patterson, 1984; Ross, Orr, Holland, & Berger, 1984). Motor learning and classical conditioning of reflexes, on the other hand, do not require the hippocampus (Berger & Orr, 1983; Mauk & Thompson, 1987; Milner, 1970; Norman, Buchwald, & Villablanca, 1977;

---

[1] By "system level" function is meant the consequence of interactions between the different populations of neurons comprising a single brain structure, as well as the consequence of interactions between different brain structures.

Solomon, 1977), and instead depend on the cerebellum and related brainstem regions (Moore, Desmond, & Berthier, 1982; Thompson, 1986). Associatively-induced changes in reflexes also can occur independently of the cerebellum in the form of classically conditioned reflex facilitation, which appears to reflect the contribution of brainstem reticular formation neurons intimately associated with the reflex pathway (Harvey, Gormezano, & Cool-Hauser, 1985; Weisz & LoTurco, 1988; Weisz & McInerney, 1990). An additional memory system which underlies classical conditioning of autonomic and "fear" responses includes the amygdala and its connections with the hypothalamus and brainstem (Jarrel, Gentile, Romanski, McCabe, & Schneiderman, 1987; Kapp, Schwaber, & Driscoll, 1985; LeDoux & Iwata, 1987; Powell & Buchanan, 1980).

One of the apparent consequences of having multiple, specialized memory systems is that conditioning of even the simplest reflex is associated with changes in neuronal activity in many different sites in the brain (Olds, Disterhoft, Segal, Kornblith, & Hirsh, 1972; Wall et al., 1985), most of which are not necessary for the development or maintenance of the conditioned response. In many instances, learning-related activity in the so-called "non-essential" brain sites has been found to be associated with neural plasticity intrinsic to those sites (Berger & Weisz, 1987; Diamond & Weinberger, 1986; Disterhoft et al., 1986; Greenough et al., 1985; Mamounas et al., 1984; Vrenson & Cardozo, 1981), and thus does not simply reflect afferent activity propagated from "essential" sites of plasticity more closely related to the reflex circuitry. The fact that multiple brain areas become engaged during learning is understandable when it is considered that each area is specialized, and that almost all tasks have multiple components. For example, classical conditioning of eyeblink using an aversive unconditional stimulus (UCS) also is accompanied by conditioned changes in heart rate, and as noted above, there are almost non-overlapping neural substrates for the two learned behaviors (in particular, see Powell & Buchanan, 1980). As another example, the hippocampus is needed for learning non-conditional discriminations, but when such discriminations are reversed or made conditional, an intact hippocampus becomes essential (Berger & Orr, 1983; Ross et al., 1984; Loechner & Weisz, 1987). Despite the requirement of the hippocampus for only a subset of such tasks, equally robust CS-evoked unit responses develop in the hippocampus throughout all types of discriminations (Berger, 1984; Deadwyler, West, & Lynch, 1979; Disterhoft & Segal, 1978). In total, these findings suggest that learning-related activity which develops in brain regions outside the circuitry essential for the conditioned response is necessary for a different learned behavior that simply is not measured, or is necessary for the concatenation of individual stimulus-response or response-reward relationships into higher-order representations.

Memory Systems with Large Numbers of Neurons and Complex Circuitries

Two additional and rather obvious characteristics of the mammalian brain that distinguish it from lower species are its size and complexity. Not only are most memory systems of the mammalian brain composed of large numbers of neurons, but there is extensive heterogeneity among principal neurons and modulatory interneurons; this wide variety of cell types interacts within complex circuitries of hierarchically organized feedforward and feedback pathways. There are several consequences of such large and complex network structures, specifically with regard to their mediation of memory functions. One is the increased possibility for "distributed representations," that is, when learning-dependent unit activity is expressed by a population of neurons and it is the combined activity of all neurons that provides the strongest correlation with the conditioned stimulus (CS) and/or conditioned response. The activities of individual cells correlate with different components of the represented event. Because many neural systems are hierarchically organized, the possibility of higher-order distributed representations also must be considered.

A second consequence is a reduced dependence of unit activity on time-locked, physical parameters of conditioned stimuli and conditioned behaviors. This lack of a precise, easily defined relationship between environmental events and unit responses can develop because of the large number of neurons comprising input/output circuits, the increased possibility for transformations of neural signals, and cross-modal integration resulting from convergence of projections from different sensory systems. When these characteristics are coupled with cellular mechanisms that allow rapid and substantial modifiability of synaptic connections, the possibility arises that neurons of more centrally located memory systems can be involved in representations of a wide range of qualitatively different classes of events. In this sense, they may function as "general" memory buffers, in contrast to lower species in which each learned behavior is stored locally as a component of the appropriate reflex circuit.

In this chapter we will review research using classical conditioning of the nictitating membrane (NM) reflex in the rabbit, a preparation first developed by Gormezano (Gormezano, Prokasy, & Thompson, 1987; Gormezano, Schneiderman, Deaux, & Fuentes, 1962) and later adapted by Thompson (Thompson et al., 1976) as a model system for studying the neurobiological basis of mammalian associative learning. We have used this preparation to study the role of the hippocampus with respect to the two issues outlined above. In one series of studies, we have investigated the representation of learned information by the population activity of hippocampal pyramidal neurons. We have attempted to determine the information content of CS-evoked firing of hippocampal pyramidal neurons, and any systematic differences in that content among individual neurons. In a second series of studies, we have attempted to define the transsynaptic propagation of learning-related activity from the hippocampus to other brain regions. The goal of these experiments is to determine how output from the hippocampus interacts with other memory systems known to contribute to conditioned nictitating membrane responding.

HIPPOCAMPAL PYRAMIDAL CELL ACTIVITY DURING CLASSICAL CONDITIONING OF THE NICTATITING MEMBRANE RESPONSE

In the studies described here, tones or lights were used as conditioned stimuli (CS; duration of 350-850 ms, depending on the experiment) and an airpuff to the cornea was used as the UCS (100 ms duration, co-terminating with the CS). Conditioned extension of the nictitating membrane (NM) over the corneal surface develops rapidly, reaching a rate of ≥80% CR rate within 1-3 days depending on the specific conditions, and with little or no non-associative contribution to CS-elicited behavior (Berger & Thompson, 1978a; Gormezano et al., 1962). Unit activity was recorded from small populations of cells (5-10 neurons) using fixed position electrodes chronically implanted in the pyramidal cell layer of the hippocampus (Berger & Thompson, 1978a). Single unit activity was recorded using chronically implanted microdrives with which recording electrodes could be lowered into the dorsal hippocampus before each conditioning session (Berger, Rinaldi, Weisz, & Thompson, 1983). The majority of recordings were from pyramidal neurons, which are the output neurons of the hippocampus; as such, their activity represents a convergent, summary measure of all neuron populations comprising the hippocampus. Antidromic activation procedures were used to distinguish pyramidal cells from other populations of neurons intrinsic to the hippocampus; different populations of non-pyramidal neurons were defined on the basis of spontaneous firing characteristics.

Learning-Induced Changes in CS-Evoked Firing Rate and Pattern of Pyramidal Cell Activity

Recordings throughout the course of conditioning in the awake animals showed that classical conditioning of the NM response is associated with a gradual increase in the within-trial firing rate of pyramidal cells; firing rate during the inter-trial intervals does not change (Figure 11.1). We also analyzed the information content of CS-evoked activity with respect to temporal pattern. Analysis of poststimulus time histograms showed that the increased firing rate of pyramidal neurons is not evenly distributed throughout the duration of each trial. Instead, there is a specific pattern of discharge that is time-locked to both onset and amplitude of the behavioral response, resulting in a highly positive correlation between the probability of cell discharge and amplitude-time course of the NM response. The learning-induced relationship between pyramidal cell activity and behavior is evident both early in training when NM movement occurs as an unconditioned reflex (Figure 11.2), and later in training when conditioned responses are expressed during the CS-UCS interval (Figure 11.2). During the development of conditioned responses, increased pyramidal cell activity occurs with a progressively shorter latency from CS onset, preceding the onset of NM movement by an average for all cells of approximately 50 ms (Berger, Laham, & Thompson, 1980; Berger et al., 1983).

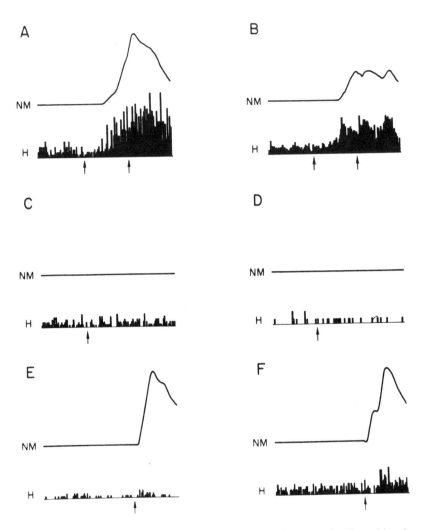

Figure 11.1. Averaged nictitating membrane (NM) responses (top traces in all panels) and peristimulus time histograms (bottom traces in all panels) of hippocampal pyramidal cell firing during delay conditioning (A and B) and unpaired training (C-F) of the rabbit NM response. Panel A and panel B show data from two different pyramidal cells, respectively, recorded from two different animals. Panels sets C and E, and sets D and F show data from two different cells, respectively, recorded from two different animals. First arrow indicates onset of tone; second arrow indicates onset of airpuff. Interstimulus interval is 250 ms. H, hippocampus. From Berger at al. (1983), copyright by the American Physiological Association. Reprinted by permission.

This positive correlation with behavior is not a fortuitous one. We found that, in addition to pyramidal cells, the firing rate of two non-pyramidal cell

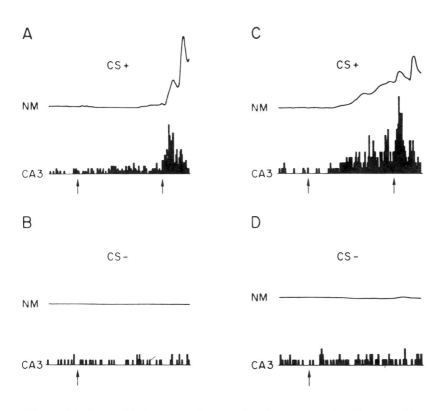

Figure 11.2. Averaged NM responses (top traces) and peristimulus time histograms (bottom traces) of hippocampal pyramidal cell firing during early (A) and late (B) phases of two-tone discrimination conditioning of the NM response. Interstimulus interval is 750 ms. From Berger (1984), copyright by Guilford Press. Reprinted by permission.

types also increased upon presentation of the CS. The within-trial firing pattern for each of the three classes of neurons was different, however, and easily distinguishable (Figure 11.3); only pyramidal cells exhibited activity paralleling the shape of the conditioned response. In addition, parameters of conditioned response shape, such as latency to peak NM amplitude, are known to be tightly coupled to the CS-UCS interstimulus interval (Schneiderman & Gormezano, 1964). Changes in the interstimulus interval (ISI) result in corresponding changes in the within-trial distribution of pyramidal cell action potentials (compare Figure 11.1A and B, 250 ms interval, with Figure 11.2A and B, 750 ms interval). Thus, the effect of NM conditioning is an enhancement of the within-trial firing rate of pyramidal cells, and an entrainment of activity to the amplitude-time course of the behavioral response. Approximately 70% of identified pyramidal cells exhibit this learning-induced change in activity (Berger et al., 1983).

The increased response of pyramidal cells reflects associative processes of conditioning. The changes in activity which occur with conditioning do not develop with explicitly unpaired presentations of the CS and UCS (Berger et al., 1976), or with paired CS-UCS presentations using very short interstimulus intervals (e.g., 50 ms) that do not support conditioned responding. The latter observation was made by Hoehler and Thompson (1980), who provided a quantitative analysis of the relationship between pyramidal cell plasticity and

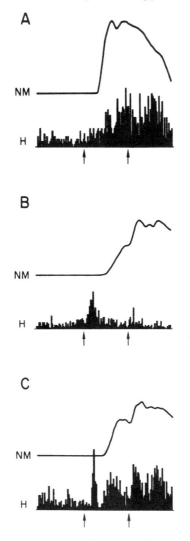

Figure 11.3. Examples of peristimulus time histograms of three different classes of hippocampal neurons recorded during delay conditioning of the NM response: identified pyramidal neuron (A), non-pyramidal neuron (B), theta cell (C). Note that all cell types exhibit increased firing rates during the trial (CS onset indicated by the first arrow; second arrow indicates airpuff onset), but all have different correlates as determined by the pattern of discharge within the trial.

ISI. They used a range of CS-UCS intervals that included both optimal (those that lead to maximum amplitude conditioned responses) and non-optimal ISIs (those that support conditioned responding, but with amplitudes that are smaller than the maximum). Results showed that magnitude of the pyramidal cell response was highly correlated with amplitude of the conditioned response. The enhanced pyramidal cell activity during the unconditioned response (UCR) also represents an associative phenomenon, and is consistent with Gormezano's finding that the first conditioned responses to appear during training have latencies equal to or greater than the interstimulus interval, and thus are obscured by the UCR (Coleman & Gormezano, 1971). During later phases of training when conditioned responses are initiated during the CS-UCS interval, maximum amplitude is reached at the time of UCS onset and so extends into the trial period associated with the UCR. Pyramidal cell activity displays these same characteristics, as revealed by CS-alone trials presented periodically throughout the course of NM conditioning (Berger, Laham, & Thompson, 1980; Berger et al., 1983). These and other investigations of hippocampal unit activity consistently have found that CS-evoked increases in pyramidal cell activity develop only when the CS-UCS configuration supports conditioned NM behavior (for a review, see Berger, Berry, & Thompson, 1986).

These learning-induced changes in hippocampal pyramidal cell activity are not specific to NM conditioning, and in this sense, appear to reflect general functional properties of the hippocampus. For example, the CS-evoked increases in pyramidal cell activity described above have been observed using several different conditioning paradigms: trace (Disterhoft, Golden, Read, Coulter, & Alkon, 1988; Solomon, Vander Schaaf, Norbe, Weisz, & Thompson, 1986), discrimination reversal (Berger, 1984), and delay (Berger, Alger, & Thompson, 1976; Moore et al., 1982). In addition, pyramidal cell plasticity during NM conditioning is independent of the modality of the CS (Thompson et al., 1980), motivational state (Berry & Oliver, 1983; Holt & Thompson, 1984), and even the species of animal (Patterson, Berger, & Thompson, 1979).

"Distributed Representation" of the Conditioned Response by the Population Activity of Pyramidal Neurons

When the within-trial firing pattern of individual pyramidal neurons was examined in greater detail, it was discovered that a "distributed representation" of conditioned NM amplitude-time course was suggested by the activity of the population of active pyramidal neurons. In our analyses of single cell activity, correlation coefficients were computed to determine the relationship between the poststimulus time histogram representing the distribution of action potentials during all trials for which a cell was recorded, and the digital representation of the averaged NM response for those same trials (Berger et al., 1983). Although many cells exhibited a statistically significant and positive correlation with the conditioned response (72%), different cells discharged maximally in correspondence with different components of the conditioned response. For example, the cell shown in panel B of Figure 11.4 fired primarily at the onset of the conditioned response; in contrast, the cell shown in panel C fired primarily with the response component occurring after onset of the airpuff. Differences in the "phase relation" between the distribution of action potentials and the amplitude-time course of NM extension for a large sample of cells ranged from +84 ms to -190 ms, indicating significant differences among pyramidal neurons despite the fact that the activity of all cells was positively correlated with the conditioned response.

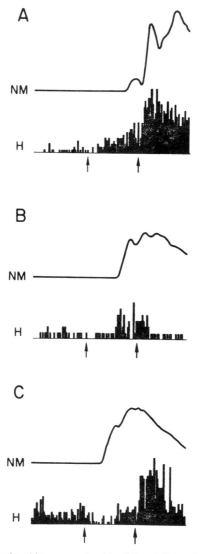

Figure 11.4. Peristimulus time histograms showing different "phase" relations between the within-trial firing of three identified pyramidal cells and conditioned NM responses. From Berger et al. (1983), copyright by the American Physiological Association. Reprinted by permission.

Additional evidence for a distributed representation of the conditioned NM response came from a comparison of the magnitudes of correlation coefficients computed as described above for recordings of single cells vs. small populations of cells. For cases in which poststimulus time histograms were generated from recordings of single cells, the values of the coefficients ranged from +0.34 to +0.80. When histograms were generated from recordings of populations of approximately 5-10 neurons, however, the values of the coefficients ranged from +0.64 to +0.95; values exceeding +0.80 and even +0.90 were frequently obtained (Berger, Laham, & Thompson, 1980). Thus, the correlation with conditioned NM behavior is greater in magnitude when the activity of more than one neuron is considered. In total, these data indicate that the amplitude-time course of the NM response represented by the CS-evoked activity of pyramidal neurons is best described as a "population correlate," given that the correlate is most accurately identified by the integrated activity of many pyramidal cells.

Multiple "Clusters" of Pyramidal Neurons Expressing the Same Population Correlate

An additional population property of hippocampal pyramidal neurons might be termed "clustering" of the correlates of single cells. The term "clustering" is used to refer to the fact that a given population correlate can be represented in an apparently complete manner by the firing of a relatively small subpopulation of spatially adjacent pyramidal neurons. As noted above, it is not unusual for the combined activity of 5-10 neurons to exhibit a within-trial distribution of action potentials which correlates at a +0.90 level or greater with the shape of the conditioned NM response (Berger, Laham, & Thompson, 1980). Such highly correlated activity is expressed by neurons that can be recorded simultaneously from the same electrode, that is, from a subpopulation of neurons that is in close proximity to one another. Thus, information sufficient to identify the population correlate is represented in the firing of a small subset of the total number of pyramidal neurons. Because the same high correlation can be found in recordings from widely varying locations in the hippocampus (at least with respect to the dorsal half of the structure), multiple representations of the population correlate appear to be distributed over many different subpopulations of cells, or "clusters." Although it remains possible that the output of each cluster varies with respect to some dimension of the population correlate, such a relationship has yet to be identified (though see Eichenbaum, Wiener, Shapiro, & Cohen, in press).

Response Specificity of Hippocampal Pyramidal Cell Correlates

At first consideration, it may seem puzzling that such a massive engagement of the majority of neurons in the hippocampus occurs as a result of acquiring one conditioned response. The changes in pyramidal cell response that accompany NM conditioning also may appear to be difficult to reconcile with other equally compelling observations of different correlates of hippocampal unit activity, for example, spatial fields exhibited during food retrieval in a maze or other well-defined environment (Muller, Kubie, and Ranck, 1987; O'Keefe, 1976). These apparent contradictions are reconciled, however, when two other well-established characteristics of the hippocampus are considered. First, the majority of input to the hippocampus (via the perirhinal and entorhinal cortices) originates from association neocortex (Van Hoesen & Pandya, 1975; Van Hoesen, Pandya, & Butters, 1975). As a result, input to the hippocampus is highly processed and sufficiently far removed from the periphery that few constraints are known to exist on the range of possible correlates of hippocampal pyramidal neurons. Second, although the hippocampus is necessary for the formation of long-term memories, it clearly is not a site of storage for long-term memories (Milner, 1970). Instead, the hippocampus appears to be involved in temporary representations of learned information (though temporary representations which are distinct from those identified with short-term memory).

This functional involvement in temporary representations is illustrated by the finding that hippocampal pyramidal cell activity correlates with the amplitude-time course of NM extension only when the ocular muscles are those activated by the UCS. When behaviors other than the NM response are classically conditioned, hippocampal activity correlates with the amplitude-time course of the response system under UCS control. Berry and co-workers have demonstrated this "response specificity" using a behavioral preparation developed by Gormezano for studying appetitive learning — classical conditioning of jaw movement in the rabbit. Using an intraoral injection of saccharin as the UCS, Gormezano and associates have shown that water-deprived rabbits display rhythmic jaw movements which are highly stereotypic in terms of amplitude and period (Smith, DiLollo, & Gormezano, 1966). Classical conditioning of this behavior occurs readily, and as with the NM response, conditioned responses can be almost purely associative in nature. Using the jaw movement preparation, Berry and Oliver (1983) found that hippocampal neurons recorded from the CA1 pyramidal cell layer develop a within-trial increase in firing rate that occurs with a progressively shorter latency from CS onset, in parallel with the development of conditioned jaw movement responses. Action potentials also occur with greatest frequency at the time of maximum jaw opening, exhibiting a rhythmic bursting in synchrony with the periodicity of the behavioral response. As with NM conditioning, these changes in hippocampal unit activity are dependent on temporal contiguity of the CS and UCS. Thus, CS-elicited firing rate of hippocampal neurons increases both during conditioning of NM extension and during conditioning of jaw movement (as well as leg flexion, see Thompson et al., 1980). The within-trial distribution of action potentials, however, is specific to the conditioned response (Figure 11.5).

The Hippocampus as a Temporary Store for Item-Specific Information

The findings reviewed above indicate that specific information about all conditioned behaviors can be represented in the activity of hippocampal pyramidal neurons. This generalization can be broadened to include specific information about "all classes of events," based on observations made by other investigators using a wide range of testing conditions (for a review, see Berger & Bassett, in press). Such a collective consideration of many findings from recordings of unit activity in the behaving animal leads to the conclusion that hippocampal neurons are not "tuned" exclusively to a narrow range of stimuli or behaviors. Instead, the major determinants of the population correlate appear to be the specific features of whatever stimuli and/or responses define the conditions for associative learning. These data justify the conclusion that the hippocampus functions as a temporary store for information about specific items relevant to ongoing learned behavior (though not necessarily being the sole determinant of behavior; see below), as suggested previously by Olton (Olton, Becker, & Handlemann, 1979) and by Rawlins (1985).

If this characterization is correct, the temporal dynamics governing functional properties of the hippocampus must allow the majority of pyramidal

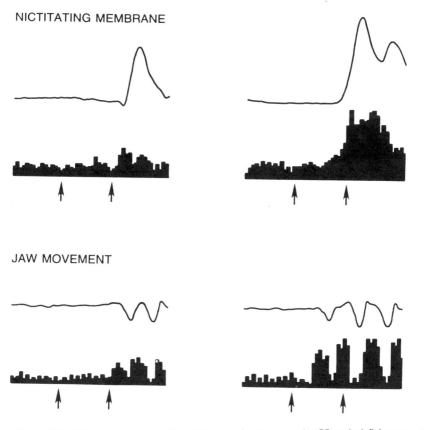

Figure 11.5. Schematic representation of the relation between the CS-evoked firing rate of hippocampal pyramidal neurons as a function of number of training trials (left: initial phase of conditioning; right: asymptotic phase of conditioning), and the relation between the pattern of pyramidal cell firing and the conditioned behavioral response (top: nictitating membrane; bottom: jaw movement).

neurons to change correlates readily. The capability for rapid alteration in activity has been demonstrated by the sensitivity of hippocampal neurons to the temporal contiguity of the CS and UCS (Berger et al., 1976; Hoehler & Thompson, 1980), and to differences in the probability of reinforcement or UCS occurrence from the previous training session (Disterhoft & Segal, 1978) and even the previous training trial (Foster, Christian, Hampson, Campbell, & Deadwyler, 1987). There also is no significant decay in the CS-evoked activity of hippocampal neurons as long as the CS remains paired with a UCS in a manner that supports learned behavior (Foster et al., 1987; Kettner & Thompson, 1982). Thus, the population correlate of pyramidal neurons has a duration determined only by the physical presence of the correlate, provided the context includes the prerequisites for associative learning.

CONTRIBUTION OF THE HIPPOCAMPUS TO CONDITIONED NM BEHAVIOR

Another major issue we have explored is the contribution of learning-induced changes in hippocampal pyramidal cell activity to conditioned NM behavior. As outlined earlier, most conceptions of hippocampal function have assumed that the structure is not necessary for more rudimentary forms of learning (Isaacson, 1974; Schmajuk, 1984). There also is little disagreement with the general notion that the hippocampus is involved in the learning of higher-order associations (Eichenbaum, Fagan, Matthews, & Cohen, 1988; Hirsh, 1974; Olton et al., 1979; Port & Patterson, 1984; Solomon, 1977). For example, damage to the hippocampus results in a failure to utilize the multiple relations among distal environmental cues specifying spatial location, though guidance of reflexive or stereotypic movements to a goal is preserved (O'Keefe & Nadel, 1975). Likewise, learning that the relationship between a tone and food depends on the relationship between that tone and a light (i.e., a conditional discrimination) is lost upon hippocampectomy. In contrast, non-conditional discriminations are learned and remembered readily (Loechner & Weisz, 1987; Ross et al., 1984). Conditional operations play a role in all learning situations that demand a change in behavior in response to a change in contingencies of reward or punishment (Hirsh, 1980). Conditional operations become particularly important when the same stimuli are involved in specifying all possible contingencies, such as during reversal of a previously learned discrimination (Fagan & Olton, 1986; Powell & Buchanan, 1980; Winocur & Olds, 1978). In such instances, cues can be sufficiently ambiguous that higher-order relationships are the only source of information about response-reward contingencies.

With this as an historical and conceptual framework, we tested the hypothesis that the changes in hippocampal pyramidal cell activity which develop with classical conditioning of the NM response also contribute primarily during the learning of higher-order associations typified by discrimination reversal. The necessity of the hippocampus for reversal learning was tested by removing bilaterally the hippocampus or the overlying neocortex as a control. After re

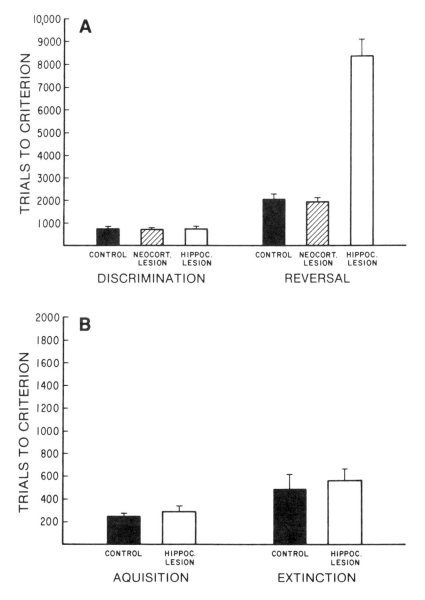

Figure 11.6. Panel A: Effects of bilateral removal of the hippocampus or overlying neocortex on the rates of discrimination and reversal conditioning of the rabbit NM response. Panel B: Effects of bilateral removal of the hippocampus or overlying neocortex on the rates of delay conditioning (Acquisition) and extinction using an explicitly unpaired paradigm. Animals in the CONTROL group received the surgical preparation only. From Berger and Orr (1983), copyright by Elsevier Science Publishers. Reprinted by permission.

covery from surgery, animals were trained using a two-tone (Berger & Orr, 1983) or tone-light (Weikart & Berger, 1986) discrimination paradigm. After reaching behavioral criterion for the initial discrimination, the tone frequencies were reversed with respect to pairing with the airpuff UCS. Hippocampectomized animals acquired the initial discrimination at the same rate as controls, but were selectively impaired during the reversal phase of the task (Figure 11.6, top panel). Animals with hippocampal damage failed at reversal by responding equivalently to both the CS+ and CS- (Figure 11.7). These data indicate that the fundamental association between the tone and airpuff was not affected by loss of the hippocampus; stated in other terms, the "motor learning" component of the task was left intact. In contrast, the ability of hippocampectomized animals to construct mnemonic labels to distinguish the CS+ and CS- properties of the two tones was greatly impaired. It should be noted that the non-differential responding during reversal conditioning did not reflect an inability of hippocampectomized animals to extinguish conditioned responding (Figure 11.6, bottom panel). Extinction rates in response to unpaired CS and UCS presentations were equivalent for control and hippocampectomized animals (for a more complete discussion of issues related to this finding, see Berger & Orr, 1983). The hypothesis that the hippocampus plays a particularly critical role in learning conditional operations also has been supported using serial feature positive discrimination tasks (Loechner & Weisz, 1987; Ross et al., 1984).

MULTISYNAPTIC PATHWAYS TRANSMITTING HIPPOCAMPAL OUTPUT TO SUBCORTICAL BRAIN REGIONS

Results from the lesion studies described above demonstrate that learning-dependent activity in the hippocampus is necessary for the modification of learned behavior in response to a particular class of environmental constraints. For this to be the case, output from the hippocampus must influence motoneurons responsible for NM movement. We are in the process of identifying the transsynaptic pathways through which hippocampal pyramidal cell activity can be transmitted to other brain regions that control striated musculature. Although extension of NM behavior is mediated by the accessory abducens nucleus of the pontine brainstem, the hippocampus contributes to learned modification of virtually all behaviors (Isaacson, 1974; Schmajuk, 1984). Two of the major premotor systems in the brain, the basal ganglia and the cerebellum, serve as control systems in providing on-line modification of virtually all reflexive and goal-directed movements related to striated musculature (Alexander & DeLong, 1985a, 1985b; Lisberger, Morris, & Tychsen, 1987; Pellionisz & Llinas, 1982; Rolls, Thorpe, & Maddison, 1983). As a result, both systems are good candidates as transsynaptic targets of hippocampal output (Figure 11.8). In addition, both the basal ganglia and the cerebellum have been identified as structures essential for conditioned reflexes and learned sequences of spe-

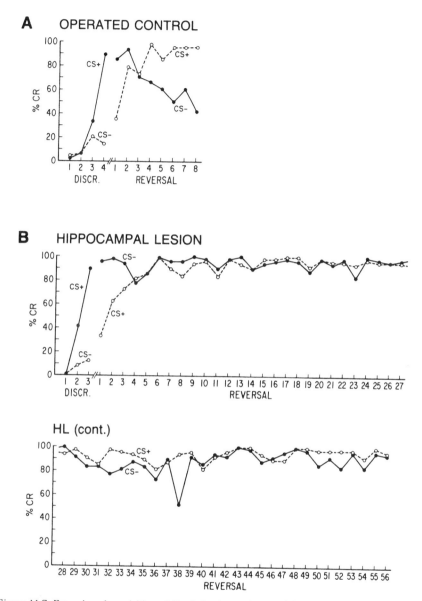

Figure 11.7. Examples of acquisition of discrimination and reversal learning rates for one representative control animal and one representative hippocampectomized animal. From Berger and Orr (1983), copyright by Elsevier Science Publishers. Reprinted by permission.

cific movements (Ito, 1974; Moore & Berthier, 1987; Saint-Cyr, Taylor, & Lang, 1988; Thompson, 1986; West, Michael, Knowles, Chapin, & Woodward, 1987), raising the possibility that the hippocampus may influence motoneurons through interactions with another memory system of the brain. In a series of anatomical studies, we have mapped multisynaptic pathways which have the potential for connecting hippocampal pyramidal cells with subcortical premotor systems, including the basal ganglia and the cerebellum.

Subicular projections to the posterior cingulate gyrus. Our initial studies focused on the subiculum (Berger, Swanson, Milner, Lynch, & Thompson, 1980), which is the target of the majority of efferents from the hippocampus. Although the subicular cortex projects to several brain regions, its reported output to the posterior cingulate gyrus (Sorensen, 1980) is of particular interest in the context of the transsynaptic influence of hippocampal output on subcortical premotor structures. The cingulate gyrus provides input to both the caudate nucleus and the ventral pontine nuclei (Domesick, 1969); the ventral pontine nuclei are the major source of mossy fiber input to the cerebellum.

The posterior cingulate gyrus has been subdivided into the cingulate cortex (of Rose & Woolsey, 1948; or the proisocortex, area 29d, of Vogt, Sikes, Swadlow, & Weyand, 1986), and the retrosplenial cortex (of Rose & Woolsey; or the periallocortex, area 29b/c, of Vogt, et al.). Using autoradiographic and horseradish peroxidase techniques, we found that the subiculum projects solely to the retrosplenial component of the posterior cingulate gyrus, terminating primarily in layer IV; virtually no terminals were detected in the more dorsal, cingulate component. These projections to the retrosplenial arise from neurons contained only in the subiculum (and not the pre- or parasubiculum), with the distribution of the cells of origin overlapping extensively with the location of terminal fields from the hippocampus.

Projections from the posterior cingulate gyrus to the ventral pons. We subsequently investigated the efferent systems of the posterior cingulate gyrus, and distinguished in our analysis between those arising from

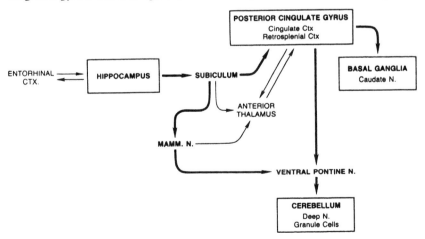

Figure 11.8. Schematic representation of the anatomical relationship between the hippocampus/subiculum and major premotor brain systems mediated by subicular projections to the posterior cingulate gyrus, and efferent projections of the posterior cingulate to the caudate nucleus and to the ventral pontine nuclei.

the retrosplenial component and those arising from the cingulate component. Because of the exclusive distribution of subicular efferents to the retrosplenial region, only brain areas receiving efferents from the retrosplenial cortex could be influenced by learning-dependent activity in the hippocampus. Although a number of different projection sites were identified (Bassett & Berger, 1990), one of the most prominent projections was that to the ventral pontine nuclei. Of the seven ventral pontine nuclei in the rabbit (Brodal & Jansen, 1946), the paramedian, lateral, and the ventral gray are the primary targets of retrosplenial (and cingulate) efferents. In contrast, the dorsolateral gray and nuclei reticularis tegmenti pontis receive a lesser innervation. Although results indicated a moderate projection to the peduncular and median gray, neither nucleus is well developed in the rabbit. Thus, the majority of retrosplenial efferents to the ventral pons terminate within the paramedian, lateral, and ventral nuclei (Figure 11.9). Studies currently in progress are determining the distribution of efferents from each of the pontine nuclei to different regions of the cerebellum to identify the cerebellar regions most likely to be influenced by hippocampal output.

The cingulate subdivision was found to provide a more widespread input to the caudate nucleus than the retrosplenial cortex. Efferents originating in the retrosplenial terminated only within a very narrow, periventricular zone. These data suggest that the two components of the cingulate gyrus influence different subcortical motor systems, with the retrosplenial cortex providing a sparse input to a very limited region of the caudate nucleus and both the retrosplenial and cingulate subdivisions sending a substantial input to the ventral pontine nuclei. Because hippocampal output projected via connections with the subiculum reaches only the retrosplenial cortex, it is uncertain how to justify conceptions of limbic system contribution to behavior that are based on hippocampal modification of basal ganglia function (Gabriel & Sparenborg, 1987; Mishkin & Petri, 1984), unless it is assumed that hippocampal/subicular output from temporal regions controls behavior through projections to the nucleus accumbens (Swanson & Cowan, 1977).

Behavioral effect of bilateral lesions of the retrosplenial cortex. These anatomical data suggest that successive projections to the subiculum, retrosplenial cortex, and ventral pons may provide an anatomical substrate for multisynaptic propagation of learning-related activity from the hippocampus to the cerebellum. We reasoned that if this hypothesis were correct, then interruption of transmission along the subiculo-retrosplenial-pontine pathway should result in a behavioral dysfunction similar to that observed after damage to the hippocampus.

Bilateral lesions of the retrosplenial cortex were performed using electrolytic techniques that spared the overlying neocortex and the cingulate portion of the cingulate gyrus. We found that damage to the retrosplenial cortex resulted in a selective deficit in reversal learning (Figure 11.10). Moreover, the deficit was as severe as that observed after bilateral damage to the hippocampus (Berger, Weikart, Bassett, & Orr, 1986). Significantly, a recent clinical report supports the generality of an apparently similar mnemonic deficit resulting from damage to either the hippocampus or the retrosplenial cortex. Valenstein

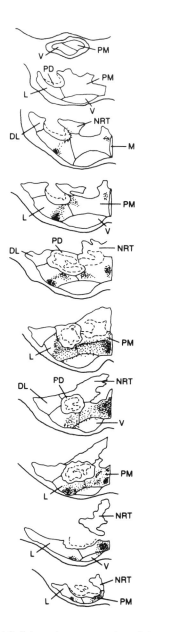
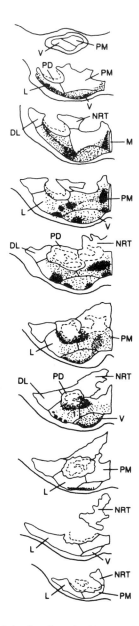

Figure 11.9. Schematic representation of the pattern and density of terminal labeling from the rostral (top) to the caudal (bottom) extension of the ventral pontine nuclei. Labeling after ^3H-proline injection in the anterior retrosplenial (left), and posterior retrosplenial (right). DL = dorsolateral gray; L = lateral gray; M = medial gray; NRT = nucleus reticularis tegmenti pontis; PM = paramedian gray; V = ventral gray.

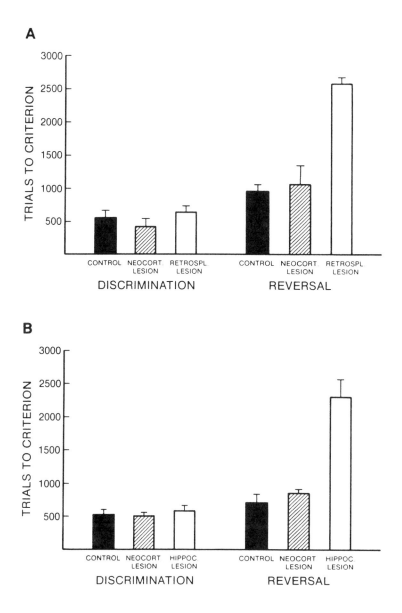

Figure 11.10. Effects of lesions of the retrosplenial cortex (panel A) and the hippocam-
pal/subicular cortices (panel B) on tone-light discrimination reversal conditioning of the rabbit NM response. Histograms indicate mean number of trials to performance criteria; error bars
indicate S.E.M. Operated control group (CONTROL); neocortical lesion control (NEOCORT.);
hippocampal lesion group (HIPPOC.); retrosplenial lesion group (RETROSPL.). From Berger,
Weikart, Bassett, and Orr (1986), coyright American Psychological Association. Reprinted
by permission.

et al. (1987) describe a patient who sustained hemorrhage-induced damage to the cingulum, retrosplenial cortex, and surrounding cortical areas. Hippocampal, parahippocampal, and thalamic regions previously implicated in mnemonic functions were not compromised, and only minimal damage of the fornix was found. Despite the temporal lobe regions being intact, the patient exhibited an anterograde amnesia for item-specific information identical to that observed after bilateral damage to the hippocampus.

Projections from the subiculum and the retrosplenial cortex to the anterior thalamus. A second prominent target of efferents originating from the posterior cingulate gyrus is the anterior thalamic complex (Bassett & Berger, 1990), a brain region that Gabriel and colleagues have demonstrated plays a central role in the development of instrumental avoidance behavior in the rabbit (Gabriel & Sparenborg, 1986). Although the anterior thalamus receives afferents from the subiculum (Sikes, Chronister, & White, 1977; Swanson & Cowan, 1977), from both components of the posterior cingulate gyrus, and from the mammillary nuclei (Berger, Milner, Swanson, Lynch, & Thompson, 1980), efferents from the anterior thalamus are distributed only to the cingulate and retrosplenial cortices (Berger et al., 1980b). As a result, the anterior thalamus is unlikely to serve as a direct component of any pathway transmitting learning-related activity from the hippocampus to the brainstem. As Gabriel has suggested, however, the anterior thalamic complex may exert a "gating" or permissive influence on transmission of information from the posterior cingulate cortex (Gabriel & Sparenborg, 1987). In such a manner, this component of the limbic system could play a role in determining the functional impact of the hippocampus on other brain systems.

Subicular-mammillary-ventral pontine projections. The subiculum is the source of a well-known projection through the postcommissural fornix to the mammillary nuclei (Swanson & Cowan, 1977). Axons of the mammillary nuclei terminate throughout several sites in the brainstem, the most medial regions of the ventral pons (Cruce, 1977). We have found that the mammillo-pontine pathway has little or no role in classical conditioning of the NM response, because lesions of the mammillary nuclei have no effect on either discrimination or reversal conditioning (Figure 11.11). Furthermore, unit recordings from either the medial or the lateral mammillary nuclei reveal no substantial CS- or UCS-related changes in firing rate or pattern throughout the course of conditioning (Figure 11.12; Berger & Thompson, 1978b).

Functional Significance of Limbic System Input to the Ventral Pons

Results of the studies outlined above support the hypothesis that learning-induced changes in hippocampal pyramidal cell activity achieve behavioral expression through multisynaptic projections involving the subiculum and retrosplenial cortex (Figure 11.13). The same results more definitively eliminate consideration of subicular projections to the mammillary nuclei as critical elements in such a circuit. The selective transmission of information to only one

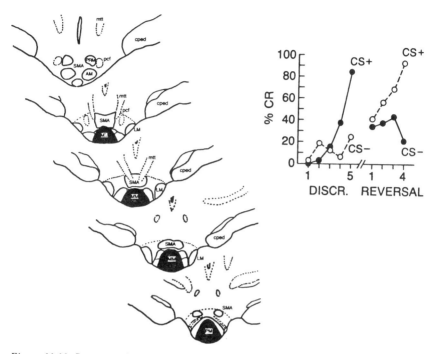

Figure 11.11. Representative example of the effects of lesions of the medial mammillary nucleus (left panel) on tone-light discrimination reversal conditioning of the NM response (right panel). Note the rapid course of both discrimination (DISCR.) and reversal phase of NM conditioning despite near-total bilateral damage of the medial mammillary nucleus. Graph shows percent conditioned response (%CR) rate as measured during the last half of each training session. Abbreviations: SMA = supramammillary area; AM = anterior mammillary area; PRM = premammillary area; MM = medial mammillary nucleus; LM = lateral mammillary nucleus; mtt = mammillo-thalamic tract; cped = cerebral peduncle; pcf = postcommissural fornix.

of the several projection targets of the subiculum is possible given the limited overlap that exists among the subpopulations of subicular neurons projecting to each target (Swanson, Sawchenko, & Cowan, 1981). More conclusive support for the hypothesized role of the subiculum and retrosplenial, however, requires resolution of at least two additional issues. The first concerns the assumption that hippocampal and retrosplenial neurons share connectivity with a common population of subicular cells, such that activation of hippocampal pyramidal neurons initiates a sequential activation of subicular and retrosplenial cells. Results of the axonal transport studies reviewed above cannot exclude the possibility that neurons projecting to the retrosplenial cortex constitute a different population of neurons than those receiving input from the hippocampus. The disruption of discrimination reversal learning following damage to the retrosplenial cortex also cannot rule out the possibility that the posterior cingulate plays a role in reversal learning independent of the role played by the hippocampus.

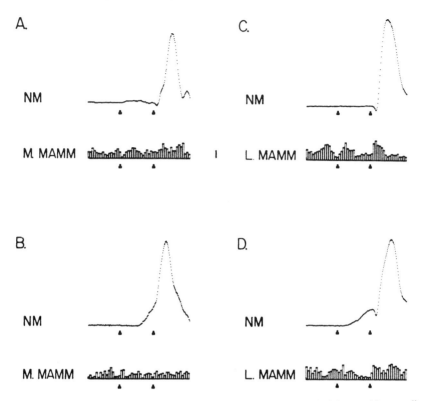

Figure 11.12. Unit recordings from the medial (left panels) and lateral (right panels) mammillary nuclei during initial (top panels) and asymptotic (bottom panels) phases of NM conditioning. From Berger and Thompson (1978b), copyright by Elsevier Science Publishers. Reprinted by permission.

Even if transsynaptic activation from hippocampus to the ventral pons were established, a second issue would concern the total propagation time through such a circuit. The average onset of CS-evoked increases in hippocampal pyramidal cell activity precedes the average onset of conditioned NM responses by approximately 50 ms. If conduction time through a hippocampal-subiculum-retrosplenial-pons-projection required less than 50 ms, it would be possible for learning-related hippocampal activity to play a role in all phases of the CR. A conduction time significantly greater than 50 ms would be more consistent, for example, with the hippocampus providing information necessary for response correction but not for "on-line" execution of the conditioned response.

Physiological characteristics of the hippocampal-subicular-retrosplenial-pontine circuit. We have begun electrophysiological investigations to address these issues, examining the latencies to orthodromic activation of neurons in each component of the proposed hippocampus-to-cerebellum circuit after electrical stimulation of one of the other components. Re-

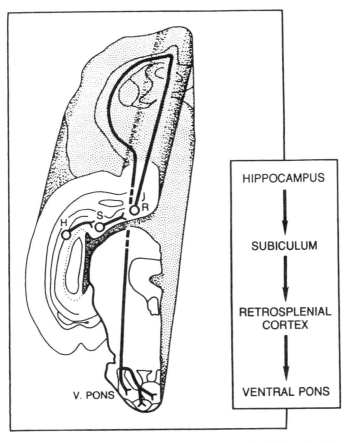

Figure 11.13. Schematic of the proposed multisynaptic circuitry linking the hippocampus, subiculum, retrosplenial cortex, and ventral pontine nuclei.

sults to date have shown that short-latency excitatory connections exist between the hippocampus and the subiculum, and between the subiculum and retrosplenial cortex. Subicular cells can be activated orthodromically within 2-3 ms of electrically stimulating the dorsal CA1 region (mean latency: 3.1 ± 1.1 ms using threshold intensity; 2.3 ± 0.8 ms using suprathreshold intensity). Electrical stimulation of the dorsal subiculum results within 3-5 ms in the orthodromic activation of layer V cells of the retrosplenial cortex (mean latency: 4.2 ± 1.6 ms using threshold stimulation; 3.5 ± 1.2 ms using suprathreshold stimulation); neurons within layer V are the cells of origin for efferents to the ventral pontine nuclei. In addition, cells in layer V of retrosplenial can be transsynaptically driven from the hippocampus at latencies (6.7 ± 2.3 ms) that are in close agreement with the additive latencies to monosynaptic activation of the subiculum and retrosplenial cortices. Finally, the same subicular neurons activated orthodromically from the hippocampus also can be antidromically activated from the retrosplenial, indicating that at least a subpopulation of subicular cells both receives input from the hippocampus and provides output to the retrosplenial cortex. The size of that subpopulation must be rather substantial, as disynaptic activation of retrosplenial neurons from the hippocampus was readily obtained. Preliminary characterization of retrosplenial input to the ventral pons indicates that cells within the ventral and paramedian gray can be driven orthodromically with latencies of approximately 4-7 ms.

In total, these findings suggest that learning-dependent responses of hippocampal pyramidal neurons are capable of modifying ventral pontine activity within 9-15 ms of the onset of hippocampal discharge, and are consistent with previous reports of short-latency responses of cerebellar neurons in response to activation of the fornix (Saint-Cyr & Woodward, 1980). Because conduction along the subicular-retrosplenial pathway is rapid and powerful, and because CS-induced changes in pyramidal cell firing rates precede NM conditioned response onset by as much as 80 ms, it is possible that output from the hippocampus modifies cerebellar function in an "on-line" manner during the expression of each conditioned response (Figure 11.14). This possibility is supported by findings that the pattern of hippocampal pyramidal cell activity predicts the shape of the conditioned NM response on the same trial (Berger, Laham, &

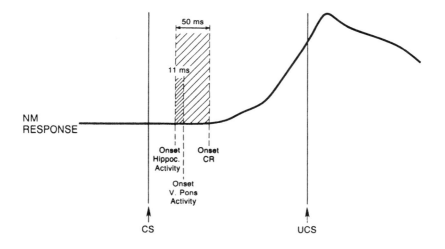

Figure 11.14. Idealized summary of our findings regarding the relationship between the NM conditioned response and latencies to activation of hippocampal and ventral pontine neurons. Studies in awake behaving animals have shown that the onset of conditioned hippocampal pyramidal cell activity precedes onset of the conditioned response (CR) by approximately 50 ms. Results of electrical stimulation and recording studies in acutely prepared animals have shown that the hippocampal-subicular-retrosplenial circuit is capable of propagating excitatory output from the hippocampal CA1 area to the ventral pons within 9-15 ms (latency of 11 ms shown). Thus, onset of ventral pontine activity may precede onset of the CR by approximately 35-40 ms.

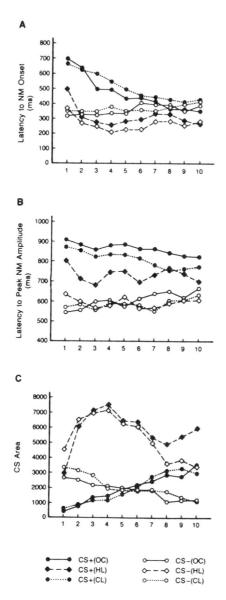

Figure 11.15. Effects of bilateral hippocampectomy on conditioned NM response shape. Results for three parameters of response shape are shown: latency to onset (A), latency to peak amplitude (B), and integrated area of the response during the CS-UCS interval (C). Data are shown for operated control animals (OC), animals with damage to the parietal neocortex alone (CL), and animals with damage to hippocampus and overlying parietal neocortex (HL). Data have been "Vincentized," that is, displayed as a function of equal nth's to performance criteria. Data from Orr and Berger (1985), copyright by American Psychological Association. Reprinted by permission.

Thompson, 1980), and that the shape of conditioned NM movements is altered by bilateral hippocampectomy (Orr & Berger, 1985; Port, Romano, Steinmetz, Mikhail, & Patterson, 1986; Solomon et al., 1986; see Figure 11.15).

Hippocampal modification of CS-related activity by transsynaptic input to the ventral pons. It has been discovered recently that information related to the CS also is transmitted to the cerebellum via the ventral pontine nuclei. Lewis, LoTurco, and Solomon (1987) have found that transection of the middle cerebellar peduncle prevents acquisition of conditioned NM responding. Furthermore, Steinmetz et al. (Steinmetz, Rosen, Chapman, Lavond, & Thompson, 1986; Steinmetz et al., 1987) have reported a direct projection to the ventral pons from the ventral cochlear nucleus, and that electrical stimulation can serve as an effective CS for the development and maintenance of conditioned NM responses. Koutalidis, Foster, and Weisz (1988) have identified the circuitry underlying visual CS information, and several of the brain sites involved also provide input to the ventral pons. It is well established that the ventral pontine nuclei receive afferents from a wide range of neocortical regions, and are a major source of sensory input to the cerebellum (e.g., Robinson, Cohen, May, Sestokas, & Glickstein, 1984). Thus, output from the hippocampus may affect behavioral responding through modification of CS information transmitted to the cerebellum through the ventral pons. The extent of convergence between retrosplenial, neocortical, and subcortical auditory input within the pons is unknown, however.

Hierarchical Organization of Multiple Memory Systems

The characterization provided here of the relationship between the hippocampus and the cerebellum is consistent with findings that damage to limbic brain regions does not eliminate the capability for learning and remembering simple associations between environmental events. As outlined above, loss of hippocampal function disrupts learned behaviors that depend on higher-order relationships among stimuli, such as when an animal is required to modify a previously learned response. As has been demonstrated by others (see Thompson, 1986), destruction of the deep cerebellar nuclei prevents acquisition and retention of conditioned NM responding and at least several other conditioned behaviors. Reflex responses, on the other hand, are unaffected or altered only temporarily, indicating that the cerebellar substrates for the conditioned response lie outside the reflex circuitry. Within this conceptual framework, we have proposed that output from the hippocampus alters behavior indirectly through modification of the cerebellum, and more specifically, that the subicular-retrosplenial-pontine projection provides the anatomical substrate for output from the hippocampus to modify and/or select among non-conditional associations stored within the cerebellum (Berger, Weikart, Bassett, & Orr, 1986). In a such a manner, learned movements may represent the combined contribution of several, hierarchically organized memory systems (Figure 11.16).

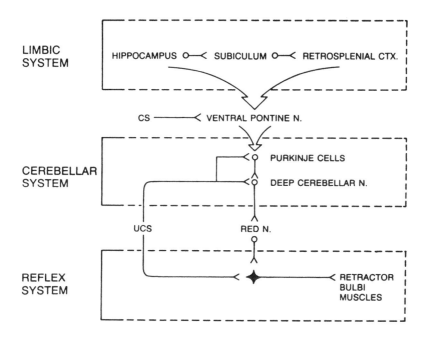

Figure 11.16. Proposed hierarchical organization of the limbic, cerebellar and brainstem re-flex systems known to underlie conditioned NM responding. Adapted from Berger, Weikart, Bassett, and Orr (1986), American Psychological Association. Reprinted by permission.

CONCLUSION

Attempts to extend the model systems approach to mammalian species have revealed several distinguishing functional characteristics of the mammalian brain which appear to derive from its larger, more complex neural circuitry. Two such functional characteristics have been discussed in the present chapter, in the context of specific examples from research with the rabbit NM prepara-tion. One characteristic is that CS- and CR-evoked activity develops in many different brain areas during conditioning of even simple reflexes, despite the fact that very little of the total mammalian brain is necessary for most condi-tioned responses. The respective contributions of the hippocampus and the cerebellum to formation of the conditioned NM response provide specific ex-amples of such "non-essential" (hippocampus) and "essential" (cerebellum) brain areas. However, they also provide examples of how neural plasticity in "non-essential" and "essential" brain regions can reflect the segregation of spe-cialized memory functions, and if our hypothesis about the functional relation between the two structures is correct, the respective roles of the hippocampus and cerebellum reveal how the output from one memory system can modify the functioning of another memory system to allow greater behavioral flexibility and adaptability on the part of the organism. This possibility suggests a reconsideration of the distinction between "essential" and "non-essential" sites of plasticity, given that the behavioral adaptability allowed by the hippocampus also can be "essential" depending on the definition of "conditioned response." A distinction such as "fundamental" and "higher-order" may be more appropriate.

The proposed hierarchical organization of the hippocampus and cerebellum raises an additional and important issue with respect to system-system interactions during learning. It is well-established that the cerebellum has a rigid, somatotopic organization with respect to the peripheral muscles groups influenced by its output. Each of the successive pathways from the hippocampus to the cerebellum also consists of highly topographic, point-to-point connections. As we have reviewed elsewhere (Berger & Bassett, in press), the activity of hippocampal pyramidal neurons can be correlated with a wide range of conditioned stimuli and conditioned responses, and as a population, pyramidal neurons appear to express a common correlate on any given trial. For the changing output of a "memory buffer" system such as the hippocampus to influence behavior through point-to-point connections with a "labeled line" system such as the cerebellum requires principles of synaptic transmission that have yet to be identified, or even conceptualized in terms that are sufficiently rigorous for an experimental analysis. The latter represents just one of many issues that undoubtedly will become apparent as the model systems approach is expanded to deal explicitly with problems related to multiple memory systems.

A second distinguishing characteristic of the mammalian brain is the greater range of learning-induced correlates that can be recorded from neurons within any one memory system. The lack of a rigid relationship with either sensory or motor events can be sufficiently great that structures like the hippocampus may function as true "memory buffers," that is, there can exist a wide range of nonetheless highly specific determinants of cell firing. If so, the possibility must be entertained that the fundamental operating principles of such a system are not revealed by a detailed analysis of the environmental events with which cell firing is correlated, given that correlates of cell activity are predictable on the basis of the stimuli and responses pre-selected for study. Instead, functional properties of a memory buffer system are more likely to be reflected by the principles for representing learned information in the population activity of its neurons. The large numbers of neurons in most mammalian brain structures and the complexity of their interconnections allow for functional levels of organization not considered previously, for example, clustering. Organizational schemes also may be dynamic, and dependent on the behavioral context (see Kubie & Ranck, 1984).

Experimental clarification of these and related issues pertinent to complex neural systems will require new experimental strategies that extend the model systems approach. In particular, strategies will be needed that are more quantitative and theoretically based. Such approaches already have been incorporated into the study of invertebrate model systems (Gingrich & Byrne, 1987; Hawkins & Kandel, 1984), but the larger number of neurons in the mammalian brain creates a greater demand for theoretically based analyses. For example, the information content of a spike train generated by a single neuron can be remarkably high (Perkel, Gerstein, & Moore, 1967). Dealing effectively with how the spike output of a single cell reflects the contribution of other neurons sharing the same network structure becomes much more difficult in the case of mammalian neurons, which typically are multi-input/multi-output elements (see Segundo, Perkel, Wyman, Hegstad, & Moore, 1968). Procedures based on concepts of signal analysis are likely to be the most useful in addressing this issue (Sclabassi & Noreen, 1981; Marmarelis, Citron, & Vivo, 1986). The importance of temporal ordering of spike events has been highlighted in recent years by the demonstration of pattern-dependent induction of synaptic plasticity (Barrionuevo & Brown, 1983; Larson & Lynch, 1986; Rose & Dunwiddie, 1986; Winson & Dahl, 1986).

The recent explosive growth of research using simulated neural networks has allowed a large number of possible schemes for distributed representations to be investigated in their abstract form, including schemes that are dynamic due to self-adaptive properties of the network (Grossberg, 1988; Hopfield, 1982; Klopf, 1988; Kohonen, 1988; Moore et al., 1986). Investigations of multi-layered neural networks, which might provide a framework for studying the problem of interactions between the hippocampus and cerebellum, also are being explored (Giles & Maxwell, 1987). As more theoretically based experimental strategies mature, however, there will be an increasing need for incorporating biological constraints of the neural systems being modeled (Burnod, 1988; Chauvet, 1986; Gluck & Thompson, 1987; Lynch, 1986; McNaughton & Morris, 1987; Zipser, 1986). As an extension of the studies reviewed here, we recently have described a theoretical framework and set of experimental procedures that allow direct measurement of the dynamic properties of real neural networks (Berger, Harty, Barrionuevo, & Sclabassi, 1989; Sclabassi, Krieger, & Berger, 1988b), and have applied this experimental strategy to characterization of the nonlinear response properties of the hippocampus (Berger, Eriksson, Ciarolla, & Sclabassi, 1988a, 1988b; Sclabassi, Eriksson, Port, Robinson, & Berger, 1988; Sclabassi et al., 1989). Procedures of this type should provide a more complete set of biological constraints for mathematical models of complex neural networks, and permit an experimental bridge between single cell recording in the learning animal and computer simulations of memory system function (see Berger & Sclabassi, 1988).

ACKNOWLEDGMENTS

This research was supported by grants from the NSF (BNS-8843368), NIMH (MH00343), ONR (N00014-87-K-0472), and AFOSR (89-0197).

REFERENCES

Alexander, G.E., & DeLong, M.R. (1985a). Microstimulation of the primate neo-striatum. I. Physiological properties of striatal microexcitable zones. *Journal of Neurophysiology, 53*, 1401-1416.

Alexander, G.E., & DeLong, M.R. (1985b). Microstimulation of the primate neo-striatum. II. Somatotopic organization of striatal microexcitable zones and their relation to neuronal response properties. *Journal of Neurophysiology, 53*, 1417-1430.

Alkon, D.L. (1979). Voltage-dependent calcium and potassium ion conductances: A contingency mechanism for an associative learning model. *Science, 205*, 810-816.

Barrionuevo, G., & Brown, T.H. (1983). Associative long-term potentiation in hippocampal slices. *Proceedings of the National Academy of Science USA, 80*, 7347-7351.

Bassett, J.L., & Berger, T.W. (1990). *Subcortical projections of the posterior cingulate gyrus in rabbit.* Manuscript submitted for publication.

Berger, T.W. (1984). Neuronal representation of associative learning in the hippocampus. In N. Butters & L.R. Squire (Eds.), *The neuropsychology of memory* (pp. 443-461). New York: Guilford.

Berger, T.W., Alger, B., & Thompson, R.F. (1976). Neuronal substrate of classical conditioning in the hippocampus. *Science, 192*, 483-485.

Berger, T.W., & Bassett, J.L. (in press). System properties of the hippocampus. In I. Gormezano (Ed.), *Learning and memory: The biological substrates.* Hillsdale, NJ: Lawrence Erlbaum Associates.

Berger, T.W., Berry, S.D., & Thompson, R.F. (1986). Role of the hippocampus in classical conditioning of aversive and appetitive behaviors. In R.L. Isaacson & K.H. Pribram (Eds.), *The hippocampus* (pp. 203-239). New York: Plenum.

Berger, T.W., Eriksson, J.L., Ciarolla, D.A., & Sclabassi, R.J. (1988a). Nonlinear systems analysis of the perforant path-dentate projection. II. Effects of random train stimulation. *Journal of Neurophysiology, 60*, 1077-1094.

Berger, T.W., Eriksson, J.L., Ciarolla, D.A., & Sclabassi, R.J. (1988b). Nonlinear systems analysis of the perforant path-dentate projection. III. Comparison of random train and paired impulse analyses. *Journal of Neurophysiology, 60*, 1095-1109.

Berger, T.W., Harty, T.P., Barrionuevo, G., & Sclabassi, R.J. (1989). Modeling of neuronal networks through experimental decomposition. In V.Z., Marmarelis (Ed.), *Advanced methods of physiological system modeling* (pp. 113-128). New York: Plenum.

Berger, T.W., Laham, R.I., & Thompson, R.F. (1980). Hippocampal unit-behavior correlations during classical conditioning. *Brain Research, 193*, 229-248.

Berger, T.W., Milner, T.A., Swanson, G.W., Lynch, G.S., & Thompson, R.F. (1980). Reciprocal anatomical connections between anterior thalamus and cingulate-retrosplenial cortex in the rabbit. *Brain Research, 201*, 411-417.

Berger, T.W., & Orr, W.B. (1983). Hippocampectomy selectively disrupts discrimination reversal conditioning of the rabbit nictitating membrane response. *Behavioural Brain Research, 8*, 49-68.

Berger, T.W., Rinaldi, P., Weisz, D.J., & Thompson, R.F. (1983). Single unit analysis of different hippocampal cell types during classical conditioning of the rabbit nictitating membrane response. *Journal of Neurophysiology, 50*, 1197-1221.

Berger, T.W., & Sclabassi, R.J. (1988). Long-term potentiation and its relation to hippocampal pyramidal cell activity and behavioral learning during classical conditioning. In P.W. Landfield & S.A. Deadwyler (Eds.) *Synaptic potentiation in the brain: A critical analysis* (pp. 467-497). New York: Alan R. Liss.

Berger, T.W., Swanson, G.W., Milner, T.A., Lynch, G.S., & Thompson, R.F. (1980). Reciprocal anatomical connections between hippocampal and subiculum: evidence for subicular innervation of regio superior. *Brain Research, 183*, 265-276.

Berger, T.W., & Thompson, R.F. (1978a). Neuronal plasticity in the limbic system during classical conditioning of the rabbit nictitating membrane response. I. The hippocampus. *Brain Research, 145,* 323-346.

Berger, T.W., & Thompson, R.F. (1978b). Neuronal plasticity in the limbic system during classical conditioning of the rabbit nictitating membrane response. II. Septum and mammillary bodies. *Brain Research, 156,* 293-314.

Berger, T.W., Weikart, C.L., Bassett, J.L., & Orr, W.B. (1986). Lesions of the retrosplenial cortex produce deficits in reversal learning of the rabbit nictitating membrane response: Implications for potential interactions between hippocampal and cerebellar brain systems. *Behavioral Neuroscience, 100,* 796-803.

Berger, T.W., & Weisz, D.J. (1987). Single unit analysis of hippocampal pyramidal and granule cells during classical conditioning of the rabbit nictitating membrane response: In I. Gormezano, W.F. Prokasy, & R.F. Thompson (Eds.), *Classical conditioning III: Behavioral, neurophysiological and neurochemical studies in the rabbit* (pp. 217-253). Hillsdale, NJ: Lawrence Erlbaum Associates.

Berry, S.D., & Oliver, C.G. (1983). Hippocampal activity during appetitive classical conditioning in rabbits. *Society for Neuroscience Abstracts, 9,* 645.

Brodal, A., & Jansen, J. (1946). The ponto-cerebellar projection in the rabbit and cat. *Journal of Comparative Neurology, 84,* 31-118.

Burnod, Y. (1988). *Cerebral cortex and behavioral adaptation: A possible mechanism.* Paris: University of Liege Press.

Chauvet, G. (1986). Habituation rules for a theory of the cerebellar cortex. *Biological Cybernetics, 55,* 201-209.

Cohen, D.H. (1969). Development of a vertebrate experimental model for cellular neurophysiologic studies of learning. *Conditional Reflex, 4,* 61-80.

Cohen, N.J., & Squire, L.R. (1980). Preserved learning and retention of pattern-analyzing skill in amnesia: dissociation of knowing how and knowing that. *Science, 210,* 207-210.

Coleman, S.R., & Gormezano, I. (1971). Classical conditioning of the rabbit's (Oryctolagus Cuniculus) nictitating membrane response under symmetrical CS-UCS interval shift. *Journal of Comparative and Physiological Psychology, 77,* 447-455.

Crow, T.J., & Alkon, D.L. (1980). Associative behavioral modification in Hermissenda: Cellular correlates. *Science, 209,* 412-414.

Crow, T., & Forrester, J. (1986). Light paired with serotonin mimics the effect of conditioning on phototactic behavior of Hermissenda. *Proceedings of the National Academy of Science, USA, 83,* 7975-7978.

Cruce, J.A.F. (1977). An autoradiographic study of the descending connections of the mammillary nuclei of the rat. *Journal of Comparative Neurology, 176,* 631-644.

Davis, M., Gendelman, D.S., Tischler, M.D., & Gendelman, P.M. (1982). A primary acoustic startle circuit: lesion and stimulation studies. *Journal of Neuroscience, 2,* 791-805.

Deadwyler, S.A., West, M., & Lynch, G. (1979). Activity of dentate granule cells during learning: Differentiation of perforant path input. *Brain Research, 169,* 29-43.

Diamond, D.M., & Weinberger, N.M. (1986). Classical conditioning rapidly induces specific changes in frequency receptive fields of single neurons in secondary and ventral ectosylvian auditory cortical fields. *Brain Research, 372,* 357-360.

Disterhoft, J.F., Coulter, D.A. & Alkon, D.L. (1986). Specific membrane changes of rabbit hippocampal neurons measured in vitro. *Proceedings of the National Academy of Science USA, 83*, 2733-2737.

Disterhoft, J.F., Golden, D.T., Read, H.L., Coulter, D.A., & Alkon, D.L. (1988). AHP reductions in rabbit hippocampal neurons during conditioning correlate with acquisition of the learned response. *Brain Research, 462*, 118-125.

Disterhoft, J.F., & Segal, M. (1978). Neuronal activity in rat hippocampus and motor cortex during discrimination reversal. *Brain Research Bulletin, 3*, 583-588.

Domesick, V.B. (1969). Projections from the cingulate cortex in the rat. *Brain Research, 12*, 396-320.

Eichenbaum, H., Fagan, A., Mathews, P., & Cohen, N.J. (1988). Hippocampal system dysfunction and odor discrimination learning in rats: Impairment or facilitation depending on representational demands. *Behavioral Neuroscience, 102*, 331-339.

Eichenbaum, H., Wiener, S.I., Shapiro, M.L., & Cohen, N.J. (in press). Functional correlates of hippocampal neurons: III. The organization of spatial coding in neural ensembles. *Journal of Neuroscience*.

Fagan, A.M., & Olton, D.S. (1986). Learning sets, discrimination reversal, and hippocampal function. *Behavioural Brain Research, 21*, 13-20.

Foster, T.C., Christian, E.P., Hampson, R.E., Campbell, K.A., & Deadwyler, S.A. (1987). Sequential dependencies regulate sensory evoked responses of single units in the rat hippocampus. *Brain Research, 408*, 86-96.

Gabriel, M., & Sparenborg, S.P. (1986). Anterior thalamic discriminative neuronal response enhanced during learning in rabbits with subicular and cingulate cortical lesions. *Brain Research, 384*, 195-198.

Gabriel, M., & Sparenborg, S.P. (1987). Posterior cingulate cortical lesions eliminate learning-related unit-activity in the anterior cingulate cortex. *Brain Research, 409*, 151-157.

Giles, C.L., & Maxwell, T. (1987). Learning, invariance, and generalization in higher-order neural networks. *Applied Optics, 26*, 4972-4978.

Gingrich, K.J., & Byrne, J.H. (1987). Single-cell neuronal model for associative learning. *Journal of Neurophysiology, 57*, 1705-1715.

Glanzman, D.L., & Thompson, R.F. (1980). Alterations in spontaneous miniature potential activity during habituation of a vertebrate monosynaptic pathway. *Brain Research, 189*, 377-390.

Gluck, M.A., & Thompson, R.F. (1987). Modeling the neural substrates of associative learning and memory: a computational approach. *Psychological Review, 94*, 176-191.

Gormezano, I., Prokasy, W.F., & Thompson, R.F. (Eds.). (1987). *Classical conditioning III: Behavioral, neurophysiological and neurochemical studies in the rabbit*. New York: Academic.

Gormezano, I., Schneiderman, N., Deaux, E., & Fuentes, I. (1962). Nictitating membrane: Classical conditioning and extinction in the albino rabbit. *Science, 138*, 33-34.

Greenough, W.T., Larson, J.R., & Withers, G.S. (1985). Effects of unilateral and bilateral training in a reaching task on dendritic branching of neurons in the rat motor-sensory forelimb cortex. *Behavioral and Neural Biology, 26*, 287-297.

Grossberg, S. (1988). Nonlinear neural networks: principles, mechanisms, and architectures. *Neural Networks, 1*, 17-61.

Harvey, J.A., Gormezano, I., & Cool-Hauser, V.A. (1985). Relationship between heterosynaptic reflex facilitation and acquisition of the nictitating membrane response in control and scopolamine-injected rabbits. *Journal of Neuroscience, 5*, 596-602.

Hawkins, R.D., & Kandel, E.R. (1984). Is there a cell-biological alphabet for simple forms of learning? *Psychological Review, 91*, 376-391.

Hirsh, R. (1974). The hippocampus and contextual retrieval of information from memory: A theory. *Behavioral Biology, 12*, 421-444.

Hirsh, R. (1980). The hippocampus, conditional operations, and cognition. *Physiological Psychology, 8*, 175-182.

Hoehler, F.K., & Thompson, R.F. (1980). Effects of the interstimulus (CS-UCS) interval on hippocampal unit activity during classical conditioning of the nictitating membrane response of the rabbit. *Journal of Comparative and Physiological Psychology, 94*, 201-215.

Holt, L., & Thompson, R.F. (1984). Hippocampal correlates of instrumental behavior. *Society for Neuroscience Abstracts, 10*, 124.

Hopfield, J.J. (1982). Neural networks and physical systems with emergent collective computational abilities. *Proceedings of the National Academy of Science, USA, 79*, 2554-2558.

Isaacson, R.L. (Ed.). (1974). *The limbic system.* New York: Plenum.

Ito, M. (1974). Recent advances in cerebellar physiology and pathology. *Advances in Neurology, 21*, 59-84.

Jarrel, T.W., Gentile, C.G., Romanski, L.M., McCabe, R.M., & Schneiderman, N. (1987). Involvement of cortical and thalamic auditory regions in retention of differential bradycardiac conditioning to acoustic conditional stimuli in rabbits. *Brain Research, 412*, 285-294.

Kandel, E.R., & Spencer, W.A. (1968). Cellular neurophysiological approaches in the study of learning. *Physiological Review, 48*, 66-124.

Kapp, B.S., Schwaber, J.S., & Driscoll, P.A. (1985). The organization of insular cortex projections to the amygdala central nucleus and autonomic regulatory nuclei of the dorsal medulla. *Brain Research, 360*, 355-360.

Kettner, R.E., & Thompson, R.F. (1982). Auditory signal detection and decision processes in the nervous system. *Journal of Comparative and Physiological Psychology, 96*, 328-331.

Klein, M., & Kandel, E.R. (1980). Mechanism of calcium current modulation underlying presynaptic facilitation and behavioral sensitization in Aplysia. *Proceedings of the National Academy of Science, USA, 77*, 6912-6916.

Klopf, A.H. (1988). A neuronal model of classical conditioning. *Psychobiology, 16*, 85-125.

Kohonen, T. (1988). *Self-organization and associative memory.* Berlin: Springer-Verlag.

Koutalidis, O., Foster, A., & Weisz, D.J. (1988). Parallel pathways can conduct visual CS information during classical conditioning of the NM response. *Journal of Neuroscience, 8*, 417-427.

Kraus, N., & Disterhoft, J.F. (1982). Response plasticity of single neurons in rabbit auditory association cortex during tone-signalled learning. *Brain Research, 246*, 205-215.

Kubie, J.L., & Ranck, J.B., Jr. (1984). Hippocampal neuronal firing, context and learning: In L.R. Squire & N. Butters (Eds.), *Neuropsychology of Memory* (pp. 417-423). New York: Guilford.

Larson, J., & Lynch, G. (1986). Induction of synaptic potentiation in hippocampus by patterned stimulation involves two events. Science, 232, 985-988.

LeDoux, J.E. (1987). Emotion. In F. Plum (Ed.) *Handbook of physiology, Volume V: Higher functions of the brain* (pp. 415-459). Baltimore: Williams and Wilkins.

LeDoux, J.E., & Iwata, J. (1987). A subcortical sensory pathway mediates emotional learning. International *Journal of Neuroscience, 32,* 598.

Lewis, J.L., LoTurco, J.J., & Solomon, P.R. (1987). Lesions of the middle cerebellar peduncle disrupt acquisition and retention of the rabbit's classically conditioned nictitating membrane response. *Behavioral Neuroscience, 101,* 151-157.

Lisberger, S.G., Morris, E.J., & Tychsen, L. (1987). Visual motion processing and sensory-motor integration for smooth pursuit eye movements. *Annual Review of Neuroscience, 10,* 97-129.

Loechner, K.J., & Weisz, D.J. (1987). Hippocampectomy and feature-positive discrimination. *Behavioural Brain Research, 26,* 63-73.

Lynch, G. (1986). *Synapses, circuits and the beginnings of memory.* Cambridge, MA: MIT Press.

Mamounas, L.A., Thompson, R.F., Lynch, G., & Baudry, M. (1984). Classical conditioning of the rabbit eyelid response increases glutamate receptor binding in hippocampal synaptic membranes. *Proceedings of the National Academy of Science, USA, 81,* 2548-2552.

Marmarelis, V.Z., Citron, M.C., & Vivo, C.P. (1986). Minimum-order Wiener modelling of spike-output systems. *Biological Cybernetics, 54,* 115-123.

Mauk, M.D., & Thompson, R.F. (1987). Retention of classically conditioned eyelid responses following acute decerebration. *Brain Research, 403,* 89-95.

McNaughton, B.L., & Morris, R.G.M. (1987). Hippocampal synaptic enhancement and information storage within a distributed memory system. *Trends in Neuroscience, 10,* 408-415.

Milner, B. (1970). Memory and the medial temporal regions of the brain. In K.H. Pribram & D.E. Broadbent (Eds.) *Biology of Memory* (pp. 29-50). New York: Academic.

Mishkin, M., & Petri, H.L. (1984). Memories and habits: some implications for the analysis of learning and retention. In L.R. Squire & N. Butters (Eds.), *Neuropsychology of memory* (pp. 287-296). New York: Guilford.

Moore, J.W., & Berthier, N.E. (1987). Purkinje cell activity and the conditioned nictitating membrane response. In M. Glickstein, C. Yeo, & J. Stein (Eds.), *Cerebellum and neuronal plasticity* (pp. 339-352). New York: Plenum.

Moore, J.W., Desmond, J.E., & Berthier, N.E. (1982). The metencephalic basis of the conditioned nictitating membrane response. In C.D. Woody (Ed.) *Conditioning: Representation of involved neuronal function* (pp. 459-482). New York: Plenum.

Moore, J.W., Desmond, J.E., Berthier, N.E. Blazis, D.E.J., Sutton, R.S., & Barto, A.G. (1986). Simulation of the classically conditioned nictitating membrane response by a neuron-like adaptive element: response topography, neuronal firing and interstimulus intervals. *Behavioural Brain Research, 21,* 143-154.

Muller, R.U., Kubie, J.L., & Ranck, J.B. (1987). Spatial firing patterns of hippocampal complex-spike cells in a fixed environment. *Journal of Neuroscience, 7,* 1935-1950.

Norman, R.J., Buchwald, J.S., & Villablanca, J.R. (1977). Classical conditioning with auditory discrimination of the eyeblink in decerebrate cats. *Science, 196,* 551-553.

O'Keefe, J.A. (1976). Place units in the hippocampus of the freely moving rat. *Experimental Neurology, 51,* 78-109.

O'Keefe, J.A., & Nadel, L. (1975). *The hippocampus as a cognitive map.* New York: Oxford.

Olds, J., Disterhoft, J.F., Segal, M., Kornblith, C.L., & Hirsh, R. (1972). Learning centers of rat brain mapped by measuring latencies of conditioned unit responses. *Journal of Neurophysiology, 35,* 202-219.

Olton, D., Becker, J.T., & Handleman, G.E. (1979). Hippocampus, space, and memory. *Brain Behavior Science, 2,* 313-365.

Orr, W.B., & Berger, T.W. (1985). Hippocampectomy disrupts topography of conditioned nictitating membrane responses during reversal learning. *Behavioral Neuroscience, 99,* 35-45.

Patterson, M.M., Berger, T.W., & Thompson, R.F. (1979). Hippocampal neuronal plasticity recorded from cat during classical conditioning. *Brain Research, 163,* 339-343.

Pellionisz, A., & Llinas, R. (1982). Space-time representation in the brain. The cerebellum as a predictive space-time metric tensor. *Neuroscience, 7,* 2949-2970.

Perkel, D.H., Gerstein, G.L., & Moore, G.P. (1967). Neuronal spike trains and stochastic point processes. I. The single spike train. *Biophysical Journal, 7,* 391-418.

Port, R.L., & Patterson, M.M. (1984). Fimbrial lesions and sensory preconditioning. *Behavioral Neuroscience, 98,* 584-589.

Port, R.L., Romano, A.G., Steinmetz, J.E., Mikhail, A.A., & Patterson, M.M. (1986). Retention and acquisition of classical trace conditioned responses by hippocampal lesioned rabbits. *Behavioral Neuroscience, 100,* 745-752.

Powell, D.A., & Buchanan, S. (1980). Autonomic-somatic relationships in the rabbit (Oryctolagus cuniculus): effects of hippocampal lesions. *Physiological Psychology, 8,* 455-462.

Rawlins, J.N.P. (1985). Associations across time: the hippocampus as a temporary memory store. *Behavioral and Brain Sciences, 8,* 479-496.

Robinson, F.R., Cohen, J.L., May, J., Sestokas, A.K., & Glickstein, M. (1984). Cerebellar targets of visual pontine cells in the cat. *Journal of Comparative Neurology, 223,* 471-482.

Rolls, E.T., Thorpe, S.J., & Maddison, S. (1983). Responses of striatal neurons in the behaving monkey. 1. Head of the caudate nucleus. *Behavioural Brain Research, 7,* 179-210.

Rose, G.M., & Dunwiddie, T.V. (1986). Induction of hippocampal long-term potentiation using physiologically patterned stimulation. *Neuroscience Letters, 69,* 244-248.

Rose, J.E., & Woolsey, C.N. (1948). Structure and relations of limbic cortex and anterior thalamic nuclei in rabbit and cat. *Journal of Comparative Neurology, 89,* 279-347.

Ross, R.T., Orr, W.B., Holland, P.C., & Berger, T.W. (1984). Hippocampectomy disrupts acquisition and retention of learned conditional responding. *Behavioral Neuroscience, 98,* 221-225.

Saint-Cyr, J.A., Taylor, A.E., & Lang, A.E. (1988). Procedural learning and neostriatal dysfunction in man. *Brain, 111,* 941-959.

Saint-Cyr, J.A., & Woodward, D.J. (1980). Activation of mossy and climbing fiber pathways to the cerebellar cortex by stimulation of the fornix in the rat. *Experimental Brain Research, 40,* 1-12.

Schmajuk, N.A. (1984). Psychological theories of hippocampal function. *Physiological Psychology, 12,* 166-183.

Schneiderman, N., & Gormezano, I. (1964). Conditioning of the nictitating membrane of the rabbit as a function of CS-UCS interval. *Journal of Comparative and Physiological Psychology, 57*, 188-195.

Sclabassi, R.J., Eriksson, J.L., Port, R.L., Robinson, G.B., & Berger, T.W. (1988). Nonlinear systems analysis of the hippocampal perforant path-dentate projection. I. Theoretical and interpretational considerations. *Journal of Neurophysiology, 60*, 1066-1076.

Sclabassi, R.J., Krieger, D.N., & Berger, T.W. (1988). A systems theoretic approach to the study of CNS function. *Annals of Biomedical Engineering, 16*, 17-34.

Sclabassi, R.J., Krieger, D.N., Solomon, J., Samosky, J., Levitan, S., & Berger, T.W. (1989). Theoretical decomposition of neuronal networks. In V.Z., Marmarelis (Ed.), *Advanced methods of physiological system modeling*. New York: Plenum.

Sclabassi, R.J., & Noreen, G. K. (1981). The characterization of dual-input evoked potentials as nonlinear systems using random impulse trains, *Proceedings of the Pittsburgh Modeling and Simulation Conference, 12*, 1123-1130.

Segundo, J.P., Perkel, D.H., Wyman, H., Hegstad, H., & Moore, G.P. (1968). Input-output relations in computer-simulated nerve cells. Influence of the statistical properties, strength, number and interdependence of excitatory pre-synaptic terminals. *Kybernetik, 4*, 157-171.

Sikes, R.W., Chronister, R.B., & White, L.E. (1977). Origin of the direct hippocampus-anterior thalamic bundle in the rat: a combined horseradish peroxidase-Golgi analysis. *Experimental Neurology, 57*, 379-395.

Smith, M.C., DiLollo, V., & Gormezano, I. (1966). Conditioned jaw movement in the rabbit. *Journal of Comparative and Physiological Psychology, 62*, 479-483.

Solomon, P.R. (1977). Role of hippocampus in blocking and conditioned inhibition of the rabbit's nictitating membrane response. *Journal of Comparative and Physiological Psychology, 91*, 407-417.

Solomon, P.R., Vander Schaaf, E.R. Norbe, A.C., Weisz, D.J., & Thompson, R.F. (1986). Hippocampus and trace conditioning of the rabbit's nictitating membrane response. *Behavioral Neuroscience, 100*, 729-744.

Sorensen, K.E. (1980). Ipsilateral projection from the subiculum to the retrosplenial cortex in the guinea pig. *Journal of Comparative Neurology, 193*, 893-911.

Steinmetz, J.E., Logan, C.G., Rosen, D.J., Thompson, J.K., Lavond, D.G., & Thompson, R.F. (1987). Initial localization of the acoustic conditioned stimulus projection system to the cerebellum essential for classical eyelid conditioning. *Proceedings of the National Academy of Science USA, 84*, 3531-3535.

Steinmetz, J.E., Rosen, D.J., Chapman, P.F., Lavond, D.G., & Thompson, R.F. (1986). Classical conditioning of the rabbit eyelid response with a mossy fiber stimulation CS. I. Pontine nuclei and middle cerebellar peduncle stimulation. *Behavioral Neuroscience, 100*, 871-880.

Swanson, L.W., & Cowan, W.M. (1977). An autoradiographic study of the organization of the efferent connections of the hippocampal formation in the rat. *Journal of Comparative Neurology, 172*, 49-84.

Swanson, L.W., Sawchenko, P.E., & Cowan, W.M. (1981). Evidence for collateral projections by neurons in ammon's horn, the dentate gyrus, and the subiculum: A multiple retrograde labeling study in the rat. *Journal of Neuroscience, 1*, 548-559.

Swartz, B.E., & Woody, C.D. (1979). Correlated effects of acetylcholine and cyclic guanosine monophosphate on membrane properties of mammalian neocortical neurons. *Journal of Neurobiology, 10,* 465-488.

Thompson, R.F. (1986). The neurobiology of learning and memory. *Science, 233,* 941-947.

Thompson, R.F., Berger, T.W., Berry, S.D., Hoehler, F.K., Kettner, R.E., & Weisz, D.J. (1980). Hippocampal substrate of classical conditioning. *Physiological Psychology, 8,* 262-279.

Thompson, R.F., Berger, T.W., Cegavske, C.R., Patterson, M.M., Roemer, R.A., Teyler, T.J., & Young, R.A. (1976). The search for the engram. *American Psychologist, 31,* 209-227.

Thompson, R.F., & Spencer, W.A. (1966). Habituation: a model phenomenon for the study of neuronal substrates of behavior. *Psychological Review, 173,* 16-43.

Valenstein, E., Bowers, D., Verfaellie, M., Heilman, K.W., Day, A., & Watson, R.T. (1987). Retrosplenial amnesia. *Brain, 110,* 163-184.

Van Hoesen, G.W., & Pandya, D.N. (1975). Some connections of the entorhinal (area 28) and perirhinal (area 35) cortices of the rhesus monkey. I. Temporal lobe afferents. *Brain Research, 95,* 1-24.

Van Hoesen, G.W., Pandya, D.N., & Butters, N. (1975). Some connections of the entorhinal (area 28) and perirhinal (area 35) cortices of the rhesus monkey. II. Frontal lobe afferents. *Brain Research, 95,* 25-38.

Vogt, B.A., Sikes, R.W., Swadlow, H.A., & Weyand, T.G. (1986). Rabbit cingulate cortex: Physiological border with visual cortex, and afferent cortical connections of visual, motor, postsubicular and intracingulate origin. *Journal of Comparative Neurology, 248,* 74-94.

Vrenson, G., & Cardozo, J.N. (1981). Changes in size and shape of synaptic connections after visual training: an ultrastructural approach of synaptic plasticity. *Brain Research, 218,* 79-97.

Wall, J.T., Gibbs, C.M., Broyles, J.L., & Cohen, D.H. (1985). Modification of neuronal discharge along the ascending tectofugal pathway during visual conditioning. *Brain Research, 342,* 67-76.

Weikart, C., & Berger, T.W. (1986). Hippocampectomy disrupts classical conditioning of cross-modality discrimination reversal of the rabbit nictitating membrane response, *Behavioural Brain Research, 22,* 85-89.

Weinberger, N.M., Diamond, D.M., & McKenna, T.M. (1984). Initial events in conditioning: Plasticity in the pupillomotor and auditory systems. In G. Lynch, J.L. McGaugh & N.M. Weinberger (Eds.), *Neurobiology of learning and memory* (pp. 197-227). New York: Guilford.

Weisz, D.J., & LoTurco, J.J. (1988). Reflex facilitation of the nictitating membrane response remains after cerebellar lesions. *Behavioral Neuroscience, 102,* 203-209.

Weisz, D.J., & McInerney, J. (1990). An associative process maintains reflex facilitation of the unconditioned nictitating membrane response during the early stages of training. *Behavioral Neuroscience, 104,* 21-27.

West, M.O., Michael, A.J., Knowles, S.E., Chapin, J.K., & Woodward, D.J. (1987). Striatal unit activity and linkage between sensory and motor events. In J.S. Schneider & T.I. Lidsky (Eds.), *Basal ganglia and behavior: Sensory aspects of motor functioning* (pp. 27-35). Toronto: Han Huber.

Winocur, G., & Olds, J. (1978). Effects of context manipulation on memory and reversal learning in rats with hippocampal lesions. *Journal of Comparative and Physiological Psychology, 92,* 312-321.

Winson, J., & Dahl, D. (1986). Long-term potentiation in dentate gyrus: induction by asynchronous volleys in separate afferents. *Science, 234,* 985-988.

Woody, C.D. (1974). Aspects of the electrophysiology of cortical processes related to the development and performance of learned motor responses. *Physiologist, 17,* 49-69.

Zipser, D. (1986). A model of hippocampal learning during classical conditioning. *Behavioral Neuroscience, 100,* 764-776.

Zola-Morgan, S., Squire, L.R., & Amaral, D.G. (1986). Human amnesia and the medial temporal region: enduring memory impairment following a bilateral lesion limited to field CA1 of the hippocampus. *Journal of Neuroscience, 6,* 2950-2967.

12 Contributions of the Amygdala and Anatomically-Related Structures to the Acquisition and Expression of Aversively Conditioned Responses

Bruce S. Kapp
Carrie G. Markgraf
Amy Wilson
Jeffrey P. Pascoe
William F. Supple
University of Vermont

For a number of years our research has been devoted to an analysis of the contribution of the mammalian amygdala to aversive conditioning processes. To analyze the contribution of this complex structure, comprised of a number of distinctly different nuclei lying deep in the temporal lobe, we adopted a well-characterized model response and conditioning paradigm; the conditioned decelerative heart rate (bradycardiac) response in the rabbit, a response which develops during Pavlovian aversive conditioning procedures. Our own results, as well as those of others, have led to our working hypothesis that the amygdaloid central nucleus (ACe) is an essential component of a forebrain-brainstem circuit which contributes, at least in part, to the motoric expression of the bradycardiac response. This function is presumably mediated via widespread projections from the nucleus and other structures with which it is associated to brainstem cardiomotor regions.

We begin our discussion by describing the reasons for our focus on the amygdala and the bradycardiac conditioned response, as well as upon the initial evidence which formed the foundation for our hypothesis. We then discuss more recent results which raise the possibility that the ACe is a component of a larger forebrain region which contributes to the motoric expression of a variety of responses to emotionally-arousing stimuli, and that this region also may be considered as a substrate for associative as well as motor functions. Finally, we elaborate upon the functions of this region in the context of a recently-presented neural theory of aversive conditioning, illustrating how this system may influence the expression of other conditioned responses which develop during aversive Pavlovian conditioning procedures.

THE AMYGDALOID COMPLEX: CONTRIBUTIONS TO AVERSIVE CONDITIONING PROCESSES

Our focus on the ACe and the rabbit bradycardiac conditioned response evolved from a variety of observations, including our own, which emerged during the late 1960s and early 1970s, and which implicated the amygdala in the acquisition and retention of aversively conditioned responses. For example, lesions administered prior to active or passive avoidance conditioning (Blanchard & Blanchard, 1972; Coover, Ursin, & Levine, 1973; Horvath, 1963; Russo, Kapp, Holmquist, & Musty, 1976; Slotnick, 1973; Ursin, 1965) or conditioned suppression training (Kellicut & Schwartzbaum, 1963; Spevack, Campbell, & Drake, 1975) were reported to produce response acquisition deficits. Consistent with these findings was a body of literature demonstrating that post-training electrical (Gold, Edwards, & McGaugh, 1975; McDonough & Kesner, 1971) or chemical stimulation of the amygdala (Gallagher & Kapp, 1978; Gallagher, Kapp, Musty, & Driscoll, 1977) immediately following aversive conditioning resulted in subsequent retention deficits, suggesting a contribution for the amygdala in memory consolidation processes for aversive events.

Despite these numerous reports, a delineation of the exact nature of the contribution(s) of the amygdala to aversive conditioning remained obscure. One was simply left with the conclusion that manipulations of the amygdala affected the acquisition and/or retention of an aversively conditioned response. Whether this effect was due to an interference with sensory, associative, motivational or motor processes, or any combination of these processes, was far from clear. A second body of literature, however, provided some insight into the nature of this contribution. Numerous reports had demonstrated that lesions of the amygdala produced placidity or tameness in a number of wild species (Goddard, 1964). Furthermore, it had been reported that such lesions decreased the species-typical fear response of freezing in the laboratory rat in response to both conditioned and innately threatening stimuli (i.e., cat) (Blanchard & Blanchard, 1972). Taken together, this literature suggested that manipulations of the amygdala attenuate the arousal of fear, commonly defined as a central motivational state which organizes a variety of species-specific defensive behaviors (Bolles & Fanselow, 1980). Given (a) the influence of the conditioning of fear in the acquisition of conditioned responses during aversive conditioning procedures, and (b) the fact that many of the conditioned responses (e.g., freezing) measured in aversive conditioning paradigms are indices of conditioned fear, the attenuation of fear could account for the response acquisition and retention deficits in aversive conditioning paradigms following manipulations of the amygdala. Indeed, the hypothesis that the amygdala contributed to the arousal of fear was consistent with additional literature demonstrating that electrical stimulation of the amygdala elicited what were described as somatomotor and autonomic components of fear-like behavior in cats, components similar to those occurring under natural fear-eliciting conditions (Fernandez de Molina & Hunsperger, 1962; Hilton & Zbrozyna, 1963; Ursin & Kaada, 1960).

While this hypothesis offered an explanation for the widespread effects of amygdaloid manipulations on acquisition and retention of aversively conditioned responses, it brought one no closer to understanding the exact neurobiological substrates by which this heterogeneous structure contributed to the arousal and conditioning of fear, nor to the acquisition of aversively conditioned responses. Rather, this proposal dictated that one incorporate into the analysis the contribution of the amygdala to fear motivation and the involvement of fear in the acquisition and retention of aversively conditioned responses. With these considerations in mind, we decided to take an neuroanatomical approach in an analysis of the contribution of the amygdala to aversive conditioning, and we adopted a well-defined model response, that of conditioned bradycardia in the rabbit, a response which develops during a Pavlovian fear conditioning procedure. Given the anatomical complexity and heterogeneity of the amygdaloid complex, we reasoned that the most fruitful approach would be to attempt to define specific nuclei and pathways within this structure which contribute to the acquisition of this response. If a specific nucleus of the amygdala could be identified which was essential for response acquisition, then a determination of its afferent and efferent projection systems would eventually lead to an identification of the entire circuit, from sensory input to motor output, essential for the acquisition of the conditioned response. The identification of the components of this circuit would obviously set the stage for analyses of their functional contributions to associative learning processes.

The Rabbit Conditioned Bradycardiac Response: A Model Response for Investigating Amygdaloid Contributions to Associative Learning

At the time that we began our investigations of the amygdala, little in the way of a systematic analysis of the exact contributions of specific nuclei of the amygdala to the acquisition of responses during aversive conditioning had been attempted. In the one attempt at such an analysis using brain lesions, it was concluded that the success of producing lesions within the rat brain which were confined to any one nucleus without damage to other nuclei was impossible due to the changing boundaries of the individual nuclei along their rostral-caudal extent (Grossman, Grossman, & Walsh, 1975). This conclusion, coupled with the relatively small size of the rat brain, suggested to us that the rat was not the most advantageous species with which to undertake an analysis of the identification of amygdaloid components which contribute to such response acquisition. What was needed was a species with a somewhat larger amygdala in order to better confine manipulations to individual nuclei. This need partially guided our choice of the rabbit.

Furthermore, investigations of the effects of manipulations of the amygdala on learning and memory processes had utilized a variety of aversive conditioning paradigms, including passive avoidance and conditioned suppression (Gallagher et al., 1977; Gallagher & Kapp, 1978; Goddard, 1969; Gold, Edwards, & McGaugh, 1975; Kellicut & Schwartzbaum, 1963; McIntyre & Stein, 1973; Slotnick, 1973; Spevack et al., 1975) as well as more complex active avoidance paradigms (Blanchard & Blanchard, 1972; Coover et al., 1973; Grossman et al., 1975; Horvath, 1963; King, 1958; Kling, Orbach, Schwarz, & Towne, 1960; Ursin, 1965). While for the most part manipulations of the amygdala resulted in marked deficits in response acquisition and retention, several reports demonstrated either little or no effect (King, 1958; McNew & Thompson, 1966), or facilitation of acquisition (Grossman et al., 1975) or retention (Gold, Hankins, Edwards, Chester, & McGaugh, 1975). These inconsistencies were most likely due to poorly understood interactions between the specific characteristics of the various conditioning paradigms used and the locale and extent of damage to, or manipulations of, various amygdaloid nuclei. Given these inconsistencies we concluded at the time that we should adopt for our analysis a simple fear conditioning paradigm which resulted in the acquisition of a species-typical response.

Our adoption of the conditioned bradycardiac response in the rabbit, a response which rapidly develops during Pavlovian fear conditioning, was guided by several considerations. First, a considerable amount of data had accumulated defining the parameters of this conditioned response in the rabbit by Schneiderman and his colleagues, including the final pathway for its expression (Schneiderman, 1972). The response was reported to emerge within ten or less paired Pavlovian conditioning trials in which a tone served as the conditioned stimulus (CS) and an electric shock as the unconditioned stimulus (US). Second, bradycardia was also demonstrated to develop during Pavlovian conditioning in other species (Bruner, 1969; Holdstock & Schwartzbaum, 1965), including the human (Obrist, Wood, & Perez-Reyes, 1965), quite possibly making the results obtained from our analysis applicable to other species. Third, the identification of the vagus nerve as the final pathway for the expression of the response rendered it far more advantageous for a circuit analysis than a variety of other conditioned responses for which the final pathway was unknown (e.g., conditioned freezing behavior in rat). The finding that vagal cardioinhibitory neurons were located in the vagal dorsal motor nucleus and nucleus ambiguus in the rabbit (Jordan, Khalid, Schneiderman, & Spyer, 1982) would be of significance in determining the sources of afferentation of the final path motorneurons. The identification of these afferents should ultimately lead to the identification of suspected components of the conditioned response circuitry which are involved in associative learning. Fourth, the choice of the conditioned bradycardiac response was based upon a variety of findings suggesting a contribution for the amygdala in cardiovascular regulation. Electrical stimulation elicited marked alterations in heart rate and blood pressure in the cat (Heinemann, Stock, & Schaeffer, 1973; Hilton & Zbrozyna, 1963), the so-called defense response, a response pattern which appeared similar to that observed in response to natural threat. These observations were consistent with the demonstration that lesions of the posterior-medial region of the archistriatum, the avian amygdalar homologue, produced a marked attenuation of a conditioned cardiovascular response in the pigeon (Cohen, 1975). These findings suggested an important contribution for the amygdala in conditioned cardiovascular responses. Fifth, it had been reported by von Frisch (1966) that bradycardia occurred in response to a predator in the rabbit. Thus, bradycardia appeared to represent one of a number of species-typical responses in the rabbit during fear, a response which is subject to conditioning via Pavlovian procedures. In this context, the bradycardiac response may be analogous to threat-induced freezing in the rat, a species-typical response which is rapidly conditioned and which is markedly attenuated by amygdaloid lesions (Blanchard & Blanchard, 1972). Finally, and of no less significance, our choice for adopting a cardiovascular response was guided by health-related issues. The choice of such a response, in combination with our analysis of a brain region which contributes to emotional arousal, may eventually yield important insights into the contributions of learned emotional states to cardiovascular disorders, including hypertension and emotionally-induced arrhythmias (see Markgraf & Kapp, 1988).

Having adopted a suitable model response system, our next task was to determine where within the amygdala to begin our analysis. Based on a number of findings, we chose to initially concentrate on the ACe. For example, Grossman et al. (1975) reported that lesions of the ACe, while facilitating the acquisition of an active avoidance response, produced a significant deficit in the acquisition of a passive avoidance response in the rat. This result was consistent with the rather severe deficit produced by such lesions in the acquisition of a passive avoidance response in the rat reported by McIntyre and Stein (1973). A lesion-induced facilitation of response acquisition in an active avoidance conditioning paradigm, accompanied by a deficit in acquisition in a passive avoidance conditioning paradigm, can be interpreted as a lesion-induced deficit in conditioned fear (Colpaert, 1975). These combined results were consistent with the results demonstrating that electrical stimulation of the amygdala of the cat, including sites within the ACe, elicited fear-like responses and autonomic correlates of these responses (Fernandez de Molina & Hunsperger, 1962; Hilton & Zbrozyna, 1963). Finally, our earlier research suggested that the ACe may be an important focal point for further research. Injections of alpha-adrenergic, beta-adrenergic, and opiate agonists and antagonists into the amygdala of rats immediately following passive avoidance conditioning resulted in significant effects upon subsequent retention performance (Gallagher et al., 1977; Gallagher & Kapp, 1978; Gallagher & Kapp, 1981a). In our procedure retention was reflected to a large extent in the amount of freezing behavior, a manifestation of conditioned fear. Since (a) enkephalins and noradrenergic systems are highly concentrated within the ACe region (Fallon, Koziell, & Moore, 1978; Sar, Stumpf, Miller, Chang, & Cuatrecasas, 1978), (b) our cannula placements were positioned at the dorsal surface of the amygdala, with the majority of placements near the ACe (Gallagher & Kapp, 1981b) and (c) our cannula placements which were positioned such that damage was evident within the region of the ACe resulted in retention deficits, we focused our analysis upon the ACe. We began with an investigation of the effects of manipulations of the ACe on the acquisition of the conditioned bradycardiac response.

Contributions of the Amygdaloid Central Nucleus to Pavlovian Conditioned Bradycardia in the Rabbit

Our initial results suggested that the ACe contributes to the acquisition of the conditioned bradycardiac response. Using a Pavlovian fear conditioning procedure in which a 5.0 second tone CS preceded the onset of a 0.5 s, 2.0 mA eyelid shock US, we first demonstrated that both large and small radio frequency lesions confined primarily to the ACe and administered prior to conditioning significantly attenuated the magnitude of the conditioned bradycardiac response (Kapp, Frysinger, Gallagher, & Haselton, 1979). The effect appeared to be selective to the conditioned response since no significant effect was observed on intertrial baseline heart rate, nor on the heart rate orienting response to a novel tone (see Figure 12.1). Also, the effects could not be explained based on a lesion-induced decrease in US sensitivity since these lesions did not attenuate the magnitude of the unconditioned heart rate response. At about the time of this initial study, Werka, Skar, and Ursin (1978) reported that lesions largely confined to the ACe reduced the frequency of a variety of open-field

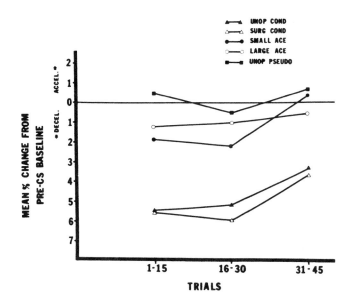

Figure 12.1. Mean percent change in heart rate to the 5.0 second CS from an immediately preceding 5.0 second baseline period for groups (ns=8) receiving 45 conditioning trials. Abbreviations: Unop Cond, Surg Cond = Unoperated and surgical control groups receiving 45 paired conditioning trials. Small ACE, Large ACE = groups with small (<50% damage) and large (>50% damage) lesions of the central nucleus and receiving 45 paired conditioning trials; Unop Pseudo = unoperated control group receiving 45 unpaired presentations of both the CS and US. Data points represent group means for 15 trial blocks. (Reprinted with permission from Kapp, Pascoe, and Bixler, 1984).

measures generally held to be indices of fear or emotionality. They concluded that such lesions reduced fear, a conclusion similar to that reached by us in our initial experiment. In a second series of experiments we demonstrated that pre-conditioning pharmacological manipulations using noradrenergic or opiate receptor agonists & antagonists administered to the region of the ACe also affected the magnitude of the conditioned response, producing an attenuation or augmentation dependent upon the agent administered (Gallagher, Kapp, Frysinger, & Rapp, 1980; Gallagher, Kapp, McNall, & Pascoe, 1981; Gallagher, Kapp, & Pascoe, 1982). These results suggested that the results of our lesion study were not due to destruction of fibers of passage. In addition, the results suggested that opiate and noradrenergic synaptic mechanisms within the region of the ACe contributed to the acquisition of the bradycardiac response.

More recently, several other reports have described results consistent with our initial studies. First, electrolytic lesions of the ACe administered to rabbits following Pavlovian aversive discriminative conditioning have been reported to attenuate the magnitude of the conditioned bradycardiac response during subsequent retention testing (Gentile, Jarrell, Teich, McCabe, & Schneiderman, 1986). Second, lesions of the ACe produced by ibotenic acid, a selective cell body neurotoxin, and administered prior to aversive Pavlovian discriminative conditioning have been reported to attenuate the magnitude of the conditioned bradycardiac response (Gentile, Romanski, Jarrell, McCabe, & Schneiderman, 1986). Third, LeDoux and colleagues have recently provided evidence which demonstrates that the region of the ACe in rats is a component of a critical circuit which contributes to the expression of conditioned freezing and blood pressure responses to the presentation of an acoustic, fear-arousing CS (Iwata, LeDoux, Meeley, Arneric, & Reis, 1986). Fourth, Hitchcock and Davis (1986) have demonstrated that a fear-potentiated, acoustic startle response elicited in the rat by a fear-arousing CS presented immediately prior to presentation of the auditory startle stimulus is markedly attenuated by lesions within the region of the ACe. Finally, it has been demonstrated that cooling of the cat ACe via cryoprobe prior to the presentation of a CS signaling an aversive US attenuates the magnitude of the conditioned blood pressure elevations normally observed in response to the CS (Zhang, Harper, & Ni, 1986).

While these results are quite consistent, it should be noted that it has recently been reported that ibotenic acid destruction of cell bodies in the ACe did not affect open field behavior nor produce deficits in the acquisition of a passive avoidance response (Riolobos & Martin Garcia, 1987). These latter results, however, are inconsistent with other recent reports demonstrating that ibotenic acid lesions primarily confined to the ACe result in deficits in passive avoidance acquisition (Jellestad & Bakke, 1985) and in increased open field behavior (Peinado-Manzano, 1988). The reasons for these discrepancies are not readily discernable and will require additional research. Nevertheless, electrolytic, radio frequency or ibotenic acid destruction of the ACe of the rabbit attenuates the magnitude of the bradycardiac response to a CS during Pavlovian fear conditioning.

Our initial experiments identified a component of the amygdala, the ACe, which appeared to make an important contribution to the acquisition of a conditioned cardiovascular response. However, the question remained concerning the exact nature of this contribution. Our own results, subsequently supported by more recent work of others (Gentile, Jarrell, Teich, McCabe, & Schneiderman, 1986), suggested that our manipulations did not render the animal grossly deficient in sensory responsiveness. Nevertheless, these results gave no insights into the extent to which our manipulations interfered with, for example, associative, motivational or performance mechanisms necessary for the expression of the conditioned response. Anatomical observations at that time, however, yielded some important clues. Hopkins and Holstege (1978) reported that in the cat the ACe projected directly to cardioregulatory nuclei in the medulla, including the nucleus of the solitary tract and the dorsal motor nucleus of the vagus, a site of preganglionic parasympathetic cardioinhibitory neurons in the rabbit (Jordan et al., 1982). We subsequently demonstrated the existence of such a projection in the rabbit (Schwaber, Kapp, & Higgins, 1981; Schwaber, Kapp, Higgins, & Rapp, 1982), a projection which has now been demonstrated in a variety of other species, including the rat and monkey (Higgins & Schwaber, 1983; Price & Amaral, 1981) (see Figure 12.2). These observations suggested to us that the ACe, via its direct as well as indirect projections (e.g., via lateral hypothalamus, the nucleus of the solitary tract, or periaqueductal gray) to the source of origin of preganglionic cardioinhibitory neurons, possessed the potential to drive the vagus for the expression of the conditioned response; in short, a premotor function. We pointed out, however, that this hypothesized function does not rule out the possibility that the nucleus also functions in associative processes (Kapp, Gallagher, Frysinger, & Applegate, 1981), a function discussed in more detail below. Nor did this hypothesis exclude the contribution of other forebrain areas to these functions, for which evidence now exists (Buchanan & Powell, 1982).

   In additional work we gathered data to test the validity of this working hypothesis. Consistent with it were our results demonstrating that short-latency, vagus-mediated bradycardia could be elicited via electrical stimulation of the ACe in the anesthetized, paralyzed, and artificially ventilated rabbit (Kapp et al., 1982), as well as in the conscious, loosely restrained rabbit (Applegate, Kapp, Underwood, & McNall, 1983) (see Figure 12.3). The most sensitive site for eliciting this response was located at the site of origin of the ACe-medullary projection; that is, the medial aspect of the nucleus. In addition, the bradycardiac response was accompanied by a longer-latency decrease in arterial blood pressure. Since a tone CS during Pavlovian fear conditioning elicits bradycardia and decreased blood pressure responses in the rabbit (Powell & Kazis, 1976), the results from these stimulation experiments were consistent with our working hypothesis. These stimulation-induced cardiovascular effects have since been replicated in the rabbit (Cox, Jordan, Paton, Spyer, & Wood, 1987). Furthermore, it has been demonstrated that stimulation of the ACe in rabbits activates vagal cardioinhibitory neurons as well as baroreceptive neurons within the nucleus of the solitary tract (Cox et al., 1986), neurons which in turn influence vagal cardioinhibitory neurons. Moreover, injections of exci-

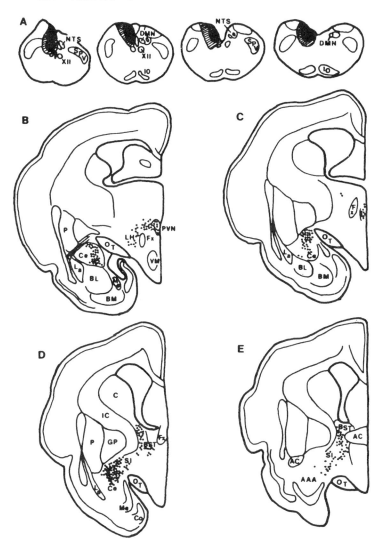

Figure 12.2. Labeled neurons in the amygdaloid central nucleus from a representative case in which four injections of horseradish peroxidase (HRP) were made at different levels along the rostral-caudal extent of the nucleus of the solitary tract and dorsal motor nucleus of the vagus (A). Each dot represents one retrogradely labeled neuron from that section alone. B-E, caudal-rostral levels through the amygdaloid complex. Abbreviations: AAA = anterior amygdaloid area; AC = anterior commissure; BL = amygdaloid basolateral nucleus; BM = amygdaloid basomedial nucleus; BST = bed nucleus of the stria terminalis; C = caudate nucleus; Ce = amygdaloid central nucleus; Co = amygdaloid cortical nucleus; DMN = dorsal motor nucleus of the vagus; La = amygdaloid lateral nucleus; NTS = nucleus of the solitary tract; OT = optic tract; P = putamen; SI = substantia innominata. (Reprinted with permission from Schwaber, Kapp, & Higgins, 1980).

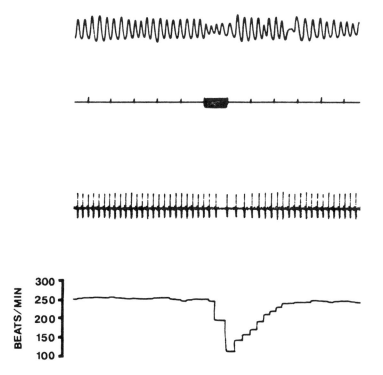

Figure 12.3. Heart rate and respiration responses produced by stimulation of the medial central nucleus in the awake, loosely restrained rabbit. The upper trace shows the respiration response, while the lower trace is the cardiotachograph response produced by a 1-second stimulus train (40 uA, 100 Hz, 0.5-msec pulse duration). (Reprinted with permission from Kapp, Pascoe, & Bixler, 1984).

tatory amino acids into the ACe elicit increased blood pressure responses in the conscious rat (Iwata, Chida, & LeDoux, 1987), responses similar to those elicited in response to a fear-arousing Pavlovian CS in this species (Iwata et al., 1986). These results, taken together with those described above, are consistent with the notion that the ACe is a premotor substrate for the expression of cardiovascular and somatomotor responses (e.g., freezing) to conditioned fear-arousing stimuli in a variety of species.

Additional findings also supported a motoric function for the ACe in the expression of the bradycardiac response. We demonstrated the development of changes in short-latency multiple unit activity within the ACe in response to the CS early during Pavlovian conditioning, the development of which was in some cases parallel to the development of the conditioned bradycardiac response (Applegate, Frysinger, Kapp, & Gallagher, 1982) (see Figure 12.4). Less than one-third of our placements within the nucleus, however, demonstrated such responses. The remaining two thirds demonstrated no obvious changes, or in many cases complex patterns of responses, prompting us to adopt a single cell recording analysis (Pascoe & Kapp, 1985a). The results of this analysis were consistent with those of our multiple unit study. A differential Pavlovian conditioning paradigm was used in which two different tone frequencies of five seconds in duration served as the CS+ and CS-. We found that the majority of ACe neurons recorded from during CS presentations during retention testing demonstrated differential responses to the two CSs, just as the heart rate demonstrated differential responses to the two CSs, with maximal bradycardia occurring to the CS+ and little or no bradycardia occurring to the CS-. Several additional, important findings emerged from this investigation. First, for some units the magnitude of the neuronal response to the CS+ was significantly correlated with the magnitude of the bradycardiac response to the CS+ (see Figure 12.5). Thus, the magnitude of the bradycardiac response could be predicted from the number of action potentials elicited in response to the CS+. Second, while some units showed differential excitatory responses to the CSs, others showed differential inhibitory responses, demonstrating the heterogeneity of response patterns in the nucleus. Finally, in an attempt to determine if neurons which demonstrated excitatory responses to the CSs were projection neurons to the lower brainstem, we identified ACe-brainstem projection neurons via antidromic activation from a stimulation electrode located within the ACe-brainstem projection pathway as it coursed through the mesencephalon. We were somewhat surprised to find that these brainstem projection neurons comprised a population of neurons which demonstrated very slow spontaneous rates (0.01-0.4 Hz), and that they did not respond in an excitatory manner to the CSs. Their slow spontaneous rates precluded statistical analysis on individual cells to determine if they demonstrated inhibition in response to the CSs. Nevertheless, the pooled data from these neurons demonstrated that when compared to the pre-CS periods, they decreased their activity more to the CS+ (by 86%) than to the CS-(by 50%). These findings suggested that during the presentation of the CS influences normally exerted by these projection neurons are withdrawn. This withdrawal may act in concert with other classes of ACe neurons which may excite cardioinhibitory neurons via multisynaptic pathways (e.g., lateral hypothalamus, midbrain periaqueductal gray). The identification of the projection fields of other ACe neurons, particularly those which demonstrate differential excitation to the CSs, is now a focus of investigation in our laboratory (Wilson & Kapp, 1987, 1988).

Identification and Analysis of a Forebrain Circuit which Contributes to the Acquisition of Conditioned Bradycardia

The combined results described above suggest a critical role for the ACe in the expression of the conditioned bradycardiac response, most probably via both direct and indirect pathways to cardioinhibitory neurons of the medulla. We have recently directed our efforts to an analysis of major afferent pathways to the ACe in the rabbit, in order to identify the possible path(s) by which CS information may access the nucleus (Kapp, Schwaber, & Driscoll, 1984, 1985a; Kapp, Markgraf, Schwaber, & Bilyk-Spafford, 1988). Table 12.1 lists the ma-

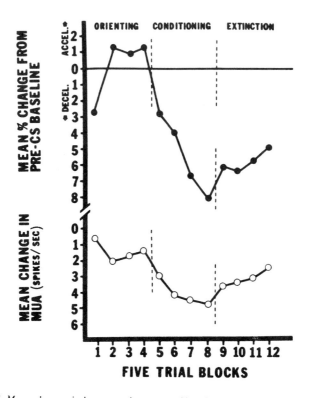

Figure 12.4. Mean changes in heart rate (upper graph) and central nucleus multiple unit activity (MUA) (lower graph) to the CS during orienting (20 CS-alone trials), conditioning (20 paired CS-US conditioning trials) and extinction (20 CS-alone trials) components of a conditioning session for one animal. Each data point represents the mean for a block of five trials. Note the increase in multiple unit activity which parallels the emergence of the conditioned bradycardiac response during the conditioning and extinction components of the session. (Adapted with permission from Applegate et al., 1982).

jor sources of afferentation based upon our own work in the rabbit as well as upon that of others in rat, cat, and primate. As is obvious, the nucleus receives afferents from a large variety of structures. In our analysis we were impressed by a particularly dense, well-defined projection which originated in the insular cortex on the lateral surface of the hemisphere and which projected to the region of the nucleus where neurons which give rise to the brainstem connections, including the NTS/DMN complex, were located (Kapp et al., 1985a). This projection has been demonstrated in a variety of species (Mufson, Mesulam, & Pandya, 1981; Saper, 1982) and was of interest to us based upon several observations. First, the insular cortex receives projections from sensory, including auditory, neocortex (Mesulam & Mufson, 1982). Second, it projects not only to the ACe, but also to a variety of subcortical structures which receive projections from the ACe and which have been implicated in car-

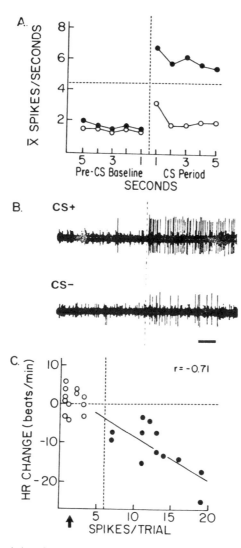

Figure 12.5. Characteristics of central nucleus neurons which demonstrate an increase in activity in response to CS+ and CS- presentations during the expression of conditioned bradycardia. A: cumulative records of the activity of 13 neurons during the course of 114 presentations each of the CS+ (●) and CS- (○). The dashed horizontal line indicates the point at which unit activity is significantly elevated over pre-CS baseline rates (p<.05). B: oscilloscope traces showing the response of one such neuron to the presentation of the CS+ and CS-Dashed vertical line depicts onset of the 5.0 second CS. Calibration bar = 1.0 second. C: the relationship between heart rate change and the activity of the neuron depicted in B during the course of 12 presentations each of the CS+ (●) and CS- (○). The correlation coefficient and regression line are based only upon those trials during which the CS+ was presented. The arrow depicts spontaneous rate and the dashed vertical line indicates the point above which the activity of this neuron is significantly increased over baseline rates (p<.05). (Adapted with permission from Pascoe and Kapp, (1985a). We thank Dr. A.D. Loewy for the adaptation).

TABLE 12.1
Amygdaloid Central Nucleus
Major Afferent Connections

CORTEX
  Agranular/granular insula

BASAL FOREBRAIN
  Substantia innominata
  Bed nucleus of stria terminalis
AMYGDALA
  Basolateral nucleus
  Lateral nucleus

THALAMUS
  Paraventricular nucleus
  Medial geniculate nucleus

MIDBRAIN
  Ventral tegmental area
  Substantia nigra

PONS
  Medial/lateral parabrachial nuclei
  Locus coeruleus
  Dorsal raphe nucleus

MEDULLA
  Nucleus solitarius
  Vagal dorsal motor nucleus

diovascular regulation (Kapp, Schwaber, & Driscoll, 1985b; Saper, 1982). Third, electrical stimulation of the insular cortex has been reported to elicit a variety of autonomic responses, including cardiovascular alterations (Kaada, 1951). Finally, lesions of the insular cortex were reported to produce deficits in the acquisition of passive avoidance (Kaada, 1951; Pare & Dumas, 1965), an effect similar to that observed following lesions of the ACe (McIntyre & Stein, 1973). These data, taken together, suggested to us that the insular cortex may, via its afferents to the ACe, convey CS information to the nucleus, information which elicits changes in the activity of neurons in the nucleus essential for the expression of the conditioned bradycardiac response.

In an analysis designed to determine the validity of this suggestion we found that electrical stimulation of the insular cortex elicited short-latency alterations in the activity of ACe neurons, including those identified to project to the brainstem (Pascoe & Kapp, 1987a). Furthermore, lesions damaging the dorsal agranular and granular insular region and located within an area of origin of insular-ACe projections and administered prior to acquisition produced a small but statistically significant attenuation of the conditioned response (Markgraf, 1984). A similar result was reported by Powell, Buchanan, and Hernandez (1985). These findings were consistent with those demonstrating that electrical stimulation of the insular cortex in the rabbit elicited short-latency bradycardia and depressor responses (Powell et al., 1985). Given these results, we initiated an investigation to determine whether insular cortex neurons which were identified to project to the ACe using antidromic activation techniques were CS-responsive, and if so, whether their latency of response to the CS was shorter than that of ACe neurons. Such a finding would be consistent with the notion that CS information accesses the insular cortex prior to the

ACe, and may be relayed from the former to the latter. In our initial investigation, however, we were unable to find CS-responsive neurons in the insular cortex, including some 21 cells which were antidromically activated from single pulse electrical stimulation of the ACe (Pascoe & Kapp, 1987b). Hence, our electrophysiological analysis to date has not yielded results consistent with the hypothesis that CS information may access the ACe via projections from the insular cortex. Our initial electrophysiological investigation, however, was directed toward the rostral insular region, and we have not yet explored the more posterior region. Any final conclusions concerning the insular cortex and CS responsivity must await further research.

Several other regions may also transmit CS information to the ACe. Another likely candidate is the magnocellular division of the medial geniculate nucleus (MGm). The MGm is recipient of auditory projections from the inferior colliculus, and short-latency, associative changes in neuronal activity have been reported to develop in the MGm in response to a CS early during the course of Pavlovian aversive conditioning in the cat. These changes occurred at approximately the same time as the development of conditioned pupillary responses (Ryugo & Weinberger, 1978). Similarly, associative changes in neuronal activity in the MGm have been demonstrated to develop in response to a CS during the early stages of differential avoidance acquisition training in the rabbit (Gabriel, Miller, & Saltwick, 1976). In addition, we have observed in rabbits that neurons within the MGm and dorsally-adjacent suprageniculate nucleus project to the region of the ACe (Kapp, Schwaber, & Driscoll, 1984). Unlike the projections of the insular cortex which enter the body of the nucleus, the projections from the MGm primarily surround the dorsal and lateral aspects of the nucleus, with some light innervation of its anterior dorsal region. A heavier innervation was observed in the lateral amygdaloid nucleus. A similar projection has been reported in the rat (Farb, Ruggiero, & LeDoux, 1988). The functional significance of projections which surround the nucleus versus those which enter the body of the nucleus is far from clear. Nevertheless, the recent data (a) implicating an MGm-amygdaloid projection in the mediation of fear-conditioned blood pressure and freezing responses in the rat (Iwata et al., 1986) and (b) demonstrating that lesions of the MGm produce deficits in the acquisition of differential heart rate conditioning in the rabbit (Jarrell, Romanski, Gentile, McCabe, & Schneiderman, 1986) prompted us to determine the CS responsiveness of MGm neurons (Supple & Kapp, 1988). For our analysis we used a differential Pavlovian conditioning procedure identical to that used in our analysis of ACe-single neuron activity. The results demonstrated that neurons located within the region of the MGm respond differentially to the CS+ and CS-. Many neurons demonstrated latencies shorter than those observed for neurons within the ACe, a finding consistent with the hypothesis that CS information may access the ACe via an MGm-amygdaloid projection. Some units demonstrated an excitatory response which was greater to the CS+ than to the CS-, while others demonstrated an inhibitory response which was greater to the CS+ than to the CS- (see Figure 12.6). These discriminative responses appeared to be associative in nature since recordings

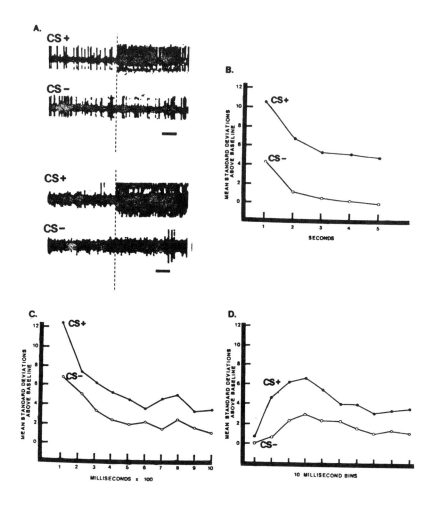

Figure 12.6. Response characteristics of neurons within the magnocellular medial geniculate nucleus which demonstrated greater responses to the CS+ compared to the CS-. A. Oscilloscope traces showing representative responses of two of these neurons to presentations of each CS. The onset of the 5.0 second CS is indicated by the dashed vertical line. Calibration bar = 1.0 second. B. Shown are the mean Z-scores of each 1.0 second period during the 5.0 second CS+ and CS- period for this group of 40 neurons. Note that responses during the CS+ (●) were increased and sustained throughout the entire CS period while responses to the CS- (○) were increased only during the first 1.0-2.0 seconds of the CS period. C. Neuronal activity during each 100-msec bin across the initial 1000 msec of the CS+ and CS-. D. Shorter latency neuronal responses. Shown is the activity during the first ten 10 msec bins following CS onset. The increased activity to the CS+ was greater and of shorter latency than to the CS-.

made in the naive rabbit demonstrated that MGm neurons, while responsive to CS presentations, did not show differential responses to the two CSs and underwent a rapid response habituation with repeated presentations of the CSs.

The results of this analysis are consistent with the hypothesis offered by Le-Doux and colleagues that the critical circuit for fear conditioning to an auditory CS involves a projection from the MGm region to the amygdala (Iwata et al., 1986).

It also should be noted that the MGm projects not only to the amygdala, but also to the region of the insular cortex which in turn projects to the ACe (Guldin & Markowitsch, 1983). LeDoux and colleagues, however, have presented data which indicate that projections from the MGm to the cortex are not essential for the acquisition of Pavlovian conditioned freezing or blood pressure responses in rat (LeDoux, Sakaguchi, & Reis, 1984). Nevertheless, the significance of a possible MGm-insula-ACe pathway in conveying CS information to the ACe during Pavlovian conditioning in the rabbit has yet to be elucidated. Finally, while the insular cortex and/or MGm are potential candidates for conveying CS information to the ACe, the possibility that other pathways mediate this function cannot be dismissed at the present time. For example, the basolateral and lateral amygdaloid nuclei send projections to the ACe (Kapp, Schwaber, & Driscoll, 1984; Krettek & Price, 1978), and neurons within these nuclei are sensory responsive (Jacobs & McGinty, 1972; Sanghera, Rolls, & Roper-Hall, 1979). Furthermore, the lateral nucleus has been demonstrated to receive a projection from the MGm (Farb et al., 1988), and when lesions are made in this nucleus, conditioned blood pressure and freezing responses to a Pavlovian conditioned auditory CS are greatly reduced (Cicchetti, LeDoux, & Reis, 1987). The contribution of these amygdaloid nuclei in transmitting CS information to the ACe in the conditioning of bradycardia in the rabbit is deserving of investigation.

That training-induced modifications of neuronal activity have been observed within the ACe and the MGm raise the possibility that one or both may be sites for such modifications—in essence, the site(s) of the engram for the conditioned bradycardiac response. Implicit in this hypothesis, and consistent with current neuronal models of Pavlovian associative learning, is the assumption that convergence of CS and US information must occur within these sites. Although the convergence of CS and US information on individual cells within the ACe has yet to be systematically investigated over the course of conditioning, we have found that cells within the ACe of naive rabbits demonstrate polymodal response characteristics, responding in an excitatory manner to visual, auditory and somatosensory stimuli (Pascoe & Kapp, 1985b). A similar polymodal response profile for ACe neurons has been reported for the cat (Schutze, Knuepfer, Eismann, Stumpf, & Stock, 1987). Furthermore, in our single unit analysis (Pascoe & Kapp, 1985b) we observed that some neurons showing discriminative, excitatory activity to the two CSs demonstrated excitatory responses to the US. Other neurons showing such activity, however, appeared unresponsive to the US, although the extent to which these unresponsive cells were inhibited by the US was not readily apparent due to their slow spontaneous rates. Thus, CS and US information does converge upon some ACe neurons. Furthermore, that a similar convergence of CS and US information occurs within the MGm is evidenced by the finding that neurons within this nucleus respond to both the CS and US during Pavlovian conditioning in cat (Weinberger, 1982).

While the pathway(s) by which the US may influence ACe neurons has yet to be delineated, demonstrated projections from several areas including the locus coeruleus (LC), MGm and parabrachial nucleus (PBN) are possible candidates. The LC is of particular importance since several lines of evidence suggest that it may represent a source of US input to the pigeon lateral geniculate homologue, an area in which conditioning-induced modification of neuronal activity develops to a visual CS during Pavlovian aversive heart rate conditioning (Gibbs, Broyles, & Cohen, 1983; Gibbs, Cohen, & Broyles, 1986). First, electrical stimulation of the LC affects the firing rate of neurons in the pigeon lateral geniculate in a manner similar to that observed in response to the aversive shock US. Second, LC neurons respond to the US. Third, lesions of the LC eliminate the US-evoked changes in neural activity in the lateral geniculate. Finally, using a standard Pavlovian conditioning procedure, presentation of a visual CS paired with electrical stimulation of the LC as a US resulted in a rapid conditioning-induced modification of lateral geniculate neuronal activity in response to the CS, a modification strikingly similar to that observed when foot shock served as a US. Taken together, these results are consistent with the hypothesis that the LC conveys US information to a site which demonstrates conditioning-induced modification of neuronal activity to a CS over repeated conditioning trials. Since stimulation of the LC also affects neuronal activity in the ACe (Schutze et al., 1987), it is conceivable that the LC may also convey US information to the ACe.

In addition to the locus coeruleus, the parabrachial nucleus (PBN) may also serve as a source of US input based on the observations that (a) PBN neurons receive a large projection from lamina I spinal and trigeminal caudalis neurons which presumably transmit nociceptive information (Cechetto, Standaert, & Saper, 1985), (b) PBN neurons respond to noxious stimuli (Bernard, Ma, Besson, & Peschanski, 1986) and (c) spinal neurons synapse upon PBN neurons which project to the ACe (Bernard et al., 1986). These results suggest that a putative nociceptive pathway may originate in lamina I and trigeminal caudalis neurons and reach the ACe via a monosynaptic relay in the parabrachial nucleus. Finally, the MGm may also transmit US information to the ACe since MGm neurons respond to somatosensory stimuli (Wepsic, 1966) and receive projections from the spinal cord (Lund & Webster, 1967). In support of this role for the MGm are the recent findings of Hitchcock and Davis (1987) which suggest that US information critical for fear-potentiated startle to an aversively conditioned CS may be relayed to the amygdala from the region of the MGm and the adjacent posterior intralaminar nucleus of the thalamus. In addition to relaying CS information, it is therefore possible that the MGm may also relay US information to the amygdala.

In summary, it should be emphasized that a variety of structures may transmit CS and US information to the ACe. No one structure may exclusively function in this capacity and information concerning these stimuli may reach the ACe via multiple pathways (see Figure 12.7). In addition, whether

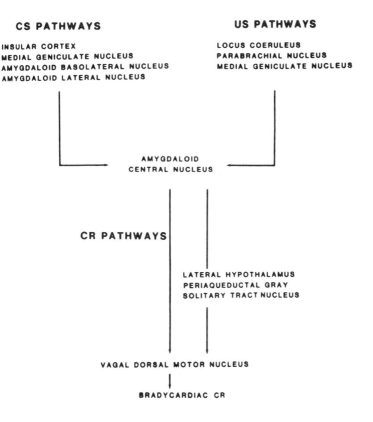

Figure 12.7. Possible pathways by which CS and US information may access the amygdaloid central nucleus and thereby contribute to the plasticity which forms the substrate for the conditioned bradycardiac response.

the site of associative change resides exclusively within the ACe and/or the MGm, or whether it resides at multiple sites throughout the critical pathway from sensory input to motor output as suggested by Cohen (1984), must await further investigation.

The ACe: A Component of an Extensive Forebrain System Contributing to the Expression of Conditioned Emotional Responses

In our anatomical and electrical stimulation experiments directed at the ACe, two interesting findings emerged. First, in experiments designed to define the source of origin of the ACe projection to the medulla (Schwaber et al., 1980), not only were the cells of origin of this projection located throughout the entire rostro-caudal extent of the medial component of the nucleus, they extended rostrally from the nucleus in an uninterrupted continuous region through the sublenticular substantia innominata and into the lateral part of the bed nucleus of the stria terminalis. At that time we suggested the anatomical unity of this continuum as a single entity, a concept supported by observations that these three regions possess common cytoarchitecture, staining properties, cate-cholamine innervation and afferentation from the solitary tract (see Schwaber et al., 1982). Recent observations have further suggested that this continuum may extend even more rostral to include the ventral most region of the nucleus accumbens (Heimer, Alheid, & Zaborszky, 1985). Additional findings, including (a) common neuropeptide immunostaining characteristics across the continuum and (b) common efferent projection fields originating from the components of the continuum, have led several others to agree with this suggestion (de Olmos, Alheid, & Beltramino, 1985; Holstege, Meiners & Tan, 1985).

Second, in our investigations using electrical stimulation to map the ACe for cardioactive sites, we observed that low-level stimulation of cardioactive sites also elicited a variety of other responses, both somatic and autonomic (Applegate et al., 1983). These included respiratory alterations reflected in increased frequency and decreased tidal volume, increased gastric motility, pupillary dilation, eyelid opening, cessation of movement, ear orientation and movements of the mouth, jaw, and tongue resembling chewing. They were of short onset latency, generally within 1.0 second or less. These observations, together with those in the cat (Ursin & Kaada, 1960), suggested that the ACe and perhaps the entire continuum exert a pervasive influence on both autonomic and somatic motor regions of the brainstem and spinal cord. In particular, the continuum may contribute not only to the expression of conditioned cardiovascular responses, but also to the expression of an entire pattern of autonomic and somatic responses to conditioned fear-arousing stimuli. Consistent with this hypothesis are the observations that during Pavlovian fear conditioning the CS elicits responses similar to those elicited by stimulation of the ACe, including (a) increased respiratory frequency and decreased tidal volume, and an inhibition of somatomotor activity (Schneiderman, 1972; Yehle, Dauth, & Schneiderman, 1967) in the rabbit and (b) pupillary dilation in the cat (Weinberger, 1982).

The emerging anatomical picture of the descending projections of this forebrain continuum is also consistent with this notion. It is well-documented that in addition to the projections to medullary cardioregulatory nuclei, various components of this continuum project to a variety of motor-related areas of the brainstem and spinal cord (see Figure 12.8). These include (a) the tegmental pedunculopontine nucleus (Swanson, Mogenson, Gerfen, & Robinson, 1984), a nucleus involved with rhythmic limb movement, (b) the ventral aspects of the periaqueductal gray (Hopkins & Holstege, 1978; Kapp, Wilson, Schwaber, & Bilyk-Spafford, 1986), which by virtue of its afferentation from motor cortex, substantia nigra, and the deep cerebellar nuclei (Meller & Dennis, 1986) suggest its alignment with the motor system, (c) the lateral tegmental field of the caudal pons and medulla, within which are located populations of interneurons which project to cranial nerve motor nuclei (Holstege, Kuypers, & Dekker, 1977; Hopkins & Holstege, 1978), and (d) the medial and ventral regions of the spinal cord, within which are located autonomic and somatic motor neurons (Sandrew, Edwards, Poletti, & Foote, 1986).

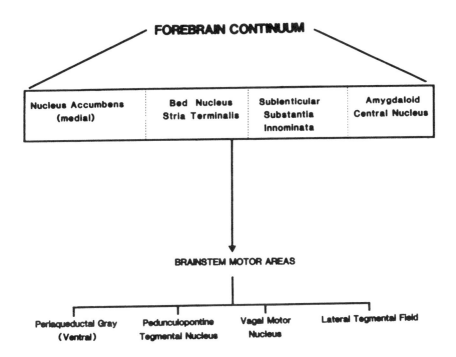

Figure 12.8. The hypothesized components of an extensive forebrain continuum which may contribute to the expression of a pattern of autonomic and somatic motor responses to emotionally-arousing stimuli. The projections of this continuum to a variety of motor-related areas of the brainstem are shown.

These projections to motor-related areas of the brainstem and spinal cord form the substrate by which electrical stimulation of the ACe evokes the responses described above. Many of these responses are most probably due to activation of interneurons within the lateral tegmental field, which in turn innervate cranial nerve motor nuclei including those innvervating the muscles of the ears, eyelid, tongue, mouth and jaw (Holstege et al., 1977; Holstege, van Ham, & Tan, 1986) (see Figure 12.9). At a conceptual level, then, the continuum can be considered as a component of the motor system which functions in part in the elicitation of a variety of species-specific responses to motivationally significant stimuli, responses which are rapidly acquired and important to the survival of the organism.

While the projections of the ACe to motor-related areas of the brainstem and spinal cord offer an anatomical substrate for the expression of a variety of responses to emotionally-arousing stimuli, additional research suggests that some of these projections may also be substrates for a more subtle function in sensory-motor integration in the presence of such stimuli. For example, Gary Bobo and Bonvallet (1975) demonstrated that stimulation sites within the lateral aspects of the ACe of cat produced an immediate, marked facilitation of the

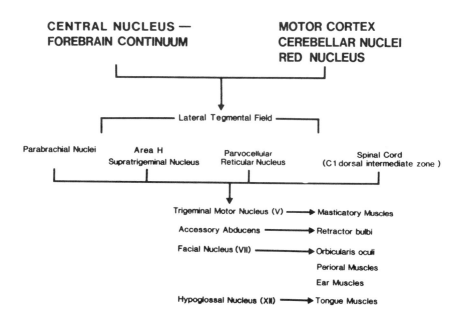

Figure 12.9. A schematic representation of the projections of the forebrain continuum to a continuous region extending from the parabrachial region to the cervical spinal cord. Within this region are the lateral tegmental fields within which are located neuronal populations which project upon a variety of cranial nerve nuclei. These nuclei in turn project to the muscles indicated. Note the overlap within the lateral tegmental field of the projections from the continuum with those from traditional motor systems.

masseteric jaw closure reflex while sites located in the more medial aspects produced an immediate inhibition of the reflex. These facilitory and inhibitory effects frequently occurred with no changes in the tonic activity of the masseteric nerve, the final pathway for jaw closure via the masseteric muscle. This suggests that modulation of the reflex may occur via presynaptic mechanisms. Since these early studies preceded the delineation of the source of origin of the descending pathways of the ACe and forebrain continuum, the relationship of these stimulation sites to the origin of the ACe brainstem pathway is not readily apparent. Nevertheless, the finding suggested a potent, modulatory influence of the ACe upon reflex sensitivity.

Modulation of reflex sensitivity by stimulation of the ACe has also been reported for the baroreceptor reflex. Schlor, Stumpf, and Stock (1984) have demonstrated that electrical stimulation of the ACe in cat reduces baroreceptor reflex sensitivity as assessed by a decreased magnitude in vagus-mediated bradycardia to baroreceptor activation. A decrease in sensitivity was also observed during arousal-eliciting situations such as confrontation with an aggressive cat. While decreased baroreceptor reflex sensitivity occurs during stimulation of the ACe in the cat, the opposite has been demonstrated in the rabbit (Pascoe, Bradley, & Spyer, 1989). Low-level electrical stimulation, while producing little in the way of bradycardia, greatly augmented the magnitude of the bradycardiac response to baroreceptor nerve stimulation.

Finally, recent work has demonstrated that electrical stimulation of the amygdala in rat, including sites within the ACe, immediately prior to an acoustic stimulus greatly enhances the acoustic startle reflex (Rosen & Davis, 1988). This finding is consistent with the observation that lesions of the ACe block the fear-potentiated startle reflex as described previously (Hitchcock & Davis, 1987). Given the projections of the ACe to the nucleus reticularis pontis caudalis (Hitchcock & Davis, 1986), an area which represents the brainstem descending limb of the startle circuit, the combined observations suggest that the ACe modulates the sensitivity of this reflex during conditioned fear.

In summary, the results suggest that the ACe and perhaps other components of this continuum, via brainstem projections, serve to modulate the sensitivity of numerous reflexes during emotional arousal, including conditioned fear. Presumably, a complex pattern of modulation of a variety of reflexes, reflected in an enhancement of some while a decrement in others, promotes the survival of the organism in the presence of a threatening stimulus. How each of the components of this pattern is adaptive must await further research.

THE AMYGDALOID ACe: ITS SIGNIFICANCE IN A TWO PROCESS THEORY OF AVERSIVE CONDITIONING

Based upon an analysis of the conditioning of the rabbit nictitating membrane (NM) response, as well as upon earlier configurations of two process models of avoidance conditioning, Thompson et al. (1987) have proposed a theory pertaining to the neural substrates of aversive conditioning. They suggest that during Pavlovian aversive conditioning trials an initial associative process, that of conditioned fear to the CS and contextual cues, develops rapidly and influences a number of brainstem motor control systems. These systems contribute to the expression of non-specific responses, responses which are (a) not specific to the nature or location of the US (e.g., conditioned bradycardia), (b) considered to be indices of conditioned fear, and (c) adaptive to the survival of the animal (see Weinberger, 1982). The theory assumes that this rapidly conditioned associative process is manifested in a specific neural substrate, different from that which represents the engram for the acquisition and expression of specific responses. The latter are those which (a) require significantly more conditioning trials to emerge than non-specific responses, (b) generally are represented by skeletal motor responses such as the NM and limb flexion responses and (c) are specific to the nature of the US (e.g., NM extension in response to corneal stimulation). While it is proposed that a separate neuronal system contains the engram for the acquisition of these specific conditioned responses, it is also proposed that the brain system which forms the substrate for the learning and performance of these specific responses is modulated by the brain system which forms the substrate for the conditioning of fear and its expression in the form of non-specific responses. That is, the non-specific engram influences the development of the specific engram, but once the latter is established, it is proposed to function in a somewhat independent manner.

Thompson et al. (1987) base their theory on a variety of observations. First, from two process models of avoidance conditioning, it is assumed that conditioned fear initially develops rapidly, followed by the acquisition of specific skeletal motor avoidance responses (Mowrer, 1947). Second, central administration of opiate agonists into the fourth ventricle during the early emergence of the conditioned NM response abolished this conditioned response (Mauk, Warren, & Thompson, 1982). These injections also abolished the conditioned bradycardiac response (Lavond, Mauk, Madden, Barchas, & Thompson, 1983). Thompson et al. (1987) suggest that opiate agonists abolish the NM conditioned response early during conditioning by affecting the system involved in the conditioning and expression of fear, as reflected in conditioned bradycardia. This interpretation is based in part on the finding that with overtraining, presumably when fear in response to the CS declines, the ability of opiates to abolish the rabbit NM conditioned response is markedly reduced (Mauk et al., 1983). The neural substrate(s) which mediate fear, therefore, is proposed to modulate the learning and performance of the specific conditioned NM response during the earlier stages of training. Consistent with the decline of fear over the course of the conditioning of the rabbit NM response are data demonstrating that the magnitude of the conditioned bradycardiac response diminishes at approximately the time that the conditioned NM response develops during Pavlovian conditioning (Schneiderman, 1972). Finally, in support of the independence of the NM response system are the observations that lesions of the dentate/interpositus nuclei of the cerebellum, while completely preventing the acquisition of the NM conditioned response, are without effect on the acquisition of the conditioned bradycardiac response in the rabbit (Lavond, Lincoln, McCormick, & Thompson, 1983).

From our discussion of the ACe-forebrain continuum, and in keeping with the above theory, the intriguing possibility exists that the ACe-forebrain continuum modulates the learning and/or performance of specific conditioned responses and their underlying neural substrates. Several interesting observations support this notion. By way of example, we will focus on the acquisition of the rabbit NM conditioned response. Recall that it develops following considerably more conditioning trials than that required for the development of nonspecific conditioned responses such as bradycardia. The question raised here concerns the difference in the number of conditioning trials required for the emergence of these two responses. While the answer is not entirely clear, certain characteristics of the ACe, as detailed above, lend some insight. In our previous discussion we proposed that the ACe and its descending projection system is a component of a forebrain continuum which represents a substrate for the expression of a variety of rapidly conditioned, non-specific responses. Of interest from our study of the various responses induced by electrical stimulation in the rabbit was the observation that such stimulation elicited an eye-opening response, suggesting that the ACe influences the musculature controlling the eyelids. In support of this notion are the anatomical observations that the ACe-forebrain continuum sends a substantial projection to the region of the lateral tegmental field of the caudal pons and medulla, a region which in turn projects to the intermediate subnucleus of the facial motor nucleus (Holstege, van Ham, & Tan, 1986). The latter innervates the orbicularis oculi muscle, the contraction of which contributes to the conditioned eyeblink response. This response occurs simultaneously with, and is highly correlated with, the conditioned NM response (McCormick, Lavond, & Thompson, 1982). The ACe, then, possesses the potential to elicit conditioned eye-opening during the early stages of NM conditioning, a response which has been reported during the early stages of NM conditioning (Maser, Dienst, & O'Neal, 1974) and which could be considered as a non-specific conditioned response incompatible with the conditioned eyeblink response. This eye-opening response could be in part mediated by an inhibition of the motor neurons innervating the orbicularis oculi, perhaps via an ACe influence on premotor interneurons in the lateral tegmental field.

Of additional importance is the observation that the same region of the lateral tegmental field which is recipient of a projection from the ACe-forebrain continuum projects not only to the motor neurons of the intermediate facial subnucleus, but also to the accessory abducens nucleus (Holstege, Tan, van Ham, & Graveland, 1986). This nucleus innervates the retractor bulbi muscle, the contraction of which produces eyeball retraction, thereby contributing to the extension of the NM across the eye (Marek, McMaster, Gormezano, & Harvey, 1984). Both the intermediate subnucleus of the facial nucleus and the accessory abducens nucleus, via their influence on the orbicularis oculi and the retractor bulbi, are major contributors to the coordinated, defensively conditioned NM/eyeblink response in the rabbit. Since stimulation at points within the region of the ACe in the cat has been reported to produce a retraction of the NM (Hilton & Zbrozyna, 1963), it is conceivable that during the early stages of NM conditioning the ACe exerts an inhibition on retractor bulbi motor neurons, manifested in a conditioned retraction of the NM. There appears to be some evidence for this in the rabbit. In an earlier study of the conditioned NM response, we noticed that in many rabbits there was a retraction of the NM to the CS which was present during the early conditioning trials (Kapp, Frysinger, Gallagher, & Bretschneider, 1977). The emergence of a retraction of the NM also appears to be present in the data presented by Berger, Alger, and Thompson (1976) and Berger and Thompson (1978) (see Figure 12.10).

In summary, within the framework of the theory proposed by Thompson et al. (1987) there is sufficient data to entertain the hypothesis that during the early stages of NM/eyeblink conditioning a conditioned competing response develops which is incompatible with and retards the emergence of the conditioned NM/eyeblink response. This retardation accounts for the increased number of trials required for the conditioning of this response when compared with those required for nonspecific responses such as bradycardia. Furthermore, this competing response may be mediated by the ACe/forebrain continuum and its descending projection to premotor brainstem regions. Thus, activation of the ACe-forebrain continuum by a fear-arousing CS may influence the performance of the specific NM conditioned response. This competing response could be considered adaptive during the early stages of conditioning, possibly by providing a mechanism for enhancing visual input. Over conditioning trials, and as

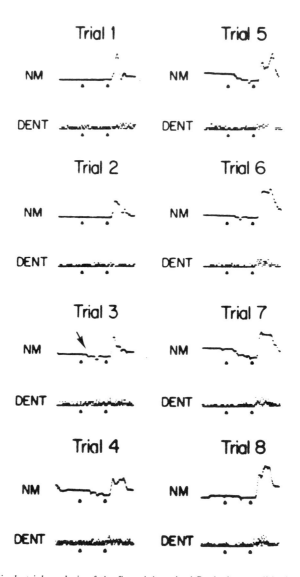

Figure 12.10. Single trial analysis of the first eight paired Pavlovian conditioning trials for an animal receiving nictitating membrane conditioning in which a 350 msec tone CS was paired with a corneal air puff presented 250 msec after CS onset. Upper trace for each trial represents the nictitating membrane response for that trial while lower trace represents the post-stimulus histogram for neuronal activity recorded from the dentate gyrus. Note that commencing on trial three presentation of the CS (first cursor) elicits a nictitating membrane response opposite in direction (arrow) to the extension or unconditioned response elicited to the airpuff unconditioned stimulus. (Reprinted with permission from Berger, Alger, & Thompson, 1976).

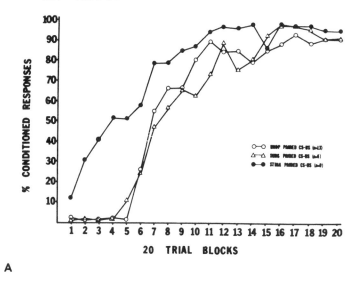

A

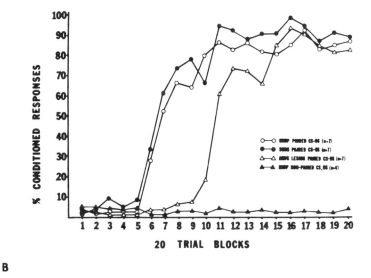

B

Figure 12.11. (A) Percent conditioned responses during nictitating membrane conditioning in which the offset of a 500 msec tone CS was coincident with the onset of a 50 msec eyelid shock US. One hundred conditioning trials were given per day for four days. Note the rapid emergence of conditioned responses in the group with stria terminalis lesions compared with unoperated and surgical control groups. (B) Percent conditioned responses during nictitating membrane conditioning for a group receiving large lesions of the amygdala when compared to surgical and unoperated control groups and a group receiving unpaired presentations of the CS and US. Conditioning parameters identical to those described in A. (From Kapp et al., 1977).

the animal learns the correlation between the CS and US, it should wane with a time course similar to the attenuation of the conditioned bradycardiac response, thereby permitting the emergence of the specific NM/eyeblink response.

While speculative, this hypothesis leads to several testable predictions. For example, destruction of the ACe and/or other components of the forebrain continuum would be predicted to affect the emergence of the conditioned NM conditioned response. While this has not been directly tested, prior to our analysis of the ACe we demonstrated that rabbits with lesions of the stria terminalis, a pathway carrying afferents and efferents of the ACe and other amygdaloid nuclei, required significantly fewer trials for the development of the conditioned NM response. On the other hand, large lesions of the amygdala, damaging an array of different nuclei, exerted the opposite effect: a prolongation of the trials required for the emergence and asymptotic performance of the conditioned NM response (Kapp et al., 1977) (see Figure 12.11). The specific area(s) of the amygdala which, when damaged, contributed to the observed effect was not readily identifiable due to the large extent of the lesions. Nevertheless, the data are consistent with the notion that the amygdaloid complex influences the learning and/or performance of the specific NM/eyeblink response.

SUMMARY AND CONCLUSIONS

Our research, as well as the research of others, has strongly suggested that the ACe is an important component of a forebrain-brainstem system which contributes to the expression of Pavlovian conditioned bradycardia in the rabbit, as well as to the expression of other rapidly-acquired species-typical conditioned responses in the presence of fear-arousing stimuli. Furthermore, the ACe and other components of this system demonstrate the required characteristics for the plasticity necessary for the development of these responses. Finally, this system possesses the potential to influence the learning and/or performance of other, more slowly-acquired, conditioned responses which emerge during aversive Pavlovian conditioning procedures; for example, the NM/eyeblink membrane response in the rabbit. The continued investigation of this system is of paramount importance in enhancing our understanding of the specific neural substrates which mediate aversively conditioned responses and the manner in which they interact during the conditioning process.

REFERENCES

Applegate, C.D., Frysinger, R.C., Kapp, B.S., & Gallagher, M. (1982). Multiple unit activity recorded from the amygdala central nucleus during Pavlovian heart rate conditioning in the rabbit. *Brain Research, 238*, 457-462.

Applegate, C.D., Kapp, B.S., Underwood, M., & McNall, C.L. (1983). Autonomic and somatomotor effects of amygdala central n. stimulation in awake rabbits. *Physiology and Behavior, 31*, 353-360.

Berger, T.W., Alger, B.E., & Thompson, R.F. (1976). Neuronal substrates of classical conditioning in the hippocampus. *Science, 192*, 483-485.

Berger, T.W., & Thompson, R.F. (1978). Neuronal plasticity in the limbic system during classical conditioning of the rabbit nictitating membrane. I. Response in the hippocampus. *Brain Research, 145,* 323-346.

Bernard, J.F., Ma, W., Besson, J.M., & Peschanski, M. (1986) A monosynaptic spino-ponto-amygdaloid pathway possibly involved in pain. *Neuroscience Abstracts, 12,* 31.

Blanchard, D.C., & Blanchard, R.J. (1972). Innate and conditioned reactions to threat in rats with amygdaloid lesions. *Journal of Comparative and Physiological Psychology, 81,* 281-290.

Bolles, R.C., & Fanselow, M.S. (1980). A perceptual-defensive-recuperative model of fear and pain. *Behavioral and Brain Sciences, 3,* 291-323.

Bruner, A. (1969). Reinforcement strength in classical conditioning of leg flexion, freezing, and heart rate in cats. *Conditioned Reflex, 4,* 61-80.

Buchanan, S.L., & Powell, D.A. (1982). Cingulate cortex: Its role in Pavlovian conditioning. *Journal of Comparative and Physiological Psychology, 96,* 755-774.

Cechetto, D.F., Standaert, D.G., & Saper, C.B. (1985). Spinal and trigeminal dorsal horn projections to the parabrachial nucleus in the rat. *Journal of Comparative Neurology, 240,* 153-160.

Cicchetti, P., LeDoux, J.E., & Reis, D.J. (1987). The lateral amygdaloid nucleus: Sensory interface of the amygdala in fear conditioning? *Neuroscience Abstracts, 13,* 643.

Cohen, D.H. (1984). Identification of vertebrate neurons modified during learning: Analysis of sensory pathways. In D.L. Alkon & J. Farley (Eds.), *Primary neural substrates of learning and behavioral change* (pp. 129-154). Cambridge: Cambridge University Press.

Cohen, D.H. (1975). Involvement of avian amygdalar homolog (archistriatum posterior and mediale) in defensively conditioned heart rate change. *Journal of Comparative Neurology, 160,* 13-35.

Colpaert, F.C. (1975). The ventromedial hypothalamus and the control of avoidance behavior and aggression: Fear hypothesis versus response-suppression theory of limbic system function. *Behavioral Biology, 15,* 27-44.

Coover, G., Ursin, H., & Levine, S. (1973). Corticosterone and avoidance in rats with basolateral amygdala lesions. *Journal of Comparative and Physiological Psychology, 85,* 111-122.

Cox, G.E., Jordan, D., Paton, J.F.R., Spyer, K.M., & Wood, L.M. (1987). Cardiovascular and phrenic nerve responses to stimulation of the amygdala central nucleus in the anesthetized rabbit. *Journal of Physiology (London), 389,* 341-356.

Cox, G.E., Jordan, D., Moruzzi, P., Schwaber, J.S., Spyer, K.M., & Turner, S.A. (1986). Amygdaloid influences on brain-stem neurons in the rabbit. *Journal of Physiology (London), 381,* 135-148.

deOlmos, J., Alheid, G.F., & Beltramino, C.A. (1985). Amygdala. In G. Paxinos (Ed.), *The rat nervous system,* (pp. 223-334). Sydney: Academic Press.

Fallon, J.H., Koziell, D.A., & Moore, R.Y. (1978). Catecholamine innervation of the basal forebrain. II. Amygdala, suprarhinal cortex and entorhinal cortex. *Journal of Comparative Neurology, 180,* 509-532

Farb, C.F., Ruggiero, D.A., & LeDoux, J.E. (1988). Projections from the acoustic thalamus terminate in the lateral but not the central amygdala. *Neuroscience Abstracts, 14,* 1227.

Fernandez de Molina, A., & Hunsperger, R.W. (1962). Organization of the subcortical system governing defense and flight reactions in the cat. *Journal of Physiology (London)*, *160*, 200-213.

Gabriel, M., Miller, J.D., & Saltwick, S.E. (1976). Multiple unit activity of the rabbit medial geniculate nucleus in conditioning, extinction and reversal. *Physiological Psychology*, *4*, 124-134.

Gallagher, M., & Kapp, B.S. (1978). Manipulation of opiate activity in the amygdala alters memory processes. *Life Sciences*, *23*, 1973-1978.

Gallagher, M., & Kapp, B.S. (1981a). Effect of phentolamine administration into the amygdala complex of rats on time-dependent memory processes. *Behavioral and Neural Biology*, *31*, 90-95.

Gallagher, M., Kapp, B.S., McNall, C.L., & Pascoe, J.P. (1981). Opiate effects in the amygdala central n. alters rabbit heart rate conditioning. *Pharmacology, Biochemistry and Behavior*, *14*, 497-505.

Gallagher, M., Kapp, B.S., Musty, R.E., & Driscoll, P.A. (1977). Memory formation: Evidence for a specific neurochemical system in the amygdala. *Science*, *198*, 423-425.

Gallagher, M., & Kapp, B.S. (1981b). Influence of amygdala opiate-sensitive mechanisms, fear motivated responses, and memory processes for aversive experiences. In J.L. Martinez, Jr., R.A. Jensen, R.B. Messing, H. Rigter, & J.L. McGaugh (Eds), *Endogenous peptides and learning and memory processes* (pp. 431-461). New York: Academic Press.

Gallagher, M., Kapp, B.S., Frysinger, R.C., & Rapp, P.R. (1980). B-adrenergic manipulation in amygdala central n. alters rabbit heart rate conditioning. *Pharmacology, Biochemistry and Behavior*, *12*, 419-426.

Gallagher, M., Kapp, B.S., & Pascoe, J.P. (1982). Enkephalin analogue effects in the amygdala central nucleus on conditioned heart rate. *Pharmacology, Biochemistry and Behavior*, *17*, 217-222.

Gary Bobo, E., & Bonvallet, M. (1975). Amygdala and masseteric reflex. I. Facilitation, inhibition and diphasic modifications of the reflex induced by localized amygdaloid stimulation. *Electroencephalography and Clinical Neurophysiology*, *39*, 329-339.

Gentile, C.G., Jarrell, T.W., Teich, A.H., McCabe, P.M., & Schneiderman, N. (1986). The role of amygdaloid central nucleus in differential Pavlovian conditioning of bradycardia in rabbits. *Behavioral Brain Research*, *20*, 263-276.

Gentile, C.G., Romanski, L.M., Jarrell, T.W., McCabe, P.M., & Schneiderman, N. (1986). Ibotenic acid lesions in amygdaloid central nucleus prevent the acquisition of differentially conditioned bradycardiac responses in rabbits. *Neuroscience Abstracts*, *12*, 755.

Gibbs, C.M., Broyles, J.L., & Cohen, D.H. (1983). Further studies of the involvement of locus coeruleus in plasticity of avian lateral geniculate neurons during learning. *Neuroscience Abstracts*, *9*, 641.

Gibbs, C.M., Cohen, D.H., Broyles, J.L. (1986). Modification of the discharge of lateral geniculate neurons during visual learning. *Journal of Neuroscience*, *6*, 627-636.

Goddard, G. (1964). Functions of the amygdala. *Psychological Bulletin*, *62*, 89-109.

Goddard, G.V. (1969). Amygdaloid stimulation and learning in the rat. *Journal of Comparative and Physiological Psychology*, *58*, 23-30.

Gold, P.E., Hankins, L., Edwards, R.M., Chester, J., & McGaugh, J.L. (1975). Memory interference and facilitation with posttrial amygdala stimulation: Effect on memory varies with footshock level. *Brain Research*, *86*, 509-513.

Gold, P.E., Edwards, R.M., & McGaugh, J.L. (1975). Amnesia produced by unilateral subseizure, electrical stimulation of the amygdala in rats. *Behavioral Biology, 15*, 95-105.

Grossman, S.P., Grossman, L., & Walsh, L. (1975) Functional organization of the rat amygdala with respect to avoidance behavior. *Journal of Comparative and Physiological Psychology, 88*, 829-850.

Guldin, W.O., & Markowitsch, H.J. (1983). Cortical and thalamic afferent connections of the insular and adjacent cortex of the rat. *Journal of Comparative Neurology, 215*, 135-153.

Heimer, L., Alheid, G., & Zaborszky, L. (1985). Basal Ganglia. In G. Paxinos (Ed.), *The rat nervous system*, (pp. 37-86). Sydney: Academic Press.

Heinemann, H., Stock, G., & Schaeffer, H. (1973). Temporal correlation of responses in blood pressure and motor reaction under electrical stimulation of limbic structures in the unanesthetized, unrestrained cat. *Pflugers Archives Gesamte Physiologie, 343*, 27-40.

Higgins, G.A., & Schwaber, J.S. (1983). Somatostatinergic projections from the central nucleus of the amygdala to the vagal nuclei. *Peptides, 4*, 1-6.

Hilton, S.M., & Zbrozyna, A.W. (1963). Amygdaloid region for defense reactions and its efferent pathway to the brainstem. *Journal of Physiology (London), 165*, 160-173.

Hitchcock, J.M., & Davis, M. (1986). Lesions of the amygdala, but not of the cerebellum or red nucleus, block conditioned fear as measured with the potentiated startle paradigm. *Behavioral Neuroscience, 100*, 11-22.

Hitchcock, J.M., & Davis, M. (1987). Proposed neural pathways for conditioned and unconditioned stimuli in the fear-potentiated startle paradigm. *Neuroscience Abstracts, 13*, 643.

Holdstock, T.L., & Schwartzbaum, J.S. (1965). Classical conditioning of heart rate and galvanic skin response in the rat. *Psychophysiology, 2*, 25-38.

Holstege, G., Kuypers, H. G. J. M., & Dekker, J.J. (1977). The organization of the bulbar fibre connections to the trigeminal, facial and hypoglossal motor nuclei. *Brain, 100*, 265-286.

Holstege, G., Meiners, L., & Tan, K. (1985). Projections of the bed nucleus of the stria terminalis to the mesencephalon, pons and medulla in the cat. *Experimental Brain Research, 58*, 379-391.

Holstege, G., Tan, J., van Ham, J.J., & Graveland, G.A. (1986). Anatomical observations on the afferent projections to the retractor bulbi motorneuronal cell group and other pathways possibly related to the blink reflex in the cat. *Brain Research, 374*, 321-334.

Holstege, G., van Ham, J.J., & Tan, K. (1986). Afferent projections to the orbicularis oculi motoneuronal cell group. An autoradiographic tracing study in the cat. *Brain Research, 374*, 306-320.

Hopkins, D.A., & Holstege, D. (1978). Amygdaloid projections to the mesencephalon, pons, and medulla oblongata in the cat. *Experimental Brain Research, 32*, 529-547.

Horvath, F.E. (1963). Effects of basolateral amygdalectomy on three types of avoidance behavior in cats. *Journal of Comparative and Physiological Psychology, 56*, 380-389.

Iwata, J., Chida, K., & LeDoux, J.E. (1987). Cardiovascular responses elicited by stimulation of neurons in the central amygdaloid nucleus in awake but not anesthetized rats resemble conditioned cardiovascular responses. *Brain Research, 418*, 183-188.

Iwata, J., LeDoux, J.E., Meeley, M.P., Americ, S., & Reis, D.J. (1986). Intrinsic neurons in the amygdaloid field projected to by the medial geniculate body mediate emotional responses conditioned to acoustic stimuli. *Brain Research, 383*, 195-214.

Jacobs, B.L., & McGinty, D.J. (1972). Participation of the amygdala in complex stimulus recognition and behavioral inhibition: Evidence from unit studies. *Brain Research, 36*, 431-436.

Jarrell, T.W., Romanski, L.M., Gentile, C.G., McCabe, P.M., & Schneiderman, N. (1986). Ibotenic acid lesions in the medial geniculate region prevent the acquisition of differential Pavlovian conditioning of bradycardia to acoustic stimuli in rabbits. *Brain Research, 382*, 199-203.

Jellestad, F.K., & Bakke, H.K. (1985). Passive avoidance after ibotenic acid and radio frequency lesions in the rat amygdala. *Physiology and Behavior, 34*, 299-305.

Jordan, D., Khalid, M.E.M., Schneiderman, N., & Spyer, K.M. (1982). The locations and properties of preganglionic vagal cardiomotor neurons in the rabbit. *Pflugers Archives Gesamte Physiologie., 395*, 244-250.

Kaada, B.R. (1951). Somato-motor, autonomic and electrocorticographic responses to electrical stimulation of "rhinencephalic" and other structures in primates, cat and dog. A study of responses from the limbic, subcallosal, orbito-insular, piriform and temporal cortex, hippocampus-fornix and amygdala. *Acta Physiological Scandinavia, 24*, Supplement 83, 1-285.

Kapp, B.S., Frysinger, R., Gallagher, M., & Bretschneider, A. (1977). Effects of amygdala and stria terminalis lesions on aversive conditioning in the rabbit. *Neuroscience Abstracts, 3*, 236.

Kapp, B.S., Frysinger, R.C., Gallagher, M., & Haselton, J. (1979). Amygdala central nucleus lesions: Effects on heart rate conditioning in the rabbit. *Physiology and Behavior, 23*, 1109-1117.

Kapp, B.S., Gallagher, M., Frysinger, R.C., & Applegate, C.D. (1981). The amygdala, emotion and cardiovascular conditioning. In Y. Ben-Ari (Ed.), *The amygdaloid complex*, INSERIM symposium no. 20 (pp. 355-367). Amsterdam: Elsevier/North Holland Biomedical Press.

Kapp, B.S., Gallagher, M., Underwood, M.D., McNall, C.L., & Whitehorn, D. (1982). Cardiovascular responses elicited by electrical stimulation of the amygdala central nucleus in the rabbit. *Brain Research, 234*, 251-262.

Kapp, B.S., Markgraf, C.G., Schwaber, J.S., & Bilyk-Spafford, T. (1989). The organization of dorsal medullary projections to the central amygdaloid nucleus and parabrachial nuclei in the rabbit. *Neuroscience, 30*, 717-732.

Kapp, B.S., Pascoe, J.P. & Bixler, M.A. (1984). The Amygdala: A neuroanatomical systems approach to its contribution to aversive conditioning. In N. Bulters & L.R. Squire (Eds.), *The neuropsychology of memory* (pp. 473-488). New York: Guilford Press.

Kapp, B.S., Schwaber, J.S., & Driscoll, P.A. (1984). Subcortical projections to the amygdaloid central nucleus in the rabbit. *Neuroscience Abstracts, 10*, 831.

Kapp, B.S., Schwaber, J.S., & Driscoll, P.A. (1985a). Frontal cortex projections to the amygdaloid central nucleus in the rabbit. *Neuroscience, 15*, 327-346.

Kapp, B.S., Schwaber, J.S., & Driscoll, P.A. (1985b). The organization of insular cortex projections to the amygdaloid central nucleus and autonomic regulatory nuclei of the dorsal medulla. *Brain Research, 360*, 355-361.

Kapp, B.S., Wilson, A., Schwaber, J.S., & Bilyk-Spafford, T. (1986). The organization of amygdaloid central nucleus projections to the midbrain periaqueductal gray and dorsomedial medulla in rabbit. *Neuroscience Abstracts, 12*, 535.

Kellicut, M.H., & Schwartzbaum, J.S. (1963). Formation of a conditioned emotional response (CER) following lesions of the amygdaloid complex in rats. *Psychological Reports, 12*, 351-358.

King, F.A. (1958). Effects of septal and amygdaloid lesions on emotional behavior and conditioned avoidance responses in the rat. *Journal of Nervous and Mental Diseases, 126*, 57-63.

Kling, A.J., Orbach, J., Schwarz, N., & Towne, J. (1960). Injury to the limbic system and associated structures in cats. *Archives of General Psychiatry, 3*, 391-420.

Krettek, J.E., & Price, J.L. (1978). A description of the amygdaloid complex in the rat and cat with observations on intra-amygdaloid axonal connections. *Journal of Comparative Neurology, 178*, 255-280.

Lavond, D.G., Lincoln, J.S., McCormick, D.A., & Thompson, R.F. (1983). Effect of bilateral lesions of the dentate and interpositus cerebellar nuclei on conditioning of heart-rate and nictitating membrane/eyelid responses in the rabbit. *Brain Research, 305*, 323-330.

Lavond, D.G., Mauk, M.D., Madden, IV J., Barchas, J.D., & Thompson, R.F. (1983). Abolition of conditioned heart-rate response in rabbits following central administration of [N-MePhe^3, D-Pro^4] Morphiceptin. *Pharmacology, Biochemistry and Behavior, 19*, 379-382.

LeDoux, J.E., Sakaguchi, A., & Reis, D.J. (1984). Subcortical efferent projections of the medial geniculate nucleus mediate emotional responses conditioned to acoustic stimuli. *Journal of Neuroscience, 4*, 683-698.

Lund, R.D., & Webster, K.E. (1967). Thalamic afferents from the spinal and trigeminal nuclei. *Journal of Comparative Neurology, 130*, 424-468.

Marek, G.J., McMaster, S.E., Gormezano, I., & Harvey, J.A. (1984). The role of the accessory abducens nucleus in the rabbit nictitating membrane response. *Brain Research, 299*, 215-229.

Markgraf, C.G. (1984). *Contributions of the insular cortex to cardiovascular regulation during aversive Pavlovian conditioning in the rabbit.* Unpublished Master's Thesis, University of Vermont.

Markgraf, C.G., & Kapp, B.S. (1988). Neurobehavioral contributions to cardiac arrhythmias during aversive Pavlovian conditioning in the rabbit receiving digitalis. *Journal of the Autonomic Nervous System, 23*, 35-46.

Maser, J.D., Dienst, F.T., & O'Neal, E.C. (1974). The acquisition of a Pavlovian conditioned response in septally-damaged rabbits: Role of a competing response. *Physiological Psychology, 2*, 133-136.

Mauk, M.D., Castellano, J.G., Rideout, J.A., Madden, IV, J., Barchas, J.D., & Thompson, R.F. (1983). Overtraining reduces opiate abolition of classically conditioned responses. *Physiology and Behavior, 30*, 493-495.

Mauk, M.D., Warren, J.T., & Thompson, R.F. (1982). Selective, naloxone-reversible morphine depression of learned behavior and hippocampal responses. *Science, 216*, 434-435.

McCormick, D.A., Lavond, D.G., & Thompson, R.F. (1982). Concomitant classical conditioning of the rabbit nictitating membrane response and eyelid responses: Correlations and implications. *Physiology and Behavior, 28*, 769-775.

McDonough, J.H., & Kesner, R.P. (1971). Amnesia produced by brief electrical stimulation of amygdala or dorsal hippocampus in cats. *Journal of Comparative and Physiological Psychology, 77*, 171-178.

McIntyre, M., & Stein, D.G. (1973). Differential effects of one vs. two stage amygdaloid lesions on activity, exploratory and avoidance behavior in the albino rat. *Behavior Biology, 9*, 451-465.

McNew, J.J., & Thompson, R. (1966). Role of the limbic system in active and passive avoidance conditioning in the rat. *Journal of Comparative and Physiological Psychology, 61*, 173-180.

Meller, S.T., & Dennis, B.J. (1986). Afferent projections to the periaqueductal gray in the rabbit. *Neuroscience, 19*, 927-964.

Mesulam, M.M., & Mufson, E.J. (1982). The insula of the old world monkey. III: Efferent cortical output and comments on function. *Journal of Comparative Neurology, 212*, 38-52.

Mowrer, O.H. (1947). On the dual nature of learning - A reinterpretation of "conditioning" and "problem solving." *Harvard Educational Review, 17*, 102-148.

Mufson, E.J., Mesulam, M.M., & Pandya, D.N. (1981). Insular interconnections with the amygdala in the rhesus monkey. *Neuroscience 7*, 1231-1248.

Obrist, P.A., Wood, D.M., & Perez-Reyes, M. (1965). Heart rate during conditioning in humans: Effects of UCS intensity, vagal blockade and adrenergic block of vasomotor activity. *Journal of Experimental Psychology, 70*, 32-42.

Pare, W., & Dumas, J. (1965). The effect of insular neocortical lesions on passive and active avoidance in the rat. *Psychonomic Science, 2*, 87-88.

Pascoe, J.P., Bradley, D.J., & Spyer, K.M. (1989). Interactive responses to stimulation of the amygdaloid central nucleus and baroreceptor afferent activation in the rabbit. *Journal of Autonomic Nervous System, 26*, 157-168.

Pascoe, J.P., & Kapp, B.S. (1985a). Electrophysiological characteristics of amygdaloid central nucleus neurons during Pavlovian fear conditioning in the rabbit. *Behavioral Brain Research, 16*, 117-133.

Pascoe, J.P., & Kapp, B.S. (1985b). Electrophysiological characteristics of amygdaloid central nucleus neurons in the awake rabbit. *Brain Research Bulletin, 14*, 331-338.

Pascoe, J.P., & Kapp, B.S. (1987a). Response of amygdaloid central nucleus neurons to stimulation of the insular cortex in awake rabbits. *Neuroscience, 21*, 471-485.

Pascoe, J.P., & Kapp, B.S. (1987b). Some electrophysiological characteristics of insular cortex efferents to the amygdaloid central nucleus in awake rabbits. *Neuroscience Letters, 78*, 288-294.

Peinado-Manzano, A. (1988). Effects of lesions of the central and lateral amygdala on free operant successive discrimination. *Behavioral Brain Research, 29*, 61-71.

Powell, D.A., Buchanan, S., & Hernandez (1985). Electrical stimulation of insular cortex elicits cardiac inhibition but insular lesions do not abolish conditioned bradycardia in rabbits. *Behavioral Brain Research, 17*, 125-144.

Powell, D.A., & Kazis, E. (1976). Blood pressure and heart rate changes accompanying classical eyeblink conditioning in the rabbit (Oryctolagus cuniculis). *Psychophysiology, 13*, 441-447.

Price, J.L., & Amaral, D.G. (1981). An autoradiographic study of the projections of the central nucleus of the monkey amygdala. *Journal of Neuroscience, 1*, 1242-1259.

Riolobos, A.S., & Martin Garcia, A.I. (1987). Open field activity and passive avoidance responses in rats after lesion of the central amygdaloid nucleus by electrocoagulation and ibotenic acid. *Physiology and Behavior, 39*, 715-720.

Rosen, J.B., & Davis, M. (1988). Enhancement of acoustic startle by electrical stimulation of the amygdala. *Behavioral Neuroscience, 102*, 195-202.

Russo, N.J., Kapp, B.S., Holmquist, B.K., & Musty, R.E. (1976). Passive avoidance and amygdala lesions: Relationship with pituitary-adrenal system. *Physiology and Behavior, 16*, 191-199.

Ryugo, D.K., & Weinberger, N.M. (1978). Differential plasticity of morphologically distinct neuron populations in the medial geniculate body of the cat during classical conditioning. *Behavioral Biology, 22*, 275-301.

Sandrew, B.B., Edwards, D.L., Poletti, C.E., & Foote, W.E. (1986). Amygdalospinal projections in the cat. *Brain Research, 373*, 235-239.

Sanghera, M.K., Rolls, E.T., & Roper-Hall, A. (1979). Visual responses of neurons in the dorsolateral amygdala of the alert monkey. *Experimental Neurology, 63*, 209-222.

Saper, C.B. (1982). Convergence of autonomic and limbic connections in the insular cortex of the rat. *Journal of Comparative Neurology, 210*, 163-173.

Sar, M., Stumpf, W.E., Miller, R.J., Chang, K.J., & Cuatrecasas, P. (1978). Immunohistochemical localization of enkephalin in rat brain and spinal cord. *Journal of Comparative Neurology, 182*, 17-38.

Schlor, K.H., Stumpf, H., & Stock, G. (1984). Baroreceptor reflex during arousal induced by electrical stimulation of the amygdala or by natural stimuli. *Journal of the Autonomic Nervous System, 10*, 157-165.

Schneiderman, N. (1972). Response system divergencies in aversive classical conditioning. In A.H. Black & W.F. Prokasy (Eds.), *Classical conditioning Vol. II: Current research and theory* (pp. 341-378). New York: Appleton-Century-Crofts.

Schutze, I., Knuepfer, M.M., Eismann, A., Stumpf, H., & Stock, G. (1987). Sensory input to single neurons in the amygdala of the cat. *Experimental Neurology, 97*, 499-515.

Schwaber, J.S., Kapp, B.S., & Higgins, G. (1980). The origin and extent of direct amygdala projections to the region of the dorsal motor nucleus of the vagus and the nucleus of the solitary tract. *Neuroscience Letters, 20*, 15-20.

Schwaber, J.S., Kapp, B.S., Higgins, G.A., & Rapp, P.R. (1982) Amygdaloid and basal forebrain direct connections with the nucleus of the solitary tract and the dorsal motor nucleus. *Journal of Neuroscience, 2*, 1424-1438.

Slotnick, B.M. (1973). Fear behavior and passive avoidance deficits in mice with amygdala lesions. *Physiology and Behavior, 11*, 717-720.

Spevack, A.A., Campbell, C.T., & Drake, L. (1975). Effect of amygdalectomy on habituation and CER in rats. *Physiology and Behavior, 15*, 199-207.

Supple, W.F., & Kapp, B.S. (1988). Response characteristics of neurons in the medial geniculate nucleus during Pavlovian differential fear conditioning in rabbits. *Behavioral Neuroscience, 103*, 1276-1286.

Swanson, L.W., Mogenson, G.J., Gerfen, C.R., & Robinson, R. (1984). Evidence for a projection from the lateral preoptic area and substantia innominata to the mesencephalic locomotor region in the rat. *Brain Research, 295*, 161-178.

Thompson, R.F., Donegan, N.H., Clark, G.A., Lavond, D.G., Lincoln, J.S., Madden, IV. J., Mamounas, L.A., Mauk, M.D., & McCormick, D.A. (1987). In I. Gormezano, W.F. Prokasy, & R.F. Thompson (Eds.), *Classical conditioning* (pp. 371-399). Hillsdale, NJ: Lawrence Erlbaum Associates.

Ursin, H. (1965). Effect of amygdaloid lesions on avoidance behavior and visual discrimination in cats. *Experimental Neurology, 11*, 298-317.

Ursin, H., & Kaada, B.R. (1960). Functional localization within the amygdaloid complex in the cat. *Electroencephalography and Clinical Neurophysiology*, *12*, 1-20.

von Frisch, O. (1966). Herzfrequenzänderung bei Drückreaktion junger Nestflüchter [Change in frequency of heart-beat during cowering responses of young nestlings]. *Zeitschrift für Tierpsychologie, 23*, 497-500.

Weinberger, N.M. (1982). Effects of conditioned arousal on the auditory system. In A.L. Beckman (Ed.), *The neural basis of behavior* (pp. 63-91). Jamaica, NY: Spectrum Publications.

Wepsic, J.G. (1966). Multimodal sensory activation of cells in the magnocellular medial geniculate nucleus. *Experimental Neurology, 15*, 299-318.

Werka, T., Skar, J., & Ursin, H. (1978). Exploration and avoidance in rats with lesions in amygdala and piriform cortex. *Journal of Comparative and Physiological Psychology, 92*, 672-681.

Wilson, A., & Kapp, B.S. (1987). The periaqueductal gray: Projections to cardioregulatory nuclei and contributions to conditioned bradycardia in the rabbit. *Neuroscience Abstracts, 13*, 644.

Wilson, A., & Kapp, B.S. (1988). The effect of stimulation of the periaqueductal gray on cardiovascular responses in the rabbit. *Neuroscience Abstracts, 14*, 192.

Yehle, A., Dauth, G., & Schneiderman, N. (1967). Correlates of heart rate classical conditioning in curarized rabbits. *Journal of Comparative and Physiological Psychology, 64*, 98-104.

Zhang, J.X., Harper, R.M., & Ni, H. (1986). Cryogenic blockade of the central nucleus of the amygdala attenuates aversively conditioned blood pressure and respiratory responses. *Brain Research, 386*, 136-145.

13 Animal Models of Alzheimer's Disease: Role of Hippocampal Cholinergic Systems in Working Memory

Thomas J. Walsh
James J. Chrobak
Rutgers—The State University

Memory allows us to benefit from the past, interpret the present, and predict the future. Elucidating the behavioral, physiological, biochemical and molecular processes involved in memory remains one of the most challenging problems in all of neuroscience. The explicit goal of this research is to provide a more complete understanding of the neurobiology of normal memory processes. However, an important corollary assumption is that this strategy will reveal the substrates of memory disorders which are associated with neurological and psychiatric diseases. For example, memory dysfunction is commonly observed in a variety of neurodegenerative disorders including Alzheimer's and Huntington's diseases (see Table 13.1).

An important approach for correlating behavioral and neurological abnormalities associated with memory disorders is through the development of appropriate animal models (Olton, 1985). Such models help to define the neurobiology of cognitive processes and suggest novel therapeutic strategies for the prevention or treatment of these disorders. While models are unable to completely reproduce the etiology, pathophysiology, or behavioral abnormality associated with diseases of the nervous system, they do provide a viable way to explore specific questions concerning structure and function (Kornetsky, 1977). A major effort of our laboratory has been to develop a model of cholinergic hypofunction that shares some of the cardinal features of Alzheimer's disease (AD) (Walsh & Hanin, 1986).

TABLE 13.1
Neurodegenerative Disorders with Accompanying Memory Impairments

Alzheimer's Disease	Adams & Victor, 1985.
Multi-infarct Dementia	"
Korsakoff's Syndrome	"
Normal Pressure Hydrocephalus	"
Huntington's Disease	"
Pick's Disease	"
Creutzfeld-Jacob Disease	"
AIDS Dementia Complex	Price, Sidtis, & Rosenblum, 1988.
Down's Syndrome	Wisniewski, Wisniewski, & Wen, 1985.
Progressive Supranuclear Palsy	Cummings & Benson, 1988.
Multiple Sclerosis	Litvan et al., 1988
Myasthenia Gravis	Tucker, Roeltgen, Wann, & Wertheimer, 1988.
Olivopontocerebellar Atrophy	Kish et al., 1988.

The goals of the present chapter are related to three interconnected themes: (1) present the salient behavioral and neurological characteristics of AD; (2) describe an animal model of cholinergic hypofunction that shares many of the features of AD; and (3) discuss the essential role of the hippocampus (HPC) and its cholinergic innervation in working or episodic memory processes.

Types of Memory Processes

A variety of sources of evidence indicate that there are two distinct memory systems that are responsible for certain types of cognitive operations and which are mediated by distinct neural systems. Amnesic disorders associated with acute brain injury or chronic neurodegeneration such as observed in Alzheimer's or Huntington's disease present with select memory deficits in which some types of memorial processes are disrupted and others are not. For example, damage to the medial temporal lobe produces an amnesic syndrome in which patients are impaired in the acquisition and retention of recently presented information but are not impaired in the acquisition of cognitive and perceptual skills (Cohen & Squire, 1980; Squire & Cohen, 1984). This dissociation of memory processes is most evident in those situations where a subject can perform a learned perceptual or motor skill in the absence of any recollection of the specific episodes in which it was acquired (Knopman & Nissen, 1987; Nissen, Knopman, & Schacter, 1987; Cohen & Squire, 1980). Although the specific tasks may vary, animals with select neural insults are also impaired in tasks in which they must maintain, over a given delay interval, representations of recently acquired information or information concerning recent events. This impairment may occur despite a sparing of the ability to acquire and perform other tasks that are characterized by slow, incremental learning where specific responses are contingently reinforced over repeated trials. This distinction between the impaired and preserved memory functions has been referred to by varying nomenclature: working versus reference memory (Olton & Pappas, 1979); representational versus dispositional memory (Thomas & Spafford, 1984); memory versus habit (Mishkin, Malamut, & Bachevalier, 1984) and others. Sherry and Schacter (1987, pg. 446) have suggested a "distinction between a memory system that supports gradual or incremental learning and is involved in the acquisition of habits and skills and a system that supports one trial learning and is necessary for forming memories that represent specific situations and episodes." These authors further suggest that the functions of these memory systems might be incompatible and thus must depend upon unique neural representations. Utilizing the terminology suggested by Olton & Pappas (1979), we have previously referred to this distinction as one between working and reference memory (Chrobak, Hanin, & Walsh, 1987) or as between working/episodic and reference/skill (Chrobak, Hanin, Schmechel, & Walsh, 1988).

Working/episodic memory is involved in temporarily maintaining representations of previously experienced events or episodes, whereas reference/skill memory contributes to the performance of learned responses in the presence of an appropriate discriminate stimulus. Working/episodic memory tasks may be designed such that the information required to perform accurately changes between trials, insuring that the animal retains information concerning a trial-unique event. The information required to perform reference/habit memory tasks typically remains constant between the trials of a particular experimental paradigm, and thus has been referred to as trial-independent. This component theory of memory serves to provide a conceptual framework for interpreting the dissociation in memory processes observed in both humans and animals following damage to the HPC or its cholinergic innervation. While several nomenclatures have been introduced to describe this dissociation, the working-reference memory distinction is attractive since each of these processes can be operationally defined within given experimental contexts. This terminology will be used throughout this chapter. However, it is recognized that other conceptual distinctions such as declarative and procedural memory share many of the features of the working-reference memory dichotomy. While dissociations in performance following experimental manipulations do not confirm the existence or independence of different memory systems they do serve to provide a conceptual framework which will direct more precise analyses of brain-behavior relationships. Furthermore, they suggest that different patterns of memory impairment in human cognitive disorders reflect the compromise of specific neural systems and that therapeutic interventions should ideally be targeted to these systems.

ALZHEIMER'S DISEASE

Alzheimer's disease affects 5-10% of the population over the age of 65 and is the most prevalent age-related cognitive disorder (Huppert & Tym, 1986; Terry & Katzman, 1983). Current estimates project that its incidence will triple over the next 75 years. The cost of institutional care for AD patients has been put at approximately 3 billion dollars per year. With no effective treatment modalities and a target group which represents the most rapidly expanding segment of the population the current and prospective strains on the nations health care system, the federal government the pharmaceutical industry, as well as the emotional and financial resources of affected families, warrants a major effort to delineate the pathobiology of the disorder and to develop treatments to prevent, ameliorate, or manage it.

A wide variety of neuropathological and neurochemical studies have shown that specific brain areas are affected in AD. Pyramidal neurons in the association cortices and in the hippocampus (HPC) are particularly susceptible to the disease process and can exhibit widespread degeneration, and other characteristic cytopathological changes such as neurofibrillary tangles and senile plaques (Coleman & Flood, 1987; Hyman, Damasio, Van Hoesen, & Barnes, 1984). Other brain areas that can be affected include the noradrenergic neurons in the locus coeruleus and the serotonergic neurons in the dorsal raphe and these alterations are reflected in changes in these transmitter systems (see Hardy et al., 1985). While these changes are evident in subpopulations of patients or late in the course of the disease they have not been shown to relate to the prevailing memory disorder (Mann et al., 1981).

A major focus for the study of AD has been the cholinergic system (see Collerton, 1986; DeFeudis, 1988). The initial neurochemical studies of AD revealed extensive loss of choline acetyltransferase (ChAT) activity in the cortex and HPC (Davies & Maloney, 1976). ChAT is an enzyme that synthesizes acetylcholine (ACh) from acetyl-coenzyme A and choline. Subsequent studies have shown that essentially all biochemical markers of presynaptic cholinergic function including ACh synthesis, high affinity choline transport, and ACh release are decreased in the HPC and neocortex in AD (Bowen, Smith, White, & Davidson, 1976; Coyle, Price, & DeLong, 1983; Henke & Lang, 1983; Rylett, Ball, & Colhoun, 1983). There is also a pronounced loss of cholinergic neurons in the basal forebrain which innervate these regions (Whitehouse, Struble, Hedreen, Clark, & Price, 1985). The functional relevance of these alterations is supported by the significant correlation between the severity of dementia, the number of senile plaques, and the loss of cholinergic markers (Mountjoy, Rossor, Iversen, & Roth, 1984; Perry et al., 1978; Wilcock, Esiri, Bowen, & Smith, 1982).

Memory Impairments in Alzheimer's Disease

Patients with AD exhibit a complex spectrum of neuropsychological changes involving the deterioration of cognitive function. The most prominent deficit early in the disease is a loss of memory for recent events (working/episodic memory). This initial deficit is followed by a progressive deterioration of cognitive function which is accompanied by additional behavioral changes including emotional volatility, aphasia, and social withdrawal (Huppert & Tym, 1986). The unremitting course of the disease results in complete cognitive dysfunction in which the individual is institutionalized for vegetative care.

Early in the course of the disease there appears to be a preferential impairment in episodic/working memory processes with a relative preservation of reference/skill memory. Patients exhibit a pronounced deficit in tasks which require the temporary internal representation of an event such as in a task whose performance is dependent upon the memory of a sample stimulus. Despite these impairments they are able to recall past events and acquire new motor and perceptual skills. Eslinger and Damasio (1986) reported that patients with AD exhibited profound deficits in the recall of a word list and in the performance of a visual delayed match to sample task but that their ability to learn and retain the perceptual motor skills necessary to perform a rotary pursuit task was not impaired. While it not possible to relate these impairments to a specific pathological change observed in AD, pharmacological evidence suggests that the loss of cholinergic systems contributes to these deficits. For example, Nissen et al. (1987) reported that the muscarinic antagonist scopolamine selectively disrupted free recall of a word list but did not alter the acquisition and retention of a visual reaction time task in adult volunteers. Furthermore, there was no disruption of general semantic knowledge (i.e., reference memory) such as the generation of city names in alphabetical order. Scopolamine selectively compromised working memory without disrupting reference memory. These observations are consistent with the animal and human literature indicating that damage or pharmacological disruption of brain cholinergic systems produces a dissociation of memory processes in which working memory processes are preferentially impaired (see subsequent sections). Therefore a disruption of cholinergic systems may contribute to the working memory deficits observed early in the course of AD (see also Collerton, 1986). A major premise of this chapter is that the cholinergic innervation of the HPC is an essential component of the neurobiological circuit supporting working memory.

ANATOMY AND PHYSIOLOGY OF THE CHOLINERGIC SEPTOHIPPOCAMPAL PATHWAY

Cholinergic neurons in the basal forebrain innervate the HPC and serve to modulate the functional activity of this structure. The advent of improved techniques to visualize cholinergic cell bodies and their projections has led to the elucidation of how brain cholinergic neurons are organized into discrete systems with specific target sites. Mesulam and colleagues have introduced a nomenclature Ch1 to Ch6 to describe the six different cholinergic systems and to provide a reference for further studies of cholinergic anatomy and function (Mesulam, Mufson, Wainer, & Levey, 1983). The cholinergic system which appears to be most important in memory processes consists of neurons in the basal forebrain which innervate the HPC and neocortical mantle. The basal forebrain cholinergic system is further partitioned into four discrete nuclei: (Ch1) the medial septal nucleus (MSN); (Ch2) the vertical limb of the diagonal band; (Ch3) the horizontal limb of the diagonal band and; (Ch4) the nucleus basalis (NB). The other cholinergic nuclei, Ch5 and Ch6, reside in the midbrain and innervate a variety of regions involved in motor control and arousal. Our discussion of cholinergic anatomy and physiology will be restricted to Ch1 which provides the primary cholinergic input to the HPC; a structure known to contribute to memory processes and to be particularly affected in AD (Ball et al., 1985; Rossor, Iversen, Reynolds, Mountjoy, & Roth, 1984).

Cholinergic neurons in Ch1 project through the fimbria and dorsal fornix to innervate the entire septo-temporal extent of the HPC and parahippocampal gyrus (see Frotscher & Leranth, 1985, 1986; Nyakas, Luiten, Spencer, & Traber, 1987). These fibers are topographically organized so that fibers in the dorsal fornix project to the septal (dorsal) pole, while fibers in the fimbria project to the temporal (ventral) pole of the HPC. Cholinergic fibers synapse on a variety of neuronal elements in the HPC including the dendrites and cell bodies of pyramidal cells in CA1-4, granule cells in the dentate gyrus, and interneurons in the hilus (Frotscher & Leranth, 1985, 1986). The distribution of septal afferents closely corresponds to the location of cholinergic receptors and to the areas of greatest AChE staining and ChAT-immunoreactive terminals (Kuhar & Yamamura, 1975; Frotscher & Leranth, 1985).

The cholinergic innervation of the HPC suggests a dual mechanism of regulation in which ACh can exert either excitatory or inhibitory effects depending on the cellular location and type of synapse formed (Valentino & Dingledine, 1981). For example, cholinergic fibers form asymmetric (excitatory) synapses on dendritic spines but only form symmetric (inhibitory) synapses on cell bodies (Frotscher & Leranth, 1985, 1986). Further, application of cholinergic agonists to hippocampal neurons can induce bidirectional effects (Rascol & Lamour, 1988; Williams & Johnston, 1988). Therefore, cholinergic afferents exert a complex integrated influence on the functional activity of the HPC. The architecture and synaptic profiles of cholinergic fibers suggest that they "modulate" hippocampal activity by exerting a discrete influence on the activity of distinct pyramidal and granule cells.

The cholinergic septohippocampal pathway appears to coordinate the neurophysiological activity of the HPC through the induction of the theta rhythm (see Bland, 1986, for review). The theta rhythm is a pattern of electroencephalographic activity characterized by rhythmic slow activity (RSA) at a cycle of 5-12 Hz. Physiological and pharmacological techniques have provided support for the role of the MSN/VLDB region (Ch1 and Ch2) in the generation of theta. For example, (1) cells within the MSN/VLDB complex discharge in phase with the hippocampal theta rhythm (Petsche, Stumpf, & Gogolak, 1962); (2) stimulation of this complex induces theta in the HPC (McNaughton, Azmitia, Williams, Buchan, & Gray, 1980), (3) damage to the MSN/VLDB, its afferent pathways, intraseptal injection of the local anesthetic procaine, and systemic injection of anticholinergic drugs such as atropine and scopolamine, can attenuate or eliminate theta (Brugge, 1965; Dren & Domino, 1968; Rawlins, Feldon, & Gray, 1979), (4) systemic or intrahippocampal injection of cholinomimetic drugs such as physostigmine and carbachol, induce theta and (5) this cholinergic enhancement of theta is blocked by lesions of the medial, but not the lateral, septum (Bures, Bohdanecky, & Weiss, 1962; Stumpf, Petsche, & Gogolak, 1962).

Recent observations indicate that theta establishes a physiological state in the HPC which is maximally compatible with the induction and expression of synaptic plasticity. Several laboratories have shown that stimulation of the Schaeffer collateral/commisural projections to CA1 in the theta frequency (5 Hz) produces an optimal condition for the induction of long-term potentiation in this pathway (Greenstein, Pavlides, & Winson, 1988; Larson, Wong, & Lynch, 1986). LTP represents a persistent increase in the amplitude of an evoked population spike that occurs following repetitive stimulation of afferent input (Bliss & Lomo, 1973). This phenomenon is currently regarded as a model of synaptic plasticity that may serve as a neural substrate for memory storage (Lynch & Baudry, 1984; Swanson, Teyler, & Thompson, 1982). Lynch and colleagues have hypothesized that "neuronal activity at this frequency (theta) is optimal for the induction of synaptic plasticity in the HPC" (Larson et al., 1986). Taken together, these observations further emphasize that the cholinergic innervation of the HPC modulates the neural activity of this structure and in particular those neural mechanisms that might subserve memory processes.

EFFECTS OF CHOLINERGIC MANIPULATIONS ON MEMORY PROCESSES

A variety of strategies have been used to examine the role of cholinergic systems in learning and memory. For example, investigators have examined whether (1) alterations in the dynamics of cholinergic neurons are associated with learning, (2) pharmacological manipulations of the cholinergic system or (3) damage to cholinergic neurons, alter memory processes in a reliable way. While no single study has used an integrated approach the results derived from these different strategies all support an important role for cholinergic systems in memory processes.

Training-induced Alterations in Cholinergic Activity

The activity of cholinergic neurons appears to be altered subsequent to a learning experience (Matthies, Rauca, & Liebmann, 1974). Time-dependent increases in ACh levels, turnover, and high affinity choline transport (HAChT) have been observed in the HPC following acquisition of a variety of tasks whose performance is dependent upon hippocampal function Wenk and colleagues observed a persistent increase in HAChT in the HPC, but not in the frontal cortex, following acquisition of a variety of tasks including: (1) a reference memory and (2) a working memory task in a t-maze, (3) an active avoidance response, and (4) a standard radial arm maze task (Wenk, Hepler, & Olton, 1984). Therefore, cholinergic indices were increased in the HPC regardless of the cognitive demands of the task. No changes in choline uptake were induced by the sensory-motor activation induced by prolonged running on a treadmill. The memorial aspect of the tasks appears to be necessary to engage the activity of the septohippocampal pathway. Other studies also support the functional significance of these changes. Rauca and colleagues reported that choline uptake was increased in hippocampal slices taken from animals exhibiting good retention of a shock-motivated visual discrimination task while no such changes were evident in the hippocampi of animals exhibiting poor retention of the task (Rauca, Kammerer, & Matthies, 1980). Thus, the degree of activation of the septohippocampal pathway is functionally correlated with the degree of retention in this paradigm. More recently, Decker and colleagues reported decreases in hippocampal HAChT in young rats and in old rats who acquired a reference memory task in a water maze, but not in old animals who were deficient in learning the task (Decker, Pelleymounter, & Gallagher, 1987). These data are consistent with the hypothesis that alterations of the septohippocampal pathway are correlated with, and perhaps necessary for, the learning and retention of a variety of tasks with differential cognitive requirements. However, these studies observed decreases in choline uptake rather than the increase reported by the other studies. This discrepancy could reflect the time dependent nature of changes in cholinergic indices induced by training and it also illustrates the problem associated with attempting to infer the functional activity of a neurotransmitter system from one temporally limited measure. Studies using in vivo analysis of cholinergic parameters such as the microdialysis of ACh release will be required to further examine the dynamic relationship between the activity of cholinergic neurons and learning and memory processes (see Damsma, Westerink, de Boer, de Vries, & Horn, 1988).

Pharmacological Analysis of Memory

There is a general consensus that drugs which compromise the functional activity of brain cholinergic systems disrupt learning and memory processes (Bartus, Dean, Beer, & Lippa, 1982). Drugs that inhibit the uptake of choline, the synthesis of ACh, or the activation of muscarinic receptors disrupt learning and retention of both appetitively and aversively motivated tasks. The behavioral substrates of this disruption are less clear and various investigators have attributed it to changes in attention, response inhibition, and stimulus control, as well as to a disruption of memory (Spencer & Lal, 1983).

The drugs most commonly used to explore this question are the muscarinic antagonists scopolamine and atropine. Many studies have also examined the peripherally active quaternary analogs of these compounds, methylscopolamine and atropine methyl nitrate, in an effort to evaluate the consequences of peripheral cholinergic blockade on behavioral parameters. These studies have consistently shown that peripherally-active muscarinic antagonists do not alter acquisition or retention of either appetitive or aversive tasks. Therefore, it is generally assumed that the disruption of central cholinergic mechanisms is responsible for the effects of anticholinergic drugs on memory.

Further support for the role of cholinergic mechanisms in memory is provided by the observation that compounds that prevent the breakdown of endogenous ACh, by inhibiting the catabolic activity of acetylcholinesterase, (physostigmine, tetrahydroaminoacridine, edrophonium), promote the release or acetylcholine (4-aminopyridine), or activate the muscarinic (arecoline, oxotremorine) or nicotinic (nicotine) cholinergic receptor directly, can facilitate memory processes under appropriate conditions (Flood, Smith, & Cherkin, 1983; Haroutunian, Barnes, & Davis, 1985).

Human Studies.   A number of human psychopharmacological studies have demonstrated a relatively selective amnesiac effect of anticholinergic drugs. The earliest pharmacological studies of the role of cholinergic mechanisms in memory revealed that scopolamine disrupted memory, and that the disruption could be attenuated by physostigmine, but not by amphetamine (Sitaram, 1984). Therefore, it was suggested that the impairments were not related to alterations in arousal or attentional mechanisms but rather to a selective disruption of cholinergic systems that participate in cognitive function. Furthermore, Drachman reported that the profile of cognitive and memory changes induced by anticholinergic drugs was similar to the pattern of neuropsychological changes observed in patients with AD (Drachman, 1977, 1979). These studies provided an important theoretical framework to guide further examination of the relationship of cholinergic mechanisms to memory processes and dementia. Subsequent studies using healthy young adults confirmed that scopolamine impaired memory in a variety of serial learning tasks and that the impairment was attenuated by direct (arecoline) and indirect acting cholinergic (physostigmine) agonists. Recent work by Rusted and Warburton (1988) found that scopolamine selectively disrupted working memory processes in young adults. In particular, they formulated their research and interpreted their results in relation to Baddeley's model of working memory (Baddeley, 1986) in which a central executive mechanism coordinates and directs two working memory systems; 1) the articulatory loop which retains verbal information and 2) the visual-spatial system which retains non verbal information. The behavioral changes observed across a number of tasks designed to differential assess these subcomponents of working memory indicated that scopolamine selectively compromised the activity of the central executive mechanism.

The human studies have demonstrated that anticholinergic drugs disrupt working memory processes and that there are formal similarities between these drug-induced memory impairments and the dementia observed in AD. Since the amnesic effects induced by anticholinergic drugs can be selectively attenuated by cholinergic agonists numerous studies have explored the efficacy of this treatment strategy for patients with AD. While this literature is complex and fraught with inconsistency, several reports have demonstrated that cholinergic agonists can facilitate memory processes in subpopulations of AD patients early in the course of the disease. A problem evident in this line of research is the inter-subject variability in the biological and behavioral response to anticholinesterase drugs. A number of laboratories are examining biological markers that might serve as an index of the effectiveness of cholinergic therapy and might be used to define a therapeutic window that is associated with enhanced cognitive function. In this regard, Thal and colleagues (Thal, Fuld, Masur, Sharpless, & Davies, 1983) reported a significant correlation between inhibition of acetylcholinesterase activity and memory performance in AD patients receiving physostigmine and lecithin. The greater the degree of cholinesterase inhibition the greater the improvement in memory. Thus, it might be possible in the future to monitor and titrate cholinomimetic regimens in each AD patient in a precise way to maximize the potential behavioral benefits.

Animal Studies. Psychopharmacological studies in both primates and rodents also consistently report that injection of anticholinergic drugs prior to acquisition or performance disrupt memory processes. A variety of experimental paradigms have been used to explore this central question but we will concentrate on studies using appetitive learning in delayed discrimination tasks and spatial learning in maze procedures. These experimental paradigms are similar to the most common tests of human cognition and can be manipulated to independently examine the subcomponents of cognitive behavior (Olton, 1983, 1987, Walsh & Chrobak, 1987).

A series of studies by Bartus and colleagues using monkeys demonstrated that scopolamine produced dose-related impairments in the performance of a visual delayed match to sample task. This task required the monkey to remember a visual stimulus and to respond to the same stimulus following a certain delay interval. Scopolamine produced no impairments at the shortest delay (0 seconds) but progressively larger impairments were evident as the delay between sample presentation and the required discriminant response increased. The drug did not disrupt the requisite sensory discrimination, but rather disrupted performance as the memory demands of the task were increased (Bartus & Johnson, 1976). The cholinergic basis of this working memory impairment was supported by the observation that physostigmine but not methylphenidate, an indirect dopaminergic agonist, attenuated the scopolamine-induced deficits (Bartus, 1978). Penetar and McDonough (1983) also using monkeys in a delayed match to sample visual discrimination task reported an atropine-induced disruption of performance with the greatest deficits observed at the longest delays (4,8,16 secs) and no impairment evident at the 0 sec delay. In contrast to the impairments induced by cholinergic antagonists a dose-related enhancement of retention by physostigmine was reported by Aigner and Mishkin (1986) in a delayed-non-match to sample task using trial-unique objects. Thus pharmacological studies in primates using delayed discrimination tasks add additional support for an essential role for cholinergic mechanisms in working memory processes.

A procedure that has been used with increasing frequency to explore memory processes in rodents is the radial arm maze task. Olton and colleagues devised this task to assess the behavioral and neurobiological characteristics of spatial memory in the rat (Olton & Samuelson, 1976; Olton, Becker, & Handelman, 1979). This task requires a food-deprived rat to obtain a single item of food from the end of each of the arms of the maze. Typically, the maze consists of a central arena from which eight equally spaced arms radiate outward. The most efficacious strategy to solve the task is to retrieve an item on food from each arm and to not reenter that arm. In most appetitive maze tasks rats adopt a win-shift strategy in which previously depleted food sources are avoided. To perform accurately the rat must remember a list of spatial locations (arms) that have and have not been entered. The dependent measures used to assess the accuracy of maze performance include the number of non-repeated arm choices in the first eight selections and the total number of choices to complete the task. Rats exhibit a remarkable capacity and duration of spatial memory in this task. The task is also similar to common tests of human memory such as serial learning which require subjects to temporarily retain a list of information (words).

An extensive series of experiments by Olton and colleagues demonstrated that the HPC is a critical neural substrate for radial-arm maze performance. Destruction of the HPC proper, its intrinsic neuronal populations, or deafferentation of either its major cortical or subcortical afferents produces a persistent disruption in radial-arm maze performance (Becker, Walker, & Olton, 1980; Olton, 1983; Olton, Becker, & Handelman, 1979; Olton & Pappas, 1979). Furthermore, these deficits are restricted to working memory processes since animals with even extensive hippocampal injury can perform reference memory problems in the maze and also exhibit unimpaired cognitive mapping abilities. Based upon the dissociation of memory performance following hippocampal injury, Olton and colleagues postulated that the HPC was a critical neurobiological substrate for working memory.

In light of the extensive cholinergic innervation of the HPC, its role in coordinating the physiology of the structure, and the similarity of behavioral deficits induced by hippocampal damage and anticholinergic drugs (Gray & McNaughton, 1983), a number of investigators have examined whether the septo-hippocampal pathway is essential for working memory processes. Several studies have demonstrated that administration of muscarinic antagonists prior to acquisition or performance of a radial-arm maze task disrupts memory in that task. Eckerman and colleagues (Eckerman, Gordon, Edwards, MacPhail, & Gage, 1980) were the first to report that scopolamine, but not other psychoactive agents such as amphetamine or pentobarbital, or methyl scopolamine, impaired maze performance. A subsequent study revealed that scopolamine only disrupted performance in rats that relied upon working memory to complete the task (Watts, Stevens, & Robinson, 1981). Animals that adopted a response strategy or algorithm that was compatible with the requirements of the task, such as choose each adjacent arm or every third arm in a clockwise pattern, were unimpaired. The use of a response strategy places a minimal demand on the working memory system while a memorial strategy requires discriminant abilities and retention over time. In this regard, Peele and Baron (1988) reported that a scopolamine-induced disruption of maze performance was most evident when rats were delayed 100 sec but not 0.5 sec following each successive arm choice. These studies indicate that scopolamine disrupts working memory depending upon the task-specific demands placed on the working memory system. In a similar context Harrell and colleagues reported that medial septal lesions disrupted radial maze performance in animals that used either a response algorithm or an apparent spatial memory strategy prior to surgery (Harrell, Barlow, & Parsons, 1987). Following the lesions all animals that were using the spatial memory strategy shifted to a response algorithm to perform the task. The animals that continued to use their preferred response algorithm recovered faster following surgery while those rats that switched their pattern of choosing required more trials to reacquire the task. These lesion-induced deficits suggest that the medial septum was required for the expression of working memory.

In order to characterize the nature and specificity of the cognitive changes induced by anticholinergic drugs several studies have explicitly examined whether these compounds differentially affect memory processes. These studies have utilized a modified version of the radial-arm maze task that allows for the independent assessment of both working memory and reference memory within the same trial. In this task, half of the maze arms are consistently baited across a series of trials, while the remaining arms are never baited. The animal enters those arms within the baited set on any given trial only once (working memory), while never entering arms within the unbaited set (reference memory). A working memory error consists of reentry into a baited arm during any given trial while a reference memory error involves entering one of the never baited arms. Studies by Wirsching and colleagues (Wirsching, Beninger, Jharmandas, Boegman, & El-Delfrawy, 1984) and Beatty and Bierley (1985) demonstrated that administration of scopolamine 20 to 30 minutes prior to testing significantly increased the number of working memory errors without increasing the number of reference memory errors in this task. Thus, low doses of scopolamine appear to preferentially impair working memory processes without affecting reference memory, spatial mapping ability, attentional mechanisms, motivation, or sensory-motor processes, necessary to perform the task.

Recent studies have shown that anticholinergic drugs can also impair performance in spatial memory tasks which lack an obvious working memory component. For example, atropine impairs performance in a Morris water maze task (Hagan, Tweedie, & Morris, 1986), in which a rat is required to locate a stationary submerged platform in order to escape from a tank of water. This represents a reference memory task since the animal learns to consistently go to the same spatial location to escape from the tank. A similar impairment has been observed following scopolamine, but not in overtrained animals even at doses that clearly disrupt radial arm maze performance and a working memory version of the water maze task (Buresova, Bolhuis, & Bures, 1986).

The available data indicate that low doses of muscarinic antagonists can selectively disrupt performance of working memory tasks, while higher doses can disrupt performance of both working and reference memory tasks. The effective dose ranges for these compounds significantly vary from study to study. These compounds can also have differential effects depending on the cognitive demands of the test and the availability of response strategies to successfully complete the task.

A number of problems are inherent in the pharmacological analysis of memory processes because anticholinergic drugs (i) have limited central nervous system specificity, (ii) they affect both M1 and M2 muscarinic receptor types, (iii) they exhibit a high degree of toxicity, (iv) they have a short duration of action, and (v) they indiscriminately affect all central cholinergic systems. Thus, it is difficult to establish causal or even suggestive relationships between specific brain mechanisms and specific cognitive processes. In light of these obstacles several studies have attempted to localize the anatomical and pharmacological specificity of the memory impairments induced by these compounds. Brito and colleagues reported that bilateral injection of scopolamine into the HPC produced a dose-related impairment in the performance of a delayed-non-match to sample task in a T-maze (Brito, Davis, Stopp, & Stanton, 1983). Some doses of scopolamine (35 µg) impaired performance in both a visual discrimination reference memory task (~20% decrement) and the working memory task (~75% decrement) while lower doses (12 µg) only affected the working memory task (~20% decrement). These data add additional support to the hypotheses that low doses of muscarinic antagonists preferentially disrupt working memory processes and that pharmacological compromise of the cholinergic innervation of the HPC is responsible for this behavioral deficit. Furthermore, a essential role for M1 muscarinic receptors is suggested by the observation that intrahippocampal injection of the selective M1 muscarinic antagonist pirenzepine impaired working memory in delayed T-maze task as much as scopolamine (Messer, Thomas, & Hoss, 1987). Another interesting approach to isolate the areas responsible for scopolamine-induced amnesia for a passive avoidance task was used by Piercey, Vogelsang, Franklin, and Tang (1987). An amnestic dose of scopolamine decreased glucose utilization in a variety of cortical areas, in the dendritic layers of the HPC, and in several thalamic nuclei. Administration of the nootropic compound piracetam prior to scopolamine attenuated the memory deficit and reversed the depressed glucose uptake in the HPC and the anterior cingulate cortex. Piracetam also enhanced glucose utilization in the medial septum in animals treated with scopolamine suggesting that it activated the septo-hippocampal pathway.

Lesions of Cholinergic Nuclei

Memory impairments have been consistently observed following experimental damage to the medial septum. Thomas and colleagues have shown that electrolytic lesions of the septum impair working memory in a delayed-non-match to sample task in a T-maze (Thomas & Spafford, 1984). These investigators subsequently replicated the effects of septal lesions on the delayed T-maze task and also found that the lesions did not alter the performance of either a reference memory visual discrimination task or a simultaneous conditional discrimination task (Thomas & Gash, 1986). The simultaneous conditional discrimination task contained an 'if-then' contingency which required the rat to enter one of two goal boxes of a T-maze depending upon the presence of a discriminative stimulus associated with each response, that is, if black, then go left. This task proved to be more difficult than either the delayed T-maze task or the visual discrimination task since animals required significantly more trials to achieve a criterion of performance on this task. In spite of the differential task difficulty, septal lesions only disrupted performance of the working memory (delayed T-maze) task. Thus it is not the difficulty but rather the cognitive demands of a task that make it susceptible to disruption following septal damage. Based upon this profile of behavioral dissociations Thomas and Gash argued that septal lesions only impair the performance of tasks that require the animal to maintain an internal representation of a previously experienced episode or event (working memory) when no external discriminative stimulus is available to direct performance.

Kesner and colleagues reported that septal lesions alter the serial position of errors in a radial arm maze task that assesses memory for the temporal order of presented information (Kesner, Crutcher, & Beers 1988; Kesner, Crutcher, & Meason, 1986). In this task rats are trained to remember the temporal order of which arms they enter in the maze. Rats exhibit a primacy-recency effect in which the items presented earliest or latest in a list are better remembered than those items presented in the middle. Septal lesions alter this pattern of errors in two distinct ways depending upon the size of the lesion and the degree of loss of acetylcholinesterase staining in the HPC. Small lesions that produce a minimal loss of staining impair memory of only those arms entered early (loss of primacy) while large lesions inducing an extensive loss of staining result in chance performance for arms entered early, middle, or late; no primacy or recency effect. Since hippocampal damage produces a similar alteration in serial position of errors it is evident that the septum and HPC act in a coordinated manner to mediate temporal as well as spatial working memory. Alterations in working memory tasks requiring the retention of temporal information (Meck, Church, Wenk, & Olton, 1987) has also been reported following administration of scopolamine. These observations demonstrate that cholinergic receptors and the septo-hippocampal pathway are involved in working memory for tasks requiring the retention of non-spatial as well as spatial information. Thus, it is not the spatial components of a task but rather the type of memory required for performance of the task that engages the septo-hippocampal pathway.

Intraseptal injection of the excitotoxin ibotenic acid impairs performance of both preoperatively acquired T-maze and radial-arm maze tasks (Hepler, Olton, Wenk, & Coyle, 1985; Hepler, Wenk, Cribbs, Olton, & Coyle, 1985; Miyamoto, Kato, Narumi, & Nagaoka, 1987) that require the use of working memory processes, but not reference memory tasks regardless of whether the tasks were acquired prior (Hepler, Wenk, Cribbs, Olton, & Coyle, 1985) or subsequent to the lesion (Knowlton, Wenk, Olton, & Coyle, 1985). Since intrastititial injection of ibotenic acid destroys cell bodies without disrupting fibers of passage these studies suggest that neurons in the medial septum, and not fibers that course through this area, are contributing to working memory processes.

A problem inherent in the lesion strategy is that the medial septum consists of a heterogeneous population of neurons of which only 35-50% are likely to be cholinergic (Mesulam et al., 1983). Other cells in this region contain GABA, substance P and other neuropeptides (Costa, Panula, Thompson, & Cheney, 1983; Kohler, Chan-Palay, & Wu, 1984; Vincent & McGeer, 1981; Woodhams, Roberts, Polak, & Crow, 1983). Furthermore, catecholamine and indoleamine projections from the brainstem ascend to the HPC and forebrain through the fimbria-fornix (Lindvall & Bjorklund, 1974; Loy, Koziell, Lindsey, & Moore, 1980). Therefore, a variety of transmitter systems are compromised by these common experimental procedures and the potential contribution of these systems to the behavioral deficits observed following hippocampal damage has often been overlooked. Clearly, it is difficult to ascribe the memory impairments induced by septal damage to the select disruption of septohippocampal cholinergic activity. A better approach for the investigation of hippocampal cholinergic processes might involve the use of selective cholinergic neurotoxins.

AF64A AS A TOOL TO EXAMINE THE BIOLOGICAL AND BEHAVIORAL PROPERTIES OF THE CHOLINERGIC SEPTOHIPPOCAMPAL PATHWAY

Selectively toxic compounds have been widely used in neurobiology to examine the functional properties of the nervous system. Toxins that disrupt specific ion channels (tetrodotoxin, saxitoxin), axoplasmic transport processes (colchicine), neuronal populations (kainic acid, MPTP) or neurotransmitter systems (6-hydroxydopamine, 5,7-dihydroxytryptamine, DSP-4) have proven useful in delineating the fundamental neurobiology of brain cells and the principles of synaptic transmission (McGeer, Eccles, & McGeer, 1987). In a related context, neurotoxins have been successfully used to examine the covariation between altered neurotransmitter dynamics and behavior and to develop animal models of neurological disorders (Sanberg & Coyle, 1984; Zigmond & Stricker, 1984)

Neurobiological Effects of AF64A

A cholinergic neurotoxin would be an important tool to further explore the central questions of cholinergic biology. In addition, such a compound would be useful for the development of animal models of cholinergic hypofunction. These considerations have prompted several laboratories to try and develop appropriate cholinotoxins. These efforts have been organized around targeting the unique synaptic dynamics and regulatory processes that characterize cholinergic neurons.

Most neurotransmitters (catecholamines, serotonin, neuropeptides, amino acids) are synthesized and packaged into synaptic vesicles within the cell body and are then transported to the nerve terminal for subsequent release (McGeer et al., 1987). In contrast, the nerve terminal of the cholinergic neuron is specialized for the synthesis of ACh. Cholinergic nerve terminals contain a sodium-dependent HAChT system which is functionally coupled to the activity of the neuron and to the activity of ChAT, the enzyme that acetylates choline to produce ACh (Jope, 1979; Marchbanks, Wonnacott, & Rubio, 1981; Simon, Atweh, & Kuhar, 1976). The HAChT system is evident only on cholinergic terminals and it serves as the rate-limiting step for the synthesis of ACh (Freeman & Jenden, 1976). A low affinity transport system is widely distributed and contributes to the synthesis of membrane phospholipids in all cell types. The characteristic presence of the HAChT system on cholinergic terminals has prompted investigators to develop compounds that selectively target this molecular site.

A few putative cholinotoxins, including several mustard analogs of choline and hemicholinium-3 (HC-3), have been developed (Hanin et al., 1987; Rylett & Colhoun, 1980; Tagari, Maysinger, & Cuello, 1986), all of which target the HAChT system located exclusively on cholinergic nerve terminals (Jope, 1979).

Fisher and Hanin (1980) explored a series of choline analogs and found that one of these compounds, ethylcholine aziridinium ion (AF64A), a nitrogen mustard analog of choline that contains a highly reactive aziridinium ring, has cholinotoxic properties that make it useful for both *in vivo* and *in vitro* studies. AF64A is structurally similar to choline and is recognized by the HAChT system. This compound irreversibly inhibits the activity of the HAChT system and also acts as an irreversible substrate for several choline-specific enzymes including ChAT, choline kinase, choline dehydrogenase and AChE (Barlow & Marchbanks, 1984; Curti & Marchbanks, 1984; Rylett & Colhoun, 1980; Sandberg et al., 1985). At low concentrations, AF64A is recognized by the HAChT system and transported into the nerve terminal where it is probably acetylated by ChAT to yield acetyl-AF64A, a putative toxic false transmitter. AF64A and its acetyl-AF64A are thought to produce a cascade of intracellular events that disrupt the viability of the cholinergic neuron (Mantione, Fisher, & Hanin, 1981, 1984). At higher concentrations, AF64A appears to irreversibly inhibit HAChT by alkylating nucleophilic sites on the HAChT carrier protein. The cholinotoxic effects of AF64A are directly due to a disruption of the HAChT system since these effects can be prevented by incubation of synaptosomes with either choline (Barlow & Marchbanks, 1984) or HC-3 (Curti & Marchbanks, 1984; Pedder & Prince, 1983). Therefore, these compounds compete for the same site and the locus of AF64A's neurotoxic action; the HAChT system.

Most studies have examined the neurobiological and behavioral effects induced by intracerebroventricular (icv) injection of AF64A. With this route of administration AF64A produces a 30-60% reduction in all indices of presynaptic cholinergic function including: (1) regional concentrations of ACh, (2) the activity of ChAT, (3) HAChT, (4) K+-stimulated release of ACh from slices of HPC, and (5) intraaxonal transport of AChE (Gaal, Potter, Hanin, Kakucska, & Vizi, 1986; Kasa & Hanin, 1985; Leventer, McKeag, Clancy, Wulfert, & Hanin, 1985; Mantione, Fisher, & Hanin, 1984; Mantione, Zigmond, Fisher, & Hanin, 1983). These effects develop over time with maximal decreases evident approximately seven days following treatment and persisting up to one year following injection (Leventer, Wulfert, & Hanin, 1987). Despite the decrease in presynaptic parameters there are no changes in postsynaptic muscarinic binding sites following AF64A treatment (Fisher, Mantione, Abraham, & Hanin, 1982; Vickroy et al., 1985).

The decreases in hippocampal presynaptic cholinergic parameters are evident without accompanying changes in regional concentrations of norepinephrine, dopamine, serotonin, their metabolites, or choline (Chrobak et al., 1988; Walsh et al., 1984). The prominent regional specificity of AF64A's cholinotoxic effect could reflect the preferential distribution of the compound to structures adjacent to the ventricles and/or to the unique vulnerability of hippocampal cholinergic nerve terminals (Potter, Harsing, Kakucska, Gaal, & Vizi, 1986).

These observations demonstrate that central administration of AF64A can produce a selective and regionally-specific decrease in presynaptic cholinergic parameters. The decreases exhibit no sign of spontaneous recovery which further supports the use of AF64A in producing a model of cholinergic hypofunction.

While most studies have observed selective cholinergic losses following Af64A (see Fisher & Hanin, 1986 for review), others have reported histological damage at the site of injection or in adjacent areas and/or persistent alterations in markers of other neurotransmitter systems (Eva, Fabrazzo, & Costa, 1987; Jarrard, Kant, Meyerhoff, & Levy, 1984; McGurk, Hartgraves, Kelly, Gordons, & Butcher, 1987). The degree to which a specific cholinotoxic effect can be induced by AF64A depends upon a multitude of interdependent variables including: (1) the purity of the starting compound, (2) the dose and concentration, (3) the rate and total volume of injection, and (4) the site of administration. Despite strict adherence to the necessary precautions icv AF64A can produce transient alterations in serotonin, norepinephrine, and dopamine in a variety of brain regions including; the HPC, cortex, striatum and hypothalamus (Eva et al., 1987; Hortnagl, Potter, & Hanin, 1987a, 1987b: Potter et al., 1986). Alterations in other neurotransmitter closely parallel changes in cholinergic markers and occur at loci distant from the injection site indicating that they are secondary to the effects of AF64A on the cholinergic system (Hortnagl, et al., 1987a, 1987b; Potter et al., 1986). In addition, it has been shown that administration of HC-3 or A-4 prior to AF64A attenuates the loss of cholinergic and serotonergic markers in the HPC (Potter, Tedford, Kindel, & Hanin, 1987). These compounds are both potent inhibitors of HAChT with inhibitory rate constants 30-100 times greater than that of the AF64A molecule (Barker & Mittag, 1975; Smart, 1981). These data indicate that the effects of AF64A on neurotransmitter systems other than ACh are probably secondary to the cholinergic hypofunction.

Behavioral Effects of AF64A

A number of studies have shown that central administration of AF64A produces behavioral impairments that are associated with persistent reductions in presynaptic cholinergic markers (Bailey, Overstreet, & Crocker, 1986; Chrobak, Hanin, & Walsh, 1987; Jarrard et al., 1984; Walsh et al., 1984). Initial studies by Walsh and colleagues examined the biochemical and behavioral effects induced by bilateral intraventricular injection of 7.5 or 15 nmoles of AF64A. ACh concentrations were reduced 45-60% in the HPC (7.5 or 15 nmoles) and frontal cortex (15 nmoles) but there were no alterations in the regional concentrations of choline, norepinephrine, serotonin, dopamine, or their metabolites. This neurochemical change was accompanied by a significant impairment in the retention of a passive avoidance response and deficient acquisition of a radial-arm maze task (Walsh et al., 1984). Since the behavioral deficits were comparable between both dose groups it was evident that the decrease of ACh in the HPC was sufficient to account for the alterations in behavior. While this study used high doses of AF64A and did not address the effects of this compound on components of memory it did demonstrate that AF64A could produce a regionally-selective decrease in ACh and impaired cognitive behavior.

A problem evident in these early studies was that the doses of AF64A were very high. Despite these cautions a similar profile of behavioral effects has been observed following icv administration of lower doses. For example,

Brandeis and colleagues reported that icv injection of 3 or 5 nmoles of AF64A produced a 35-50% decrease in hippocampal ChAT activity and HAChT and impaired the acquisition of a passive avoidance response and the performance of both radial-arm maze and Morris water maze tasks (Brandeis et al., 1986).

Effects of AF64A on Working and Reference Memory

Subsequent studies in our laboratory revealed that the memory impairment induced by AF64A reflects a selective compromise of working, as opposed to reference, memory. To assess the differential effects of AF64A on memory processes we developed a T-maze task that independently assessed working and reference memory within the same trial (see Figure 13.1 and Chrobak et al., 1986). In this task each trial was initiated by placing the rat into either the left or the right start/goal box of the T-maze for 15 seconds. The food-deprived rat was then rewarded with a single chocolate-flavored pellet for turning into and traversing the stem of the maze and for subsequently returning to the alternate start/goal location. The choice of start box varied randomly, with the provision that no more than 3 of the 5 daily trials could begin from the same location. The different facets of this task may be characterized as (1) a trial-independent component (reference memory) which involves an invariant response of running down the stem of the maze and (2) a trial-dependent response (working

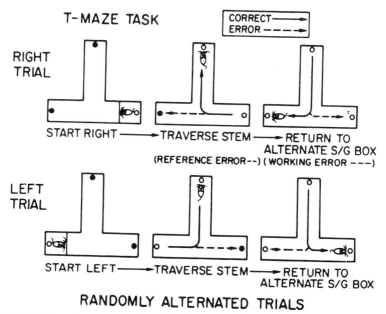

Fig. 13.1. A schematic representation of the T-maze task is presented. The rat is initially placed into either the right (Right Trial) or left (Left Trial) start compartment. The reference memory component of the task consists of turning into and traversing the stem of the maze. The working memory component consists of running to the alternate start/goal box. From Chrobak, Hanin, & Walsh (1986). Copyright by Elsevier. Used with permission.

memory) in which the animal must maintain a representation of the start location in order to perform accurately.

All animals acquired the task prior to surgery and at the end of 120 trials
were performing with 90-100% accuracy on both the reference and working
memory components. Rats were subsequently bilaterally injected icv with
cerebrospinal fluid (CSF) or 3 nmoles of AF64A. Following a two week recovery period animals were retrained on the T-maze task. The CSF-injected rats
rapidly reacquired both components of the task. The AF64A group however
exhibited a transient decrease in reference memory that recovered within 30 trials and a persistent decrease in working memory that was evident throughout
the 75 post-operative trials (Figure 13.2). Working memory was impaired in
this group even when their reference memory performance was comparable to
controls and close to 100% accurate (Figure 13.3). AF64A-treated rats navi-
gated through the maze, consumed the pellets after a correct response, completed each trial in the same amount of time as the CSF-injected controls, and
were able to discriminate and perform the appropriate response to complete the
reference memory component of the task. This behavioral dissociation was apparently related to a disruption of the cognitive and neural mechanisms required
to perform the trial-dependent working memory aspects of the task. Neurochemical analysis revealed that these behavioral deficits were associated with a
42% decrease in ChAT activity in the HPC with no alterations in striatum or
frontal cortex.

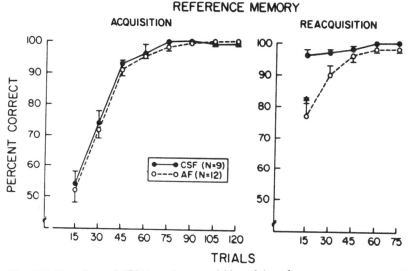

Fig. 13.2. The effects of AF64A on the reacquisition of the reference memory component of
the T-maze task described in Figure 13.1. Following 120 acquisition trials rats were injected
with AF64A (3 nmoles/side,icv) or CSF, allowed 14 days to recover from surgery; and were
then given 75 reacquisition trials. This figure presents mean (± SEM) percentage of correct responses summarized over each 3-day block of sessions in which there was 5 trials per day. (*p
< 0.01 vs CSF controls, Spjotvall-Stoline t-test.) From Chrobak et al. (1986). Used with
permission.

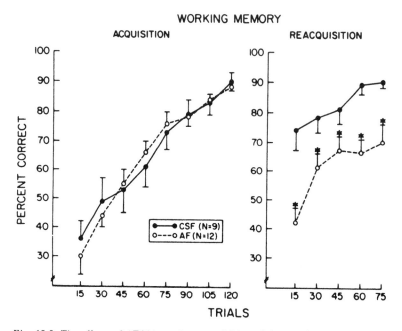

WORKING MEMORY

Fig. 13.3. The effects of AF64A on the reacquisition of the working memory component of the T-maze task described in Figure 13.1. Following 120 acquisition trials rats were injected with AF64A (3 nmoles/side,icv) or CSF, allowed 14 days to recover from surgery; and were then given 75 reacquisition trials. This figure presents mean (± SEM) percentage of correct responses summarized over each 3-day block of sessions in which there was 5 trials per day. (*p < 0.01 vs CSF controls, Spjotvall-Stoline t-test.) From Chrobak et al. (1986). Copyright 1986 by Elsevier. Used with permission.

This study demonstrated that intraventricular AF64A produced a permanent disruption of working memory and a chronic decrease of ChAT activity in the HPC. The following experiment further examined the behavioral and neurobiological correlates of the AF64A-induced working memory impairment.

Behavioral, Neurochemical, and Histological Correlates of AF64A-Induced Working Memory Impairments

The previous experiments demonstrated that icv injection of AF64A produced a selective impairment of working memory. The following experiment examined the behavioral specificity of this observation and its neurochemical and histological correlates.

Rats were tested in a series of behavioral tasks involving the sequence of events described below (Chrobak et al., 1988).

a. Preoperative Radial-Arm Maze Training. Rats were initially trained for 15 trials on a standard radial-arm maze task in which each of the 8 arms was baited with food and re-entry into a previously visited arm constituted an error. Animals were subsequently trained for 30 trials on a version of the task in which a one hour delay was imposed between the fourth and fifth arm choices. In this task barriers are used to force the animals to select a predetermined set of four arms. Four arms are open and baited with food and four arms are blocked. After entering all 4 open arms rats are returned to their home cages for a one hour delay period. Following this period the animal is returned to the maze and all 8 arms are now open but only those arms that were blocked during the pre-delay sessions now contain food. This represents a delayed-nonmatch to sample task in which the rat must use a win-shift strategy to complete the task. The number of correct choices during the first four arm entries following the delay served as the dependent measure. The pattern of open and closed arms varied in a random manner from day to day. Therefore, the animals was faced with a new working memory problem each day. Further, this task prevents the development of response strategies or algorithms that are compatible with completion of the task and which can complicate the analysis of memorial processes.

All rats acquired this task prior to surgery and were making 80-85% correct choices during their first 4 post-delay selections during the last block of 5 trials. Following acquisition they were bilaterally injected icv with CSF or 3.0 nmoles of AF64A and given a 14 day recovery period before being retested on the maze task.

b. Post-operative Radial-Arm Maze Training (14-70 days). The animals were tested for 30 post-operative trials with delays of 0, 0.5, 1, 5, 15 or 30 minutes randomly imposed between the fourth and fifth arm choices. The animals injected with CSF exhibited excellent performance (80-85%) at each of the delay intervals. However, the AF64A-injected group was performing at approximately chance levels (50-60%) of accuracy under each delay condition (see Figure 13.4). This working memory deficit showed no signs of diminishing over time.

Locomotor activity was assessed 60-61 days after surgery during the phase of radial-arm maze testing. The activity levels of the CSF or AF64A -injected rats were comparable when they were tested in either a food-deprived or non-deprived state. Both groups exhibited similar number of activity counts and a similar rate of motor habituation. Thus, AF64A had no effect on locomotor activity.

c. T-maze Reference Memory Task (70-72 days after surgery). Subsequent to testing on the delay task animals were trained to perform a simple discrimination task in a radial-arm maze in which five arms of the maze were removed to produce a T-configuration. Animals were trained with food reward to go to the initially non-preferred arm of the T-maze over 60 trials given over two consecutivedays. Animals learned to perform an invariant trial-independent response of always going to the same spatial location. All animals required a comparable number of trials to achieve a performance criterion of 70%, 80%, or 90% correct in any 10-trial block. Thus, while AF64A impaired performance of the working memory task, even at very short intervals, it did not interfere with the learning of a reference memory task. These data confirm the specificity of the behavioral deficit induced by icv injection of

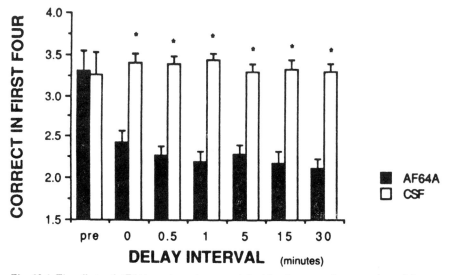

Fig. 13.4. The effects of AF64A on the performance of the delayed-non-match to sample radial-arm maze task described in the text. Delays of 0.0, 0.5, 1, 5, 15 or 30 minutes were imposed between the fourth and fifth arm choices. The figure presents the mean (± SEM) number of correct choices made in the first 4 post-delay arm selections. (* $p < 0.001$ vs CSF controls, Spjotvall-Stoline t-test.) From Chrobak, Hanin, Schmechel, & Walsh (1988). Copyright 1988 by Elsevier. Used with permission.

AF64A. Further, the dissociation of memory processes indicates that the cholinergic innervation of the HPC is an essential substrate for working memory processes.

d. Neurochemical Analysis. Animals were sacrificed 90 days following surgery. ChAT activity and the regional concentrations of norepinephrine, dopamine, DOPAC, serotonin and 5-HIAA were determined in the HPC, the frontal cortex, the parietal cortex, the cingulate, the amygdala, and the striatum. AF64A reduced ChAT activity in the HPC by 50% but did not alter the activity of this enzyme in any other region or the concentrations of the other neurotransmitters or their metabolites in the HPC or any other region. This further illustrates the unique neurochemical and regional specificity of AF64A's effects following icv injection.

e. Histological Analyses. To assess the morphological effects induced by AF64A a separate group of rats was injected with 3.0 nmoles of AF64A into the right lateral cerebroventricle and sacrificed 14 days later for histological analysis. Serial sections of the medial septal area and the HPC were stained with (1) thionin for inspection of gross histological changes, (2) antibodies to ChAT; an enzyme only found in cholinergic neurons, and (3) antibodies to neuron-specific enolase (NSE), a glycolytic enzyme present in all types of neurons. Sections stained for both ChAT and NSE in the septal area were used to determine whether AF64A only affected the population of cholinergic (ChAT-positive cells) neurons in this region or all neuron types (NSE-positive cells).

Intraventricular injection of AF64A produced a slight ventricular dilatation in most animals without damaging the HPC or the fimbria-fornix. There was however an approximate 35% decrease in the number of ChAT-immunoreactive neurons on the injected side in the region of the medial septum/ventral limb of the diagonal (Ch1 and Ch2) without a concomitant decrease in the number of NSE-immunoreactive neurons following AF64A. Therefore, AF64A only affected the population of cholinergic neurons in the medial septum/vertical limb of the diagonal band area. This effect was regionally specific since there was no apparent decrease in the number of ChAT-immunoreactive neurons in the striatum, the nucleus accumbens, or Ch3 and Ch4 in the basal forebrain.

The results of this study demonstrate that the intraventricular injection of low doses of AF64A produces a selective impairment of working processes which is associated with a decrease in ChAT activity in the HPC and a loss of cholinergic neurons in the medial septum. Thus, the HPC and its cholinergic innervation appears to be a critical neurobiological circuit that is necessary for working memory. The following experiment further addressed the cholinergic specificity of the behavioral and neurochemical effects induced by AF64A.

Mechanism of AF64A-Induced Working Memory Impairments

The present study examined whether the behavioral deficits induced by icv administration of AF64A are a specific consequence of the compound's cholinotoxic properties. Preliminary data in our laboratory indicated that intraventricular administration of HC-3 prior to AF64A could attenuate the AF64A-induced decreases in HAChT. HC-3 is a short-acting inhibitor of HAChT with an inhibitory rate constant 100 times greater than that of AF64A (Barker & Mittag, 1975; Smart, 1981). Therefore, if the behavioral and neurochemical deficits induced by AF64A result from a disruption of the HAChT system then pretreatment with HC-3 should block or attenuate these effects.

Animals injected icv bilaterally with 3 nmoles of AF64A exhibited a decrease in HAChT in the HPC and were significantly impaired in their ability to perform the delayed-non-match to sample radial-arm maze task previously described. Icv administration of HC-3 prior to AF64A completely prevented these behavioral and the neurochemical alterations (Chrobak, Spates, Stackman, & Walsh, 1989).

These data confirm the previously reported working memory deficits induced by AF64A and demonstrate that they are a direct consequence of the compound's cholinotoxic properties. They also demonstrate that disrupting the septohippocampal projection is sufficient to impair these memory processes which further supports the hypothesis that this system is a critical neurobiological substrate of working memory.

Use of AF64A to Model Alzheimer's Disease

A central cholinergic hypofunction is believed to underlie the cognitive impairments observed in AD. Patients with AD exhibit decreases in presynaptic cholinergic indices and a loss of cholinergic neurons in the basal forebrain both of which are correlated with the degree of cognitive impairment. These observations have inspired investigators to develop animal models of AD by inducing a chronic central cholinergic hypofunction. Since a disruption of cholinergic afferents to the HPC may be the locus for the cognitive impairments observed in AD (Rossor et al., 1984), AF64A may be used to model this aspect of the disease. In fact, AF64A does produce a profile of neurobiological and behavioral changes in the rat which closely resembles the changes observed in AD. Whether these changes are homologous or analogous with the pathophysiology manifest in AD requires a more complete understanding of the etiology and temporal dynamics of the disease process. The AF64A model, however, can be used to evaluate the efficacy, and assist in the development, of treatment modalities that may prove useful in the prevention, remediation, or management of the disorder (Emerich, Spates, & Walsh, 1988). In addition, AF64A appears to be a selective and powerful tool for examining the relationship between the activity of the cholinergic septohippocampal pathway and cognitive function.

CONCLUSION

The literature reviewed in this chapter indicates that drug, lesion, or neurotoxin-induced compromise of the central cholinergic system preferentially impairs working memory processes without necessarily affecting reference memory. The studies using AF64A demonstrate that a selective impairment of the cholinergic septohippocampal pathway is sufficient to permanently impair working memory processes. Taken together, these observations support the hypothesis that the cholinergic septohippocampal pathway is a critical neurobiological circuit that allows an animal to retain information concerning recently experienced events, that is, working or episodic memory.

ACKNOWLEDGMENTS

Supported in part by a Biomedical Research Support Grant (RR 07058-23) and a Rutgers University Research Council Grant to T.J.W.

REFERENCES

Adams, R. D., & Victor, M. (1985). Dementia and the amnesic syndrome. In R.D. Adams & M. Victor (Eds.), *Principles of neurology* (3rd ed., pp. 311-322). New York: McGraw-Hill.
Aigner, T.G., & Mishkin, M. (1986). The effects of physostigmine and scopolamine on recognition memory in monkeys. *Behavioral and Neural Biology, 45*, 81-87.
Baddeley, A.D. (1986). *Working memory*. Oxford: Clarendon Press.
Bailey, E.L., Overstreet, D.H., & Crocker, A.D. (1986). Effects of intrahippocampal injections of the cholinergic neurotoxin AF64A on open-field activity and avoidance learning in the rat. *Behavioral and Neural Biology, 45*, 263-274.
Ball, M.J., Hachinski, V., Fox, A., Kirshen, A.J., Fishman, M., Blume, W., Kral, V.A., Fox, H., & Merskey, H. (1985). A new definition of Alzheimer's disease: a hippocampal dementia. *Lancet , i*, 14-16.

Barker, L.A., & Mittag, T.W. (1975). Comparative studies of substrates and inhibitors of choline transport and choline acetyltransferase. *Journal of Pharmacology and Experimental Therapeutics, 192,* 86-94.

Barlow, P., & Marchbanks, R.M. (1984). Effect of ethylcholine mustard on choline dehydrogenase and other enzymes of choline metabolism. *Journal of Neurochemistry, 43,* 1568-1573.

Bartus, R.T. (1978). Evidence for a direct cholinergic involvement in the scopolamine-induced amnesia in monkeys: effects of concurrent administration of physostigmine and methylphenidate with scopolamine. *Pharmacology, Biochemistry and Behavior, 9,* 833-836.

Bartus, R.T., & Johnson, H.R. (1976). Short-term memory in the rhesus monkey: disruption from the anticholinergic scopolamine.*pharmacology, Biochemistry and Behavior, 5,* 31-39.

Bartus, R.T., Dean, R.L., Beer, B., & Lippa, A.S. (1982). The cholinergic hypothesis of geriatric memory dysfunction. *Science, 217,* 408-417.

Beatty, W.W., & Bierley, R.A. (1985). Scopolamine degrades spatial working memory but spares spatial reference memory: Dissimilarity of anticholinergic effect and restriction of distal visual cues. *Pharmacology, Biochemistry and Behavior, 23,* 1-6.

Becker, J. T., Walker, J.A., & Olton, D.S. (1980). Neuroanatomical bases of spatial memory. *Brain Research, 200,* 307-320.

Bland, B.H. (1986). The physiology and pharmacology of hippocampal formation theta rhythms. *Progress in Neurobiology, 26,* 1-54.

Bliss, T.V.P., & Lomo, T. (1973). Long-lasting potentiation of synaptic transmission in the dentate area of the anesthetized rabbit following stimulation of the perforant path. *Journal of Physiology, 232,* 331-356.

Bowen, D.M., Smith, C.B., White, P., & Davidson, A.N. (1976). Neurotransmitter-related enzymes and indices of hypoxia in senile dementia and other abiotrophies. *Brain, 99,* 459-496.

Brandeis, R., Pittel, Z., Lachman, C., Heldman, E., Luz, S., Dachir, S., Levy, A., Hanin, I., & Fisher, A. (1986). AF64A-induced cholinotoxicity: behavioral and biochemical correlates. In A. Fisher, I. Hanin, & C. Lachman (Eds.), *Alzheimer's and Parkinson's diseases: Strategies for research and development* (pp. 469-478). New York: Plenum Press.

Brito, G.N.O., Davis, B.J., Stopp, L.C., & Stanton, M.R. (1983). Memory and the septo-hippocampal cholinergic system in the rat. *Psychopharmacology, 81,* 315-320.

Brugge, J.F. (1965). An electrographic study of the hippocampus and neocortex in unrestrained rats following septal lesions. *Electroencephalography and Clinical Neurophysiology, 18,* 36-44.

Bures, J., Bohdanecky, Z., & Weiss, T. (1962). Physostigmine induced hippocampal theta activity and learning in rats. *Psychopharmacologia, 3,* 254-263.

Buresova, O., Bolhuis, J.J, & Bures, J. (1986). Differential effects of cholinergic blockade on performance of rats in the water tank navigation task and in a radial water maze. *Behavioral Neuroscience, 100,* 476-482.

Chrobak, J.J., Hanin, I., Schmechel, D.E., & Walsh, T.J. (1988). AF64A-induced working memory impairment: Behavioral, neurochemical and histological correlates. *Brain Research, 463,* 107-117.

Chrobak, J.J., Hanin, I., & Walsh, T.J. (1987). AF64A (ethylcholine mustard aziridinium ion), a cholinergic neurotoxin, selectively impairs working memory in a multiple component T-maze task. *Brain Research, 414,* 15-21.

Chrobak, J.J., Spates, M., Stackman, R.W., & Walsh, T.J. (1989). Hemicholinium-3 prevents the working memory impairments and the cholinergic hypofunction induced by ethylcholine aziridinium ion (AF64A). Manuscript submitted for publication.

Cohen, N.J., & Squire, L.R. (1980). Preserved learning and retention of pattern analyzing skill in amnesia: dissociation of knowing how and knowing that. *Science, 210,* 207-209.

Coleman, P.D., & Flood, D.G. (1987). Neuron numbers and dendritic extent in normal aging and Alzheimer's disease. *Neurobiology of Aging, 8,* 521-545.

Collerton, D. (1986). Cholinergic function and intellectual decline in Alzheimer's disease. *Neuroscience, 19,* 1-28.

Costa, E., Panula, P., Thompson, H.K., & Cheney, D.L. (1983). The transynaptic regulation of the septal-hippocampal cholinergic neurons. *Life Science, 32,* 165-179.

Coyle, J.T., Price, D.L., & DeLong, M.R. (1983). Alzheimer's Disease: a disorder of cortical cholinergic innervation. *Science, 219,* 1184-1190.

Cummings, J.L., & Benson, D.F. (1988). Psychological dysfunction accompanying subcortical dementias. *Annual Review of Medicine, 39,* 53-61.

Curti, D., & Marchbanks, R.M. (1984). Kinetics of irreversible inhibition of choline transport in synaptosomes by ethylcholine mustard aziridinium. *Journal of Membrane Biology, 82,* 259-268.

Damsma, G., Westerink, B.H.C., de Boer, P., de Vries, J.B., & Horn, A.S. (1988). Basal acetylcholine release in freely moving rats detected by on-line transstriatal dialysis: Pharmacological aspects. *Life Sciences, 43,* 1161-1168.

Davies, P., & Maloney, A.F.J. (1976). Selective loss of cerebral cholinergic neurones in Alzheimer's disease. *Lancet, 2,* 1403.

Decker, M.W., Pelleymounter, M.A., & Gallagher, M. (1987). Effects of training on a spatial memory task on high affinity choline uptake in hippocampus and cortex in young adults and aged rats. *Journal of Neuroscience, 8,* 93-99.

DeFeudis, F.V. (1988). Cholinergic systems and Alzheimer's disease. *Drug Development Research, 14,* 95-109.

Drachman, D.A. (1977). Memory and cognitive function in man: does the cholinergic system have a specific role? *Neurology, 27,* 73.

Drachman, D.A. (1979). Central cholinergic system in memory. In M.A. Lipton, A. DiMascio, & K.F. Killam (Eds.), *Psychopharmacology: A generation of progress* (p. 651). New York: Raven.

Dren, A.T., & Domino, E.F. (1968). Effects of hemicholinium-3 on EEG activation and brain acetylcholine in the dog. *Journal of Pharmacology and Experimental Therapeutics, 161,* 141-154.

Eckerman, D.A., Gordon, W.A., Edwards, J.D., MacPhail, R.C., & Gage, M.J. (1980). Effects of scopolamine, pentobarbital, and amphetamine on radial arm maze performance in the rat. *Pharmacology, Biochemistry and Behavior, 12,* 595-602.

Emerich, D.F., Spates, M.J., & Walsh, T.J. (1988). Ganglioside AGF2 promotes recovery of AF64A-induced behavioral and neurochemical deficits. *Society for Neuroscience Abstracts, 14* .

Eslinger, P.J., & Damasio, A.R. (1986). Preserved motor learning in Alzheimer's disease: implications for anatomy and behavior. *Journal of Neuroscince, 10,* 3006-3009.

Eva, C., Fabrazzo, M., & Costa, E. (1987). Changes of cholinergic, noradrenergic and serotonergic synaptic transmission indices by ethylcholine aziridinium ion (AF64A) infused intraventricularly. *Journal of Pharmacology and Experimental Therapeutics, 241,* 181-186.

Fisher, A., & Hanin, I. (1980). Minireview: choline analogs as potential tools in developing selective animal models of central cholinergic hypofunction. *Life Science, 27,* 1615-1643.

Fisher, A., & Hanin, I. (1986). Potential animal models for seniledementia of Alzheimer's type, with emphasis on AF64A-induced cholinotoxicity. *Annual Review of Pharmacology and Toxicology, 26,* 161-181.

Fisher, A., Mantione, C.R., Abraham, D.J., & Hanin, I. (1982). Long-term cholinergic hypofunction induced in mice by ethylcholine aziridinium ion (AF64A) in vivo. *Journal of Pharmacology and Experimental Therapeutics, 222,* 140-145.

Flood, J.F., Smith, G.E., & Cherkin, A. (1983). Memory retention: Potentiation of cholinergic drug combinations in mice. *Neurobiology of Aging, 4,* 37-43.

Freeman, J.J., & Jenden, D.J. (1976). The source of choline for acetylcholine synthesis in brain. *Life Sciences, 19,* 949-962.

Frotscher, M., & Leranth, C. (1985). Cholinergic innervation of the rat hippocampus as revealed by choline acetyltransferase immunocytochemistry: a combined light and electron microscopic study. *Journal of Comparative Neurology, 239,* 237-246.

Frotscher, M., & Leranth, C. (1986). The cholinergic innervation of the rat fascia dentata: identification of target structures on granule cells by combining choline acetyltransferase immunocytochemistry and golgi impregnation. *Journal of Comparative Neurology, 243,* 58-70.

Gaal, G., Potter, P.E., Hanin, I., Kakucska, I., & Vizi, E.S. (1986). Effects of intracerebroventricular AF64A administration on cholinergic, serotonergic and catecholaminergic circuitry in rat dorsal hippocampus. *Neuroscience, 19,* 1197-1205.

Gray, J.A., & McNaughton, N. (1983). Comparison between the behavioural effects of septal and hippocampal lesions: a review. *Neuroscience and Biobehavioral Review, 7,* 119-188.

Greenstein, Y.J., Pavlides, C., & Winson, J. (1988). Long-term potentiation in the dentate gyrus is preferentially induced at theta rhythm periodicity. *Brain Research, 438,* 331-334.

Hagan, J.J., Tweedie, F., & Morris, R.G.M. (1986). Lack of task specificity and absence of posttraining effects of atropine on learning. *Behavioral Neuroscience, 100,* 483-493.

Hanin, I., Fisher, A., Hortnagl, H., Leventer, S.M., Potter, P.E., & Walsh, T.J. (1987). Ethylcholine mustard aziridinium (AF64A; ECMA) and other potential cholinergic neuron-specific neurotoxins. In H.Y. Meltzer (Ed.), *Psychopharmacology — The third generation of progress* (pp. 341-349). New York: Raven.

Hardy, J., Adolfsson, R., Alafuzoff, I., Bucht, G., Marcusson, J., Nyberg, P., Perdahl, E., Wester, P., & Winblad, B. (1985). Transmitter deficits in Alzheimer's disease. *Neurochemistry International, 7,* 545-563.

Haroutunian, V., Barnes, E., & Davis, K.L. (1985). Cholinergic modulation of memory in rats. *Psychopharmacology, 87,* 266-271.

Harrell, L.E., Barlow, T.S., & Parsons, D. (1987). Cholinergic neurons, learning, and recovery of function. *Behavioral Neuroscience, 101,* 644-652.

Henke, H., & Lang, W. (1983). Cholinergic enzymes in neocortex, hippocampus and basal forebrain of non-neurological and senile-dementia of Alzheimer type patients. *Brain Research, 267,* 281-291.

Hepler, D.J., Olton, D.S., Wenk, G.L., & Coyle, J.T. (1985). Lesions in nucleus basalis magnocellularis and medial septal area of rats produce qualitatively similar memory impairments. *Journal of Neuroscience, 5*, 866-873.

Hepler, D.J., Wenk, G.L., Cribbs, B.L., Olton, D.S., & Coyle, J.T. (1985). Memory impairments following basal forebrain lesions. *Brain Research, 346*, 8-14.

Hortnagl, H., Potter, P.E., & Hanin, I. (1987a). Effect of cholinergic deficit induced by ethylcholine aziridinium on serotonergic parameters in rat brain. *Neuroscience, 22*, 203-213.

Hortnagl, H., Potter, P.E., & Hanin, I. (1987b). Effect of cholinergic deficit induced by ethylcholine aziridinium (AF64A) on noradrenergic and dopaminergic parameters in rat brain. *Brain Research, 421*, 75-84.

Huppert, F.A., & Tym, E. (1986). Clinical and neuropsychological assessment of dementia. *British Medical Bulletin, 42*, 11-18.

Hyman, B.T., Damasio, A.R., Van Hoesen, G.W., & Barnes, C.L. (1984). Alzheimer's disease: cell specific pathology isolates the hippocampal formation. *Science, 225*, 1168-1170.

Jarrard, L.E., Kant, G.J., Meyerhoff, J.C., & Levy, A. (1984). Behavioral and neurochemical effects of intraventricular AF64A administration in rats. *Pharmacological & Biochemical Behavior, 21*, 273-283.

Jope, R.S. (1979). High affinity choline transport and acetyl CoA production in brain and their roles in the regulation of acetylcholine synthesis. *Brain Research Reviews, 180*, 313-344.

Kasa, P., & Hanin, I. (1985). Ethyline mustard aziridium blocks the axoplasmic transport of acetylcholinesterase in cholinergic nerve fibres of the rat. *Histochemistry, 83*, 343-345.

Kesner, R.P., Crutcher, K., & Beers, D.R. (1988). Serial position curves for item (spatial location) information: role of the dorsal hippocampal formation and medial septum. *Brain Research, 454*, 219-226.

Kesner, R.P., Crutcher, K., & Meason, M. (1986). Medial septal and nucleus basalis magnocellularis lesions produce order memory deficits in rats which mimic symptomatology of Alzheimer's disease. *Neurobiology of Aging, 7*, 287-295.

Kish, S.J., El-Awar, M., Schut, L., Leach, L. Oscar-Berman, M., & Freedman, M. (1988). Cognitive deficits in olivopontocerebellar atrophy: Implications for the cholinergic hypothesis of Alzheimer's disease. *Annals of Neurology, 24*, 200-206.

Knopman, D.S., & Nissen, M.J. (1987). Implicit learning in patients with probable Alzheimer's disease. *Neurology, 37*, 784-787.

Knowlton, B.J., Wenk, G.L., Olton, D.S., & Coyle, J.T. (1985). Basal forebrain lesions produce a dissociation of trial-dependent and trial-independent memory performance. *Brain Research, 345*, 315-321.

Kohler, C., Chan-Palay, V., & Wu, J.Y. (1984). Septal neurons containing glutamic acid decarboxylase immunoreactivity project to the hippocampal region in the rat brain. *Anatomical Embryology, 169*, 41-44.

Kornetsky, C. (1977). Animal models: Promises and problems. In I. Hanin & E. Usdin (Eds.), *Animal models in psychology and neurology* (pp. 1-7). New York: Pergamon Press.

Kuhar, M.J., & Yamamura, H.I. (1975). Light autoradiographic localization of cholinergic muscarinic receptors in rat brain by specific binding of a potent antagonist. *Nature, 253*, 560-561.

Larson, J., Wong, D., & Lynch, G. (1986). Pattern stimulation at the theta frequency is optimal for the induction of hippocampal long-term potentiation. *Brain Research, 368*, 347-350.

Leventer, S., McKeag, D., Clancy, M., Wulfert, E., & Hanin, I. (1985). Intracerebroventricular administration of ethylcholine mustard aziridinium ion (AF64A) reduces release of acetylcholine from rat hippocampal slices. *Neuropharmacology, 24*, 453-459.

Leventer, S.M., Wulfert, E., & Hanin, I. (1987). Time course of ethylcholine aziridium ion(AF64A)-induced cholinotoxicity in vivo. *Neuropharmacology, 26*, 361-365.

Lindvall, O., & Bjorklund, A. (1974). The organization of the ascending catecholamine neuron systems in the rat brain. *Acta Physiologica Scandanavia Supplement, 412*, 1-48.

Litvan, I., Grafman, J., Vendrell, P., Martinez, J.M., Junque, C., Vendrell, J.M., & Barraquer-Bordas, J.L. (1988). Multiple memory deficits in patients with multiple sclerosis. *Archives of Neurology, 45*, 607-610.

Loy, R., Koziell, D.A., Lindsey, J.D., & Moore, R.Y. (1980). Noradrenergic innervation of the adult rat hippocampal formation. *Journal of Comparative Neurology, 189*, 699-710.

Lynch, G., & Baudry, M. (1984). The biochemistry of memory: a new and specific hypothesis. *Science, 224*, 1057-1063.

Mann, J.J., Stanley, M., Neophitides, A., de Leon, M., Ferris, S.H., & Gershon, S. (1981). Central amine metabolism in Alzheimer's disease: in vivo relationship to cognitive deficit. *Neurobiology of Aging, 2*, 57-60.

Mantione, C.R., Fisher, A., & Hanin, I. (1981). AF64A neurotoxicity: a potential animal model of central cholinergic hypofunction. *Science, i*, 579-580.

Mantione, C.R., Fisher, A., & Hanin, I. (1984). Possible mechanisms involved in the presynaptic cholinotoxicity due to ethylcholine aziridinium (AF64A) in vivo. *Life Science, 35*, 33-41.

Mantione, C.R., Zigmond, M.J., Fisher, A., & Hanin, I. (1983). Selective presynaptic cholinergic neurotoxicity following intrahippocampal AF64A injection in rats. *Journal of Neurochemistry, 41*, 251-255.

Marchbanks, R.M., Wonnacott, S., & Rubio, M.A. (1981). The effects of acetylcholine release in choline fluxes in isolated synaptic terminals. *Journal of Neurochemistry, 36*, 379-393.

Matthies, H., Rauca, C.H., & Liebmann, H. (1974). Changes in the acetylcholine content of different brain regions of the rat during a learning experiment. *Journal of Neurochemistry, 23*, 1109.

McGeer, P.L., Eccles, J.C., & McGeer, E.G. (1987). *Molecular neurobiology of the mammalian brain*. New York: Plenum Press.

McGurk, S.R., Hartgraves, S.L., Kelly, P.H., Gordons, M.N., & Butcher, L.L. (1987). Is ethylcholine aziridinium ion a specific cholinergic neurotoxin? *Neuroscience, 22*, 215-224.

McNaughton, N., Azmitia, E.C., Williams, J.H., Buchan, A., & Gray, J.A. (1980). Septal elicitation of hippocampal theta rhythm after localized deafferentation of serotonergic fibers. *Brain Research, 200*, 259-269.

Meck, W.H., Church, R.M., Wenk, G.L., & Olton, D.S. (1987). Nucleus basalis magnocellularis and medial septal area lesions differentially impair temporal memory. *Journal of Neuroscience, 7*, 3505-3511.

Messer, W.S., Thomas, G.J., & Hoss, W.P. (1987). Selectivity of pirenzepine in the central nervous system. II. Differential effects of pirenzepine and scopolamine on performance of a representational memory task. *Brain Research, 407*, 37-45.

Mesulam, M.M., Mufson, E.J., Wainer, B.H., & Levey, A.I. (1983). Central cholinergic pathways in the rat: An overview based on an alternative nomenclature (Ch1-Ch6). *Neuroscience, 10*, 1185-1201.

Mishkin, M., Malamut, B., & Bachevalier, J. (1984). Memories and habits: Two neural systems. In G. Lynch, J.L. McGaugh, & N.M. Weinberger (Eds.), *Neurobiology of learning and memory* (pp. 65-67). New York: Guilford Press.

Miyamoto, M., Kato, J., Narumi, S., & Nagaoka, A. (1987). Characteristics of memory impairment following lesioning of the basal forebrain and medial septal nucleus in rats. *Brain Research, 419*, 19-31.

Mountjoy, C.Q., Rossor, M.N., Iversen, L.I., & Roth, M. (1984). Correlation of cortical cholinergic and GABA deficits with quantitative neuropathological findings in senile dementia. *Brain, 107*, 507-518.

Nissen, M.J., Knopman, D.S., & Schacter, D.L. (1987). Neurochemical disociation of memory systems. *Neurology, 37*, 789-794.

Nyakas, C., Luiten, P.G.M., Spencer, D.G., & Traber, J. (1987). Detailed projection patterns of septal and diagonal band efferents to the hippocampus in the rat with emphasis on innervation of CA1 and dentate gyrus. *Brain Research Bulletin, 18*, 533-545.

Olton, D.S. (1983). Memory functions and the hippocampus. In W.Seifert (Ed.), *Neurobiology of the hippocampus*. New York: Academic Press.

Olton, D.S. (1985). Strategies for the development of animal models of human memory impairments. *Annals of The New York Academy of Sciences, 444*, 113-121.

Olton, D.S. (1987). The radial arm maze as a tool in behavioral pharmacology. *Physiology and Behavior, 40*, 793-797.

Olton, D.S., Becker, J.T., & Handelman, G.E. (1979). Hippocampus, space, and memory. *Behavioral Brain Science, 2*, 313-365.

Olton, D.S., & Pappas, B.C. (1979). Spatial memory and hippocampal function. *Neuropsychologia, 17*, 669-682.

Olton, D.S., & Samuelson, R.J. (1976). Remembrances of places passed: spatial memory in rats. *Journal of Experimental Psychology (Animal Behavior), 2*, 97-116.

Pedder, E.K., & Prince, A.K. (1983). The reaction of rat brain choline acetyltransferase (ChAT) with ethylcholine mustard aziridinium ion (ECMA) and phenoxybenzamine (PB). *British Journal of Pharmacology, 80*, 134.

Peele, D.B., & Baron, S.P. (1988). Effects of scopolamine on repeated acquisition of radial-arm maze performance by rats. *Journal of the Experimental Analysis of Behavior, 49*, 275-290.

Penetar, D.M., & McDonough Jr., J.H. (1983). Effects of cholinergic drugs on delayed match-to-sample performance of rhesus monkeys. *Pharmacological & Biochemical Behavior, 19*, 963-967.

Perry, E.K., Tomlinson, B.E., Blessed, G., Bergmann, K., Gibson, P., & Perry, R.H. (1978). Correlation of cholinergic abnormalities with senile plaques and mental test scores in senile dementia. *British Medical Journal, 2*, 1457-1459.

Petsche, H., Stumpf, C., & Gogolak, G. (1962). The significance of the rabbit's septum as a relay station between the midbrain and the hippocampus: 1. The control of hippocampal arousal activity by the septum cells. *Electroencephalography and Clinical Neurophysiology, 14*, 202-211

Piercey, M.F., Vogelsang, G.D., Franklin, S.R., & Tang, A.H. (1987). Reversal of scopolamine-induced amnesia and alterations in energy metabolism by the nootropic piracetam: implications regarding identification of brain structures involved in consolidation of memory traces. *Brain Research, 424,* 1-9.

Potter, P.E., Harsing, L.G,, Kakucska, I., Gaal, G., & Vizi, E.S. (1986).Selective impairment of acetylcholine release and content in the central nervous system following intracerebroventricular administration of ethylcholine mustard aziridinium ion (AF64A) in the rat. *Neurochemistry International, 8,* 199-206.

Potter, P.E., Tedford, C.E., Kindel, G.H., & Hanin, I. (1987). Inhibition of high affinity choline transport with A-4 attenuates the effect of ethylcholine mustard aziridinium (AF64A) on both cholinergic and serotonergic parameters. *Society for Neuroscience Abstract, 13,* 326-327.

Price, R.W., Sidtis, J., & Rosenblum, M. (1988). The AIDS dementia complex: Some current questions. *Annals of Neurology, 23(Suppl.),* S27-S33.

Rascol, O., & Lamour, Y. (1988). Differential effects of M1 and M2 muscarinic drugs on septohippocampal, hippocampal, and cortical neurons in the rat. *Brain Research, 446,* 303-313.

Rauca, Ch., Kammerer, E., & Matthies, H. (1980). Choline uptake and permanent memory storage. *Pharmacology, Biochemistry & Behavior, 13,* 21-25.

Rawlins, J.N.P., Feldon, J., & Gray, J.A. (1979). Septo-hippocampal connections and the hippocampal theta rhythm. *Experimental Brain Research, 37,* 49-63.

Rossor, M.N., Iversen, L.L., Reynolds, G.P., Mountjoy, C.Q., & Roth, M. (1984). Neurochemical characteristics of early and late onset types of Alzheimer's disease. *British Medical Journal, 288,* 961-964.

Rusted, J.M., & Warburton, D.M. (1988). The effects of scopolamine on working memory in healthy young volunteers. *Psychopharmacology, 96,* 145-152.

Rylett, R.J., Ball, M.J., & Colhoun, E.H. (1983). Evidence for high affinity choline transport in synaptosomes prepared from hippocampus and neocortex of patients with Alzheimer's disease. *Brain Research, 289,* 169-175.

Rylett, R.J., & Colhoun, E.H. (1980). Kinetic data on the inhibition of high affinity choline transport into rat forebrain synaptosomes by choline-like compounds and nitrogen mustard analogues. *Journal of Neurochemistry, 34,* 713-719.

Sanberg, P.R., & Coyle, J.T. (1984). Scientific approaches to Huntington's disease. *CRC Critical Reviews in Neurobiology, 1,* 1-44.

Sandberg, K., Schnaar, R.L., McKinney, M., Hanin, I., Fisher, A. & Coyle, J.T. (1985). AF64A: an active site directed irreversible inhibitor of choline acetyltransferase. *Journal of Neurochemistry, 44,* 439-445.

Sherry, D.F., & Schacter, D.L. (1987). The evolution of multiple memory systems. *Psychological Review, 98,* 439-454.

Simon, J.R., Atweh, S., & Kuhar, M.J. (1976). Sodium-dependent high affinity choline uptake: a regulatory step in the synthesis of acetylcholine. *Journal of Neurochemistry, 26,* 909-922.

Sitaram, N. (1984). Cholinergic hypothesis of human memory: review of basic and clinical studies. *Drug Development Research, 4,* 481-488.

Smart, L. (1981). Hemicholinium 3-bromo mustard: a high affinity inhibitor of sodium-dependent high affinity choline uptake. *Neuroscience, 6,* 1765-1770.

Spencer, D.G., & Lal, H. (1983). Effects of anticholinergic drugs on learning and memory. *Drug Development Research, 3,* 489-502.

Squire, L.R., & Cohen, N.J. (1984). Human memory and amnesia. In G. Lynch, J.L. McGaugh & N.M. Weinberger (Eds.), *Neurobiology of learning and memory* (pp. 3-64). New York: Guilford Press.

Stumpf, C., Petsche, H., & Gogolak, G. (1962). The significance of the rabbit's septum as a relay station between the midbrain and the hippocampus: II. The differential influence of drugs upon the septal cell firing pattern and the hippocampus theta activity. *Electroencephalography and Clinical Neurophysiology, 14*, 212-219.

Swanson, L.W., Teyler, T.J., & Thompson, R.F. (1982). Hippocampal long-term potentiation mechanisms and implications for memory. *Neuroscience Research Program Bulletin, 20*.

Tagari, P.C., Maysinger, D., & Cuello, A.C. (1986). Hemicholinium mustard derivatives: Preliminary assessment of cholinergic neurotoxicity. *Neurochemistry Research, 11*, 1091-1102.

Terry, R.D., & Katzman, R. (1983). Senile dementia of Alzheimer's disease. *Annals of Neurology, 14*, 497-506.

Thal, L.J., Fuld, P.A., Masur, D.M., Sharpless, N.S., & Davies, P. (1983). Oral physostigmine and lecithin improve memory in Alzheimer's disease. *Psychopharmacology Bulletin, 19*, 454-456.

Thomas, G.J., & Gash, D.M. (1986). Differential effects of posterior septal lesions on dispositional and representational memory. *Behavioral Neuroscience, 100*, 712-719.

Thomas, G.J., & Spafford, P.S. (1984). Deficits for representational memory induced by septal and cortica lesions (singly and combined) in rats. *Behavioral Neuroscience, 98*, 394-404.

Tucker, D.M., Roeltgen, D.P., Wann, P.D., & Wertheimer, R.I. (1988). Memory dysfunction in myasthenia gravis: Evidence for central cholinergic effects. *Neurology, 38*, 1173-1177.

Valentino, R.J., & Dingledine, R. (1981). Presynaptic inhibitory effect of acetylcholine in the hippocampus. *Journal of Neuroscience, 1*, 784-792.

Vickroy, T.W., Watson, M., Leventer, S.M., Roeske, W.R., Hanin, I., & Yamamura, H.I. (1985). Regional differences in ethylcholine mustard aziridinium ion (AF64A)-induced deficits in presynaptic cholinergic markers for the rat central nervous system. *Journal of Pharmacology and Experimental Therapeutics, 235*, 577-582.

Vincent, S.R., & McGeer, E.G. (1981). A substance P projection to the hippocampus. *Brain Research, 215*, 349-351.

Walsh, T.J., & Chrobak, J.J. (1987). The use of the radial arm maze in neurotoxicology. *Physiology and Behavior, 40*, 799-803.

Walsh, T.J., & Hanin, I. (1986). A review of the behavioral effects of AF64A, a cholinergic neurotoxin. In A. Fisher, I. Hanin, & C. Lachman (Ed.), *Alzheimer's and Parkinson's diseases: Strategies for research and development* (pp. 461-467). New York: Raven.

Walsh, T.J., Tilson, H.A., DeHaven, D.L., Mailman, R.B., Fisher, A., & Hanin, I. (1984). AF64A, a cholinergic neurotoxin, selectively depletes acetylcholine in hippocampus and cortex, and produces long-term passive avoidance and radial-arm maze deficits in the rat. *Brain Research, 321*, 91-102.

Watts, J., Stevens, R., & Robinson, C. (1981). Effects of scopolamine on radial maze performance in rats. *Physiology and Behavior, 26*, 845-851.

Wenk, G., Hepler, D., & Olton, D. (1984). Behavior alters the uptake of [3H]choline into acetylcholinergic neurons of the nucleus basalis magnocellularis and medial septal area. *Behavioral Brain Research, 13*, 129-138.

Whitehouse, P.J., Struble, R.G., Hedreen, J.C., Clark, A.W., & Price, D.L. (1985). Alzheimer's disease and related dementias: Selective involvement of specific neuronal systems. *CRC Critical Review in Clinical Neurobiology, 1*, 319-339.

Wilcock, G.K., Esiri, M.M., Bowen, D.M., & Smith, C.C.T. (1982). Alzheimer's disease: Correlation of cortical choline acetyltransferase activity with the severity of dementia and histological abnormalities. *Journal of Neurological Science, 57,* 407-417.

Williams, S., & Johnston, D. (1988). Muscarinic depression of long-term potentiation in CA3 hippocampal neurons. *Science, 242,* 84-87.

Wirsching, B.A., Beninger, R.J., Jharmandas, K., Boegman, R.J., & El-Delfrawy, S.R. (1984). Differential effects of scopolamine on working and reference memory of rats in the radial maze. *Pharmacological & Biochemical Behavior, 20,* 659-662.

Wisniewski, K.E., Wisniewski, H.M., & Wen, G.Y. (1985). Occurrence of neuropathological changes and dementia of Alzheimer's disease in Down's Syndrome. *Annals of Neurology, 17,* 278-282.

Woodhams, P.L., Roberts, G.W., Polak, J.M., & Crow, T.J. (1983). Distribution of neuropeptides in the limbic system of the rat: the bed nucleus of the stria terminalis, septum and preoptic area. *Neuroscience, 8,* 677-693.

Zigmond, M.J., & Stricker, E.M. (1984). Parkinson's disease: Studies with an animal model. *Life Sciences, 35,* 5-18.

14 Brain, Emotion, and Cognition: An Overview

Charles F. Flaherty
Rutgers—The State University

Lawrence Dachowski
Tulane University

In this chapter we will provide an integrated precis of each of the other chapters, indicating how different authors have treated similar issues and, to some degree, relevance to current literature not represented in this collection.

COGNITION

The Expression of Learning

The study of "latent learning," historically linked to Blodgett, Tolman, and maze behavior, has undergone a renaissance in contemporary Pavlovian conditioning research. Current interest in the expression of prior learning was derived from concern with conceptualizations of memory rather than from motivational issues of learning and performance characteristic of work from Tolman's laboratory. Although it is probably fruitless to search for the exact origin of the recent focus, Underwood's consideration of memory in terms of multidimensional attributes (e.g., Underwood, 1969) and Spear's application of this model to animal memory (e.g., Spear, 1973, 1978) in terms of retrieval processes rather than consolidation processes were clearly very influential. Early signs of the "retrieval" approach were evident in the analysis of amnesia produced by electroconvulsive shock (Lewis, 1969, Miller & Springer, 1973) and in Spear's analysis of interference patterns obtained in animals trained in both active and passive avoidance tasks (e.g., Spear, 1978; Spear, Miller, & Jagielo, 1990).

Another important influence was Konorski's (1967) representation interpretation of Pavlovian conditioning and subsequent experimental and theoreti-

cal consideration of the issues raised by representation and contingency interpretations of conditioning (e.g., Dickinson & Boakes, 1979).

Both of these influences may be seen in the first four chapters of this volume, all of which are concerned with aspects of postacquisition "processing."
The shift in emphasis from acquisition to postacquisition has revealed a perhaps unexpected richness and complexity to conditioning. This research also
serves to remind us of how difficult it is to get any animal to tell us all that it
has learned.

Reinstatement. Each of the first four chapters is concerned with how
aspects of the training context may serve to reinstate the memory for original
learning when animals are exposed to these context cues following extinction.
The context that Richardson and Riccio are concerned with is the hormonal
state of the animal. They show that administration of adrenocorticotrophic
hormone (ACTH) after extinction will lead an extinguished animal to perform
as it did in acquisition. This effect was demonstrated in both passive avoidance
and active avoidance tasks thereby showing that the effects of ACTH were not
simply motoric—making the animal more or less active.

Does ACTH function as a retrieval cue—reminding the animal of the conditions that existed in acquisition—thus interfering with the memory of extinction? As a test of this interpretation, Richardson and Riccio administered dexamethasone during acquisition of an avoidance task. Dexamethasone is a synthetic glucocorticoid which suppresses the release of ACTH. The results
showed that ACTH, administered after extinction, did not produce acquisition-
like behavior in animals treated with the dexamethasone during initial training.
Thus, in order for ACTH administration to interfere with the memory of extinction, endogenous ACTH had to be present during acquisition.

Bouton, Miller and Grahame, and Delamater and LoLordo are all concerned
with the role of traditional exteroceptive contextual stimuli in reinstatement.
Previous research had demonstrated that a single exposure to the US could reinstate responding to an extinguished CS. An earlier interpretation of this effect
was that the US exposure strengthened the memory of the US that had been
weakened by extinction (Rescorla & Heth, 1975). However, Bouton argues that
this is not the case because there is little evidence that the memory of a US is
lost in extinction. If, for example, the same US is associated with two CSs,
the extinction of one CS-US association does not lead to the loss of the other
(discussed both by Bouton and by Delamater and LoLordo).

Bouton presents evidence that the mechanism of reinstatement produced by
the US presentation is a new context-US association and he concludes that "...
in a newly dangerous context, the CS again arouses fear." The conditioning
interpretation is interesting because one of the puzzles of the ACTH effect reported by Richardson and Riccio is that ACTH was equally effective in restoring acquisition performance whether it was administered 15 minutes or seven
days before the test session. Since the half life of injected ACTH is a matter of
minutes, the long term effects of the drug present a puzzle—unless the effects
were mediated by the formation of a new context-arousal association. Delamater and LoLordo's review generally leads to the same conclusion. However,
they raise other issues that remain to be resolved. These issues include the ef-

fect of degree of extinction on reinstatement, and the role of context-US associations in reinstatement after the extinction of training which had initially involved either partial reinforcement or latent inhibition.

Renewal. Bouton also considers another context-extinction relationship, one he refers to as "renewal." If a CS and US are paired in Context A, then the CS is extinguished in context B, the return to context A will renew responding to the CS. A change in context with an excitatory CS has little effect on responding but a change for an extinguished CS has a substantial effect. Evidence presented by Bouton suggests that renewal, unlike reinstatement, does not depend on Context-US associations. Instead, the context acts like a conditional cue or "occasion setter." It may modulate performance without having a direct association with the US—it may serve to "disambiguate" a CS which sometimes signals a US and sometimes signals the absence of a US.

Revaluation. Postacquisition modifications of the US influence responding to non-extinguished CSs. Since these modifications occur in the absence of CS-US pairings the subsequent change in responding to the CS is thought to reflect non-associative processes. As reviewed by Delamater and LoLordo both the repeated presentation of the same US used in conditioning and the presentation of a less intense US result in a weaker CR, but neither of these effects are particularly robust. Presentation of a more intense US after conditioning generally leads to an enhanced CR the next time that the CS is presented. The standard interpretation of these revaluation effects (after Konorski, 1967) is that the CS, upon its re-presentation, now elicits the altered representation of the US—hence, the altered CR.

Other methods of producing revaluation, such as postconditioning changes in motivational state, post-conditioning manipulations of contingency events, and counterconditioning, are reviewed by Delamater and LoLordo. The general conclusion is that revaluation does occur, although it is usually incomplete. Revaluation also seems to be different from reinstatement in that it occurs with non-extinguished CSs and, most importantly, revaluation is not dependent on context-US associations. Among the evidence that Bouton reviews in regard to the latter statement is that context manipulations that influence reinstatement do not influence revaluation.

The fact that revaluation is often only partial leads Delamater and LoLordo to muse about the number of associations that are formed when a CS is paired with a US. There may, for example, be separate associations formed between the CS and "sensory" and affective aspects of the US. Subsequent modification of the affective qualities of the US may lead to revaluation in that regard but leave unaltered the "sensory" association.

Other postacquisition modifications. In the acquisition-extinction experiments considered above, the CS was associated with different events in different phases of the experiment. There are a variety of other Pavlovian paradigms in which this is also true. How is the notion of postacquisition processing related to these other paradigms? Bouton argues that procedures such as latent inhibition, Hall-Pearce transfer, and transfer across motivational states are similar to the sequence acquisition-extinction-CS presentation in that they present a retrieval problem for the subject—the CS has signalled different events at different times. Thus, from this perspective, a variety of Pavlovian "interference" procedures reflect a problem in retrieval, because of an ambiguous CS, rather than a problem in initial acquisition.

A similar interpretation is favored by Miller and Grahame, who offer a model to incorporate a variety of such results. A number of studies, many from Miller's laboratory, have demonstrated that postacquisition treatments, such as the presentation of reminder cues, can alleviate apparent acquisition failures that occur in blocking, overshadowing, latent inhibition, and retrograde amnesia procedures. The model, termed the "comparator hypothesis" portrays a zero sum scenario in which the CS competes for expression with other stimuli present during acquisition. Similar positions have been adopted before in theories of attention and discrimination learning but the model from Miller's laboratory is different in that the comparison of the associative strengths of the CS and its comparator stimuli occurs at the time of testing. The model assumes that CS presentation elicits a representation of both the US and the context. The context representation then also activates a representation of the US and the two representations of the US are compared. The comparison of the two determines the response to the CS.

In addition to the results described above, Miller has shown that other phenomena previously thought to represent acquisition effects or failure of acquisition (e.g., US pre-exposure effect, conditioned inhibition) are also capable of interpretation in terms of postacquisition comparator operations. Working within the framework of the model, Miller's laboratory has also found that the simultaneous conditioning procedure, often thought to lead to little in the way of associative learning, does in fact lead to the formation of associations, but special conditions are necessary for the expression of these associations.

Memory and Concept Formation

Memory. As behaviorist restrictions began to fade in the 1960s, there developed a resurgence of interest in animal memory (e.g., Honig & James, 1971; Spear, 1978), and the interest continues unabated. The chapter by Zentall, Urcuioli, Jackson-Smith, and Steirn illustrates two aspects of newer research on memory—the apparent flexibility of memory and the marked spatial memory ability of animals.

One current view of animal memory, as suggested by the use of "strategies" in the title of Chapter 5, is that alternative ways of remembering material, perhaps dependent on task demands, are available to an animal. Sometimes, as tradition would have it, animals seem to store memories in terms of past events (retrospective memory). But, at other times, an animal's memory seems to consist of what it will do when confronted with a specific situation in the future (instructional or prospective memory). Zentall et al. provide evidence for both of these processes with the suggestion that a retrospective process dominates when the stimuli are highly discriminable for the pigeon, but a prospective process may be favored when sample discriminability is not high and, in particular, when there are a small number of comparison stimuli. Another interesting suggestion from these experiments is that pigeons may group sample stimuli as similar to one another if they predict the same outcome.

Zentall et al. also present data on spatial memory in pigeons using two different key-pecking task developed to incorporate spatial aspects of the radial arm maze used with rats. Results obtained in these studies also demonstrated evidence of both retrospective and prospective memory, with the animals shifting from retrospective to prospective when it was advantageous, in terms of memory load, to do so. The data also indicate working memory of substantial durations for this task in pigeons and they indicate that memory may be enhanced by increasing either the spatial or visual distinctiveness of the items to be remembered.

Concepts. Harry Harlow's pioneering work with the "learning set" paradigm (e.g., Harlow, 1949, 1959) suggested that monkeys could form concepts or at least rules for responding that were not amenable to interpretation in terms of simple associative and reinforcement processes. For many years this field of study did not progress much beyond Harlow's work. However, studies of discrimination learning in pigeons by Herrnstein and his colleagues revived interest in the question of the conceptual abilities of lower animals. These studies used photographs of natural objects and showed that pigeons had either an extraordinary memory for different instances of such stimuli or else had formed concepts that allowed them to identify correct instances without ever having seen that particular stimulus before. The memory versus concept issue is not resolved, although evidence is often interpreted as favoring the conceptual view (e.g., Herrnstein, Loveland, & Cable, 1976; Wasserman, Kiedinger, & Bhatt, 1988). However, if a concept is formed, it is not at all clear what the nature of the concept would be for the animals (D'Amato & Van Sant, 1988).

The chapters by Pearce and D'Amato are concerned with this issue of conceptual behavior in pigeons and monkeys. Pearce used a categorization task in which pigeons were exposed to a series of computer-generated television images containing three bars of different heights. The mean height of these bars defined the correctness or incorrectness of each sample. Pearce found that pigeons could readily learn to categorize the stimuli as correct or incorrect. The nature of the results suggested that this categorization was not based on any particular simple feature of the patterns, nor was it based in any obvious way on the relationship between the heights of the bars in different samples (although humans seemed to readily use this cue as a basis for categorization). The evidence also indicated that the pigeons did not form a prototype pattern, as might be expected from conceptual interpretation of their performance. A similar failure to respond to a prototype was recently reported by Watanabe (1988).

How then did the pigeons learn the categorization task? Pearce offers a conservative interpretation. He develops a generalization model which owes much to Spence's theory of discrimination learning (Spence, 1937), to Kornorski's representational view of conditioning, and to the Pearce-Hall representational model of conditioning (Pearce & Hall, 1980). Essentially, Pearce assumes that the birds learn an association between each stimulus and a representation of either US or of no-US. Excitatory and inhibitory gradients then develop around stimuli eliciting these representations and the response to any particular stimulus presented then is determined by the similarity of that exemplar to those that the animal has previously experienced and to the interaction of the gradients. Pearce recognizes that this interpretation requires that the animal remember all or many of the exemplars that it has experienced but he argues that evidence in regard to the pigeon's ability in this regard indicates that it has a very large capacity, at least when photographs of natural objects are used as stimuli (e.g., Vaughan & Greene, 1984). Whether or not Pearce's model can be extended to the study of "natural" concepts that develop with the photographic stimuli remains for the future and, perhaps, for a better analysis of just what aspects of natural photographs the animals are using as the basis of their categorization.

The chapter by D'Amato is concerned with another aspect of the cognitive ability of animals—their ability to learn serial patterns. This issues has arisen in a variety of guises; the rats' ability to learn patterns of reward magnitude (e.g., Hulse & Dorsky, 1979) the ability of songbirds and monkeys to learn sequences of tones (melodies) (Hulse & Page, 1988; D'Amato & Salmon, 1984); and perhaps the ability of animals to "count" (Capaldi & Miller, 1988).

Of particular relevance to D'Amato's work is a paper by Straub and Terrace (1981) which showed that pigeons were capable of learning to peck four differently colored response keys in a specific order and that they performed well, except on interior pairs, when two-item samples were presented to them. D'Amato subsequently showed that capuchin monkeys could learn a five item serial order task and that they performed well on all paired item tests, including the interior pairs on which pigeons fail.

In order to account for this species difference, D'Amato suggested that monkeys form an internal representation of the sequence, which they resort to for comparison purposes when presented with test items, whereas pigeons do not form such a representation. As a test for this hypothesis, D'Amato examined the monkeys' latency to respond to the first item in each test pair. If the monkeys have formed a representation of the five item sequence, then the latencies should be increased the deeper into the series the first item in each test pair is. He found that was the case, whereas it is not the case for pigeons (Terrace, 1986). D'Amato reasoned that a similar increase in latency should occur when non-adjacent items are presented in pairs—the greater the number of intervening items, the greater the latency to respond should be (as the animals search through their representation). Again, this was the case for monkeys but not for pigeons.

Although these data supported a representational account of learning, at least by the monkey, D'Amato considered an alternative hypothesis. He reasoned that it was possible that the animals formed associative chains (A associated with B which is associated with C, etc.) rather than forming a true representation. In order to test this, he utilized a "wild card" procedure in which a novel item or items would sometimes substitute for any of the usual stimuli in the sequence. His reasoning here was that the wild card items could not enter into stable associative chains. The results of this experiment indicated that the monkeys could still respond on the basis of serial order—indicating that they had formed spatial representations of the ordinal position in the sequence held by each item.

D'Amato suggests that many species are capable of acquiring serial information. However, the degree to which such information is associatively based as opposed to more cognitive or relationally based may vary with the species. For example, he suggests that the rats ability to track serial changes in reward magnitude (e.g., Capaldi & Miller, 1988) may be interpreted in terms of a serial association converted into a spatial ordering—it is not necessary to assume that the animals have developed an abstract representation of quantity or of serialization. In a conclusion similar to that drawn by Pearce for his data, D'Amato argues that other evidence suggesting tonal pattern discrimination or reward magnitude transitivity does not yet demand the assumption that lower animals are able to learn abstract concepts based on pattern. Instead, the learning may be based on a mechanism which allows random access to items organized serially, which is perhaps, in turn, based on a spatial transformation of the associative chain.

EMOTION

Fear

The study of fear has played an important role in experimental psychology. From the Watson and Raynor (1920) study through Mowrer's two-factor account of avoidance learning (Mowrer & Lamoreaux, 1946) to recent studies of the observational learning of fear (e.g., Cook & Mineka, 1987), the selective breeding for fear or emotionality (e.g., Brush, 1985; Brush et al., 1988), and the relationship among fear, anxiety, and frustration (Gray, 1982, 1987) the study of fear has proved to be a fertile stimulus to conceptual development in the field.

In Chapter 8, Fanselow, Helmstetter, and Calcagnetti explore the applicability of one of the newer developments in pharmacology to conditioned fear. Several pharmacological compounds have been shown to function at the binding site of the benzodiazepine tranquilizers to produce pharmacological and psychological effects opposite to those produced by the tranquilizers. The discovery of these agents has afforded the opportunity to investigate the relationship between emotional states and behaviors produced by these "inverse agonists' and corresponding states and behaviors produced by traditional aversive events.

One of the benzodiazepine inverse agonists, DMCM, was found to enhance freezing elicited by conditioned fear stimuli; to elicit freezing on its own when administered without a fear stimulus; and to function as a US to produce evidence of conditioned fear. Other studies showed that DMCM, like shock, produced analgesia and that this analgesia could be blocked by the benzodiazepine antagonist flumazenil (Ro 15-1788). Thus, substantial evidence suggests that inverse agonist activity at the benzodiazepine receptor produces states analogous to fear and/or conditioned fear. However, Fanselow et al., also report evidence suggesting some differences between the effects of DMCM and standard fear manipulations. For example, the startle response to acoustic stimuli is typically enhanced by fear and conditioned fear stimuli (e.g., Davis, Hitchcock, & Rosen, 1988) and this response is moderated by benzodiazepine tranquilizers (e.g., Davis, 1979). However, Fanselow et al., found that DMCM reduced rather than potentiated the magnitude of startle. These results were obtained with both central and peripheral administration of the drug. Another discrepancy occurred in the case of analgesia. The opiate antagonist naltrexone, which will typically block analgesia produced by conditioned fear stimuli, had a relatively small effect on DMCM-produced analgesia.

Thus, although there are many parallels, the psychological condition produced by the anxiogenic DMCM seems not to be isomorphic with conditioned fear states.

Disappointment, Frustration and Anxiety

Chapters 9 and 10 are concerned with incentive contrast effects produced by reward shifts. Although a variety of interpretations have been offered for contrast, a prominent role for the causal involvement of emotional behavior (disappointment and frustration, as suggested by Crespi, 1942; see also Gray, 1982), remains the most viable explanation, at least for some aspects of contrast.

The analysis of consummatory contrast presented in Chapter 9 by Flaherty has two foci. In the first section, three types of contrast—successive, simultaneous, and anticipatory—are differentiated on pharmacological and procedural grounds. Successive negative contrast (Crespi's "depression" procedure) is further analyzed and shown to consist of at least two stages: the initial occurrence of contrast and then recovery from contrast. These stages appear to differ in terms of the effects of novel (disinhibitory) stimuli, in terms of corticosterone elevation correlated with contrast, and in terms of the effectiveness of the benzodiazepine tranquilizers and ethanol in alleviating contrast. The suggestion is made that the initial occurrence of contrast may reflect a process of searching for the missing reward, whereas the recovery phase, which occurs after an unsuccessful search is completed and which is probably driven by the deprivation condition of the animal, may involve a period of approach-withdrawal conflict elicited by the absolute and relative rewarding properties of the postshift reward. It is during the conflict stage that ethanol and the benzodiazepines may be effective in facilitating recovery.

The second focus is a comparison of the psychopharmacology of negative contrast with that of three animal models of anxiety: operant conflict, potentiated startle, and punished drinking. The benzodiazepines and barbiturates seem to affect all four models in a qualitatively similar fashion, suggesting some commonality in the emotional states elicited by these diverse procedures. There are also differences. For example, buspirone, a serotonin type 1_A agonist and purported tranquilizer, has no effect on contrast, mixed effects on punished drinking and operant conflict, and anxiolytic effects in the potentiated startle procedure. Differences in drug effects such as these and others reviewed in the chapter suggest that it may be fruitful to correlate pharmacological profiles with behavioral paradigms as an approach to differentiating among emotional states. That this enterprise is likely to be complex is suggested by the results reported by Fanselow et al. (chapter 8) that the effects of the anxiogenic

DMCM are not consistent across different procedures that all ostensibly measure fear.

How complex is contrast? A wide range of phenomena associated with contrast has been explored in recent reviews (e.g., Flaherty, 1982; Williams, 1983). In Chapter 10, Dachowski and Brazier offer a taxonomy of contrast, a methodological scheme which could help to integrate the array of empirical findings. They then present data which may be regarded as addressing the boundary conditions under which Flaherty's findings regarding consummatory contrast prevail. In particular, they suggest that the recovery from contrast that is influenced by anxiolytic drugs may be specific to animals under relatively high levels of food deprivation; nondeprived rats seem to show much more persistent negative contrast.

In attempting to integrate these data with Flaherty's findings, Dachowski and Brazier advocate a more detailed theoretical account of negative contrast effects which may relate in a general way to event revaluation procedures (cf. Delamater & LoLordo, chap. 3 of this volume) and specifically to Miller's comparator hypothesis (see Miller & Grahame, chap. 4 of this volume). Achieving a theory that can successfully deal with the details of both positive and negative contrast effects remains an elusive goal, however. Dachowski and Brazier found positive consummatory incentive contrast in deprived animals, but not with nondeprived animals, a result that poses problems which still resist theoretical solution.

BRAIN

It has been a long and sometimes lonely road from the early physiologists measuring "animal electricity," to Helmholtz, to Fritsch and Hitzig, to Lashley, to Hebb, to Olds, to the current large group of behavioral neuroscientists investigating the neural basis of learning and motivation. There have been many obstacles in this road including technological inadequacies, opposition from anti-vivisectionists and current animal rights groups, and sometime disparagement and/or condescension from radical behaviorists or the "it's-too-soon-for-physiology" school. However, remarkable progress has been made and this progress is now proceeding at an ever quickening pace. Chapters 11-13 provide perspectives on three aspects of this work.

Amygdala

The chapter by Kapp and his colleagues traces their efforts to identify brain circuits involved in the conditioning of heart-rate deceleration in rabbits. It has been known for some time that lesions of the amygdala have a taming effect on animals and interfere with the conditioning of emotion-related behaviors (e.g., Blanchard & Blanchard, 1972). Subsequent research, reviewed by Kapp et al., suggested that the central nucleus of the amygdala may be important in the arousal or expression of fear-related behaviors. Kapp's laboratory then went on to show that radio frequency lesions of the central nucleus attenuated the magnitude of the decelerative CR and that a variety of pharmacological agents administered in the region of the central nucleus also modulated conditioning. A role for the central nucleus in cardiac conditioning was further supported by studies of Gentile, Jarrell, Teich, McCabe, and Schneiderman (1986) showing that the cell body neurotoxin ibotenic acid administered to the central nucleus also attenuated conditioning.

Given that the central nucleus is involved in cardiac conditioning, questions remained regarding the circuitry and function of this involvement. A combination of neuroanatomical and neurophysiological studies, reviewed in this chapter, suggest that the nucleus is involved in the expression of the CR, probably through multiple projections to cardioinhibitory neurons located in the medulla. Kapp and his colleagues also review evidence concerning the many inputs to the central nucleus.

A requisite for conditioning is convergence of CS and US information. On the basis of electrophysiological data, Kapp et al., suggest that such convergence may occur both in the medial geniculate and in the central nucleus of the amygdala. The US information may be conveyed to the amygdala via at least three routes—from the locus coeruleus, the parabrachial nucleus, and the magnocellular area of the medial geniculate.

The finding that the central amygdala nucleus is involved in cardiac conditioning in the rabbit is consistent with other research indicating an important function for this nucleus in other aspects of conditioned fear including blood pressure changes, behavioral freezing, and potentiated startle (LeDoux, 1987; Davis, Hitchcock, & Rosen, 1988). The data are also consistent for a role for the avian homolog of the amygdala in pigeon cardiac conditioning (Cohen, 1975).

Kapp et al. suggest that the central nucleus of the amygdala, and neurons in closely related structures, may exert a pervasive influence on both autonomic and somatic responses elicited by conditioned fear stimuli. Possible pathways for this influence are outlined in their chapter.

In closing, Kapp et al. consider the relevance of this apparent extensive influence of the central nucleus to the "two process" view of aversive conditioning offered by Thompson and his colleagues (e.g., Thompson et al., 1987). Briefly, this theory proposes that conditioned fear develops rapidly and is expressed in terms of responses that are not specific to the location of the CS. A second association, which reflects specific characteristics of the US and which involves a different neural substrate, requires considerably more trials to develop. Evidence supporting this model, which has much in common with Konorski's preparatory-consummatory response dichotomy of conditioning, is reviewed by Kapp et al. They also go on to suggest that the central nucleus of the amygdala, and related structures, may not only be fundamentally involved in fear conditioning, but may also modulate the performance and/or the learning of the specific CRs. In particular, they suggest that this system mediates an early retraction of the nictitating membrane, a response which competes with, and retards, the eventual development of the nictitating membrane closure response.

Hippocampus, Cingulate Cortex, and Cerebellum

The circuit controlling nictitating membrane conditioning itself has been extensively investigated and current data indicate that deep cerebellar nuclei (dentate/interpositus) are essential for the performance of the nictitating membrane and for conditioning hind limb flexor reflex in rabbits, but not for heart-rate conditioning (e.g., Moore, Desmond, & Berthier, 1982; Thompson et al., 1987). Until recently, it appeared that the dentate/interpositus nuclei were essential for nictitating membrane conditioning, but recent data from Harvey's laboratory have suggested a performance-modulating effect of these structures (Welsh & Harvey, 1989).

One of the enigmas regarding nictitating membrane conditioning concerns the correlate of such conditioning that develops in the hippocampus. Recordings from the pyramidal cells of the CA3 and CA1 areas have shown that a model of the behavioral UR and CR develops in these cells during the course of conditioning. The development of this model precedes behavioral evidence of conditioning and, on each trial, the model of the CR appears in the hippocampus some 50 ms prior to the occurrence of the nictitating membrane closure (e.g., Berger & Weisz, 1987; Thompson et al., 1987). The puzzle is that the hippocampus is unnecessary for such conditioning (e.g., Berger & Orr, 1983; Solomon, 1977). This riddle is the concern of the Chapter by Berger, Bassett, and Orr. Their approach is that the brain has multiple memory systems. For example, there are the aforementioned differences in loci for heart rate/fear conditioning on the one hand and nictitating membrane conditioning on the other. In addition, it is known that the hippocampus is necessary for nictitating membrane conditioning when procedures more complex than simple delay conditioning are used—procedures such as trace conditioning, conditional discrimination, or discrimination reversal training (e.g., Berger & Orr, 1983; Fagan & Olton, 1986; Ross, Orr, Holland, & Berger, 1984).

Berger and his colleagues argue that these data suggest that a function of the neural engram that develops in the hippocampus during "simple" delayed conditioning is, in a way, preparatory. The hippocampal memory may be necessary in order for the animal to demonstrate flexibility if the conditions of reinforcement change (e.g., are reversed). Thus, this memory trace, while seeming "non-essential" for simple conditioning, is essential for adaptive change.

In considering the general role of multiple memory traces in the brain, Berger et al. review the advantages of distributed engrams. Differentially localized memory traces may be correlated with different aspects of the event being represented in memory and/or with different levels of processing or abstraction of that event. They also consider in detail the hierarchical organization for distributed memory traces that appears to be the case regarding nictitating membrane conditioning. Within the hippocampus the CR model that develops in the activity of the pyramidal neurons (the hippocampal output system) is independent of the modality of the CS and, within the limits so far investigated, the conditioning paradigm and the species. This level of independence suggests a high level of processing. Even within the pyramidal neurons, the memory trace seems to be distributed in that different clusters of neurons show different correlations with the CR, possibly reflecting the encoding of different aspects of the CS and US.

The hierarchical aspects of the hippocampal memory trace were investigated by searching for the circuit by which the hippocampus could influence the cerebellar basic memory function. Berger et al. describe in detail their elegant studies of potential pathways, particularly the circuit leading from hippocampus to subiculum to posterior cingulate gyrus to ventral pontine nuclei to the cerebellum. The results of these studies, including the temporal aspects of transmission through this multisynaptic circuit, suggest that the hippocampus may modify cerebellar activity in an "on-line" fashion. Thus, both hierarchical and non-hierarchical aspects of distributed memory processing involving the hippocampus have been demonstrated by Berger and his colleagues.

The hippocampus is many things to many people. The sometimes bewildering variety of behaviors that seem to involve this structure has led to the conceptualization that the hippocampus serves as a temporary memory buffer for multiple psychological processes (Berger et al., chap. 12 in this volume; Rawlins, 1985). A memory function for the hippocampus, and the relationship of this memory function to some of the symptoms of Alzheimer's disease, is the subject of the chapter by Walsh and Chrobak.

Hippocampus, Septum, and Cholinergic Systems

Alzheimer's patients have a deficit in the ability to recall recent events, but their memory for past events and their retention of motor skills is normal. These cognitive symptoms of Alzheimer's disease have been related to a deterioration of the cholinergic transmitter system which innervates the hippocampus and septal area. The study of the relationship of acetylcholine function to memory in animals has been pursued using a variety of tasks, many of which are reviewed by Walsh and Chrobak in conjunction with consideration of the anatomy and physiology of the cholinergic systems involved in memory.

Much of the recent research on hippocampal and cholinergic involvement in memory has utilized the radial arm maze, a task reintroduced by Olton to study spatial learning and memory. Olton had previously shown that the rats' excellent spatial memory for the location of food items in the eight-arm maze was disrupted by lesions of the hippocampus (e.g., Olton, Becker, & Handelman, 1979). Of particular interest was the finding that memory of recent events was compromised considerably more than the ability to learn the maze per se. A procedure frequently used to test these different memory functions is to train the animals in the eight arm maze with four of the eight arms blocked and the other four baited. After the animal has successfully obtained the food from the four baited arms, it is removed from the maze for a retention interval and then replaced with all eight arms open but the only arms baited are the four which were initially blocked. The number of errors made in locating these food items is taken as a measure of "working" memory—the memory for recent events. Error rate in learning the initial four arms is taken as a measure of "reference" memory—the memory of how to solve the maze.

Walsh and Chrobak review evidence showing that lesions of the septum or hippocampus, or the administration of anticholinergic drugs directly to these structures, interferes with working memory but not reference memory. However, both of these techniques, lesion and pharmacological, have problems regarding the specificity of their action: Gross lesions destroy cells using transmitters other than acetylcholine and anticholinergics may have general toxic effects. In their own research, Walsh and Chrobak have used the compound AF64A, a neurotoxin reportedly selective for cholinergic neurons. They found that low doses of this compound administered intraventricularly produced substantial interference with working memory in the radial arm maze and in a T-maze working memory task, but did not affect activity levels or the learning of a spatial discrimination in the T-maze. In a neurochemical analysis, Walsh and Chrobak showed that this AF64A treatment produced a substantial reduction in cholinergic activity in the hippocampus but did not affect cholinergic activity in other areas of the brain analyzed nor did it influence the levels of other neurotransmitters in the hippocampus.

Thus, their work suggests a specific relationship between hippocampal cholinergic activity and working memory. As the authors suggest, the exact relationship of these deficits to the apparently similar deficits associated with Alzheimer's disease remains to be determined.

CONNECTIONS

Like distributed memories in the brain, investigators of psychological processes have different locations and concern themselves with different aspects of psychology. Connections are often difficult to perceive because of the necessity to concentrate on the immense volume of specialized literature in each field, because of differences in training and interest, and because of the multiplicity of procedures used in psychological research. What connections may be abstracted from the research represented in this volume?

In regard to emotion, there is a substantial degree of correspondence between the pharmacological studies of fear, disappointment and anxiety described by Fanselow and Flaherty and the neural mechanisms of heart rate and fear conditioning described by Kapp et al. The amygdala, perhaps the central nucleus, is unquestionably a nodal point for the conditioning and/or expression of all of these negative emotions. Lesions of the structure antagonize cardiac conditioning, various aspects of fear conditioning (Davis et al., 1988; LeDoux, 1987), and eliminate negative contrast (Becker, Jarvis, Wagner, & Flaherty, 1984). Furthermore, the administration of anxiolytic drugs directly to the amygdala produces anti-conflict effects (e.g., Hodges, Green, & Glenn, 1987; Shibata, Yamashita, Yamamoto, Ozaki, & Ueki, 1989). However, this relationship cannot be simple because the pharmacological studies reviewed by Fanselow and Flaherty suggest emotional subdivisions that have not been distinguished as yet in studies of amygdala function.

The interrelationships between emotion and cognition, and brain substrates subserving such interrelationships, are less well understood than each of the areas considered independently. Gray (1982) and Gray and Rawlins (1986), considering data from partial reinforcement studies and other animal models of anxiety, have suggested that the hippocampal-septal system and aspects of the Papez circuit function as an "interface between cognition and emotion" (Gray & Rawlins, 1986, p. 180). Kapp et al. in this volume, and Thompson and colleagues (1987) suggest interactions between the diffuse, emotional conditioning subserved by the amygdala and the discrete skeletal responses subserved by the cerebellum, but their suggested interactions are quite different—antagonistic in the case of Kapp et al., and facilitating in the case of Thompson et al. Also, the data that are available suggest that damage to the amygdala does not prevent nictitating membrane response conditioning and that damage to the cerebellum does not prevent heart-rate conditioning. Furthermore, the finding that nictitating membrane conditioning apparently proceeds normally if the US and CS inputs to the cerebellum are directly stimulated (Thompson et al., 1987) suggests that a separate emotion-eliciting function of the US, mediated by other structures, is not necessary for this discrete motor reflex to be conditioned. Arousal that would normally accompany such conditioning may be adaptive for other reasons, such as generally alerting the animal or preparing it to meet other adverse circumstances that may accompany the noxious interference with its eye.

Relatively little is known regarding brain mechanisms subserving the types of animal cognition described in the early chapters of this book. The hippocampus is most likely involved in the contextual effects described by Bouton and by Miller and Grahame because recent data suggest the necessity of the hippocampus for filtering punctate CSs from a contextual background in conditioning studies (Winocur, Rawlins, & Gray, 1987). Miller and Grahame's model rests heavily on the role of a "comparator" in determining the expression of a conditioned response. There have been many suggestions of a comparator function for the hippocampus and related circuitry (e.g., Gabriel, Sparenborg, & Stolar, 1986; Gray, 1982). Comparisons are often made to memory of past events such as what a CS has been paired with previously (cf. chapters 1-4) or with rewards previously experienced (cf. chapters 9 and 10), thus a comparator function would require ready access to a memory system—which also may involve the hippocampus (e.g., Walsh & Chrobak, Chapter 13).

Some localized role for aspects of memory in the hippocampus is suggested by the finding that accurate performance of delayed matching to sample in rats seems to require the hippocampus but not the amygdala (Raffaele & Olton, 1988). However, other data suggest other "localizations" of memory for complex behavior. For example, there is evidence of modality-specific memory in cortical areas subserving auditory and visual functions in studies of delayed matching to sample tasks with monkeys as subjects (Colombo, D'Amato, Rodman, & Gross, in press).

Although there is substantial evidence for varying localizations of function in the hippocampus, amygdala, and other structures, there is little doubt that, in the end, the full understanding of psychological processes will require a systems approach. In perhaps the most ambitious attempt to detail interacting systems underlying memory and cognition, Mishkin has described a circuit involving aspects of the temporal cortex, the amygdala, the hippocampus, and thalamic areas that function to subserve visual recognition memory in delayed non-matching-to-sample tasks (e.g., Mishkin, 1982). Mishkin (1982) also suggested that similar cortical-limbic circuits might underlay memory in other modalities since ". . . the highest cortical level in each modality appears to project to both the amygdala and the hippocampus. . ." (p. 93).

All-in-all, there is reason to be optimistic that millennia-old questions regarding brain function and psychological phenomena are in fact soluble by experimental techniques through the use of a combination of behavioral and neurobiological procedures. At the present time, it seems that the study of the neural basis of conditioning and learning lags behind the subtleties demonstrated in behavioral studies over the past two decades or so. But that is probably the way it must be.

REFERENCES

Becker, H. C., Jarvis, M., Wagner, G., & Flaherty, C. F. (1984). Medial and lateral amygdala lesions differentially influence contrast with sucrose solutions. *Physiology & Behavior, 33,* 707-712.

Berger, T. W., & Orr, W. B. (1983). Hippocampectomy selectively disrupts discrimination reversal conditioning of the rabbit nictitating membrane response. *Behavioral Brain Research, 8,* 49-68.

Berger, T. W., & Weisz, D. J. (1987). Single unit analysis of hippocampal pyramidal and granule cells during classical conditioning of the rabbit nictitating membrane response. In I. Gormezano, W. F. Prokasy, & R. F. Thompson (Eds.), *Classical conditioning III: Behavioral, neurophysiological and neurochemical studies in the rabbit* (pp. 217-253). Hillsdale, NJ: Lawrence Erlbaum Associates.

Blanchard, D. C., & Blanchard, R. J. (1972). Innate and conditioned reactions to threat in rats with amygdaloid lesions. *Journal of Comparative and Physiological Psychology, 81,* 281-290.

Brush, F. R. (1985). Genetic Determinants of avoidance learning: Mediated by emotionality? In F. R. Brush & J.B. Overmier (Eds.), *Affect, conditioning, and cognition: Essays on the determinants of behavior* (pp. 27-42). Hillsdale, NJ: Lawrence Erlbaum Associates.

Brush, F. R., Del Paine, S. N., Pellegrino, L. J., Rykaszewski, I. M., Dess, N. K., & Collins, P. Y. (1988). CER suppression, passive avoidance learning, and stress-induced suppression of drinking in the Syracuse High-and Low-Avoidance strains of rats *(rattus norvegicus). Journal of Comparative Psychology, 102,* 337-349.

Capaldi, E. J., & Miller, D. J. (1988). Counting in rats: Its functional significance and the independent cognitive processes that constitute it. *Journal of Experimental Psychology: Animal Behavior Processes, 14,* 3-17.

Cohen, D. H. (1975). Involvement of avian amygdalar homolog (archistriatum posterior and meduale) in defensively conditioned heart rate change. *Journal of Comparative Neurology, 160,* 13-35.

Colombo, M., D'Amato, M. R., Rodman, H. R., & Gross, C. G. (1990). Auditory association cortex lesions impair auditory short-term memory in monkeys. *Science, 247,* 336-338.

Cook, M., & Mineka, S. (1987). Second-order conditioning and overshadowing in the observational conditioning of fear in monkeys. *Behavior Research and Therapy, 25,* 349-364.

Crespi, L. P. (1942). Quantitative variation in incentive and performance in the white rat. *American Journal of Psychology, 55,* 467-517.

D'Amato, M. R., & Salmon, D. P. (1984). Tune discrimination in monkeys (*Cebus apella*) and in rats. *Animal Learning & Behavior, 10,* 126-134.

D'Amato, M. R., & Van Sant, P. (1988). The person concept in monkeys (*Cebus apella*). *Journal of Experimental Psychology: Animal Behavior Processes, 14,* 43-55.

Davis, M. (1979). Diazepam and flurazepam: Effects on conditioned fear as measured with the potentiated startle paradigm. *Psychopharmacology, 62,* 1-7.

Davis, M., Hitchcock, J. M., & Rosen, J. B. (1988). Anxiety and the amygdala: Pharmacological and anatomical analysis of the fear-potentiated startle paradigm. In G. Bower (Ed.), *The psychology of learning and motivation* (Vol. 21, pp 263-305). New York: Academic Press.

Dickinson, A., & Boakes, R. A. (Eds.). (1979). *Mechanisms of learning and motivation: A memorial volume to Jerzy Konorski.* Hillsdale, NJ: Lawrence Erlbaum Associates.

Fagan, A. M. & Olton, D. S. (1986). Learning sets, discrimination reversal, and hippocampal function. *Behavioural Brain Research, 21*, 13-20.

Flaherty, C. F. (1982). Incentive contrast: A review of behavioral changes following shifts in reward. *Animal Learning & Behavior, 10*, 409-440.

Gabriel, M., Sparenborg, S. P., & Stolar, N. (1986). An executive function of the hippocampus: Pathway selection for thalamic neuronal significance code. In R.L. Issacson & K.H. Pribram (Eds.), *The hippocampus* (Vol. 4, pp. 1-39). New York: Plenum Press.

Gentile, C. G., Jarrell, T. W., Teich, A. H., McCabe, P. M., & Schneiderman, N. (1986). The role of the amygdaloid central nucleus in differential Pavlovian conditioning of bradycardia in rabbits. *Behavioral Brain Research, 20*, 263-276.

Gray, J. A. (1982). *The neuropsychology of anxiety: An enquiry into the function of the septo-hippocampal system.* Oxford: Oxford University Press.

Gray, J. A. (1987). *The psychology of fear and stress.* Cambridge: Cambridge University Press.

Gray, J. A., & Rawlins, J. N. P. (1986). Comparator and buffer memory: An attempt to integrate two models of hippocampal function. In R. L. Isaacson & K. H. Pribram (Eds.), *The hippocampus* (Vol. 4, pp. 159-199). New York: Plenum Press.

Harlow, H. F. (1949). The formation of learning sets. *Psychological Review, 56*, 51-65.

Harlow, H. F. (1959). Learning set and error factor theory. In S. Koch (Ed.), *Psychology: A study of a science (Vol. 2).* New York: McGraw-Hill.

Herrnstein, R. J., Loveland, D. H., & Cable, C. (1976). Natural concepts in pigeons. *Journal of Experimental Psychology: Animal Behavior Processes, 2*, 285-302.

Hodges, H., Green, S., & Glenn, B. (1987). Evidence that the amygdala is involved in benzodiazepine and serotonergic effects on punished responding but not on discrimination. *Psychopharmacology, 92*, 491-504.

Honig, W. K., & James, H. P. R. (Eds.). (1971). *Animal memory.* New York: Academic Press.

Hulse, S. H., & Dorsky, N. P. (1979). Serial pattern learning by rats: Transfer of a formally defined stimulus relationship and the significance of nonreinforcement. *Animal Learning & Behavior, 7*, 211-220.

Hulse, S. H., & Page, S. C. (1988). Toward a comparative psychology of music perception. *Music Perception, 5*, 427-452.

Konorski, J. (1967). *Integrative activity of the brain: An interdisciplinary approach.* Chicago: University of Chicago Press

LeDoux, J. E. (1987). Emotion. In F. Plum (Ed.), *Handbook of physiology, Volume V: Higher functions of the brain* (pp. 415-459). Baltimore: Williams and Wilkins.

Lewis, D. J. (1969). Sources of experimental amnesia. *Psychological Review, 76*, 461-472.

Miller, R. R., & Springer, A. D. (1973). Amnesia, consolidation and retrieval. *Psychological Review, 80,* 69-79.

Mishkin, M. (1982). A memory system in the monkey. *Philosophical Transactions of the Royal Society of London, 298,* 85-95.

Moore, J. W., Desmond, J. E., & Berthier, N. E. (1982). The metencephalic basis of the conditioned nictitating membrane response. In C. D. Woody (Ed.), *Conditioning: Representation of involved neuronal function* (pp. 459-482). New York: Plenum.

Mowrer, O. H., & Lamoreaux, R. R. (1946). Fear as an intervening variable in avoidance conditioning. *Journal of Comparative Psychology, 39,* 29-50.

Olton, D. S., Becker, J. T., & Handelman, G. E. (1979). Hippocampus, space, and memory. *Behavioral Brain Science, 2,* 313-365.

Pearce, J. M., & Hall, G. A. (1980). A model for Pavlovian learning: Variations in the effectiveness of conditioned but not unconditioned stimuli. *Psychological Review, 87,* 532-552.

Raffaele, K. C., & Olton, D. S. (1988). Hippocampal and amygdaloid involvement in working memory for nonspatial stimuli. *Behavioral Neuroscience, 102,* 249-355.

Rawlins, J. N. P. (1985). Associations across time: The hippocampus as a temporary memory store. *Behavioral and Brain Sciences, 8,* 479-496.

Rescorla, R. A., & Heth, C. D. (1975). Reinstatement of fear to an extinguished conditioned stimulus. *Journal of Experimental Psychology: Animal Behavior Processes, 1,* 88-96.

Ross, R. T., Orr, W. B., Holland, P. C. & Berger, T. W. (1984). Hippocampectomy disrupts acquisition and retention of learned conditional responding. *Behavioral Neuroscience, 98,* 221-225.

Shibata, S., Yamashita, K., Yamamoto, E., Ozaki, T., & Ueki, S. (1989). Effects of benzodiazepine and GABA antagonists on anticonflict effects of antianxiety drugs injected into rat lateral amygdala in a water-lick suppression test. *Psychopharmacology, 98,* 38-44.

Solomon, P. R. (1977). Role of the hippocampus in blocking and conditioned inhibition of the rabbit's nictitating membrane response. *Journal of Comparative and Physiological Psychology, 91,* 407-417.

Spear, N. E. (1973). Retrieval of memory in animals. *Psychological Review, 80,* 163-194.

Spear, N. E. (1978). *The processing of memories: Forgetting and retention.* Hillsdale, NJ: Lawrence Erlbaum Associates.

Spear, N. E., Miller, J. S., & Jagielo, J. A. (1990). Animal memory and learning. *Annual Review of Psychology, 41,* 169-211.

Spence, K. W. (1937). The differential response in animals to stimuli varying within a single dimension. *Psychological Review, 44,* 430-444.

Straub, R. O., & Terrace, H. S. (1981). Generalization of serial learning in the pigeon. *Animal Learning & Behavior, 9,* 454-468.

Terrace, H. S. (1986). A nonverbal organism's knowledge of ordinal position in a serial learning task. *Journal of Experimental Psychology: Animal Behavior Processes, 12,* 203-214.

Thompson, R. F., Donegan, N. H., Clark, G. A., Lavond, D. G., Lincoln, J. S., Maden, IV, J., Mamounas, L. A., Mauk, M. D., & McCormick, D. A. (1987). Neuronal substrates of discrete, defensive conditioned reflexes, conditioned fear states, and their interactions in the rabbit. In I. Gormezano, W. F. Prokasy, & R. F. Thompson (Eds.), *Classical conditioning* (pp. 371-399). Hillsdale, NJ: Lawrence Erlbaum Associates.

Underwood, B. J. (1969). Attributes of memory. *Psychological Review, 76,* 559-573.

Vaughan, W., Jr., & Greene, S. L. (1984). Pigeon visual memory capacity. *Journal of Experimental Psychology: Animal Behavior Processes, 10,* 256-271.

Wasserman, E. A., Kiedinger, R. E., & Bhatt, R. S. (1988). Conceptual behavior in pigeons: Categories, subcategories, and pseudocategories. *Journal of Experimental Psychology: Animal Behavior Processes, 14,* 235-246.

Watanabe, S. (1988). Failure of visual prototype learning in the pigeon. *Animal Learning & Behavior, 16,* 147-152.

Watson, J. B., & Raynor, R. (1920). Conditioned emotional reactions. *Journal of Experimental Psychology, 3,* 1-14.

Welsh, J. P., & Harvey, J. A. (1989). Intra-cerebellar lidocaine: Dissociation of learning from performance. *Society for Neuroscience Abstracts, 15,* No. 258.1.

Williams, B. A. (1983). Another look at contrast in multiple schedules. *Journal of the Experimental Analysis of Behavior, 39,* 345-384.

Winocur, G., Rawlins, J. N. P., & Gray, J. A. (1987). The hippocampus and conditioning to contextual cues. *Behavioral Neuroscience, 101,* 617-625.

Author Index

Numbers in *italics* refer to pages on which the complete references are listed.

K

Subject Index

A

Z

This book was prepared on a microcomputer-based publishing system and submitted to Erlbaum in camera-ready form. Chapter authors submitted their chapters in electronic form (on floppy disks) and editorial revisions were made to the electronic manuscripts. Chapters were formatted on an Apple® Macintosh™ computer using Microsoft® Word. Camera-ready pages were printed in Times, Helvetica, and New Century Schoolbook typefaces using Adobe Postscript™ on an Apple LaserWriter II NT™ printer. The use of trade, firm, and corporate names is for the information and convenience of the reader and does not constitute official endorsement of any product or service to the exclusion of others.